To my dear friend and mentor

WILLIAM REUBEN FARMER

*"Happy are those who hunger and thirst
for what is right; they will be satisfied."*

THE ANCHOR BIBLE REFERENCE LIBRARY

PUBLISHED BY DOUBLEDAY
a division of Random House, Inc.
1540 Broadway, New York, New York 10036

THE ANCHOR BIBLE REFERENCE LIBRARY, DOUBLEDAY,
and the portrayal of an anchor with the letters ABRL are trademarks of
Doubleday, a division of Random House, Inc.

Book design by Ellen Cipriano

Library of Congress Cataloging-in-Publication Data

Dungan, David L.
A history of the synoptic problem: the canon, the text,
the composition, and the interpretation of the Gospels / by
David Laird Dungan. — 1st ed.
p.   cm. — (The Anchor Bible reference library)
Includes bibliographical references and indexes.
1. Synoptic problem—History. I. Title. II. Series.
BS2555.2.D85   1999
226'.066—dc21   97-49895
CIP

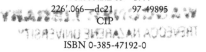

ISBN 0-385-47192-0

3   5   7   9   10   8   6   4

• THE ANCHOR BIBLE REFERENCE LIBRARY •

A HISTORY OF THE SYNOPTIC PROBLEM

*The Canon, the Text, the Composition, and
the Interpretation of the Gospels*

DAVID LAIRD DUNGAN

ABRL

Doubleday
New York London Toronto Sydney Auckland

A HISTORY OF THE SYNOPTIC PROBLEM

THE ANCHOR BIBLE REFERENCE LIBRARY is designed to be a third major component of the Anchor Bible group, which includes the Anchor Bible commentaries on the books of the Old Testament, the New Testament, and the Apocrypha, and the Anchor Bible Dictionary. While the Anchor Bible commentaries and the Anchor Bible Dictionary are structurally defined by their subject matter, the Anchor Bible Reference Library will serve as a supplement on the cutting edge of the most recent scholarship. The series is open-ended; its scope and reach are nothing less than the biblical world in its totality, and its methods and techniques the most up-to-date available or devisable. Separate volumes will deal with one or more of the following topics relating to the Bible: anthropology, archaeology, ecology, economy, geography, history, languages and literatures, philosophy, religion(s), theology.

As with the Anchor Bible commentaries and the Anchor Bible Dictionary, the philosophy underlying the Anchor Bible Reference Library finds expression in the following: the approach is scholarly, the perspective is balanced and fair-minded, the methods are scientific, and the goal is to inform and enlighten. Contributors are chosen on the basis of their scholarly skills and achievements, and they come from a variety of religious backgrounds and communities. The books in the Anchor Bible Reference Library are intended for the broadest possible readership, ranging from world-class scholars, whose qualifications match those of the authors, to general readers, who may not have special training or skill in studying the Bible but are as enthusiastic as any dedicated professional in expanding their knowledge of the Bible and its world.

David Noel Freedman
GENERAL EDITOR

ACKNOWLEDGMENTS

As I explain in the Introduction, I first began gathering the material for this book in a course on the Synoptic Problem that I was invited to teach at the Pontifical Biblical Institute in Rome in 1977. I still remember the open-mindedness, exuberance, and brilliance of the international students in that class. It will always be my happiest teaching experience in biblical studies.

Whatever knowledge of the Synoptic Problem I might have brought into that course was gained in large part from years of working with a number of colleagues in the International Institute for the Renewal of Gospel Studies: William Farmer and Bernard Orchard (codirectors), Lamar Cope, David Peabody, Allan McNicol, and Philip Shuler. In addition to what I learned from these friends and colleagues, I was also deeply educated by the numerous reports and publications of the members of the Synoptic Problem Seminar in the Studiorum Novi Testamenti Societas. Out of more than a score of participants, I wish to express my debt in particular to Frans Neirynck, Christopher Tuckett, Marie-Émile Boismard, Bo Reicke, Michael Goulder, William O. Walker, Joseph Tyson, Thomas Longstaff, and Ed Sanders. Even though we may have found ourselves locked in sharp debate on many occasions, I would like to take this opportunity to express my profound admiration for each of these men and to thank each one for bearing with my personal faults and scholarly weaknesses. I have truly felt myself generously included within a lifelong community of learning, and I am deeply grateful.

To a number of colleagues I owe a special debt of gratitude for their willingness to read portions of this manuscript and to provide helpful critique. Above all, I wish to thank Allan McNicol for reading the entire manuscript in an earlier form and assisting me to find the essential "story line" and lift it out of what was a maze of detailed arguments, so as to clarify the whole presentation. I would also like to mention my dear friend Ben Meyer († 1993) whose publications on biblical interpretation helped me formulate my own ideas and whose personal encouragement by letter and telephone meant everything to me. I also wish to give special thanks to Sean McEvenue, William Petersen, Sam Preus, and David Linge for reading chapters of the book and providing helpful criticism.

I am indebted to several libraries for their support. I wish to name especially Dr. Maria Grossmann and Mr. Charles Woodbury, formerly of the Andover Harvard Library, for their gracious support when I visited Harvard on my periodic visits over the years. Dr. Page Thomas of the Bridwell Library of the Perkins School of Theology, Southern Methodist University, also made Bridwell's excellent holdings available on a number of occasions. As for the staff in my own library at the University of Tennessee, Knoxville, I have nothing but complete admiration and gratitude for their courteous, swift, and unstinting service. Ours is a library to gladden the scholar's heart.

I am happy to take this opportunity to express my gratitude to the deans and officers of the Faculty Research Program at the University of Tennessee, Knoxville, for several grants in support of this project, particularly one in 1985 that provided advanced computing equipment and software.

I also thank the officers in the National Endowment for the Humanities for a fellowship which made possible a leave of absence from my teaching duties in 1993–1994 to work on this book.

As director of the International Institute for Renewal of Gospel Studies, I am happy to take this occasion to thank many friends and interested persons in the Knoxville area, in particular Condon Bush and Baxter Lee, who generously provided the institute with funding to carry out our research and publication agenda. The scholars of the Church have always looked to learned and interested laypeople for support in their scholarly endeavor; these wonderful people join a great and honorable tradition in this respect.

Neither this book nor the recently published volume entitled *Beyond the Q Impasse: Luke's Use of Matthew* would have seen the light of day were it not for the decades of unstinting support, encouragement, and timely guidance of my department chairman, Charles H. Reynolds. He is one of those rare department heads whose letters of support in grant applications are usually more interesting and convincing than the author's original statements. I would also like to express my great appreciation to our two superb department secretaries, Mrs. Debbie Myers and Mrs. Joan Riedl, for their years of consistent performance of the many chores that make ours a busy, productive department.

In this connection, I cannot fail to express my gratitude to Michael McGuire, senior applied computing analyst in the university's Department of Computing and Academic Services, for his consistently helpful advice on computing hardware and software and above all his unfailing ability to unscramble my computer after I have done my level best to destroy it.

I was privileged to take a course in Old Testament from David Noel Freedman in 1958 at McCormick Seminary in Chicago. He was at the time on the faculty of Western Seminary in Pittsburgh, and he used to commute twice a week by train to McCormick. Over the years, Noel kept up his interest in my work, and this eventually resulted in an invitation to contribute an article on the Griesbach hypothesis for the *Anchor Bible Dictionary*. When I turned in an article that was ten times longer than the original page limit, Freedman and the editorial staff were kind enough to accept it. He must have sensed that this detailed treatment was drawn from a well that contained more, since he also sent me a letter asking if I would be willing to write a full-length book on the Synoptic Problem for the Anchor Bible Reference Library. I said that, as a matter of fact, I already had just such a book almost completed. That was in 1991. I sent a proposal to Noel and it was accepted. Seven years later, I am finally ready to release this manuscript, even though there are many, many places that need further work. Over the years since, Mark Fretz and Andrew Corbin, religion editors for Doubleday, have been more than patient. To all, but especially to Noel Freedman, I am glad to express my real gratitude for their generous approach to this project and for their patience and encouragement.

Finally, my wife and sons know the many times I felt defeated and hopeless before the enormous task I had undertaken. They always stepped up and encouraged me to keep going. To them I express my love and gratitude for their understanding and support.

David Laird Dungan
University of Tennessee, Knoxville

CONTENTS

PART THREE. *Current Trends in the Post-Modern Period*

LIST OF ABBREVIATIONS

SIGLA

In the quotations in this book,
    ( ) contain either the author's additions for better understanding of
       the meaning of the original or inserted references;
    [ ] contain conjectural emendations to the text, that is, conjectures
       as to what the original text contained.

ABBREVIATIONS

The following volumes have been referred to without giving full
bibliography *in situ.*

HS	E. Hennecke and W. Schneemelcher, eds., *New Testament Apocrypha*, 2 vols., rev. ed. (Louisville: W/K 1991–1992)
IDB	*The Interpreters Dictionary of the Bible*, 4 vols. (Nashville: Abingdon Press, 1962)
Liddell-Scott *Lexicon*	Henry G. Liddell and R. Scott, *A Greek-English Lexicon*, rev. ed. (Oxford: University Press 1996)
OCD	*The Oxford Classical Dictionary*, rev. ed., ed. Simon Hornblower and Antony Spawforth (Oxford: University Press 1996)
ODCC	*The Oxford Dictionary of the Christian Church*, rev. ed., ed. F. L. Cross and E. A. Livingstone (Oxford: University Press 1997)
Quasten, *Patrology*	Johannes Quasten, *Patrology*, 4 vols. (Allen, TX: Christian Classics, 1983)
PG	*Patrologia graeca*, J. Migne
CSEL	*Corpus scriptorum ecclesiasticorum latinorum*

INTRODUCTION

This history of the Synoptic Problem originated in a course I taught while I was Catholic Biblical Association of America visiting professor at the Pontificio Istituto Biblico (part of the Università Gregoriana) in Rome in 1976–77. I had been invited by the faculty and former rector Carlo Martini to give a course entitled Introduction to the Synoptic Problem. This subject had never been taught at the Biblicum and, in view of the increased interest provoked by recent prominent challenges to the Two Source Hypothesis, the subject seemed quite timely. Roman Catholic scholars had just begun to adopt the Two Source Hypothesis in large numbers, and the fact that I, a Harvard-trained, Two Source Protestant, belonged to a small group of renegades working to overthrow this Protestant hypothesis may have appealed to their Italian love of ironic contrast.

Whatever the reason, it was a memorable year. My superb, hardworking international class of students had complete freedom to analyze the synoptic material and propose any hypothesis they wanted in their class reports. And make full use of their freedom they did; the whole gamut of theories came to expression sooner or later. In the end, I was educated far more than they were. For one thing, I saw at first hand how the cultural backgrounds of the students—they included Asians, Africans, Indians, Europeans, Irish, and one American—could predispose toward a particular hypothetical solution. I dare say this aspect of the Synoptic Problem is still unknown to my white, Euro–North American, male colleagues, who pay little heed to the cultural assumptions influencing their scholarly work.

Again, it was in this course that two students first presented me with evidence that all synopses were biased toward one solution to the Synoptic Problem or another. Until then I had never thought twice about using Huck or Aland. Like everyone else, I naively thought they were "neutral" with respect to the presentation of the synoptic phenomena. It never dawned on me that there were major differences between them, hinting at important biases that no one had ever noticed.

Why Another History of the Synoptic Problem?

Given the hundreds of handbooks introducing the New Testament and Bible study guides being used around the world, as well as the scores of commentaries on the Gospels and the dozen or so histories of New Testament scholarship, why should I feel impelled to add another lengthy study of this subject, especially since there is such unanimity regarding the solution to the Synoptic Problem, namely, the almost universal acceptance of the Two Source Hypothesis? What more could be said that hasn't been already, more than once? My account will differ from all others in four important ways:

- Most accounts do not tell the whole story; they begin around 1800 instead of at the beginning. As a result, they privilege the most recent form of the Synoptic Problem, treating it as if it were somehow self-evident. Thus, they do not notice that there are earlier forms of the Synoptic Problem, and, by comparison with them, they do not notice how destructive to traditional Christianity the modern form is. This skewed situation is instead regarded as morally and politically neutral and objective, when precisely the opposite is the case.
- No history of source criticism correlates the four basic components of the full Synoptic Problem to each other or explains their intrinsic interrelationships. This history will show how the Synoptic Problem has always involved much more than just the question of how the Gospels were composed and what sources were used. The complete Synoptic Problem has always also involved the question of *which Gospels* to consider (the question of canon), *which text* of the normative Gospels to use (text criticism), and how to interpret the Bible as a whole and the Gospels in particular (hermeneutics). The full Synoptic Problem, strictly speaking, always includes these four components.
- This history is unique in that it discusses the history of each of these four components as they arise within each of the major Forms of the Synoptic Problem.
- No history of the Synoptic Problem has tried to indicate the cultural, political, economic, and technological presuppositions undergirding and shaping the debate in every historical period. Instead, most biblical scholars naively believe that their discipline is free of such mundane concerns, as if their biblical research had no economic agenda and did not serve fundamental political objectives. It

will be the task of this history to make these political and economic aspects clear for each of the major Forms of the Synoptic Problem.

Overview of Part One

This book is a chronological narrative divided into three parts that roughly correspond to three major epochs in the debate over the interrelations among the Gospels. Part One covers the period from the first century to the fifth. It takes its start with the first signs of anxiety regarding the multiplicity of differing accounts of the Lord Jesus Christ and the early attempts by Christian leaders to marginalize rival versions (the Apostle John regarding the Gospel of Mark and Church leaders in Rome refusing to use the Gospel of John) or just to exclude them altogether (Marcion).

This phase was followed by a second phase, coinciding with the rise of the canonization process during the middle of the second century (a response to the first phase in some respects), in which—since *four* Gospels were universally accepted among the orthodox faction as normative—more and more elaborate accounts were produced to provide solid intellectual explanations for the many differences among the four, so that they could retain their credibility as authoritative accounts of the Lord Jesus. An early sign of this process is the use by Justin of a Gospel harmony resulting in Tatian's *Diatessaron*.

A key point to watch for in Part One is the way Origen handled the divergencies and similarities among the Gospels in a multivalent, multicentered manner, as compared with Augustine, who represents the apex of the authoritarian, literalist approach to the Gospels. These two approaches are so different in their hermeneutical methods and political assumptions that I distinguish them as the First and Second Forms of the Synoptic Problem, respectively.

Perhaps a further word of explanation about their differing political assumptions is in order at this point. Origen and Augustine worked within very different political and religious periods of the Christian Church vis-à-vis the Roman Empire. In Origen's time, the Christian movement was an embattled minority within a hostile, religiously pluralistic, competitive environment. I believe this minority status accounts in part for Origen's irenic tone in his debates and writings. Moreover, there was no centrally authorized canon of the Scripture in existence, although the outlines of such a standard collection were beginning to be recognized among the orthodox. But it is well known that Origen occasionally used more than the four Gospels in his exegetical and critical writings. In this regard, Origen's tendency to *avoid* literal harmonizations of the differences among the Gospels will require very careful explanation, since it is based in his general biblical hermeneutics. Finally, probably more than any other scholar of the early Church, Origen was aware of the *textual variations* among the many copies of the sacred writings in circulation. All told, Origen was the first to confront every aspect of the Synoptic Problem: canon, text, composition, and hermeneutics. As such, he may rightly be regarded as the paradigm for all later attempts to account for the differences among the Gospels.

Augustine, on the other hand, had two momentous events behind him that radically transformed the Church's political situation. By his day, the highest levels of Roman officialdom had long since accorded the Christian religion the status of a *religio licita* and opened to Christian use the large public basilicas in the downtown areas of the great cities of the Roman Empire. The emperor had also ordered reparations to be paid out of the public *fiscus* to Christians who had suffered property loss or other damages during the persecutions under Diocletian. In view of this imperial favor, Augustine could assume that what he, as Bishop of Hippo, said regarding Scripture, or theology, or Church practice had, at least in principle, the power of the Roman sword behind it. This may account for the edge detectable in *his* arguments with Christian opponents.

Second, at least two major councils of bishops had met, one of which Augustine attended personally. Among other actions that council adopted a "standard set" of sacred writings to be read in the Church's worship services throughout the empire on Sunday mornings and at other times. As far as Augustine's perception of the Synoptic Problem was concerned, these councils effectively shut the door on the need for him to take into consideration any other Gospels than Matthew, Mark, Luke, and John. This in part explains why he treated them like a single block of text and embraced whatever assumptions he needed to make possible a literalist harmonization of their words into a single meta-narrative. The Gospel harmony is the telltale sign of the Second Form of the Synoptic Problem.

I mentioned earlier that there were a number of other attempts by Christian thinkers to cope with the similarities and differences among the Gospels. Justin Martyr and his student Tatian created combinations of Gospel texts for use in their polemical contests with philosophical critics of the Christian Gospels. Justin referred to the Gospels with the label "memoirs of the apostles" so as to confer upon them a well-known Platonic and/or Pythagorean genre.

The Pontic shipmaster and Christian philosopher Marcion took a very different tack, conducting a kind of "ethnic cleansing" of Christianity by throwing out everything Jewish, including the Old Testament and all Gospels except for his sanitized version of Luke—which told of a non-Jewish Jesus. Marcion's agenda resurfaced 1,750 years later when, in the early decades of the twentieth century, German Lutherans, led by such world-famous scholars as Adolf von Harnack, called for a new Marcionite Christianity minus all Jewish elements including in particular the Old Testament.

The differences among the Gospels eventually attracted the attention of the numerous critics of Christianity, who saw in them ample ammunition for destroying the credibility of the Christian religion. In this respect, Part One briefly examines statements by Celsus, Porphyry, Hierocles, and the Manichaeans concerning the differences among the Gospels. I go on to describe how the most important Christian theologians, particularly Eusebius and Augustine, responded to these attacks. Another reason for noting what the early Greek and Roman critics of Christianity said is the fact that their arguments came back into the discussion 1500 years later when Enlightenment opponents of traditional religion mined their writings—along with those of Sextus Empiricus, Cicero, and Lucretius—for arguments to use in their attacks against religious bigotry and superstition.

Overview of Part Two

Augustine set the pattern that persisted for a thousand years. Indeed, his influence was felt even longer than that, since neither the Protestant Reformers nor the Roman Catholic biblical scholars and theologians of the Reformation deviated from his harmonistic approach. Part Two begins with the Reformers, then, not because they differed in any marked degree from Augustine but because the seeds of the "modern spirit" were planted then, in the breakdown of late nominalist Scholasticism that heralded some of the new epistemological assumptions of the Reformers.

The Modern Period, covered in Part Two, lasted until World Wars I and II, a single horrendous event in two cataclysmic spasms. Albert Schweitzer believed in 1914 that he was witnessing "the suicide of civilization." During the nineteenth century, a completely new, Third Form of the Synoptic Problem appeared, accompanied by a revolutionary new instrument for the comparison of the Gospels known as a *synopsis*.

All four components of the Third Form of the Synoptic Problem did not arise in their new configurations overnight. The first component to break down and begin the process of reformulation was the *text* of the Gospels. This occurred as a result of the collapse of confidence in the great *Vulgata latina* of Jerome. By 1500, its manuscript tradition had become so corrupt that numerous reform efforts were under way to purify it. However, a more drastic solution soon appeared. The Roman Catholic classical scholar and theologian Erasmus of Rotterdam was persuaded to bring out a *Greek* edition of the New Testament in 1516—the first text of the Greek New Testament to appear in the West in almost one thousand years. Ironically, because of the great haste with which it was done, Erasmus' Greek New Testament was riddled with mistakes, omissions, misprints, and faulty readings. One chapter describes just the remarkable circumstances surrounding Erasmus' publication of the Greek New Testament, and a second chapter is devoted to the textual chaos that ensued. A third traces the gradual appearance of a consensus regarding a new *textus receptus* of the Greek New Testament.

The next component of the Synoptic Problem to break down was the canon of Scripture. Doubts about the validity of the canonization process had circulated among Church scholars behind closed doors since the late fifteenth century. It broke out into the open when Martin Luther refused to accord canonical status to certain books in both the Old and the New Testament in his German translation of the Bible. Skepticism regarding the biblical canon was especially pronounced in English deism.

I provide an illustration of this development with John Toland's notorious *Nazarenus*, published in 1718, in which he announced to shocked readers on both sides of the Channel that none of the canonical Gospels contained the true historical account of Jesus of Nazareth. Instead, he pointed to *The Gospel of Barnabas*, a mysterious document Toland had just seen in Amsterdam, as the real truth. This Gospel, he said, contained the startling information that Jesus, when challenged by the High Priest to declare whether he was the Son of God or not, announced not only that he was *not* the Son of God—the true God had no sons—but that neither was he the true Prophet. That title belonged to the one coming after him named Mohammed. Outrage greeted Toland's book, but it opened the door to skepticism regarding the credibility of the fourfold Gospel canon. By the mid-nineteenth century, the Gospel canon was considered passé in historical-critical scholarship—a view still widely held.

Two chapters are devoted to the third component of the Third Form of the Synoptic Problem: the hermeneutical principles underlying the "modern, historical-critical method." Contrary to most histories of historical criticism, I show that it was actually set in motion by Baruch Spinoza, an earlier contemporary of Richard Simon, the French biblical scholar usually granted that honor. It is true that Simon did publish a number of books that proved to be models of their kind of historical-critical scholarship, but it was Spinoza who provided the philosophical *and political* intellectual justification for the new historical-critical method.

The chapter on Spinoza is especially significant in the overall design of this book, since it lays out for the first time, as far as I can tell, the *political* agenda animating the modern historical-critical method. Few modern biblical scholars realize that their biblical scholarship serves a definite political agenda, namely, the creation and maintenance of political democracy. Even rarer is the realization that Spinoza's main purpose for inventing the historical-critical method was to destroy the Bible's usefulness for traditional religious and political purposes. Since this claim will undoubtedly strike my colleagues as unlikely in the extreme, I have laid out the evidence from Spinoza's writings with particular care.

The chapter on Spinoza is followed by a second chapter on the rise of modern biblical hermeneutics. It treats another side never discussed in modern histories of biblical scholarship, namely John Locke's contribution to the *economics* of modern historical biblical scholarship. This chapter shows how modern fundamentalist scholarship and critical biblical scholarship act both as precursors and as sustainers of the modern bourgeois class with its twin aspirations: political democracy and laissez-faire capitalism.

I mentioned modern fundamentalism. Few scholars have noticed the tight link between modern fundamentalism's literal interpretation of the Bible and the antihierarchical, voluntary religious associations, consisting of equally authoritative individuals, that Locke thought churches should be. The chapter on Locke concludes by showing how his dictum that the Bible should be interpreted literally was picked up by Scottish theologians and taken to America, where it rooted in Protestant denominations like the Baptists, the Assemblies of God, and the Churches of Christ. These churches avoid various forms of hierarchical connection, some reject all creeds, and otherwise adhere to a strictly literal interpretation of the Bible, in order that no elite will ever rise again and regain control. As such, these fundamentalists are neither blind to reason (anyone who has ever heard them debate a point of doctrine or Church polity can see that they are rationalist to the core) nor oblivious to the virtues of modern science, democracy, and capitalism. In short, these denominations—regardless of all claims to being "strictly based on the New Testament"—are all *Enlightenment voluntary associations* which in principle eschew historical-critical hermeneutics for *political* reasons.

Part Two concludes with the breakdown and reorganization of the fourth component of the Third Form of the Synoptic Problem, the composition of the Gospels. After an early phase of widespread methodological exploration, a revolutionary new tool for comparing the Gospels was invented by J. J. Griesbach, called a Gospel *synopsis,* to distinguish it from the traditional Gospel *harmony.*

Griesbach's own solution—but not the synopsis concept—was eventually abandoned in favor of the Two Source Hypothesis. The chapter traces the evolution of this hypothesis among leading thinkers of Germany's new bourgeois class to its classic expression at the hands of Heinrich Julius Holtzmann. It then became the accepted hypothesis in the main German universities during the 1870s *Kulturkampf,* where it became another club with which German Protestant scholars could beat the Roman Catholic Church.

Toward the end of the nineteenth century, the Two Source Hypothesis leaped across the English Channel, where it was taken into William Sanday's Oxford Seminar on the Synoptic Problem. The fruit of the Seminar's lengthy investigation was Burnett Hillman Streeter's epoch-making book *The Four Gospels: A Study of Origins,* published in 1924, which set the stage for fifty years of source criticism in English-language scholarship.

This chapter also documents a major factor in the success of the Two Source Hypothesis. Scholars in both Germany and England inadvertently became entangled within a vicious cycle whereby the scholarly instruments used to examine the Gospels (the new synopses) were first created to illustrate the Two Source Hypothesis and then used to defend it.

Overview of Part Three

Part Three takes up the story in the post–World War II period and examines current trends and developments. It notes that, while the First Form of the Synoptic Problem—associated above all with Origen—has just about disappeared entirely, the Second Form—the Augustinian, as modified by the political philosophy of John Locke—is very active in modern Western fundamentalism. Armed with its talisman, the Gospel harmony, fundamentalists insist on a strictly literal harmonization of the differences among the Gospels.

Meanwhile, the Third Form continues to flourish and expand, as modern historical criticism—armed with *its* talisman, the Gospel synopsis—rises to ever new heights of complexity and historical detail.

Part Three does not attempt to discuss the current trends within each of the four components of the Third Form of the Synoptic Problem as completely as Parts One and Two. Instead, it focuses on a few significant illustrations of current trends and developments for each component part of each Form of the Synoptic Problem still active in the contemporary scene.

PART ONE

*The First to the Fifth Century:
Conflict and Consolidation*

CHAPTER I

Responses to Multiple, Differing Gospels in Early Christianity

Overview of Part One

During the first decades of the Christian movement, Gospels were produced and disseminated in response to the needs of the missionary expansion leadership. It was a bountiful, creative period, and Gospel narratives—without names or titles—flowered innocently and prolifically. Our first example, the preface to the Gospel of Luke, illustrates the spirit of the earliest period.

The abundance of differing accounts quickly exacerbated the tensions already roiling the loosely connected, far-flung religious movement. Our second example, the record of Papias' explanations of how Mark and Matthew were written, clearly reflects the tensions in this increasingly ominous situation. By the mid-second century, possibly as many as two dozen Gospels had been produced and were in circulation in different parts of the empire, causing serious friction and confusion.

Various stratagems had also emerged to cope with the dilemma of these many, differing Gospels. One was to produce a composite of several accounts and use that, especially when dealing with hostile outsiders who would instantly mock the Christians' confusion should they learn about it. The approach of Justin Martyr and his famous pupil Tatian is the most important example of this kind of harmonization.

Another emerging stratagem was a complete surgical strike: *cut off and throw away all but one, authoritative account.* This was the approach taken by Marcion of Sinope, and he had many followers. However, Marcion went much farther, jettisoning everything Jewish about the Christian religion as well—a sort of "ethnic cleansing" of Christianity.

Such fratricide within the Christian movement is a clear indication of just how dangerous the differences among the Gospels were. The biblical scholars were quite aware of them, however little they said to the laity. Origen of Caesarea, the most gifted and accomplished text critic of the early Church, spent considerable time attempting to deal with the differences among the Gospels while preserving the integrity of their composition process. As such, he was the first person to deal with all four parts of the Synoptic Problem in the history of the Church and thus becomes the model for all later treatments.

Toward the end of the second century, stung by Christian attacks on the Greek and Roman religious traditions, pagan philosophers began to counterattack. Central to their strategy was a ridiculing examination of the Scriptures of the Christians. The plethora of differing Gospels presented a fat target. At first little more than a side issue (Celsus), this feature of the Christian Scriptures soon attracted greater attention, until the differences among the many Gospels became the centerpiece of a frontal assault on the entire Christian religion conducted by the most dangerous critic of them all—the third-century Neoplatonic philosopher Porphyry.

Efforts at damage control by orthodox Christian theologians increased in proportion to the greater intensity and scope of the pagan philosophical critique. In this regard, the Emperor Constantine's Edict of Toleration (312) gave sufficient breathing space to Eusebius of Caesarea to publish four monumental treatises answering each of the main allegations of Porphyry.

One century later, Augustine of Hippo—goaded by the continued criticisms of his former Manichaean coreligionists—decided to provide an exhaustive explanation of *all* of the differences and discrepancies in the Gospels. Entitled *On the Harmony of the Evangelists,* Augustine's work provided such cogent justification for the differences among the Gospels that it remained the last word for a thousand years. He differed enough from both Origen and Eusebius that I find his harmonistic approach to be worth the title the Second Form of the Synoptic Problem.

CHAPTER 2

Luke's Preface

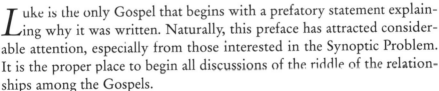

*L*uke is the only Gospel that begins with a prefatory statement explaining why it was written. Naturally, this preface has attracted considerable attention, especially from those interested in the Synoptic Problem. It is the proper place to begin all discussions of the riddle of the relationships among the Gospels.

If we consider Luke's preface from the perspective of the turmoil and anguish caused by the creation and circulation of multiple, differing Gospels over the first five hundred years, certain features stand out. I will give a translation that brings them out, followed by explanatory comments keyed to the numbers in < >. (The superscript numbers refer to notes at the end of the book.)

Since many have tried <1> to make narratives <2> about the events <3> which have taken place among us, it seemed appropriate for me (to make one also). And just as those who were the original eyewitnesses[1] guarded the accounts[2] <4> and passed them on <5> accurately to us, so also I— who have investigated <6a> everything accurately <6b> for a long time <6c>—will write a correctly ordered account <7> for you, My Excellent Theophilus <8>, so that you may know the truth concerning the things you've heard <9>.[3]

Comments

The general argument consists of two parallels, with the author at the receiving end of each one:

(a) "Many" have tried to create narratives so I will do the same. This is especially appropriate since they weren't as qualified, while I . . .

(b) like the authoritative cadre of eyewitnesses who personally saw everything from the beginning and who maintained the accuracy of the tradition they handed on "to us," so also I, who have for a long time accurately studied all these things, in contrast to "many," will write a narrative having the correct order, which you, Theophilus, can be certain is the truth.

<1> The word ἐπιχειρέω can have a positive connotation, but that is probably not the case here. If we look at its use elsewhere in Luke/Acts, we find two (more) negative uses:

> Acts 9:29: ". . . preaching boldly in the name of the Lord. And he spoke and disputed against the Hellenists; but they were *seeking* to kill him" (οἱ δὲ ἐπεχείρουν ἀνελεῖν αὐτόν) (RSV).
>
> Acts 19:13: "Then some of the itinerant Jewish exorcists *undertook* to pronounce the name of the Lord Jesus (ἐπεχείρησαν δέ τινες καὶ τῶν περιερχομένων Ἰουδαίων ἐξορκιστῶν ὀνομάζειν) over those who had evil spirits . . ." (RSV) with disastrous (i.e., comical) consequences.

In the LXX (the Greek Old Testament), the word mostly occurs in phrases describing attempts at evil, outrageous, or foolish objectives.[4] Origen interpreted this whole opening phrase negatively when he commented on the "many" heretics who had "taken in hand to write" heretical Gospels.[5]

<2> The word used to designate what "Luke" created was the widely used technical term διήγησις, signifying an artfully constructed historical narrative.

<3> The term here is the generic word πράγματα, the standard term for historical events or happenings.

<4> The reference to the "eyewitnesses and guardians of the record" uses technical terms that refer to a specific cadre of trained tradition-tradents whose professional responsibility was to preserve and hand on the authoritative tradition.[6] These were probably Apostles and/or their assistants (including relatives). Note the structure of the logic in this preface: (a) *since* many have already composed narratives about the Lord, *therefore* I can too. Why should *I* do it? Because (b) just as original eyewitnesses handed accurate tradition to "us," "so also it seemed appropriate

that I, who have made myself accurately informed of all things for some time past now," should write an "orderly account" for you, most Excellent Theophilus. The author has explained why he *should* do it and then why *he* should do it.

<5> "To hand on" παραδίδωμι was another widely used technical term signifying the handing on of normative tradition, in this case probably oral.

<6a> Another technical term: παρακολουθέω, "to investigate, trace something," implying direct investigation by the author.

<6b> "Accurately" ἀκριβῶς, another technical term widely used in such diverse fields as mathematics, philosophy, and historiography.

<6c> "For a long time" ἄνωθεν or "from the beginning."

<7> "To write (an) orderly (account) for you" καθεξῆς σοι γράψαι. The term translated "orderly" raises the question what kind of order? Is the writer thinking of *chronological* order or *narrative* order, i.e., having the proper sequence of events? The question of the *right order* will eventually plague every discussion of Gospel comparisons, as we will see in the next chapter.

<8> A real person, in this case "Theophilus," addressed by name in the preface as the recipient of a writing was a common feature in Hellenistic literature, continuing to the end of the eighteenth century. In our times we name a specific person on the dedication page.

<9> "... in order that you might know the truth . . ." ends the preface with an implied criticism of the rival narratives—another characteristic of Hellenistic prefaces. The author must explain, in view of the existence of other possibly well-known narratives, why his should be bothered with. "Mine is far more accurate" and "mine is both more complete and entertaining" were typical justifications.

Conclusion: The Age of Innocence

Every feature of this preface—the claims to greater accuracy, reliance on eyewitness testimony, the name of the intended recipient, and so on—can be found in prefaces throughout the literature of the Hellenistic-Roman period. Good examples include Arrian's preface to his *History of Alexander the Great* (early second century C.E.), Philo of Alexandria's preface to his *Life of Moses* (beginning of the first century C.E.), and Philostratus of Lemnos' *Life of Apollonios of Tyana* (early third century C.E.).[7]

If the preface does not reveal anything unique about the way the Gospel of Luke was created, recent study has demonstrated that the *diegesis* "Luke" created was not a unique kind of writing either.[8] This conclusion parallels the evidence that the *portrait* the author created within the Gospel presenting Jesus of Nazareth as the "savior of the world" was not a unique concept either: the familiar wandering philosopher/sage.[9]

In short, while some of the specific contents of the Gospel of Luke were unique, the author was not conscious of producing a unique kind of writing; "many" others had composed narratives about Jesus of Nazareth. If anything, his was going to be more orderly, accurate, and true. Such claims would be fiercely contested in later times.

One striking feature of this preface is what it does *not* say: its author makes no claim to having been instructed by the Holy Spirit to write this narrative nor mentions a divine omen to finish it[10] or a heavenly sign approving it, once completed, such as we find in the Gospel prefaces of the second and third centuries. There is a complete lack of any nimbus of glory around the creation of the Gospel of Luke, as far as the preface is concerned. Instead, this earliest explanation given by an author of a Gospel sounds surprisingly ordinary, describing the kinds of things Hellenistic writers in those days did (or at least claimed to do) when they composed laudatory historical narratives about famous sages or generals or statesmen for a discriminating and educated audience. There is a confident assurance that "Theophilus" will be pleased with the new narrative.

The innocence of this aspiration is what one might expect at this early date. It will fall to later generations to deal with the problems caused by the early confident assurance that each new narrative or collection of sayings was going to be helpful, given the spectrum of cultural audiences to whom the Gospel was preached. The "many" quickly grew and expanded into *dozens* of Gospels, causing the Christian movement a monumental headache and presenting its enemies with a huge and tempting target.

Looking back from the vantage point of two thousand years of history, it is ironic that the only Gospel preface that gives any information at all about matters of composition and authorial intention begins by revealing the potentially ominous existence of "many" other narratives already in circulation.[11] Equally ironic is the fact that the author is not daunted in the least by this fact. The "many" others are treated by the author of Luke as justification for adding one more because his will be written in the correct narrative order.

Part One describes some of the repercussions of the flowering of Gospels, identifies the dilemmas caused by the superabundance of differing narratives about Jesus Christ. It examines the massive efforts at "damage control" by later bishops and theologians as they fought to separate the original apostolic Gospels from all later Gospels and, once they found themselves saddled with *four* apostolic narratives, attempted to demonstrate their integrity and overarching harmony in spite of all evidence to the contrary.

We will see in the next chapter that the existence of "many" narratives exacerbated an already existing conflict, not between Christians and Jews or non-Christians, but between two powerful factions within the early Christian leadership—specifically between the Apostle John and the Apostle Peter.

Papias of Hierapolis Reports the Apostle John's Criticism of Peter's Gospel (Mark)

The oldest surviving comments on how the Gospels were produced—outside of the Gospels themselves—come from an obscure early-second-century Church leader named Papias, bishop of Hierapolis in Asia. Nothing of his writings have survived except a few brief quotations by Eusebius in his *Ecclesiastical History.* These quotations have attracted scholarly comment for centuries, since they are most puzzling.

What do we know about the man? Very little. Papias (ca. 75–140) was a bishop of Hierapolis, a Greek city in eastern Asia Minor. Hierapolis was one of a number of Christian communities that looked to Ephesus as their center. The Revelation of John 1–2 mentions seven of these communities, including Ephesus, Smyrna, Pergamum, Thyatira, Sardis, Philadelphia, and Laodicea. In Papias' day, Hierapolis was the home base for a famous Christian preacher named Quadratus and two elderly daughters of a first-generation Christian evangelist named Philip, women who were revered for their prophetic gifts.[1]

Papias belonged to the third Christian generation. He was taught the Christian tradition mainly by those who were followers of Jesus' disciples. However, according to Irenaeus (ca. 115–ca. 200), the Bishop of Lugdunum in Gaul and a native of Asia Minor, Papias was a "hearer" of an unusually long-lived disciple of Jesus named John, the son of Zebedee, who spent his last years in Ephesus after the destruction of Jerusalem in 70.[2]

Papias said that he loved to listen to the stories of those who personally knew the disciples of the Lord, preferring their oral accounts to anything he had in writing. Note that Papias used the term "the Elders" to designate Jesus' disciples.

> "I shall not hesitate also to put down for you ... whatsoever things I have at any time carefully learned from the Elders and carefully remembered, guaranteeing their truth. For I did not, like the multitude, take pleasure in those that speak much, but in those that teach the truth ... If, then, any one came (to Hierapolis) who had been a follower of the Elders, I questioned him in regard to the words (i.e., teachings) of the Elders—what Andrew or what Peter said, or what was said by Philip, or by Thomas, or by James, or by John, or by Matthew, or by any other of the Disciples of the Lord ... For I did not think that what was to be gotten from the books would profit me as much as what came from the living and abiding voice."[3]

What did Papias do with the stories he heard? Eusebius reports that Papias wrote a treatise called *Interpretations of the Lord's Oracles.* I suggest that the "books" Papias refers to in the quotation were ones written by the disciples, such as the Gospels, and that his *Interpretations* consisted in elaborating these books with the oral traditions he obtained from the followers of the disciples.

Unfortunately, nothing of Papias' *Interpretations of the Lord's Oracles* has survived except some quotations in Eusebius' *Ecclesiastical History.* These include two priceless statements describing the creation of the Gospels of Matthew and Mark. They are the oldest surviving explanations of any kind on how the Gospels of Matthew and Mark were produced. Both are surprising in what they say and don't say.

Papias' Statement About the Gospel According to Mark

Papias' explanation of how the Gospel of Mark was produced is curiously defensive. The source of the information quoted by Papias is someone he simply calls "the Elder." (This is my own translation; explanations of contested renderings are in the footnotes. Words in ( ) have been added by me to clarify the meaning.)

> This also the Elder used to say:[4] since Mark became the interpreter of Peter,[5] he wrote accurately though not indeed in order whatever he (Peter) remembered of what was said or done by the Lord. For he (Mark) neither heard the Lord nor followed him, but afterwards, as I

said, (heard and followed) Peter, who made his teachings fit the needs of the moment, but not as if he (Peter) were making[6] a connected account of the Lord's oracles,[7] so that Mark did not sin when he wrote thus some things as he (Peter) remembered.[8] For he (Mark) was careful of one thing, to leave out none of the things that he heard (Peter say), nor to falsify any of them. These things are related by Papias concerning Mark.[9]

There are a number of remarkable features in this account. Note the complete lack of any glorifying or miraculous elements here, just as we saw in the last chapter with Luke's preface. Not only are all hagiographic features missing, but "the Elder" makes a number of surprisingly derogatory statements about his fellow disciple, Simon Peter. Let us identify some of them.

The first thing "the Elder" does is to exonerate Mark of all responsibility for the contents of his Gospel. Mark, he says, had no firsthand knowledge of what he wrote, since he had never personally heard the Lord Jesus nor followed him; he just copied whatever Peter said. So if any faults exist in the Gospel, they are not Mark's responsibility.

Then come the criticisms. First "the Elder" says that, although the stories Mark wrote were accurate (in some sense), they were not written "in (the proper) order." I wish to postpone for a moment the question of what "the Elder" is comparing Mark's Gospel to, so that it seems "out of order." "The Elder" goes on to explain, with a curious phrase, that the lack of correct order in Mark's Gospel was not his fault but was caused by the disciple Peter who, in McGiffert's translation, "adapted his teachings to the needs of his hearers." The Greek here is terse: πρὸς τὰς χρείας ἐποιεῖτο τὰς διδασκαλίας. A more literal translation might be "Peter used to give his teachings as demanded by necessity" (Koester), or "off the cuff."[10] The phrase πρὸς τὰς χρείας conveys a slightly negative connotation of want or need.[11] On this reading, Peter told of the sayings and doings of the Lord *as the occasion demanded,* not systematically, not in order, following no chronological plan, and *not complete.*[12]

This leads "the Elder" to add that "Mark did nothing wrong" (Koester translating ἁμαρτάω) because he wrote down only *"some of"* (ἔνια) the Lord's sayings and doings as they were remembered by Peter. The implication is that some people thought Mark had sinned for not having written a complete account. "The Elder" exonerates Mark: "Mark made one thing his concern, to not leave out anything he heard (Peter say) nor to *lie about, falsify* (ψεύσασθαι) anything he heard (from him)." Here is an additional objection: some people said that Mark's Gospel contained falsehoods, lies. "The Elder" distances Mark from Peter: "Don't accuse

Mark of wrongdoing. Mark was just the interpreter of Peter and faithfully copied down whatever Peter said. *He* didn't falsify or omit anything."

Reflections on the Papias Tradition Regarding the Gospel of Mark

If what "the Elder" said was meant to be a defense of the Gospel of Mark, it is a most peculiar one. On the one hand, "the Elder" seemed concerned to shield Mark from certain grave accusations regarding his Gospel—without denying any of them—while shifting the blame squarely onto Peter. Peter was responsible for the flaws in the Gospel of Mark by his lack of organization, since he impulsively spoke according to the needs of the moment. It was Peter's fault that the Gospel of Mark seems disorganized, truncated, and riddled with falsehoods.

Before we ask why "the Elder" would say these things about Peter, let us pause for a moment and ask, Do these accusations regarding Peter sound familiar? Have we encountered them elsewhere?

Let us recall the picture of the Apostle Peter as given by the Apostle Paul in the second chapter of his letter to the Galatians:

> But when Cephas (Peter) came to Antioch I opposed him to his face because he was manifestly in the wrong. Before certain people came (to Antioch) from James (the Lord's brother living in Jerusalem), he ate regularly with the Gentile (Christians). But as soon as they showed up he quit and kept himself apart from them, out of fear (of what they would tell James) . . . Even Barnabas was carried away by . . . (the same kind of) insincerity![13]

Are these not the same accusations: impulsiveness (inconstancy) and insincerity (lying)? And now we find "the Elder" accusing Peter of similar behavior when it came to producing a written account of the Lord's sayings and actions through his interpreter Mark.

Who exactly was "the Elder"?

We noted earlier that Irenaeus, a native of the same part of Asia as Papias, said that Papias was personally acquainted with, "a hearer of," the aged disciple of Jesus, John the son of Zebedee. In Papias' description of his meetings with the *followers* of the Lord's disciples, he refers to the latter as "the Elders." However, in the quote regarding the Gospel of Mark, he simply mentions "*the* Elder." Which disciple was it?

From the context in Eusebius' *Ecclesiastical History* where this quote occurs, it is clear that this "Elder" was John, the traditional author of the Gospel named after him. So we may translate: "This is what the Elder

John used to say about the Gospel of Mark."[14] Why would John say these negative things about *Peter* as the one who was responsible for the Gospel of Mark? Was there some sort of hostility or rivalry between these two disciples of Jesus?

This question is exceedingly difficult to answer. However, there is some evidence within the Gospels themselves. It is well known that Peter's brashness, impulsiveness, and betrayal of Jesus are repeatedly mentioned in all of the Gospels. Less well known is the evidence about the Apostle John's negative side. For example, there are the two little vignettes in Luke where John's exclusiveness and vengeful nature are described. In Luke 9:49f., the text explicitly identifies John as the one who stopped an outsider from healing in Jesus' name (even though he and the other disciples had just failed to do the same thing) because he "was not in their company." Immediately after this, Luke 9:54f. relates that John and James angrily ask Jesus to bring down fire from heaven on some Samaritan villagers who would not welcome them, causing Jesus to rebuke John twice in quick succession.

More could be said about the portrait of John and Peter in the Synoptic Gospels, but it is the Gospel of John that contains the most striking evidence of friction between John and Peter. If John was the "author" of this Gospel, he has portrayed himself as "the beloved disciple," the one to whom the Lord gives his most direct teachings, the one who "lay upon the Lord's breast" at the Last Supper, the one who instead of fleeing like the rest of the disciples is present with Jesus at his crucifixion and therefore is the one disciple to whom the Lord, with his dying breath, can entrust his own mother, in effect making John a member of Jesus' own family.

Peter, in contrast, is shown in the Gospel of John to be impulsive, fickle, uncomprehending, cowardly, and traitorous, on the level of or even below Judas Iscariot. He misunderstands Jesus (e.g., the foot washing); he denies he ever knew him at the trial; he races John to the tomb but comes in second; once both are inside, Peter just looks around and nothing happens while John looks around, sees the empty place where Jesus lay, "and believed." The list could be considerably extended, but this gives some idea of the sharp contrast between the portraits of Peter and John in the Gospel of John.[15]

Why would the author of the Gospel of John want to say such negative things about the Apostle Peter? I know of no in-depth discussion of this question. It looks as if John wanted to set the record straight in his Gospel regarding Peter's deplorable behavior during the ministry of Jesus and, later, in his teaching in Ephesus, to set the record straight again regarding the shortcomings of Peter's account of the Lord (out of order,[16] truncated, false), in the narrative known as the Gospel according to Mark.

If these conjectures have any validity, they provide a striking glimpse into the tension between two of the most prominent Apostles within the first generation of the Christian movement. However, we cannot stop here. This hostile portrait of Peter in the Gospel of John is so pronounced it should have left an impact somewhere. But where?

A Ban of Silence on the Gospel of John?

There is a long-standing riddle in the field of Gospel studies: Why did it take so long for the Gospel of John to become accepted and used in Rome as well as Asia Minor, the place where most scholars agree that it was written?[17] One way to approach this riddle is to ask: Why are there *no quotations* from the Gospel of John in any writings coming from Asia Minor before the middle of the second century?[18] There are many quotations from the other Gospels in these same writings, but none from the Gospel of John.

This lack of quotations is particularly striking in the case of Polycarp, the early-second-century Bishop of Smyrna, a day's walk up the coast from Ephesus, where John spent his last years. Tradition is definite that Polycarp was a personal "hearer" of the Apostle John. Yet in his famous *Epistle to the Philippians,* Polycarp does not quote a single word from the Gospel of John, despite the fact that his letter is a carefully constructed mosaic of quotations, allusions, and echoes of numerous Christian writings: the Gospels of Matthew, Mark, and Luke/Acts, nearly all of the epistles of Paul, the Pastoral Epistles, and many epistles of Ignatius. He also quotes or alludes to passages from such Old Testament books as Isaiah, Jeremiah, Ezekiel, Psalms, Proverbs, and Tobit. His favorite sources were 1 Clement (nineteen quotations from all parts) and 1 Peter (thirteen quotations from every chapter). In short, his letter is a compendium of the favorite writings of the orthodox Church in Asia. Nevertheless, there is not one word from the Gospel according to John, despite the fact that Polycarp can weave in *two unmistakable allusions to John's letters.*[19]

Another early writer from whom references or quotations to the Gospel of John are completely missing is the early-second-century father Ignatius, third Bishop of Antioch.[20] It is barely conceivable that he had never heard of the Gospel.

The situation in Rome is different. Neither 1 Clement nor Justin Martyr reveals any knowledge of it, although each writer uses quotations from other Gospels, as well as the Old Testament.[21] But there is evidence that Bishop Caius of Rome and others *knew* of both the Gospel and Revelation of John and *refused to accept them.* In other words, the situation in Rome was not ignorance of the Gospel of John but a *ban of silence* on it. In view of the Roman Church's proud claim to be the location of Peter's martyrdom, any use of the Gospel of John—given its negative portrait of the Apostle Peter—might have been difficult.

There may have been other reasons as well. Epiphanius reports that the "alogoi" (those who rejected both the Gospel of John and the Revelation of John) took offense at the *narrative inconsistencies* between John and the Synoptic Gospels. The following quotation is typical of the criticisms they made:

> (These alogoi), not understanding the meaning of the gospels, say: How is it that the other evangelists say that Jesus fled from Herod's face to Egypt and after his flight came and stayed in Nazareth, and then having received baptism went off into the desert, and after that returned and after returning began to preach while the Gospel in John's name lies? For after saying that the Word became flesh and dwelt among us and a few other things, it immediately says that a wedding took place at Cana of Galilee . . .[22]

Epiphanius also mentions a major chronological contradiction between John and the Synoptics:

> These same people find further fault with the holy evangelist or rather with his gospel, saying: "John says that the Savior kept two Passovers in a period of two years, whereas the other evangelists speak of one Passover."[23]

It will not suffice to argue that the Gospel of John was not written until after Polycarp and Papias and other third-generation Christian leaders in Asia had died. The discovery of early-second-century fragments of the Gospel of John in Egypt, such as Pap. 52, rules this out.

Another flaw in this argument is that it assumes that these orthodox leaders would have quoted it if they had known of it because they would have had the same profound respect for the Gospel of John that we do. This assumption is probably unfounded. Polycarp and the others probably knew of the Gospel of John *and avoided using it.* At least in Polycarp's case, judging from his strong preference for the Petrine tradition, as evidenced by his repeated quotations of 1 Peter, he might well have been so offended at the portrayal of Peter in the Gospel of John that he chose not to use it. We know of others who were opposed to the Gospel of John.[24]

This concludes our analysis of Papias' statements about the Gospel of Mark. We have discovered a deep and pervasive pattern of antagonism between John and Peter (more precisely, John toward Peter), their respective followers, and the Gospels later given in their names. In view of the powerful role the Roman clergy later played in the canonization process, it is not too much to say that if they had had their way, the New Testament might not have contained any of the writings of the Apostle John!

With this we take leave of the earliest known explanation of the creation of the Gospel of Mark. Let us now examine Papias' other tradition, namely, how the Gospel according to Matthew came into being.

Papias' Statement on the Gospel of Matthew

Such then is the account given by Papias concerning Mark, but concerning Matthew the following was said (by him): "So then Matthew composed the oracles (λόγια) in the Hebrew language (Ἑβραΐδι διαλέκτῳ), and each one interpreted (ἡρμήνευσεν) them as he could."[25]

It is probable that Papias meant by "Matthew" what we today know as the canonical Gospel according to Matthew. The very fact that he passes on the information that "Matthew" was originally composed in "Hebrew" suggests that the Gospel of Matthew *he* knew was not written in Hebrew but in *Greek*.[26]

It should be noted that the word διαλέκτος, which gives us the English word "dialect," does not necessarily mean "language." It can also be translated "way of speaking" or "mode of expression."[27] In this sense, Papias' statement would be translated "Matthew composed the (Lord's) oracles *in a Hebrew mode of expression.*"[28] This would make sense, since the Gospel according to Matthew focuses on issues concerning the Torah of Moses, uses obscure Hebrew phrases without explanation, contains important but typically Hebrew ideas (like "Son of Man," "Day of Judgment"), and so on.

The trouble with that translation is that it doesn't fit with what Papias says next: "and each person ἡρμήνευσεν as he was able." The verb used here can also be translated in at least two ways: "translate" or "interpret." The person who translates someone's statements into another language is called an interpreter. If we take it in the sense mentioned above, the meaning would be something like this: "Matthew composed the oracles *in the Hebrew mode of expression* and each translated—*into his own mode of expression*—as well as he could." There is nothing inherently wrong with this translation; it just is probably not what Papias meant. He probably meant that Matthew was composed in the Hebrew *language* and "each" *translated* it as well as he could into his own language: Greek, Latin, Syriac, and so on.

Who "each" refers to here is completely unknown. Each of the other disciples of Jesus? Each of the traveling evangelists (like Paul) who needed the story of Jesus Christ in other languages? The open-endedness of this term is reminiscent of the "many" in Luke's preface: "since *many* have undertaken to compile a narrative . . ." (NRSV). Here again, we have no idea whom Papias meant by "each."

The vagueness of the rest of the statement, "each translated *as well as he could*," while refreshingly candid, suggests that some translations were better than others. Which ones were better and which were worse? We cannot answer this question, either. All we can say is that there appear to have been numerous Syriac, Latin, and Greek versions or portions of "Matthew" (Hebrew or not) circulating under other titles (or with no title at all).[29]

There has been an enormous discussion of Papias' use of the term λόγια to designate the Gospel of Matthew. This word should not be confused with λόγοι "words, sayings." A λόγιον was a technical term that was used of the supernatural prophecies of a divinity, such as the *oracles* given by Apollo at Delphi.[30] It could be used generically to refer to supernatural sayings of all kinds.[31] Hence it probably should not be translated by "sayings"[32] but by "oracles." This is no light matter, since the meaning shifts considerably depending on which translation is adopted. If Papias meant to say, "Matthew composed (the Lord's) *sayings* in the Hebrew language and each translated them as he was able," then we would tend to think of a collection of Jesus' teachings (like the Sermon on the Mount; Mt 5–7). But if Papias meant "Matthew composed the Lord's *oracles*," then a more heterogeneous text could be meant, because "oracles . . . may be used to describe a work containing a narrative of events." In this case, he could have been thinking of the whole Gospel of Matthew.[33]

In either case, we are confronted with the question: Where is this original "Hebrew" Matthew? No trace of such a writing has survived; no Hebrew fragments found in caves along the Dead Sea, no mention by scholars of the second century (such as Origen) or fourth century (such as Jerome) saying that they had seen copies of the original Hebrew Matthew, nothing—apart from this one statement of Papias. The absence of any other solid evidence for an original Hebrew Matthew is so complete that some modern scholars conclude that this report of Papias must be erroneous.[34]

Conclusion

This brings to a close our discussion of the earliest second-century explanations of the way the Gospels of Mark and Matthew were created. They are maddeningly brief and elliptical. For this reason, I have no confidence that I have rightly understood them.

If I may return to a point I made earlier, it is striking to observe what is *not* said by Papias. There is no nimbus of glory surrounding the creation of the Gospels of Mark or Matthew in Papias' reports—as was also the case with Luke's preface. This will change as time goes by. But here, at the very beginning, the actions reported in these terse statements seem surprisingly mundane. Two or three disciples or their immediate assistants, under various circumstances, composed historical narratives that described the life and teachings of Jesus Christ. Some were frankly better at the task than others, but there seems to have been no unwillingness to try. This soon produced a situation where the many different Gospels led to a dangerous situation of confusion and polarization. As we will see in the next chapter, some attempted to paper over the differences by producing composite narratives or harmonies. Others, such as Marcion, reacted by seizing upon one Gospel and making it the lone standard narrative.

CHAPTER 4

Justin Martyr Uses a Gospel Harmony; Tatian's Diatessaron

A s new Gospel narratives appeared toward the end of the first century and continued to multiply during the second, all designed in one way or another to be "more accurate" or "more true," a new problem emerged: their details rarely matched up. In most cases, the differences were enormous, causing an immediate dilemma. Which ones should be used? They couldn't all be equally accurate and true!

One answer suggested itself immediately: create composite narratives built up out of the details of two or more earlier, differing Gospels. Sometimes called a "harmony," this was the solution of Justin Martyr, a prominent Syrian philosopher-theologian to be discussed in this chapter. His student Tatian, however, carried his teacher's approach one step further and created a classic of the genre, the *Diatessaron*. To see why these experiments were first undertaken, I will give a little background.

Justin—Champion of the "Barbarian Philosophy"

Around the middle of the second century, an "Assyrian" philosopher named Tatian appeared in Rome and attached himself to a small group of students gathered around a Christian teacher, also originally from Syria/Palestine, who called himself "Justin the philosopher." Who was this Justin?

In one of his writings, Justin described his native land and family.[1]

He said that he was a native of the city of Flavia Neapolis in Palestine (modern Nablus) and that his father was Priscus and his grandfather Bacchius. From this brief sentence, we may deduce certain additional information. The city of Justin's birth was the ancient Hebrew city of Shechem in the region of Samaria, just north of Judea. It had been destroyed during the Jewish revolt of 66–70 C.E. by Vespasian's Roman legions and then reestablished and renamed Flavia Neapolis, "the New City of Flavia," in honor of then Emperor Vespasian's clan name, Flavia. At this same time, the region, which had been called Samaria, was officially renamed Syria Palestina.

From the Greek names of his father and grandfather and from the good Greek education Justin must have received (to judge from his later writings), we can deduce that he belonged to one of the wealthier families of the new city. His father may have been among the new Greek or Syrian settlers brought in to repopulate the city after its destruction by the Romans.[2] It is obvious that Justin never had to work for a living but was able to indulge his quest for truth, i.e., live the life then fashionable among those who saw themselves as *philosophers*, "lovers of wisdom." So Justin traveled around to the great cities of Asia and Greece looking for opportunities to converse with other "lovers of wisdom." He stayed in Ephesus for a period of years and visited Athens, before he inevitably came to Rome, where he remained from approximately 155 until his death in 165.

Somewhere along the way, he does not say where but it may well have been in Ephesus, Justin became a Christian. He describes this conversion in idealized terms,[3] saying that after spending years studying the doctrines of the Platonists and the Pythagoreans and the other currently popular "schools of thought," one day he was wandering alone, out "in a certain field, not far from the sea" (he does not say where), wondering what he should do, when he unexpectedly met a mysterious, kindly "old man," who entered into a long philosophical discussion with him about God. Eventually, says Justin, the old man kindled in him "a love of the prophets and of those men who are friends of Christ."[4] Thus Justin describes his conversion to Christianity. Put differently, Justin found a way to combine his love of Greek "philosophy" with the desire, deeply rooted in his native Syrian culture, to experience salvation personally.[5]

Having become a Christian, or, as he put it, an adherent of the "barbarian philosophy," by which he meant *non-Greek* philosophy, Justin came to Rome and began debating adherents of the other philosophies, including representatives from other Christian schools of thought. Who might some of these persons have been that Justin encountered in mid-second-century Rome?

Among the Romans, the reputation of the famous Stoic philosopher

Musonius Rufus (ca. 30–101 C.E.) still resonated among all schools, regardless of orientation. He had taught in Rome in the previous century, and his equally renowned pupil Epictetus had continued teaching after him until he was banished by the mad Emperor Domitian only a few decades before Justin got to Rome.[6] Both had earned reputations for complete fearlessness. This was no small achievement because then, as now, Rome was a strikingly contentious city. In the course of his own public and private debates, Justin tells us that he got into such violent arguments with the Roman philosophers that one in particular, a certain Crescens (Lat. Criscus), about whom we otherwise know nothing, sought to have him killed. As he wrote at the time, "I expect to be plotted against (by him) and (burned) at the stake."[7]

As it turned out, this is exactly what happened. Crescens had friends in high places and, not many years later, was able to persuade a Roman prefect to carry out Justin's execution on the grounds that he was a Christian. Nor was Crescens the only pagan philosopher to be mightily offended by Justin. The Platonist philosopher Celsus may well have been so provoked by Justin's attacks that he wrote the first refutation of Christianity.[8]

Moreover, Justin did not hesitate to take on the other Christian philosophers of his time. Such figures as Valentinus,[9] Saturninus of Antioch,[10] Basilides,[11] and Marcion[12] were all there in Rome during Justin's day, teaching their various doctrines and pitting their interpretations of Christianity against one another.[13] Justin battled each one of them with the same conviction that he had the pagan philosophers, defending what he understood to be the genuine, apostolic tradition as represented by such predecessors as Polycarp—who may have briefly visited Rome while Justin was there[14]—and Ignatius of Antioch.

The year of Justin's death is well documented.[15] Eusebius says that Justin was executed because of the philosopher Crescens, who apparently gained the ear of the Emperor Antoninus Pius (ruled 138–161), the same emperor to whom Justin had directed his still extant defense of Christianity known today as the *First Apology*.[16] But Antoninus Pius died before the sentence could be carried out, and the trial and execution occurred early in the reign of another emperor even more ruthless toward the Christians, Marcus Aurelius (161–180), probably in the year 165.[17]

Justin Pins a New Label on the Gospels

What kind of writing did Justin think the Gospels were? Did he think they fit into any well-known categories? Apparently so, since he regularly used a well-known label when he referred to the Gospels, calling them the *memoirs* written by Jesus' disciples.

For example, near the end of the *First Apology,* which he dedicated to the Emperor Antoninus Pius, Justin describes a Christian worship service (it is one of the earliest such descriptions we have), in order to convince the emperor that the services were not—contrary to popular opinion—occasions for hatching plots to overthrow the government. In the midst of this explanation, Justin comes to the part of the service where the worship leader is supposed to read something from the Christian Gospels, and this is how Justin describes them:

> ... And on the day called Sunday, there is a meeting in a certain place of those who live (nearby) in cities or the country, and the *memoirs of the apostles* and the writings of the prophets are read as long as time permits. When the reader is finished, the man presiding urges and invites us in a sermon to imitate the noble things (described in them) ... For the apostles, in the *memoirs* composed by them which are called Gospels, handed down (to us) what was commanded of them (by the Lord Jesus) ...[18]

This designation of the Gospels as the "memoirs of the apostles" was not accidental; Justin used the same term in other writings also. It was his preferred way of identifying the Gospels of Matthew, Mark, and Luke—at least in his writings intended for interested or hostile outsiders.[19]

Why did he choose the term *memoirs?* The answer is not hard to find. Among the philosophers with whom he did battle were those who held the Platonic tradition in high esteem. Central to it was the immensely popular image of Socrates, who had left nothing in writing. However, his disciples, chiefly Plato and Xenophon, had supposedly recorded their master's words for posterity. Xenophon's *Memoirs of Socrates* was well known, while Plato's "Socratic dialogues" were internationally famous.[20]

In addition, he may have encountered philosophers belonging to the Pythagorean tradition, among whom the "memoir" was a special type of writing believed to contain the authentic doctrines of the Master.[21] Justin undoubtedly knew of the *Pythagorean Memoirs* circulated by the prominent historian Alexander Polyhistor around the middle of the first century C.E. in Rome.[22] Regarding these disciples' memoirs, the learned third-century Syrian philosopher Iamblichus wrote in his *Life of Pythagoras:*

> On (the topic of Pythagoras' own) wisdom, to state it briefly, let there stand as the greatest testimony *the memoirs written down by the Pythagoreans,* since they contain the truth about all things. In comparison

with all other statements, they are outstanding for being succinct and redolent of the ancient and venerable style of transcendent elegance (since they have been) compiled with (his) unutterably inspired wisdom.[23]

Other memoirs known in Justin's time were the *Memoirs* of Diodorus Siculus (ca. 30 B.C.E.)[24] and the *Memoirs of the Sayings of Famous Men* collected by Dioscurides (ca. 10 C.E.).[25] A contemporary of Justin's in Rome, the court philosopher Favorinus of Arelate (Arles), known personally to the Emperor Antoninus Pius and possibly a "debate partner" of Justin's, published his own *Memoirs* about the time Justin was in Rome.[26]

In short, this type of writing was both common and well respected in Justin's time, evoking the familiar tableau of the sage old philosopher surrounded by loyal disciples who drank in every word and later faithfully recorded their "memoirs" extolling the master's wisdom and giving verbatim examples of it. This is precisely what occurred in the well-known case of the first-century C.E. Stoic philosopher Epictetus. It could be the image Justin wanted to evoke in his readers' minds by using this label for the homely and personal writings by Jesus' disciples containing his most memorable sayings and acts.

In other words, Justin's choice of this term probably reflects his desire to give the Christian Gospels a kind of philosophically respectable aura, so that he could appeal to them without fear of ridicule as he pursued his professional career in the pagan-Christian-Jewish debate over God, the world, morals, and so forth. In this freewheeling debate, the designation "memoirs of the apostles of Christ" would have had an immediate and desirable recognition value that Justin needed. If he can tell the emperor that

> Christ is the first-begotten of God ... the Divine Reason (*logos*) of which every race of man partakes. All those who have lived in accordance with the Divine Reason are Christians ... such as, among the Greeks, Socrates and Heracleitus and others like them; among the barbarians (= the Jews), Abraham, Ananiah, Azariah and Mishael,[27] and Elijah, and many others,[28]

then it is obvious that, at one level at least, in his attempt to enculturate the Gospel, Justin did not draw a sharp line among Christian, Jew, and Greek. From this inclusive perspective, to be able to refer to the Christian Gospels of Matthew, Mark, and Luke under the label "memoirs of the apostles" would have communicated precisely what Justin wanted to his audience. For one thing, it lent an air of eyewitness immediacy and validity to the Gospels that was considered to be extremely valuable. In fact, in one of his published debates Justin went out of his way to stress precisely this feature: "(These are) memoirs which I say were composed by his (Jesus') apostles and those who followed them."[29] And he pointed to the preface to Luke's Gospel as proof.[30] A century later, the famed Alexandrian Christian philosopher Origen did precisely the same thing. Writing against Celsus' claim that Jesus could not foretell the future, he asks,

> is it conceivable that Jesus' own pupils and hearers handed down the teaching of the gospels without writing it down and that they left their own disciples without their reminiscences (ὑπομνήματα) of (Jesus' predictions of the destruction of Jerusalem) in writing?[31]

There may also be another reason behind Justin's choice of label. He may have learned, while he was living in Ephesus before coming to Rome, the same tradition that his earlier contemporary Papias got from the Apostle John, namely, that Mark the interpreter of the Apostle Peter wrote down in the Gospel bearing his name *what he remembered Peter saying during his final sermons in Rome.*[32] This kind of thing was precisely what disciples did, and this tradition alone could have provided Justin with sufficient warrant to refer to these Gospels as "memoirs of the apostles and those who followed them."

Justin's Disciple Tatian

Not long after Justin arrived in Rome and began teaching and debating, a young philosopher named Tatian (ca. 110–185), also a native of the East—probably Syria—joined his "school." Tatian may have been drawn to Justin at first because of their similar Middle Eastern origins. But Tatian says he was attracted to Justin's exposition of the message of the Hebrew prophets.[33] We can see from his own writings that he would have been quite at home with Justin's currently fashionable method of allegorical interpretation of the sacred books of the Jews.[34] Finally, Justin's blend of popular Neoplatonic metaphysics, Stoic/Epicurean ethics, and orthodox Christian theology would have proved a fascinating challenge to this budding philosopher. So Tatian became a Christian; or, rather, he adopted this "barbarian philosophy" as the basis for attacking the more traditional Greek philosophies. In Tatian's own words,

> I was persuaded by these barbarian writings (the LXX = Greek Old Testament) because of their lack of arrogance, the artlessness of the

speakers, the easily intelligible account of the creation of the universe, etc., etc.[35]

It must have been an exciting time for Tatian to live in "the great city," arguing and debating with the leading philosophical lights of his age. Justin must have seemed to him a brave and skillful teacher, the way he courageously took on the more powerful philosophers in Rome. But then disaster struck. Justin and a few others were arrested, examined, and executed, for no more reason than that they were Christians. Later Christian historians identified the Roman philosopher Crescens as the person responsible for Justin's execution. This is certainly the view of Tatian. But we also learn from Tatian that there was more to the situation; *Tatian's own name was also on the hit list.* In his *Oration to the Greeks,* where he ridicules Greek philosophers' so-called courage, he says:

> You say that you despise death and practice self-sufficiency? Ha! You are so far from that practice that some of you take 600 gold coins a year from the Roman emperor for no useful purpose but to be paid for letting your beards grow long. Crescens, at any rate, who built his nest in the great city, surpassed all others in his passion for boys and addiction to money. He who (said he) despised death was so afraid (of us) that he conspired to cause the death, not only of Justin, *but me too.*[36]

How did Tatian escape? We do not know. All we do know is that Tatian abruptly left Rome around the time Justin was executed and fled to Palestine.

Assuming the general accuracy of this reconstruction of events, what would have been the feelings in Tatian's heart at this time? Would he have been filled with rage at the philosophers who were the pets of the Emperors Antoninus Pius and his "son" Marcus Aurelius, those who were responsible for Justin's death? Would he have been disgusted by this group's ostentatious affection of the old-fashioned Attic Greek and their bland harping on tired philosophical clichés? Would he have harbored any feelings of guilt that he did not do more to help his master avoid execution? Or, which is more likely, did he feel intense shame that he too did not suffer death for the Lord Jesus?[37] We cannot answer questions like these, but this much we can say: Tatian poured out his feelings not much later in a writing that we still have—the *Oration to the Greeks.* I think it may give us a glimpse of his feelings at this time, for I see it as his rage-filled, grieving defense of himself and his revered master, Justin.[38]

Scholars have long noted that Tatian's *Oration* is a very angry writing. Where Justin was irenic, Tatian burns the bridges and heaps unremitting abuse on all "Greeks." In place of Justin's "come and see" attitude, Tatian brandishes his "barbarian philosophy" defiantly at the "Greeks," daring them to come and get him. Why is this? Perhaps we can find a clue in the way he ends the *Oration:*

> All these (points in my oration) I have composed for you, O men of Greece. (Behold, I am) Tatian, philosophizing in the barbarian way.[39] (I was) born in the country of the Assyrians and educated first in your ways and secondly in what I now profess to proclaim to you. As for the rest, knowing who God is and what is his creation, I offer myself to you, prepared for an examination of doctrines, while I remain entirely unwilling to renounce living according to God's way![40]

Who wanted Tatian to renounce living according to his barbarian philosophy? Could it be that this was precisely the demand addressed to *Justin,* which he bravely refused, thereby hastening his execution? Did Tatian know that exactly the same demand would have been addressed to him if he had been captured? Whatever the answer to these questions may be, it is certainly no accident that Tatian's *Oration to the Greeks* ends with this defiant refusal.

Later, the Church Father Irenaeus wrote that after Tatian left Rome, he became the founder of a heretical sect called the Encratites (from *encrateia,* Greek for "self-control"). This view has passed down through the centuries and can now be found in all our textbooks as the conventional wisdom regarding Tatian—that after Justin died, Tatian went crazy theologically and became a heretic. This is Irenaeus' sarcastic description of what happened to Tatian:

> (Tatian) was a disciple of Justin's, and as long as he continued with him, he expressed no (heretical) views. But after Justin's martyrdom, Tatian separated from the (orthodox) Church and, excited and puffed up by the thought of being a teacher, as if he were superior to others, he composed his own peculiar type of doctrine.[41]

Irenaeus points to Tatian's teaching of celibacy as the chief error introduced by him. He goes on to mention other quirks as well, such as Tatian's avoidance of meat and wine. "He also," says Irenaeus, "invented a system of certain invisible Aeons like the followers of Valentinus."[42]

How mistaken was Irenaeus? I believe that blind adherence to Irenaeus' judgment not only has prevented a correct understanding of Tatian's monumental accomplishment called the *Diatessaron* but also has skewed our perception of his other activity as well. Irenaeus' central error lay in saying that *Tatian departed from Justin's teachings* and became a heretic.

Let us begin with Tatian's *Oration to the Greeks.* If we compare it with two writings traditionally ascribed to Justin, the *Oration to the Greeks* and the *Cohortatory Address to the Greeks,*[43] we can see in them precisely the same sharp-tongued attack against the immoral behavior of the Greek gods, the contradictions and absurdities of the Greek philo-sophical schools, and the lascivious and wasteful lifestyles of the rich and powerful Greeks (as well as the Romans who imitated them) that are so prominent in Tatian's *Oration.* If anything, Tatian's draft has more rage in it. It also has references to being "delivered from tyrants" that are not found in Justin's writings but that would make sense given Tatian's recent experience in Rome.[44]

What about Tatian's alleged founding of the sect of the Encratites and his program of celibacy and abstention from eating meat and drinking wine? Did Tatian do these things because he lost his grip on orthodoxy or because, as some say, unlike Justin he had a crabbed and abstemious nature? I say, "neither of the above." Tatian was, at every point, faithfully adhering to Justin's teachings.

For example, let us consider his strict insistence on celibacy. Where did it come from? If one looks carefully at the list of the "noble teachings of Christ"[45] that Justin displays before the Emperor Antoninus in his *First Apology,* to give him a better idea of the contents of Jesus' "philosophy," one cannot but notice that they consist mainly of the celibate, ascetic, and non-retaliation sayings in the Sermon on the Mount. Indeed, the very first "noble teaching" that Justin lifts up is Jesus' recommendation of lifelong celibacy. Justin goes on to mention Jesus' warning against lust, then Jesus' approval of celibacy (again), and he ends with the proud claim that, as a result of this "noble teaching," "many (Christian) men and women who have been disciples of Christ from their childhood have preserved their (sexual) purity (i.e., celibacy) into their sixties and seventies."[46]

From this it is obvious that it was not Tatian who invented the early Christian ideal of sexual abstinence or the stress on celibacy for which he later became notorious. It was his teacher Justin who had recommended it to the Roman emperor as the very pinnacle and goal of the ideal Chris-tian life. How could Tatian do otherwise?[47]

Again, Irenaeus and others make it sound as if Tatian's asceticism was the raving of a demented rigorist. But if we look closely at what Tatian himself says about his own lifestyle, we find nothing that is unusual in the Syro-Palestinian context. Consider the following passage from his *Oration:*

> I have no desire to rule, I do not wish to be rich, I do not seek command, I hate fornication, I am not driven by greed to go on voyages, I am not . . . tormented by ambition; I scorn death, rise above every kind of sickness, I do not let grief consume my soul. If I am a slave, I put up with slavery; if a free man, I do not boast of my good birth. I see that the sun is the same for everybody, and through pleasure and want there is one death for everybody.[48]

In its defiant rhetorical style, and in what he boasts of, Tatian sounds exactly like the Apostle Paul[49] as well as any number of Stoic and Epicurean philosophers of his time.[50] In other words, there is no heretical innovation here either. Indeed, such teachings soon became the staple of the monastic movements in Syria and Egypt and eventually the clergy of the Roman Catholic Church.

What of Irenaeus' accusation that Tatian introduced "certain invisible Aeons" after the manner of Valentinus? When Tatian does present a brief conspectus of Christian theology in his *Oration*, it has been noted that he never mentions the name of Jesus Christ. Instead he consistently speaks of "the Savior," or "the heavenly Word,"[51] or "the power of the Word."[52] Why did he do this? He was just following Justin's example. For this is precisely Justin's language: "The first power after God the Father and Master of all, even (his) Son, is the Word . . . " In his *Dialogue with Trypho,* Justin explains the nature of God in such a way as to posit a sharp distinction between God, the First Cause, and a lower divine principle in the universe that Justin calls "the ruling mind"(νοῦς βασιλικός). This idea is very similar to the Logos concept in the first chapter of the Gospel of John and in Philo of Alexandria.[53] If Tatian used these concepts, he may well have sounded to Irenaeus like Valentinus or one of the other Egyptian Gnostics who taught in Rome, but he would not have departed from his teacher's doctrines. However, there is more.

Irenaeus and later Epiphanius both accused Tatian of being heretical and hating God's creation because he advocated abstention from eating meat. Was this heretical? Could it have simply been Tatian's drawing the logical consequence of Justin's doctrine that the souls of all living creatures, both men and animals, partake of the cosmic "ruling mind"? In Justin Martyr's *Dialogue with Trypho,*

> (the old man asks Justin,) "And do *all the souls of all living beings comprehend God*? Or are the souls of men of one kind and the souls of animals another kind?" "No, *the souls which are in all are similar,*" I answered.[54]

It requires no great act of the imagination to see Tatian, having adopted this teaching of his master, taking the next logical step and refusing to kill and eat creatures whose souls comprehended God, as a way of honoring both them and God. None of this is particularly biblical in origin. On the contrary, teachings of this sort were very common in his day, being found all the way from Italy (the early Pythagoreans) across Greece, Syria, Palestine, down to Egypt, and over to India (where they probably came from). All of the ascetic branches of Christianity and Judaism shared these conceptions, as did every kind of Gnostic, Pythagorean, and Orphic initiate.[55] Wherever Justin may have gotten these teachings, at least Tatian was simply being faithful to him.

Tatian's Harmony of the Gospels

Can we see any hint in Justin's example of the one thing which Tatian later made famous, a harmony of Matthew, Mark, Luke, and John into one continuous narrative? Yes, we can. However, Justin's practice does not explain the name which, according to all reports, Tatian gave to his composition: the Greek term *diatessaron*.

Let us probe these matters further. To understand what was at stake, we must first note that Justin (and Tatian) constantly criticized the Greek philosophical schools for their many contradictions, absurd teachings, and inconsistent behavior. They insisted that harmony and consistency were the prime hallmarks of veracity. Consider this typical attack upon the inconsistencies of the Greeks' myths from Tatian's *Oration to the Greeks:*

> How are those (divine) beings to be worshipped among whom there exists such a great contrariety of opinions?[56] For Rhea, whom the inhabitants of the Phrygian mountains call Cybele, enacted emasculation on Attis of whom she was enamored; but Aphrodite is delighted with the embraces of marriage. Artemis is a poisoner; Apollo heals diseases. After the decapitation of the Gorgon, ... Athene and Asklepios divided between them the drops of blood. He saved men's lives by them while she by the same blood became a homicide and the instigator of wars.[57]

This kind of objection was commonplace in the philosophical debates of that time. Irenaeus levels precisely the same kind of criticism against the Gnostics: they teach all sorts of doctrines and contradict each other and themselves in the process. On the other hand, Irenaeus adds, we orthodox Christians are entirely free from all self-contradiction:

The Universal Assembly (καθολικὴ ἐκκλησία) ... proclaims and hands down her traditions with perfect harmony, as if she possessed only one mouth.[58]

The Christians did not invent this kind of rhetoric. In the previous century, when a Jewish historian wished to impress his Roman audience with the advanced level of Jewish culture, he insisted:

Unity and identity of religious belief, perfect uniformity in habits and customs, produce a very beautiful concord in human character. Among us alone will be heard no contradictory statements about God such as are common among other nations.[59]

Given this widespread belief in the importance of exhibiting consistency and harmony in one's religious doctrines, it is not surprising to see Justin Martyr attempting to smooth over the differences among the Gospels whenever he quoted them in writings intended for interested or hostile outsiders.[60] Far from being meant to replace the Christian Gospels, his harmonized quotations were part of Justin's outreach efforts, if you will, a simplification intended to keep the Christian message as clear as possible. Such harmonizations of the Gospels can be found in every missionary field, from medieval Persia to modern China.[61] They are, properly understood, *missionizing tools,* not replacements for the canonical Gospels.[62]

In creating his harmonizations, Justin seems to have relied most heavily on the Gospel of Matthew. Why was this? He may have been guided by the Christian religion's important claim that the "ancient prophets" of the Hebrew nation had predicted the coming of the Christ of God as well as the events that had happened subsequently. This "proof from prophecy" was offered by Justin as the central argument in defense of the truth of the Christian religion.[63] The Gospel according to Matthew was made to order for this kind of argument; more than sixty times it cites the ancient Hebrew prophecies as being fulfilled in the life and ministry of Jesus Christ. In thus relying upon Matthew as his foundation, Justin was actually following widespread custom in the second century.[64]

How did the other Gospels of Mark, Luke, and John fit in? Judging from his two public defenses of Christianity (the *First* and *Second Apology*) and the *Dialogue with Trypho the Jew,* Justin blended the Gospels of Mark and Luke into Matthew; he rarely cites them separately. Nor does he ever quote the Gospel of John or include its words in his harmonizations, although he was probably well aware of its existence.[65]

If Justin (and undoubtedly other Christian philosophers of his time) dealt with the superabundance of differing narratives of the Lord Jesus by means of harmonizations, then it is clear that Tatian was just following his example when he produced, immediately after returning to Palestine, his own harmonization—of *four* Gospels including John—in a new Syriac translation.[66] In the process, Tatian dropped the label *memoirs of the apostles* used by Justin and adopted a new title instead: *diatessaron.* Can we discover any explanation for this new designation?[67]

Why Did Tatian Entitle His Harmony Diatessaron?

At the simplest level, *diatessaron* was a well-known term in Greek music. It referred to the first four notes in the octave.[68] The word *diatessaron* was actually part of a longer phrase: ἡ διὰ τεσσάρων χορδῶν ἁρμονία, "the fitting-together through the (first) four notes." According to Greek musical terminology, the *diatessaron* contained the first four notes and the *diapente* the second five notes (one note overlapping with the first set) that together made up the eight note *diapason:* διὰ πασῶν "through all (eight notes)" or, in Latin, *octave* ("eighth"). To this day the octave is the basic interval in Western music.

The term ἁρμονία (*harmonia*) in the above phrase, which gives us our English word "harmony," could suggest the modern practice of *blending notes* in a polyphonic chord. This would be a mistake. Ancient Greek music was always sung in unison (or octaves, if there were boys in the choir), never in parts. Nor did the stringed accompaniment play while the singers sang, but before and after each phrase.[69]

The term ἁρμονία (*harmonia*) was not originally a musical concept. It came into music by way of a secondary extension of its original meaning in the domain of *woodworking.* In that context, it referred to boards that a craftsman had carefully joined together.[70] For example, Odysseus (*Od.* 5.248) made his raft out of boards that he had *fitted together* in carved joints (like tongue-and-groove) called *harmonies,* using pegs to fasten the overlapping sections together.[71] Central to the concept is the notion that the craftsman aspired to create such a close or snug fit between two or more boards that they seemed to be a single piece of wood. "Anything fashioned with joints such that they make the original pieces part of a unified structure is called a *harmony*" (ἁρμονία).[72]

When applied to music, the term did not signify notes which were "harmonious" in the modern sense. Rather, the notes (i.e., strings) had the *proper intervals between them;* they were *in tune* with each other. They "fit next to each other" according to one of the four traditional scales.[73]

At the simplest level, then, we are in a position to grasp Tatian's intention: his *Diatessaron* signified the meticulous *fitting together* of four Gospels into a single seamless narrative, *harmonizing* them. The full title of his work was probably what Epiphanius calls it: λέγεται δὲ τὸ διὰ τεσσάρων εὐαγγελίον, "It is called the Gospel (harmonized, fitted together) through (the) four (individual accounts);" or simply "the fourfold (harmony) of the Gospel."[74]

Why did he give his Syriac harmony of the Gospels a Greek title? Later Syrian Christians quickly dropped his title. They used the Syrian term "the Mixed" (*da-Mehallete*). The canonical Gospels they called "the Separated" (*da-Mepharreshe*). In view of this evidence that the term meant nothing in Syriac, why did Tatian choose it? Did it have important *philosophical* significance?

The Pythagorean Significance of Diatessaron

The term *diatessaron* was in fact a major concept in Pythagorean musical theory (much of the theory of Greek music was believed to have been invented by the Pythagoreans).[75] It was thought to embody musically the sacred Pythagorean *tetraktys*, the fundamental equation containing the four smallest whole numbers: $1 + 2 + 3 + 4 = 10$. The number 10, called the *"decad,"* was thought to be the perfect number symbolizing the entire universe.[76]

Did this Pythagorean concept influence Tatian? Possibly. Just as Justin used the Platonic/Pythagorean concept of *memoirs* to refer to the three Christian Gospels he had harmonized, Tatian might have selected the Platonic[77]/Pythagorean term *diatessaron* to identify his new fitting together of the four sacred books of the "barbarian philosophy."

Would Tatian have been aware of the Pythagorean connotations of this term in Syria-Palestine at this time? Possibly. Although Pythagorean speculation had died down somewhat during the centuries after Plato, there was a great revival of interest in Pythagorans and things Pythagorean in the first and second century c.e.[78] In Syria, three decades prior to Tatian's return, a leading Pythagorean philosopher and mathematician named Nicomachus of Gerasa (60–145 c.e.), published a treatise entitled *Handbook on Harmony* that discussed all of these terms, giving them deep religious significance.[79] For example, chapter three is dedicated to the relationship between the harmonious sound of the planets and human music: "Among objects of perception, the music associated with the planets is considered to be the prototype of our music by virtue of our imitation of it."[80]

When Tatian returned to his home country after fleeing Rome, he would undoubtedly have heard of Nicomachus' writing. He would have met people attracted by its number mysticism among those to whom he intended to proclaim the Christian faith. Could he have decided to co-opt a famous Pythagorean technical term *diatessaron* to place at the head of his meticulous fitting and jointing *harmony* of the four Gospels? If so, he provided his literate Syrian compatriots with the Christian *tetraktys,* the true meaning of the universe.

There may be an additional reason. Tatian may have decided to abandon Justin's term *memoirs of the apostles* because it suggested that the Gospels were in some sense unfinished, incomplete, a bit rough around the edges. According to ancient literary standards, memoirs, like diaries, were intrinsically private writings; they were never regarded as polished literary products (or if they were highly polished, precisely that made them suspect). If they were to be publicly circulated, they had to be set within proper historical narratives, where they could provide vivid, eyewitness details (such as the "we-passages" in Acts).[81] Did Tatian abandon this possibly negative label in favor of one that was more impressive, a concept that would underline the Christian Gospels' essential consistency and reliability?

Judging from scholarly reconstructions of the *Diatessaron,* Tatian did not limit himself to just the four (eventually canonical) Gospels. He appears to have included other Jewish-Christian Gospel traditions that he found in Syria-Palestine among the flourishing Jewish-Christian communities.[82] As for his inclusion of the Gospel of John (again in contrast to Justin's custom), this may have been possible (or necessary) because that writing was held in much higher esteem in Syria-Palestine than it was in Asia Minor and Italy.[83]

The Influence of the Diatessaron

The *Diatessaron* was instantly popular. There is no evidence that Tatian intended that his composition *replace* the original Greek Gospels. Nevertheless, his version of the Gospels soon began to be read in worship services, at least in the eastern countries, instead of the "separated Gospels." Before long, Tatian's *Diatessaron* had traveled the silk route east to Persia and on to China, even as it spread south to Egypt and Ethiopia and west to Christian churches in north Africa, Italy, and beyond, all the way to England and perhaps Iceland.[84]

In the process, it carried with it a priceless treasure: *a second-century Palestinian text of the Gospels.* This text stands in the closest proximity to the original writings of the Apostles of anything that we have. As such, it is superior in importance even to the stately fourth-century masterworks: the Codex Sinaiticus and Codex Vaticanus.[85] This fact is all the more important in view of the powerful anti-Jewish reaction that swept through western Christianity beginning in the mid-second century, affecting many Christian practices including the copying of the Gospels. It is only in Tatian's *Diatessaron,* a few very early Greek papyri, and the Syriac and old Latin translations that we can still detect the faint, original Jewish echoes of many of Jesus' sayings—turns of speech and specific teachings—that were modified in all later copies of the Gospels. As such, it has rightly been said that all attempts to reconstruct the original text of the Gospels must begin with Tatian's gift to his fellow Syrians, the *Diatessaron.*[86]

CHAPTER 5

Marcion Carries Out an "Ethnic Cleansing" of Christianity

C hristians had difficulty explaining their central religious beliefs from
the beginning. Fellow Jews would become enraged when they were
told that Jesus of Nazareth really had been the long-awaited Messiah of
Israel, but that, rather than accepting and following him, the citizens and
priests of Jerusalem had instigated his crucifixion.[1] Greeks and other foreigners regarded it as lunacy when they were told by Christian missionaries that Jesus of Nazareth, the Son of God and Savior of the world, had
been crucified like a vile criminal by the Jewish and Roman authorities in
Jerusalem and had not demonstrated any divine power in self-defense.[2]
By the mid-second-century a full-blown political crisis had emerged to
compound the Christians' difficulties.

The relationship between Roman officialdom and the Christian
movement had also been problematic from the start. It was well-known
that the Christians worshipped a man whom the Roman governor of Judea
had crucified on suspicion of treason: "Jesus of Nazareth, King of the
Jews" the sign had read on his cross. Less well-known was the Christian
belief that this Jesus was going to come back in full divine power accompanied by great angelic armies when he would destroy all evildoers everywhere, including the Romans. Such beliefs may have led some to accuse
Christians of "hatred of humanity."[3]

The uneasy relationship between Christians and the Imperial government reached a crisis in 66 c.e. when armed Judean and Galilean forces
liberated Jerusalem and proclaimed an independent state. The Christian

leadership, who had been waiting in Jerusalem for Jesus to return, fled across the Jordan, wanting no part of this rebellion.[4] It took four years for Roman forces to completely pacify Galilee and Judea, and in 70 C.E. Titus defeated the rebel coalition holding Jerusalem with great loss of life and considerable destruction to the city and temple.

The rebellion of 66–70 (or 73), with its strong overtones of Messianic jubilation, proved to be a watershed event. As punishment the Jewish people had the privilege of sending the Temple Tax annually to Jerusalem revoked. Instead, they had to pay tribute to Rome like other captured nations (the *fiscus Iudaicus*). As a result, the Temple was never rebuilt— even though Vespasian caused no edicts to be enacted forbidding it. With their power base destroyed, the traditional Israelite priestly families lost their hereditary privileges. The Jewish people now had no political center and no cultic center. What was left to hold them together?

With the permission of Vespasian, the Pharisees assumed the status of national leaders from their center at Jamnia (Yavneh) under the leadership of Rabban Johanan ben Zakkai. Immediately after hostilities ceased, first Johanan and then Gamliel II (Hillel's grandson), his successor, vigorously set about reorganizing the people around neighborhood synagogues, reestablishing economic and political links between the Pharisaic leadership at Jamnia and the Jewish communities in the Diaspora, and codifying the Jewish law (Torah).

A striking feature of the rebellion of 66–70 was the fact that not a single one of the large and prosperous Diaspora Jewish communities in Cyrenaica, Egypt, Asia, Syria, or even Parthia, sent any food, money, weapons, or soldiers to help their kinsmen defeat the Romans. Were they so pleased with their lot under the Romans that they were unsympathetic to the rebels' cause? Were they caught off-guard and unable to do much before the revolt ended?

This much is clear. The Pharisaic leadership under Johanan ben Zakkai and Gamliel II eschewed all signs of political machinations that might cause the postwar Roman officials in Syria-Palestine to become suspicious. Thus it is not surprising that the next Jewish rebellion—the Diaspora Rebellion of 116–117[5]—arose outside Palestine in the Roman provinces of Cyrenaica, Egypt, Cyprus, and Mesopotamia.

This rebellion probably began in the summer of 116 when the Emperor Trajan was poised at the mouth of the Tigris-Euphrates rivers, presumably musing on being another Alexander and taking the forces with him to conquer India.[6] The moment must have seemed opportune to the just-defeated Parthian and Armenian cities behind him—along with their large Jewish communities—because they suddenly threw off their new Roman yoke and slew the soldiers guarding them. Trajan raced back to recapture the cities when suddenly Jewish colonists in a number of central Mediterranean provinces—Cyrenaica, Egypt, and Cyprus—simultaneously rose up and killed their Roman masters. Once the local Roman forces had been exterminated, these Jewish rebels then went on unprecedented rampages, killing local inhabitants (especially Greeks), burning, looting, and destroying temples, farmlands, buildings, and even roads— clearly a scorched-earth policy.

Once their local surroundings were decimated, armed contingents of Jewish soldiers, led by what the records describe as a Jewish "king" or messiah, left Cyrenaica and Cyprus en masse for Egypt, where they apparently intended to unite with Jewish insurrectionists in Alexandria. This would certainly have happened if the local Roman general had not nipped the strategy in the bud by quickly suppressing the Jewish revolt and forcing the rebels out of Alexandria into the Egyptian interior, where they met with the forces from Cyrenaica and Cyprus, burning and looting and killing for months before they were bloodily suppressed.

The Roman general in Alexandria probably prevented a rebel Jewish invasion of Judea. The ultimate goal of the rebels from Cyprus, Cyrenaica, and Egypt, once they had destroyed their former communities, seems to have been to return to Palestine. One army was going to attack the Roman forces in Judea from the south, while a second Jewish army may have planned to come down through Syria and attack the Roman garrisons in Galilee from the north. Fighting on two fronts, the Roman forces in Palestine would certainly have been defeated and the Jews would have been free once more.[7]

As soon as the broad outlines of this multiple, international, coordinated uprising became clear to Trajan, he saw that the whole Roman empire was in grave danger. If the Jews succeeded, rebellions of other subject nations (the Germans, the Gauls in eastern Asia) were sure to follow. Hastily leaving his counter-offensive in the hands of his generals in Syria and Judea, Trajan sought to hurry back to Rome where he could rally his forces. However, he died suddenly and unexpectedly (under suspicious circumstances) *en route* in Cilicia and the eastern armies immediately proclaimed Hadrian, Trajan's commander-in-chief, their new emperor. It was the summer of 117.

Hadrian promptly withdrew all Roman forces back into Syria and gave up Trajan's just retaken territories in Mesopotamia. He also beefed-up the Roman legions in Judea and strengthened roads and fortifications against future attack. His concerns eventually proved to be justified. Fifteen years later in 132, about seventy years after the first revolt in 66, a second, massive rebellion broke out in Judea once again, led by a coalition of Pharisaic leaders and a Jewish "king" or messiah named Bar Kokhba.

Recent archaeological discoveries indicate that there was substantial advance preparation for this revolt, including the digging of underground staging centers, food and weapons storage depots, and the like.[8] The Bar Kokhba rebellion took the Romans three years to suppress, at great expense and bloodshed.

This time, the Roman Senate was not inclined to be lenient. Circumcision was made a crime, Jews were forbidden to serve in any civic positions anywhere in the empire, Jerusalem was turned into a colony of Rome with a new legal foundation and a new temple and a new name—Aelia Capitolina (thus destroying the old shekel-based Jewish economy), and Jews were forbidden on pain of death to come even within eyesight of their former capital city.

If there had been popular anti-Jewish sentiment around the Empire before, it now became official governmental policy.[9] This posed an acute problem for Christians, who felt no sympathy for the nationalism which inspired the Jewish rebellions. In fact, the Christians tended to side with the Romans in being angry at Bar Kokhba, since he apparently went out of his way to kill Christians.[10]

However, the Christians had a problem: to most people they were indistinguishable from Jews. Neither group would participate in the public sacrifices to the gods, neither would serve in the local armies, they both revered a single divine being and not the plethora of divinities worshipped by everyone else, and they both utilized the same divine Scriptures. It was not easy to tell them apart. For example, Suetonius could report that the Emperor Claudius had expelled "the *Jews* from Rome because they constantly made disturbances at the instigation of (someone named) Chrestus" (which would have been pronounced like *christus*).[11]

By the middle of the second century, in view of the widespread popular and official hostility against the Jews, it became a prime objective of post-Bar Kokhba, Christian public relations to make crystal clear the enormous differences between Christians and Jews. This took several forms. Some Christians sought to outdo local pagan leaders in protestations of subservience to the emperor and denunciations of the impious and rebellious Jews, such as Melito of Sardis (120–185)[12] who addressed an *Apology* to the Emperor Marcus Aurelius (ca. 170) advocating solidarity between Christianity and the Empire, and an *Easter Homily* blaming the Jews *of Sardis* for Jesus' crucifixion.[13] Other Christians argued that pagans were one race, Jews a second, and Christians a third, brand-new race within the human family (the *Epistle to Diognetus,* mid-second century). Still other Christians insisted that true Christianity never had anything to do with Judaism in the first place.

This third option was championed by the subject of this chapter:

Marcion of Pontus. Marcion went far beyond simply rejecting the Jewish roots of Christianity, however. Let us recall the two worrisome aspects of Christian belief mentioned at the outset:

- the embarrassing fact that Jesus of Nazareth was supposedly the promised King of the Jews but had been crucified by his own people;
- the confusing way in which Jesus had not demonstrated any divine powers when he was arrested, tried under false pretenses, and executed like a common criminal.

Marcion emphatically rejected each of these Christian beliefs, claiming that they rested on false traditions. The truth of the matter, he insisted, was that Jesus had not been Jewish himself, nor was he the Son of the God of the Jews, nor was he going to return in the future to liberate the Jews. Instead, Jesus had come to reveal a totally new, previously unknown God, and all followers of Jesus were destined to leave this evil world and travel to a realm of pure light far above the heavens. Consistent with this position, Marcion totally rejected the "Jewish Scripture" (i.e., the Old Testament) as having any role to play in the Christian religion.

Second, Marcion claimed that Jesus, the Son of the Unknown Good God, had not been crucified. The mob of the Jews mistakenly crucified someone else (possibly Simon of Cyrene) and ignorant Christian writers got the truth completely garbled in their accounts called the Gospels. Moreover, added Marcion, Jesus had never been born—he simply appeared out of the blue as a full-grown man in the synagogue at Capernaum—nor did he die. At the end of his "life" Jesus had simply vanished and then reappeared to a select few (such as the Apostle Paul) to encourage them to carry his teachings to the elect among the Gentiles.

Marcion dealt with the knotty problem of the many conflicting writings called Gospels by claiming that there was in fact only one true account, not four or more, namely *his* version, which he simply called "the gospel" (*to euanggelion*). Marcion's orthodox opponents accused him of having obtained his gospel by bowdlerizing the Gospel according to Luke, removing the first two chapters (containing references to birth and infancy) as well as all references to things Jewish, but Marcion and his followers always rejected this accusation. To "the gospel" Marcion appended ten letters of Paul—beginning with Galatians—on the grounds that they alone contained the correct *interpretation* of "the gospel."

In short, Marcion removed all Jewish elements from the Christian religion, carrying out an "ethnic cleansing" of Christianity. Who was this remarkable person and where did he come from? Before we look more closely into Marcion's doctrines and the Scripture based upon them (or vice versa), let us briefly examine his biography.

Marcion's Biography

According to a number of well-attested traditions, Marcion was the son of the Christian bishop of Sinope, the largest port city in the ancient Roman province of Pontus (on the northern shore of modern Turkey).[14] Born around 85 C.E., as an adult he took up the trade of shipmaster, a vocation that afforded him the opportunity to travel widely so that he could devote attention to his real interest: completely reforming the Christian Church. He was very successful in both endeavors. When he came to Rome around 140 C.E., during the reign of Antoninus Pius (ruled 138–161), he was able to give the bishop of Rome a cash gift of 200,000 sesterces, which was roughly the equivalent of a man's wages for 166 years.[15] As for his reform efforts, his contemporary Justin Martyr said,

> There is a certain Marcion of Pontus who is still teaching his converts that there is another God greater than the Creator. By the help of demons he has made many in every race of men to blaspheme and to deny God the Creator of the Universe, professing that there is another Who is greater and has done greater things than He.[16]

By the end of the second century, Marcion's reform movement had spread far and wide, probably outnumbering all other types of Christianity combined.[17] Nor did the orthodox counterreaction succeed in eradicating it in subsequent centuries. As late as 400, Epiphanius (310–402) could report:

> The sect may still be found in Rome and in Italy, Egypt, Palestine, in Arabia and in Syria, in Cyprus and the Thebaid, and even in Persia and other places.[18]

Marcion's Distinctive Doctrines

Marcion's conception of the Christian Gospel was ostensibly based on the letters of the Apostle Paul. This Apostle, the only one in Marcion's eyes to successfully withstand what Marcion saw as the overwhelming trend toward Judaizing that occurred in the first generation, was his hero and mentor. The following doctrines are an example of what Marcion thought he found in the Apostle's letters.

First, Marcion believed that Paul had taught an entirely unheard of, brand-new Deity, called "the Father of Jesus Christ."[19] He could have taken his lead from a passage like this from Paul's first letter to the Corinthian Christians:

> Among the perfect we do speak wisdom (*sophia*), though it is not a wisdom of this age or of the rulers of this age, who are doomed to perish. But we speak God's wisdom, secret and hidden ... As it is written, "What no eye has seen, nor ear heard, nor the human heart conceived, what God has prepared for those who love him." (1 Cor 2:6–9 RSV)

Christ revealed this God,[20] a God of supreme goodness (or, in Marcion's terms, *deus optimus; maximus optimus*),[21] indeed, according to Marcion, this God had one single attribute: goodness.[22] It was through goodness alone that He was prompted to save those who belonged to the other, the evil Creator.[23] This God of Goodness had had nothing to do with Creation, that is, nothing to do with Matter in any way. The Marcionites were fond of gibing:

> Sufficient to our God is this one single work, that he has by his great and particular kindness set man free, a kindness of more value than (the creation of) any number of destructive insects.[24]

The Good God's sole act was to save the souls of the elect.[25] By the same token, it was not his nature to punish sinners, for he is "incapable of judgment, a stranger to all emotions of severity and reproof."[26] Instead, the Good God shuns sinners.[27] The Marcionites scorned those who claimed to fear their God, saying, "we do not at all fear our God, for ... a bad god needs to be feared but a good one loved."[28]

Over against this Good God revealed by Jesus is the Creator God revealed in the pages of the Jewish Scriptures. This Creator God made his own world and his own heaven[29] and is totally ignorant of the Good God higher than he.[30] In fact, he is an evil, sordid fashioner,[31] who likes to dabble in evil, foul, eternal Matter. This evil Creator somehow tricked souls to occupy bodies of material flesh,[32] so that they would suffer in his "prison house."[33] He created contradictory laws and cruelly punished those who broke them.[34]

Beyond this, each God has his own Christ, the one totally opposed to the other.[35] The Creator's Christ will be warlike and belligerent and named Emmanuel.[36] He was never predicted to be crucified,[37] he has not come yet, and when he does, his sole task will be to gather all Jews everywhere back into one nation in Palestine.[38] The Good God's Christ was not expected and had never been heard of;[39] he was an "alien."[40] He did not come in real flesh,[41] he did not suffer,[42] and he did not die or rise in the flesh.[43] Instead, he inhabited a humanlike, ghostly form,[44] like an angel, the same nonmaterial "body" the elect will have in the resurrection. For, as Christ says in the Gospel, "they will be like angels."[45]

> Jesus said to them, "Those who belong to this age marry and are given in marriage; but those who are considered worthy of a place in that age and in the resurrection from the dead neither marry nor are given in marriage. Indeed, they cannot die anymore, because *they are like angels* and are children of God, being children of the resurrection." (Lk 23: 34–36 NRSV)[46]

Finally, in line with this teaching of Jesus preserved in the canonical Gospel of Luke, Marcion held that marriage was evil. As is evident from this passage, Jesus condemns all those who marry and are given in marriage as not being worthy of the Age to Come. Since marriage was tantamount to eternal "destruction,"[47] Marcion insisted that all who wanted to be baptized had to be virgin, or widowed, or unmarried, or divorced.[48] In all this, Marcion surely believed that he was following the real desires of the Apostle Paul, when he said:

> It is well for a man not to touch a woman, but to prevent fornication, let each man have his own wife ... but I wish all were as I myself am (i.e., single). (1 Cor 7:1, 7)

In this and his other rigorously ascetic practices, Marcion believed he was taunting the evil Creator and flouting his rule over the realm of matter.[49]

Marcion's Antitheses

Marcion's Scripture sparked controversy from the moment it appeared. Not only did he reject the entire Old Testament, his "new testament" (he did not use that term) was prefaced by a writing attacking the Old Testament in a way guaranteed to enrage the orthodox. This prefatory writing was entitled Αντιθέσεις ("antitheses" or "contradictions"), and it consisted of a series of contrasts between his version of Christianity and Judaism.[50] Some examples of the kinds of contradictions Marcion included are the following:[51]

· Contradictions within the Jewish Scripture, especially Genesis:

> (It is) absurd for the first and greatest God to command, Let this come into existence, or something else, or that, so that He made so much on one day and again so much more on the second, and so on with the third, fourth, fifth and sixth.[52]

> (How) silly it is to have allotted certain days to the making of the world before days existed. For when the heaven had not yet been made, or the earth yet fixed, or the sun borne round it, how could days exist?[53]

> The Jews . . . composed a most improbable and crude story (in Genesis) that a man was formed by the hands of God and given breath, that a woman was formed out of his side, that God gave commands and a serpent opposed them and even proved superior to (the Creator)—a legend which they expound to old women . . . making God into a weakling from the beginning (who was) incapable of persuading even the one man he had formed (to obey his laws).[54]

> The God of the Jews is accursed, being the God who sends rain and thunder (and other calamities), (he) who is the Creator of this world and the God of Moses. (He deserves to be accursed) because he himself cursed the serpent which imparted to the first men the knowledge of good and evil.[55]

· The God of the Jews is the opposite of the God of Jesus Christ:

> Marcion sets up unequal gods, the one a judge, fierce and warlike, the other mild and peaceable, solely kind and supremely good.[56]

> The prophets of the God of the Jews (gave) laws by Moses that they were to become rich and powerful and to fill the earth and to massacre their enemies, children and all, and slaughter the entire race (of the Canaanites) . . . And if they were not obedient, He threatened to do to them what He did to their enemies. Yet his Son, the man of Nazareth, gives contradictory laws, saying that a man cannot come forward to the Father if he is rich or loves power or lays claim to any intelli-

gence or reputation and that he must not pay attention to food . . . or to clothing more than the lilies . . . Who is wrong? Moses or Jesus?[57]

(The Creator) himself claims to be the creator of evil when he says, "It is I who create evil things" (Isa 45:7),[58] (whereas the God of Jesus Christ is) supremely good.[59]

· The God of the Jews (the Creator) was inconsistent and contradictory:

The Creator differs (from himself) commanding what he has forbidden and forbidding what he has commanded, smiting and healing.[60]

So also in the rest of his acts (we) accuse him (the Creator) of inconsequence and inconsistency, alleging that his instructions are in contradiction with one another: he forbids labour on the Sabbath days, and yet at the storming of the city of Jericho he commands the ark to be carried around during eight days which include the Sabbath . . . (Likewise, the) Creator forbids making the likeness of any of the things in heaven and on earth, then commands Moses to make a bronze snake (Exod 20.9ff.).[61]

The Creator proved capricious concerning persons as well as institutions, when he expresses disapproval of men previously approved of (Saul [2.24.1–2] and Solomon [2.24.1]), or else lacking in foresight . . . (We) allege that he is either reversing his previous judgments or is ignorant of those he will afterwards make (e.g., regarding Nineveh: "And God repented of the wickedness which he had said he would do unto them" Jon 4:2 [2.24.3]).[62]

· The Christ of the Creator is the opposite of the Christ of the Good God:

Marcion lays it down that there is one Christ who in the time of Tiberius was revealed by a God formerly unknown, for the salvation of all nations; and another Christ who is destined by God the Creator to come at some time still future for the reestablishment of the Jewish kingdom. Between these two he sets up a great and absolute opposition, such as that between justice and kindness, between law and gospel, between Judaism and Christianity.[63]

Neither for that matter can you establish that suggestion of yours whereby you differentiate between two Christs, the Judaic Christ (who) was intended by the Creator for the regathering out of dispersion of the people (of Israel) and no others, whereas your Christ has been advanced by the supremely good God for the deliverance of the whole human race.[64]

· The absurdity of the idea that Jesus Christ was a Jew:

This is an absurd idea that the God of the Universe would send the Savior to humanity through the Jewish race. "If God ... wanted to deliver the human race from evils, why on earth did he send this (divine) spirit into a (such a) corner (as Judaea)? ... Do you not think it is ... ludicrous to make the Son of God to be sent to the *Jews*?"[65]

· Opposition between the Law of the Old Testament and the Gospel of the New Testament:

The separation of Law and Gospel is the primary and principal exploit of Marcion ... Such are Marcion's Antitheses or Contrary Oppositions, which are designed to show the conflict and disagreement of the Gospel and the Law.[66]

Marcion's Scripture

Having thus distinguished what was unique about Christianity, what was the rest of Marcion's Scripture like? As you might expect, *it was a completely non-Jewish book.* There was no "Old Testament," no Matthew-Mark-Luke-John; no Acts of the Apostles (too "Jewish"), no Catholic epistles (1 Peter, 1 John, etc.), no Revelation of John, and no other Gospels or Acts or Revelations or Secret Teachings or Church Orders. What then did he have in it?

First of all, it contained a single Gospel, with no name attached to it.[67] Marcion dubbed this document simply *Evangelion,* "Gospel."[68] As justification for such radical minimalism, Marcion quoted the words of Paul: "But if we or an angel from heaven should proclaim to you a gospel contrary to what we proclaimed to you, let him be accursed!" (Gal 1:8 *NRSV*). Marcion took these words to mean that, *originally, there was only one Gospel narrative.*[69] When Paul spoke of comparing his "gospel" with what the Jerusalem Apostles were teaching (cf. Gal 2:1–2), Marcion assumed that he was referring to an actual *text* of the story of Jesus. In the third century, Origen knew of Marcionites who still insisted on this point:

> Marcion's followers ... reject the (other) Gospels. (Why?) When the Apostle (Paul) says, "according to my Gospel in Christ Jesus" (cf. Rom 2:16) "he does not say gospel*s*." They fix their attention on this point and say that the Apostle said "gospel" in the singular because there were not any more gospels (in existence at that time).[70]

What was in Marcion's *Evangelion*?[71] It seems to have resembled the Gospel according to Luke, at least to some extent. There were major differences: Marcion's Gospel lacked the first three chapters in Luke, beginning with the appearance of Jesus in the synagogue at Capernaum (cf. Lk 4:31f.[72]), and all traces of Jesus' Jewish ancestry were absent, as well as all references to Israel's God being Jesus' "Father," in the rest of the narrative.

These differences between Marcion's *Evangelion* and the orthodox Gospel of Luke prompted the orthodox theologians, beginning with Irenaeus and Tertullian, to accuse Marcion of *creating his Gospel* by cutting what he did not agree with out of the original text of Luke.[73] However, as far as I can determine, neither Marcion nor any of his followers ever admitted that this was how they had obtained their *Evangelion*.[74] In fact, they claimed exactly the opposite: they consistently held that they alone preserved the pure original Gospel while it was *the orthodox Christians who had corrupted their Gospels*.[75] This debate continues to this day, with most scholars taking the view that there just is not enough evidence to decide definitively what the source of Marcion's *Evangelion* may have been.

Marcion's Scripture included a second part that consisted of ten letters of Paul. These he called simply "letters of the apostle."[76] Marcion held that Paul, of all the Apostles, had not adulterated the Gospel with Jewish doctrines. As Tertullian reports:

> They object that Peter and those others, pillars of the apostleship, were reproved by Paul for not walking uprightly according to the truth of the Gospel (cf. Gal 2:11–14).[77]

As might be expected, Marcion's set of Paul's letters was also distinctive. It began not with Romans but the epistle to the Galatians, Paul's most vehemently anti-Judaizing letter. It included nine of the rest, omitting 1 and 2 Timothy, Titus, and Hebrews, which Marcion evidently took to be nongenuine.[78] Furthermore, the text of his version of Paul's letters differed from the text of the same letters in use among the orthodox. Close examination reveals numerous variations, all reflecting Marcion's theological agenda.[79]

Marcion's Legacy

The appearance of Marcion and his political and theological agenda coincided with the emergence of mild to virulent anti-Judaism within all factions of the Christian movement from the middle of the second century onward. As evidence of this, we may point to the *Gospel of Peter,* which seems to have appeared for the first time in Syria about this date.[80] Based on older Gospel accounts, it retold the crucifixion of Jesus in such a way as to exonerate the Romans of all guilt while fastening the blame exclusively upon the Jerusalem leaders and mob. It is first explicitly attested as being used by a congregation of Marcionites in Rhossos, the port city of Antioch in Syria.[81] Its heterodox portrayal of Jesus' crucifixion ("My Power ... why have you forsaken me?") also fit in with the Docetists' (and Marcionite) claim that *Christ* was never crucified.

Similar in its strong anti-Jewish, pro-Roman outlook is the mid-second century *Acts of Pilate,* later incorporated into the *Gospel of Nicodemus.* It also exonerated Pilate of all wrongdoing, paving the way for his beatification by the Roman Catholics during the Middle Ages.[82]

The new Christian hostility toward Jews was expressed in a wide variety of dialogues, tracts, and diatribes, from the mid-second-century onward. Known generally as *adversus Iudaeos* literature, these ranged from stilted dialogues between a Christian and a Jew to lengthy treatises denouncing Jewish customs and beliefs in contrast to Christian.[83]

Finally, anti-Jewish hostility came to expression within the liturgy for Easter, as Melito's *Easter Homily* demonstrates. In this development, all Jews—not just first-century Jews—were accused of deicide every Easter.[84]

International hatred of the Jews seems to have been a trend that arose primarily in the eastern Mediterranean regions, an understandable response to the widespread destruction caused by the Jews during the two rebellions of 116–117 and 132–135. Marcion's brand of Christianity coincided with and capitalized upon this widespread popular, originally non-Christian, fury.

There were other Christian theologians who preached a similar hate-filled message. Saturninus of Antioch, an earlier contemporary of Marcion's, also taught that there were two Gods, a Creator God of the Jews and an Unknown Higher God of pure spirit revealed by Jesus. This Saturninus also taught that Jesus had not been born, had no real body and never suffered or died. He taught, furthermore, that Jesus had come to destroy the God of the Jews. Finally, Saturninus inculcated the same kind of rigorous personal asceticism that Marcion insisted upon: abstinence from sex, from wine, and from all forms of luxury.[85]

Was there any contact between Saturninus and Marcion? Probably not, but there was between Marcion and another contemporary Syrian anti-Jewish theologian named Cerdo (Κέρδων). According to Irenaeus, it was Cerdo who went to Rome and instructed Marcion when they met there around mid-century.[86]

If Irenaeus' statement is correct, it demonstrates how Christian anti-Jewish polemics sprang up in the eastern Mediterranean and spread far and wide.[87] This was the beginning of the terrible story of centuries-long hatred and persecution of Jews by Christians, orthodox and unorthodox, official and lay. When Marcion's anti-Jewish agenda surfaced again seventeen hundred years later in Europe, during the rise of late nineteenth-century German imperialism, it was no accident that Church historian Adolf von Harnack chose Marcion as his hero.[88]

Some of Marcion's ideas even penetrated other religions, such as Manichaeism and Islam. For example, the *Qur'an* teaches the Marcionite doctrine that Jesus Christ was never crucified.[89]

If Marcion precipitated a major crisis within the Christian movement, we must add that he was probably responsible for the fourfold Gospel canon we have today in our New Testament. His meat-cleaver approach to issues in Christian theology and the multiplicity of differing Gospels provoked an outraged, vociferous reaction among the defenders of orthodoxy regarding Christianity's need for the Old Testament. It was Marcion's attempt to jettison all Gospels save his one, politically correct version, that prompted the orthodox to defend *all* (four) Gospels known to have been composed by Jesus' disciples or their assistants as the true apostolic foundation of Christianity. The irony of Marcion's life is that he, far more than external opponents like Celsus and Porphyry, forced the orthodox theologians to create the anti-Marcionite *canon* and the anti-Marcionite Apostles' *credo* still in use among the orthodox to this day.

After Marcion, there is a noticeable trend among orthodox fathers to avoid using any other than the four Gospels of Matthew, Mark, Luke, and John. This trend culminated in the placing of these four at the head of the orthodox New Testament as a result of the canonization process, something I will discuss more fully in the rest of Part One. What needs to be noted here is that the early, naive period of Gospel formation and reformation that we have examined up to this point ended with Marcion's drastically reduced Bible. His example caused the keepers of orthodoxy to realize the dangers of unfettered Gospel creation and awoke in them an awareness of the need to ascertain which Gospels were authoritative and which were not.

Thus it came about that, after Marcion, the orthodox Christian Church tenaciously clung to *four* Gospels—despite their all-too-obvious differences. This commitment in turn led to redoubled efforts by the fathers of the third, fourth, and fifth centuries to provide coherent explanations of how these differences came to be, in such a way as to preserve the credibility of these four as the basis of Christian faith and life. These heroic efforts, against the background of the discovery by the philosophical opponents of Christianity of these same glaring Gospel differences, have been elaborated in the remaining chapters in Part One.

CHAPTER 6

Celsus Attacks Christianity in True Doctrine

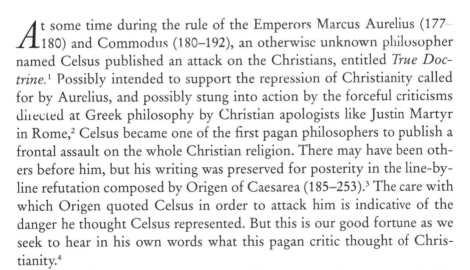

*A*t some time during the rule of the Emperors Marcus Aurelius (177–180) and Commodus (180–192), an otherwise unknown philosopher named Celsus published an attack on the Christians, entitled *True Doctrine*.[1] Possibly intended to support the repression of Christianity called for by Aurelius, and possibly stung into action by the forceful criticisms directed at Greek philosophy by Christian apologists like Justin Martyr in Rome,[2] Celsus became one of the first pagan philosophers to publish a frontal assault on the whole Christian religion. There may have been others before him, but his writing was preserved for posterity in the line-by-line refutation composed by Origen of Caesarea (185–253).[3] The care with which Origen quoted Celsus in order to attack him is indicative of the danger he thought Celsus represented. But this is our good fortune as we seek to hear in his own words what this pagan critic thought of Christianity.[4]

In the discussion that follows, I will list some of Celsus' general criticisms of the Christian religion and then a few of his statements regarding the Gospels, including the problem of multiple, differing accounts.

Celsus' Main Criticisms of the Christian Religion

Celsus' *True Doctrine* adopted a tone of haughty sarcasm toward the upstart Christian religion. Rejecting out of hand the Christians' claim to uniqueness, Celsus characterized Christianity as a hodgepodge of other religions' ideas, customs, and rituals, albeit in a diseased and distorted condition.[5] Here is a sampler of Celsus' comments and criticisms in this regard.

- The Christian refusal to tolerate images and temples and altars is derived from the Scythians, Libyans and Persians. If they say that God is a spirit, that is borrowed from the Stoics.[6]
- Their idea of the Kingdom of God is taken from the Platonic saying "God is King of all."[7]
- Their belief in heaven as a place of bliss is taken from the ancient belief in the Islands of the Blest or the Elysian Fields.[8]
- The Christian belief in seven heavens is plagiarized from the Mithraic mysteries.[9]
- The Christian notion of hell misunderstands the ancient beliefs about judgment beneath the earth.[10]
- The fantastic concept of Satan was stolen from the myths of the Titans, of Osiris and Tryphon.[11]

Nor were the healing powers of the man Jesus unique. The Greeks all believed that Heracles, Asclepius, and Dionysius are Gods "even though they were humans in the first place."[12] Indeed, "a great multitude of men, both Greeks and barbarians, confess that they have often seen and still do see ... Asclepius himself healing men and doing good and predicting the future."[13]

Nor was Jesus' resurrection unusual. "Aristeas the Proconnesian ... vanished miraculously from men and again clearly appeared and ... visited many parts of the world"[14] whereas "after Jesus died he just appeared to his own religious club (θίασος)."[15]

> Many other cults produce (resurrections) like this to convince simple hearers whom they exploit by deceit. They say that Zamolxis, the slave of Pythagoras, did the same among the Scythians and Pythagoras himself in Italy and Rhampsinitus in Egypt ... (and) that Orpheus (was raised from the dead) among the Odrysians ... and Heracles at Taenarum and Theseus.[16]

On the other hand, says Celsus, it is impossible to tell what the Christians actually do believe, since they disagree among themselves so much. "When they were beginning ... they were few and of one mind, but since then they have spread to become a multitude and are divided and rent asunder because each wants to have his own party."[17]

Some of them will agree that they have the same God as the Jews while others (the followers of Marcion) think there is another God to whom the former is opposed and that the Son came from the latter ... There are some, too, who profess to be Gnostics ... And some who accept Jesus although they still want to live according to the law of the Jews (e.g., the Ebionites) ... And there are some who are Simonians who reverence ... Helena or Helenus, ... (and) Marcellians who follow Marcellina and Harpocratians who follow Salome and others who follow Mariamme and ... Marcionites who take Marcion as their leader ... And these (different sects) slander one another with dreadful and unspeakable words of abuse ... for they utterly detest each other.[18]

Celsus' Statements about the Gospels

Christian claims about Jesus Christ seemed especially irritating to Celsus. Regarding the incarnation through the Virgin Mary, Celsus said,

if God did wish to send down a spirit from Himself, why did he have to breathe it into the womb of a woman? He already knew how to make men. He could have formed a body for this one also without having to thrust his own spirit into such foul pollution.[19]

Given this disgusting beginning point, the human issue, Jesus, was not impressive.

If a divine spirit (took up residence) in a (human) body, it must certainly have differed from other bodies in size or beauty or strength or voice or striking appearance or powers of persuasion. It is impossible that a body which had something more divine than the rest should be no different ... yet Jesus' body was ... little and ugly and undistinguished.[20]

But anyone can tell that the birth accounts in the Gospels are pure fabrications. What actually happened was that Jesus

invented the story of his birth from a virgin. (His mother) was driven out by her husband, who was a carpenter by trade, since she was convicted of adultery ... (After this) she was wandering about in a disgraceful way and gave birth to Jesus in secret. (Later,) because he was poor, he (Jesus) hired himself out as a workman in Egypt and there tried his hand at certain magical powers on which the Egyptians pride themselves. (So he eventually) returned full of conceit because of these powers and on account of them gave himself the title Son of God.[21]

In other words, the Christian doctrine of the "virgin birth" was no more than an elaborate façade to disguise the shameful fact that Jesus was a bastard. Celsus drew on Jewish sources to add that Jesus "was the son of a certain Roman soldier named *Panthera*."[22]

Jesus' alleged miraculous powers recounted in the Gospels were nothing more than those of a small-time country sorcerer, the type who swindle gullible peasants and fishermen with snake oil and tall tales. His so-called miracles (the health cures, raising people from the dead) and the story of

> a few loaves feeding many people, as well as other monstrous tales related by the disciples . . . (are no different than) the Egyptians, who, for a few coins, make known their sacred lore in the middle of the marketplace. (They are all a pack of charlatans who) drive demons out of men and blow away diseases and invoke the souls of heroes, and display expensive banquets . . . (with) cakes and dishes which are non-existent . . . Since these men do these wonders, ought we to think of them as Sons of God? Or ought we to say that they are . . . wicked men possessed by evil demons?[23]

If the birth stories and miracle accounts irritated Celsus, the account of Jesus' crucifixion drove him into a fury.

Come then, O Christians, cried Celsus, name some "fine action that Jesus did like a God? Did he despise men's opposition and laugh and mock at the disaster that befell him?"[24] Quite the opposite! When disaster loomed over him, Jesus cringed in terror, begging his God to let the calamity not strike him, as if he were powerless to avoid it himself, "uttering loud laments and wailings and praying that he may avoid . . . death."[25] Once he was captured, why didn't he simply "disappear from the cross" like Apollonios of Tyana, who boldly disappeared right in the middle of Domitian's cross-examination of him?[26]

The Gospel account of Jesus' death is pathetic, said Celsus. Who would want to believe that a real God was arrested and brutally executed like that?

> If he were a God he could not . . . be led away under arrest (against his will). Least of all could he who was regarded as Savior and Son of the greatest God . . . be deserted and betrayed by his own associates who

had privately shared everything with him and had been under him as their teacher.[27]

Celsus went on to claim that the Gospels were full of many other incredible, indeed bizarre, stories. Instead of bringing forward evidence of "a pure and holy Logos (they depict) a man who . . . when he was alive won over only ten (*sic*) sailors and tax-collectors of the most abominable sort and not even all of these."[28] They reveal that Jesus was no more than a dirty, unkempt vagabond[29] who "was arrested most disgracefully and crucified."[30]

The Gospels' accounts of Jesus' resurrection are ridiculous, being cheap imitations of the well-known accounts of more honorable gods. Worst of all is the disgusting idea that Jesus Christ came back from the dead in the same physical body, wounds and all, in which he had been tortured and killed and which had been decomposing for three days, like a ghoul from the Netherworld. And who saw him? Some hysterical women and disreputable beggars.

> But we must examine this question whether anyone who really died ever rose again with the same body . . . While he was alive he did not help himself (evade death) but then after death he (supposedly) rose again and showed the marks of his punishment and how his hands had been pierced. But who saw this? A hysterical female . . . and perhaps some other one of those who were deluded by the same sorcery, who either dreamt in a certain state of mind and through wishful thinking had a hallucination . . . (an experience which has happened to thousands) or, which is more likely, (someone) wanted to impress the others by telling this fantastic tale and so by this cock-and-bull story to provide a chance for other beggars (to make some money).[31]

Finally, said Celsus, if anyone objects to their stories, the Christians do not hesitate to alter their writings so as to evade criticism. "Some believers as though from a drinking bout go so far as to oppose themselves and alter the original text of the gospel three or four or several times over and they change its character to enable them to deny difficulties in face of criticism."[32]

This brief summary gives some idea of the nature and tone of Celsus' attack on Christianity. We will conclude with one final insult: "Let no one educated, no one wise, no one sensible draw near" to the abominable Christians. Their ravings make sense "only to the foolish, dishonorable and stupid (among men), (and to) slaves, women and little children."[33]

Conclusion

The words reported here are only a small part of his whole writing. I have completely skipped his attack on the Old Testament (especially Genesis). What I have presented illustrate his two-pronged attack on the credibility of the Gospels:

- the Christians' stories are not new but distorted imitations of more noble accounts in other religions.
- Christians constantly tamper with their writings so that it is impossible to tell what they actually believe.

The latter criticism comes out clearly in the quotation given above. A closer inspection reveals a potentially important clue. Celsus is quoted as saying that the Christians "alter the original text of the gospel three or four or several times over and . . . (thereby) change its character." It looks as if he was aware of multiple, differing narratives that comprised "the gospel" in the Christians' Scripture and assumed that these were successively altered accounts of basically the same story. Celsus questioned the morality of those who would intentionally alter the original narrative. He apparently assumed that there should have been only one narrative—the original.

Celsus' reaction seems similar to the Marcionites who accused the other Christian factions of corrupting "the gospel" by introducing "Jewish" alterations into it. As is well known, the Marcionites insisted that they alone possessed the one, uncorrupted, *original* "gospel."

Whatever Celsus meant, this much is clear. He discovered a particularly vulnerable spot in the Christian religion, one that would be mercilessly exploited by critics of the Christian religion after him. As we will see in Chapter 8, the next major opponent, Porphyry, the follower of Plotinus, took up Celsus' criticisms and expanded them into a much longer and more detailed list of even more damaging questions and accusations in his *Fifteen Books against the Christians*.

In the next chapter, we will see that, while Origen could in his *Against Celsus* mount an elaborate refutation of such outside criticism of the Gospels, within the safety and trust of his own school and in his Gospel commentaries, he could raise many of the same questions himself.

CHAPTER 7

Origen Confronts All Four Aspects of the Synoptic Problem for the First Time

*N*o matter how bitterly they disagreed in other respects, Christian theologians and their Stoic, Neoplatonic, and Epicurean opponents shared many assumptions concerning proper philosophical debate. They employed the same methods for interpreting their own Scriptures—and attacking rivals. Each fought for particular ideas within a common hermeneutical context. This happened because the most prominent Christian philosophers of the second through the fifth century had received "classical" educations and were personally conversant with the philosophical systems against which they contended.

For this reason, the criticisms of Celsus in the previous chapter would have been nothing new to Origen. Judging from Origen's commentaries on the Gospels and the hermeneutical portion of his treatise *On First Principles* (Περὶ ἄχρων), we can see that he was quite aware of the kinds of questions Celsus and others raised about the Gospels. His Christian school in Alexandria would have dealt with these and others as a matter of daily debate and discussion. In fact, I wouldn't doubt that Origen and his students had a long list of such objections, complaints, and criticisms of Old Testament books, the miracles of Jesus, the significance of the many parallels between Christian beliefs and rituals and those of other religions,[1] the grossness of an unnuanced statement of the physical resurrection of Jesus, and many other topics not mentioned by Celsus.

What is especially noteworthy for the purposes of this book is that Origen is the first Christian thinker to raise and answer, in a logical and systematic manner, the set of questions about the Gospels which later scholars came to call the Synoptic Problem. My discussion will track logical stages along which Origen progressed, as he moved deeper and deeper into this great Gospel riddle. By the end of the chapter, I will show that Origen's methodical approach is so carefully thought out that it is worthy of being made the paradigm for all later discussions in the book.

Let us begin with an overview of Origen's life.

Origen's Biography

Origen of Caesarea (185–253) was a native of Alexandria, at that time the most affluent and progressive city in the entire Mediterranean area.[2] His father was sufficiently wealthy to give Origen a good education in both Christian doctrine as well as the standard Greek curriculum of mathematics, rhetoric, philosophy, and history. When he was still in his teens, his father was martyred for being a Christian, an event that deeply influenced him. After the persecution died down, the Bishop of Alexandria, Demetrius, appointed the young eighteen-year-old Origen to teach Christian subjects at the same school where the famous Alexandrian theologians Clement and Pantaenus had taught. He stayed there until he was forty-six (203–231), attracting considerable numbers of students.

During this period, Origen made several journeys. In 212, he visited Rome and met Hippolytus. In 214, he visited Arabia at the invitation of the Roman governor. He also visited Antioch at the invitation of Julia Mamaea, the mother of the Emperor Alexander Severus. Around 216, Caracalla looted the city of Alexandria, prompting Origen to leave the city and spend some time in southern Palestine. During this period, Origen was invited by the bishops of Caesarea to lecture to them on Scripture, which he did although he was not ordained. When Bishop Demetrius of Alexandria heard of it, he was outraged that a layman should lecture bishops and forbade Origen from doing so again. About fifteen years later, two bishops, Alexander of Jerusalem and Theoctistus of Caesarea, ordained Origen while he was passing through their area on a mission for Demetrius, so that he could give them lectures. In 230–231, Demetrius excommunicated Origen and suspended his ordination.

Origen returned to Alexandria in 232 upon hearing of Bishop Demetrius' death, hoping to be reinstated. But Demetrius' successor, Origen's former assistant Heraclas, upheld the excommunication. At this, Origen departed from Alexandria and went to Caesarea where he found far more congenial surroundings. He took his extensive library with him and, in the relative peace of Caesarea, labored for the next twenty years.

During this period, Origen's fame spread and he was often invited to settle theological and scriptural disputes. We have a priceless stenographic transcript of one such debate, conducted in a church in Arabia in 245.[3]

When he was in his sixties, the fires of persecution began to rage once again. The Emperor Decius, in an effort to revive the faded glory of imperial Rome, ordered a systematic suppression of Christianity. Origen was arrested and tortured. He survived and lived a year or two, but his health had been broken. He died in 253 at the age of sixty-eight.[4]

Origen's Writings

Origen is generally regarded to have been the most original, advanced, and prolific theologian and biblical scholar in the early Christian Church. His output was enormous, partly because a wealthy patron in Alexandria named Ambrose placed his considerable financial resources at Origen's disposal at an early date. By the end of his life, Origen had as many as seven stenographers working in shifts to take down his dictation, plus numerous copyists and calligraphers in his library workshop. According to one count, he produced nearly two thousand treatises.[5] Unfortunately, few survived the witch-hunts of the fifth century, led by such as Epiphanius of Salamis.

The vast majority of Origen's work dealt in some fashion with the Christian Scriptures. His most impressive creation was a massive, six-column copy of the Old Testament called the *Hexapla.* In the far right column was a Hebrew text and next to it was a column giving the correct Hebrew pronunciation utilizing Greek letters. Then next to that were four columns of various Greek translations, beginning with the widely used Septuagint (LXX).[6] By comparing the three next Greek translations with the LXX, and comparing them all with the Hebrew original, Origen was able to *stabilize the text* and produce an extraordinarily reliable Greek Old Testament that was widely used.[7] His student Eusebius of Caesarea probably used it when he created the fifty copies of the Bible ordered by Constantine for the new churches in his new imperial capital of Constantinople.[8]

Origen also wrote hundreds of sermons, commentaries, and scholarly treatises on nearly every book of the Bible. Of these, the most important for our discussion of the Synoptic Problem are his famous commentaries on the Gospels of Matthew and John.[9]

Otherwise, Origen's most famous writing is his refutation of the Stoic philosopher Celsus, *Against Celsus,* which he composed in his old age in Caesarea.[10]

Origen's Quest: Reliable Tradition regarding the Lord Jesus Christ

Throughout his life, Origen's goals in his work on every aspect of the Bible were

> · accurate, reliable texts of Scripture and
> · true, self-consistent, and harmonious interpretation of those texts.

We can obtain a good sense of these aspirations from a passage in his *Commentary on Matthew,* where he commented on Jesus' statement "Blessed are the peacemakers." Origen interpreted "peacemaking" to be an apt description of his endeavors as a biblical scholar. Note the basic metaphor of the Bible as a harp or lyre:

> "Blessed are the peacemakers . . ." To the man who is a peacemaker . . . there is nothing in the Divine oracles that is crooked or perverse . . . (Such a man) sees an abundance of peace in all the Scriptures, even in those which seem to be at conflict and in contradiction with one another . . . He becomes a peacemaker as he demonstrates that that which appears to others to be in conflict in the Scriptures is no conflict. (Rather) he exhibits their concord and peace, whether of the Old Scriptures with the New, or of the Law with the Prophets, or of the Gospels with the Apostolic Scriptures . . . For as each different string of the . . . lyre gives forth a certain sound of its own, which seems unlike the sound of another string, is thought by a man who is not musical . . . to be inharmonious, . . . so those who are not skilled in hearing the harmony of God in the sacred Scriptures think that the Old is not in harmony with the New, or the Prophets with the Law, *or the Gospels with one another,* or the Apostle (Paul) with the Gospel, or with himself, or with the other Apostles. But he who comes instructed in the music of God, . . . like another David . . . will bring out the sound of the music of God, having learned at the right time to strike the strings . . . of the Law, then the Gospel strings in harmony with them, and again the Prophetic strings . . . For he knows that all the Scripture is the one perfectly tuned instrument of God, which from different strings gives forth one saving voice to those willing to learn . . . (Such a person is indeed) a peacemaker who

sees in accordance with the Scripture the peace of it all and implants this peace in those who rightly seek . . . in a genuine spirit.[11]

This beautiful passage is all the more interesting, coming as it does from a person who traveled widely and argued regularly with Greek and Roman philosophers, Marcionites, and other non-orthodox Christians and compared notes with learned Jewish rabbis. From these discussions, Origen was quite aware of the seeming naiveté, disjointedness, and inconsistency exhibited by the Christian Scriptures!

The problems became particularly acute in view of the many differing Christian Gospels. Here, Origen pursued one objective: where may one obtain reliable, authentic testimony to the Lord Jesus Christ? To reach this objective, Origen cycled among four, closely related questions:

- Which Gospels are the authentic records of the life and ministry of Jesus Christ?
- Which texts of the authentic Gospels must be used?
- How were these authentic Gospels composed and how were they originally related to one another?
- How should they be rightly interpreted?

In the discussion that follows, I will track Origen's steps as he dealt with each of these questions in his exegetical work. I will show how he delineated, for the first time, the standard component parts of what later scholars call the Synoptic Problem.

We are fortunate that it was Origen who was the first to deal with this profound Gospel dilemma. He was that rare combination, a first-rate technical philologian who also happened to be a profound theologian. As such, we may be confident that nothing he did, no matter how strange or misguided it may seem to us, was an accident or a superfluous step. We are also fortunate that Origen handled each of these questions himself, *in situ,* so that each problem *was organically related to the others* in his discussion. As such, he will serve as the model for all later discussions of the Synoptic Problem in this book.

Let us now turn to a closer examination of Origen's step-by-step encounter with the Synoptic Problem and the pioneering strategies he employed to cope with each aspect. In the discussion that follows, I have abstracted Origen's statements from the living context in which they appear. The idea is to clarify his methods and conclusions, at the cost of rendering them in an unnaturally schematic manner.

First, Which Gospels Are the Authentic Records of the Life and Ministry of Jesus Christ?

Origen did not need his learned philosophical opponents to tell him that there was a serious problem with the multiple, differing Gospel narratives. His extensive travels had brought him into contact with the entire gamut of Christian literature of his day, orthodox and unorthodox. Origen himself occasionally made use of Gospels other than the four, later canonized, Gospels.[12] In the preface to his first *Homily on the Gospel of Luke,* he commented on this plethora of Gospels in regard to the statement in Luke 1:1: "many have undertaken to compose a narrative" of Jesus' life:

> So also today "many" have wanted to write gospels, but not all (of them) have been sanctioned (by the Assembly). Indeed, everyone knows that not four gospels alone but very many have been written, from which these which *we* have were selected and handed down in the Assembly[13] . . . So the *Assembly* has *four* gospels, the *heretics many.* They have such titles as "Gospel according to the Egyptians," and another one is entitled "According to the Twelve Apostles." Indeed Basilides dared to write a "Gospel according to Basilides." Many have "undertaken" (to write gospels). I also know of a "Gospel according to Thomas," and another called "According to Matthias" and many others. These are those which (the heretics) have "undertaken" (to write), but the *Assembly of God* has granted authority only to four.[14]

Here we see the critical first step: *examine your sources.* Origen lived at a time when the separation between genuine apostolic writings and spurious, non-apostolic writings was in full swing. The primary question was: How genuine is the writing? In the preface to his *Commentary on Matthew,* Origen made the obligatory division between *genuine* and *spurious* Gospels:

> Among the four Gospels, which are the only *undisputed* Gospels in the Assembly of God under Heaven,[15] I have learned by tradition that the first was written by Matthew, . . . the second was (written) by Mark who composed it according to the instructions of Peter, . . . and the third (was written) by Luke (and is) the Gospel commended by Paul, (and) last of all (is) that (one) by John.[16]

How did he know which Gospels were genuine and which were spurious? By inquiring of the only authoritative line of tradition back to the apostles, namely, the bishops in churches originally founded by them. They alone would be in a position to know.

Irenaeus of Lyon, some fifty years earlier, dealt with the plethora of Gospels circulating in Rome using precisely the same strategy:

> We have learned from none others the plan of our salvation than from those through whom the (four) Gospels have come down to us,[17] (namely) that tradition which originates from the apostles and which is preserved by means of the successions of presbyters in the (orthodox) Assemblies.[18]

Nor is this *apostolic tradition* difficult to find:

> It is within the power of all in every Assembly who may wish to see the truth, to contemplate clearly the tradition of the apostles manifested throughout the whole world. And we are in a position to reckon up those who were by the apostles instituted bishops in the Assemblies and (to demonstrate) the succession of these men down to our own times.[19]

And which Gospels did these orthodox Assemblies all use? The same four as mentioned by Origen.

As part of this apostolic tradition, there were brief statements *how each Gospel had been composed.* The traditions quoted in Chapter 3 from Papias seem in evidence in this statement from Irenaeus:

> Matthew issued a written Gospel among the Hebrews in their own dialect, while Peter and Paul were preaching in Rome and laying the foundations of The Assembly. After their departure, Mark, the disciple and interpreter of Peter, did also hand down to us in writing what had been preached by Peter. Luke also, the companion of Paul, recorded in a book the Gospel preached by him. Afterwards, John, the disciple of the Lord, who also had leaned upon his breast, did himself publish a Gospel during his residence at Ephesus in Asia.[20]

Irenaeus wrote these words around the year 190. Some twenty years later, Tertullian, the brilliant Roman lawyer turned Christian, said, in his indictment of the heretic Marcion:

> I lay it down, to begin with, that the documents of the gospel record (*evangelicum instrumentum*) have the apostles for their authors, and that this task of promulgating the gospel was imposed upon them by our Lord himself. If they also have for their authors apostolic men, yet these

stand not alone, but as companions of apostles or followers of apostles ... by the authority of Christ. In short, from among the apostles the faith is introduced to us by *John* and *Matthew,* while from among apostolic men *Luke* and *Mark.*[21]

It is evident that Origen stood within a consistent tradition supported by orthodox theologians in many different parts of the Roman Empire. Matthew, Mark, Luke, and John were the four *undisputed* Gospels in use among all orthodox Assemblies everywhere. They were *the only Gospels* unanimously handed down in the apostolic tradition as having been written by the Apostles of Jesus Christ or their assistants.[22]

Thus the stage is set. The orthodox bishops and theologians have no choice but to use four different narrative Gospels. We will come back to the canonization process again in the discussion of Eusebius' *Ecclesiastical History* in Chapter 9.

Second, Which Text of the Four Undisputed Gospels Should We Use?

One might think that, once the field had been narrowed down to four genuine Gospels, the main part of the battle was over. Far from it. It was one thing to ascertain which were the original apostolic Gospels; it was another thing altogether to be certain that the texts of those writings in one's possession were *exactly identical to the texts of the originals* composed by the Apostles. Book reproduction technology being what it was in those days, this could never be assumed.

Origen's commentaries on Matthew and John often mention the difficulty of obtaining the original text of a particular passage. At one point, where he is dealing with a particularly knotty problem, he pauses to say with some weariness:

> Indeed there are many other (differences of this kind) so that many copies of the Gospel of Matthew do not harmonize with each other. The same thing (is true) also with the other Gospels ... For it is clear that there has been much alteration of these writings, whether due to the carelessness of certain scribes, or due to boldness on the part of some who intentionally alter them, such as those who insert (something) or remove the proper reading in order to support their own beliefs.[23]

To tackle this problem, Origen drew upon his training in the methods, concepts, and tools of the sophisticated Greek text-critical tradition at Alexandria. There, in the many libraries maintained by the Greek kings and their priests, scholars labored to preserve faithful copies of the Greek classics: Homer, Hesiod, Plato, Aristotle, and the Greek playwrights. Tertullian reports that the great Temple of Serapis in the ancient precinct of Rhacotis housed the library of Ptolemy Philadelphus in which could be found the sacred books of the Hebrews and the famous translation into Greek.[24] The most famous library was the Museion, reputedly the largest library in the ancient world, especially after it received the 200,000 volumes stolen from the libraries of Pergamum by Mark Antony and given to Cleopatra.[25]

These libraries were not just repositories of books, as ours are today. They were repositories of writings where communities of learned men lived and worked, copying, correcting, and producing learned treatises of interpretation. The Museion was originally organized under the guidance of the Peripatetic philosopher Demetrius of Phaleron to resemble the Lyceum of Aristotle in Athens.[26] It was located within the Royal Quarter or Sema, directly on the main avenue connecting the eastern and western gates of the original (Alexandrian) city plan. Strabo's description of the Museion clarifies its character as a philosophical community with a cloister, arcade (for strolling about during discussions, the Aristotelian custom), and a large guest house with a common room for meals of the learned men using the Museion.[27]

Origen and his scholarly predecessors in the Christian school in Alexandria participated in this philosophical tradition, living and teaching in some of the same libraries. Within this context, Origen would have been well trained in the sophisticated Alexandrian methods of text-criticism, to establish a reliable text for each book of the Christian Scriptures. To this end, he diligently collected as many manuscripts of Old and New Testament writings as he could, eventually bringing together "every then existing type of text" for analysis.[28] His endeavor had a very practical goal. As part of his constant activity in settling disputes within the Church and debating critics outside it (both Jewish and pagan), Origen needed to be certain he was not basing his arguments on faulty texts of Scripture.[29] This is one reason why he spent most of his life producing the *Hexapla.*

Unfortunately, he never produced anything like this for the New Testament Gospels. However, in his commentaries on Matthew and John, he went a long way toward establishing a reliable text for these two Gospels.

What were some of the methods he used?

After he moved from Alexandria to Caesarea, Origen had an unparalleled opportunity to travel about in the Holy Land, familiarizing himself with the places, buildings, and terrain mentioned in the Bible. This firsthand, personal investigation frequently served him in good stead in his text criticism. Place names were notoriously difficult for scribes ignorant of Palestinian geography to keep straight. For example, one of his copies of Matthew 8:28 said that Jesus crossed the Sea of Galilee and came ashore at "the land of the Gerasenes." Another said that he came to "the land of the Gergasenes," a third said "Gadarenes." Which was it? Origen's personal knowledge of Palestinian geography provided the answer: Gadara was not even in Galilee but in Judaea, far from the Sea of Galilee. Gerasa (biblical Jerash) was likewise impossible, since it was situated fifty miles away from the Sea of Galilee on the other side of the Jordan River (the pigs would have had to sprout wings to make it to the Sea of Galilee when they threw themselves over the cliff into the lake and drowned!). Gergesa, however, "is a little old village lying on the edge of the lake (= Sea of Galilee) now named (in honor of the Emperor) Tiberias." The original Gospel authors would hardly have used either of the first two names, said Origen, but copyists unfamiliar with the Galilean countryside might well have altered "Gergesene"—a word they probably thought was mistaken because of its unfamiliarity—to something they knew, such as "Gerasene" or "Gadarene."[30]

On another occasion, Origen found the name "Bethany" in all the manuscripts known to him for John 1:28; yet he commented, "We are convinced that we should not read "Bethany" but "Bethabara." Why the certainty that "Bethany" is an error?

> *We have visited the places to enquire as to the footsteps of Jesus and his disciples* ... Now Bethany (where the text says John was baptizing in the Jordan), ... was the town of Lazarus and of Martha and Mary; it is only 15 stadia (about two miles) from Jerusalem but about 180 stadia (about 25 miles) distant from the Jordan River ... Nor is there any other place of the same name (i.e., Bethany) in the neighborhood of the Jordan ... but (local inhabitants) say that Bethabara is located ... on the banks of the Jordan and that John is said to have baptized there.[31]

Taking a step deeper into the Synoptic Problem, Origen occasionally *compared one Gospel to another to decide upon a contested reading.* Thus, for example, one of his copies of Matthew contained the statement "Thou shalt love thy neighbor as thyself" in the list of injunctions from the Ten Commandments (Mt 19:19) that formed part of Jesus' reply to the young man who asked what good deed he must do to have eternal life. Not finding this phrase in the parallel accounts of Mark 10:19 and Luke 18:20, Origen decided that *it was not in the original version of Matthew.* He gave three reasons for this conclusion: first, it clashed with the sense of Jesus' reply; second, the parallel versions in Mark and Luke did not have it; third, if it had been in Matthew's text originally, reasoned Origen, "Mark and Luke would hardly have omitted this comprehensive and most excellent commandment."[32] Note the assumption here: the latter two evangelists were somehow familiar either with the original text of Matthew or—like him—with a common tradition that described the actual event.

Sometimes (like Celsus), Origen brought his *sense of historical probability* to bear upon a questionable text. For example, all of the Gospels narrate that the sun was darkened during Jesus' crucifixion. But Origen noticed that some copies of Luke read, "There was darkness all over the land, the sun being *eclipsed*" (23:44–45), while other copies of Luke read, "and a darkness came over the whole land until the ninth hour, and the sun was *darkened*." In his comment, Origen noted that none of his copies of Matthew or Mark mentioned an eclipse, and "neither did Luke, according to many (other) copies which we have."[33] He then added that there was no record of an eclipse at that time among Greek or Roman records. "It is more likely," concluded Origen, "that the original text of Luke did not include any reference to an *eclipse*."[34]

These are some examples of Origen's procedure in establishing a reliable text of the Gospels through comparative study. Most often, he just turned to what he considered to be the oldest, most reliable manuscript(s) to settle a contested reading, as he did with the text of the Old Testament:[35]

> Moreover, the discrepancies in the various texts of the Old Testament we are, with God's assistance, endeavoring to remedy, using various editions so that we might make from them one correct text.[36]

As always, his motivation was to obtain the most reliable text, whether in the books of the Old Testament or the books of the New Testament.[37]

Third, How Were the Authentic Gospels Composed and How Were They Originally Related to One Another?

Sometimes, when Origen was comparing the Gospels with each other, he found large *structural* differences that could not be explained as the result of scribal error. They were too large or too embedded in their respective narratives to be mere scribal mistakes. They had to be the result of the evangelists' *own compositional activity*.

For example, when Origen came to Jesus' statement in Matthew that, after his crucifixion, he would spend *three days and nights* in the heart of the earth (Mt 12:40), he was unable to reconcile this with Jesus' promise to the thief on the cross in Luke, "*This day* you will be with me in *Paradise*" (Lk 23:43), a location Origen believed—with many Greeks—to be somewhere up in the sky.

> This (passage in Luke) so distresses some people by its discrepancy (with the other statement of Jesus in Matthew) that they make bold to suppose that the words, "Today you will be with me in Paradise" were an addition to the Gospel (of Luke) made by some (later) unscrupulous hand.[38]

Then there was the well-known problem of the many women who anointed Jesus with ointment. Different accounts are told in all four Gospels: Mt 26:6–13; Mk 14:3–9; Lk 7:36–50; and Jn 12:1–8. After noting the similarities, Origen listed the differences:

- The ointment is poured on Jesus' head in Matthew and Mark; on his feet in John and Luke.
- In Luke she is a sinner; in John she is Mary the sister of Martha and Lazarus.
- In Luke she weeps; in John she does not.
- In Matthew, Mark, and Luke the event takes place in "Simon's house"; in John somewhere else.
- In Matthew the event takes place two days before Passover; in John it is six days before Passover.[39]

Are all of these variations to be explained as intentional or unintentional alterations caused by *scribes?* Hardly. Origen believed that these differences were of a complexity and scope that transcended copyists' alterations. He decided that the Evangelists had described three different women, each of whom anointed Jesus on three different occasions.

This kind of literal, historicizing explanation was one standard approach in Origen's day, not only for him but for most biblical commentators before and after. Similarly, the two feedings mentioned in Matthew and Mark, one to a company of five thousand followed by another to four thousand, were viewed by many as descriptions of two different historical events.

However, Origen knew of other differences between the Gospels, such as the two different genealogies of Jesus as given in Matthew 1 and Luke 3, where a literal, harmonizing approach seemed impossible.

Or take the story of Jesus' temptation. In his *Commentary on John,* when Origen came to the place in Chapter 2 of John's Gospel where—judging from the other three Gospels—John should have mentioned Jesus' temptation, John's Gospel is silent; no temptation. To make matters worse, there is no baptism either.[40] Instead, John's narrative speaks of other things altogether. There is a very different account of the calling of the first disciples, after which Jesus returns to Galilee, and "six days later" he goes to Cana of Galilee to attend a wedding. There is no "chronological room" in John's order for a temptation that lasted forty days according to the other three authentic Gospels.

Origen then ran into the different explanations given by the Evangelists as to why Jesus went to Capernaum in the first place:

> How can people show both to be true, that is, the statements of Matthew and Mark, who say that Jesus first went to Capernaum *because he heard that John had been arrested,* with that of (the Gospel of) John, who says that Jesus returned to Capernaum *while John was not yet cast into prison but still baptizing in Aenon near Salim?*[41]

These and other differences were patiently laid out by Origen in his *Commentary on John.* Then he announced: there can be only one answer that will fit all of the literary facts: *sometimes the Gospel authors wrote in a symbolic or spiritual manner; at other times they wrote in a literal, historical manner; and they alternated between the two with no warning.*

> The truth of these matters must lie in that which is seen by the mind.[42] If (such) discrepancies between the Gospels are not solved, we must give up our trust in the Gospels as being true and written by a divine spirit,[43] or as records worthy of credence, for both these characteristics are held to belong to these writings.

Those who accept these four Gospels (as the truth), and who do not think that their apparent discrepancies are to be solved by ... appeal to mystical interpretation,[44] will have to (find some other way to) clear up the difficulty mentioned above, namely (what) about the forty days of the temptation (mentioned by Matthew, Mark and Luke), a period for which no room can be found in any way in John's narrative. (Moreover,) they will have to tell us exactly when it was that the Lord first came to Capernaum. If it was (as John says) six days after his baptism, ... then (the other Evangelists have lied and) Jesus was never tempted (for forty days).[45]

Fourth, the Basic Hermeneutical Level: The Gospels Contain Two Types of Truth

This statement brings us to the foundation of the Synoptic Problem: How were the Gospels composed? Origen's answer to this question will involve giving a general hermeneutical theory regarding all of the Gospels. Having seen him descend, step by step, from canon to text to composition, we are now confronted by his claim that the Gospels contain much more than literal truth.

Was this something Origen said just because there were so many intractable differences between the Gospels? Hardly. At times Origen decided that an account must have originally been intended symbolically *even though all four Gospels contained literally similar versions of it.*

For example, Origen didn't think the account of Jesus' temptation described a historical event, even though two very similar versions are found in Matthew and Luke and an echo is found in Mark. Why? Because taken literally Origen saw two factual impossibilities:

> When the devil is said to have placed Jesus on "a very high mountain" in order to show Him from there "all the kingdoms of the world" (Mt. 4:8). How could it possibly happen according to the letter either that the Devil *led Jesus* to a high mountain or that to His *physical* eyes Satan showed, as though they were below and next to that one mountain, "all the kingdoms of the world," including the (extremely far distant) kingdoms of the Persians, the Scythians, and the Indians?[46]

There are other multiply-attested accounts that Origen did not accept as literally true, including the triumphal entry and the cleansing of the temple.[47] Let us consider what he says about them.

In his *Commentary on John,* Origen began his analysis of Jesus' entry with a list of parallels to the other three Gospels, particularly Matthew.[48] Matthew's account seemed particularly outrageous and Origen subjected it to a withering critique.

- Matthew says that Jesus' entry was supposed to fulfill the words of the prophet Zechariah (9:9). But the words quoted are not from Zechariah. "Instead, he abbreviates the prophetic passage" and inexplicably inserts words taken from Isaiah 62:11[49]
- Matthew claims that Jesus fulfilled Zechariah's prophecy, but Zech 9:10 continues: "and he shall destroy chariots from Ephraim and

horse from Jerusalem, and the bow of the warrior shall be destroyed, etc." When did Jesus fulfill this warlike prophecy? "The Jews," Origen added, "when they examine with us the connection of this prophecy with the things recorded about Jesus, exert great pressure on us when they demand to know when Jesus destroyed the chariots out of Ephraim and the horse out of Jerusalem?"[50]

· Why does Matthew say that Jesus ordered his disciples to get *two* beasts of burden for so short a journey? Surely the Son of God would not need to *ride* such a short distance![51] And why does Matthew say that Jesus, in ridiculous fashion, seated himself on *both animals at once* as if he were a circus rider? For the text plainly says: "*He sat on them.*" (Mt 21:7).[52]

· And what about the irrational behavior of the crowd, throwing branches in Jesus' path? The text says: "The branches were cut down from the trees and thrown on the road before him . . . Surely they were a hindrance to Jesus' passage rather than a well-devised reception."[53]

Origen concluded:

> (For these reasons) it seems to me to indicate a certain degree of stupidity on the part of (Matthew) to enjoy telling such things, if *all he meant to describe were literal events.*[54]

At this point, Origen launched into a mystical interpretation of the story, even taking into account the differences between John and the other Gospels: "Now to see into the *real* truth of these matters . . ." the two animals are the Old and New Testament and Jesus is the Word of God that rides into the soul called Jerusalem. The two Testaments are not allowed to "touch the ground" because they tread on "branches," that is, upon Origen's insightful expositions, which he flings in the path of the Word of God to facilitate its passage. The crowds signify the angelic hosts announcing the Word of God, and so on.[55]

The cleansing of the temple is another story contained in *all four Gospels,* but that did not convince Origen that it was an actual historical event.

· The story is factually "incredible" (Greek: ἀπίθανος) if interpreted literally. Jesus would not have driven out animals needed for the sacrifices ordained by God.[56]

· It is hard to believe that Jesus, "reputed to be the lowly son of a carpenter, would venture upon such an outrageous act as to drive out the merchants from the temple,"[57] who were only doing their duty since pilgrims needed victims to offer to God on behalf of their fathers' houses.

· The story is not literally credible for a third reason. Jesus couldn't have succeeded. The crowd would have instantly stopped him, not knowing who he was and seeing that they greatly outnumbered him, who was armed with nothing more than a little whip.[58]

· Origen also raised a moral objection. When Jesus is described as upsetting the tables of the money-changers, if this were taken literally, Matthew described Jesus "doing something quite unwarranted when he dashed the money belonging to the money-changers to the floor."[59] Were they also not performing a necessary service to pilgrims who had come from abroad with foreign currencies and needed temple shekels to buy their victims?

· Finally, on the literal level, it is bad theology. To think of the Son of God taking small pieces of string in his hands and plaiting a little whip to hit people with, . . . does this not suggest foolishness and arrogance and even a measure of lawlessness (on Jesus' part)?[60]

Origen concluded, "if this event really happened,"[61] the exegete should ignore the literal sense and interpret it mystically: the Son of God came to purify Israel's corrupt religious leadership, etc. etc.[62]

The Whole Bible Is a Mixture of Symbolic (Pneumatic) and Literal (Bodily) Truth

The dual nature of the Gospels was part of Origen's view of the entire Bible. As a young theologian in the catechetical school in Alexandria, Origen was taught this hermeneutical principle by his forefathers, Clement and the founder Pantaenus, who had adopted it from Greek philology.[63] Given this basic assumption, the central hermeneutical task was to detect the literal *and* the spiritual sense of every passage in the Bible.

Lest some think this approach dissolved the Bible into thin air, Origen gave this clarification in his methodological treatise *On First Principles:*[64]

Some may . . . suspect us of saying that because some (parts) of the (Old Testament) history did not happen (as recorded), therefore none of it happened. Or that because (we say that) a certain law (of Moses) is irrational or impossible when interpreted literally, therefore no laws ought to be kept to the letter. Or that the records of the Savior's life are not true in a physical sense, or that no law or commandment of His ought to be literally kept. We must assert therefore that in regard to some things (in the Bible) we are clearly aware that the literal account is true: such as that Abraham was buried in the double cave at Hebron, together with Isaac and Jacob ... and that Shechem was given as a portion to Joseph, and that Jerusalem is the major city of Judaea, in which a temple of God was indeed built by Solomon; and thousands of other facts. *For the passages which are historically true are far more numerous than those which were composed with purely spiritual meaning.*[65]

Origen went on to list a number of ethical commands which were clearly meant to be taken literally, such as the Ten Commandments. But then he qualified his position carefully:

Nevertheless, the exact reader will often come to passages where he cannot decide, without considerable further investigation, whether a particular incident, believed to be history, actually happened or not; or whether a particular law is to be literally obeyed or not. Accordingly, he who reads in an exact manner must, in obedience to the Savior's precept which says "search the scriptures," carefully investigate how far the literal meaning is true and how far it is impossible.[66]

How Can One Know When to Interpret Scripture Literally and When Not To?

One way to know when not to interpret something literally was when the Bible said something impossible on the literal or historical level. Origen believed that the Holy Spirit put descriptions of *impossible events* in the Scripture to warn us to interpret them symbolically:

Divine wisdom has (frequently) arranged for certain stumbling-blocks and interruptions of the historical sense ... by inserting in the midst (of a passage or story) a number of impossibilities and incongruities, in order that the very interruption of the narrative might as it were present a barrier to the reader and lead him to refuse to proceed along the pathway of the ordinary meaning and so, by shutting us out and debarring us from that, (it) recalls us to the beginning of another way and thereby brings us, through the entrance of a narrow footpath, to a higher and loftier road, laying open the immense breadth of the divine wisdom.[67]

Another basic way to know was when the text said something offensive, absurd, or immoral if taken literally. These also are hints to interpret the text exclusively on the spiritual level. For example, when Matthew described the Son of God asking for *two animals* to ride on just to go from Bethany into Jerusalem (about five hundred meters), Origen reacted:

> It does not appear to me to be worthy of the greatness of the Son's divinity (for Matthew) to say that such a nature as His confessed that it had need of an ass to be loosed from its bonds and of a foal to come with it; for everything the Son of God has need of should be great and worthy of His goodness.[68]

What about situations where there are elements *within* a story that look as if they were meant to be interpreted spiritually, but they are surrounded by other elements clearly intended to be taken literally?

Here Origen set forth a complex maneuver: First of all, compare the suspected mystical words with similar expressions found elsewhere in Scripture. Then find a way to correlate what the whole passage means literally with what is being said mystically, *in order to find a spiritual meaning for the whole passage:*

> When a passage as a connected whole is literally impossible, but the most important part of it is not impossible but even (literally) true, the reader must endeavor to grasp the entire meaning, connecting by an intellectual process the account of what is literally impossible with the parts that are not impossible but are historically true, these being interpreted allegorically in common with the parts which, so far as the letter goes, did not happen at all. *For our contention with regard to the whole of Divine Scripture is that it all has a spiritual truth but not all of it has a literal truth, for often the bodily meaning is proved to be impossible* ... Consequently, the man who reads the divine books reverently, believing them to be divine writings, must exercise great care (to interpret each passage correctly).[69]

Distinguishing between Spiritual and Literal Interpretation Is Not a Task That Can Be Avoided

Origen realized how vulnerable to misunderstanding this complex approach was. But he did not back down at any time from it, because the evidence in the Bible and the Gospels would not let him.

Consider the following passage from his *Commentary on John*. After carefully comparing the first chapters of John with the first dozen or so chapters of the other Gospels, Origen found that there was scarcely any similarity in order or content. So he laid down this triple either/or:

> Indeed, there are many more (such examples), if one were to carefully examine (all of) the Gospels looking for the discrepancies of historical fact—and we will attempt to present each one to the best of our ability (as we go along).
>
> But whoever has been made dizzy (by these discrepancies) will give up (the attempt) to obtain literal truth from (all four) Gospels and will *either* elevate one of them at random (to be historically true), not daring to abandon completely the faith in our Lord, *or* he will admit, regarding (all) four, that their truth is not (exclusively) in bodily images.[70]

Origen was convinced that the Gospels contained both kinds of truth, but the spiritual was both more extensive and more important:

> I believe that the (Gospel) historians, after their minds had understood (God's revelation), decided to teach us by means of an (spiritual) image the things had been beheld by their minds[71] ... Naturally, they made full use for their purpose of things (actually) done by Jesus ... as well as (his) sayings. But they also interwove into their writing of *sensory* things *other things* that were made clear to them *purely mentally*.[72] Indeed, I do not condemn them if they even sometimes *altered history* in the service of some *mystical object* they had in mind, so that they spoke of a thing which happened in a certain place as if it happened in another, or of what took place at a certain time as if it happened at another time, or otherwise introduced into what was spoken (by Jesus) in a certain way some changes of their own.[73] It was set before them to disclose the truth spiritually and literally together, but when both were not allowed, to prefer the spiritual over the literal, *often preserving the spiritual truth in the, as one might say, literal falsehood.*[74]

A striking statement. Note the inexorable logic which drove Origen to make it. First, he used the apostolic succession to identify the (four) authentic records of Jesus Christ. Second, he used his extensive research facility to obtain the most reliable texts possible of those (four) records. Having done that, Origen and his students undoubtedly examined the Gospels repeatedly to resolve the many differences and inconsistencies in which they abounded. Out of this exhaustive research arose Origen's basic triple either/or: once one has fully grasped all of the differences among the four authentic Gospels,

> · *either* one will give up all faith in Christ (because of a failed attempt to make them make sense literally),
> · *or* one will select one Gospel as the norm of literal truth and reject the rest where they literally differ from it,
> · *or* one will accept all four (as capital *T* True) but realize that their contents are only partially true on the literal level while wholly True on the spiritual level.

There are no other options. Origen chose the third:

> The truth of these matters (in the Gospels) *must lie in that which is seen by the mind.* If the discrepancies between the Gospels is not solved (in this way), we must give up our trust in the Gospels as being true and written by a more divine spirit, or successfully recorded (by the apostles).[75]

Origen's Description of How the Gospels Were Written

In this way, Origen descended, step by step, down to the deepest question of all, the question lying at the very center of the Synoptic Problem—and, arguably, the Christian religion as well: *How did the Evangelists learn what to put in their Gospels?*

The explanation we are about to read must have been holy knowledge in Origen's school at Alexandria. As we look at this account, we should not be misled by the oblique terminology. Origen is treading on sacred ground; he is describing the moment *in illo tempore* when the Holy Spirit caused the Gospel authors to *"see God"*—each in a unique way.

> Let it be supposed that certain men by the Holy Spirit see God (i.e., Jesus) and his holy words and his appearance, which he prepared for them, to be revealed (to them) at chosen times for their (spiritual) progress, (these men) who are several in number and in *different places.*
>
> They are *not* blessed by wholly similar visions and benefits (but) each one, in his own way, announces what he *sees in the spirit* concerning God (Jesus) and his words, concerning his appearances to his saints, so that the first one announces certain things said to his righteous one and done by God (Jesus) at a certain time and place, but to another (second man He reveals other things) concerning oracles and divine fulfillments,

and to a third man (who) wants to teach (us) other (things) than what has just been said concerning the two just mentioned; and let there also be a fourth (man) doing something analogously to the (other) three. But let these four agree with each other concerning certain things revealed to them by the Spirit and let them disagree a little concerning other things.[76]

In short,

> *Jesus is many things, according to the conceptions of Him,* of which it is quite likely that the Evangelists took up different notions, while yet they were (still) in agreement with each other (despite) the different things they wrote.[77]

At one level, this statement seems surprisingly modern, resembling reader-response hermeneutics. However, there is a profound difference in the respective starting points. Origen's whole theology is based on a conception of God's self-revelation and participation in creation as a multiple-stage, increasingly diversified, progressively physical, spiritual activity. The spiritual side, that is, God, is in control throughout. The differing visions God bequeathed to each of the Evangelists led to four different Jesuses since God *adjusted the vision* according to the needs of each, and yet all were also perfect, in some sense, since they were all visions of *God/Jesus.*

Given this starting point, it finally becomes obvious why Origen never produced a harmony of the literal words of the Gospels. *The real harmony already existed on the spiritual level,* while the literal differences were both less important and at the same time precious indications of God's gracious condescension to the specific differences of his saints. Any egregious disagreements between them were simply hints planted by the Holy Spirit to seek the spiritual Truth.

> Whoever thinks the writing of these four (Gospels) is (just literal) history, or a representation of real things through historical images, and who supposes God to (literally) be within certain limits in space, and to be unable to present to several persons in different places *several versions of Himself at the same time* . . . (will find) it impossible (to maintain) that our four writers are writing the truth.[78]

Conclusion

This brings to a close our examination of Origen's way of dealing with the similarities and differences in the Gospels. Guided by the central question:

Where may reliable testimony to the Lord Jesus be found?, Origen sorted through the many Gospels for the four, authoritative, apostolic Gospels, compared texts of these for the most reliable text of these Gospels, proposed a general theory of composition that would account for their similarities and differences, and used a method of interpretation consistent with his understanding of how the Gospels (and the entire Bible) had been written.

It is obvious, given his understanding of how the Gospels were originally composed, that the *order of composition* played no role in his thinking. All four Evangelists had *seen God* and received what God revealed to their minds. The *order* in which this happened was immaterial. Origen said they received their visions in different places, presumably in isolation.

Origen's main concern, given the dual character of the truth within the Gospels, was to pay close attention to what the Gospel authors *meant to say:*

> We must (always) . . . try to obtain some impression of the intention of the Gospel authors and guide ourselves by it.[79]

Unlike a modern interpreter, who would take this principle and begin to look for linguistic parallels and historically conditioned ranges of meaning, Origen and his contemporaries set off in a radically different direction. They reasoned that the intention of the authors was precisely coextensive with the *"mind of Christ"* who had originally inspired them to write. This led to a very different kind of biblical research, as we saw in the passage quoted above where Origen explained how to cope with situations where literal and spiritual truth are mixed together in the same passage.

We will see this watchword echoed by Augustine,[80] whence it passed into medieval interpretation generally and from there into Protestantism and modern biblical interpretation. It came to expression most recently in the great document on biblical interpretation of Vatican II, *Die Verbum.* I will discuss the modern attack on the principle of "authorial intention" in Part Three. I mention it here in order to point out that it was a logical part of patristic scriptural interpretation, given their conception of the divine inspiration of Scripture.

Having said thus, I must add that the Fathers' idea of "authorial intention" was quite different from modern conceptions of authorial intention, so that the postmodern critique doesn't even touch the ancient conception at all. The ancient concept held that, since all of Holy Scripture had the Holy Spirit as its primary author, the human contribution, while real enough, in no sense resembled a "modern" writer's self-conscious and autonomous "intended meaning."

Furthermore, given the patristic concept of Holy Spirit–as–author, the *spiritual requirements of the interpreter* were very different from post-modern theories of interpretation. The patristic conception of "God-as-author" caused the act of interpretation to be seen not as an isolated individual seeking to guess at the meaning intended by the biblical writer ("what it meant"), nor did it allow the exegete to impose his or her own meaning upon it (reader response). In patristic exegesis, the interpreter worked within a dynamic, spiritual relationship joining the community of faith with the active presence of the Holy Spirit, in the course of which the interpreter actively asked God to reveal God's meaning as Scripture was read and pondered. Origen's commentaries are filled with pauses where he momentarily stopped expounding the text and turned directly to God in prayer with a plea for assistance.[81]

This awareness that the hidden, spiritual meaning in the Bible *always* transcended the capacities of the interpreter to discover, also explains Origen's characteristic humility in his interpretive activity. He often ended his discussions with an appeal to the reader to offer a better explanation. For example, at the conclusion of his explanation of the triumphal entry story, Origen added:

> I have written out long sections from the Gospels, . . . in order to exhibit the discrepancy in this part of our Gospel of John. Three of the Gospels place these incidents, which we suppose to be the same (event) as that narrated by John, in connection with the one visit of the Lord to Jerusalem, while John, on the other hand, places it in connection with two visits which are widely separated (in time) from each other and between which were various journeys of the Lord to other places. I conceive it to be impossible for those who admit nothing more than literal history in their interpretation (of the Gospels) to show that these discrepant statements are in harmony with each other. *If any one considers that we have not given a sound exposition, let him write a reasoned rejoinder to this declaration of ours.*[82]

We should remember that appeals of this sort were by no means intended solely for the Christians in his audience. Origen was always prepared to debate his conclusions with Jewish scholars as well as pagan philosophers. Nor did he end his arguments with a veiled threat against those who disagreed with him, as we will see Augustine do. Witness these closing words in his famous *Against Celsus:*

> And so you now have, holy Ambrose, the conclusion of the task you set me, according to the ability possessed by and granted to me. We have

concluded in eight books everything we have thought fit to say in reply
to Celsus' book entitled *The True Doctrine.* It is for the reader of his
treatise, and of our reply against him, to judge which of the two breathes
more of the spirit of the true God and of the temper of devotion towards
Him and of the truth attainable by men, that is, of sound doctrines
which lead men to live the best life.[83]

Origen's carefully reasoned approach to the Gospels was too complex and risky for most of his contemporaries. Within a hundred years,
severe criticisms were brought forward against his theology and, within
two hundred years, most of his writings had been taken out and burned.
When we encounter the next major attempt by Augustine to cope with
the differences among the four canonical Gospels, an enormous effort will
be made to demonstrate the complete lack of inconsistency—and therefore the Truth—of their literal level.

CHAPTER 8

Porphyry—"the Deadliest Foe"—Has Read the Gospels, Carefully

The year 248 witnessed great celebrations as Rome commemorated the thousandth anniversary of its founding. Ironically, the Roman Empire had never been in worse economic, political, or moral condition. Cries of alarm could be heard coming from all directions, calling for revival of the ancient traditions. Their disappearance was blamed on the Christians, who were now found in every city and town. Occasionally, this popular resentment was used by desperate officials to mollify the populace; nothing like a bloody purge of a hated minority to take people's attention off their troubles.

These sporadic persecutions of the Christian Church had occurred from time to time, beginning with Nero in the first century. The second century was relatively quiet, but conflict broke out again in the time of Caracalla (211–217) and Maximinus (235–238). It receded in the brief reigns of Gordian (238–244) and Philip the Arabian (244–249), and Christians returned to normal conditions. When the Emperor Decius came to the throne in 249, however, storm clouds once again appeared on the horizon. A former Roman senator who firmly believed in the traditional Roman virtues, Decius set out in 250 to destroy the Christian religion as a way of rectifying the empire's rotten condition.

He began with public executions of two prominent Christian bishops, in Rome and Antioch.[1] In a sweep through the eastern provinces, thousands of Christians—including Origen—were arrested, tortured, and killed, and their property was confiscated by the state. Scriptures were burned, clergy driven away, church buildings destroyed, and property seized.

Decius' persecution ended in 251 when he unexpectedly died on a military campaign against the Germans. It was renewed in 257 by his eastern associate Valerian. More Christians were killed, including the beloved Cyprian, Bishop of Carthage. By the time this persecution was stopped in 260 by Valerian's successor, Gallienus (260–268), the Christian movement had suffered enormous damage. Congregations were bankrupt and leaderless, clergy lost or discredited, and accurate copies of Scripture hard to find.

In the period of calm after the last onslaught, just as Christians were beginning to hope that the worst was over, a prominent Roman philosopher named Porphyry published a lengthy denunciation entitled *Against the Christians.* It was the prelude to the most devastating persecution the Church ever experienced.

Porphyry of Tyre (ca. 233–304) was the most famous disciple of the great Egyptian Neoplatonic philosopher Plotinus (ca. 205–269). Not an original thinker himself, Porphyry excelled at collecting and summarizing the doctrines of others. The massive writing *Against the Christians in Fifteen Books*[2] was just such a compendium of previous attacks upon the Christians, with considerable additional material of his own. It was composed during a lull in the persecutions sometime around 270, while he was living on the island of Sicily.[3]

Word of this latest philosophical attack spread among Christian thinkers, prompting the Christian Bishop Methodius of Patera to publish an immediate refutation of it. It had little effect. Porphyry's damaging arguments continued to foment anti-Christian sentiment among pagan philosophers and officials. In 303, court officials, led by Galerian (293–311), the associate emperor with Diocletian (284–305) and an inveterate enemy of the Christians, urged Diocletian to renew the attack.[4]

At first Diocletian began cautiously, banning Christians from all ranks of government. In 303, after a number of uprisings and riots in Melitene and Syria convinced him that this selective policy would not succeed, he issued two far more sweeping edicts, ordering churches to be burned, sacred books to be confiscated, and Christian leaders to be arrested and forced to worship the Roman gods. Once more, as with Decius and Valerian, the goal was the complete extermination of the powerful Christian Church.[5]

During this persecution, the Roman governor of the province of Bithynia, Hierocles, took large chunks from Porphyry's text and issued his own attack on the Christians. The new element in his writing was a series of laudatory statements about the famous first-century Pythagorean sage

Apollonios of Tyana, paralleled with a series of deprecatory statements about Jesus of Nazareth and the Gospel writers.[6]

The persecution of Diocletian ended in 312 C.E. with the Edict of Toleration issued by the new, pro-Christian Emperor Constantine. Not long after that, the Church historian Eusebius of Caesarea published a reply attacking Hierocles in a tract entitled *Against Hierocles.*[7] Later, Eusebius wrote a series of refutations of Porphyry (to be considered in the next chapter).

But the effects of Porphyry's writing were not ended by these measures. When the anti-Christian Emperor Julian the Apostate gained control of the empire in 361, he jumped into the fray with *Three Books against the Galileans,* most of which was lifted from Porphyry. Julian was answered by the Christian theologian Apollinarius of Laodicea, who published *Thirty Books against Porphyry.*[8]

In the fourth century, Porphyry's criticisms of the Christians were taken up and refined by the Manichaeans. When a bishop in north Africa came across a "Porphyrian list" of criticisms of the Bible, he passed them on to Augustine to answer—prompting Augustine's massive tome *On the Harmony of the Evangelists.*[9]

Even after that, Porphyry's carefully constructed criticisms did not go away. Explosions and repercussions continued for centuries, proof of the claim that Porphyry "was regarded by the early Fathers as the bitterest and most dangerous enemy of the Church . . . (His treatise) was looked upon as the most powerful attack there had ever been."[10] His name became a kind of insult, as when Pope Leo X said of Martin Luther, "a new Porphyry has arisen!"[11]

A Reconstruction of Porphyry's Against the Christians

Unlike most earlier philosophical critics, Porphyry read the entire Christian Scriptures carefully. Out of this painstaking study emerged page after page of embarrassing questions pinpointing hundreds of inconsistencies, absurdities, and morally objectionable episodes. He drew heavily on earlier critiques of the Bible, both Christian (especially Marcionite and Gnostic) and non-Christian (Jewish, Neoplatonic [Celsus] and Manichaean), thus distilling the concentrated venom directed against the Bible over the previous two hundred years. His attack was especially dangerous in that his Neoplatonic orientation was similar to that of many Christian theologians of his day; his objections were often ones they secretly shared.[12]

He did have one major problem. His writing was so lengthy that it was cumbersome and expensive to reproduce. As a result, it circulated very slowly. That ended abruptly in 324 when Constantine personally ordered all existing copies gathered and burned.[13] The imperial ban was apparently successful in destroying the few copies that were in circulation, since modern scholars and archeologists have yet to find a single copy of the original. But Porphyry's imitators and critics quoted him extensively and it is on these echoes that the following reconstruction is based. I have paid special attention to what he said about the Gospels and their authors.[14]

Book 1

Book 1 echoed Celsus' *True Doctrine* in praising Jesus as a good if weak man who was victimized by rebellious and unprincipled disciples. Among many examples, we may note the following.

· Why did Peter draw and use his sword at Jesus' arrest instead of forgiving as Jesus had commanded?
· Paul shamefully squabbled with Peter in public at Antioch, although the latter deserved punishment for his insincerity.[15]

Book 2

This book is entirely lost. It may have had other attacks on the Apostles.

Book 3

In this book, Porphyry listed the inconsistencies and absurdities in Genesis. His points are a compendium of previous criticism similar to those of Celsus, who in turn probably borrowed from Marcion. Some of these ideas have a Marcionite ring:

> The Jews, being bowed down in some corner of Palestine, were totally uneducated and had not heard (of the noble poetry of the Greeks. Instead) they composed a most improbable and crude story that a man was formed by the hands of God and given breath, that a woman was formed out of his side, that God gave commands and a serpent opposed them . . . making God into a weakling who was incapable of persuading even one man whom He had formed.[16]

But it is far more silly to have allotted certain days to the making of the world before days existed. For when the heaven had not yet been made, or the earth yet fixed, or the sun borne round it, how could days exist? . . . Would it not be absurd for the first and greatest God to command, "Let this come into existence," or something else, so that he made so much on one day and again so much more on the second, and so on?[17] If these are the Creator's works, how can it be that God should make what is evil (the serpent)? And . . . how can he find fault and threaten and destroy his own offspring (e.g., in the Flood)?[18]

Book 4

The fourth book discussed the history of the Jews given in the Bible, arguing that a far more credible history was written by Sanchuniathon of Byblos.

Note on Books 5–11

No quotations from these books have been found in any of the extant writings composed against Porphyry. However, we may reconstruct the contents of Books 5–11 from the *Apocriticus* of Macarius Magnes.[19]

Book 5: Criticisms of Jesus Christ

- In John 7:6–10,[20] Christ said he would not go up to the feast and then contradicted himself by going.
- Why did Christ not appear to Pilate and Herod and other trustworthy witnesses after the resurrection, and not merely to women and peasants? He had told the high-priest . . . that they would see him in his glory. Had he shown himself (to them) it would have caused belief and saved (the Christians) from Jewish persecution.
- Why did he allow himself to be mocked and crucified, not saying anything worthy for the benefit of his judge or his hearers, but tolerating insults like the meanest of men?
- Why, after saying "Fear not them that kill the body," did he pray in his agony that his suffering might pass from him?
- Why did he not cast himself down when his tempter told him to? Did he fear danger?

Book 6

This book listed inconsistencies and absurdities in the teachings of Christ as quoted in the four canonical Gospels.

- In John 5:31, Christ said, "If I bear witness of myself, my witness is not true"; and yet he did bear witness of himself, as when he said, "I am the light of the world."
- In John 5:44, he said, "If you believed Moses you would believe me, for he wrote concerning me." But the stupidity of the saying is shown, first, in that no writings of Moses have been preserved; and second, in that, even if Moses did write them, they cannot be shown to speak of Christ as God.
- In Matthew 19:24, he said, "It is easier for a camel to go through the eye of a needle than for a rich man to enter into the kingdom." But if this is the case, all practical morality disappears and salvation depends not on virtue but on poverty, which is ridiculous.
- In Matthew 26:11, he said, "Me you have not with you always," but elsewhere he says the exact opposite, "Lo, I am with you always."
- The saying in John 6:54 about eating his flesh and drinking his blood is worse than the cannibals in its savagery. The first three Gospel writers probably omitted it because it was so repulsive.
- The saying in Mark 16:18 about the signs following true believers, such as receiving no harm from drinking poison—if this is true, it ought to be made the test of church membership and of appointing Church officers.
- Similarly in Matthew 17:19, he said, "You shall say to this mountain, be thou lifted up," etc. But not even the clergy can do it.
- His words to Peter are utterly inconsistent, for first he said, "Get thee behind me Satan," and then he said, "On this rock I will found my Church."

Book 7: Untrustworthiness of the Gospel Writers

- In Matthew 9:9, the account of the call of Matthew/Levi is most improbable, making him follow the first man he casually meets. Either the Gospel writer is untruthful or the Savior's first followers had no sense.
- The Gospel writers, in their desire to make the miracle of Christ walking on the sea seem more amazing, call Genezareth (i.e., Galilee) a "sea" even though it is no more than a little lake.

· There are numerous discrepancies in the four accounts of the crucifixion of Jesus. Mark says someone offered Jesus vinegar and he uttered the cry "My God, My God," etc. Matthew says it was wine mixed with gall which he tasted and refused. John says they gave him vinegar with hyssop which he took and said, "It is finished," and died. Luke says the great cry was "Father into thy hands," etc. These discrepancies show that the Gospels are not historically reliable.

Contents of Books 8–13: General Objections

Book 8. An examination of the shabby Christian ideas about God.

Book 9. The obscene and foolish Christian rituals.

Book 10. The unreasonableness of Christian doctrines.

Book 11. Special objections to the idea of the incarnation of the word of God.

Book 12. Investigation into Old Testament prophecies (particularly the Book of Daniel which is a complete fraud).

Book 13. Rejection of the Christian hope for the end of the world. It proves that the Christians hate both themselves and the world.

Book 14: The Gospel Writers Did Not Interpret the Old Testament Correctly

· Mark in his opening verses confuses two Old Testament quotations, one taken from Malachi and the other from Isaiah. He wrongly attributes both to Isaiah.

· Matthew 13:35 quotes Christ speaking in parables as fulfilling the prophecy of Isaiah, "I will open my mouth in parables," etc., but in fact the words of the "prophecy" come from Asaph in Psalm 78:2.

Book 15: The Christian Church Has Had an Evil Effect upon the World, Causing Untold Misery

· The Gods have given up helping men since the honoring of Jesus began.

· The plague raging for so long in Rome is because Asclepius and the other Gods have abandoned it.

Conclusion

This concludes our summary of the main points in Porphyry's writing. Such a summary can provide at best only a faint impression of the power of the original. One scholar who spent decades attempting to isolate Porphyry's words said this about it:

> *Against the Christians* was the work of a man who knew the language of the Bible from one end to the other, and who annotated a great deal of it with the shrewd and biting criticism of skeptical common sense . . . He relentlessly attacked the Christian miracles (described in the Gospels) as not resting on sufficient evidence . . . He seems to have regarded them as pious fictions intended to glorify Jesus, whom he considered a good but weak enthusiast, a man who often said and did what was inconsistent and unwise. He laid the chief blame for the propagation of this false and dangerous cult, not upon Jesus but upon his followers. These he branded as a pack of fools and knaves, (men who) gave themselves up to unworthy quarrels and bitter controversies.[21]

This reconstruction, while hopefully faithful to the original, does not fully convey the alarming force of his arguments. In the following list, I attempt to add what I believe to be is a fair replica of Porphyry's rhetoric. His objections are summarized under four main heads:

Objection 1

Christians are social misfits who reject their own venerable Greco-Roman heritage in order to adopt the crabbed and alien tradition of the Jews. But why would anyone want to adopt the Jewish conceit of being the supreme race? The idea of the particular choice of the Jews by God is offensive to international etiquette and is absurd theologically. Why would the God who created the entire universe favor one nation and ignore the rest? This concept is just Jewish arrogance dressed up in religious jargon. In fact, the Jews have precious little to be proud of.

> Jewish literature and tradition are inferior to the Greek; the Ten Commandments, where there are parallels to the non-Jewish world, are of lesser value; the Jewish God is seen to be vengeful and jealous. The Jews had no wise men, their generals were mediocre, they knew no science, and their laws were barbarous and savage. From this pathetic nation the Christians have chosen for themselves the most inferior elements.[22]

Objection 2

Not satisfied with being traitors, Christians madly go on and abandon even Judaism, concocting for themselves monstrous fables about a crucified Savior who had a bodily resurrection. These ideas are offensive to all reasonable and decent people.[23]

Objection 3

Having thus separated themselves from all mankind, Christians make a mockery of the teachings of their Founder in the way they fight against and oppose each other. Indeed, they seem to hate each other more than those who do not share their insane beliefs. Because of their constant bickering, it is impossible to say what the Christian religion actually does teach.

Objection 4

The Scriptures used by the Christians are full of contradictions and inconsistencies, particularly their fables about Jesus they call Gospels. It is common knowledge that Christians constantly alter their sacred Scriptures to make them say whatever they please.

Porphyry summed up his arguments by vehemently rejecting the Christian claim to be good citizens of the empire, a claim first made by Justin Martyr in the mid-second century. "On the contrary," Prophyry said in effect, "you are traitors! You conduct barbarous and unspeakable rites! You are atheists who teach insane superstitions! You are fools who corrupt your own sacred writings! It is because of you that the great gods are offended and are punishing us! Your insanity will bring down ruin upon the whole empire! You must be exterminated or Rome will be totally destroyed!"

CHAPTER 9

Eusebius of Caesarea's Four-Part Response to Porphyry

As we noted in the previous chapter, the Christian responses to Porphyry went on for centuries, if one takes into consideration all that was written against him by Methodius of Tyre, Eusebius of Caesarea, Apollinarius of Laodicea, Augustine of Hippo, and other fifth- and sixth-century orthodox theologians. Augustine's response will be discussed in the next chapter. But by far the most comprehensive reply to Porphyry came from a contemporary of his, the Emperor Constantine's preeminent historian and biblical scholar, Eusebius of Caesarea (260–340). In the process, Eusebius dealt with most aspects of the Synoptic Problem, albeit in a very roundabout way.

Eusebius was born in Palestine around the year 260 and grew up in or near Caesarea, a prosperous seaport on the Palestinian coast. He says in one of his writings that he was taught and baptized according to the creed used by the Church in Caesarea.[1] As a young man he was given an extensive education in both pagan philosophy and Christian theology by a leading Christian scholar in the city named Pamphilus. Eusebius also learned from the other scholars who congregated in Pamphilus' library during the period of peace between the persecutions of Decius/Valerian (250–259) and Diocletian (303–312). Origen came to Caesarea in 233 and remained there for nearly twenty years, greatly adding to the library's collection. Eusebius based many of his own biblical publications on Origen's research. Finally, it was probably at Caesarea that Eusebius first met the young Emperor Constantine when the latter went through the city on his way to Egypt with Diocletian in 296.[2]

When Eusebius first heard of Porphyry's book *Against the Christians,* there would have been little doubt that he and the circle of Christian scholars at Caesarea would reply to it. For one thing, they had Origen's magnificent example to go by, *Against Celsus* having been written there in Caesarea not long before.[3] Eusebius hastily dashed off a refutation, called *Against Porphyry,* in twenty-five books.[4] However, he seems to have realized that a much more substantial counterattack was needed. Eventually, he produced major responses to each of Porphyry's four main criticisms.[5] Although Porphyry is not named explicitly very often in Eusebius' pages, he definitely is the key opponent in view throughout Eusebius' great *Preparation for the Gospel* (fifteen books) and his even larger *Demonstration of the Gospel* (twenty books).[6] I suggest that his third largest writing, the *Ecclesiastical History* (ten books) and his *Gospel Canons* are actually the third and fourth parts of Eusebius' overall defense of Christianity against the accusations of Porphyry. Let us briefly examine each of these writings to see how they were carefully shaped to rebut each of Porphyry's four major objections.

The Preparation for the Gospel *and the* Demonstration of the Gospel

The *Preparation for the Gospel* was the first part of Eusebius' response to Porphyry. It was probably written during the latter years of the persecution (ca. 305–310). In it, Eusebius set out to refute *Porphyry's first main objection,* that Christians had unreasonably abandoned the honorable heritage of the Greeks to take up Jewish customs.[7] Eusebius replied that the Christians were fully justified in rejecting the religion and philosophy of the Greeks and turning to the religion and sacred writings of the Hebrews. Eusebius defended this position by means of a shrewd device: turning the Greek philosophers' criticisms of their own mythology and each others' philosophical schools back against them. This turned the *Preparatio* into a priceless series of quotations taken from Greek philosophers whose writings have otherwise perished.

Having undermined the credibility of the Greek heritage, Eusebius went on to urge the reasonableness of the Jewish alternative. Next came the much larger *Demonstration of the Gospel,* which probably appeared after the Edict of Toleration in 312.[8] Its goal was to refute *Porphyry's sec-*

ond objection that the Christians, having exchanged Greek ways for Jewish, foolishly abandoned them also for some sort of outrageous nonsense about a crucified messiah.[9] Eusebius' reply consisted of lengthy discussions of the Hebrew Scripture interpreted so that they prophesied Jesus Christ as the promised Messiah and Savior of the world.[10] We may be sure the decades of exegetical labor by Origen and others in the library of Pamphilus contributed richly to this complex and lengthy reply. Eusebius also took this opportunity to respond to contemporaneous Jewish critique of the Christian interpretations of Jewish sacred books.

Part three of Eusebius' response to Porphyry was embodied in the *Ecclesiastical History*. It probably appeared in 324, just before the Council of Nicaea.[11] Its purpose was to refute the *third objection of Porphyry*, Celsus, and the other pagan skeptics, that the Christian Church was such a hodgepodge of sects, divisions, hostile factions, and correspondingly bewildering variations of their sacred texts that no one could tell—least of all the Christians themselves—exactly what they believed. Eusebius sought to refute this criticism by laying out a detailed record of all who belonged to the orthodox or "catholic" tradition on the one hand and the names of those who belonged to the deviant, heretical branches of the Christian Church on the other.

The fourth part of Eusebius' response focused on *Porphyry's fourth objection*,[12] that even if the Christians could agree on their beliefs and on their sacred Scriptures, the orthodox Gospels were so riddled with inconsistencies and contradictions that they were useless for establishing a system of doctrine. Since the third and fourth parts of Eusebius' response to Porphyry bear directly on the history of the Synoptic Problem, I will discuss them more fully.

The Ecclesiastical History

To adequately answer Porphyry's last objection, Eusebius had to prove two points. First, the orthodox faction was guided by an unbroken succession of authorities going back to Jesus Christ himself and therefore was in undoubted possession of Divine Truth. Second, in contrast to the heretics, the orthodox network used only the four Gospels written by actual disciples of Jesus or their assistants, and they were perfectly consistent with each other.

As for the first point, the goal of Eusebius' *Ecclesiastical History* was to provide a historical record of all those who belonged to the true Church founded by Jesus and the Apostles and all who belonged to false and deviant forms of Christianity. This purpose is explicitly announced in the very first sentence of the book.[13]

> It is my purpose to write an account of the successions of the holy apostles,[14] as well as of the times (i.e., historical events) which have elapsed from the days of our Savior to our own; and to relate the many important events which are said to have occurred in the history of the (orthodox) Church; and to mention those who have governed and presided over the (orthodox) Church in the most prominent parishes,[15] and those who in each generation have proclaimed the divine word either orally or in writing. It is my purpose also to give the names and number and times (history) of those who through love of innovation have run into the greatest errors, and, proclaiming themselves discoverers of knowledge falsely so-called, have like fierce wolves unmercifully devastated the flock of Christ.[16]

Eusebius intended that his history be nothing less than a detailed, name-by-name separation of the sheep from the wolves. He intended to identify by name those who belonged to the few orthodox congregations that possessed an unbroken succession of bishops back to the first convert appointed by the founding Apostle for that region.[17] This was the essence of his reply to Porphyry: "as an outsider you have made an elementary mistake. You lumped all Christians together in one pot, but in fact there are enormous differences among us. Many so-called Christians have invented their doctrines whereas the true Christians have received theirs from the Apostles of Jesus Christ. I will now give you a record of the names of those who belong to each group . . ." and he went on to do just that in crushing detail.

Eusebius' Debt to Irenaeus

Eusebius did not invent this method of identifying the holders of true doctrine by tracing the lineage of their "school." It had already been used for centuries as a potent weapon in the polemics between (and within) the Greek philosophical schools. Irenaeus used it against the heretics of his generation.[18] In his *Refutation and Overthrow of Knowledge, Falsely So-called,*[19] written during the episcopate of Eleutherus at Rome (182–188), Irenaeus traced the succession of the Gnostics teaching in Rome (mainly the schools of Valentinus, Saturninus, and Basilides) back to the archheretic Simon Magus.[20] Irenaeus argued that each heretic had mixed foreign ideas into his Christian theology.[21] Orthodox Christians, on the other hand, said Irenaeus, clung faithfully to the apostolic tradition, so that even though they were "dispersed throughout the whole world, even unto the ends of the earth, (they have kept the teachings they) have received from the apostles and their disciples."[22] This is the reason why true Christians all believe the same thing . . .

> as if (they) had one soul and one and the same heart, and (they) proclaim (these teachings) and hand them down with perfect harmony, as if (they) possessed one mouth . . . For the (orthodox) churches of Germany do not believe or hand down anything different (from those) in Spain, (or) those in Gaul, (or) those in the East . . . But as the sun is one and the same throughout the whole world, so also the preaching of the truth shines everywhere and enlightens all men.[23]

Irenaeus was not the first bishop to combat heretics by relying upon the network of orthodox bishops. Precisely the same sort of institutional bulwark against false doctrine had been advocated several decades earlier by Ignatius, the early-second-century bishop of Antioch (fl. ca. 110). The germ of this concept can be seen in a letter sent near the year 100 from the Church at Rome to the Corinthian Christians, admonishing some of their members to give up their rebellion. Notice how the "succession" goes straight back to God.

> The Apostles received the Gospel for us from the Lord Jesus Christ; Jesus, the Christ, was sent from God. Thus Christ is from God and the Apostles from Christ . . . And so the Apostles after receiving their orders . . . went out in the confidence of the Holy Spirit to preach the Good News . . . They preached in country and city and appointed their first converts . . . to be bishops and deacons of future believers.[24]

Coming back to the *Ecclesiastical History,* Eusebius was very aware that his goal of compiling a record of all of the names of all of the bishops and theologians in all of the churches that traced their lineage back to one of the Apostles was not only something that had never been done before, it was an impossible goal.

> At the outset I must crave for my work the indulgence of the wise, for I confess that it is beyond my power to produce a perfect and complete history, and since I am the first to enter upon the subject, I am attempting to traverse as it were a lonely and untrodden path. I pray that I may have God as my guide and the power of the Lord as my aid, since I am unable to find even the bare footsteps of those who have traveled

the way before me, except in brief fragments which, some in one way, others in another, have transmitted to us particular accounts of the times in which they lived ... (These fragments) we shall endeavor to embody ... in an historical narrative, content if we preserve the memory of the successions of (bishops from) the Apostles of our Savior, if not indeed of all, yet of the most renowned of them in those churches which are the most noted and which even to the present time are held in honor.[25]

The Inner Logic of the Canonization Process

Having seen the purpose Eusebius had for recording the names, dates, and activities of bishops who belonged to churches originally founded by the Apostles—namely, to establish a legitimate authority whose decisions were normative in all matters pertaining to Scripture and doctrine, we can now examine his second goal. This was to explain how this authoritative network decided which writings should be accepted as divinely inspired Scripture to be used in public worship and which writings should not.

As we saw in Origen's case, establishing which were the authentic Gospels was the first step. However, Origen lived at a time when the process was still somewhat informal. He did not dwell on how he knew which Gospels were authentic. Eusebius went a step beyond Origen and established in writing the names, dates, and addresses of the authentic network of orthodox authorities from whom a reliable judgment could confidently be obtained.

Because this step is so crucial to a full understanding of how the Great Assembly came to rest with *four* (and not one or ten or twenty) Gospels, I will dwell a bit on what we can learn from Eusebius' pages. There are certain elements of the logic of the orthodox canonization process which have not been, to my knowledge, adequately recognized. These will be clarified as I examine a few statements from Eusebius and conclude with a crucial statement from Tertullian.

Apart from the opening sentences quoted above, the first explicit statement of the Great Assembly's basic canonization logic occurs at the beginning of Book Three. Book Two was concerned with events in Palestine and the East. Eusebius was now ready to begin describing the—idealistically symmetrical—dispersion of Jesus' disciples throughout the known world:

Such was the condition of the Jews. Meanwhile the holy apostles and disciples of our Savior were dispersed throughout the world. Parthia, according to tradition, was allotted to Thomas as his field of labor;

Scythia to Andrew, Asia to John, who, after he lived some time there, died at Ephesus. Peter appears to have preached in Pontus, Galatia, Bithynia, Cappadocia, and Asia (to the Jews of the Dispersion) . . . (while) Paul preached the Gospel from Jerusalem to Illyricum and afterwards suffered martyrdom in Rome under Nero.[26]

Eusebius then gave the name of the first bishop of Rome after describing the deaths of the Apostles Paul and Peter. The reference to Peter becomes the occasion for Eusebius to go off on a tangent, as he summarized the consensus regarding the genuine and spurious writings associated with the Apostle Peter:

One Epistle of Peter, that called "the First," is acknowledged as genuine. And this the ancient elders used freely in their own writings as an undisputed work. But we have learned that his extant Second Epistle does not belong to the canon.[27] Yet, as it has appeared profitable to many, it has been used[28] with the other Scriptures.[29] However, the so-called Acts of Peter and the Gospel which bears his name[30] and the Preaching and the Apocalypse as they are called,[31] we know have not been accepted (anywhere) in the whole (collection of) catholic (writings),[32] because no ecclesiastical writer,[33] ancient or of our own time, has made use of . . . them.[34]

Eusebius went on to describe the basic strategy he followed for all writings that were at any time considered to be candidates for inclusion in the Great Assembly's canon of Scripture.

But in the course of my history I shall be careful to show, in addition to the official successions,[35] what use the ecclesiastical (i.e., orthodox) writers have made, from time to time, of any of the disputed works, and what they have said in regard to the canonical and accepted writings.[36]

I will discuss the special meaning of the terms "disputed" and "accepted" in a moment. But first let us summarize the logical elements described thus far in the canonization process.

- The only decisions that count come from a specific network of bishops and theologians who belonged to churches that had been founded by one of the Apostles.
- Eusebius will trace the successions of every one of these churches in order to identify the names of the bishops and theologians who

alone must be consulted regarding any matters of Scripture (canon) or doctrine (creed).[37]

· Eusebius will include in his narrative whatever these authorities have said about all candidate writings, whether indirectly, by making "use" of it, or directly, by expressing an explicit judgment on its canonical status, from the first generation down to his own time.

· He has given a little preview of what this historical survey will produce: three logical options. Some writings with the name of the Apostle Peter on them will be put into the category *universally accepted* (in this case, the First Epistle); others will be put into the category *disputed* (the Second Epistle); and still others will be put into the category *universally rejected* (the *Gospel of Peter*, the *Apocalypse of Peter*, and the *Preaching of Peter*).[38]

The most important passage in the entire *Ecclesiastical History* for clarifying the logic of the canonization process does not occur in a prominent location at the beginning or end of any of his chapters or "books." It is buried two-thirds of the way through Book Three. Nevertheless, it is the center and pivot of Eusebius' entire survey of the canonization process in the first six books of the *Ecclesiastical History*. Up to this point, he has focused on the "universally accepted" writings. After this point, he will spend more time on the "disputed" writings.

> (Let us now) sum up the writings of the New Testament[39] which have been already mentioned. First, then, must be put the holy quartet of the Gospels; following them the Acts of the Apostles. After this must be reckoned the epistles of Paul; next in order the Epistle of John called "the First,"[40] as also the Epistle of Peter should be recognized[41] . . . These then belong among the accepted writings.[42] Among the disputed writings,[43] although they are recognized by many, are the so-called (Epistles) "of James" and "of Jude," also the Second Epistle of Peter, and those that are called the Second and Third (Epistles) of John . . . Among the spurious[44] must be reckoned also the Acts of Paul . . . and the Apocalypse of Peter . . . also the Gospel according to the Hebrews . . . (and) such books as the Gospels of Peter, (and) of Thomas . . . and the Acts of Andrew and John . . . To none of these has any who belonged to the succession of the orthodox ever referred in his writings.[45]

Let us briefly summarize the logical elements in the canonization process disclosed by this important passage. All the way through the *Ecclesiastical History*, Eusebius recorded the votes yea or nay regarding writings which were candidates for the New Testament canon by authorities who belonged to churches that were founded by one (or more) of the Apostles. When all was said and done, a small number (probably twenty)[46] of the total number of potential candidates for inclusion in the New Testament canon (under one hundred)[47] received unanimous affirmative votes from all of the authorities in the apostolic succession churches. These few writings Eusebius labeled "acknowledged" (ὁμολογουμένοι). Note that he means *universally* acknowledged, because the next category, "disputed" (ἀντιλεγομένοι) meant precisely that the same authorities were *split* in their decision regarding certain writings, some having voted yea while others voted nay about them.

Finally, the term "spurious, counterfeit" refers to writings that all of the orthodox authorities in churches having apostolic successions *unanimously* agreed were not genuine. Despite the presence of Apostles' names in the titles of these candidate writings, they were universally rejected as νόθοι spurious, illegitimate.

On the basis of this discussion, let us add three more logical elements to the list we began above:

- Since the revelation of God is perfectly self-consistent,[48]
- all churches having valid successions back to the Apostles will teach self-consistent (i.e., non-self-contradictory) doctrine,[49]
- and they will all use the same, original, apostolic writings in their worship and theology.

Eusebius used these logical concepts both positively and negatively throughout the first six books of the *Ecclesiastical History*. When used positively, they certified certain writings as apostolic and therefore canonical. When applied negatively, they certified many more writings as never having been used in churches founded by Apostles or as having been explicitly rejected by authorities belonging to the churches founded by Apostles. The latter immediately excluded them from the final set; the former raised a question mark against them.

Thus prepared, Eusebius could confront Porphyry and his ilk with an ironclad defense: our Gospels are verifiably apostolic in origin. As such, they are naturally completely consistent with each other in content.

Tertullian Adds a Clarification to the Logic of Canonization

There was one crucial element of the fundamental logic of canonization that did not, to my knowledge, explicitly appear anywhere in Eusebius' writings. The clearest instance of it can be found in the legal brief composed by the Roman lawyer turned Christian theologian Tertullian (ca. 155–220), entitled *The Prescription of Heretics.*[50]

Tertullian's argument ran as follows:

1. Heretics should be excluded from the Great Assembly because they abuse the Scriptures in the way they interpret them.
2. Why do heretics misinterpret the Scriptures? Because their theology was not formed by deep, sustained contact with apostolic orthodoxy. How can one objectively verify this contention?
3. Because

   ... their doctrine, after comparison with that of the apostles, *will declare by its very diversity and contrariety,* that it had for its author neither an apostle nor an apostolic man, because the apostles would never have taught things which were self-contradictory, (nor would) the apostolic men have inculcated teachings different from the apostles.[51]

4. Contrary to the heretics' repeated accusation that the Great Assembly is filled with error, the exact opposite is the case: the churches belonging to the apostolic successions teach pure apostolic truth. And how can one objectively verify this contention? Precisely by the fact that they do not have any variation or contradiction among them in what they teach and believe.
5. This is no accident.

   Is it likely that so many churches, and they so great, should have (accidentally) gone astray into one and the same faith? *No casualty distributed among many men issues in one and the same result* ... When, therefore, that which is deposited among many is found to be one and the same, it is not the result of error *but of tradition.*[52]

Tertullian's principle (in italics) is important because it spells out an important element in the logic of the whole canonization process employed by the Great Assembly. This logical principle brought the whole canonization process out of the realm of abstract logic and rooted it firmly within the world of flesh-and-blood Church politics, binding theological orthodoxy firmly to the institutional bulwark of historic, apostolic succession.[53]

One final point. As might be expected, Eusebius' *Ecclesiastical History* had a powerful impact on the Church authorities of his day and, through them, on the canonization process itself. It probably paved the way for the Emperor Constantine to request that Eusebius prepare "fifty copies of the sacred Scriptures . . . written on parchment in a legible manner . . . by professional transcribers thoroughly practiced in their art,"[54] to be used in the churches in his new imperial city of Constantinople. In turn, Eusebius' choice of what to put into these "magnificent and elaborately bound volumes"[55] undoubtedly influenced the canonization process as well.[56]

The Question of the Internal Harmony and Consistency of the Gospels

Now that the Great Assembly was stuck with *four* apostolic Gospels, there still remained the major problem of how to cope with their obvious differences. Porphyry's fourth criticism still haunted everyone: the inconsistencies among the Gospels were so flagrant that it was impossible to found any system of Christian doctrine on them.

Porphyry was not the first to raise this objection. Celsus and probably Marcion before him had said much the same thing. What was new was Porphyry's nasty habit of actually reading the Gospels and comparing them point by point. He had been followed by Hierocles in mocking and deriding specific passages in the Gospels. Origen's skillful allegorizations were greeted with scorn and derision. Clearly, something definitive had to be done.

Characteristically, Eusebius' defense of the truth and harmony of the four Gospels came out in several installments. First, he wrote a reply against Hierocles not long after the Edict of Toleration in 312.[57] Then around 320,[58] he composed two small writings that dealt with the most troubling inconsistencies in the Gospels. The *Questions and Answers on the Genealogy of Our Savior Addressed to Stephanus* sought to resolve certain discrepancies in the infancy narratives of Matthew and Luke (including the strikingly divergent genealogies), and the *Questions and Answers on the Resurrection of Our Savior Addressed to Marinus* set out to reconcile the resurrection accounts. These writings dealt with questions such as the following:[59]

- How does the Savior appear after his resurrection "late on the Sabbath" in Matthew, but "early on the first day of the week" in Mark?
- How, according to Matthew, have Mary of Magdala and the other Mary seen, while standing *outside* the tomb, *one* angel sitting (outside) on the slab of the tomb, and how according to John does Mary of Magdala see *two* angels sitting *inside* the tomb, whereas according to Luke *two men* appeared to the women, and accord-

ing to Mark *a young man* was there sitting on the *right side* of the tomb visible to Mary of Magdala and Mary the wife of James and Salome?

Eusebius responded to questions of this type by postulating additional persons of the same name or additional events of the same description until all had been accommodated in one harmonious narrative on the literal level. "Thus he explicitly infers that there were two women with the name Mary of Magdala, in order to avoid any suspicion that the evangelists may have erred."[60]

The differences between infancy accounts were handled in a similar fashion:

> After Jesus was born, he was circumcised in the temple and taken to Nazareth (Luke), but two years later Joseph and Mary went to Bethlehem again, whence they fled to Egypt (Matthew).[61]

These writings show Eusebius poised to provide a complete harmony of the Gospels in answer to the philosophical detractors of his day. Instead, he pulled back and set off in an entirely novel direction, creating an elaborate chart listing by a simple numerical code system every parallel paragraph in the Gospels. Did Eusebius invent this system? Possibly. He says in the preface that he already had a synopsis-like chart created by Ammonius, an Alexandrian scholar and contemporary of Origen's.[62] He also knew of Tatian's *Diatessaron*, although he appears never to have seen an actual copy of it.

Ammonius' chart contained Matthew broken up into paragraphs, with the parallel texts of Mark, Luke, and John rearranged so that they corresponded to Matthew's order. Eusebius did not like Ammonius' disruptive rearrangement. But he probably took over Ammonius' paragraph divisions (*sectiones*), numbered them in different color inks, and then created ten tables (or *canones*) listing all of the parallels in differing sets: four Gospels, three Gospels, etc.[63] When he was done, he sent his chart to a friend with a letter explaining the way it worked.[64] Here is Eusebius' letter almost in full:

> Eusebius, to Carpianus his beloved brother in the Lord, greeting.
> Ammonius the Alexandrian, having employed much industry and effort—as was proper—has left us the fourfold Gospel,[65] placing the corresponding passages[66] of the other evangelists beside the Gospel of Matthew so that the continuous thread of the other three is necessarily broken,[67] preventing a continuous reading. So that you may know the

individual passages of each evangelist,[68] in which they were led to speak truthfully on the same subject, with the whole context and order of the other three still preserved,[69] I have taken my point of departure from the work of the man already mentioned, but proceeded by a different method,[70] and have produced for you ten canons which follow:

The first (table or canon) contains numbers in which the four, Matthew, Mark, Luke, and John have said similar things.

The second in which the three, Matthew, Mark, and Luke.

The third in which the three, Matthew, Luke, and John.

The fourth in which the three, Matthew, Mark, and John.

The fifth in which the two, Matthew and Luke.

The sixth in which the two, Matthew and Mark.

The seventh in which the two, Matthew and John.

The eighth in which the two, Mark and Luke.

The ninth in which the two, Luke and John.

The tenth in which each of them wrote about something in an individual manner.

This then is the underlying purpose of the following canons; their clear application is as follows: before each section of the four Gospels[71] stands a number in the margin, beginning with the first, then the second and third, and proceeding in order throughout until the end of the books. And underneath each number is a mark in red,[72] indicating in which of the ten canons the number occurs ... Hence, if you were to open any one of the four Gospels, and wish to light upon any chapter whatever,[73] to know who else has said similar things and to find the relevant passages in each, in which they treated of the same things, then find the number marked against the passage which you have before you, look for it in the canon which the mark in red has suggested and you will immediately learn ... those passages which say similar things.

This letter has been quoted almost in full for two reasons. Eusebius' novel method for dealing with the differences among the Gospels had revolutionary significance. It provided a quick and simple way for all who lacked the leisure and mental capacity to memorize the Gospels to find their parallel passages. Eusebius inserted this new scheme in every Bible produced in his scriptorium and, before long, other scriptoria adopted it as well. It was copied at the beginning of virtually all Gospel manuscripts in the West down to the Reformation. After that, it still found a place in the critical editions of Mill, Bengel, Griesbach, Tischendorf, Nestle, and Aland.

In the second place, Eusebius intentionally created a scheme of parallelization *that did not disturb the original order or contents* of the four

Gospels. In this sense, he was a true student of Origen, who also did not attempt—beyond a certain point—to harmonize the texts on the literal level since he believed that the essential harmony of the story contained in the four Gospels already existed on the spiritual (πνευματικός), i.e., symbolic, level. Furthermore, Origen viewed their literal, surface differences as important evidence of the *accommodations of the Holy Spirit* to different human capacities and needs.[74] As such, they were to be honored, not wiped away.

In other words, Eusebius may have realized that the very act of literal harmonization, far from being an appropriate defense of the credibility of the Gospels, was actually a misguided attempt to improve upon God's self-giving within the diversity of human forms or shapes. For these reasons, Eusebius may have sensed the danger here and avoided physically harmonizing the Gospel texts. Instead, he left them in their original literal diversity and at the same time pointed out the impressive mass of material they shared (thereby partially depriving the critics of this major objection). It was a brilliant solution to an exceedingly thorny problem.

CHAPTER 10

Augustine Refutes the Manichaean Critique of the Gospels; the Second Form of the Synoptic Problem

⌐⌐⌐⌐

*A*ugustine of Hippo (354–430) gave one direct explanation as to why he attempted to carry out something as difficult as harmonizing all four Gospels. In his final writing, the *Retractions*, he said:[1]

> During the years (from 400–416) in which I was gradually composing the (ten) books for the *On the Trinity*,[1] by unceasing labor I also wrote other things ... Among these are four books, *On the Harmony of the Evangelists*, composed because of those who falsely accuse the Evangelists of lacking agreement.[2]

Beginning from this single clue, historians have pieced together some of the circumstances that led to the writing of what is, by all accounts, the most sophisticated and comprehensive explanation of the writing of the Gospels in all of early Christianity.

For a number of years, Augustine had been deeply involved in biblical exegesis, working in particular on the first chapter of Genesis. Out of this intense exegetical activity there came a small handbook called *On Christian Doctrine*, published in 397. It set forth, for the first time in the Church's history, the principles and methods of biblical interpretation. It reveals that Augustine was quite aware of the obscurities, inconsistencies, inaccuracies, and morally offensive passages in the Bible. We will return to this writing in a moment, to show how its guidelines were applied to the Gospels.

Augustine was not particularly well prepared to be a biblical exegete. For one thing, he could not read Greek very well and had no knowledge of Hebrew. Normally, he used the *Vetus Itala,* the early Latin translation found among the Christian churches in Italy, although he sometimes used different Latin translations found just in north Africa.[3] However, for this particular task, he used Jerome's recently completed "critical edition" of the Latin New Testament, the Vulgate, which saved him from some of the more egregious inaccuracies in the Latin translations of his day.[4]

Although he was not fluent in Greek, he was familiar with the great Greek biblical commentators in the Latin translations by Ambrose, Hilary, and Lactantius. He made use of the Eusebian sections and canons, which were included in his Latin text of the Gospels by Jerome.[5]

However, Augustine more than made up for his lack of linguistic expertise by his superb philosophical training and aptitude for rigorous theological thought. To these he added a depth and power of expression borne out of his painful conversion to the Christian faith as an adult.

So much for his technical background and preparation. What about the reason he gave for tackling the question of the inconsistencies and differences among the Gospels? Who exactly were "those who falsely accuse the evangelists of lacking agreement"?

Augustine's Constant Strife with the Manichaeans

The opponents primarily in view were certain learned Manichaeans, possibly former friends of his in Italy (mainly Rome) and north Africa. They were adept at embarrassing their learned Christian colleagues by ridiculing the Gospels. They never tired of pointing out the inconsistencies and contradictions between the Gospels as proof that Christianity was essentially muddle-headed.

> Those holy chariots of the Lord (= the four Gospels), by which he is carried through the earth subjugating peoples to his lenient yoke and his light burden, certain persons falsely and maliciously attack, either because of godless arrogance or ignorant boldness, in order to detract from the trust in those truthful narratives by which the Christian religion has been disseminated through the world.[6]

During the period from about 386 on, he composed a series of counterattacks against these Manichaeans, focusing on their morals and their theosophical system.[7] Why was Augustine so obsessed with these Manichaean critics? Because, not many years before, he had been one of them himself.

> For my part, I, who after much and long-continued bewilderment, attained at last to the discovery of the simple truth (of the Gospel) ... who barely succeeded by God's help in refuting the vain imaginings of my mind ... who long wept that the immutable and unviolable Being would vouchsafe to convince me inwardly of Himself in harmony with the testimony of the sacred books (of the Christians),—I can on no account rage against you, for I must ... be patient with you as formerly my associates were with me when I went madly and blindly astray in your beliefs.[8]

This polemical activity culminated in the year 400 when Augustine published a lengthy attack on the Manichaeans' most prominent philosopher, entitled *Against Faustus the Manichaean* (in thirty-three books).[9] In this work, although Augustine battled relentlessly against the Manichaean dualistic doctrines, he was nevertheless forced by Faustus to go back again and again to the inconsistencies and contradictions among the four Gospels, particularly the two shockingly different genealogies of Jesus.

> Faustus: "Do I believe the Gospel? Certainly! Do I therefore believe that Christ was born? Certainly not!"[10] ... "Do I also believe in the incarnation? ... I have long tried to persuade myself of (this), that *God was born;* but the discrepancy in the genealogies of Luke and Matthew caused me to stumble, as I knew not which to follow."[11]

Having hit upon this sore point, Faustus came back repeatedly to the great discrepancy between these two genealogies as proof that the Gospel writers were fundamentally untrustworthy in everything they wrote.[12]

As a further example of the kind of penetrating questions the Manichaeans brought to bear on the Gospels, consider this question put by Faustus:

> Faustus: "You ask why we do not receive the law and the prophets, when Christ said that he came not to destroy them, but to fulfill them. Where do we learn that Jesus said this? From Matthew, who declares that he said it on the mount. In whose presence was it said? In the presence of Peter, Andrew, James, and John—only these four. The rest, including Matthew himself, were not yet chosen. Is it not the case that one of these four—John, namely—wrote a Gospel? It is. Does he mention this saying of Jesus? No. How, then, does it happen that what is not recorded

by John, who was on the mount, is recorded by Matthew, who became a follower of Christ long after He came down from the mount?"[13]

This is the sort of close comparison of the Gospels that was introduced by Porphyry. Once the learned critics of Christianity found out how much havoc could be wrought by closely comparing the Gospels to each other, they began tearing them to shreds. When Christian scholars tried to give convincing explanations, they merely invited further attacks.

The "Porphyrian List"

Augustine said that, after he had written part of *On the Trinity*, he stopped and wrote other things, including the four books *On the Harmony of the Evangelists*. What triggered this change in course?

There may be a clue in *On the Trinity* itself. Why did Augustine write *On the Trinity*? To answer this question, we must go back and look at *Against Faustus*. In this writing, Augustine replied to criticisms from the learned Neoplatonic and Manichaean critics regarding the Christian doctrine of the incarnation. Augustine's answers bristle with complicated exegetical, philosophical, and theological concepts. However, the format he adopted in the *Against Faustus* was one of question-and-answer, which prevented him from giving a systematic treatment of the complex issues involved. So he immediately began another writing, this one arranged along more systematic lines. This *second reply* to Faustus (and the rest of the Manichaeans and Neoplatonists) he began in 400 under the title *On the Trinity.*

But then, once he was well into it (around 404), a letter came to him from a bishop in Carthage containing a copy of a list of "Porphyrian" criticisms of the Gospels that was circulating in the learned circles in Carthage, with the request that Augustine reply to them. So he halted work on the *Trinity* long enough to dash off a reply, the "Epistle to Deogratias."[14] Then he seems to have decided that his flimsy and cursory arguments were not sufficient, so he wrote two more short tracts,[15] which dealt with two of the most troublesome areas in the Gospels, the infancy narratives and the resurrection appearances.[16] Meanwhile, he resumed *On the Trinity.* Not much later, Augustine seems to have gotten word back from Carthage that his reply to the "Porphyrian list" not only had not stopped the criticisms but, had opened the door to many new questions and criticisms of the same type, i.e., detailed criticisms of the inconsistencies between the Gospels. At this time (404 or 405), Augustine preached three sermons in which he explicitly attacked Porphyry by name, calling him "the most bitter enemy of the Christian religion."[17]

This seems to have been the moment when Augustine concluded that something decisive, something *comprehensive* needed to be done. And so, as he wrote years later, he abruptly dropped *On the Trinity* and took up the monumental task of providing convincing, rational explanations not just for the genealogies in Matthew and Luke, but for *all* of the Gospel inconsistencies from beginning to end.

General Characteristics of Augustine's Approach

The general outline of *On the Harmony of the Evangelists* is fairly straightforward. Book One is a lengthy defense of the Christian view of God, as opposed to the Neoplatonic spiritual "Being" and Manichaean dualistic Good and Evil principles. It shows that Augustine's attention was very much focused on theological issues, as would be expected of someone currently writing a treatise on the Trinity.

Book Two enters into the problem area proper, namely, whether the four authoritative and divinely appointed historians wrote anything contradictory about Jesus, the Son of God. To answer this question, Augustine undertook a detailed analysis in which he compared the other three Gospels to Matthew, beginning with the genealogies and going all the way to the Last Supper, following the sections and canons devised by Eusebius.

Book Three carries on the comparisons from the Last Supper through the resurrection. In this part, Augustine abandoned his previous method of comparing the other three to Matthew and instead constructed a single, harmonized narrative. Book Four considers the material unique to each Gospel, in the order Mark, Luke, John.

Throughout all four books, Augustine never explicitly cited any earlier Christian scholar. He did make use (without attribution) of viewpoints originated by others, such as the reference in Book One to the four animals signifying the Evangelists, but as a whole the work is largely his own.

Thus considered, it must be viewed in the first instance as a *theological construct* from start to finish. This is not to say that it was not a *historical construct* as well, in the sense that it was an unsurpassed attempt to explain the human dimension in the writing of the Gospels. But the human dimension was viewed from the perspective of God's activity. In this sense, the *Harmony* was a theological construct, invented out of Augustine's doctrine of the revelation of the Word of God.

At the same time, it was profoundly *political* in orientation. A comparison with Origen's position will show what I mean. Origen was a prominent figure in a persecuted religious movement which clung to the fringes of society, when it was not actively fleeing persecution. Furthermore, Origen belonged to a minority faction within the Christianity of his day, a group that called itself the "Great Church" and which prided itself on its direct descent from the Apostles of Jesus Christ, as did most other Christian factions.

As far as the Scriptures were concerned, Origen lived in a veritable jungle of sacred writings. He had to contend with more than two dozen Gospels and versions of Gospels, all claiming to be the truth about Jesus Christ. In this confusing situation, Origen stoutly maintained that four of them were "universally accepted" by the "Great Assembly" as having been written by one of the Twelve Apostles of Jesus Christ or their immediate followers.[18] Nevertheless, Origen also used a number of other Gospels from time to time,[19] a practice which fatally compromised him. He could never say positively that he had used *only* the universally accepted historical testimonies to the Lord Jesus. He was always open to the criticism that his favorite Gospels needed to be augmented by others or that he had altogether the wrong set, and so on.

Augustine's situation was completely different. He lived in the wake of the enormous impact created by the emperor's decree in 312 that Christianity was a *religio licita*—a legitimate religion. Except for a brief relapse under Julian, persecution was a thing of the past.

Second, there had been a series of ecumenical Church councils that had, among other things, closed off all further discussion regarding the four Gospels, as well as most of the other books in the Old and New Testament. Augustine himself had been present (while still a priest) at the Council of Hippo in 393, which promulgated a catalog of the books of the Bible that is identical to the list he put in his handbook on biblical interpretation in 397.[20] Parallel to this growing consensus regarding the contents of Holy Scripture (canon) there had been a relentless standardization of the faith (creed) and centralization of the bureaucracy (magisterium), carried out by the orthodox Church leadership under the vigilant gaze of one devout Christian emperor after another. In short, the line dividing orthodoxy and heresy in Church governance, canon, and creed was much sharper than it was in Origen's day.

Buttressed by these Church councils and confident of the growing power of orthodox Christianity vis-à-vis the sacred and secular authorities, Augustine had no difficulty deciding which Gospels to discuss. Origen's choice of the universally accepted four out of a shapeless, indeterminate cloud of Gospels was a thing of the chaotic past. Augustine could take a decisive, monolithic approach toward the problem of contradictions between these four canonical Gospels, since they had been ratified by Church decree. Where Origen saw the harmony of the four primarily on the spiritual level, and Eusebius identified the verbal similarities among the four Gospels without attempting to combine them physically, as it were, Augustine was the first major theologian since Tatian to treat all verses and stories in the four Gospels as if they were fragments of a jigsaw puzzle that could be combined in one, continuous, literally true super-narrative. As such, Augustine set a pattern that flourished in the Church for more than a thousand years; indeed, it continues to this day.

Augustine's different political situation shows up in other ways, such as in his tone of voice. Where Origen explored the mysteries of divine revelation, his mind following the luminous pathways partly hidden in the physical words of Scripture, open to suggestion from others, Augustine's language has a striking dual tone. On the surface there is the vigorous philosophical argumentation; directly beneath it (and sometimes not so far down), there is a harsh peremptoriness, a threatening tone, which implies that he would not hesitate to bring in the sword of the state if need arose. As a result, Augustine's writing seems curiously smug, as if he secretly believed that all he needed to do was put forth a convincing show of rational explanations regarding the Gospels, and the imperial police would imprison any who dared dispute with him.

Augustine's Basic Guidelines for Biblical Interpretation

As mentioned above, Augustine based his approach to the Gospels on a number of fundamental assumptions that had been spelled out several years earlier in his handbook on biblical interpretation, *On Christian Doctrine.*

Before we summarize some of the points made in that writing, we must take note of his fundamental concept of truth and its relation to human reason, since, in one sense, Augustine would never have conceived of the problem in the way that he did, were it not for the concept of truth that he (and his opponents) assumed. For Augustine, "true knowledge" can be discovered through the operations of "reason." The study of the Bible, however, is a special case. Here, the mind must first be thoroughly "cleansed" and, even then, will attain its goal of knowledge of the truth (i.e., the correct interpretation of Scripture) only if the Holy Spirit assists it.[21]

The goal of human reason in all of its operations, including biblical interpretation, resembles mental vision; "the object must be clearly manifested (to the mind's eye) and must have no features which might lead it to be confused with something else."[22] There is no truth if what it "sees" is self-contradictory, because everything that is inconsistent or self-contradictory cannot be either true or false. But since every word of Scripture comes from God, who is Truth, it necessarily follows that all Scripture is completely free from error, self-contradiction, and inconsistency.[23] Hence one task of scriptural interpretation is to remove all *apparent* contradictions or inconsistencies in Scripture.

Given this understanding of truth, the basics of biblical interpretation are as follows. First, since all human signs (words) point to or intend (mean) intelligible objects,[24] the purpose of all interpretation of Scripture is to ascertain correctly the intelligible objects intended by the authors' signs:[25]

> In reading (Holy Scripture) men seek nothing more than to find out the thought and will of those by whom it was written, and through these, to find out the will of God, in accordance with which they believe these men to have spoken.[26]

Therefore, revelation per se does not consist of the signs (words) contained in the Bible, but what one knows or perceives if one interprets the Bible correctly, namely, the intentions of the writers, who were informed by the Mind of God.[27]

Second, all difficulties in interpreting the biblical signs (words) arise from signs (words) which are either *unknown* or *ambiguous*.[28] The best way to solve problems caused by the *unknown* signs or words is by acquiring a knowledge of ancient languages and customs, such as words for trees, shrubs, animals, local geography, and so forth. Moreover, since the Bible is full of human artistry, a knowledge of ancient artistic and literary genres will help the interpreter to obtain the correct interpretation of the *unknown* signs (words) used by the original authors.[29]

More difficult are the passages of Scripture in which the author expressed himself intentionally or unintentionally in *ambiguous* signs (words), i.e., where the original author expressed himself using figurative or mystical signs (words). A number of guidelines should be followed for the proper interpretation of these passages,[30] but the basic guideline is that no interpretation should ever contradict the "rule of faith."[31]

Analysis of Augustine's On the Harmony of the Evangelists

The Defensive Tone of Book One

Augustine began Book One by noting that the Gospels occupy the preeminent position in all of Holy Scripture. They deserve this status, he said, because they are the carefully prepared records of what the Lord and Savior Jesus Christ said and did. Two of them, Matthew and John, are faithful eyewitness reports. The other two, Mark and Luke, are writings by men who "with due credit received facts with which they became acquainted in a trustworthy manner through the instrumentality of these former (i.e., the disciples of the Lord)."[32]

These opening statements prepared the ground for two questions of fundamental importance for Augustine's whole approach. The first question was: Where can reliable tradition about the Lord Jesus be found? As we saw in the discussion of Origen, it led to a profound grasp of the Gospels in their relationships with each other. But where Origen lived in the midst of sectarian conflict over the many Gospels, Augustine could take a decisive stand based on the edicts of several recent Church councils that conferred canonical status exclusively on the Gospels of Matthew, Mark, Luke, and John. As for the other so-called Gospels, said Augustine,

> All those other individuals who have attempted or dared to offer a written record of the acts of the Lord or the apostles, failed to commend themselves in their own times as men of the character which would induce the Church to yield them its confidence, and to admit their compositions to the canonical authority of the Holy Books.[33] (Instead) they were condemned by the catholic and apostolic rule of faith[34] and by sound doctrine.[35]

Finished! The door is firmly closed on the past. No other Gospels! The past has spoken and from now on its door will remain tightly locked—until the seventeenth century unlocked it again.[36]

Having thus dealt with the opening question of which Gospels to consult (canon), Augustine went on to a closely related question that Origen never discussed, although Eusebius (following Irenaeus) had. Why did it please God to authorize precisely *four* records of the sayings and doings of Christ? Wouldn't *one* have been preferable?

Augustine gave two kinds of answers. The first echoed what Irenaeus said (although he doesn't mention his name). There are four Gospels for the simple reason that there are four divisions of that world through the universal length of which they, by their number as by a mystical sign, indicated the advancing extension of the Church of Christ.[37]

To this Augustine added another suggestion reminiscent of the approach of Origen: the Holy Spirit prompted each of the Gospel authors to *create a unique general portrait of Jesus,* the Son of God. Matthew undertook to "construct the record of the incarnation of the Lord according to the royal lineage."[38] Mark played a courtier's role in Matthew's royal portrait because he "follows (Matthew) closely and looks like his attendant and summarizer, for in his narrative . . . he has a very large number of passages in concord with Matthew."[39] "Luke seems to have occupied himself rather with the priestly lineage and character of the Lord."[40] These three are closer to each other than they are to John, who is in a class by himself. They sought to portray Christ after the flesh and in temporal terms. But John

> had in view that true divinity of the Lord in which He is the Father's equal, and directed his efforts above all to the setting forth of the divine nature in his Gospel . . . Therefore he is borne to loftier heights, in which he leaves the other three far behind, (passing) beyond the cloud in which the whole earth is wrapped and reaching to liquid heaven from which, with clearest and steadiest mental eye, he is able to look upon God the Word, who was in the beginning with God, and by whom all things were made.[41]

Ignoring for the moment the quaintness of this imagery, let us observe what Augustine is doing: giving a justification guided by the *regula fidei* for a question in Scripture concerning which tradition is silent. He found a *suitable answer.* At the same time, his suggestions were consistent with a real concern of any author, namely, to write something that had a central, organizing focus or image. Taken together, Augustine provided a perceptive and useful *point d'appui* for analyzing each writing as a literary whole.

Augustine then went on to give what historical information he had concerning their current placement vis-à-vis each other in the New Testament. The Gospels, he said, are arranged according to their *order of composition*: Matthew wrote first, then Mark, then Luke the companion of Paul, and finally John.[42] Matthew wrote his Gospel in Hebrew, the rest wrote their Gospels in Greek.[43] Then he asked, Why are Matthew and John not placed together?—and again his historical information is silent. No doubt, said Augustine, because these two, who were actual followers of the Lord, should take first and last place, with the other two in the middle, being embraced by them as it were, like sons by a father.[44] Nice answer—clearly prompted by little more than the *regula fidei.*

Notice how Augustine brought in the issue of the order of composition—as part of a general explanation of how the Evangelists sought to organize their writings. This is the third aspect of the Synoptic Problem, and Augustine is the first theologian in western history to suggest that the author of Mark made direct use of the Gospel of Matthew. Did Augustine not know what Papias had said about the origin of Mark? Not likely. It appears that, in the course of preparing his notes for this volume, based on Eusebius' sections and canons, Augustine took it for granted that Matthew was written first and that the extensive similarities between Matthew and Mark were due to the latter having borrowed from Matthew. He went on to say that Luke was written third, but later, after he had finished exhaustively comparing the Gospels, Augustine changed his mind and suggested that *Mark also borrowed from Luke.*[45]

Having dealt with these preliminary questions regarding the Gospels, Augustine then came to the reason for writing his current treatise: certain malicious persons have attacked the credibility of the Gospels.[46] They advance two basic objections. First and most important, they claim that the Gospel authors are not in harmony with each other.[47] As we noted above, given Augustine's concept of truth, there could be no more serious accusation than this. If it could be proved that the Gospel authors contradicted each other or themselves, then *ipso facto* their writings would be false and Christianity would rest on a foundation of sand. Augustine devoted the rest of his treatise to a comprehensive refutation of this accusation.

Augustine then mentioned the second charge brought up by these same "malicious persons," namely, that Jesus wrote nothing himself to provide a check against the lies and fabrications of his ignorant and unscrupulous followers:[48]

> But first we must discuss a matter which is apt to present a difficulty to the minds of some. I refer to the question why the Lord has written nothing Himself and why He has left us to the necessity of accepting the testimony of other persons who have prepared records of his history.[49]

These objections are pure hypocrisy, said Augustine. Is it not the case that these same detractors accept without question what the disciples of Socrates wrote, as well as the disciples of Pythagoras, neither of whom ever wrote anything themselves? Why then do they object to us doing precisely the same thing they do?[50]

Furthermore, these unbelievers do not understand that Christ did "write," first as a man teaching his disciples and then as the Holy Spirit guiding each Evangelist, so that in effect Christ alone wrote as if with four hands.[51]

> When those (Gospel authors) have written matters which He declared and spake to them, it ought not by any means be said that He has written nothing himself. The truth is His members have accomplished only what they became acquainted with by the repeated statements of the Head. For all that He was minded to give for our perusal on the subject of His own doings and sayings, He commanded to be written by those disciples, whom He thus used as if they were His own hands.[52]

Thus, the four Gospel authors were incapable of writing any false or contradictory statements since they were divinely influenced by him who said, "I am the Way, the Truth, and the Life."[53]

The Logic of Augustine's Proof of the Harmony of the Gospels' Authors

With these fundamental clarifications in Book One behind him, Augustine was ready to attack the question of the inconsistencies and contradictions among the Gospels in Books Two through Four. I will not attempt to follow his discussion through each of the remaining books. Instead, I will present his arguments in a logical structure, with brief examples, which will simplify what he said.

Augustine divided all variations between the Gospels into two main categories: differences in the orders of events and differences in the details of the same event. I will arrange his comments under each category in succession.

Category One: Variations in the Order of Events

Augustine adopted *six basic principles* to explain the variations in order of events.

1. All of the Gospel authors had full and correct knowledge of the original order of historical events of Jesus' life. This knowledge is not to be confused with what they wrote.

These (four) had one order (of events) determined among them with regard to the matters of their personal knowledge ... but a different order in reference to the task of giving the written narrative.[54]

2. When they came to the task of writing a narrative, sometimes they recorded events not in their proper chronological order, but in the order in which they remembered them, making them appear as if they were in correct chronological order. When the order of narration is found to differ among the Gospels, as it frequently does, this is not due to any error or forgetfulness on the part of the Gospel authors. These different orders of events were caused by the Holy Spirit.

> (The Gospel authors frequently) record at a subsequent point things which have been omitted at a previous stage, or bring in at an earlier point occurrences which (actually) took place at a later period, according as they had incidents suggested to their minds by the heavenly influence.[55]

No one should find fault with the Gospel authors in this respect. It happens to anyone who remembers: past events do not come before one's memory in their original, historical order but in a curiously jumbled fashion. This is what happened to the Gospel authors. Nor can anyone help it.

> It is not in one's own power, however admirable and trustworthy may be the *knowledge* (one) has once obtained of the (original) facts, to determine the order in which (one) will *recall them to memory*—for the way in which one thing comes into a person's mind before or after another is something which proceeds not as we will but simply as it is given to us. (Hence) it is reasonable enough to suppose that each of the Gospel authors believed it to have been his duty to relate what he had to relate, in that order in which it had pleased God to suggest to his recollection the matters he was engaged in recording.[56]

Occasionally we can prove that the Gospel author's personal knowledge of the historical succession of events was different from his order of narration. In Luke's account of the rejection of Jesus at Nazareth, he has Jesus say to the townspeople:

> "Ye will surely say to me, Physician, heal thyself! What we have heard you did in Capharnaum, do also here in thy country!"[57] But so far as the narrative of this same Luke is concerned, we have not yet read of Him as having done anything at Capharnaum ... What then can be more

manifest than that he has knowingly introduced this notice at a point antecedent to its historical date? (Hence it is shown) that Luke knows of certain mighty deeds done by Him in Capharnaum which . . . he has not yet narrated.[58]

Let no one criticize the Gospel authors for writing in this manner. Who could do better than they did?

Let (us) therefore be content to reckon (our) own notion (of what to write in what order) inferior to Mark . . . who judged it right to insert (this account) just at the point at which it was suggested to him by divine inspiration. For the recollections of those historians have been ruled by the hand of Him who rules the water, as it is written, according to His own good pleasure. For the human memory moves through a variety of thoughts,[59] and it is not in any man's power to regulate either the subject which comes into his mind or the time of its suggestion.[60]

3. The variations in order among the Gospels sometimes means that one (or more) is proceeding according to the order of recollection while another is proceeding according to the original historical succession of events. For example, in the story of Jesus teaching parables to the crowds by the seashore, Matthew's version begins, "In that same day, Jesus went out of the house and sat by the seashore."[61] It is clear that Matthew connects the following account with what had just happened in the previous account, "retaining the historical order in his version of these events (because he says) in passing from one subject to the other . . . 'In that same day.'"[62] That Matthew is following the historical order of events "is confirmed by the fact that Mark keeps by the same order."[63] Luke, however, does not follow this order in his narrative.

Luke, on the other hand, after his account of what happened with the mother and brethren of the Lord passes to a different subject. But at the same time, in making that transition, he does not institute any such transition as bears the appearance of a want of consistency with this (i.e., Matthew's//Mark's) order.[64]

These variations in order do not mean these writers contradicted each other.

In the matter of the order of narration[65] although it is presented somewhat differently by the various Gospel authors, according as they have proceeded severally along the line of historical succession,[66] or along that of the succession of recollection,[67] I see as little reason for alleging any discrepancy of statement or any contradiction between any of the writers.[68]

4. Some of the time, the Gospel authors adopted the order of events found in the other Gospels. This is particularly true of Mark.

Mark follows (Matthew) closely and looks like his courtier and *summarizer.*[69] For, (generally speaking,) in his narrative he gives nothing in concert with John apart from the others. By himself separately he has little to record. In conjunction with Luke, as distinguished from the rest, he has still less. But in conjunction with Matthew, he has a very large number of passages. Much too he narrates in words almost numerically and identically the same as those used by Matthew. (That is,) the agreement is either with that Gospel author alone, or with him in conjunction with the rest.[70]

This sophisticated statement, which remains unchanged in modern Gospel study, is clearly borne out of Augustine's own close investigation of the texts. As he went on and learned more about the Gospels, however, he changed his mind. In Book Four, Augustine revised what he said in Book One about Mark being Matthew's summarizer:

Mark . . . either appears to prefer to be Matthew's companion . . . as I stated in Book One, *or else, in accord with the more probable account of the matter, he holds a course in conjunction with both (Matthew and Luke).* For although he is at one with Matthew in the larger number of passages, he is nevertheless at one rather with Luke in some others.[71]

Again, this important conclusion was unknown to Gospel scholars prior to Augustine. We will discuss its fate in later centuries in Parts Two and Three.[72]

5. At other times, a Gospel author will avoid unnecessary repetition and simply pass over what his predecessor(s) wrote.

However much they are seen to hold at times to a unique order of narration (i.e., one completely unlike the others), this (did) not (happen because) each of them chose to write in ignorance of what another predecessor had written, or to omit out of ignorance what the other is found to have written. But just as each was inspired not to add superfluous cooperation to his work (he silently passed over what the other(s) had written).[73]

When a Gospel author is following the order of another but then decides to omit one or more events mentioned by the other so as to avoid unnecessary repetition, he never gives any warning that he is skipping over anything.

> (These) writers, in many instances, leave unnoticed much that intervenes and, *without any express indication of the omissions they are making,* proceed precisely as if what they subjoin followed actually in literal succession.[74]

That is, each Gospel author constructed his narrative in such a way as to

> *give it the appearance* of being a complete and orderly record of the events in their (original historical) succession. While preserving silence on those incidents of which he intends to give no account, he then connects those which he does wish to relate with what he has been immediately recounting, in such a manner as to make the recital *seem continuous.*[75]

This procedure is one of the main explanations for the differences in orders of narration in the Gospels. For example, when Matthew says the healing of the paralytic took place "in his city" (Mt 9), i.e., Nazareth, but Mark says it occurred in "Capharnaum" (Mk 2.1), while Luke does not say where the event took place (Lk 5.17), the problem can easily be resolved by taking into consideration all that Matthew has passed over before telling this story, which Mark has covered, and that therefore, Matthew clearly *meant to say* Capernaum.[76]

To give a much more important example, if one looks at the succession of events in all four Gospels prior to the miracle of the feeding of the five thousand, one can see *all four* Gospel authors following diverse routes until they come together to relate this particular event. Even John,

> who differs greatly from (the other) three in this respect, that he deals more with the discourses which the Lord delivered than with the works which He so marvelously wrought, after recording how He left Judaea and departed the second time into Galilee, which departure is understood to have taken place at the time to which the other evangelists also refer when they tell us that on John's imprisonment He went into Galilee,—after recording this, I say, John inserts in the immediate context of

his narrative the considerable discourse which He spake as He was passing through Samaria (with the woman at the well). Then he states that,
two days after this He departed for Galilee, coming to Cana of Galilee
where he turned the water into wine. But as to the other things which
the rest have told us He did and said in Galilee, John is silent (although
he does mention other miracles they don't). Then John tells the miracle
of the five loaves and the two fishes; which story is given us also by the
other Gospel authors. And this makes it certain that he has passed by
those incidents which form the course along which these others have
come to introduce the story of this miracle into their narratives. (Thus)
while different pathways of narration,[77] as it appears, are followed, and
while the first three Gospel authors have left unnoticed certain matters
which the fourth has recorded, we see how those three who have been
keeping nearly the same course have found a direct meeting point with
each other at this miracle of the five loaves, while the fourth writer, who
is conversant with the profound teachings of the Lord's discourses, in
relating some matters on which the others are silent, has sped round in
a certain method on their track and, although about to soar off from
their pathway into . . . loftier subjects, has found a meeting-point with
them in this narrative of the five loaves, which is common to them all.[78]

6. After the Gospel authors had written down what they remembered, they did not change, correct, or in any way alter, what the Holy
Spirit had prompted them to write.

Seeing then, that those holy and truthful men, in this matter of the order
of their narrations, committed the casualties of their recollections (if
such a phrase may be used) to the direction of the hidden power of God,
to whom nothing is casual,[79] it does not become any mere man (like us)
. . . far removed from *the vision of God* and sojourning distantly from
Him,[80] to say, "This ought to have been introduced here (rather than
there)"; for (such a person) is utterly ignorant of the reason which led
God to will its being inserted in the place it occupies.[81]

From these six basic principles regarding the order of events, Augustine deduced *six corollaries* to resolve apparent contradictions or inconsistencies in the order of events among the several Gospels.

1. These divergencies have been created by the Holy Spirit and are
an invitation to figure out the original, historical order of events.

Wherever the order is apparent, if one Gospel author presents anything
which seems to be inconsistent with his own statements or with those

of another, we must certainly take the passage into consideration and endeavor to clear up the difficulty.[82]

2. Where there are three orders and two agree against the third, the two are preserving the original, historical order while the third is following the order of recollection. For example, after relating the account of Jesus teaching in parables, Matthew proceeds to tell of Jesus' rejection at Nazareth.

> But we see how Mark passes on from these parables to a subject which is not identical with Matthew's directly succeeding theme, but quite different from that, agreeing rather with what Luke introduces. (And we can see) how he has constructed his narrative in such a manner as to make the balance of credibility rest on the side of the supposition that what followed in immediate historical sequence was rather the occurrences which these two latter Gospel authors both insert in near connection (with the parables), namely, (the story of the stilling of the storm).[83]

3. There is no necessity to suppose that, just because a Gospel author has connected events in a seemingly continuous, chronological narrative, that the individual events cannot be broken apart and *recombined in reverse order*, or interleaved with events mentioned in other Gospels in a new, *hybrid narrative*, combining stories from all the Gospels that more closely approximates the original, chronological order.

> We are certainly under no necessity of supposing that, because (some incident) is recorded after a certain event, it must also have happened in actual matter of fact after that event.[84]

It is always legitimate to *posit chronological gaps* in the Gospel accounts where there don't seem to be any. If one notices events mentioned in other Gospels that seem to be roughly chronological with events in the one under consideration, but are not mentioned there, this is evidence that the author of the latter knew of those other events but is silently passing over them.

> When one of them mentions factors of which the other has given no notice, the order of narration, if carefully considered, will be found to indicate the point at which the writer by whom the omissions are made has taken the leap in his account ... On this principle, therefore, we understand that, where (Matthew) tells us how the wise men were warned in a dream not to return to Herod and how they went back to

their own country by another way, Matthew has simply omitted all that Luke has related respecting all that happened to the Lord in the temple, and all that was said by Simeon and Anna. And, on the other hand, Luke has omitted in the same place all notice of the journey into Egypt, which is told by Matthew, and has introduced the return to the city of Nazareth as if it were immediately consecutive (to the prophetess Anna).[85]

4. At other times it is legitimate, when similar events are mentioned in different contexts, to assume that this similar event actually happened two or three different times.

> In good truth I must repeat here once more an admonition which it behooves the reader to keep in mind, . . . namely, that in various passages of His discourses, the Lord has reiterated much which He had uttered already on other occasions. It is needful, indeed, to call this fact to mind, lest, when it happens that the order of such passages does not appear to fit in with the narrative of another of the Gospel authors, the reader should fear that this establishes some contradiction between them. Instead he ought to understand it to be due to the fact that something is repeated a second time . . . that had already been expressed elsewhere. And this (principle) is applicable not only to his words but also to His deeds. For there is nothing to hinder us from believing that the same thing may have taken place more than once.[86]

Augustine mentions several cases of similar events recorded in differing contexts which probably occurred twice: two sermons (one on the mount and a similar one on the plain);[87] two feeding miracles;[88] two cleansings of the temple;[89] Mary putting ointment on Jesus two different times;[90] and, as for the resurrection of Jesus, four angels at the tomb: one outside sitting on the stone (Matthew), one sitting inside the tomb at the right (Mark), and two others standing inside the tomb who spoke to the women in words similar to the other angels' (Luke).[91]

5. Sometimes, however, we simply cannot decide which Gospel preserves the original, chronological order. For example, the time when John the Baptist was imprisoned is described one way by Matthew and a different way by Luke. Nor is it

> clear which of them gives the order of his own recollections and which keeps by the historical succession of the things themselves.[92]

There is one instance where it seems impossible to find any explanation for the chronological discrepancy between the Gospels or to discover the original, historical order. This is the apparent contradiction between Mark 15:25: "It was *nine o-clock* in the morning when they *crucified* him," and John 19:14: "Now it was the Day of Preparation for the Passover . . . about *twelve noon*" when Jesus was *sentenced* to be crucified.[93]

When such an apparent direct contradiction is discovered, we should not be unduly concerned. Since the Gospel authors now and then ignored strict chronological order, we have permission to disregard it also.

> (Our goal) is to demonstrate that not one of the Gospel authors contradicts either himself or his fellow historians, whatever be the precise order in which (the Gospel authors) may have had the ability or may have preferred to compose his accounts of the sayings and doings of Christ . . . For this reason, when the order of times is not apparent, we ought not to feel it a matter of any consequence what order any of them may have adopted in relating the events.[94]

Given this dual kind of order adopted by them all, it is wrongheaded to find fault with the orders of events narrated in the four Gospels.

> For of what consequence is it in what place any of them may give his account? Or what difference does it make whether he inserts the matter in its proper order or brings in at a particular point what was previously omitted, or mentions at an earlier stage what really happened at a later (time), provided only that he contradicts neither himself nor a second writer in the narrative of the same facts or others?[95]

Gaps in order or apparent contradictions in order should serve to excite our pious curiosity rather than our anger.

> The reason why the Holy Spirit, who divideth to every man severally as He will . . . has left one historian at liberty to construct his narrative in one way and another in a different fashion, that is a question which any one may look into with pious consideration, and for which, by divine help, the answer may possibly be found.[96]

6. In any case, we should always proceed with fear and trembling, for Divine Providence intentionally created these variations in the Gospels' orders and those who find fault with them are going to hell. The Gospels are a trap to ensnare the arrogant and godless, while giving mental exercise to the pious and elect.

Who, then, knows the mind of the Lord? (Who will explain why) He has in such wise ruled the hearts of the Gospel authors in their recollections . . . (so that their writings) present the appearance of contradictions (and so) become the means by which many are made blind, deservedly given over to the lusts of their own heart; and by which many others are exercised in the thorough cultivation of a pious understanding, in accordance with the hidden righteousness of the Almighty?[97]

Category Two: Variations in the Descriptions of the Same Event

Augustine adopted *four basic principles* to explain the variations in the details of the same event.

1. Sometimes the variation is no more than a flaw in the *text* of one of the Gospels. In the well-known difference between the Gospels as to what the voice from heaven said at Jesus' baptism (Mt 3:17; Mk 1:11; Lk 3:22), some copies of the Gospel of Luke say something different from the others, having words that are an echo of Psalm 2:7. Augustine notes: "(these words are) said not to be found in the more ancient Greek codices (of Luke)."[98]

2. Sometimes the variations are more apparent than real, involving the use by one of the Gospel authors of an *unfamiliar cultural idiom*. When Matthew wrote that Jesus rode into Jerusalem on two animals, an ass *and a colt*, the foal of an ass,[99] while the others mention only one animal,[100] there is no contradiction involved. Matthew's words are simply an example of the parallelism typical of Hebrew poetry; he *meant* one animal.

> The explanation of this variation seems to me to be found in the fact that Matthew is understood to have been written in the Hebrew language (while the others were written in Greek).[101]

3. Sometimes the Gospel authors used different words to express the same idea. When two authors are apparently describing the same event and there seem to be some direct contradictions between them involving details, as when Matthew has John the Baptist say, "The one who comes after me is mightier than me; *I am not fit to take off his shoes*" (3:11), while Luke has John say "*I am not fit to unfasten his shoes*" (3:16), this variation in wording is not a contradiction, since different writers normally relate the same idea using different words.

We ought not to suppose that any one of the writers is giving an unreliable account if, when several persons are recalling some matter either heard or seen by them, they fail to follow the very same plan or use the very same words while describing nevertheless the self-same fact.[102]

In general, when reading and comparing the Gospels, it doesn't matter if their words are different, or if the word order is different, or if some words are entirely omitted, or even if one of the Gospel authors added some words of his own to the original. We must remember that the Gospel authors

were not entirely successful, however much they made it their aim, in calling to mind and reciting anew with the most literal accuracy, the very words they heard on (this or that) occasion.[103]

4. Occasionally, one or more of the Gospel authors, when recording an incident also found in another Gospel, intentionally changed the telling of it so as to communicate a mystical meaning. For example, in the accounts of the healing of the centurion's servant, while "Luke has unfolded the whole incident just as it occurred,"[104] Matthew didn't follow Luke but "adopted . . . a certain mystical depth in the phraseology"[105] of his account, when he says the centurion came to Jesus, while Luke rightly says that the Centurion sent friends to Jesus.

In this general category, Augustine brought up the second major aspect of the Synoptic Problem: the correct text. In this way, we can see how he has methodically focused on all four major aspects of the Synoptic Problem: canon, text, composition, and hermeneutics.

From these four basic principles, Augustine deduced *five corollaries* to resolve the *variations in details in the same story.*

1. Always pay careful attention to the reliability of the text. Whenever there is a disagreement in a particular passage so that it is uncertain what the original Gospel author wrote (example given above), always follow the reading of the oldest and most reliable Greek manuscripts.

2. Learn and become familiar with the idioms of the biblical writers. The apparent mistranslations in the Greek Old Testament (the Septuagint), when compared with the Hebrew original, are instructive in this regard (see General Conclusion 4, below).

3. Often, such variations in wording are of no real significance, provided the meaning intended by the several authors is clearly understood to be the same.

In what most seriously concerns the faithfulness of doctrinal teaching,[106] we should understand that it is not so much in mere words as rather truth in the facts themselves that is to be sought and embraced.[107] For as to writers who do not employ precisely the same modes of statement, if they only do not present discrepancies with respect to the facts and the sentiments themselves, we accept them as abiding by the same truth.[108]

4. Always keep in mind that there are two distinct and radically different realms: the eternal Word of God and the temporal words of men. The purpose of the latter is to point toward the former, which the Gospels do without error.

> The truth of the Gospel (is) conveyed in that Word of God which abides eternal and unchangeable above all that is created, but which at the same time has been disseminated throughout the world by the instrumentality of temporal symbols and by the tongues of men. (Nor, just because they are temporal symbols,) ought we to suppose that any one of them gave an unreliable account . . .[109]

It is wrongheaded to wish that the Gospels were "more perfect" (i.e., less variable). These Gospels are the perfect Word of God in human words.

> It is evident that the Gospel authors have set forth these matters just in accordance with the memory each retained of them, and just according as their several predilections prompted them[110] to employ greater brevity or richer detail on certain points, while giving, nevertheless, the same account of the subjects themselves.[111]

So we should be satisfied with them the way they are. In any case, we mortals cannot know ultimate Divine Truth without the aid of their words. Only God and the angels can do this.

> The harmonious diversity which marks the four gospel authors (does not mean there has been any) failure from strict truth, although one historian may give an account of some theme in a manner different indeed from another . . . (In fact, we must always remember that) the theme itself which is to be expressed[112] is (of such) superior importance to the words in which it has to be expressed, that we would be under no obligation to ask (anything) about them at all if it were possible for us *to know the truth without the words,* as God knows it and as His angels also know it in Him.[113]

5. Finally, we must remain alert to the fact that the Gospel authors chose to speak in figurative expressions in certain places, while in other places they spoke in literal terms, while giving no warning when they were changing from the one to the other. Nor should this habit of theirs surprise us, for they were simply doing what the Lord Himself did, for He often combined literal with figurative expressions, giving no warning which was which. This is the explanation of the seemingly contradictory instructions about tunics and purses and coats and shoes that the Lord gave the Twelve when He sent them out on their first evangelistic mission.

> It is not by any means to be made a matter of doubt that the Lord Himself spoke all these words, some of them with a literal import and others of them with a figurative, although the Gospel authors may have introduced them only in part into their writings, one inserting one part and another giving a different portion. Certain instructions, moreover, have been recorded in identical terms either by two of them, or by three, or even by all the four together . . . Moreover, if anyone thinks that the Lord could not in the course of the same discourse have used some expressions with a figurative application and others with a literal,[114] let him but examine His other addresses and he will see how rash and inconsiderate such a notion is.[115]

Summary of the Arguments

All told, it is a complex and sophisticated picture of the activity of the Gospel authors when they wrote the Gospels. It may be helpful to summarize Augustine's arguments up to this point, in order to get a better picture of what he said.

- The Gospel authors were holy and truthful men who had been personally instructed by the Lord Jesus Christ during his ministry (Matthew and John) or were close followers of those who were his disciples (Mark and Luke).
- When they wrote, the Spirit of Christ willed and moved their minds and memories to write what they wrote, so that everything they wrote was completely without error. What they wrote reflected the Mind of Christ who is the Word of God; he was the real author of the four canonical Gospels.
- As regards full knowledge of the original historical events, none of the Gospel authors was lacking in any way.

· Each wrote about Christ in a unique way, to bring out some particular virtue of the Son of God: Matthew the royal element, Mark the
human, Luke the priestly, and John the divine Word.
· Each wrote in full awareness of what his predecessor(s) had written.
Mark in particular made use of the accounts of Matthew and—to
some extent—Luke.
· Sometimes the Gospel authors supported what the other(s) had
written, sometimes they departed from it.
· When they supported (repeated) what a predecessor had written,
this was to confirm the historical or literal succession of events.
· When they departed from what another author had written, they
did so for a number of reasons.

—They avoided repeating what the other had sufficiently described.
—They silently passed over what the other(s) had already described, making their narratives seem continuous.
—They recorded events as the Holy Spirit prompted them to
their memories, with no attention to chronological order.
—They were not always able to give an exact literal account of
what actually happened.
—Each author used his own words, employing richer or lesser
detail.
—They occasionally employed cultural idioms to rephrase
something another had said.
—They sometimes used figurative language to describe something another had described literally.

· Although each pursued a somewhat different path, with John being
the most dissimilar, all four intended to give truthful accounts of
what the Lord said and did.
· When they were finished, they did not rewrite or correct anything
that had been written under the guidance of the Holy Spirit.

General Conclusions

On the basis of these arguments proving the essential harmony among the
Gospel authors, Augustine propounded *six general conclusions* regarding
these variations in order and detail among the Gospels.

1. The diversity among the various accounts has been intentionally
brought about by Divine Providence as an aid to the Church's better un-

derstanding of the Lord's teachings and actions. Four different Gospel narratives provide a much richer, more nuanced portrait of the Lord Jesus Christ, which is a better safeguard against misunderstanding and heresy. We should therefore be grateful and not embarrassed that there are four and not just one Gospel (or four precisely identical Gospels, which is the same thing).[116]

2. The apparent contradictions are a standing invitation to the pious reader to seek for explanations. With the help of the Holy Spirit, he may find them. In any case, it is not so difficult a problem; where there are variations, one of the Gospels will contain the literally true account, and "you can fix on whichever account you will."[117] Occasionally, however, none of them contains the literal account, nor does it really matter because most variations are merely differences in wording about the same thing. For example, in the case of the variation of what the disciples cried out to Jesus during the storm at sea (Mt 8:25; Mk 4:38; Lk 8:24),

Matthew gives us "Lord, save us: we perish." Mark has: "Master, carest Thou not that we perish?" And Luke says simply, "Master, we perish." These different expressions, however, convey one and the same meaning on the part of those who were awaking the Lord and who were wishful to secure their safety. Neither need we inquire which of these several forms is to be preferred as the one actually addressed to Christ.[118] For whether they really used the one or the other of these three phraseologies, *or expressed themselves in different words which are unrecorded by any one of the evangelists,*[119] but which were equally well adapted to give the like representation of what was meant, what difference does it make in the fact itself?[120]

When it is impossible to decide which order or form of words to accept as the literal, historical account, this is nothing to become overly concerned about. The Gospel authors themselves did not always keep to a hard-and-fast rule in this respect.

3. We must never let the apparent mistakes in the Gospels shake our trust in their veracity. If an apparent mistake is not a textual error, i.e., a mistake caused by a careless copyist, but is clearly wording that was in the original, then we must be prepared to acknowledge that it was intended by the Holy Spirit and a good reason can usually be found for the apparent mistake. For example, when Matthew, telling of the fate of Judas, writes, "Then was fulfilled what was spoken by the prophet Jeremiah," he quotes not Jeremiah but Zechariah.[121]

Now, if anyone finds a difficulty in the circumstance that this (quote) is not found in the writings of Jeremiah (but in Zechariah),[122] let him first take notice that this ascription of the passage to Jeremiah is not contained in all codices of the Gospels, and that some of them state simply that it was spoken *"by the prophet."*[123]

However, this "mistake" may have been intended by the Holy Spirit. In the example just mentioned, it may be that this apparent mistake

was done in accordance with the more secret counsel of the providence of God by which the minds of the Gospel authors were governed. For it may have been the case that when Matthew was engaged in composing his Gospel, the word Jeremiah occurred to his mind instead of Zechariah, in accordance with a familiar experience (that we all have had). Such an inaccuracy, however, he would most undoubtedly have corrected (since someone would have immediately called his attention to it. But, since that obviously didn't happen, we must conclude that Matthew) reflected that it was not without a purpose that the (wrong) name of the prophet was suggested instead of the other (right one) ... That being the case, was it not the proper course for him to bow to the authority of the Holy Spirit, under whose guidance he certainly felt his mind to be placed in a more direct sense than is the case with us? Consequently he left untouched what he had thus written, in accordance with the Lord's counsel and appointment.[124]

4. To be sure, there are those who insist

that the Gospel writers ought certainly to have had that kind of capacity imparted to them by the power of the Holy Spirit which would secure them against all (mistakes and all) variation the one from the other.[125]

But we must remember, these apparent mistakes are like all human foibles. If we say that the Gospels are "false" because they do not exhibit a superhuman perfection, then what we are really saying is that we think the Holy Spirit should have turned the Gospel authors into nonhuman robots. And if we say that, *we simultaneously condemn every human foible as evil and false also.*

For just as we are prohibited by divine law from thinking or saying that any of the Gospel authors were untruthful, so also another writer will not appear to be untruthful, when he recorded something, and it can be shown that the same thing happened to him as to them (i.e., he made mistakes).[126]

Rather than leap to the conclusion that there is some sort of mistake, it is better to inquire further and see if they are not mistakes at all, but Hebrew cultural signs (words) with which Latin-speaking readers might be unfamiliar. For example, it is well known that if one compares the Hebrew original of the Old Testament with the Greek translation called the Septuagint, one can find many apparent mistakes. But they aren't really mistakes. They are only Hebrew cultural forms of expression that were translated as well as possible by the seventy inspired Greek translators.

> It is obvious that the (Greek) translation which bears the name of the Septuagint . . . in many passages diverges from the rendering of the truth which is discovered in the Hebrew (originals, but we don't for this reason call these divergencies mistakes).[127]

The Church has accepted all of these mysterious "mistakes" in the Greek translation of the Hebrew Old Testament as having been prompted by the Holy Spirit. Therefore, let us adopt this same approach with respect to the Gospels as well.

5. In all cases, here as well as elsewhere, one must seek to comprehend the meaning intended by the original author, for that is what the Holy Spirit intends. *What the Holy Spirit intends is the Word of God.*

> From this universal variety of words (in the Gospels), which is (at the same time) a harmony in objects and thoughts (referred to), it is sufficiently clear that nothing is to be sought in words except the will (intention) of the speaker . . . whether (he says something) about humanity or about the angelic realm or about God.[128]

6. In general, when all else has failed and one is still confronted by a seemingly intractable problem, remember that all questions of doubt and uncertainty in scriptural interpretation must ultimately be resolved in such a way as to conform to the rule of faith.

Using these principles and corollaries, Augustine carefully removed all seeming contradictions from the Gospels.

Conclusion

Augustine's comprehensive and sophisticated analysis ended the debate. Nothing more was heard from the Manichaeans or the Porphyrians or the Neoplatonists. The increasing suppression of these religions may have had something to do with it, but, whatever the reason, Augustine's exhaustive discussion of the similarities and differences among the Gospels became the last word on the subject for more than one thousand years. It also paved the way for countless harmonies, especially in the sixteenth century and after,[129] down to the present time.

As such, Augustine must be said to have created a second general form of the Synoptic Problem and provided it with its appropriate solution.

It is instructive to compare Augustine's approach with Origen's.

For one thing, we can see the same fourfold structure in dealing with the similarities and differences among the Gospels pioneered by Origen. As for the first aspect, the canonical question Where can I find reliable Gospels about the Lord Jesus?, we noted that Augustine was able to confront and resolve this issue decisively at the very beginning of Book One, in a way that Origen—living as he was in the midst of the canonization struggle—could not.

As for the second question, Where can I find reliable *texts* of the canonical Gospels?, Augustine was on less certain ground than Origen because of his lack of expertise in Greek and Hebrew. However, he used the best Latin translations available and turned to the best Greek manuscripts when serious disputes over the Latin text arose.

As for the third question, How were the holy Gospels actually composed?, Augustine towered far above anyone else in the entire history of early Christianity. His complex, articulate, and theologically sophisticated series of answers to this question were more advanced than anything anyone else had written. Here, quite unlike Origen, Augustine sought to *weave together* the actual words of the four Gospels, to prove that the Gospel authors were in harmony in their outward, physical writings *as well as* at their spiritual level. In the course of doing this, he noticed the close similarities in wording and order between Matthew, Mark, and Luke, prompting him to revise his original statement about the order of composition that Mark was the abbreviator of Matthew, to the new idea that Mark had used Luke as well. In this, Augustine anticipated the discovery of Henry Owen and Johann Griesbach, many centuries later.

Be that as it may, this issue had no real interest for him either. Augustine's complex approach to the physical words of the Gospels negated the importance of the historical order of composition as effectively as Origen's spiritual approach had done.

As for the fourth question, How do the Gospels express and reveal the central mystery of the Christian faith?, Augustine touched on this here and there, at one point making a statement that sounded strikingly similar to Origen: the Gospel authors each had visions of God.[130] As a result, once they were finished, they did not dare tamper with what they had written, nor should any lesser mortal criticize what Christ through the Holy Spirit had prompted them to write.

PART TWO

The Creation of the Modern
Historical–Critical Method

CHAPTER 11

The Rise of the Modern Period and Its Consequences, 1500–1950

*I*t took more than three hundred years, from the Italian Renaissance to Johann Jakob Griesbach's synopsis, for the Third Form of the Synoptic Problem to emerge. It will be the task of Part Two to document some of the main trends, developments, and people involved in that process.

Since this way of dealing with the differences among the Gospels was so radically unlike anything seen before, I have devoted a major portion of Part Two to the task of clarifying the hermeneutical and theological assumptions that gave rise to it and preordained its conclusions.

Again, since most histories of biblical scholarship pay no attention to parallel economic, political, and technological developments, preferring to give the impression that "biblical science" is immune from such extraneous considerations, I have devoted what may seem to be an inordinate amount of space to precisely these factors as well. It is my hope that the reader will see that these factors were anything but extraneous in determining the success of the most widely accepted solution to the Third Form of the Synoptic Problem: the Two Source Hypothesis.

Historians of western culture say that the Enlightenment fundamentally transformed every institution in western society. This was certainly true of biblical research. Everything that had been taken for granted about God, the Church, and the Bible was flung to the winds. As far as the Synoptic Problem was concerned, Enlightenment scholars dismissed all traditional assumptions—that the Gospels were written under the guidance of the Holy Spirit, that Matthew, Mark, Luke, and John were the only Gospels that needed to be taken into account, that scholars had a reliable text of the Gospels, and that the Bible should be investigated in light of what the Church's tradition (Roman Catholic or Protestant) had to say about it in an attitude of trust that the Holy Spirit would reveal further truth (if necessary).

As each of these foundation stakes was pulled up and cast aside, the entire tent of Gospel interpretation fell to the ground, carrying with it Augustine's famed demonstration of the harmony of the evangelists.

Part Two documents the specific points of demolition that paved the way for the slow reconstruction of an entirely different structure of Gospel interpretation, this one built out of modern steel and concrete. But as before, its core girders are certain fundamental assumptions about each aspect of the Synoptic Problem: canon, text, composition, and hermeneutics. When it was completed, it housed the Third Form of the Synoptic Problem, complete with a third kind of solution.

In the past, biblical scholars have been inclined to begin histories of the Synoptic Problem in the late seventeenth century. It is one of the main contentions of this book that this is a major mistake. Not only does this procedure ignore the monumental achievements of the early Church, it hinders a balanced assessment of the novel features of the modern historical-critical approach. Given the picture in Part One of the mighty struggle the early Church waged to demonstrate the integrity of the four, differing Gospels, I will attempt to provide this balanced assessment of the strikingly different approach toward the four, differing Gospels typical of the historical-critical method.

This part begins with a dual introduction. Chapter 11 gives a broad overview of the main political, economic, and philosophical developments after the Middle Ages down through World War II, what I and many others term the "modern period." Chapter 12 focuses specifically on the main trends of modern historicist biblical hermeneutics that flowed from the modern assumptions about nature, God, humanity, history, and the state, outlined in Chapter 11.

Defining "Modern Period"

Although in some fields "modernity" may aptly refer to things that have occurred exclusively in the twentieth century, for something as broad as the "modern period," historians must use a much longer time frame. American historian Robert Anchor says it requires a three-century perspective:

The modern world-view is closely bound up with a number of significant developments, many of which link the eighteenth with the nineteenth and twentieth centuries. Among them are the geographical unification of the world, . . . the triumph of capitalism and modern science and their application to agriculture and industry, . . . the rise of the ideas of national sovereignty and inviolable human rights, the liberal and democratic doctrines, (the rise) of socialism and communism . . . These bonds are so numerous and significant that many, if not most, historians view the last two and a half centuries as forming a single historical unit.[1]

An American historian of philosophy, Louis Dupré, has recently argued, however, that one cannot fully understand the modern worldview without going back even further to the breakdown of the medieval synthesis during the fourteenth and fifteenth centuries. This process, says Dupré, paved the way for the emergence of the modern worldview.[2] German Church historian Klaus Scholder agrees, especially if one wishes to understand the origins, methods, and goals of modern historical criticism of the Bible:

In the great controversy over the understanding and significance of the Bible which began with the rise of modern thought in the West, the most important positions were staked out around 1680. The Enlightenment may have changed the historical balance, but it did not introduce anything essentially new. Orthodoxy died out slowly and with it the last group which held resolutely to the universal claim of scripture. By contrast, rational criticism was extended and made more radical. In between, there were mediating positions of all degrees and shades . . . (By our time,) the Bible has become a handbook of morality whose doctrines are acceptable to any reasonable person.[3]

For the purposes of the discussion in Part Two, therefore, I will take the modern worldview to refer to those ideas and goals which originated in the breakdown of the medieval synthesis during the late fourteenth century, that reached their fulfillment in the world empires of the European nations during the nineteenth century, and which died a fiery death in the catastrophic World War in Two Acts: 1914–1918 and 1939–1945.

Modern Historical Criticism Destroys the Bible?

Scholder's statement suggests that modern historical criticism of the Bible inflicted a mortal wound upon Christian orthodoxy, one which included denaturing the Bible so that it became no more than a handbook of morality any decent person could accept. This assessment may surprise those who view modern historical criticism of the Bible as an unambiguous improvement over the morass of medieval allegorization and the rigid dogmatism of Roman Catholic and Protestant scholasticism.

Certainly there is nothing in recent histories of the rise of modern biblical criticism to suggest that it is destructive in any way.[4] Indeed, it is my impression that my colleagues in Europe and North America are quite ignorant of the political and economic agendas their scholarship serves. Speaking for myself, I had always thought that the historical-critical study of the Bible had nothing to do with politics, that it was a pure and noble calling requiring years of apprenticeship followed by decades of dedicated service in the vineyards of archaeology, comparative philology, historical reconstruction, sophisticated literary analysis, fearless theological critique, and so on. I never knew that I was a foot soldier in a great crusade to eviscerate the Bible's core theology, smother its moral standards under an avalanche of hostile historical questions, and, at the end, shove it aside so that the new bourgeois could get on with the business at hand.

I had read Albert Schweitzer's warning that the historical study of the Bible originally had nothing to do with a genuine interest in history but appeared "as an ally in the struggle against the tyranny of dogma."[5] But I dismissed his warning, perhaps because neither he nor any other historian ever spelled out in explicit detail how modern historical criticism of the Bible was originally forged as a weapon in the furious battle between the Enlightenment and the Christian Thrones and Altars of Europe. No one told me precisely how the inventors of the new historical method first eviscerated the Bible, then secretly packed it with their own values so that, after the defenders of orthodoxy had dragged this strange Trojan horse inside their city, the hidden soldiers could rule the city under the guise of biblical criticism.

A full explanation of that process far exceeds the limitations of this book. However, in this and the next chapters, I will explain a few of the most salient developments, particularly as they bear on the modern historical criticism of the Gospels. In the remainder of this chapter, I will sketch the main features of the origins, basic concepts, and terrible consequences of the modern worldview. Chapter 12 will give a brief overview of the three main operations contained within modern historicist biblical hermeneutics. These two chapters will form the background for subsequent discussions in Part Two on the breakdown of the medieval criterion of truth, the increasingly literal interpretation of the Bible as a whole and the Gospels in particular, the collapse of confidence in the text of the New Testament, the breakup of the Gospel canon, the emergence of a new method of historical biblical criticism based on the new physical understanding of the universe, the insistence that biblical criticism be consistently democratic, and finally the engulfing of all European culture in the horrible cataclysms of World Wars I and II.

The Beginnings of the Modern Worldview

To understand what happened to the study of the Bible in the modern period, we must begin with the theological controversies that broke out toward the end of the Middle Ages. On the one side were Neoplatonic theologians who, in their enthusiasm for the realm of the spirit, insisted that physical objects had no real existence. On the other side were "nominalist" theologians who claimed that the so-called spiritual realities of the Neoplatonists were no more than names (Lat. *nomen*, hence "nominalist"), empty verbal abstractions, and that the only real entities were physical things. When the Neoplatonic theologians said that God, Jesus Christ, the angels and saints, humans, and the whole created universe all formed a glorious, hierarchical harmony, with the earth in the center, the nominalists replied that God's relation to the universe could not be known beyond the fact that he created it.[6] They defined God as pure, unlimited power and said all other traditional attributes, such as goodness, rationality, mercy, and so on, were just human inventions.

As this view gained adherents during the fourteenth and fifteenth centuries, God became progressively more unknowable, the natural world was perceived to be separate and distinct from God, and true knowledge of nature came from human reason, not divine revelation (i.e., the Bible). This split produced the unintended side effect of removing all moral quality or purpose from the realm of nature. Now that God had nothing more to do with nature beyond creating it, it fell to humans to decide what nature's purpose was. Thus arose the practical character of modern science and technology, accompanied by modern laissez-faire capitalism and bourgeois democratic politics. I will spell each of these changes out in more detail in the sections that follow.

Modern Thinkers Reinvent Nature

Nothing is rightly understood about the rise of modern biblical criticism if close attention is not paid to the shifting meanings given to the term "nature" throughout this period. A static, mechanical meaning was given to "nature" during the first, rationalist phase of the Enlightenment (1600–

1700). This changed to a dynamic, organic meaning during the Romantic period (1770–1860).

By the beginning of the Reformation, the traditional, biblical understanding of nature as having been created by God according to his purposes was being challenged by a radically different conception of nature.[7] Nicholas of Cusa (1401–1464), a Roman Catholic bishop who devoted much of his time to philosophy and mathematics, argued that the earth had to revolve around the sun while rotating on its own axis. He envisioned an infinite universe ruled by mathematically derived laws.[8] His theory was given mathematical support by Nicolaus Copernicus in *De revolutionibus orbium caelestium,* published in 1543. Copernicus opposed the Bible's view of the earth as the center of the cosmos. A few decades later, Galileo Galilei (1564–1642) backed up Copernicus with empirical demonstrations using a revolutionary new piece of technology, the telescope. Galileo claimed that it enabled him to see mountains on the moon and moons around Jupiter. His examiners in the Inquisition were so terrified that they refused to look through his instrument, fearing demonic influences. Galileo also argued that the Bible's view of the earth's relation to the sun was mistaken, for which he was tried for heresy and imprisoned until he recanted.

What was so disconcerting about the new scientists was their use of an alternative source of knowledge to attack the Bible: empirical observation aided by mathematics. Defenders of the Bible were hard pressed to respond, since few among them knew anything about mathematics. "The truth," insisted Galileo,

> is written in this grand book—I mean the universe which stands continuously open to our gaze—but it cannot be understood unless one first learns to comprehend the language and interpret the characters in which it is written. *It is written in the language of mathematics* and its characters are triangles, circles, and other geometrical figures.[9]

As mathematics became widely used to understand the physical universe, "nature" necessarily took on a strict uniformity.[10] The hierarchical universe of the Bible became passé. The new "physical philosophers" were uninterested in anything they could not measure. To them, the universe was a giant machine, a view given definitive expression by Isaac Newton in his *Philosophiae naturalis principia mathematica* (1687). Newton's celestial mechanics ended any credibility the Bible's earth-centered cosmos may still have retained, a credibility that had already been seriously compromised by the use of torture to defend it.[11]

The quantification of nature led to a purely *physical* view of the universe. Having lost its divine center, the universe became a centerless, infinitely extended *thing* containing an immense number of smaller things. Among such smaller things were humans, whom Descartes called "thinking things" (*une chose qui pense*).[12]

Although small in size, these thinking things—aided by mathematics—could know with perfect accuracy, independent of Scripture or divine revelation, all there was to know about the entire universe (as they defined it). This new type of knowledge, freed from Church control, presented the Christian establishment with a major challenge: the new view of nature said God had no further role beyond getting it all started. This undercut the Church's claim over all practical knowledge of nature as well as God. Church officials attacked the blasphemous new science and tried to stamp it out. That failed, and new discoveries and hypotheses continued to be produced. In the end, the defenders of orthodoxy abandoned the field completely. Inventing the concept of the "supernatural," they retreated into the placid waters of scholasticism, leaving modern culture to the materialists.[13]

Modern Thinkers Reinvent Human Reason

As the universe came to be seen as a vast machine operating under its own laws, all thought of reason or purpose gradually drained out of it until finally it was just *there*. At that point, nature suddenly began to seem strange and unfamiliar. Things happened in it, triggering multitudes of other things, in a vast and infinite series of interlocking mechanisms, extending backwards and forwards in infinite time. How did it all work? Humans decided it was up to them to observe things and piece together clues that might explain how nature worked. For this quest, mathematics was indispensable. On the other hand, the usual business of proving how *good* or *beautiful* nature was began to seem quaint and old-fashioned. The main issue now was, how did it all work? Gradually, that question became: How can *we make* nature work *for us*? Thus human reason—guided by mathematics—came to be seen as an instrument to be used for purely utilitarian purposes.[14]

The classic spokesman for this new point of view was Francis Bacon (1561–1626). In his famous *Novum Organum* (1620), Bacon dismissed the traditional medieval method of studying nature by reading the Bible and travel books written by classical authors. Instead, he called for a direct empirical analysis of natural phenomena using mathematics to quantify the results. By this means, Bacon hoped, humanity would conquer nature and thereby bring about its God-given right to universal happiness.[15]

Bacon laid repeated emphasis on the theme of *conquering nature*. His assumption was that nature had no purpose of its own and must be *conquered*, i.e., given a purpose by humans. Bacon was certain that this would make human life richer and more secure. He was influenced by Utopian writings such as Thomas More's *Utopia* (1516), which envisioned the "unlimited ability of humans to conquer nature by rational means (and usher in) a state of universal happiness."[16]

In this way, the human capacity for understanding (reason) was taken out of its ancient community context, where (a) its innate powers were believed to be divinely given and (b) its main purpose was the formation of community, i.e., relatedness with God, with other human beings, and with the entire created order. In the modern worldview, human reason was perceived to have its power from itself (like God) and to contain no moral or aesthetic core. It became flat and featureless, one-dimensional: *usefulness* was its goal and *quantity* was its guide.

Modern Thinkers Reinvent Time

The modern conception of nature as consisting of a totally uniform, featureless, infinitely extended space, having no center, devoid of goodness, purpose, beauty, or anything that could not be quantified, necessarily involved a similar transformation of the traditional concept of *time*. Modern time became pure chronological extension, demarcated by tiny, medium, and large mathematical periods. This new concept was given physical form by an invention called a *clock*, from the German *Glocke* or "bell," so called because the early clocks, which were put up on church steeples everywhere, had bells that were struck with little hammers announcing the hour.

The most important feature of these new mechanical measurers of time was not noticed in the general enthusiasm over their accuracy; they could tell you precisely when it was but never *why*. In traditional Greek cosmology, the bare passage of time (Greek *chronos*) was rarely thought of. Like the biblical view, time was thought of in terms of *seasons* (Greek *kairos*), such as in the famous passage from Ecclesiastes 3.

> For everything there is a season
>   and a time for every occupation under heaven.
> A time to be born and a time to die;
> A time to plant and a time to pluck up what is planted;
> A time to kill and a time to heal;
> A time to break down and a time to build up;
> A time to weep and a time to laugh;

A time to mourn and a time to dance; . . .
A time to seek and a time to lose; . . .
A time to rend and a time to sew;
A time to keep silence and a time to speak;
A time to love and a time to hate;
A time for war and a time for peace. (RSV)

This "time to" concept fit within a ceaseless temporal rhythm of day/night, which fit within week/month, which fit within the great annual cycle of planting and harvest. Cutting across all of these, there were the "times" of the human community, demarcated by reigns of kings: Israel, Babylon, Assyria, Rome. These were invariably remembered as times of victory or devastation, good times or evil. Containing and sustaining and giving meaning to all of these overlapping times was the great, all-controlling power and wisdom of God, guiding all things from creation to the end of history. Thus one always knew not only when it was but why it was that time as well. Human events transpired within and were identified by numerous temporal intersections, all remembered and passed down from generation to generation by the elders in the community. And all of these times needed to be skillfully woven together if the full picture were truly told. Hence the rich, dense feeling of time in ancient epics like the *Epic of Gilgamesh,* the *Iliad,* the saga of Joseph in Genesis, the *Niebelungenlied, Beowulf,* the *Bhagavad-gita.*

In the worldview being invented by the modernists, this all disappeared. For them, time became a mathematics-friendly linear continuum: centerless, featureless, infinite. Since no transcendental agency could—by definition—get involved in this kind of time, events in the modern concept of time had no transcendent meaning or purpose; they *just happened.*

Before long, an interesting twist began to emerge: the present time of the modern scientists seemed to be invariably *better* than any previous time. The word "modern" began to be used. These thinkers called their present the *modern age,* the "now" age (from the Latin *modo,* meaning "now"), as opposed to the past or "then" age. Whereas traditional western culture had made a virtue of holding on to the past and remaining true to tradition, the "now" age began to assert its superiority over the past.[17] The concept of "progress" became popular as a general time designator. In this view, the present is always superior to the past and the future is going to be even more glorious than the present.

This concept was not entirely new. It drew on both traditional Christian as well as classical Greek ideas. In the Middle Ages, Augustine's *City of God* had helped shape the view of human history as a continual struggle between good and evil, ending only when the Lord Jesus would return with all the saints to establish the Kingdom of God on earth for one thousand years. In the Italian Renaissance, humanists replaced this view with a concept of history based on ancient Greek sources that viewed human history as unceasing progress because of the increments of human knowledge accumulating generation by generation.[18] During the Reformation, millenarian groups looked for the Kingdom of God to arrive at any time, and by the late sixteenth and early seventeenth centuries, "new light" communities were found in many parts of Europe and England. The Quakers in England and the Collegiants in Holland were among the best organized. All these trends fed the modern concept of progress, making the "modern" age superior to all past ages.

Modern Thinkers Reinvent Human Nature

In the Bible, human beings are understood to be part of a great, ordered harmony or *kosmos*. The basic question facing humans always was how to "fit in" to this great, divinely ordered harmony. In the Old Testament, a term for a human act that did not fit in was *ra'*, which literally meant "to injure or hurt." The proper recompense for an act of *ra'* was to do an equal injury to the offender: "an eye for an eye." Underlying this conception of justice as revenge lay an ancient sense of the divine balance in creation. The divinely given law code helped society rectify imbalances caused by those who injured or hurt anything or anyone, restoring the original divine harmony and returning the social order to a right relation with the Creator (hence the term "righteousness"). Similarly, in classical Greek and Roman ethics, personal virtue was always defined in terms of social obligation. A definition of the divine/human community always preceded and conditioned discussions of human virtue, freedom, and privilege.[19]

This ancient synthesis persisted through the Middle Ages until it broke up during the theological battles between the Neoplatonists and the nominalists. For one thing, Christian theology had never been able to resolve the antinomy between an all-powerful Creator and human freedom.[20] Late medieval nominalism came down on the side of God's absolute power to control all things in such a way that God's will acted in and through the human will.[21] This solution had the curious effect of raising the freedom of the human will to divine levels. Nicholas of Cusa (1401–1464) called the human "a contraction of God's all-comprehensive nature."[22] Wrote Cusa:

> Human nature includes everything within itself and attains all things by the power of its sense, intellect, and will. *The human person is a god,* yet

not absolutely, because he is human; *a human god*, then. Person is also the world, but not in the world's contracted existence, because he is human. Hence the person is a *microcosmos* or a human world.[23]

Cusa was not the only fifteenth-century thinker to view humans in this exalted manner. In the Italian Renaissance, Marsilio Ficino (1433–1499), an Italian philosopher and protégé of Cosimo de Medici, taught that "the power of the human person almost resembles that of God's nature."[24] Pico della Mirandola (1463–1494), another leader of the Italian Renaissance and one of the most learned men of his time, stated in his "Oration on the Dignity of Man" that God gave Adam his own *unlimited freedom* to define himself however he wished:

> We have not made you either celestial or terrestrial, mortal or immortal, in order that you may as it were become your own maker and former and *shape yourself in whatever form you like best*.[25]

It should be emphasized that such exalted ideas about the divine essence of humans were not all that new. They had been around in one form or another for over two thousand years. Aristotle taught that human reason partook of the divine reason underlying the entire cosmos and therefore was in some sense itself divine.[26] In Christian theology, the concept of the human being as "the image of God" contained a lofty estimation of its own. Consider these famous lines from Psalm 8:

> O Lord, our Sovereign,
>   how majestic is your name in all the earth!
> You have set your glory above the heavens.
> When I look at your heavens, the work of your fingers,
>   the moon and the stars that you have established;
> What are human beings that you are mindful of them,
>   mortals that you care for them?
> *Yet you have made them a little lower than God,*
>   *and crowned them with glory and honor.*
> You have given them dominion
>   over the works of your hands;
> You have put all things under their feet,
>   all sheep and oxen, and also the beasts of the field,
>   the birds of the air, and the fish of the sea,
>   whatever passes along the paths of the seas.
>   (8:1–8, RSV; italics added)

Precisely the same thoughts are found in the famous speech of the chorus in the roughly contemporaneous Greek tragedy *Antigone* by Sophocles: "many wonders there be, but naught more wondrous than man"— and the chorus goes on to marvel at human dominion over the earth and the sea and all animals.[27]

These traditional concepts were reformulated by late medieval nominalism and then heightened during the Italian Renaissance into an exalted vision of the magnificent powers of human reason, possessing godlike sovereignty over all of nature. This potent dream spread northward from Italy to France, to northwestern Europe and to Great Britain, accompanied by sweeping demands for radical changes in all of the old-fashioned ways of doing commerce, politics, and religion.

Humanist Optimism Changes into Radical Skepticism

The tide of optimism did not last long. By the year 1500, one foundation stone of the traditional, biblical worldview after another had been questioned by the new scientists and humanists. Equally disconcerting were new geographical discoveries brought home by Portuguese and Spanish adventurers, which challenged the traditional view of the makeup of the inhabited world. Meanwhile, Muslim scholars were teaching long-lost Greek classics in architecture, mathematics, medicine, and philosophy to enthusiastic students in Italy and Spain. This led to an eager search for other classical writings, including the Greek and Roman skeptics, such as Sextus Empiricus and Lucretius.[28] Their withering critique of tyranny and traditional religion was immediately turned against the Roman Catholic Church and the institution of monarchy. All of these developments combined to foster an atmosphere of confusion and mistrust toward all established norms and values.

In the midst of this rising tide of skepticism and confusion, a young German monk named Martin Luther (1483–1546) began attacking the practice of selling "indulgences"—papal certificates guaranteeing the bearer of God's forgiveness for sins, past or future, so that little or no time would have to be spent in the torments of Purgatory. These indulgences were being hawked about Europe by agents of the Pope to raise cash for a huge cathedral he wanted to build in Rome in honor of the Apostle Peter. Luther complained that these disgusting documents undermined Christian piety and made a mercenary transaction out of God's free gift.

After several unsuccessful lower-level attempts to shut him up, in 1521 Luther was ordered to cease and desist by the Pope himself. He refused, saying that he had Scripture and tradition on his side and the Pope had neither. One thing led to another until finally Luther was ordered to appear before the emperor at a specially convened hearing at the imperial city of Worms on 17 April 1521. Standing before the assembled royalty, papal emissaries, clergy, and nobility, Luther was shown a row of his books and ordered to retract them. He requested a day to consider his reply. The next afternoon, he was once again ordered to recant them. He replied as follows:

> Your Imperial Majesty and Your Lordships demand a simple answer. Here it is, plain and unvarnished. Unless I am convicted of error by the testimony of Scripture or clear reason, I remain convinced by the Scriptures to which I have appealed, since I put no trust in the unsupported authority of Popes or councils because they have often erred and contradicted themselves. My conscience is taken captive by God's Word. I cannot and will not recant anything, for to act against our conscience is neither safe nor open to us. On this I take my stand. I can do no other. God help me. Amen.[29]

At this point, says American historian Richard Popkin, Martin Luther raised the dispute to an entirely new level.

> Luther ... presented a radically different criterion of religious knowledge. He developed from just one more reformer attacking the abuses and corruption of a decaying bureaucracy into the leader of an intellectual revolt that was to shake the very foundations of Western civilization.[30]

What does it mean to "present a radically different criterion"? In classical Greek philosophy, it had been shown that nothing could be proved unless all parties in a dispute agreed upon some preestablished rule or criterion for knowing when something was true or false (in Greek, κριτήριον, or *kriterion,* means "that by which to judge"). Absent such a prior agreement, the disputants would argue past one another indefinitely, an exercise in futility.

When Luther stood before the emperor and representatives of the Pope and rejected the final authority of popes and councils where they differed from the Scripture, he denied the criterion of the medieval Roman Catholic Church. When he went on to say that he was going to be *his own criterion* guided by *his own interpretation of Scripture,* he put into place a brand-new criterion that seemed shockingly crazy. What could ensue but chaos if everyone did the same? One way to look at the religious controversies that erupted immediately after Luther's stand before Charles V is that they were pitched battles between rival criteria.[31]

As word of what Luther had done spread across Europe, a chain reaction broke out, greatly exacerbating already existing frictions between the Pope and the kings of France, Spain, England, and Bavaria. Local uprisings occurred in Bavaria and south Germany. Eventually, whole nations, such as Switzerland, England, the Netherlands, Norway, and Sweden, declared their independence from Rome. In Germany, fierce struggles broke out between pro-Lutheran and pro-Catholic territories that were to last more than a century. A temporary halt to the fighting came in 1555 with the Peace of Augsburg, which settled on the compromise that each prince could determine the religion of his own territory (*cujus regio ejus religio*). This represented a *political* solution to the religious controversies flaming on all sides. As such, it signaled a definitive breakdown of the traditional religious unity of western Christendom. Skepticism about all traditional religious norms grew apace as modernism won new followers, particularly in France, England, and the Netherlands.

It wasn't long before war broke out again, as nations and territories across Europe were drawn into a protracted series of bitter conflicts. This bloody period has come to be known as the Thirty Years' War. It lasted down to the middle of the seventeenth century. In 1648 at the Peace of Westphalia, representatives of the emperor and Lutheran, Reformed, Anglican, and Roman Catholic territories divided up Europe along religious lines once and for all.

The fighting ended mainly because all sides were too exhausted to fight any longer, not because any decisive victory was won. Whole regions lay in ruins, but the German territories were most devastated. Armies had plundered and looted them for a full generation. The population had fallen from around sixteen million to less than six million, with few men anywhere. The regional economies lay in shambles; poverty and starvation were everywhere. Well into the next century, when industrialization brought new wealth and power to France and England, Germany remained disorganized, backward, and fearful.

Most significant for our purposes is the explicit recognition in the treaty signed at Westphalia that the religious issue could not be resolved. Article V declared that Protestants and Roman Catholics would hereafter cease any attempt to change a territory's confessional status by force "until an understanding has been achieved about religion by God's grace."[32] Skepticism about religion had finally achieved the status of international policy.

René Descartes Finds a Path out of Skepticism

In the midst of this turbulent period of doubt, fanatical certainty, and politically motivated religious persecution, a French philosopher and mathematician named René Descartes (1596–1650) suggested a solution to the problem of the missing criterion: make skepticism itself the path to a new criterion. In his most famous writing, the *Discourse on Method* (1637), Descartes laid down as the first of his four rules for ascertaining the truth:

> Never accept anything as true that I did not evidently know to be such
> . . . (i.e.) to include in my judgments nothing more than that which
> would present itself to my mind so clearly and so distinctly that I would
> have no occasion to put it in doubt.[33]

With this, Descartes ushered in one of the most characteristic features of the modern worldview: its profound subjectivism. In Book I of the *Discourse,* Descartes listed and then swept aside all previous systems of thought, all previous theological doctrines, all art and poetry, and all past tradition, because in them existed no clear and indubitable truth. He alone was all he could rely on.

If Descartes seems strikingly individualistic, keep in mind that Martin Luther had pioneered the self-as-ultimate-authority criterion more than one hundred years earlier. Subsequent religio-political wars had spread this individualistic criterion across Europe. It was only a question of time before the principle that *each prince* should decide the religious fate of his subjects would cave in to democratic criticism that *each individual* should decide his own religious fate.[34]

Beyond this, the similarity between Luther and Descartes ends. Whereas Luther had based himself on his *conscience* as guided by *Holy Scripture* and thereby remained firmly within the Church's tradition (at least the early part of it), Descartes substituted *abstract reason* as the guide for his *mind.* Klaus Scholder explains:

> Now reason has nothing but itself on which it can rely. No tradition
> may stand as the truth for it, no (external) authority give it the certainty
> which it achieves solely through its own judgment.[35]

Luther escaped Descartes' total subjectivism by remaining firmly committed to the Bible. Descartes had nothing but his own mind and the artificial world of geometry.

Having cut himself off from all authorities, Descartes went on to propose a way out of what now threatened to become infinite skepticism. As simple as it was daring, Descartes turned the act of doubt itself into an affirmation. Could he in fact doubt *everything?* he asked himself. No, logical analysis showed that he could not possibly doubt *that he was doubting.* Upon this razor-thin affirmation, Descartes constructed a series of additional affirmations:

- Since something is doubting, that something must exist. "I think, therefore I know that I exist."[36]
- Since I exist and can conceive of my existence clearly and distinctly, "clear and distinct ideas" must be true.
- Since I have a clear and distinct innate idea of something greater than myself, something than which nothing greater can be conceived, that something—which I will call God—must also exist.
- This clear and distinct innate idea of God logically means that God has so constructed reality that all clear and distinct ideas, whether innately present in my mind or conveyed by my senses, are true without possibility of error. God has so constructed the world that clear and distinct ideas must be true.[37]

Later in Part Two, I give a few examples of thinkers who exhibit total disregard for Christian tradition in answering historical questions about the Bible or who ignore the plain meaning of the biblical text when they interpret it. To adequately understand how they could act in this manner, it is essential to grasp the self-centeredness of Descartes' solution to the problem of skepticism. He did not ask the traditional question What is reality? Rather, he asked, *How can I know* reality? Then he grounded the basic guarantee that he could know reality not in the traditional manner, namely, by appealing to God's providence, but squarely within the nature of his own individual mind. Thus, Descartes set in motion a kind of self-centered subjectivism which became a key feature in modern western culture: it is the individual who establishes the truth.[38] Past tradition no longer has any authority. The modern individual freely decides everything for himself or herself, based on nothing more than his or her own experience. This is the root of the sweeping subjectivism typical of modern western culture: art, ethics, education, religion, economics, politics—and biblical interpretation.

On the basis of this starting point, Descartes spelled out a system of ideas that brought together all of the leading themes of the developing modern European worldview up to that point.

First, true knowledge of external reality consisted of "clear and distinct ideas" present in the mind from itself and from physical sensations. This principle applied to both physical and spiritual reality (there was no difference between them).[39]

Second, what was his model for "clear and distinct ideas"? The logical demonstrations of classical geometry. Dupré comments on the momentous significance of Descartes' choice.

> While attempting to secure indubitable certainty, Descartes *transformed the concept of knowledge itself* . . . (He posited) as the universal norm of knowledge . . . mathematics. The demand for an unshakable foundation together with the mathematical model that followed from it gave the "idea of science" . . . its definitive orientation in the modern age.[40]

Descartes' choice had a profound effect: anything *not* known with mathematics-like certainty *was not true*. Mathematics became the norm for all true knowledge: if something can be quantified, it can be known. Otherwise, it is just a guess.[41]

Third, mathematics works best with physical objects. True to his nominalist education, Descartes accepted the definitions of God and nature created by the classical nominalist thinkers: Duns Scotus (1265–1308) and William of Ockham (1290–1350).[42] In Descartes' system, God is defined by no other characteristics than pure power; "God is incomprehensible power" (*puissance incompréhensible*).[43] This definition left God's relationship to the universe barren of any other characteristics than being the ultimate cause. The image widely used at the time was that of the clockmaker and the clock. Like the new physical scientists of his day, Descartes viewed the universe as if it were a giant machine, a thing ruled by a "system of invariable forces causally imposed at the beginning."[44] This idea deprived all things in the universe, animate and inanimate, of intrinsic meaning or value; they just *were*.[45] That is, they just were *things*. The universe was no more than a vast collection of things. Humans were "thinking things" (*une chose qui pense*).[46]

Fourth, this "physicalization" of everything drove spiritual and moral concerns out of the picture completely. All that was left was *force*. Since none of the things in the universe had any purpose, it was up to humans to give it to them. What was the main criterion? Usefulness to humans. Nature had no other purpose than what was useful to humans. The human mind, guided by geometrical reason, had the godlike freedom[47] to impose purpose on things in the natural environment.[48] Discovering what things, like animals, were good for required personal observation. Arguing that animals were no more than machines, Descartes recommended experimenting on *live* animals, such as cutting them open to see how their respiratory systems worked, since he believed that animals had no minds and could not feel pain.[49]

Fifth, in Descartes' view, the human mind had no content beyond its godlike freedom to choose.[50] Descartes' "self" was devoid of all moral or artistic or spiritual elements. It was a featureless, thinking thing; *will* was its sole activity. Nothing guided the will save whatever physically satisfied the thinking thing: avoidance of pain and pursuit of pleasure. In this way, Descartes gave a powerful impetus to the development of modern materialistic hedonism. The irony of this empty self seeking its own pleasure was noted by Nietzsche, Kierkegaard, and others at the time. "Separated from that totality which once nurtured it and deprived of that (interior vitality) which once defined it, (the modern self became) an indigent self."[51] As protection against this terrible feeling of emptiness and poverty, there arose the typical bourgeois appetite for consumer goods, for more and more things to fill up inner emptiness. The shopping mall, with its endless display of potential possessions, and the credit card, with its promise of sufficient wealth, are the central realities of this lost soul's desperate quest for substance. Such craving for physical possessions was never seen in earlier days in western culture, when the self saw itself as rich, full, bathed in divine favor.

Sixth, this isolated, featureless, individual thinking thing lacked all awareness of anything beyond itself except for the huge physical universe created and then abandoned by God. The only thing left to do was to join itself with other thinking things to improve each one's physical well-being. Thus Cartesian philosophy gave a powerful boost to egocentrism in politics (self-rule = "democracy") and egocentrism in commerce (capitalism). We will now examine these two developments.

Individualism in Commerce and Politics

The traditional Christian conception of society held out the ideal of the good life in such a way that it was always based on

> the good of the community . . . The (community) trained and educated individuals as well as morally fulfilling them: it functioned both as end and as means. From that perspective, the good of human nature consisted in the first place in a *common good,* and the virtuous life aimed, above all, at building and maintaining a good society.[52]

With the collapse of traditional political theory during the Italian Renaissance, a harsher theory of human community was forged in the crucible of the brutal, internecine conflict following the Reformation. The most stark expression of the new conception of the state was the *Leviathan,* published in 1651 by the eminent English philosopher and mathematician Thomas Hobbes (1588–1679).

Hobbes based his theory of the state squarely on the new, mechanical, amoral, physical conception of nature. Since this view of nature was so flat and one-dimensional that it permitted none of the usual explanations as to why humans left off roaming in the wilds to form societies, Hobbes had to invent a new one. In a "state of nature," Hobbes theorized, humans had unlimited freedom and unlimited "rights" to do whatever they wanted. There were no moral constraints of any kind. As these individuals pursued their various pleasures, strife inevitably broke out, leading to a constant state of war of the strong against the weak. This meant that human existence "in nature," said Hobbes in a famous phrase, was "nasty, brutish, and short."

Out of a desire for self-preservation, humans gave up some of their unlimited freedom to join together in societies governed by rulers and laws. Thus the state was formed, not because of any innate drive for companionship (the traditional explanation[53]), but purely out of fear and a need for security.[54] Once gathered together in a state, humans had no obligations beyond that of obeying the ruler, who had absolute power. The good life for any individual still consisted of satisfying "the object of any man's appetite or desire"[55] within the laws.

Hobbes' explanation became widely accepted among physical thinkers in the seventeenth century. As this view took hold, it caused a momentous shift in the modern understanding of rights and obligations. By beginning with the individual human isolated "in nature" (as they understood that term) and ascribing infinite rights to that individual, they defined rights *prior to* obligations. In this way, the logic of Hobbes' theory radically transformed the modern discussion of rights and obligations. In the classical view, the individual's obligation to the community came first and conditioned any subsequent discussion of the individual's rights and privileges. Hobbes began by defining human rights in isolation from obligations to the community, which then meant that it was the task of the government to guarantee to the individual as many of the original "natural" rights as possible. From this perspective, we can understand the peculiarly nebulous and unbounded character of the modern western conception of "human rights," as well as the strident demand that the state "guarantee" all sorts of "human rights"—such as "life, liberty, and the pursuit of happiness"—that had never been heard of before.

As far as the state's moral obligation to other states was concerned, in Hobbes' view it had none. The ruler's sole concern was the efficient application of power. This view makes Hobbes a chief spokesman of modern, amoral power politics (*Realpolitik*), in a direct line that runs from Machiavelli to Marx and Lenin.[56] By the same token, the law in Hobbes' state no longer had any intrinsic moral character either. Its sole purpose was technical efficiency; i.e., "law" became whatever the sovereign decreed.[57]

John Locke and the Egocentric Commercial Aspirations of the New Bourgeois Class

Until the modern age, the traditional basis of wealth in western culture had always been land and the products it produced. Owners of the land owned everything on it as well as the peasantry who lived and worked on it. The lord of the estate in turn was obligated to provide his serfs with protection in times of trouble. This basic system of wealth persisted across Europe until the discovery of the New World. Then new forms of wealth having nothing to do with land began to pour into the coffers of merchant entrepreneurs in Spain, Portugal, Holland, and England. These were trade commodities, such as spices, hardwoods, silk, gold, and silver.

This new form of wealth was soon augmented by still another: manufacturing. As new inventions in agriculture and metalworking made it more profitable to clear the land of peasants (e.g., the Enclosure Act in England 1788), cash crops became available.[58] Other inventions speeded the process of industrialization, especially in England, and more marketable commodities flowed into the marketplaces of Europe. By the late eighteenth century, merchant capitalism had reached the point where "money ceased to be merely a means of exchange and became a form of private property."[59]

Merchant capitalists in the maritime nations formed corporations with local industrialists to exploit foreign resources, trade, and territorial acquisition. Inevitably, these new trade corporations became embroiled in international power politics, leading to conflict in far-off countries, such as between England and Holland for control of New Amsterdam/New York. These "new rich" (*nouveaux riches*) acquired powerful positions in government where their interests and aspirations collided with the hereditary landed aristocracy. The aristocracy banded together with the ecclesiastical establishment, while the new "middle class" (bourgeois in France, Whigs in England) prided themselves on being the "modern" party of reform. They were interested in the latest scientific discoveries (as long as they undermined the power of the aristocracy), they called for toleration in religious matters (it was good for their business), and they insisted on representative democracy (i.e., representation of their interests) in government.

John Locke (1632–1704) was the foremost expositor of the new capitalist political agenda. In his *Essay on Human Understanding* (1690), Locke had successfully refuted Descartes' notion of "innate ideas," saying that the mind was no more than a "blank slate" (*tabula rasa*) until it received sense impressions. Thus Locke removed the last vestiges of traditional metaphysics from Descartes' worldview, leaving the human mind barren of any ideas whatsoever.[60] The practical effect of this argument was to cut the present off from any admixture of the past more thoroughly than even Descartes had done.

Locke's *Epistle on Toleration* (1690) contained a powerful argument for the complete separation of religious organizations from the civil government, a view that eventually found its way into the United States Constitution. In his *Letter*, Locke defined both religious associations and states as voluntary associations. Each had a central goal from the individual person's point of view, which is why he joined it. The state's purpose was to make it possible for the individual to obtain "life, liberty, bodily health, and freedom from pain, and the possession of outward things, such as lands, money, furniture, and the like."[61] The religious association's purpose was "the public worship of God and, by means thereof, the acquisition of eternal life."[62] Note the egocentric, acquisitive character of each activity.

Locke's ideas became popular in England and the English colonies. They also found a ready reception in France among the materialist philosophers, such as La Mettrie (*Man a Machine*, 1748), Étienne Condillac, and Claude Adriene Helvétius. The last-named said in *On the Mind* (1759) that humans were

> purely egoistic creatures, and, if left to pursue their private interests unimpeded, would automatically serve the general good because natural law implies a natural harmony of interests. This view became the basis of *laissez-faire* economics.[63]

In 1776, the Scottish economist Adam Smith (1723–1790), having traveled in France and met some of the better-known French political thinkers, published what has become the classic statement of the new laissez-faire economics: *An Inquiry into the Nature and Causes of the Wealth of Nations*. Taking as his starting point Locke's assertion that private property was the most basic "natural right," Smith provided this "natural" right with a theoretical justification. (He argued) that the competitive pursuit of self-interest, if not interfered with (by government regulation), not only results in a "natural" social order, but also leads to a rapid increase of wealth, which was assumed to be the best way to bring about the greatest happiness of the greatest number ... Capitalism, therefore, was as "natural" as progress and the best way to promote it.[64]

Much more should be said about Locke's contributions to the rise of the modern worldview, but this must suffice for now. In Chapter 17, I provide a detailed examination of the close link he forged between the literal interpretation of the Bible and democratic politics under a secular government.

Impact of the Modern Worldview on European Civilization and the Planet

As the middle-class families espousing these ideas became more numerous and powerful, especially in the mercantile nations of England, Holland, France, Spain, and Portugal, an era of unprecedented physical aggrandizement began, guided by the amoral, hedonistic, individualistic, bourgeois worldview. The sole aim was to make physical existence more profitable and pleasurable.

Corresponding to what is widely known as the industrial revolution in the eighteenth and nineteenth centuries, these ideas opened the gates for changes in energy production (steam power, then coal-fired electricity), new methods of refining (iron, copper, bronze, and glass), transportation (railroads, automobiles, airplanes), communication (radio, telephone-telegraph), incandescent lights, synthetic plastics (Bakelite), the typewriter, mass-circulation news, military technology, and more.[65]

The new methods of refining iron, steel, nickel, and aluminum produced immense wealth for powerful industrial families: in Germany, the Krupps; in England, ICI and Vickers Armstrong; in France, Schneider Creusot; in the United States, Ford and J. P. Morgan. The new metals provided the means for expanding transportation shipping beyond anything previously imagined.

Scientific discoveries in medicine and nutrition (Beyer, Ross, Salvarsan), in antisepsis (Pasteur), anesthesia, and surgical instruments revolutionized the ordinary citizen's life expectancy. New methods of artificial fertilizer produced from petroleum, refrigerated transportation, and sterilization of milk products made possible enormous increases of cheap, plentiful food, widely distributed.

The building of new industrial plants for coal mining, iron and steel production, factories for food production (canning), textiles, furniture, and automobile manufacturing caused a great shift of the rural population into what had been cities, but now became "vast urban agglomerations."[66] This urban migration was hastened in part as farmers went bankrupt, being unable to compete with cheap, imported food. Soon a "proliferation of social conditions sprang up unknown at any time in the planet's past—the rise of what is usually called 'mass society.'"[67]

As a result of these sweeping changes, Europe's population soared to disastrous heights. In aggregate figures, Europe's population rose 30 million between 1850 and 1870. It increased a further 100 million between 1870 and 1900.[68] Europe's whole population *doubled* in one century, between 1800 and 1900, sending *40 million emigrants* to all parts of the planet. Where these Europeans encountered opposition, they overcame it by means of superior technological force. After the local armed resistance had been sufficiently crushed, cultural suppression followed as local languages, arts, and religions were replaced by European equivalents. Protected by the ensuing hybrid indigenous-European infrastructure, powerful European corporations inserted smaller hybrid companies whose sole purpose was to extract the valuable natural resources needed by Europe's voracious industries: from Chile nitrates, copper; from Australia copper, gold, lead, zinc; from West Africa hardwoods; from South Africa gold, diamonds; from the Congo copper, bauxite; from Southeast Asia rubber, tin; from the Middle East petroleum.[69]

This sudden mass migration of armed and predatory Europeans into all of the regions of the planet was paralleled in world history only by the armed expansion of Islam to South Asia in the east and to North Africa in the west during the sixth to ninth century and the Mongol-Turkic expansion across central Asia during the thirteenth century. By 1900, *one-tenth of the planet's inhabitants had seized control of most of the rest of the planet:*

· Africa by Germany, England, France, Belgium
· South and southeast Asia by France, Britain, Holland, Portugal
· China by France, England, Russia
· South America by Spain, Portugal
· Middle East and Iran by France, England, Russia

The sudden influx of immense amounts of wealth into Europe during the latter part of the nineteenth century certainly fanned the feverish visions of world conquest among Europe's imperialist powers and fueled their burgeoning weapons industries. But there were also cries of alarm. One thinks of Oswald Spengler, Friedrich Nietzsche, Honoré de Balzac, and Charles Dickens, to name just a few of the most famous nineteenth-century Continental and British figures in literature and philosophy who rose up to condemn the imperialist and materialist trend. Indeed, expressions of fear and loathing were heard already in the late eighteenth century when bourgeois imperialistic capitalism was still in its infancy. Consider this biting assessment by the idealistic leader of the French Revolution Maximilien Robespierre (1758–1794). Laissez-faire capitalism, he said, was

> a practical philosophy which, reducing selfishness to a system, looks on human society as the battle-ground of cunning, which measures right and wrong by the yard-stick of success, and which regards personal integrity as a matter of taste or decorum, and the world as the heritage of the astute egoist.[70]

A few years earlier in 1774, his equally famous countryman Jean-Jacques Rousseau (1712–1778) could already see that the "modern" way of living, if allowed to continue unchecked, would lead to catastrophe:

> I see all the states of Europe rushing headlong to ruin; monarchies, republics, all those nations whose origins are so glorious and whose governments were built up with so much wisdom, are falling into decay and are threatened by an imminent death. All the great nations are moaning, crushed by their own weight.[71]

Did Rousseau's prophecy come to pass a few years later in the French Revolution and the bloody, destructive wars of Napoleon Bonaparte? Or did Rousseau somehow detect the faint rumblings of a far greater cataclysm, one that needed 140 years to gather its fury before it exploded over Europe: the Great War of 1914–1918?[72]

No one foresaw, during the climax of the modern period in late-nineteenth-century Europe, not even Rousseau, that it all would lead not just to one brutal war but to two great wars in quick succession and that the second would be the most destructive war in the planet's history. Involving the same highly educated, wealthy, powerful Christian nations of Europe, it was conducted by the sons of the men who had fought and died in the first war. Writing from Lambaréné just after the outbreak of World War I, theologian Albert Schweitzer cried in dismay, "We are living today under the sign of the collapse of civilization! . . . It is clear now to everyone that the suicide of civilization is in progress."[73]

If American literary historian Paul Fussell rightly said that irony was the great cultural result of the First World War,[74] then absurdity was the cultural result of the Second, evident in post–World War II French and Italian cinema, German and British literature. It reflected the pervasive feeling that western civilization had gone crazy, that nothing was what it seemed to be, *nor did it really matter.* These twin emotions are still prevalent in the "postmodern" west (see Part Three).

These two wars were the funeral pyres that burned the "modern worldview" to ashes, ushering in the postmodern world of planetwide leagues and governments (the United Nations), planetwide companies (multinational corporations), planetwide terrorism, and planetwide communications (the "global village" with its "worldwide web"). The Second World War marked the first appearance in human history of planetwide war, a war which continued, after armed hostilities had ceased among the original belligerents, among a new set of belligerents for another fifty years as the "cold war." This planetwide struggle witnessed the emergence of the Soviet Union and the United States as history's most powerful industrial-military nations. They were also the first nations in history willing to use weapons that might result in *irreversible planetary destruction* to achieve their military-political objectives.[75]

As the twentieth century draws to a close, it is becoming increasingly evident that the enormous annual increase in human population among the less-developed countries, the ceaseless international conflicts, the grinding socioeconomic conditions of the Third World, the ugly and superficial mass communications in the industrialized nations, and the planetary species and environmental destruction are the unintended but inevitable consequences of the values and aspirations of the modern western worldview with its technological consequences. Yale historian Louis Dupré identifies these effects of two hundred years of modernism:

> unprecedented ecological disasters . . . in (an era of) increasing hazards of a yet uncontrolled technology, (in an era marked by a) dismaying lack of aesthetic harmony in our human-made environment.[76]

Dupré could also have mentioned the crippling of religious life in Europe and North America, or anywhere else that the modern spirit is found. He could have mentioned the corruption of education caused by decades of utilitarian efficiency in an educational context already weakened by rampant subjectivism. He could have mentioned the potentially dreadful consequences of amoral, utilitarian reason employed in the service of aggressive bioengineering corporations looking to manipulate any living tissue, human or otherwise, for a profit.

In the next chapter, we will see what the modern period produced in terms of a distinctive approach to the Bible in general and the Gospels in particular.

CHAPTER 12

Main Features of the Modern Historical-Critical Approach to Biblical Interpretation

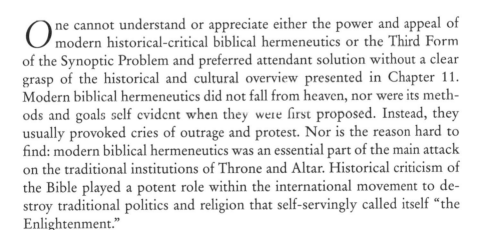

One cannot understand or appreciate either the power and appeal of modern historical-critical biblical hermeneutics or the Third Form of the Synoptic Problem and preferred attendant solution without a clear grasp of the historical and cultural overview presented in Chapter 11. Modern biblical hermeneutics did not fall from heaven, nor were its methods and goals self evident when they were first proposed. Instead, they usually provoked cries of outrage and protest. Nor is the reason hard to find: modern biblical hermeneutics was an essential part of the main attack on the traditional institutions of Throne and Altar. Historical criticism of the Bible played a potent role within the international movement to destroy traditional politics and religion that self-servingly called itself "the Enlightenment."

The Basics of Modern Historical-Critical Biblical Interpretation

To prepare the reader for the chapters that follow, I summarize here at the beginning of Part Two an outline of the three fundamental operations or steps I see as typical of modern, historicist—"Enlightenment"—biblical hermeneutics, founded on the broad philosophical, political, and economic assumptions described in Chapter 11. These are presented here schematically and as part of a logical progression; in actual practice, they are always more ambiguous and mixed together.

The First Step: Begin by Changing the Subject

Baruch Spinoza is widely regarded as the father of modern histori-cal criticism of the Bible. He insisted that the Bible should be studied *his-torically.* At the time, this did not seem an unusual thing to say, since sixteenth- and seventeenth-century Protestant pastors and theologians said the same thing. What Spinoza did was to *substitute the new ex-clusively physical conception of history for the complex and rich biblical conception.* Thus when Spinoza said, "The Bible must be studied *histori-cally,*" he meant a very different kind of *history* than that assumed by the defenders of traditional orthodoxy.

When Spinoza went on to say, "One cannot be sure of the theological meaning of any passage of the Bible until one has first answered certain historical questions," it sounded reasonable enough. But then he set forth a great, long list of questions directed at the *physical history* of the Bible and its writers. Where did all these books of the Bible come from? Who wrote them? How did they come into this collection? Were those who collected them also inspired? Were any books left out that should have been included? Who are the characters in these writings? Did they actually exist? What do all these miracle stories mean? Did they actually happen? What do the *words* mean, i.e., what *did they mean* in the original lan-guages? Does anybody really know the ancient languages anymore? How reliable are the texts of these writings? Where are the originals? Who made the translations? Were the translators also inspired? How accurate are they? And on and on and on.

Spinoza and his followers multiplied questions about the physical history of the text to the point that the traditional theological task could never get off the ground. That, however, was precisely the intended effect of the first step: to create an endless "nominalist barrage," if you will, an infinitely extendable list of questions directed at the physical history of the text, to the point where the clergy and the political officials allied with them *could never bring to bear their own theological interpretations* of the Bible. In other words, Spinoza switched the focus from the *referent* of the biblical text (e.g., God's activity, Jesus Christ) to *the history of the text.*[1] In so doing, he effectively eviscerated the Bible of all traditional theological meaning and moral teaching.

The Second Step: Make Oneself the Norm and Source of All Truth

While the all-important questions concerning the physical history of the Bible were still being discussed, the modern historical critics would add the paradoxical claim that—ultimately—answers to all these questions were not that important; the most important moral and religious truths—"love God and your neighbor"—were already well known to everyone through the operation of the "inner light" of human reason.

Here we can see a fundamental impact of Descartes' *cogito ergo sum.* Having rejected all traditional "systems of divinity," as well as the entire ancient tradition of biblical interpretation, modern historical critics insisted that each individual should be his or her own ultimate authority on ball questions. Guided by nothing more than one's own personal experience and the operation of "divine reason," each person was free to give any answers to any questions—or ignore them altogether. I see here the insertion of Cartesian *subjectivism* into modern historical criticism of the Bible.

This produced a very important corollary. Descartes' epistemology rested on the ancient Platonic distinction between *uncertain opinions* based on untrustworthy sense impressions of shifting external phenomena and *certain knowledge* of eternal truths known by reason alone. Given this radical disjunction, the lack of connection between shaky opinions regarding external historical data and certain knowledge of eternal truths *is simply a deduction from the original a priori disjunction.* This disjunction was given famous expression in the eighteenth century by G. E. Lessing: "The contingent truths of history can never become the proof of the necessary truths of reason."[2]

Since then, this idea has become commonly accepted within the writings of modern Protestant theologians and biblical critics, namely—in a more recent way of phrasing it—the inability of historical "facts" to guarantee the truth of the kerygma and faith (e.g., Barth, Bultmann).

What has *not* been recognized widely enough, in my view, is that this principle is no more than a deduction from Descartes' a priori disjunction between mind and physical reality. Reject this a priori disjunction and the inference immediately falls to the ground. Instead of realizing that this idea is no more than a philosophical axiom invented in the heat of opposition to ecclesiastical tyranny in the seventeenth century, modern historical critics and theologians *naively assume that it is a fact of reality.* The widespread application of this disjunction within modern historicist biblical interpretation has been *profoundly destructive* of the understanding of the interaction between God, humans, and the whole of creation as presented by the Bible itself. In short, Lessing's "ugly ditch" is just an *assumption* created by modern historicist biblical hermeneutics.

The Third Step: Make Pious Moralism the "True Meaning of the Bible"

Having changed the subject so as to strip out the Bible's core theology and moral teaching and having repudiated all authority (biblical or traditional) except oneself, Spinoza and his followers called for a new secular, rational society as the ideal haven for modern economic prosperity (capitalism) and political activity (democracy, i.e., representative government).

For these ambitious goals to be realized, however, they well knew that it would require the full cooperation of citizens and intellectuals formerly loyal to Throne and Altar. What about those reactionary citizens who were unwilling to make the leap to the modern worldview? Spinoza held out to them a simplistic moralism—"love God and your neighbor as yourself"—as "the true meaning of the Bible." In other words, they could still read their Bibles, but he made sure that these two traditional concepts were all they found.

By this devious route, Spinoza hoped that the profound institutional changes in the economic and political spheres espoused by the modern agenda could work their way unimpeded into eighteenth- and nineteenth-century Protestant society. No longer were the spheres of politics and commerce considered part of the Bible's core teaching; instead, it was henceforth restricted exclusively to the personal, private sphere of "love." Even so, the modernist philosophers took no chances that the old monarchy/priesthood monsters would rear their ugly heads again, so they insisted that *all* religious activity—regardless of its content—be under the strict control of the newly *secular* state.

In short, the net effect of what historical critics have accomplished during the past three hundred years—apart from accumulating an enormous heap of data about the physical history of the biblical text—has been to eviscerate the Bible's core religious beliefs and moral values, preventing the Bible from questioning the political and economic aspirations of the new bourgeois class.

The Modern Study of the Gospels and the Third Form of the Synoptic Problem

How did all this play out in the arena of Gospel studies? Specifically, what happened to the traditional explanations of the interrelations among the Gospels? Part Two documents the demolition by modern historical critics of all traditional elements of the Synoptic Problem and the erection of a totally new Third Form of the Synoptic Problem. How did this take place?

First of all, as modern skepticism eroded the Church's most cherished assumptions, sixteenth- and seventeenth-century theologians produced increasingly strident defenses of traditional religion. This included, among other things, sweeping assertions that the entire Bible was historically—i.e., literally—true. Ironically, they never noticed the trap they had fallen into: with such claims they had unwittingly given up the biblical and adopted the new scientific view of truth.

This inadvertent adoption of the modern scientific standard of truth may explain in part why there arose such a powerful concern about the purity and stability of the physical *Gospel text.* Among Protestants and Roman Catholics alike, this resulted in a great hunger to acquire the *original text* of the biblical writers—or, as far as our theme is concerned, to actually have what Matthew, Mark, Luke, and John *originally* wrote. Given this hunger, it was inevitable that the medieval Latin text of the Gospels would be set aside in favor of the *Greek original.* What no one anticipated was the unimaginable turmoil that ensued the day Erasmus published his attempt at a Greek New Testament, as scholars realized that it was riddled with flaws and tried to improve it.

So the first aspect of the traditional Synoptic Problem to crumble before the onslaught of the modern spirit was the *text* of the Gospels. Chapters 14, 15, and 19 describe the arc from certainty down into mass confusion and the slow ascent out of chaos back into a relatively stable consensus regarding the text of the Gospels.

The *canon* was the next aspect of the Synoptic Problem to collapse under the strains of modern skepticism, combined with new information pouring into Europe from Asia and the Middle East. As a complete history of text criticism during the modern period is not necessary for this book, so also Chapter 18 describes just the opening blast against the traditional canon of the Gospels by the forces of modernism. After this point, the canon remained an area of constant dispute, even down into the postmodern period discussed in Part Three.

The fundamental debate about the appropriate hermeneutics for biblical interpretation raged during the entire modern period. My account treats this all-important trend exclusively from the side of the modernists. I show that, at first, the modernists engaged in a static, blocklike approach to the Gospels (closely resembling the static, blocklike approach of their orthodox foes). Chapters 16 and 17 describe the methods and results of two of the most important creators of modern historical interpretation during this early, rationalist period: Baruch Spinoza and John Locke.

In the wake of the Romantic revolt of the late eighteenth and nineteenth centuries, a new, dynamic conception of history appeared which called for a *developmental* understanding of history. Within this trend, the signal moment for the emergence of the Third Form of the Synoptic Problem finally arrived with Johann Jakob Griesbach's invention of a synopsis, based on his decisive refusal to create yet another traditional harmony. The synopsis made it possible for Griesbach and his fellow modernists to examine the differences among the Gospels in terms of a *serial, progressive scenario of their composition.* Within this context, the question of the order of composition became of prime importance, for the first time in western history. I document and explain these momentous developments in Chapter 20, showing how Griesbach's synopsis made possible a completely new approach to the differences among the many Gospels, ultimately leading to the Third Form of the Synoptic Problem, attended by its own solution to the age-old question of how and why the Gospels were created.

Here again, I have documented a general movement from certainty down into mass confusion and chaos, followed by a slow ascent back up into clarity, definition, and consensus around a new fundamental approach.

At the dawn of the twentieth century, with the single exception of the issue of canon—or, rather, having disposed of the canonical status of any biblical writing—modernist biblical research had reached a high point of sorts. The moment of triumph was short-lived, however. In the second decade of the twentieth century, the mighty nations of Europe erupted into war, bringing upon themselves four catastrophic decades that nearly destroyed European and British civilization. But these terrible events were no surprise; the conditions for them had long since been prepared by the modern spirit, and it died in the fiery catastrophe that it created.

Signs of Things to Come: The Protestant Reformers on the Differences among the Gospels

It should not be surprising to find the chief Protestant Reformers, Luther and Calvin, exhibiting a mixture of old and new in their interpretations of the Gospels. In this chapter I will discuss a few passages from some sermons of Martin Luther (1483–1546) and a commentary on the Gospels by John Calvin (1509–1564), to show how they stood on the dividing line between tradition and innovation when it came to explaining the differences among the Gospels.

Luther's Slight Interest in the Synoptic Gospels

It is widely recognized that, for Martin Luther, the hermeneutical center of the New Testament—indeed of the whole Bible—was not the Gospels but the writings of the Apostle Paul. Among them, Romans and Galatians were his favorites. They functioned like a "canon within the canon," guiding Luther's approach toward the rest of the Bible. Basically, whatever biblical text agreed with Paul's doctrine of justification by faith alone as set forth in these two letters, that Luther happily quoted and approved of. Writings that clashed with this doctrine, Luther disagreed with or urged that they be removed from the New Testament. For this reason Luther questioned the canonical legitimacy of the Epistle to the Hebrews, the Epistle of James, the Epistle of Jude, and the Revelation of John.[1] Although he was unsuccessful in having these removed from the top rank of canonical New Testament writings, he did succeed in pushing a number of Old Testament writings into deuterocanonical status.

Luther's use of the Gospels reveals another one-sided situation. Although he never questioned the canonical status of the first three Gospels, he was much more attracted to the Gospel of John. While he preached on and discussed the Gospel of John on numerous occasions, he published only one work on the first three Gospels, and it did not deal with all parts of them. In 1534 he allowed some sermons on the Sermon on the Mount to be published, more or less unretouched.[2]

The reason for his slight interest in the Synoptic Gospels is not hard to find. It was one of Luther's main contentions that Christ was a Savior, not a Lawgiver. As a result, Luther refused to use the teachings of Christ in the Gospels as a guide to Christian holiness, as did the Roman Catholics, John Calvin, and rest of the Protestant Reformation. The Synoptic Gospels were filled with moral injunctions—which seemed to fly in the face of Luther's central tenet, justification by faith alone. We should not be surprised, therefore, to find some convoluted explanations of passages like Mt 5:18f.:

> (Our Savior) will not let (the Pharisees) get away with the accusation that He intends to abolish the law. Instead He will turn the attack back upon them by proving that they have weakened and abolished the Law with the glosses they have smeared over it. Our mob of papists have done the same with the Gospel and Scripture. They have completely ignored that most important doctrine, the righteousness of faith through Christ.[3] . . . I shall not go into the question now of how the Law is to be fulfilled so that no iota or dot of it is lost, though at the same time we teach that no man can fulfill it. I have said that here Christ is not talking primarily about life but about doctrine. He is not dealing with the great chief doctrine of what He is and what He gives us. We cannot be justified or saved through the teaching of the Law, which only brings us to knowledge of ourselves . . . that by our own ability we cannot properly fulfill an iota of it.[4]

Throughout his discussion of the Sermon on the Mount, Luther invoked his doctrine of the Two Realms as a way of placing Jesus' moral injunctions outside the sphere of Christian sanctification. Commenting on Christ's sayings about nonretaliation (Mt 5:38–42), Luther said:

> This text has also given rise to many questions and errors among nearly all of the theologians who have failed to distinguish properly between

the secular and the spiritual, the kingdom of Christ and the kingdom of the world.[5]

Turning to Augustine's distinction between the private and public spheres of morality, Luther went on to argue that these teachings belonged to the private sphere, while in the public, retribution for evil was always justified and necessary to maintain order.

> (In this passage Christ) is not tampering with the responsibility and authority of the government, but He is teaching His individual Christians how to live personally, apart from their official position and authority.[6]

Luther on the Differences among the Gospels

In dealing with the differences among the Gospels, Luther adhered to the Augustinian harmonistic approach, although Augustine's sophisticated nuances occasionally get lost in Luther's rough and ready treatment. Here are a few examples to illustrate what I mean.

In a series of sermons on the Gospel of John delivered in Wittenberg, Luther discussed the conflicts between John and the Synoptic Gospels. For example, Jesus' baptism is portrayed one way in Matthew but is ignored in the first chapter of the Gospel of John. The exchange between John and Jesus at the Jordan River is recorded in two different forms in Mt 3:13–17/Jn 1:29–34. Luther commented:

> The record in Matthew gives the impression that these words between John and the Lord were exchanged before the Baptism. I shall let it pass without quibbling, although it may well be that the conversation took place after this event. *Occasionally the evangelists reverse the order of events; they often report them out of their chronological sequence.*[7]

Luther went on to point out that the calling of the first disciples in John 1 was not like the same account in the other Gospels. "This may give the impression," he said to his flock,

> that Matthew and John contradicted each other, for Matthew's record of the calling of the four apostles does not coincide with John's.[8]

Such is not the case, Luther assured them, and went on to show how the two could be harmonized in good Augustinian fashion.

Luther ran into heavier weather when he got to John's account of

Jesus' cleansing of the temple (Jn 2:13–25). Not flinching from the challenge, Luther presented the gist of the problem to his congregation:

> How do we harmonize the accounts of the two evangelists, Matthew and John? For Matthew writes that all this happened on Palm Sunday, when the Lord made his (final) entry into Jerusalem. But here in John we read that it occurred at the Passover which followed Christ's Baptism (at the beginning of his public ministry).[9]

Groping around for a solution, Luther proposed a few ideas without much success. Feeling vulnerable, he abruptly lashed out at certain invisible enemies who used such discrepancies to discredit the Bible:

> These are problems and will remain problems. I shall not venture to settle them. Nor are they essential. It is only that there are so many sharp and shrewd people who are fond of bringing up all sorts of subtle questions and demanding definite and precise answers, etc. etc.[10]

Who these unnamed persons were need not detain us. After berating these impious knaves, Luther summarily dismissed the whole problem in typical Augustinian fashion:

> Our inability to answer such questions is of little consequence. *The evangelists do not all observe the same chronological order.* The one may place an event at an earlier, the other at a later time . . . Be that as it may, whether it happened sooner or later, whether it happened once or twice, this will not prejudice our faith.[11]

Having cast the literal discrepancies to one side, one would think Luther was ready to go on. But no; he went back to them again, this time concocting a chronology based on Christ's age when he was baptized and then the number of years his ministry must have lasted from that date, in order to fit in *two* cleansings. Then, abruptly abandoning this third attempt, Luther finally declared:

> But when it took place is really immaterial. If one account in Holy Writ is at variance with another, and it is impossible to solve the difficulty, *just dismiss it from your mind* . . . In their accounts of Christ's deeds and miracles they do not observe a uniform order and often ignore the proper chronological sequence.[12]

Even after we make allowances for Luther's inimitable style—and how many of us would take such risks in our sermons?—it is evident that Augustine's legacy is alive and well in Luther, the ex-Augustinian monk.

John Calvin and the Differences among the Gospels

Of the front-rank Protestant Reformers, John Calvin and Martin Bucer (1491–1551) are generally recognized as having the deepest training in the new humanist disciplines. Among these elite scholars, skepticism was privately expressed regarding the canon of the Bible. They wondered if Paul actually wrote the Epistle to the Hebrews, or the Apostle John the Second and Third Epistles of John and the Apocalypse.[13] Typically, the famed Humanist Erasmus (1469?–1536) said he would accept them as canonical because the Roman Catholic Church had traditionally believed it.[14]

Calvin scorned this kind of argument, saying that no one had the authority to alter the canon, as it was under the control of the Holy Spirit.[15] However, beneath the hard crust of Calvin's theology lurked the cancer of doubt. While he never questioned the canonicity of the four Gospels, there are ominous signs of stress.

Perhaps the best place to observe Calvin at work on the Gospels is in his commentary *A Harmony of the Gospels Matthew, Mark, and Luke*.[16] The reason Calvin gave for writing the commentary was characteristically arrogant:

> As limited minds find the comparison (among the Gospels) hard to grasp, continually having to turn up this place and that, I thought it would be a welcome and useful short-cut to treat the three narratives together in a continuous line, on one form so to speak.[17]

Who were these "limited minds"? Skeptical questions were coming from somewhere and Calvin decided it was time to rise to the defense of . . . *three* of the canonical Gospels. It is surprising to see him—this early—entirely abandon the attempt to harmonize the first three Gospels with the Gospel of John. Nor did Calvin, to my knowledge, ever explain this decision, so clearly a harbinger of what Johann Jakob Griesbach would do two hundred years later when he created the first synopsis.

Nor did Calvin explain that *he* did not do the work of comparing the Gospels for those of "limited minds," but that he got it from Martin Bucer.[18] Nor did he explain why he harmonized Mark and Luke to the order of Matthew (it could have been the influence of Eusebius' sections and canons in a Greek Gospel manuscript in Bucer's possession).

With this de facto decanonization of John behind him, Calvin went on to explain how the Gospels were written. First he set aside the contention (the source is never identified; it was Papias as reported in Eusebius) that Mark was Peter's hearer and copyist. Instead Calvin favored a new theory: each Gospel was dictated directly from heaven.

> As regards the three writers of Gospel story whom I am taking as my subject, Matthew is well enough known, while Mark is believed by some to have been the close disciple of Peter, and to have written down the Gospel as Peter dictated it to him, thus serving merely as amanuensis or secretary. We need not make a great fuss over this, as it has little significance for us, once we realize he was a witness of standing and of divine appointment, publishing nothing except by the previous dictation of the Holy Spirit.[19]

Calvin went on to reject Augustine's statement—incorrectly attributing it to Jerome—that Mark borrowed from Matthew. The reason given hints at a belief in the Gospel writers' literal exactness coupled with a new sense of authorial initiative.

> But Jerome's (*sic*) comment makes no sense at all, that (Mark) was a shortened form of the Gospel written by Matthew. He (Mark) does not consistently follow Matthew's order, and from the very start has a different approach in his handling; he relates certain matters omitted by the other and at times gives a fuller account of the same event. I think it is much more likely, and a conjecture closer to fact, that he never set eye on Matthew's book when he wrote himself: so far was he from wishing to put down a set condensation of that work.[20]

The logic seems to be something like this: since the Gospel narratives differ so much on the literal level, it is inconceivable that their authors would have copied from each other and made so many changes. They would have tried to copy more accurately. Since that obviously is not the case, it must have been that the Holy Spirit dictated the Gospels, giving more or less to each Evangelist independently. This left exegetes with one option: to blend all of the literally true details into one harmonious whole—à la Augustine.

Calvin went on to examine Luke:

> I should make the same judgment regarding Luke. We should not say that the diversity which appears between the three *was consciously simulated,* but that as each in good faith determined to put to writing *what*

he accepted as certain and factual, so each arranged it *as he thought would be best.* There was nothing fortuitous about it, of course, for it all happened under the control of divine providence. The Holy Spirit has given such wonderful unity in their diverse patterns of writing that this alone would almost be enough to win them authority if a greater authority from another source did not supply it.[21]

Notice the uniform expectation that what the Gospel authors wrote was entirely "certain and factual." The symbolic or spiritual level of the Gospels, so important to Origen and Augustine, did not exist for Calvin.

Nor did Calvin mention other key features of Augustine's harmonistic theory, such as that the Gospel authors wrote not in chronological order but *in ordo recordationis*—as they remembered the events—and that the Gospel authors skipped what had already been written by others to avoid superfluous repetition. In other words, Calvin stripped Augustine's nuanced and sophisticated hypothesis down to a single claim: all of the writers were (independently) aided by the Holy Spirit to write the literal truth.

When he began the commentary, Calvin had been using Erasmus' new Greek text for some time. One reason he used the Greek was his desire to obtain the literal meaning of the text—a goal rendered more difficult if he relied on the Latin. Why was he so intent on the literal sense? Because he firmly believed that the *verus Scripturae sensus*, "the true meaning of Scripture," or the "genuine meaning" (*genuinus sensus*), was sure to lead him to the "real meaning" (*germanus sensus*), which was nothing else than the "simple meaning" (*simplex sensus*). The "simple meaning," said Calvin, was identical to the author's intended meaning,[22] and *that* was the truth inspired in the biblical writer by the Holy Spirit. Calvin had little use for allegorical or figurative interpretation. If necessary at all, it was to be confined to a few passages in the Old Testament; it was never appropriate, in his opinion, for the New.[23]

Conclusion

Compared with Martin Luther's, Calvin's approach to the Gospels reveals a striking hardening of insistence upon their literal truth. There is very little room left for any symbolic or spiritual interpretation, such as we saw was the cornerstone of Origen's exegesis. Calvin was determined to demonstrate the harmony of the first three Gospels on the literal level. He seems to have had no awareness of the glaring contradiction in which he was trapped, by ignoring the Gospel of John without so much as a word of explanation. Nor does he betray any inkling of the disastrous consequences lurking just ahead for all who thought it honored God to insist that the Gospels were one hundred percent literally true. Spinoza, a century later took up this claim and used it with devastating effect (see Chapter 16).

Again in contrast with Luther, who was obviously not worried by the verbal inconsistencies among the Gospels since his center of gravity—the Pauline epistles of Romans and Galatians—was high and dry, Calvin exhibited a striking *narrowing of focus* as far as the composition of the Gospels was concerned. In Chapter 11, I said that late medieval nominalism reduced God's role in creation to a single point: power. This can be seen quite clearly in Calvin's reduction of the contribution of the Evangelists to that of passive automatons, as it were, while the power of the Holy Spirit caused thing-like thoughts to enter their minds and flow thence into their quill pens to become thing-like words that became, in the aggregate, a literally divine or supernatural thing called the Bible.

These beliefs were to last another hundred years—albeit under increasing stress. When the first explosion rocked the house of Gospel studies, it came from a thing-like source: Erasmus' *text.*

CHAPTER 14

The Text Reemerges as a Problem: Erasmus and the Return to the Greek New Testament

*I*f John Calvin inadvertently gave a hint that the canon of the Gospels was about to crack open, nothing really happened on that front for another two hundred years, until John Toland published *Nazarenus* (see Chapter 18). The first aspect of the traditional, Augustinian solution to the Synoptic Problem to actually break down was also the least anticipated. Neither the interpretation of the Gospels nor how they were composed, but the *text* became the focus of intense modification in the early sixteenth century. Two major factors were responsible.

First, it was a central desideratum of the Protestant Reformers to have a Bible as faithful to what the biblical authors originally wrote as possible.[1] But this goal proved to be unexpectedly difficult to achieve. The invention of printing facilitated the preparation of Bibles in the vernacular—a key factor in spreading the Protestant Reformation. But the first Bibles printed were in Latin. John Gutenberg's first major publication was a magnificent folio edition of Jerome's Latin version of the Bible, the Vulgate,[2] published at Mainz between 1450 and 1456. Other publishers soon acquired the new technology and, within the next fifty years, more than one hundred printed editions of the Vulgate appeared.

The speed and flexibility of the printing press also facilitated the publication of the Bible into languages other than Latin. In 1488, the first Hebrew text of the Old Testament was printed by the great Jewish publishing firm Soncino in Lombardy.[3] By 1500, printed translations of the Latin Bible had appeared in French, German, Italian, and Czech. But no one had published a Greek edition of the New Testament, possibly out of reverence for Jerome's Latin version.[4]

A second major factor was at work encouraging publishers to print Bibles in their original languages. The Protestant Reformers abandoned the medieval Roman Catholic theological tradition in favor of strict reliance upon the Bible as the source and norm for preaching and theology. But as we saw was the case with John Calvin, the Protestant *sola scriptura* meant a strictly *literal* interpretation of the Bible, as opposed to traditional Roman Catholic allegorization. Given this intense focus on the text of Scripture, Protestants were plagued by the knowledge that their Vulgate text was not an exact and reliable copy of what the original biblical writers had written.

The spark that set the tinder ablaze came from Italy. Since the beginning of the Italian Renaissance in the fourteenth century, the north Italian cities of Venice, Milan, Ravenna, and Genoa had been Europe's frontier ports in dealings with the Ottoman Empire. Alongside a thriving mercantile exchange went a flourishing transfer of ideas. The Italian intelligentsia could not get enough of the ancient Greek and Roman classics brought in by the traders, many of them existing only in Arabic translations. From Italy (and from Moorish Spain as well) these new intellectual impulses poured into the universities of northern Europe: not only the older ones in Paris, Seville, Cologne, Prague, Basel, Oxford, and Cambridge, but also the newer centers of learning in Valencia, Turin, Nantes, Freiburg, Trier, Glasgow, and St. Andrews.[5] For the first time in a thousand years, scholars read Plato and Aristotle in the original Greek, Seneca and Cicero in classical Latin, and the Old Testament in Hebrew and the New Testament in Greek. It was a thrilling experience, as we can see from this statement from the most important pre-Reformation New Testament textual critic, Lorenzo Valla (1407–1457). Noting how Jerome had complained about the texts of his time, Valla added:

> Now if after 400 years (from the beginning of the Church Jerome could complain of) so muddy a stream which flowed from the original fount, what marvel if after 1,000 years—for so many there are between Jerome and the present age—this stream, no part of which has been cleaned or tidied up, has become scummy and squalid?[6]

The First Printed Edition of the New Testament in Greek

Thus pressure was building for a comprehensive reform of the text of the Bible. The most ambitious attempt soon emerged in Spain.

Around the turn of the century, the powerful bishop of Toledo and Cardinal primate of Spain Francisco Ximénez de Cisneros (1437–1517) began gathering a team of scholars who would bring out a magnificent six-volume edition of the Bible in four languages.[7] Deciding to imitate Origen, he set about collecting all of the most important texts and translations of the Bible he could find.[8] The first four volumes were to contain the Old Testament in three columns per page: the "original" Hebrew on the right, the Greek LXX (Septuagint) on the left, and Jerome's Latin in the middle. The first volume also included the Aramaic Targum Onkelos (ancient Aramaic translation of the Hebrew) across the bottom accompanied by a Latin translation.[9] The New Testament was to occupy the fifth volume. It would have two columns per page: the "original" Greek on the left and Jerome's Latin translation on the right.[10] A sixth volume would contain a Hebrew-Aramaic-Latin lexicon, a glossary of names, and a brief Hebrew grammar.[11] Centered in the University of Alcalá, near Madrid, which Ximénez had founded to foster humanistic studies, especially in the three biblical languages, Latin, Greek, and Hebrew, the undertaking was massive, requiring the efforts of numerous scholars.[12]

The New Testament was completed first, in 1514,[13] but was held back from publication until the rest was ready. But then the great project suddenly ground to a halt. The Pope refused to allow anything to be published until the Greek manuscript of the New Testament he had loaned to the project was back in the Vatican Library. For some reason, this took five years. Finally, on 28 March 1522, the six-volume *Complutensian Polyglot* was unveiled, amidst much fanfare.[14]

Unfortunately, they were beaten to the market by an enterprising Swiss publisher. Froben of Basel knew of the Spanish project and decided he would be the first to publish the New Testament in Greek. His choice to carry out the task: Desiderius Erasmus of Rotterdam (1469–1536), the best-known scholar of his time.[15]

For his part, Erasmus had been interested in New Testament textual issues ever since 1504 when he discovered a copy of Valla's critical annotations of Jerome's Vulgate. He was so impressed by it that he republished it that same year.[16] Prior to that, he had been analyzing the text of Paul's epistles for some years.[17] By 1506 he was working on a new Latin translation using Valla's notes. By 1507 he decided that a new Greek New Testament was imperative and asked the famed Venetian publisher Aldus Manutius if he was interested.[18]

In 1511, Erasmus went to Cambridge, where he lectured on Greek and began a tentative collation of New Testament Greek manuscripts he found there.[19] Word of Erasmus' activities spread in scholarly back corridors, whence his publisher friend Froben learned what he was up to. When

Erasmus came to Basel in August of 1514 to talk to Froben about other projects Froben was doing for him, Froben asked Erasmus if *he* was interested in preparing a Greek New Testament. Erasmus demurred, saying he was too busy. He may have been in consultation with Aldus or other publishers looking for a better deal.

In any case, he returned to Cambridge without giving Froben a definitive reply. Shortly afterward, Froben importuned a mutual friend to ask Erasmus again. This time, Froben had an offer Erasmus could not resist. "I will pay you," said Froben through his intermediary, "as much as anyone else might offer" (*se daturum pollicetur quantum alius quisquam*).[20] That got Erasmus' attention.

He returned to Basel in July 1515, ready to work. He first made sure his other three projects were coming along (a series of moral instructions, an edition of the works of Seneca, and an edition of the works of Jerome). Then he began preparations on a new Greek New Testament. His method was simple and direct. He went to the university library and got out two Greek New Testament manuscripts: one had the Gospels and the other the letters of Paul and the Catholic Epistles. He *made corrections directly on these texts* (based on what?) and gave them to Froben to put into print.[21] He appended Jerome's Latin on facing pages. The printing process was one of mass confusion: proofreaders disappeared and could not be found; Erasmus kept bringing in last-minute changes and additions to his annotations of Jerome's Vulgate; galleys from the other three projects were examined with those of his Greek New Testament. Says one scholar, "the chaos of Froben's shop during those months hardly bears thinking about."[22]

The two Greek manuscripts Erasmus used were hardly optimal for the task. Late-twelfth-century copies of other late-medieval copies, they were riddled with misspellings and incorrect punctuations and frequently lacked words and even whole phrases. How did Erasmus deal with their errors? He corrected them against Jerome's Vulgate. A worse dilemma arose when he could not find a Greek manuscript containing the Revelation of John. At last, he obtained one from a friend, but when he examined it the last page, containing the last six verses, was missing. Not to be deterred, Erasmus *invented a Greek text* by retranslating Jerome's Latin into Greek.[23]

In this way, Froben and Erasmus rushed it through the press in less than six months. Erasmus later admitted that his text had been "thrown together rather than (carefully) edited."[24] The resulting thousand-page manuscript saw the light of day on 1 March 1516, long before the Spanish finally put theirs on the market. Froben's dream was accomplished and orders poured in. According to one count, he sold more than 3,300 copies in the first three years.

The Value of Erasmus' Text

No sooner was Erasmus' New Testament released than complaints began to be heard. Irate scholars found misspellings, broken sentences, missing words, and incorrect punctuation on every page. It was so full of mistakes that one nineteenth-century English text critic called Froben's first edition "the least carefully published book ever printed."[25] But Froben saw a money-making opportunity even in this adversity. Propelled by the chorus of complaints, Froben published a series of gradually corrected editions, so that scholars had no choice but to buy several editions before it was over.

The thousands of misprints and misspellings were not the most important shortcoming of Erasmus' text, however. The fatal flaw lay in his original choice of manuscripts. The "most serious defect of the first edition of the Greek New Testament ever printed was that it represented *a type of text* which was . . . the most recent and the poorest (quality) of all types of text of the New Testament ever recorded."[26]

The Later History of Erasmus' Text

Of course, this is twenty-twenty hindsight. At the time, Erasmus' Greek New Testament was considered a major breakthrough, and scholars from all over Europe eagerly bought it. Pirated versions appeared in Venice, Strasbourg, and Paris.[27] He had successfully broken the monopoly of Jerome's Latin New Testament. Luther used the second edition of Erasmus' Greek text to make his famous translation into the German, although there is some question how far he actually depended on it and how much he still relied on the Vulgate.[28] Calvin, Beza, and Zwingli also made use of it.[29]

However, Erasmus' deed called down a torrent of wrath and abuse from tradition-minded Roman Catholic scholars and Church officials, especially after the second edition contained Erasmus' own Latin translation rather than Jerome's.[30]

But the process of working directly from the Greek original had been set in motion, and publishers everywhere jumped on the bandwagon. In 1550, the eminent French publisher Robert Estienne of Paris prepared a beautiful folio edition of the Greek New Testament.[31] Based largely on Erasmus' text, this edition was the first to publish variant readings from other Greek manuscripts in the margins.[32] His next edition (1551) was the first to divide the text into numbered verses—a practice which has continued up to the present.[33] Each new publication contained a major advance in the conception of the New Testament as a working instrument for understanding the Word of God.

Among the Protestants, Theodore Beza (1519–1605), the close friend and successor of Calvin in Geneva, published nine editions of the Greek New Testament between 1565 and 1604.[34] Although he had two very ancient and valuable manuscripts in his personal library (Codex Bezae and Codex Claromontanus), Beza refused to rely on them because they differed so much from Erasmus' text. Instead, he printed Erasmus' text with a few alternative readings from these older manuscripts in the margin. The work of this respected biblical scholar and linguist did much to establish the international reputation of Erasmus' Greek New Testament as the text of choice for Protestant biblical scholarship.

In 1624, the Elzevir brothers of Leiden published a handy popular version of the Greek New Testament utilizing mainly Beza's text (itself based on Erasmus'). In the preface to their second edition, they boasted, "The text you have is now received by all" (*textum ergo habes nunc ab omnibus receptum*).[35] This phrase caught on, giving this text the name *textus receptus,* and the rest was history.

> Partly because of this catchword, the form of the Greek text incorporated in the editions that Stephanus (Estienne), Beza, and the Elzevirs had published, succeeded in establishing itself as "the only true text" of the New Testament, and was slavishly reprinted in hundreds of subsequent editions. It lies at the basis of the King James Version and all of the principal Protestant translations in the languages of Europe prior to 1881.[36]

The *textus receptus* was used by the faithful in countless sermons, theological disputations, handbooks on theology, Church educational materials, as well as by writers and poets. In the form of the King James Version, it became the "infallible and inerrant" bedrock upon which Protestant piety confidently rested. So great was the reverence directed toward the King James Version that later

> attempts to criticize or emend it were regarded as akin to sacrilege. Yet its textual basis is essentially a handful of late (medieval) and haphazardly collected manuscripts *and in a dozen passages its reading is supported by no known Greek witness.*[37]

CHAPTER 15

The Overthrow of Erasmus' "Standard Text" and the Descent into Textual Chaos

The hasty embrace of Erasmus' flawed text caused the Protestants to stumble around for centuries as they tried to rectify the situation. While it was only a question of time before the so-called *textus receptus* was replaced by a better Greek text based on earlier manuscripts, the process turned out to be long, confusing, and difficult.

As the first "original Greek" New Testament used in the West in more than a thousand years, Erasmus' Greek New Testament was immediately surrounded by a halo of sacredness. This veneration was enhanced by the enormously popular translations based on it: Martin Luther's in 1531 and the King James Authorized English Version in 1611. The popularity of these translations made any challenge to the *textus receptus* difficult.

Another reason why improvements to the *textus receptus* were so slow in coming was that the enormous breadth and staggering complexity of the work necessary to do it dawned only gradually on everyone.

From the perspective of a history of the Synoptic Problem, the discovery of massive numbers of harmonized readings in the medieval manuscripts—alterations that made the Gospel texts more closely resemble one another—must have come as a shock. That discovery and others that led to a better Greek text than the *textus receptus* are the focus of this chapter.

Amassing Variant Readings: A Dangerous Occupation

Erasmus and other biblical scholars in the sixteenth century had little idea of the boundless swamp they had plunged into the instant they abandoned Jerome's familiar Vulgate in quest of the "Greek original." Erasmus even boasted of having

> used many manuscripts, both Greek and Latin, and not just any sort but *the oldest and most correct,* to produce a text faithful to the true Greek, to the Greek *original (ad Graecam veritatem, ad Graecae originis fidem).*[1]

One wonders how Erasmus dared to say this, given what we know about his methods. In any case, to *really* do what he claimed would take the combined efforts of hundreds of scholars more than four hundred years. Chapter 19 tells the story of the presumed achievement of that goal, as the world beheld the appearance of a *new textus receptus* in the mid-twentieth century.

The process began tentatively enough. Estienne printed a New Testament (Paris 1550) in which words and phrases from fifteen manuscripts that differed from Erasmus' text were displayed in the margins to alert scholars to the fact that a few manuscripts did not agree with those used by Erasmus. But the fifteen manuscripts had not been chosen in any particular way; they were just "assembled at random."[2]

Fifty years later, a more systematic approach was used. In 1600, Brian Walton published in London the Polyglot Bible in six volumes: Estienne's Greek New Testament was in volume 1, two Latin New Testaments (including the Vulgate) were in volume 2, and Syriac, Ethiopic, Arabic, and Persian New Testaments (each accompanied by a literal Latin translation) appeared in volumes 2–5. At the bottom of each page of volume 1, Walton placed words and phrases differing from Estienne's text that he had found in the fifth-century Codex Alexandrinus, recently acquired and presented to King Charles I by the Patriarch of Constantinople as a gesture of friendship. Volume 6 contained words and phrases that differed from Estienne's text which Walton laboriously collected from fifteen other manuscripts.[3]

From this beginning, the number of words and phrases that disagreed with Erasmus' text began to mount, as new manuscripts of the Greek New Testament were discovered and compared with Erasmus' text. In 1675, John Fell (1625–1686), Dean of Christ Church, Oxford, published an edition of the Greek New Testament (using the Elzevir 1633 edition)[4] in which he listed hundreds of differing words and phrases from the fourth-century Codex Vaticanus, as well as one hundred other manuscripts,[5] and two ancient versions: the Coptic and the Gothic.[6] But Fell did not attempt to decide the relative importance of all these words and phrases; he merely added them together: "thirty-two manuscripts have such and such a word, but twenty-two others have two different words in the same place," etc.

The reason he could not recognize the relative value of the differing readings was that he had no idea where each manuscript had originally come from, nor when each one had been created. So he just lumped together variants from the Codex Vaticanus with others from medieval manuscripts. Fell's labors were not unnoticed. He was attacked by John Owen, the Puritan Dean of Christ Church College, Oxford, for carrying out an "assault on the Word of God," and the Roman Catholics put his New Testament on the Index of Prohibited Books.[7]

As disturbing as they were, these few investigations were minor warning shocks and advance tremors for the real earthquake that hit thirty years later. In 1707, John Mill (1645–1707), fellow of Queen's College, Oxford, published an epoch-making edition of the New Testament in which he listed nearly *thirty thousand* words and phrases differing from Erasmus' text.[8]

To produce such an astonishing list, Mill had worked for three decades studying as many Greek manuscripts as he could find, laboriously comparing each word of each manuscript with Erasmus' text. He examined the quotations from most of the Church Fathers and compared them with Erasmus' text. He compared every earlier printed edition of the Greek New Testament with Erasmus' text.

When he was done, he laid out this enormous database in a lengthy introduction to the *textus receptus* (in this case, Estienne's 1550 edition). He did not attempt to change a single word in the *textus receptus,* but the shocking number of words and phrases that differed from it—Mill discussed no less than 3,041 out of the total 8,000 verses in the New Testament[9]—sounded a warning bell heard all over Great Britain and Europe. Naturally, defenders of the *textus receptus* rose up and denounced Mill for casting doubt on the authority of the Bible. But the damage to its credibility was irreversible.

In hindsight, we can see that the hostile reaction of the defenders of the *textus receptus* stemmed in part from the near-divine status to which Protestants of this period had elevated the Bible. They firmly believed that the text of the Bible in their hands was precisely the same thing as the divine Word of God—a conclusion that Church Fathers from Origen and Eusebius to Augustine would have regarded with horror. Here we must observe a creeping *physicalization* of the Word of God consistent with the progress of seventeenth- and eighteenth-century natural science.

In addition, because of this idolization of the Bible, few Protestants were capable of admitting that *no one knew for certain what the original biblical authors actually wrote.* To ask that question risked undermining the Protestants' cherished doctrine of the *infallibility of Scripture.* For if *no one* possessed the text of the exact words the original New Testament writers actually wrote and nothing else, then what degree of corruption infected the text everyone used? One percent? Ten percent? Twenty percent? No one knew the answer to this question. Worse yet, having burnt the Roman Catholic bridge of Tradition ("Scripture *and Tradition*"), Protestant theologians and pastors had painted themselves into the logical corner of *sola Scriptura.* They had no choice but to resist all efforts to correct Erasmus' text. As a result, the process of improving it took far longer than it might have.

To the open-minded, Mill's enormous collection of variant readings was convincing proof that the *textus receptus* was riddled with defects. It also made it glaringly clear that the task of recovering a text one hundred percent identical with what the inspired writers of the New Testament originally wrote was going to be far more complicated an undertaking than anyone had dreamed.

One sign of Mill's caution was the striking fact that, having collected his huge number of alternative words and phrases, even he did not dare to change a single word in Erasmus' text. Although in his discussion he frequently indicated that he thought he had found a more original word or phrase in some early manuscript, Mill did not feel that he was in a position to actually change the *textus receptus,* largely because he was reluctant to make such piecemeal alterations. He did not have any general principle or method to guide his decisions because no one had proposed a general geographical and chronological scheme for evaluating all of the variant readings.

Mill's caution was soon to be abandoned. Two New Testaments simultaneously appeared two years later in France and England that did make changes in Erasmus' text. In 1709 an Oxford scholar named Edward Wells (1667–1727) began publishing portions of the New Testament in which he introduced more than two hundred changes in the text of Erasmus (Elzevir edition) based on earlier manuscripts.[10] That same year a French scholar named Toinard published a Greek-Latin harmony of the Gospels in which he made numerous changes in the text of Estienne on the basis of two early Greek manuscripts that he had examined in the Vatican Library, as well as Jerome's Vulgate (where it agreed with them).[11]

In this way the race began to see who could produce the first complete alternative to Erasmus' *textus receptus.* In 1719, Richard Bentley (1662–1742), an eminent classical scholar and Master of Trinity College,

Cambridge, announced with great fanfare an ambitious project to do away with the *textus receptus* in favor of a combined Greek and Latin New Testament. His goal was to produce parallel texts that would be as close as humanly possible to the New Testament as it existed in the fourth century.[12] Scholars were signed up, manuscripts were collected, money was raised. Before anything really got under way, however, defenders of the *textus receptus* rose up and attacked Bentley's project, drawing him into a protracted controversy. At one point, he was even suspended from his duties at Cambridge. Ultimately nothing came of it, but his idea did attract widespread interest.[13]

Fifty years later, in 1776, Edward Harwood (1729–1794) made good on Bentley's dream. His method was rather crude by modern standards, but it did the job. Harwood simply picked three excellent early Greek manuscripts (the Codex Bezae for the Gospels and Acts and the Codices Claromontanus and Alexandrinus for the Pauline Epistles) and followed their wording virtually every time their words diverged simultaneously from the *textus receptus.* Meanwhile, more sophisticated instruments were being readied in Germany for another assault on the *textus receptus.*

Systematic Preparations to Dispense with the Textus Receptus *in Germany*

A young German scholar named Johann Albrecht Bengel (1687–1752) was impressed by John Mill's Greek New Testament and set out to make effective use of his mass of evidence. Missing from Mill's data was any systematic analysis for weighing the value of the variants. Eighteen years after Mill, in 1725, Bengel published a "forerunner" to his edition of the New Testament in which he proposed certain principles to objectively evaluate the evidence.[14] Two important principles were the following:

- Manuscripts should be grouped according to geographical provenance in "companies, families, tribes and nations" (Bengel's terms).[15]
- The best words and phrases should be identified by means of reliable guidelines; for example, the seemingly crude word or phrase is likely to be closer to the original than a smooth, "correct" Greek version of the same sentence.[16]

Bengel's research into the *history of the text* reached two important conclusions. Most manuscripts belonged to what he called the "Asiatic" text: smooth, good Greek style, typical of medieval copies like those on which the *textus receptus* was based. He suggested that it came from master copies created during the fourth and fifth centuries at Constantinople (later Byzantium) and was of progressively less value the further into the Middle Ages one went. The other text type he named "African." It included manuscripts going back to the Greek text used at Alexandria during the fourth and fifth centuries as well as Latin translations of it made in north Africa (on which Jerome's Vulgate was based). These manuscripts Bengel regarded as extremely valuable.[17]

As for his list of text-critical guidelines, many are still in use to this day.

Bengel's ideas proved to be a major breakthrough in the nascent science of text criticism. Even so, he himself was reluctant to insert alternative readings into the *textus receptus*. When he finally did publish his own Greek New Testament in 1734, he used Erasmus' *textus receptus* without any alterations. It was in the margins that his ideas were placed: hundreds of alternative words and phrases differing from Erasmus' text, with little marks indicating how much superior they were to the words in the *textus receptus.*[18] Once again, the defenders of the *textus receptus* were enraged and attacked Bengel as "an enemy of the Holy Scriptures."[19]

A couple of decades later, an even more sophisticated Greek New Testament appeared in Amsterdam, published by Johann Jakob Wettstein (1693–1754). Originally a pastor in Switzerland, Wettstein had been amazed by Mill's pile of evidence, and he also determined to see what use could be made of it. However, his parishioners did not like him spending so much time "undermining the Bible," and they drove him from his pastorate.[20] Migrating to that bastion of freedom, Holland, Wettstein was offered a position at the Arminian (Remonstrant) College in Amsterdam, where he became the successor to the famous Jean LeClerc. Laboring there for forty years, Wettstein finally published in 1751 a magnificent two-volume Greek New Testament in which hundreds of words or phrases that differed from the *textus receptus* (the Elzevir edition) were placed in the margins next to relevant portions of the text. The footnotes—taking up more than half of each page—contained thousands of similar words and phrases drawn from classical Greek and Roman authors, from rabbinic writings, and from the Church Fathers. This enormous mine of information has remained unsurpassed to this day.[21]

Meanwhile, the eminent German philosopher Johann Salomo Semler (1725–1791) continued Bengel's and Wettstein's research. He turned to the frontier marked out by Harwood and Bengel—the text of the New Testament in the fourth century—and sought to push further back toward the beginning. His detailed analysis led him to conclude that there were in fact *three different archetypes* existing in the fourth century: the "Eastern" (centered in Constantinople and Antioch), the "Western" (north Africa), and the "Alexandrian" (centered in Origen's workshop).[22] He also argued that any early representative from any of these three archetypes *could contain words and phrases that stemmed from the original first-century autograph.* Thus Semler set the stage for modern text criticism, which has relentlessly attempted to press behind the fourth century toward the first.[23]

By the end of the eighteenth century, enormous pressure had built up against the *textus receptus.* Thousands of manuscripts had been discovered and collated against it. Tens of thousands of quotations had been collected from the Church Fathers and compared with it. Twenty or more ancient translations of the Greek New Testament had been discovered and carefully compared with the words of the *textus receptus* (the Vulgate and the Syriac being the most important). Finally, biblical quotations in early lectionaries were compared with the *textus receptus.* Out of this bewildering mass of data, brilliant minds had begun to piece together the broad outlines of an enormously complicated history of the transmission of the Greek text of the New Testament in different geographical locations of the early Church. This history would become the indispensable chronological framework for evaluating all manuscripts, to see which ones should be used in the delicate task of reconstructing what the New Testament authors had originally written.

The stage was set for the final challenge. Who would succeed in pushing back behind the great fourth-century manuscripts like Vaticanus and Sinaiticus to the third century, from which only a handful of manuscripts of the Greek New Testament have survived, and then behind *it* to the text of the second century, from which only a few scraps of papyrus have survived (and these reveal strikingly divergent texts), and then finally to the first century—from which *nothing* has survived—to the "original Greek" words of the Apostles of Jesus Christ?

We have seen in this and the preceding chapter the fall into chaos once Jerome's Latin Vulgate was abandoned. As the hostile reactions greeting every attempt to improve the *textus receptus* indicate, this period was one of constant anxiety for those inclined toward certainty in Gospel interpretation.

Ironically, it was the quest for textual certainty that propelled the whole debate deeper and deeper into chaos. Thus the first of the four aspects of the traditional Form(s) of the Synoptic Problem to break down was, as I said at the outset of Chapter 14, the least anticipated: the *text* of the Gospels. The attack upon the *canon* of the Gospels did not arise until much later (see Chapter 18). Meanwhile, a frontal attack upon the third and fourth aspects of the traditional Form(s) of the Synoptic Problem, the *composition* and *proper interpretation* of the Gospels, was to occur first. I describe these developments in Chapters 16 and 17.

CHAPTER 16

Baruch Spinoza and the Political Agenda of Modern Historical-Critical Interpretation

*E*ven if the enormously influential *Ethics* of Baruch Spinoza (1632–1677) had been destroyed before it could be published posthumously, his foundational importance for another discipline—modern biblical criticism—would have been established by his *Theological-Political Treatise.*[1] Together with his younger Roman Catholic contemporary Richard Simon of France (1638–1712), the two set the course and provided the first full-fledged examples of the kind of modern historical criticism of the Bible now used in seminaries and universities around the world.[2]

It is commonly believed that the historical investigation of the Bible pioneered by Spinoza and Simon represented a major breakthrough for the spirit of scientific objectivity, releasing the Bible to speak for itself after centuries of dogmatic allegorical exegesis in medieval Roman Catholicism and the equally doctrinaire readings of the Bible employed by Protestant scholasticism.

Over against the older tradition of arbitrary and subjective styles of interpretation, it is commonly said, the Enlightenment represented a great advance because of its rigorous adherence to historical objectivity and consistent application of philological research to verify the original meanings of words, in a general posture of reserved skepticism regarding "assured results," so as to keep an open mind to new evidence. The essential requirement demanded by Enlightenment-style historical criticism of the Bible, so it is commonly believed today, is diligent and open-minded pursuit of objective evidence, regardless of the theological consequences.

The entire operation is deemed to be "value-free," that is, devoid of any particular theological agenda or political ideology. It is "scientific."

There is a grain of truth to these beliefs. However, as will become evident from this account of how and why Spinoza came to write the *Theological-Political Treatise,* disinterested objectivity and a nonideological purpose for his method of "historical criticism" were the furthest things from Spinoza's mind. Albert Schweitzer was much closer to the truth when he said, with respect to the quest for the historical Jesus, that the historical study of the Bible did not spring from a disinterested regard for historical accuracy. It was invented, as he put it, "as an ally in the struggle against the tyranny of dogma."[3] It will be one of the main objectives of this chapter to explain precisely how the method of historical criticism was utilized by Spinoza as an ally in the struggle against the tyranny of dogma (both Jewish and Christian) and also to identify the political ideology that was its ultimate rationale.

Spinoza and Simon did not carry through this agenda alone. Their publications were part of the seventeenth and eighteenth centuries' attempt to reinvent the universe along non-Christian/Jewish lines, carried out by such philosophers and statesmen as Thomas Hobbes, John Locke, David Hume, Gottfried Wilhelm von Leibniz, and Immanuel Kant. They drew heavily on the Greek and Roman classics for their ideas, along with recent discoveries in mathematics, astronomy, and physics. Biblical criticism played a key role in their program—especially the earliest writers like Hobbes and Spinoza—namely, *as a weapon to destroy or at least discredit the traditional metaphysics of Christianity and Judaism.* Its major purpose was to "clear-cut" all of the political-religious structures growing out of the Bible so that the Enlightenment's new reconception(s) of the universe could be elaborated unimpeded by reactionary attacks from the forces of orthodoxy using the Bible as their sacred authority.[4]

The Biographical Setting of the Theological-Political Treatise

During the early seventeenth century, the newly liberated Dutch provinces developed economically at an amazing pace. Dutch traders established colonies in the East and West Indies, as well as in South and North America. Spices, exotic woods, teas, coffees, tobaccos, silks, precious gems, and delicious fruits were shipped back to the bustling Dutch ports. By 1620, the Dutch provinces were the most powerful maritime power in Europe, and, of all the Dutch cities, Amsterdam was the leading political and economic center.

Along with the rise in economic prosperity went a series of political reforms instituting religious toleration and political democracy. As a result, political refugees and freethinkers from all parts of Europe and the British Isles flocked to the Netherlands. Mennonites, Quakers, Collegiants, Anabaptists, and Dissenters all found a place to live there, as did the occasional political fugitive—like John Locke—running one jump ahead of foreign police.

Among the political refugees were large numbers of Spanish and Portuguese Jews fleeing the ravages of the Inquisition in their home countries. Around 1593, the first of several hundred Jewish families were permitted to settle in Amsterdam. They were even allowed to set up their own schools, govern their own internal affairs, and join the flourishing commercial enterprises in Amsterdam. Some of the more affluent families soon owned enough shares in the West India Company to affect its policies.[5]

It was into this developing economy and fledgling democracy that Baruch Spinoza was born on 24 November 1632, the second son of four children. His father and mother were Portuguese Marranos, that is, Jews who had escaped the Inquisition by pretending to convert to Roman Catholicism. Having escaped that torturous existence, they had come to Amsterdam and joined the other expatriate Jews who were trying to put their lives back together and recapture some semblance of their erstwhile Jewish identity. His father, Michael D'Espiñosa, ran a small export/import business that provided his family with a respectable, if not lavish, lifestyle.[6]

The education of young Bento (as he was called) was conducted at the local synagogue. His teachers were the chief rabbi, Saul Levi Morteira, a Venetian Jew well versed in medicine but whose theological tastes tended toward the mystical medieval Jewish Kabbalah. He and a large number of the Amsterdam Jews later got swept up in the disastrous Sabbatai Z'vi messianic movement. Spinoza's other teacher, Rabbi Manasseh ben Israel, was an energetic and broadly educated man who had spent most of his life in Amsterdam. He taught young Bento Hebrew, memorization of Scripture and Torah, Latin, and a smattering of mathematics.[7] At age thirteen, Bento began helping his father in the family business.

Spinoza's youth was punctuated by a number of extraordinary events. When he was eight years old, he saw his teacher Manasseh ben Israel excommunicated but then reinstated and then fined and suspended from rabbinical duties. Why? Because he had dared to challenge openly the economic stranglehold on the Jewish community by a few of its leading families.[8] That same year, Bento was present at the public humiliation of Uriel Acosta, a recently arrived Marrano from Portugal. His crime consisted of privately uttering certain unorthodox religious beliefs and publicly criticizing the community's leading elders. For this he was flogged, trampled on by the entire male community in a ritual act of shaming, and then released. The following week Acosta wrote his autobiography and then shot himself.[9] When Bento was ten years old, he witnessed the Jewish community's lavish welcome to a prince of Orange and then a queen of England. These events were an expression of the Jewish community's gratitude for their welcome in Amsterdam. They did not want to do anything that would alienate either the national Orange royalists or their powerful allies, the Calvinist clergy. When William of Orange responded to the widespread discontent under James II of England (1685–1688) and went over in 1689 to become William III, King of England, the Amsterdam Jewish community celebrated jubilantly along with thousands of Dutch royalists.[10]

Spinoza's mother, Hannah Deborah, died when he was quite young, as did his older brother, Isaac. His father died in March 1654, when Bento was twenty-two, leaving everything to a stepsister so she would have a dowry. Thrown onto his own resources, Bento formed another trading company with his younger brother, Gabriel, but it did not do very well.[11] After two years of struggling, he sold his share.

Not long after his father died, Spinoza had gone to live with an ex-Jesuit freethinker named Frans Van den Enden. Van den Enden owned a private school for sons of the more open-minded Dutch citizens of Amsterdam, and Spinoza assisted with teaching. In turn, Van den Enden taught him the philosophy of Descartes. It was also in the circle of thinkers associated with Van den Enden that Spinoza first came into contact with the more radical political and religious ideas circulating in Europe.[12]

During this period Spinoza drifted steadily away from Judaism. His growing disaffection did not go unnoticed. In June 1656, he was brought before the council of elders for questioning. Boldly defending his freedom to think as he chose, he was excommunicated on 27 July 1656. He was twenty-four years old.

Spinoza was not grief-stricken at the sentence. As he told a friend, "They do not force me to do anything that I would not have done of my own accord if I did not dread the publicity. But since they want it that way, I gladly enter on that path that is open to me."[13]

To erase the Jewish element from his name, Spinoza adopted Benedictus[14] and moved in with a small colony of Christian freethinkers known as Collegiants. They believed in inspiration from the "inner light" and practiced complete democratic equality. A small group of these men became his lifelong friends and supporters, in particular Peter Balling, a merchant who translated his first publication on Descartes into Dutch, and Jan Rieuwertsz, a bookseller who printed all of Spinoza's writings, at considerable personal risk.[15]

When he was twenty-eight, Spinoza moved to Rijnsburg, a small village outside the university city of Leiden, which housed the main community of the Collegiant sect. Here he spent the next three years in peace and safety, writing and working out the main lines of his philosophy.[16] One of his earliest writings, a Latin essay entitled *Treatise on the Emendation of the Intellect* (1661), is an exploration both in method and in writing style.[17] He also composed at this time *A Short Treatise on God, Man, and His Well-being*, which was so radical that only a few close friends were permitted to see it. Published posthumously, it contains hints of many of his mature conceptions. I will list a few here by way of illustration:

· There is no divine being or "God" apart from nature or the physical universe. The entire physical universe *is* God.[18]
· Nature (or God) was never created; it is eternal and unchanging.[19]
· Man's true happiness consists in knowing God, that is, the whole of nature.[20]
· God does not make God known to man by any words or signs (recorded in the Bible) but only by itself (i.e., through scientific study of nature).[21]
· Miracles do not happen. Nature or the universe acts solely according to necessity, or what may be called the "laws of nature."[22]
· The Universe (God) is not good in any sense; it is, however, unchangingly and infinitely perfect.[23]
· The terms "good" and "evil" cannot be applied to persons or events in a state of nature. All particular aspects of nature are perfect according to their causes.[24]
· Beings such as Satan or the Devil, who are by definition beings or things completely contrary to God, are precisely nothing.[25]
· All particular things in nature are composed of the same infinite, eternal substance. Modes of substances, such as the soul, which is a mode of the body, disappear when the body dies. There is no "afterlife."[26]
· One should try to form a society that will accept and live by these principles.[27]

It was during this time that he began writing the first drafts of his great *Ethics Demonstrated in Geometric Order*, using the then fashionable style of geometrical reasoning.[28]

These and other ideas show that Spinoza was well versed in the mathematics, physics, and astronomy of his time, as well as classical Greek and Roman philosophy.[29] He was particularly attracted to the teachings of Epicurus as interpreted by Lucretius; there he found a congenial mixture of opposition to religious superstition combined with a serene naturalism.[30]

While Spinoza was living with the Collegiants, he met and discussed theology with other spiritualist groups, such as the Quakers, who claimed to know God directly without the need of clergy or the Bible.[31] When he was still living with Van den Enden, Spinoza may have had the opportunity to meet the prominent Quaker thinker Samuel Fisher. Fisher argued that the Word of God was known by "the inner light," not the Bible, since the Bible was a human product filled with errors and obscurities, put together by no one knows who or why, the text of which is completely uncertain, as the many different biblical manuscripts prove.[32] This kind of fundamental attack on the traditional source of the knowledge of God in Judaism and Christianity made a deep impression on Spinoza and led to the radical skepticism toward the Bible visible in his *Theological-Political Treatise*.

He heard discussions of contemporary political philosophy, from Machiavelli's *The Prince* (1532) to Thomas Hobbes' *Leviathan* (1651). Machiavelli amazed him. Instead of discussing the subject of political power in the traditional philosophical manner by asking what men should do, Machiavelli began by looking at what powerful men actually did. In addition, he ignored the religious truth of theological arguments made by kings and princes to defend their claim to rule, treating them as so many propaganda weapons to seize and keep political power.[33] Years later, Spinoza commented that he could not understand why Machiavelli had published his book, unless it was because Machiavelli secretly admired democracy and decided to warn everyone of the underhanded tricks tyrants used to prevent people from enjoying liberty.[34]

Hobbes influenced Spinoza in a different way. His basic question was What is it that drives men to accept civil order? His answer came from the ancient Greek Sophists and the skeptic Carneades: fear of other men.[35] In this perspective, the state is founded not on justice but on raw power.[36] Hobbes argued that the state must have ultimate power over everything, including religion, a view we will see emerge prominently in Spinoza's conclusion to the *Theological-Political Treatise*.[37] Nor did Spinoza overlook the destructive role historical biblical criticism played in Hobbes' political treatise, the *Leviathan*, where he dealt the credibility of the Bible a series of massive blows in order to weaken England's religious belligerents.[38] This weapon was later utilized by Spinoza in his *Theological-Political Treatise* for precisely the same purpose.[39]

But where Hobbes sought for a solution to religious strife in an all-powerful monarch, Spinoza preferred a different political solution. The doctrine of the "divine light" that Spinoza heard from his spiritualist friends suggested the possibility of an entire society where all would be completely equal and none would exercise undue power over anyone else, because all would possess the same "divine light." The Collegiants and other "inner light" groups like the Quakers used this doctrine to justify their radically democratic social organization and Spinoza was deeply impressed by their peaceful serenity.

As a corollary to this doctrine, the spiritualists rejected the concept of original sin, envisioning each human being as containing a spark of the divine life within him or her. Spinoza termed this "the divine light of reason" or "the natural light," arguing that each human being participates in the divine life of Nature by innate reason and can live with other humans in a society ruled by divine reason alone. It was fervently believed that such a society would reflect the serenity and order of Nature itself.[40]

In 1663, when he was thirty-one, Spinoza felt he was ready for a more active life, so he left Rijnsburg and moved to Voorburg, just outside The Hague. This brought him closer to his friend Jan de Witt, then at the peak of his career as the prime minister of the Dutch provinces. De Witt had put the financial affairs of the country in order, worked to establish political democracy, and defended religious toleration.[41] In addition, he was himself an internationally known scientist and mathematician.[42]

Since Spinoza began writing the *Theological-Political Treatise* about a year after the move, we may surmise that he felt impelled to take a more direct role in the political struggle then going on between the party in favor of a Dutch republic (the Remonstrants) and the royalists who wanted to reinstate the monarchy under the House of Orange, as did the Calvinist clergy and most of the common people. Things came to a head when representatives of the various Dutch states met at the Grand Assembly at The Hague in 1651, and a majority refused to appoint the heir of the just-deceased William II of Orange to the traditional role of the nation's de facto sovereign and formed themselves into a republic instead.

This decision caused a national uproar. Several Dutch provinces repudiated the decision of the Grand Assembly, forming themselves into the Orange Party, which included wealthy landholders, Calvinist clergy, old military families, and a majority of the citizens. Their political agenda demanded that the House of Orange be viewed as the legitimate heir to the thrones of England and Holland and as the only reliable protection against the onslaughts of the hated French and Spanish.

The leaders of the Dutch states in favor of a republican form of government and more liberal religious and economic practices were often on the defensive. People still remembered the arrest and public execution of the great Dutch statesman and advocate of religious toleration Johan van Oldenbarneveldt and the banishment of the eminent jurist and biblical critic Hugo Grotius in 1619.[43] At the time Spinoza moved near The Hague in 1663, the Dutch political situation was at another crisis point. With the restoration of Charles II to the throne in England in 1660, a new era of hostility toward Holland began. In 1663, English militiamen seized New Holland (including New Amsterdam) and King Charles offered it to his brother the Duke of York as a present.[44] Simultaneously, on the other side of the planet, English agents seized Dutch territories in the East Indies. De Witt and the States General immediately declared war on England and England responded in 1665. The German provinces lying on the eastern border of the Dutch states, allies of the English, jumped into the fray.

It was during this three-sided brawl—in the summer of 1665—that Spinoza abruptly stopped working on his masterpiece, *Ethics Demonstrated in Geometric Order,* and began writing the *Theological-Political Treatise.*[45] He saw it as his contribution to the struggle for democracy and liberalism in his adoptive country. Little did he suspect the disastrous consequences that would ensue after it was published.

The war with England consisted mainly of a number of naval battles. After an initial disastrous defeat on 13 June 1665 at the mouth of the Thames,[46] the Dutch rallied and, under the leadership of Jan's brother Cornelius de Witt, fought a number of indecisive naval battles during the rest of 1665 and early 1666. Then Jan de Witt decided that the Dutch should attack the British fleet at its heart, up the Thames beyond London in the shipbuilding docks and weapons depots. No one had ever attempted such a daring raid before. Preparations were made in absolute secrecy and, in mid-1666, Cornelius de Witt and eighty Dutch ships conducted a devastating raid that destroyed nearly the entire English fleet. The Dutch provinces erupted in jubilation and the de Witt brothers were national heroes.[47]

The Dutch triumph was short-lived. No sooner had war ended (in May 1667) than Louis XIV, who had intervened on behalf of the Dutch against the German army, demanded the entire southern tier of Dutch provinces as payment for "services rendered." The Dutch parliament refused and Louis declared war. De Witt scrambled to mobilize the Dutch army, but it was in no condition to respond, thanks to his policy of undermining the military factions loyal to the House of Orange. In desperation, he sent an ambassador to England with the unlikely request for assistance against the French.[48]

While all this was going on, the public situation suddenly became ominous for Baruch Spinoza. In 1668, a wealthy Amsterdam physician named Adrian Koerbagh was arrested and tried by an ecclesiastical court on the grounds of publicly advocating atheism and hedonism. He was closely questioned as to his relationship with one Baruch de Spinoza, Jew of Amsterdam. Koerbagh admitted knowing Spinoza but denied that the ideas in his books were anyone's but his own. The court found Koerbagh guilty and sentenced him to have his right thumb cut off (so he could never practice medicine again), to have his tongue bored through with a red hot iron (so he could never talk again), to pay a crushing fine of 6,000 florins (so he would be ruined financially), and to serve a prison term of thirty years, followed by banishment, if he survived prison. He died after one year in prison.[49] It is difficult to imagine what effect this punishment of one of his friends and disciples had on Spinoza, who was at this time in the midst of writing the *Theological-Political Treatise*.[50]

Meanwhile on the national scene, de Witt's proposed scheme with the English had backfired, bringing the Dutch provinces into a situation of deadly peril. When he broached the subject of a treaty with the English, they immediately began back-channel negotiations with the French. This led to both countries suddenly declaring war on the now completely isolated Dutch provinces in 1670, just when Spinoza was putting the finishing touches on the preface to his *Theological-Political Treatise*.

The prospect of war against both France and England panicked the Dutch. The royalists pushed through a resolution in the parliament re-instituting the young Prince of Orange as the national sovereign and sent emissaries to England to make a separate peace. De Witt's career was on the brink of extinction.

That was the moment when Spinoza's *Theological-Political Treatise* went on sale in Amsterdam in late 1670. The timing could not have been worse. Since his book was a frontal attack on everything the forces of orthodoxy and monarchy held dear, it caused a violent reaction. Numerous attempts were made to suppress it, but these were foiled by de Witt. The following year, as translations appeared in other countries, more cries of outrage could be heard in France and Germany and England against the atheist Jew in Amsterdam.

Meanwhile, de Witt was fighting for his life. The Orange Party had succeeded in gathering the votes necessary to oust him from his position as head of the government and he was thrown into prison. Despite frantic attempts to get him released, on 20 August 1672 a mob stormed the prison where de Witt was being held, bludgeoned him and his brother Cornelius to death, and then dragged the bodies outside where they hacked them into pieces. Thus ended the first Dutch experiment with republican government.[51]

When Spinoza heard of de Witt's death, he flew into an uncontrollable rage and tried to rush down to where the mob was ranting over the pieces of his friends' bodies. He had a sign he intended to put up that read—in *Latin*—"you are the worst of barbarians." His landlord, suspecting that Spinoza might do something like this, locked his door so that he could not get out, unquestionably saving Spinoza's life.[52]

De Witt's death marked the complete termination of all attempts by

Spinoza to participate in the politics of his adopted country. He passed his last years in almost complete isolation. He returned to the task of completing the *Ethics,* but by now his public reputation was so bad he was afraid to publish it. When he finished the *Ethics,* he worked on a few other projects, such as a Dutch translation of the Hebrew Bible (which he threw into his fireplace as soon as he finished it) and various scientific efforts.

Spinoza's international reputation was not entirely negative. In February of 1673, he was offered a professorship of philosophy at the recently founded University of Heidelberg by the Elector Palatine, Karl Ludwig, a liberal-minded advocate of the new reforms and an enthusiastic supporter of Descartes.[53] He had known and admired Jan de Witt, had often visited Holland, and was "a strong advocate of the republican philosophy of religious and economic freedom."[54] Spinoza politely declined the invitation.

Not long after this, in 1674, Spinoza learned that his old friend Frans Van den Enden had been hanged in France after the collapse of a utopian scheme there.[55] Things became more bleak with each passing day. The return to power of the Prince of Orange, aided by the Calvinist clergy, seemed to crush Spinoza's "republican optimism" completely.[56] One wonders to what extent Spinoza blamed himself during these years for being partly responsible for the brutal death of Jan de Witt. In any case, his last days were marked by profound grief. His health deteriorated rapidly and, on 21 February 1677, he died at age forty-five.

The Purpose for Writing the Theological-Political Treatise

It is clear from Spinoza's biography that he moved to Voorburg and decided to play a role in the turbulent maelstrom of Dutch politics just when it was entering a period of national crisis. I believe we can discern veiled references to this period in the Preface (written in 1670), as well as in the concluding, political portion of the *Treatise,* where he warns his readers not to attempt a transition back to monarchy.[57] I will note these places in my comments.

When he began writing the *Treatise* in mid-1665, Spinoza sent a letter to his trusted friend Henry Oldenburg to inform him of his new project.

> I am now writing a Treatise about my interpretation of Scripture. This I am driven to do for the following reasons:
>
> 1. The Prejudices of the Theologians; for I know that these are among the chief obstacles which prevent men from directing their mind to philosophy . . .

2. The opinion which the common people have of me, who do not cease to accuse me falsely of atheism; I am also obliged to avert this accusation as far as it is possible to do so.
3. The freedom of philosophizing and of saying what we think; this I desire to vindicate in every way, for it is always suppressed through the excessive authority and impudence of the preachers.[58]

It is obvious from this list that Spinoza had reached the point where he could no longer remain uninvolved in national politics. He clearly felt compelled to take on the theologians and preachers and do whatever he could to break their power, discredit them, and convince people to turn away from them. He accused the theologians of hindering the progress of "philosophy," which I am inclined to interpret broadly as referring to the progressive lifestyle espoused by the liberal party in the Netherlands. He specifically accused the "preachers" of suppressing freedom of thought, sometimes brutally (as we saw in the case of Adrian Koerbagh). Finally, he was clearly irritated by the constant harping on his alleged atheism and intended to set the record straight on that score as well.

Overview of the Main Features of the Theological-Political Treatise

When Spinoza began the *Theological-Political Treatise,* all of his major conceptual categories had been thought out for some time. To really understand what he hoped the *Treatise* would accomplish, a preliminary understanding of these categories is indispensable.

Rather than provide a summary of Spinoza's thought in the usual abstract history-of-ideas manner, I am persuaded by Israeli scholar Yirmiyahu Yovel's recent research that one must begin by examining Spinoza's Marrano-Jewish heritage.[59]

First, one must note and honor Spinoza's profound moral rage. As a Marrano Jew whose heritage included two hundred years of brutal persecution, first in Spain and then in Portugal, Spinoza and his fellow Amsterdam Marrano Jews were only too aware of the precariousness of their existence in the presence of autocratic Christian sovereigns and powerful and prejudiced Christian preachers. Centuries of vicious treatment, encouraged and led by Christian clergy, bred in many Jews, including Baruch de Spinoza, an all-consuming rage. But what could they do? Word came back monthly from Spain and Portugal that friends or relatives unwilling or unable to leave had been arrested and burned alive "to the glory of God." Yet the Amsterdam Jews seemed powerless to stop this constant murder in the name of the Christian God. Even as Spinoza was writing the *Theological-Political Treatise,* his friend and disciple Adrian Koerbagh was hideously tortured by the local Calvinist consistory. What was Spinoza's reaction? Fury at such arrogant, vicious prejudice? Did he want to fight back? But in every direction he looked, whether toward Cromwell's England, or Luther's Germany, or Amsterdam itself, Spinoza's eyes beheld countless images of murderous religious fanatics, especially Christian but also (and on a much lesser scale) Jewish. What was Spinoza's reaction? His reaction is there for all to see on the very first page of the Preface to the *Theological-Political Treatise.* But just because his rage disappears from sight after that does not mean it is not still there. Far from it. I will point out its continued activity beneath the seemingly cool logic of the *Treatise* as, chapter by chapter, Spinoza systematically destroyed the entire medieval religious worldview, repeatedly putting one thing in its place: the commandment to love God and *love your neighbor.*

A second aspect of Spinoza's Marrano-Jewish heritage helps us understand his philosophical vision. From the very beginning, the readers of Spinoza's writings were stunned by his ability and willingness to go beyond both Judaism and Christianity toward some new vision of the universe. How did he get the internal freedom to do this? We are told that when the young German philosopher Leibniz first read the *Theological-Political Treatise* (not knowing who the author was), he told a friend, "(It) is an unbearably free-thinking book."[60] How was it psychologically possible for Spinoza to produce such a work?

Yovel suggests that one of the bitterest experiences of the Jews in Spain and Portugal was watching, from 1391 on, thousands of their fellow Jews "convert" to Christianity in order to save themselves from having their property confiscated, from being thrown from the upper levels of society down to its dregs. They went through Baptism and attended Mass, but in the privacy of their homes, these *conversos* vented their rage and frustration by mocking and ridiculing Christian customs and beliefs. But this was very dangerous; they could be found out, arrested, and tortured by the Inquisition as backsliders into Judaism (a capital offense punished by the royal authorities).

In Spinoza and other Jews, the behavior of both the hated Spanish monarchs and Jesuit Inquisition, as well as the miserable hypocrisy of the *conversos,* produced an utter skepticism regarding all religious claims. It was this skepticism, added to the Jews' age-old cultural rootlessness, that made possible Spinoza's "unbearable freedom of thought."

What were the essential elements of his new vision of the universe?

At first, Spinoza was deeply attracted to the system of René Descartes. Descartes' bold intention to sweep from his mind everything that could not be known with certainty—which included all medieval metaphysical and theological systems—struck Spinoza as remarkably refreshing, as did Descartes' rational, geometrical style of writing.[61] No hidden agenda permitted here; no illicit logical leaps.[62] But almost from the beginning, Spinoza also noticed serious problems in Descartes' philosophy. Yet he paid him the honor of learning his system thoroughly . . . and then he left it behind.

He especially disliked Descartes' too-easy identification of the God of traditional Christian theism with the "God" knowable as a necessary concept of reason. For Spinoza, a different "basic idea" beckoned: nature (or, we might say, the universe). From almost the time he began to study Descartes, Spinoza was working out a way whereby a few of the traditional attributes of theism's "God" could be attributed to nature or the physical universe. In Spinoza's view, nature is supremely orderly; it is eternal; it is ruled not by free will but by "laws," i.e., absolute necessity. Above all, it is "knowable by the human mind," since both share the same rational structure. All of this led Spinoza to his first basic negation and affirmation: there is no God *above* nature. There is no personal God of any kind. There is simply—nature. It was a breathtaking act of reduction:

> No Creator-God is necessary to explain the work of nature. No divine Legislator is allowed to prescribe the laws of morality. Religion itself must exclude the idea of God from its foundations and be grounded exclusively in the autonomy of the rational human will. Nor is there room, other than rhetorical (to educate the masses), for revelation, or the Law of Moses, or the love and passion of Christ. The human mind itself, when exercising its rationally structured spontaneity, prescribes the basic laws of morality and religion to itself, just as it legislates the universal and necessary lawlike patterns that nature itself obeys.[63]

This depersonalization of the traditional concept of God and reduction of God to nature was perceived as a great loss by Spinoza's contemporaries and was probably the cause of most of the accusations of atheism.[64]

Not so clearly perceived, perhaps, but registering seismically at the visceral level, was Spinoza's daring elevation of human reason to the level of divine reason (evident in the last quotation). Human knowledge at its highest level was absolutely identical with God's knowledge. Hence, human reason could comprehend the precise nature of God/reality. But the standard for such knowledge was mathematics, that is, perfectly objective reasoning. Spinoza's goal was nothing less than "through the proper use of intellect . . . to become aware of one's place in the infinite and necessary scheme of things."[65] Knowledge of the universe was the path to rational happiness. Spinoza's philosophy "can be seen as the most fully developed defense of the ideal of scientific objectivity as a life task that is to be found in the history of western thought."[66]

This conception of the power of human reason was accompanied by a categorical rejection of the notion of original sin and all traditional understandings of good and evil.[67] Since human beings share with each other and with the universe at large "the divine light of reason,"[68] there can be no innate good or evil, much less sin. This too was perceived as a great loss by the orthodox. Whom would good people like them hate if there weren't any sinners and wicked people in the world? It is likely that Spinoza's elevation of humanity to the divine level may have caused some of the accusations of blasphemy.

Finally, instead of the traditional notions of grace and redemption, whether Jewish or Christian, Spinoza held out a most peculiar definition of true blessedness: "to arrive at . . . the knowledge of the union that the mind has with the whole of nature."[69] This concept seemed so bloodless, so bizarre, that most of his contemporaries couldn't understand it clearly enough to accuse him of anything except insanity. Since Spinoza's time, however, this peculiar notion has gradually begun to make sense. Akin to unitive mysticism,[70] the feeling of oneness with the All can indeed lead to a life of serenity and service to all sentient beings. In a note added to the *Theological-Political Treatise*, Spinoza clarified this idea:

> We have shown that the divine commandments appear to us as commandments or ordinances only as long as we do not know their cause. Once this is known, they cease to be commandments and we embrace them as eternal truths; . . . that is, obedience passes into love which arises from true knowledge by the same necessity as light arises from the sun. Therefore by the guidance of reason we can love God, but not obey him.[71]

American philosopher James Collins says that the act of adopting Spinoza's philosophy is no purely mental exercise, but also

> involves a transformational process. What were regarded by veiled (unenlightened) revelational faith as commandments for our obedience are now clearly known as eternal truths for our love . . . (Thus we see) a specific instance of Spinoza's philosophical meaning (leading to) a human loving response to the truth about the mind's union with nature in its fullness.[72]

Finally, the goal of Spinoza's whole philosophical program was to create "a new social and cultural universe, based upon reason, secularization, mechanical science, social tolerance, and political freedom . . . thus opposing the medieval world in its most essential aspects."[73]

Blocking the way to this beautiful, new universe and the peaceful social order that mirrored it loomed the mountain of wreckage and chaos generated by fifteen hundred years of Christian and Jewish religious superstition and prejudice. Someone had to break it down and blow it away. This Spinoza resolved to begin. He attacked both historic religions at their common root: the Bible, as interpreted within a hierarchical social order and universe.

The Five Basic Operations within Spinoza's "Historical Method"

Detailed analysis of the *Treatise* reveals a program of demolition and reconstruction consisting of five distinct but closely related basic operations.

1. Negation of the traditional interpretation of all major biblical concepts
2. Redefinition of these same concepts so that the Bible would be in accord with the worldview of seventeenth-century mechanistic science
3. Prescription of a new method of "historical" biblical interpretation that would forever block people from finding the traditional concept of God in the Bible again
4. Repetition of a few simple moral principles for people to cling to as "the teaching of the Bible"
5. Which, if followed, would render them capable of living together, enjoying freedom of thought and speech, all firmly under the control of a secular, democratic state

Let us examine each of these more carefully.

Negation of the Traditional Interpretation of All Biblical Concepts

Spinoza's activity in this regard may be best summarized by saying that he categorically rejected the Bible's entire supernatural worldview. Here is a partial list of specific *negations* taken from the *Treatise:*

· There is no God "above" nature. This is a fantasy of childish, prescientific minds.

- Early Hebrews had no knowledge of natural causes, therefore no knowledge of the power of God.[74]
- The Hebrew prophets were endowed with vivid imaginations, not intellectual understanding of God. No one has ever obtained true knowledge of God through prophecy.[75]
- Miracles never happen; no event can contravene the eternal, unchanging order of nature.[76] It is impossible to know God from so-called miracles.[77]
- God never chose the Hebrew nation or any other nation for special favor.[78]
- Belief in historical narratives (such as Exodus or the Gospels) has nothing to do with knowledge of God and does not lead to happiness or salvation.[79]
- Ceremonial rituals contribute nothing to our knowledge of God or personal holiness.[80]
- The Bible is not and cannot be the Word of God.[81]
- There is no good or evil in nature. Sin against the eternal decrees of nature is impossible.[82]
- The Holy Spirit does not lead to any knowledge of truth but only to good works. Truth and certainty of philosophical knowledge are aided by no spirit other than reason.[83]
- No biblical law has any place in a modern society.
- The New Testament writings are of an entirely different character from the Old Testament prophets; they are just personal speculations by Jesus' followers. As such, they are of little value.[84]

Taken together, these negations constitute a sweeping repudiation of every major tenet of traditional Jewish and Christian faith. Even the apparent holdovers (such as the existence of God and the love commandment) are not really founded on the Bible anymore; they have become the necessary truths of reason. It is important to bear this list of denials in mind when considering the real (as opposed to the stated) purpose for Spinoza's "historical exegesis."

Redefinition of These Concepts So That the Bible Will Be in Accord with Science

Throughout the *Treatise*, Spinoza undertook a systematic transformation of all major biblical concepts into seventeenth-century scientific ideas, which, in turn, came mostly from ancient Stoicism and Epicurean naturalism.[85]

Why didn't Spinoza simply throw the Bible out along with the outmoded medieval religion in general? He realized he had to accommodate
to some extent to the views of his audience. Yovel explains this aspect of
the *Theological-Political Treatise* as follows: Spinoza was only too aware
that the

> major obstacles in the way of a (purifying) critique of religion were be-
> lief in the Bible's suprarational authority, in the literal truth of its stories,
> and in the sacred validity of the vast dogmatic, ritual and institutional
> apparatus that grew up around it. But to be effective, the critic must
> have an affinity with the mind of his audience. As long as the public is
> immersed in (what Spinoza called) *vana religion* (religious superstition),
> no dialogue is possible, much less a change in attitude . . . This is where
> biblical exegesis becomes instrumental, serving as a *fictitious common
> ground* between the critic and his audience. Since the believer in revealed
> religion cannot share the philosopher's first principles, the latter, by ap-
> pealing to the Bible, must *appear* to share the first principles of the be-
> liever, while actually turning them against themselves . . . In this sense,
> (Spinoza used) biblical hermeneutics as an aggressive activity . . . an of-
> fensive weapon . . . A major avenue for the social and practical involve-
> ment of the philosopher.[86]

What are some of the *redefinitions* that Spinoza embeds within the
traditional biblical concepts?[87]

- Natural knowledge of God is like prophecy in the Bible in that it
  involves knowledge of God's "eternal decrees," which are nothing
  else than the laws of nature and the causes of natural events.[88]
- The term "God's decrees" just means the natural order.[89]
- "'God's direction' does not mean divine providence. It means the
  fixed and unchanging order of Nature."[90]
- The natural light of reason teaches us about "God's commands,"
  which are nothing else than natural phenomena. The more we learn
  about natural phenomena—gravity, the weather, the stars, and the
  like—the more we learn about "God's commands" and the more
  blessed we are.[91]
- Christ's teachings can be summed up in the Sermon on the Mount.[92]
  But there is no need for the Gospels. "The whole of Christ's doctrine can be readily grasped by everyone by the natural light of
  reason."[93]
- God's Word and covenant and true religious faith arise in our minds
  through natural reason as we learn more about the universe. They

do not come from our imaginations or from what we read in religious writings like the Bible.[94]

· Saying the Bible, a thing of paper and ink, is God's eternal word is a form of idolatry.[95]

· The Christian Gospel has nothing to do with rituals or doctrines; it is simply belief in and obedience to God/Nature.[96]

· "The Holy Spirit is nothing other than the peace of mind that results from doing good."[97]

· A heretic is not the person who believes unorthodox things about God but "the person who promotes obstinacy, hatred, strife and anger."[98]

This list is meant to put the reader on guard, so that, when I quote from the text where Spinoza sets forth his method of "historical exegesis," no one will naively assume that the traditional biblical language he uses has the traditional meanings. *It never does.*

New Method of "Historical" Interpretation That Will Block People from Finding the Traditional Concept of God in the Bible

In his younger years, Spinoza had personally experienced the negative impact historical questions had on his faith in the Bible. He also saw Hobbes use historical criticism of the Bible to good effect in his political treatise, the *Leviathan*.[99] How could this experience be transferred to the masses, so that they would give up their outmoded belief in the supernatural God of the Bible? Spinoza decided they needed a good dose of historical skepticism. This was Spinoza's true objective:

> When the mind vacillates back and forth in a state of doubt and confusion, (this) can help *destroy entrenched beliefs* and clear the way for philosophy.[100]

Thus Spinoza proposed a "new method for discovering the truth of Scripture," which consisted of piling up hundreds and thousands of particular historical[101] questions, all focused on the physical history of the biblical books: How can we ascertain the original sense of early Hebrew words? Who were the original authors? What were they like? Was each book of the Bible written by one person or several? How can we tell? What about the multitude of historical inconsistencies and scientific absurdities in the Bible? Do they affect our confidence in its theological reliability? And so on and so on. Then, as soon as he was finished piling up all of these questions, Spinoza surprisingly went on to conclude that, because so many of them were unanswerable, no one can ever be certain that he or she knows what the Bible teaches. This conclusion, far from upsetting Spinoza, was precisely what he wanted. As we can see from the summary of his early beliefs above, he had long since given up any thought that he could learn anything about God/Nature from the *Bible*. Science and reason were the only true guides for learning about God/Nature.[102]

Repetition of a Few Simple Moral Principles for People to Cling to As "the True Meaning of the Bible"

Having thrown up a blockade consisting of a boundless swarm of historical questions, each one of which can be broken down into still further questions, the general effect of which is to paralyze the would-be user of the Bible, Spinoza then offered a way out: the *moral* doctrines of Scripture are well known, easily understood, and generally agreed upon. They can be summed up in one sentence: Love God and love your neighbor. The essence of the moral teachings of the Old Testament and the New Testament, said Spinoza, comes down to justice, mutual help, tolerance of the beliefs of others, and obedience to the laws of the state.[103] In other words, the "historical method" is really meant for nothing else than to create room for an alternate politically safe substitute, a simple universal morality masquerading as religion.[104]

This Pious Moralism Will Result in Social Harmony and Free Thought and Speech in a Democratic State

With the Bible thus shackled and popular religion "purified" of its tendencies toward prejudice, strife, and tyranny—and here we come to the concluding chapters of the *Theological-Political Treatise*—the new democratic state envisioned by Spinoza must be the ultimate arbiter as to what will be permitted as a legitimate religious expression. Drawing on his experience of living among the Collegiants, and in accord with the popular millenarian philosophies flourishing at the time,[105] Spinoza held out the prospect of an *entire society* living more or less according to the dictates of natural reason, or the "inner light." If all this could come to pass, there would be a new era of peace and prosperity and security for all.

With this preparation, let us observe these five operations at work in the chapters of the *Treatise*.

THEOLOGICAL-POLITICAL TREATISE

In the discussion that follows, I intersperse quotations (indented in regular type) with my comments (*in italics*). I also present expository paraphrase (not indented, in regular type) interspersed with my comments (*in italics*). In other words, my interpretive comments are always set off *in italics*.[106]

Preface

The Preface reveals all of the passionate concerns within Spinoza's heart more clearly than any other writing of his. In summarizing his text, I will give some parts in quotation and otherwise paraphrase the most pertinent aspects of his argument. I will omit all detailed biblical illustration since it is not essential to this analysis. This is how the *Treatise* begins:

> If men were able to exercise complete control over all their circum-
> stances, or if continuous good fortune were always their lot, they would
> never be prey to superstition. But since they are often reduced to such
> straits as to be without any resource, and their immoderate greed for
> fortune's fickle favors often makes them the wretched victims of al-
> ternating hopes and fears, the result is that, for the most part, their
> credulity knows no bounds . . . This being the case, we see that it is par-
> ticularly those who greedily covet fortune's favors who are the readiest
> victims of superstition of every kind, and it is especially when they are
> helpless in danger that they all implore God's help with prayers and
> womanish tears. Reason they call blind because it cannot reveal a sure
> way to the vanities they covet . . . while the delusions of the imagination,
> dreams, and other childish absurdities are taken to be the oracles of God
> . . . It is fear, then, that engenders, preserves, and fosters superstition.[107]

Note the characteristic psychological analysis of human behavior, an approach that runs throughout Spinoza's philosophical activity.[108] He dedicated all of his effort not to the erection of an elaborate philosophical system but to the achievement of happiness for as many of his fellow beings as possible.[109] The primary obstacle to this happiness is superstition. In a very significant clarification (not given in the Treatise), *Spinoza says that quest for "final ends" or ultimate purposes in human history is the root of all superstition.[110]*

If anyone seeks particular examples to confirm what I have said, let him consider Alexander. It was only when he first learnt to fear fortune at the Gates of Susa that superstition drove him to employ seers.[111]

At first glance, the choice of the first-century Roman historian Quintus Curtius Rufus to make his point seems far-fetched. But there may be more here than meets the eye. Curtius' History of Alexander *5:4.1 refers to a harrowing event in Alexander's campaign against the Persians. His armies had just captured a neighboring city and Alexander was leading a small, lightly armed company through a narrow pass to attack the great imperial city of Susa itself when he was ambushed by 25,000 well-armed Persians deployed on both sides of the pass, which was called the Gates of Susa (Pylae Susidis). Most of his troops were slaughtered and he barely escaped with his life. That evening, Curtius informs us, a badly shaken "Alexander not only began to take counsel on what was to be done (in view of the loss of so many of his best soldiers) but also, from a feeling of superstition, to summon soothsayers." Is Spinoza commenting on the crisis of 1670 and the panic caused by the simultaneous declarations of war by England and France? In this case, "Alexander" might be the Dutch people and the "soothsayers" the Calvinist clergy then crying out for God's deliverance from the godless leadership of Jan de Witt.*

This being the origin of superstition . . . it clearly follows that all men are by nature liable to superstition. It also follows that superstition, like all other instances of hallucination and frenzy, is bound to assume varied and unstable forms, and that, finally, it is sustained only by hope, hatred, anger and deceit. For it arises not from reason but from emotion, and emotion of the most powerful kind . . . Indeed, as the multitude remains ever at the same level of wretchedness, so it is never long contented (with one particular superstition) and is best pleased only with what is new and has not yet proved delusory.[112]

The "powerful emotions" and "hallucination and frenzy" mentioned here will come into play later in Chapter 6 when Spinoza explains the psychological basis of biblical miracle stories. For Spinoza, "emotion" represents what is unpredictable and dangerous in human behavior. It, together with another code word—"enthusiasm"—connotes all those surging, overmastering inner impulses that turn groups of humans into frenzied mobs, burning and destroying everything in their path, a terrifying experience with which Jesus were only too familiar. Spinoza intends to remove "emotion" in all of its dangerous manifestations from religion, once and for all. Reason will be the new Savior; it will be the Guide on the sure

path toward safety, order, calm, and happiness. Having identified the root
cause of superstition, Spinoza turns now to those chiefly responsible for
propagating and manipulating it behind the false face of religion.

> This inconstancy has been the cause of many terrible uprisings and wars,
> for—as Curtius says so well in Book 4,10—"the multitude has no ruler
> more potent than superstition."[113] So it is readily induced, under the
> guise of religion, now to worship its rulers as gods. To counteract this
> tendency (toward fickleness), immense efforts have been made to invest
> religion, true or false, with such pomp and ceremony that it can sustain
> any shock and constantly evoke the deepest reverence in all its wor-
> shippers.[114]

Behind Spinoza's whole critique of superstition lies the ancient Jewish
opposition to idolatry. "Thou shalt have no other Gods before me" means
reverence due only to God must not be demanded for any person, institu-
tion, political cause, or material object. To this he adds the classical Greek
and Roman suspicion of the methods used by tyrants and absolute rulers—
whether religious or political—to manipulate the religious impulses of the
gullible masses to bend them to their will.[115] Spinoza now turns his atten-
tion to the situation in Holland at the time of writing.

> Granted then that the supreme mystery of despotism, its prop and stay,
> is to keep men in a state of deception, and with the specious title of
> religion to mask the fear by which they must be held in check, so that
> they will fight for their enslavement as if for salvation, and count it no
> shame but the highest honor to spend their blood and their lives for the
> glorification of one man. Yet no more disastrous policy can be devised
> or attempted in a free commonwealth (like ours) . . . Since we have the
> rare good fortune to live in a commonwealth (*republica*) where freedom
> of judgment is fully granted to the individual citizen and he may wor-
> ship God as he pleases, and where nothing is esteemed dearer and more
> precious than freedom, I think I am undertaking no ungrateful or un-
> profitable task in demonstrating that not only can this freedom be
> granted without endangering piety and the peace of the commonwealth,
> but also that the peace of the commonwealth and piety depend on this
> freedom. *This then is the main point which I have sought to establish in*
> *this treatise: to indicate the main false assumptions that prevail regarding*
> *religion . . . and then again the false assumptions regarding the right of*
> *civil authorities.* There are many who, with an impudence quite shame-
> less, seek to usurp much of this right, and under the guise of religion,
> to alienate from the government the loyalty of the masses, still prone to

heathenish superstition (*Gentilium superstitioni*), so that slavery may return once more.[116]

In the italicized sentence, Spinoza summarizes his whole religious and political agenda. The reference to "Gentile superstitions" is a rare hint of Spinoza's Jewish orientation. Having identified the enemy, namely religious functionaries of every stripe, he moves over to the attack, all guns blazing.

> I have often wondered that men who make a boast of professing the Christian religion, which is a religion of love, joy, peace, temperance and honest dealing with all men, should quarrel so fiercely and display daily the bitterest hatred towards one another *so that what kind of people they are is recognized more easily by these things than by their supposed "faith."[117]

Why do the clergy display such bitter hatred? Because everyone has gotten the twisted belief that religious vocations should be a pathway to political and financial aggrandizement. As a result of this deplorable conviction,

> . . . every worthless fellow feels an intense desire to enter holy orders, and eagerness to spread abroad God's religion degenerates into base avarice and ambition . . . (which) inevitably gives rise to great quarrels, envy and hatred . . . Little wonder, then, that nothing is left of the old religion but the outward cult—wherein the common people seem to engage in base flattery of God rather than his worship—and their "faith" is nothing more than credulity and prejudice.[118]

Having characterized all religious offices and vocations, whether Jewish or Christian, as thoroughly infected by "base avarice (sordidam avaritiam) and ambition," Spinoza goes on to denounce the prejudices these religious functionaries parade as God's Truth.

> But what prejudice! Degrading rational man to beast, completely inhibiting man's free judgment and his capacity to distinguish true from false, and apparently devised with the set purpose of utterly extinguishing the light of reason! Piety and religion—O everlasting God!—take the form of ridiculous mysteries, and men who utterly despise reason, who reject and turn away from the mind as naturally corrupt—these, these are the men who are believed to possess the divine light![119]

There is no angrier rhetoric in Spinoza's pages than this passage. In a fury of purification, he sweeps into one great pile all of the accumulated rubbish of fifteen hundred years of Jewish and Christian theological specu-lation, calling them "ridiculous mysteries" (arcana absurda), and heaves them overboard. All of the old-fashioned metaphysical systems, hoary reli-gious rituals, dusty books, tomes, and commentaries—dragged to the ship's rail and tossed overboard into the sea with a curse. Still furious, Spinoza returns to his opening theme:

> Surely, if they possessed but a spark of the divine light, they would not indulge in such arrogant ravings, but would ... surpass their fellows in love, as they now do in hate. They would not persecute so bitterly those who do not share their views. Rather would they show compassion, if their concern (really) were for man's salvation and not for their own standing.[120]

Spinoza, suddenly ice cold, is ready to begin the Treatise. *In it he will do everything in his power to make sure that such hate in the name of religion, such arrogance, and such superstition will never again be able to base themselves on the Bible.*

> When I pondered over these facts, that the light of reason is not only despised but is condemned ... that merely human superstitions are re-garded as divine doctrine ... and that disputes of philosophers are raging with violent passion in Church and Court ... I deliberately resolved to examine Scripture afresh, conscientiously and freely, and to admit noth-ing as its teaching which I did not most clearly derive from it.[121]

Watch out.

Part One: Preliminary Definitions (Chapters 1–4)

Chapters 1 and 2: The Knowledge of God

Spinoza begins the *Treatise* proper with four chapters of definitions focusing on the concepts of the knowledge of God and the law of God. Apart from their being similar to major philosophical categories such as epistemology and ethics, which could be logical places to begin a philo-sophical treatise, my impression is that the real factor at work in prompt-ing Spinoza to begin where he does is his Jewish heritage. He begins where all Jews should begin: with Moses (the prophet par excellence; Chapters

1–2), then God's election of Israel (Chapter 3), and the Torah or Law of Moses (Chapter 4). The definitions (or I should say redefinitions) he gives to these three categories—prophecy, election, and law—will function throughout the *Treatise* as basic touchstones for every level of his argument.

His first major objective, which is not explicitly stated until the beginning of Chapter 16, is to disentangle and completely separate faith from reason, theology from philosophy, and the Bible from science, so that he will be able, in the last four chapters, to show how they can function harmoniously in the ideal democratic state. So, beginning with these all-important four opening chapters, Spinoza will lay out a whole series of definitions and redefinitions of the familiar biblical terms that will serve to distinguish and separate these two great domains.

Chapter 1 starts with the fundamental question What is the end and goal of all human effort? Spinoza gives a seemingly traditional answer: to know and love God; the more one knows and loves God, the happier one is.

However, Spinoza proceeds to load this seemingly familiar answer with so many redefinitions that the answer quickly takes on very untraditional connotations.

He asks first of all: What is the nature and function of prophecy? Prophecy, he answers, may be defined as "sure knowledge of some matter revealed by God."[122] But if this be correct, then the "natural knowledge (of God) can also be called prophecy because the knowledge we obtain by the natural light of reason depends solely on knowledge of God and of his eternal decrees."[123] Since the natural light of reason is present in all humans, "this knowledge (of God) is common to all men"[124]—not just the few prophets in the Bible.

This redefinition is a critical step in Spinoza's strategy of democratizing all knowledge of God/Nature. Later, Chapter 7 will extend this principle to argue that it is the individual (and not the state or the clergy) who is the sole judge of religious truth. These affirmations will provide the basis for his conclusion that the ideal form of state is a political democracy, in which each person can think and say whatever he or she pleases, religiously or politically.

Granted, most people think the biblical prophets had superior knowledge of God, but in fact their prophecies were all based on imagination, which has nothing to do with knowledge.[125] The Old Testament prophets saw God entirely with their imaginations; they "were not endowed with a more perfect mind but with a more vivid power of the imagination."[126] Therefore one cannot learn anything about God from the writings of the prophets. Knowledge of God can be obtained only through the natural light of reason, which is superior in every way. Indeed, our natural knowledge is itself divine because "the human mind contains the nature of God within itself in concept and partakes of it."[127]

Consistent with Spinoza's definitions of "God," "mind," and "reason," it should not come as any surprise to see him say that the "natural mind" contains the concept and essence of God within it. Note the "divinization of the human mind" which is at the same time a democratization of divine reason, both of which are central to Spinoza's understanding of the basis of democracy in human nature.[128]

Moreover, one cannot understand the prophets because their prophecies differ from each other according to personal temperament, the time in which they lived, their level of education, their style of speaking, and audience.[129] The same variability can be found in the New Testament as well, where the Apostles' writings differ widely for the same reasons.[130] This complete absence of consistency proves that all prophetic passages in the Bible have nothing to do with reason, only with imagination.

This fundamental distinction will be used throughout the Treatise *to deprive all prophetic and historical writings of intellectual value save the minimal idea: a God exists. Beyond that, everything will be cast into the domain of imagination, "beyond the intellect," where each person can interpret them however he or she pleases. So we have, in Chapters 1–2, the first step in making it possible for individuals to interpret whole portions of the Bible in any way they wish, or not at all.*

Chapter 3: Of God's Election of the Hebrew Nation

Just as prophecy "properly understood" refers to the natural capacity of every person to know God, it follows that God is not related to one individual person or nation any differently than to all others. "God is the God of all nations; he is equally gracious to all."[131]

One might describe Spinoza's purpose here as the "democratization of God's love." In contrast to the biblical view, where Israel's national God loves his nation more than the others, and certain individual Jews more than others, Spinoza proposes a radically different level of "God" (i.e., Nature) and therefore a radically level way in which all humans—indeed, all physical phenomena—relate to "God": they are all equal parts of "God/Nature."

When it says in the Old Testament that God loved the Hebrew nation above all other nations, this is merely a sign of "the immaturity of their understanding."[132] As far as knowing God and obtaining true happiness, the Hebrews "were on the same footing as other nations."[133]

Of course, many Jews think they still are the Chosen People. They attempt to prove this by arguing that their continued existence after so many centuries of suffering and persecution is nothing less than a miracle, proof of God's special favor toward them. Nothing could be further from the truth. The truth is that there is precisely nothing to which the Jews can point so as to set themselves above all other nations in the eyes of God. Their original nation disappeared long ago with the destruction of the First Temple by the Babylonians. And

> . . . as to their continued existence (as a people) for so many years when scattered and stateless, this is in no way surprising since they have separated themselves from other nations to such a degree as to incur the hatred of all . . . They are preserved largely through the hatred of other nations.[134]

This conclusion is easily proved by historical evidence. When the King of Spain decreed in 1492 that all Jews had to become Roman Catholics, within a short time the converted Jews disappeared into the population, having received all the privileges of citizenship.[135] So "in respect of understanding (God) and (knowing how to obtain) true virtue . . . God has not chosen one nation before another."[136]

The statement that the Jews' continued existence has nothing to do with divine favor, but is a result of the hatred caused by their own stand-offish behavior, like that other international pariah group the gypsies, is a striking illustration of Spinoza's searing experience of separateness and the desire to give it up. As a calculated insult, this sentence undoubtedly infuriated his former Jewish compatriots.

The explicit rejection of a basic biblical category like election is rare in Spinoza's book. The other case will come up in Chapter 6 where he categorically rejects the biblical concept of supernatural miracles. The reason there are not more of these open, direct rejections is that they undermine Spinoza's strategy of clothing old, biblical concepts in new dresses. But in a few cases, he apparently saw no way to redefine the biblical concept and so he just made it walk the plank.

Chapter 4: Of Human and Divine Law

But how does natural reason teach the path to true virtue? The answer to this involves a distinction between human and divine law. Human law may be described as "a prescribed rule of conduct whose sole aim is to safeguard life and the (state or) commonwealth."[137] Divine law is "that which is concerned only with the supreme good, the true knowledge and love of God."[138] How does a person obtain this supreme good? Not by reading the Bible or any other literature. One must know God directly by the natural light, and the more one knows God, the more perfect one is, because the more of God is in one. Since "God" is nothing more nor less than the universe or nature,

> everything in nature involves and expresses the conception of God in proportion to its essence and perfection. Therefore, we acquire greater and more perfect knowledge of God as we gain more knowledge *of natural phenomena.*[139]

To state it precisely: the more one is able to understand natural phenomena, the more one is able to "love" God/Nature *intellectually.*

> He who loves above all the intellectual cognition of God, the most perfect Being, . . . is necessarily the most perfect and partakes most in the highest blessedness.[140]

This brief section in Chapter 4 is a dense, quick introduction to Spinoza's concept of God and is the only place in the Treatise *where Spinoza attempts to set out, for laypeople, what he explains at length for scholars in his other writings. It is also one of the best examples of Spinoza's strategy of taking the familiar biblical concepts through a mind-bending series of redefinitions so that they come out meaning something completely different.*

How is a person to carry this out in her or his life? The means come from the human mind, guided as it is by the divine light of reason, which is nothing other than God's Mind. Therefore, everyone can know by nature, that is, by the natural light, how to live and know God. If we must use biblical terminology,

> the means required to achieve this end of all human action . . . *may be termed* God's commands, for they are ordained for us by God himself, as it were, in so far as he exists in our minds.[141]

And the rules for living a life directed toward this goal of ultimate human happiness *"can fitly be called* the Divine Law."[142]

Since this knowledge of God comes from knowledge of natural phenomena and is produced by the natural light of reason, obtaining the highest good and ultimate stage of human happiness in no way entails belief in any historical narratives in the Bible or elsewhere.

> Belief in historical narratives, however certain (which they aren't), give us (no) knowledge of God nor of the love of God. For . . . the knowledge of God (derives) from general axioms that are certain and self-evident (to human reason), so belief in historical narratives is by no means essential to our attainment of our supreme good.[143]

Nor does it require a person to adhere to any ceremonial laws or religious rituals of any kind, biblical or otherwise.

> The *natural* Divine Law does not enjoin ceremonial rites, that is, actions which in themselves are of no significance and are termed good merely by tradition.[144]

Finally, adherence to these rules does not spring from either fear of punishment or desire for reward, but "the supreme reward of the Divine Law is the law itself."[145]

This remarkable series of negations of whole portions of the biblical laws in the Old and New Testaments spring from a single root: there is a better way—the natural light of reason brings us into deeper and clearer knowledge of Nature/God than faith or the Bible will. It alone unites us with "God" or the whole of the universe. This way does not require any religious rituals, nor does it envision some Male Parent in the Sky who will punish you if you fail. Not doing "God's law" is itself the punishment. By the same token, living one's life in a process of deeper and deeper closeness with All That Is is itself the ultimate reward; there is no "afterlife."

Nor need we be in any doubt that all of the above is taught by Scripture itself: "Scripture unreservedly commends the natural light and the Divine Law" (as defined above).[146]

This is surely one of Spinoza's cheekier statements. But it fits in with his strategy of adopting a fictitious common ground so that his readers will listen to him long enough to "understand the Bible properly." With this preliminary "ground clearing" behind him, Spinoza is ready to tell

*his readers how to interpret the Bible so that they will understand it
"properly."*

Part Two: The Historical Method of
Interpreting the Bible (Chapters 5–11)

Chapter 5: The Value of Ceremonial Laws and Historical Narratives

In the previous chapter, it was argued that "the Divine Law, which makes men truly blessed and teaches the true life, is of universal application to all men; . . . (being) innate in the human mind."[147] However, the ceremonial laws in the Old Testament "were instituted for the Hebrew (nation) alone . . . and do not pertain to the Divine Law and therefore do not contribute to blessedness and virtue."[148] The New Testament supports this view, for the Apostles of Jesus gave up all Jewish ceremonial observances as soon as they took the Gospel to other nations. From this it follows that, since the ancient Hebrew nation no longer exists, the Old Testament ceremonial laws are obsolete for Jews as well as Christians. "Jews (today) are no more bound by the Mosaic Law than they were before their political state came into being."[149]

What was their purpose originally? Like any other nation, when the Hebrew nation was founded, the people continually disobeyed the laws of the state and did whatever they pleased. Now a state should be so constructed as to encourage its citizens to obey the laws, but not out of a craven fear of punishment. Instead they should do it out of a desire for the common good and prosperity.

> This was the reason why Moses . . . introduced a state religion: it was to make the people do their duty from devotion rather than fear.[150]

Thus it is evident that "ceremonial observances contribute nothing to blessedness and that those specified in the Old Testament and indeed the whole Mosaic law were relevant only to the original Hebrew state."[151] As for all of the

> Christian ceremonies, namely, baptism, the Lord's supper, festivals, public prayers, and all the other ceremonies that are . . . common to all Christendom, if they were ever instituted by Christ or the Apostles, of which I am not yet convinced, they were instituted only as external sym-

bols of a universal Church, not as conducing to blessedness or as containing an intrinsic holiness.¹⁵²

With this, Spinoza firmly sets to one side all traditional religious rituals as obsolete, at least for those who live according to reason. Like many Enlightenment rationalists, Spinoza viewed religious ceremonies with deep suspicion, if not outright disgust. Too often they consisted of little more than superstitious mumbo jumbo foisted off on a gullible public by cynical priests and rabbis seeking money, power, and prestige. Spinoza much preferred the quiet simple worship of the Quakers and Collegiants, who eschewed all exterior trappings of ritual.

Turning now to the historical narratives in the Bible, what is their purpose? First, since they play such a prominent role in the Bible, we must inquire what led Divine Providence to put so much of the Bible into this form. The answer is quite simple: since the vast majority of people are not capable of living a life according to reason, nor of knowing God intellectually, they must do everything according to their imaginations. Thus the Bible, which was originally written for the whole Hebrew people, not just the intellectual elite, is full of fanciful visions and astonishing stories, all couched in terms that appeal to the popular imagination. Their sole purpose is to arouse the emotions of awe, wonder, and devotion, from which will spring obedience to God and a lifestyle resembling one lived according to reason.¹⁵³

What are the few basic philosophical doctrines taught in the historical narratives?

> The teachings of Scripture that are concerned only with philosophical matters can be summed up as follows: that there is a God or Being who made all things, and who directs and sustains the world with supreme wisdom; that he takes the utmost care of men, that is, those of them who live moral and righteous lives, and that he severely punishes the others and cuts them off from the good.¹⁵⁴

Scripture teaches these simple truths by striking and impressive historical narratives so as to inculcate obedience and devotion in the minds of common people "who lack the ability to perceive things clearly and distinctly."¹⁵⁵

There are the few who already know these truths by the light of natural reason. Their life is superior to that of ordinary people, since they, although perhaps unacquainted with these (historical) writings, nevertheless know by the natural light that there is a God having the attributes we have recounted, and (if they) also pursue a true way of life, (they are) altogether blessed—indeed, more blessed than the multitude, because in addition to true beliefs they also have a clear and distinct conception of God (i.e., Nature).[156]

Granted, therefore, that the masses need the Bible's historical narratives; but they don't need to read all of them, just the ones that make the most "striking impression on men's minds."[157]

The suggestion that most of the historical narratives can safely be ignored will be developed further in Chapters 11 and 12 to include the Gospels.

Chapter 6: Of Divine Actions or Miracles

A major shortcoming of the historical narratives is that they are filled with stories of supernatural acts of God called miracles. How should we interpret these accounts?

This problem is such a huge obstacle to Spinoza's whole program of desupernaturalizing the Bible that he devotes an entire chapter just to it. He begins by building a bridge back to the notion of "divine law" and associates it with the concept of "divine work" as a way of getting at the subject of miracles. The opening sentence thus reads:

Just as men are accustomed to call divine the kind of knowledge that surpasses human understanding, so they call divine or the work of God any work whose cause is generally unknown . . . particularly if such an event is to their profit or advantage . . . (Such) unusual works of Nature are termed miracles or works of God by the common people.[158]

Driven by their irrational hopes and fears, people leap to all sorts of superstitious nonsense, guided as always by religious functionaries who never miss the opportunity to reiterate to the ignorant masses that "the clearest possible evidence of God's existence is provided when Nature deviates . . . from her proper order."[159] As a result, since the deceitful are leading the blind, it is impossible to find a sound conception of God anywhere. "(People) consider that God is inactive all the while Nature pursues her normal course." But, like Old Testament prophecy, "neither God's essence nor God's existence . . . nor God's providence can be known from (stories about) miracles"[160] because they are all false if taken literally. "No event can occur to contravene Nature."[161] "A miracle either contrary to Nature or above Nature is a mere absurdity,"[162] since Nature has observed the same unchanging order from all eternity. All such stories, whether they are in the Bible or anywhere else, must "be understood only with respect to men's beliefs," that is, they are nothing more than mental fantasies of "common people who are quite ignorant of the principles of science."[163]

The opening polemical fireworks in this chapter hark back to the flaming prose in the Preface and indicate that we are near a storm center in Spinoza's agenda. But we should not let the powerful rhetoric obscure the fact that, for all of his revolutionary theology, Spinoza is leveling a traditional Jewish accusation at his miracle-mongering opponents: you are idolaters. You have for centuries led the people after false gods. The people believe in idols because of you; "their children have forsaken Me and have sworn by those who are no Gods" (Jer 5:7).

The reference to "science" in the last sentence can be misunderstood. Spinoza is not thinking of modern, twentieth-century science founded on Heisenberg's principle of indeterminacy and Einstein's general relativity. Spinoza lived in the seventeenth century when the universe was just coming to be thought of as a vast machine operating according to certain rational "laws." The universe of Newton, Boyle, Kepler, and Galileo was a physical, mechanical, cause-effect, living substance of some sort.[164] Whereas the older universe was finite, teleologically and hierarchically ordered, the universe (of seventeenth-century science) is infinite, mechanically ordered, and governed by a single set of universal laws that apply to all phenomena, celestial and terrestrial alike. The key to this new conception is the role given to mathematics in scientific explanation. In the famous and oft-quoted words of Galileo:

> Philosophy is written in that great book which ever lies before our eyes—I mean the universe—but we cannot understand it if we do not first learn the language and grasp the symbols, in which it is written. This book is written in the mathematical language, and the symbols are triangles, circles, and other geometrical figures, without whose help it is impossible to comprehend a single word of it; without which one wanders in vain through a dark labyrinth.[165]

Spinoza went a step further and insisted that this gigantic living substance was "God." To say that this machinelike Substance sometimes intervened within itself against its own eternal workings to cause a miracle somewhere was of course complete nonsense. But it should be noted that Spinoza's repudiation of the mythical world of supernatural Gods and miracles originates in his religiously motivated adoption of a scientific worldview, not just observation of "empirical facts." The "facts" were produced by his worldview, not vice versa.

The biblical accounts of miracles should never be interpreted literally because the writers were imprisoned within all sorts of personal biases and superstitions. To take what they wrote as fact would be complete foolishness. In any case,

> it rarely happens that men relate an event exactly as it took place without introducing something of their own judgment.[166] Indeed, when they see or hear something strange, they will generally be so much influenced by their own preconceived beliefs. . . that what they perceive is quite different from what they really see or hear . . . In consequence, the (biblical) chronicles and histories reflect the writer's own beliefs rather than the actual facts.[167]

This psychologizing reduction of miracle stories to the superstitions and personal prejudices of the storyteller was a favorite weapon in the arsenal of ancient Greek and Roman religious polemics. Rediscovered by Enlightenment scholars like Hobbes, Spinoza, and Hume, it played a big part in the destruction of Europe's trust in traditional Jewish and Christian supernaturalism in the Bible as well as in personal faith.[168]

Another reason not to take the ancient writers literally is that we forget the ancient Hebrew love of paradox, metaphor, and exaggeration. "He who does not pay sufficient attention to this will ascribe to Scripture many miracles which Scriptural writers never intended as such."[169]

In general, "there can be no doubt that all events narrated in Scripture occurred naturally."[170] Whenever the biblical writers use such words as "God's decrees and volitions and . . . providence . . . (this) means nothing other than Nature's order."[171] Thus we must arm ourselves with exact knowledge of the makeup of the biblical writers in order to know how to interpret the stories they told.

> To interpret Scriptural miracles and to understand . . . what really took place, one must know the beliefs of those who originally related them . . . and one must distinguish between . . . what really happened and what was imagined and was no more than prophetic symbolism. *For many things are related in Scripture as real and were believed to be real*

which were merely symbolical and imaginary—such as that God, the Supreme Being, came down from Heaven (to speak with Moses).[172]

This explicit, categorical rejection of miracle is striking and does not fit well with Spinoza's strategy of accommodating to the primitive minds and childish concepts of his readers, so it was bound to arouse opposition. With this passage in Chapter 6, Spinoza blows up the last remaining partitions holding up the Bible's supernatural infrastructure. He circles around the Bible, eyeing the wreckage. How can he give a sop to all those ignorant people who still want to "believe" in this mess? Ah yes, he remembers his favorite answer: the Bible was meant for the unphilosophical majority and, "properly interpreted," can still be useful. Maybe it's even better this way. Let the masses think the desupernaturalized Bible really does teach nothing else but "love your neighbor."

Be assured, there is no reason to worry about the historical narratives. The Bible was produced for the entire Hebrew nation and so no attempt was made to phrase anything philosophically. It is all aimed at the imagination so as to excite the common people's emotions to devotion and obedience toward God. In this frame of mind, people will obey the few simple rules of morality that will bring happiness to them and stability to the state.[173]

Chapter 7: How to Obtain Clear, Distinct, and Universally Acceptable Philosophical Doctrines and Moral Teachings from the Bible

Men often say the Bible is the Word of God, but their lives prove that they "make no attempt whatsoever to live according to the Bible's teachings."[174] Or, which is still worse, all kinds of so-called scholars "parade their own ideas as God's word,"[175] and, using religion as a pretext, seek secular power by pretending their fabrications are God's truth and must be obeyed by everyone in the country. But their lives prove that such people are false to the core. They are not really religious. They spend their time quarreling and fighting, looking for any pretext to accuse people of heresy so they can torture them into submission. Their so-called

religion is manifested not in charity but in spreading contention among men and in fostering the bitterest hatred, under the false guise of zeal in God's cause, and a burning enthusiasm.[176]

The emotionally charged series of accusations in the opening lines of Chapter 7 again recall the flaming rhetoric of the Preface, but here Spinoza focuses on two specific accusations against the forces of orthodoxy: hypocrisy and capricious interpretation of the Bible. The first condemns them for not living by their own moral standards. The second accuses their theologians of teaching as the Word of God fantastic concoctions made up of strange and novel doctrines drawn from everywhere else and foisted off onto the Bible.

> To free our minds from the prejudices of theologians . . . we must discuss the true method of Scriptural interpretation . . . For unless we understand this, we cannot know with any certainty what the Bible or the Holy Spirit intends to teach.[177]

Here, then, in brief compass, is the only true and correct way to interpret the Bible. One must imitate the way scientists study natural phenomena. That is the guide.

> Just as the method of interpreting nature consists essentially in producing a history of nature from its phenomena, that is from certain and definite facts to infer definitions of natural things, so also it is necessary for the interpretation of Scripture to discern the real purpose of the historians, that is from certain and definite facts and principles to draw legitimate conclusions regarding the intention of the authors of Scripture.[178]

To understand what Spinoza has in mind, it is essential to remember that for him, the study of nature was always the study of physical substances, individual physical substances. He was a thoroughgoing nominalist; abstractions and "spiritual realities" did not exist. Only things exist. Thus what he is suggesting is that all of the physical aspects of the Bible's history should be studied in order to understand the intention of the authors. What becomes apparent immediately is that this method, borrowed from physics and having mathematical certainty as its standard of knowledge, can hardly—contrary to Spinoza's claim—provide much insight into the mental intentions of anyone, much less the ancient authors of the biblical books. It is a glaring breakdown in logic on Spinoza's part to suggest otherwise. But if that be true, why does he hold out this hope? We will learn more of this conundrum in a moment.

As we continue, it is necessary to remember that Spinoza uses the key terms "history" and "nature" in peculiar ways. As noted in the introduction, "history" refers to the this-worldly, cause-effect chain of natural events over time, located within the all-encompassing web of necessary events in the physical universe. There is nothing supernatural about this history. Similarly, as we noted in the five basic operations within Spinoza's "historical method," "nature" is nothing "created by God," nor is it a cosmos with a definite time span bounded by a beginning and an end, as the Bible teaches. It is an infinite, eternal, mechanically driven, mathematically precise, closed physical continuum, having neither purpose nor moral value. Every single one of these adjectives is the opposite of what is found in the Bible. Thus, what Spinoza is proposing here is that we should radically redefine everything in the Bible into these two categories—"history" and "physical nature"—in order to understand better the intentions of the authors!

If this method is followed, "steady progress can be made without any danger of error," for "this is not merely a sure way but the only way open to us."[179] "As for the moral doctrines that are also contained in the Bible," these also must be understood historically, that is naturally.[180] In short, "all knowledge of Scripture must be sought from Scripture alone."[181]

If we want to break this historical method of biblical interpretation down into its component parts, "what are the chief topics it should include?"[182]

First, there is the whole area of the original meanings of the words of each book of the Bible—what might be called historical philology. We need to know

> the nature and properties of the language in which the Bible was written and which its authors were accustomed to speak. Thus we should be able to investigate from established linguistic usage, *all possible meanings* of any passage.[183]

Second, we must begin collating the statements in various books under specific doctrinal topics; this might be called *biblical* theology in contrast to philosophical or systematic theology.

> The pronouncements made in each book should be assembled and listed under headings so that we can have to hand all the texts that treat of the same subject.[184]

Third, we need a complete, exact biography of the author of each book in the Bible. We must find out the circumstances relevant to all the extant books of the prophets, i.e., the life, character and pursuits of the author of every book, detailing who he was, on what occasion and at what time and for whom and in what language he wrote.[185]

Fourth, we must obtain a detailed, exact history of each book in the Bible. We must find out

what happened to each book, how it was first received, into whose hands it fell, how many variant versions were created, (and so on).[186]

Fifth, we must learn how and by whom each book was brought into the Bible, that is, "by whose decision it was received into the canon."[187]

Sixth, we need a history of the *text* of each book. It is pointless to base any eternal doctrine or definition of God on a statement or verse in a book of the Bible if no one knows for sure whether the original inspired author actually wrote that statement or not. The general task will be to form an opinion concerning

the authenticity of each book, . . . whether or not it may have been contaminated by spurious insertions, whether errors crept in (over the centuries, and so on).[188]

After we have all this information in hand, the history of the writers, the books, the canonization process, and the text of the books of the Bible,

when we possess this historical account of Scripture and are firmly resolved not to assert as the indubitable doctrine of the prophets anything that does not follow from this study . . . *then it will be time to embark on the task of investigating the meaning of the prophets and the Holy Spirit.*[189]

But, here again, we must stick to the method as outlined above.

For this task we need the method . . . similar to that (described above) which we employ in interpreting nature . . . In examining natural phenomena we first of all try to discover those features that are most universal and common to the whole of Nature, such as (the laws of gravity) . . . In just the same way we must first seek from our study of Scripture that which is most universal and forms the basis and foundation of all Scripture, . . . that which is commended . . . by all the prophets as doctrine eternal and most profitable for all mankind.[190]

In fact, a few universally accepted doctrines are already well-known:

> i. that God exists . . .
> ii. one alone and omnipotent . . .
> iii. who alone should be worshipped . . .
> iv. who cares for all . . .
> v. who loves those who worship him and love their neighbors as themselves.

These and similar doctrines . . . are taught everywhere in Scripture so clearly and explicitly that no one has ever been in any doubt as to its meaning on these points.[191]

Notice in the italicized words in the quotation above the use of traditional exegetical terminology, followed by a transfer of the whole process into the realm of physics. Spinoza then bridges from the notion of "natural laws" to "universally valid doctrines taught throughout Scripture" which are somehow like natural laws. Then he lists these universally valid axioms—before he has done any historical research. What is going on?

Spinoza is following a carefully devised strategy. Having insisted that the necessary place to begin is by answering a long list of questions regarding the physical history of the Bible, the ostensible goal of which is to prepare the researcher to infer clear and distinct and (morally) certain generalizations about the intentions of the authors, Spinoza suddenly leaps forward and says, well, actually, everyone already knows the basic doctrines of Scripture, and he lists them. The immediate effect of this move is to create an impulse in the interpreter to dispense with the theological synthesis step promised at the conclusion of the historical research. But he is not finished. He proceeds to isolate this list and set it apart from any potentially damaging theological speculation if anyone is foolhardy enough to hazard that step after some research. He goes on to say . . .

Beyond these few basic doctrines, it is very difficult to obtain any clear and distinct results "because the prophets differed among themselves in matters of philosophical speculation . . . and their narratives conform especially to the prejudices of their particular age."[192] With this warning

we have (finished) setting out our plan for interpreting Scripture, at the same time demonstrating that it is the only sure road to the discovery of its true meaning.[193]

Thus Spinoza completes the skeleton outline of his "historical method." He has also given the short list of "clear and distinct and universally accepted" basic doctrines taught throughout the Bible. It is beginning to become clear what role this list plays. But Spinoza is not finished. There is one more especially devious twist to his strategy. Having described his method and naming some of the major conclusions it will produce (before using it), he goes on to point out certain problems that will make it impossible for his method to reach any definite results.

> At this point I have to discuss any difficulties and shortcomings in our method which may stand in the way of our acquiring a complete and assured knowledge of the Holy Bible.[194]

First of all, we do not know nearly enough about the original meanings of the Hebrew words to be certain how to translate them in countless numbers of passages (many examples). Second, we do not know the biographies of any of the biblical writers, nor do we know anything definite about the histories of the books they wrote. Lacking this kind of information, "we cannot possibly know what was, or could have been, the author's intention" when we read a particular passage.[195] Third, we don't have certain books of the Bible in the language in which they were originally written.

> Such then is a full account of the difficulties involved in this method of interpreting Scripture from its own history. These difficulties . . . (are) so grave that I have no hesitation in affirming that in many instances we either do not know the true meaning of Scripture or can do no more than make a conjecture.[196]

But of course no definite and certain theological principles can rest on mere conjectures. It must be added that these difficulties have to do only with ascertaining clear, distinct, and definite ideas about *philosophical doctrines* taught by the prophets beyond the simple axioms listed above, not moral instruction.[197] As far as the latter are concerned, "with the help of such an historical study . . . we can grasp the meaning of (the Bible's) moral doctrines and be certain of their true sense."[198]

What is the meaning of this sudden distinction? Why aren't the moral teachings of the Bible every bit as ambiguous and inconsistent as the "philosophical doctrines"? The answer is that Spinoza simply intends to leave the reader with an essential moralism as the "teaching of the Bible." He will stress this repeatedly later in Chapters 12–14.

But since the writings of the prophets are filled with so many wild and fanciful stories whose meaning we are in no position to understand rationally, each person is free to make up her or his mind about them.[199] After all, "the interpretation of religion is vested above all in each individual."[200]

> The rule that governs interpretation must be nothing other than the natural light that is common to all, and not to any supernatural right nor to any external authority. Nor must this rule be so difficult as not to be available to any but skilled philosophers. It must be suited to the natural and universal ability and capacity of mankind . . . our rule fits this description.[201]

This passage could be regarded as the "Magna Charta" of modern historical biblical scholarship. It seems to place the entire enterprise of biblical scholarship within the same domain as all scientific knowledge and seems to open the door to anyone to enter within and take up the task of scientific interpretation of the Bible. Gone is the need to belong to the specially equipped (male) religious elite who alone understand the esoteric knowledge necessary for unlocking the secrets of "God's Holy Word."

However, nothing is ever what it seems to be in the Theological-Political Treatise. *To be sure, Spinoza is definitely concerned to deprive all religious functionaries of authority over anyone and anything. But, as we will see later in Chapters 16–20, he does not really intend to give the masses much freedom in matters religious.[202] As a matter of fact, in his later writing, the* Political Treatise, *he gives "the people" even less freedom than he does in this* Treatise. *What Spinoza really means here is that, beyond certain basic theological doctrines and moral principles* that will be enforced by the state, *individuals may interpret the fanciful portions of the Bible any way they wish.*

Chapters 8–10: Illustration of the Method's Use on the Old Testament

To see how the historical method works, let us focus for a moment on one central issue: Who wrote the books of the Old Testament? What about the first five books; how reliable is the widely accepted belief that they were all written by Moses? In fact, there is no hard evidence to support this belief (lengthy discussion follows).[203] The same conclusion must be reached regarding the books of Joshua, Judges, the books of Samuel, and the books of Kings; we have no evidence of any sort as to who their original authors were.[204] In fact, all of them look as if they were written by many different authors over a considerable period of time. But of this history of each book, we again have no hard evidence of any kind. As for their present status as a collection and then location in the Old Testament, I am inclined to believe this was the work of Ezra, after he returned from the Exile around the mid-fifth century B.C.E., long after most of them were written (several pages of argument follow).[205] Of their status before that, we know nothing. They may not have existed.

What about the whole question of the reliability of the texts of these writings? Here we must say that . . .

It is obvious from the numerous marginal notations and interlinear markings in the Masoretic Hebrew text that the text we now have of these writings is full of uncertainties.[206]

Leaving the prophetic writings, if we examine the other writings, such as the Psalms, Proverbs, and latter prophetic writings, it is clear that they also are riddled with uncertainties concerning authorship, authenticity, and textual corruption. Nor is there any sign that all of these writings were formed into a canon prior to the Maccabean period (ca. 134–63 B.C.E.). Hence anyone who appeals to the older books as divine Scripture must defend, on a book by book basis, whether each one has the necessary qualifications for being the eternal Word of God.[207]

The preceding summary of Spinoza's historical method does not do justice to the complex, detailed, and learned series of observations offered by Spinoza in defense of his arguments at each step. Let it only be said that every single problem he identifies here is still being investigated by biblical scholars three hundred years later. Indeed, they have become whole scholarly disciplines and have resulted in mountains of historical, archaeological, and philological information, pyramids of historical data. Biblical scholars at the end of the twentieth century can give detailed answers to every single question he raises about authorship, date of writing, presumed author(s), and history of the text of each book of the Old and New Testaments.

Has this immense historical knowledge resulted in immensely better theological understanding of the Holy Scripture? Not in the least. Spinoza reduces the theological content of the Bible to emotion, fantasy, and illusion on the one hand and, on the other, denies that historical knowledge per se has anything to do with the necessary truths of reason. Furthermore, it cannot be said that we have enough historical knowledge, since it is the nature of Spinoza's nominalistic, physical inquiry regarding historical data that for every question answered, ten new questions spring up in its place. This produces the paradoxical effect of an infinite regression: the more we learn, the less we know. Therefore we can never know enough to get to the point where Spinoza pretends we can stop and infer the general theological interpretations we undertook all this labor to get. Hence the entire process is endless and the alleged theological payoff is a mirage. But if this be true, then what is the real purpose for all those questions?

As we have seen, Spinoza himself shows no interest in pursuing the synthetic, theological step supposedly to come at the end of the historical preliminary step. Instead, he leaps from history into the realm of reason and lists certain axioms everyone should learn from the Bible. He then repeats this list a number of times. In fact, he does this often enough that one suspects some sort of covert purpose in the very repetitions.[208] Perhaps they are meant as a sort of mantra: "The Bible says: God exists. Love your neighbors! God exists. Love your neighbors! God exists. Love your neighbors!"

We might be tempted to conclude from this that Spinoza's barrage of historical questions has no positive purpose. Perhaps it doesn't on the level of cognitive content. But if one's goal is to create confusion and uncertainty in a person or group using the Bible to tyrannically enforce its religious beliefs upon one, these historical questions can be very powerful. They can lure the unsuspecting tyrant into a trap. Taking the tyrant's very factual dogmatism as a starting point, one can mount a diversionary assault by getting the oppressor to begin debating all sorts of factual questions. These can easily be multiplied to the point where an impasse is created, derailing the tyrant's theological train.[209]

When Spinoza finally gets around to discussing the New Testament in the next chapter, the opening paragraph is such a superb example of his sleight-of-hand argumentation that it is worth quoting in full.

Chapter 11: The New Testament

Nobody who reads the New Testament can doubt that the Apostles were prophets. However, prophets did not speak at all times from revelation, but only on rare occasions, as we showed towards the end of chapter 1; and so the question may be raised as to whether the Apostles wrote their Epistles as prophets, from revelation and express mandate like Moses, Jeremiah and others, or as private individuals or teachers.[210]

Although the Apostles themselves may have been prophets, a close examination of their writings shows that they were not composed under divine inspiration; they were just friendly advice or consolation for their acquaintances. Nowhere does anyone say, "Thus saith the Lord," as we find in the books of Moses. Instead, the Apostle Paul repeatedly says things like "it seems to me" and "I do not have a word of the Lord, but this is my advice," and so on.[211] Furthermore,

> Moses, the greatest of the prophets, never engaged in logical argument, whereas in the case of Paul the lengthy chains of logical argumentation such as we find in the Epistle to the Romans were most certainly not written from supernatural revelation.[212]

Thus we may conclude that the Apostles' writings "originated not from revelation and God's command but from their own natural faculty of judgment."[213]

Furthermore, the story of Christ as told by them in the Gospels surpasses the bounds of the rational intellect. But Christ's moral teachings do not.

> Religion, as preached by the Apostles—who simply related the story of Christ—does not come within the scope of reason. Yet its *substance,* which consists essentially in *moral teachings,* as does the *whole* of Christ's doctrine, can be readily grasped by everyone by the *natural light of reason.*[214]

Three operations of fundamental importance have taken place before our eyes.

First, not the Apostles but all of their writings—i.e., the entire New Testament—has been taken outside the bounds of "prophecy" and put into the vast domain of common human writings (one can detect a special animus directed against the Apostle Paul in this context, someone the Enlightenment philosophers all loved to hate). In the next chapter, Spinoza will build on this chapter to prove that the Bible cannot be the Word of God. These arguments, in short, lead to a decanonization of all biblical writings, including the Gospels.

Second, Spinoza gives a fleeting glance at the Gospels, but it is, if you will, a withering look. These writings he sweetly calls "the story of Christ" and says that they do not come within the scope of reason. Now in Spinoza's code language this is never a compliment, although it might sound like one. What he really means is that the Gospels are obscure and ambiguous stories of fantastic events that, like the other childish stories in the Old Testament, can safely be interpreted by anyone any way they wish or simply be ignored. The main teachings of Christ are exclusively moral and can be known equally well by human reason (next point). Thus the Gospels—being histories—cannot be looked to for theological truth. That can be supplied only by the divine light of reason. This is the second general principle of Enlightenment biblical hermeneutics: truth cannot be found in the Bible but in the proper exercise of one's own intellect.[215]

Third, Spinoza says the "whole of Christ's doctrine" can be summed up in the Sermon on the Mount. Actually not the whole *Sermon on the Mount, but just the Beatitudes and the love commands in Matthew 5.*

Everything Jesus Christ taught summed up in Matthew 5? Spinoza never explains this claim. All he does is insist that the whole of the Christian religion is summed up in Love God and love your neighbor. At one stroke, Spinoza cancels most of the rich theological content of the New Testament, handing out a moral platitude instead. This is the third general principle of Enlightenment biblical hermeneutics: reduce traditional religion to basic morality. He is following his original strategy: give the masses who want to "believe" in God and Jesus according to the New Testament something safe and nondestructive to cling to: the love commandment.

In summary, there can be no doubt that the obvious differences between the many writings of the Apostles gave rise to serious disputes and constant strife in the early Church, which has lasted down to our own times. This will continue until people "*separate philosophical speculation from religion* and (stick to) the few simple (moral) doctrines that Christ taught his people."[216]

Here Spinoza touches on the differences among the Gospels. The inconsistencies and differences among them cannot be ignored. They are, he says, the cause of centuries of strife and bloodshed. His solution? Stop using the Bible to find the truth about God and salvation. More negative comments on the Gospels will come in the next chapter.

With this, Spinoza completes the massive simplification and reduction necessary to his program of removing almost everything theologically authoritative from the New Testament and thus from the Christian religion, leaving a simple pious moralism for the masses to cling to. Spinoza was among the first to posit the essential difference between Jesus and Paul that, more than three hundred years later, can still be seen in modern investigation of early Christianity.

Part Three: Separation of Theology from Philosophy (Chapters 12–15)

Chapter 12: The Bible Is Not the Word of God

The next three chapters round out what Spinoza has to say about the Bible, in preparation for his final section, where he considers the place of religion in a democratic state. The beginning of Chapter 12 is uncharacter-istically defensive; Spinoza may be feeling a bit guilty at the mayhem he has wrought, so he challenges his opponents directly:

> Those who look upon the Bible in its present form as a message for mankind sent down by God from heaven will doubtless cry out that I have committed a sin against the Holy Ghost in maintaining that the Word of God is faulty, mutilated, adulterated and inconsistent, that we possess it only in fragmentary form, and that the original of God's cove-nant with the Jews has perished.[217]

That's quite a list. Spinoza does not mince his words. It is not in his interest to mince words. If he is going to destroy confidence in the Bible's general credibility, he has got to paint it in the worst colors possible because he is about to return to what he claimed earlier, that the Bible cannot be the "Word of God." The "Word of God" is what God has written in our hearts and minds.

On the contrary, the whole Bible teaches that *it* is not the Word of God itself. God has placed his Word in our hearts, "that is, in our minds," and sealed it with his own seal, which means that we have "the idea of himself, the image of his own divinity, as it were," in our minds.[218]

Those who are firmly convinced that, even though God may reveal himself to us directly through the Holy Spirit, "Scripture is nevertheless the Word of God and it is not ... permitted to say that it is mutilated, contaminated (and truncated)."[219]

> In reply to this, I have to say that such objectors are carrying their piety too far, and are turning religion into superstition; indeed, instead of God's Word they are beginning to worship likenesses and images, that is, paper and ink.[220]

A constant theme in Spinoza's critique of both Jewish and Christian traditionalists is that they have for too long devoted a reverence toward humans, rituals, institutions, and, here, the Bible, which they should have been giving only to the Uncreated and Eternal God. In this way, Spinoza repeatedly comes back to the ancient taboo against idolatry. His religious opponents are all deeply immersed in fostering and propagating idolatry. One might call this Spinoza's "de-deification of the Bible."[221]

He can do this because for him the Bible has no divine attributes. Indeed, it has no relevance at all. This chapter will summarize all Spinoza has said to prove this point.

In what follows, Spinoza presents four reasons why the Bible cannot be the "Word of God." Each directly challenges the traditional claims defended at great length by Origen, Eusebius, and Augustine.

1. Inspiration. The biblical writers, including the Apostles, were not inspired when they wrote. Whatever they produced was for particular situations (this is the nominalist reduction) and is largely irrelevant to any others.

2. Canon. The councils that canonized the books were not inspired and therefore no one can be certain that the Bible is anything more than a chance collection. Henceforth, the biblical canon may be disregarded in historical study of the Bible.

3. Text. The manuscripts of the Bible are full of inaccuracies and cannot certainly be known to contain what the original authors wrote. Henceforth, great caution must be exercised in the historical investigation of the biblical texts.

4. Composition. As for the Gospels, their great differences prove that they were independently written for particular audiences at different times (the nominalist reduction), with no attempt at mutual coordination. They can be reconciled by scholars, but only because of chance similarities.

General conclusion. Ergo, the Bible is not the "Word of God." Ultimate truth about God is knowable outside the Bible. Morality is the essence of religion.

Let us now see how Spinoza sets forth his arguments.

The Bible cannot be the Word of God for a number of reasons. First of all, the books of both testaments

> were not written at one time for all ages. They were the fortuitous work of certain men who wrote according to the requirements of the age and of their own particular character.[222]

This also applies to the prophets. I said in Chapters 1 and 2 that the mind of the prophets is not at all the same thing as the mind of God.[223]

Moreover, the books of the Bible were collected by councils of men who were not themselves prophets; hence the collection has no prophetic authority as a collection.[224]

Again, I said in Chapter 11 that the Apostles wrote as teachers, not prophets. Hence their writings "contain many things that are no longer relevant to religion."[225] In this respect, the authors of the Gospels did not write as prophets, nor were they inspired to write for all time. Instead, they wrote whatever they felt necessary for specific audiences, with no attention to what the others had written.[226]

Who can believe that God willed to tell the story of Christ and impart it in writing to mankind four times over? ... If a comparison of their different versions sometimes produces a clearer understanding, this is a matter of chance.[227]

This chapter is the only place Spinoza says anything about how he thinks the Gospels were produced. His skeptical assessment is clear: they were mere human writings, produced for various particular audiences. It seems ludicrous in the extreme to him that God would want four of these "stories of Christ"—especially inconsistent and conflicting stories. Aware that there are numerous Gospel harmonies intended to cover up this problem, Spinoza strikes at the root of the argument first uttered by Augustine,[228] that God's Divine Providence had led to the creation of four accounts so that they would illuminate each other.

Each Gospel author preached his message in a different place and each wrote down what he had preached with a view to telling clearly the story of Christ, not with a view to explaining the other Evangelists.[229]

A critical statement. With it, Spinoza splits the Gospels apart and alleges differing historical situations for each. Thus, at one stroke, he dismisses Augustine's traditional starting point, that all four had in fact been written by the one, divine hand of Jesus Christ, so that there could be no real inconsistency, nor any falsehood. Instead, Spinoza creates a scenario of confusion, ambiguity, and petty human difference as the reason for four different Gospels. He is not finished.

Finally, one should not forget that the manuscript copies of the biblical writings are full of inaccuracies and can in no wise be certainly known to resemble what the authors originally wrote. For all these reasons then, it is utterly futile to think of the Bible as being itself the eternal Word of God.

Not only were the Gospels composed in four different historical contexts, but there is no certainty that the texts of them in use today are exactly what the original authors wrote.

Note how Spinoza has by now dealt with each of the constitutive aspects of the Synoptic Problem—canon, text, hermeneutics, and composition—in radically nontraditional ways. He thus lays the groundwork and identifies the basic elements of a new conception of the Synoptic Problem, departing profoundly from the two previous conceptions of it. Present here only in nuce, it will take about one hundred years for his ideas to develop

and be further refined—especially in the seminal research of Johann Gries-
bach in Germany—until, by the beginning of the nineteenth century,
Enlightenment-inspired historicism brings forth a fully articulated Third
Form of the Synoptic Problem.

    Spinoza is now ready to offer, in place of the theological confusion
evident in the Bible, a simple moralism knowable to human reason as the
essence of all religion.

But this does not mean that we are without all knowledge of the
divine law. The "universal divine law" has come down to us outside the
Bible uncorrupted. It is simply this: "to love God and one's neighbor as
oneself."[230] Or, to be more explicit, we know from all of the writings of
Scripture these basic doctrines:

> that (God) exists, that He provides for all things, that He is omnipotent,
> that by His decrees the good prosper and the wicked are cast down, and
> that our salvation depends solely on His grace.[231]

In addition to these we also know from the entire Scripture the following
moral principles: "to uphold justice, to help the helpless, to do no murder,
to covet no man's goods, and so on."[232] Nothing has corrupted these teachings or caused them to become lost. Especially "the doctrine of charity
which is everywhere commended in the highest degree in both testaments" is a sure guideline to hold onto.[233]

    We may therefore be absolutely certain that the essential aspects of
religion, both doctrine and morals, have come down to us uncorrupted
in Scripture, as well as outside Scripture through our natural knowledge
of God.[234]

    We are nearing the conclusion of Spinoza's demolition derby. He has
pretty well destroyed the religious usefulness of the Bible while pretending
that "the whole Bible" teaches the above-mentioned basic moral principles.
Lest there be some seriously dull-witted readers in his audience, he proceeds
to repeat the whole message once more in the next chapter. Only now he
begins to flavor his arguments with democratic idealism, saying that anyone
can see what he is talking about, not just the experts.

Chapter 13: *What Scripture Teaches Is Basically Very Simple*

It is inconceivable that the Bible should attempt to teach anything
complicated theologically because it is meant for all to read and under-

stand, not just the few trained intellectuals.[235] Its miracles and histories are not intended to teach advanced philosophical doctrines but to impress the ignorant and simple minds of the masses to the point of adoration and willingness to be obedient to God.[236]

> Scripture demands nothing from men but obedience and condemns not ignorance but only obstinacy. Furthermore, since obedience to God consists solely in loving one's neighbor . . . it follows that Scripture commands no other kind of knowledge than that which is necessary for all men before they can obey God according to this commandment.[237]

Having spent several chapters pointing out all of the problems in obtaining certain and distinct conclusions from Scripture, Spinoza now rounds out his position by insisting that, as far as a religion suited to the masses is concerned, the Bible is clear enough: love God and love your neighbor as yourself. This is the conclusion of Spinoza's campaign to provide the ignorant masses with a suitable "purified" substitute universal religion which will never become the seedbed of intolerance or hatred.

This knowledge has already been repeated several times—that God exists, that he is omnipotent, etc. Beyond these simple doctrines,

> other philosophic questions . . . have nothing to do with Scripture and should therefore be dissociated from revealed religion.[238]

Philosophic questions should be left to philosophy. "The intellectual or exact knowledge of God is not a gift shared by all the faithful,"[239] so the masses need a substitute. They can get this from the general message of the Bible which emphasizes God's "justice and charity, that is, such attributes of God as men find possible to imitate by a definite rule of conduct."[240]

Here is the veiled reference to Spinoza's concept of popular religion that is an imitation of the life entirely according to natural reason, without any support from the Bible or historic religion whatsoever. As defined here, this popular universal moralism in the name of religion will be completely safe to have in a democratic society. As we will see in the next chapter, Spinoza wants to leave all other theological matters up to the private opinion of the individual and out of the purview of organized religion.

Chapter 14: Complete Separation of Faith from Philosophy

Taking our cue from the extraordinary variety within Scripture, which is composed of books written by different individuals over an enormously long period of time, "two thousand years and perhaps longer,"[241] it is obvious that not all of it can be considered divine revelation. Moreover, since so much of the Old Testament was "adapted to the intellectual level . . . of the fickle and unstable Jewish multitude,"[242] it has been disastrous to try to make what was given to them as binding on all people for all time. On the contrary, the basics of universal faith are clear enough. "The chief aim of Scripture in its entirety. . . is simply to teach obedience."[243] This applies also to the message of Jesus.

> The message of the Gospel is one of simple faith; that is, belief in God and reverence for God, or—which is the same thing—obedience to God.[244]

Since Scripture is designed to be read and obeyed by "all men of every time and race," this means that we have to pay attention only to that which is meant to be universal.

> Therefore this (love) commandment is the one and only guiding principle for the entire common faith of mankind, and through this commandment alone should be determined all the tenets of faith that every man is in duty bound to accept.[245]

If that be understood, then it follows that everything else, all other theological questions, advanced speculations, and so forth, are completely independent of the common faith and religion of the masses and can be interpreted by individuals in any way they wish without anyone attacking them for doing so. We must never again try anyone before a court of law for having unorthodox beliefs or dissenting opinions. Just as the judges themselves formed their own opinions freely,

> my accusation against them is that they refuse to grant this freedom to others. (Instead) they persecute as God's enemies all those who do not share their particular opinions, however righteous and virtuous the dissenters may be . . . Surely, nothing more damnable than this and more fraught with danger to the state, can be devised.[246]

This violent outburst could well be a hint of Spinoza's reaction to the torture of Adrian Koerbagh. It could also be a general reaction to all reli-

gious persecution of anyone; the preceding centuries were full of equally hideous examples.

With the universal religion thus clearly prescribed, it should be clear that there is no relation between the intellectual knowledge of God (philosophy) and faith.

Philosophy rests on the basis of universally valid axioms and must be constructed by studying Nature alone, whereas faith is based on history and language and must be derived only from Scripture and revelation.[247]

The aim of philosophy is truth; the aim of religion is obedience. Each occupies its own sphere and should remain there. The person of faith may philosophize to her or his heart's content with no prohibitions or penalties. But the new "heretic" will be the person who accuses and attacks others for believing differently than he does. Likewise, the new "orthodox" persons will be those who "promote justice and charity to the best of their intellectual powers and capacity."[248]

Chapter 15: *Theology Not to Be Confused with Philosophy*

Just as faith and reason have their separate domains, so also religion and philosophy have theirs. They do not overlap, nor do they contradict one another. Philosophy is for the scientific-minded few; religion is for the masses. As we have said, religion is based on a few essential doctrines as taught throughout the Bible and consists primarily of obedience to the joint command to love God and neighbor. Philosophy focuses on nature or God and seeks to grasp clear, true, and distinct conceptions of God through learning about natural phenomena. Finally, it is not for religion to ascertain the truth of its doctrines; that is the task of philosophy.[249]

With this, Spinoza slips in one final safeguard against religious tyranny. Religion cannot be responsible for the truth of its own doctrines. That is the task of philosophy, since religion is not the domain of ultimate Truth, but of obedience to God. What Spinoza is doing is to prepare for the final part of his Treatise. *There he will argue that religion should be under the absolute control of the state, even down to the hiring and firing of pastors and the admission and excommunication of church members.*

By this point, Spinoza has reached the end of his discussion of the Bible. The last two chapters have been spent laboriously defining and separating faith from reason, religion from philosophy, Scripture from nature, revelation from the natural light. Now that they are thus totally separated and nonoverlapping, Spinoza will go on to argue (in the last four chapters) that the entire domain of popular religion/faith should be under the control of the state as guided by reason/philosophy.

Part Four: Religion in a Democratic State (Chapter 16–20)

Chapter 16: What Is the Best Form of State and Citizens' Rights?

At this point, Spinoza reaches the rhetorical climax of his entire Trea-tise. All that remains is to describe the ideal state and the way religion, now thoroughly "purified" of its most dangerous elements, should fit into it. In other words, now that Spinoza has (a) thoroughly destroyed the Bible's su-pernatural infrastructure and set up a method that will henceforth make it impossible to use the Bible for any theological enterprise, Christian or Jew-ish, and (b) altered the conventional notion of religion so that it consists primarily of obedience to a few simple moral truths, he is ready to take the final step and explain how all of this should become institutionalized. What is the best form of state, what are the ideal citizens' right within it, and how does popular religion fit into all this? The beginning of Chapter 16 says:

> Up to this point our object has been to separate philosophy from theol-ogy and to show that the latter allows freedom to philosophize for every individual. It is therefore time to enquire what are the limits of this free-dom of thought, and of saying what one thinks, in a well-conducted state.[250]

First, we must understand what forces compel humans to associ-ate together in states at all. Why don't they simply remain in a state of nature?

In the state of nature, there are no laws and no institutions. Each person has the "right" to do whatever his or her power and capacity en-ables him or her to do. In this state, there is no right or wrong, good or bad, sin or evil. There is only power and the rights conferred by the pos-session of power.[251] Whatever is to one's advantage one does.

Since all humans act according to their own advantage, there are two overriding advantages that cause humans to come together in societies or cities: safety from attacks by others and the desire to secure a good life.[252] But when people do come together, they give up their natural freedom and transfer it to the state, which now acts on behalf of all. In coming together, the citizens agree to be guided in all matters only by the dictates of reason ... and to keep appetites in check in so far as it tends to another's hurt, to do to no one what they would not want done to themselves,[253] and to uphold another's rights as they would their own.[254]

This little list is a bit peculiar, not resembling what Hobbes said in his description of the origins of civil society, which Spinoza has just repeated. The reason for this bit of improvisation is that Spinoza is headed in a very non-Hobbesian direction—toward democracy as the ideal society.

The name of that state which comprises citizens who have all passed their natural freedom in to the central government, and who therefore share equally in its power, actions, rights, and obligations, is *democracy*. As it is not our intention to describe all forms of government but only that one which is in our judgment the best, we will not go further than this.

The state is sovereign over each citizen in all things,[255] and the general obligation of each citizen is to act in accordance with the laws of the state. But one of the chief features of a democracy is that each citizen has the liberty to think and speak freely. How can this be accomplished without upsetting the common peace or infringing on the authority of the state?

Chapter 17: Ways States Have Sought to Control Citizens in the Past

Now that the *theory* of democratic states and the rights of citizens has been discussed, what are the realities? Is it in fact possible to have a peaceful, stable state with freedom of speech and thought and still ensure the full authority of the state?

In reality, no one can or will transfer all allegiance to the state. There are countless opportunities for citizens to evade the state's power and authority. And in view of everyone's natural tendency to prefer the untrammeled freedom of the state of nature, there is always a certain level of resentment and hostility toward the central authorities, no matter how well they rule.

Spinoza is about to weave in a bit of Carneades and the ancient Sophists' explanation for the origins of religion—as an underhanded means tyrants used on gullible citizens to keep their passions in check.

In view of this inveterate tendency of citizens to disregard the laws and seek their own advantage, how have states tried to coerce obedience?

Since what tyrants want are subjects who wholeheartedly do their will, they will use any means available to rule over their minds and hearts.

> It was for this reason that kings who in ancient times seized power, tried to persuade men that they were descended from the immortal gods, thinking that if only their subjects and all men should regard them not as their equals but should believe them to be gods, they would willingly suffer their rule and would readily submit.[256]

Many examples come to mind: Augustus and Alexander are two of the more famous. In recent times, kings and monarchs have succeeded in "convincing men that royalty is sacred and (that they are) God's regents on earth and their government is established by God, not by the votes and consent of men."[257]

> *This must have been intended as a jab at all those Dutch clergy and common people who supported the House of Orange with the traditional arguments about the "divine right of kings." Spinoza gives this one his best shot. Wary that an argument could be brought from the Old Testament theocracy, he demolishes its relevance (again).*

But all claims like these are bogus, being covert extortions of people's trust.[258] Equally despicable is it for religious functionaries to have political power and make political decisions on the basis of their religious beliefs. In this regard, the ancient Hebrew theocracy was entirely different. There Moses did indeed act as God's appointed overseer, but this was entirely with the consent of the people, nor did he do it for any personal aggrandizement. Moreover, it came to an end when the monarchy was established, and the reasons for its collapse are most instructive.[259]

Chapter 18: Lessons to Be Learned from the Hebrew Theocracy

The Hebrew nation *prior* to the establishment of the monarchy was a period noted for its peace and stability. *This disappeared as soon as kings arose,* and, after they were overthrown, the nation was ruled (or, rather, misruled) by priests. From the sorry example of the collapse of the Hebrew theocracy we may take the following lessons: First, never permit religious functionaries to exercise any of the affairs of state. Before long they want to be called kings and attract to themselves outrageous powers and privileges.[260]

Second, governments should never intervene in a theological dispute or attempt to legislate in philosophical matters.[261] The Pharisees incited Pilate to do their dirty work for them when he crucified Christ. Since then, the Pharisees,[262]

> these vile hypocrites, urged on by that same fury which they call zeal for God's law, have everywhere persecuted men whose blameless character and distinguished qualities have excited the hostility of the masses, publicly denouncing their beliefs and inflaming the savage crowd's anger against them. This shameless license, sheltering under the name of religion, is not easy to suppress.[263]

This passage is so furious that I surmise we are in the presence of Spinoza's rage at his excommunication by the Amsterdam Jewish elders, as well as that of several others, such as Acosta, Juan de Prado, and Daniel Ribera.[264]

How avoid such entanglements? There is only one way, and it has been repeatedly stressed throughout this *Treatise*.

> To avoid these evils, the safest course for the commonwealth is to define piety and religious observance as consisting only in works, that is simply in the exercise of charity and just dealing and to allow free thinking in all other matters. But more of that later.[265]

Here Spinoza tips his hand so that the broader strategy he is pursuing is for a fleeting second completely transparent. Give the masses nothing more than the love commandment for their religion and forbid (by state law) any conflict over doctrine. Thus emasculated, popular religion will be little more than the Golden Rule, which, admittedly, would be a safe religion for any state if the masses could ever be persuaded to adopt it and stick to it.

Third, the state must have absolute authority over everything that takes place within its boundaries, including religion. There cannot be any talk of "obeying God, not man" or "We are loyal to the Pope first, Holland second." What people say is one thing, but in their actions, they must obey the laws of the state.[266]

Finally, once a people has tasted liberty, as the ancient Hebrews did, it is exceedingly dangerous to try to establish a monarchy.

Here is another slap at those who wanted to reestablish the House of Orange as the legal monarch of the Dutch states.

Chapter 19: Behavior, Not Doctrine, Is under the State's Control

Having pointed out the fraud of turning kings into gods and having shown the disastrous results of letting priests or ministers run government affairs, it is now time to say that the only safe course is for religion to have nothing to do with running the state, but to place it under the complete control of the state.

This does not mean that people are not free to believe whatever they wish, or even nothing at all. Personal *belief* is up to each individual, as we noted in Chapter 7. But the "external forms of religion . . . must accord with the peace and preservation of the commonwealth."[267] Specifically, this means such things as the hiring and firing of ministers, the foundations of churches, the establishment of church doctrine (within broad guidelines), determining the standards of church membership, carrying out admission and excommunication of members, and providing for the poor. All these should be under the control of the state.[268]

Arranged in this manner, the state must be totally indifferent to the various sectarian beliefs and religious institutions operating within it, conducting all of its business according to the dictates of reason alone.[269] If the common religion of all citizens is one of mutual toleration, justice, and concern for the common good, then neither the civil religion nor the state government will conflict with the other. There will be general peace and concord.[270]

Here at the very end, Spinoza returns to another idea of Hobbes, namely, the so-called secular state that conducts all of its affairs with nothing higher to guide it than human reason. Religious concerns, sectarian strife, none of these are to have any role in secular government.

With this, Spinoza reaches the conclusion of the kind of society he calls for in the Preface to the Treatise.

This then is the main point which I have sought to establish in this treatise, (namely) to indicate the main false assumptions that prevail regarding religion . . . and then again the false assumptions regarding the right of civil authorities. There are many who, with an impudence quite shameless, seek to usurp much of this (civil) right and, under the guise of religion, to alienate from the government the loyalty of the masses.[271]

All that remains now is Spinoza's brilliant peroration and conclusion.

Chapter 20: Freedom of Speech in a Secular Democracy

In conclusion, now that the best form of state has been identified (democracy) and the rights of the citizens explained, and the state separated from and put in control of religion, it is time to conclude by explaining how citizens may speak and think freely without causing discord or infringing on the authority of the state.

Since it is obvious that a state which is not in complete control of all of its citizens cannot long endure, it must first of all be taken as a given that the citizens, no matter what they think or feel, must *act* in conformity with the laws. But this does not mean that they are not free to speak their minds, or express how they feel about the government or anything else.

> Moses had gained the strongest of holds on the minds of his people . . . yet even he was not exempt from their murmurings and criticisms.[272]

It is the fundamental purpose of a democracy

> not to restrain men by fear and deprive them of independence but on the contrary to free every man from fear so that he may live in security and so far as is possible . . . develop their mental and physical faculties in safety, to use their reason without restraint and to refrain from the strife and the vicious mutual abuse that are prompted by hatred, anger or deceit. Thus the purpose of the state is, in reality, freedom.[273]

Individual citizens can and should express their differing opinions on every imaginable subject without fear of reprisal, from either their fellow citizens or the government. And they can do so without infringing on the right of the government or violating the peace of the commonwealth if they do so "decently and in order."[274]

Just as "every man's loyalty to the state can be known only from his works—just as his devotion to God can be known only by his works, that is, his charity to his neighbor,"[275] it is obvious that the state will give each citizen the same freedom to think and speak that he enjoys in the common religion. Our own country has many sad examples when the opposite was attempted, with disastrous results.

> What greater misfortune can be imagined for a state than that honorable men should be exiled as miscreants because their opinions are at variance with authority and they cannot disguise the fact?[276]

This could be a direct reference to the exile of the famed jurist and biblical scholar Hugo Grotius (see p. 204).

> Therefore, if honesty is to be prized rather than obsequiousness, and if sovereigns are to retain full control and not be forced to surrender to agitators, it is imperative to grant freedom of judgment and to govern men in such a way that the different and conflicting views they openly proclaim do not debar them from living together in peace. This system of government is undoubtedly the best . . . because it is in closest accord with human nature.[277]

Since it is in harmony with human nature, such a state will go on to be the most stable that humans can devise. And it will enjoy the highest degree of prosperity as well. Consider the glorious example of the

> city of Amsterdam, which enjoys the fruits of this freedom, to its own considerable prosperity and the admiration of the world. In this flourishing state, a city of the highest renown, men of every race and sect live in complete harmony; and before entrusting their property to some (merchant), they will want to know no more than this, whether he is rich or poor and whether he has been honest or dishonest in his dealings. As for religion or sect, that is of no account, because such considerations are regarded as irrelevant in a court of law. And no sect whatsoever is so hated that its adherents—provided that they injure no one, render to each what is his own, and live upright lives—are denied the protection of the civil authorities.[278]

With this, we may conclude our *Theological-Political Treatise,* for we have shown how the religious and secular spheres should be defined and kept distinct, how the freedom of the individual to say what he thinks can take place without injury to others or infringement on the authority of the government, and, last but not least, how such freedom and mutual toleration will lead to a stable and prosperous state.[279]

The Reception of the Theological-Political Treatise

As noted in the introduction to this chapter, Spinoza began working on the *Treatise* in 1665, when Jan de Witt was riding high and yet the forces of monarchy and orthodoxy were also threatening. It was a time of crisis, and the son of Jewish immigrants, Baruch de Spinoza, felt called to do what he could to strengthen the cause of liberty and science in his new homeland. So he stopped work on his *Ethics* and began writing this treatise on biblical interpretation, intended to refute those who used the Bible to defend monarchy and religious oppression.

His *Treatise* took much longer to finish than he expected. If we take his youthful self-defense before the Jewish elders of Amsterdam into account, he labored longer and more assiduously over this writing than he did the *Ethics,* usually considered his magnum opus. From the perspective of the length of time devoted to it, it would not be unfair to call *this* writing his masterpiece, his most important writing, not the *Ethics.*[280]

When he finally gave it to his publisher, the political situation in the Netherlands had become ominous, for Spinoza personally as well as for the liberal coalition nationally. Spinoza took the precaution of having the *Treatise* published anonymously, with the title page listing Hamburg, rather than Amsterdam, as the city of origin.

No one was fooled. It soon became common knowledge who the author was.[281] Within months it was translated from his original Latin into Dutch, and all sorts of people were reading it whom he never meant to do so. The outcry rose to heaven.[282] Calls to suppress it came from several quarters; in 1671 the Calvinist Synod of North Holland passed a recommendation demanding an official ban.[283] These attempts were all foiled at the national level by Jan de Witt.[284]

The verbal abuse heaped on Spinoza can be gauged from the following example: "(This is a wicked instrument) forged in Hell by a renegade Jew and the Devil and issued with the knowledge of Mr. De Witt."[285]

The work also spread rapidly abroad. By the end of 1670, there had been four reprints in Germany and the Dutch provinces, with many others under false titles. The international reaction was equally abusive. In England, Spinoza was lumped together with Hobbes as a henchman of the devil and destroyer of revealed religion. In Germany, a pamphleteer wrote:

> the abominable doctrines and hideous errors which this shallow Jewish philosopher has—if I may say so—shit into the world.[286]

Attacks on the *Treatise* were published in Denmark and France (Bossuet). One of the most surprising negative responses came from the French skeptic Pierre Bayle, who called it "a pernicious and detestable book in which he (Spinoza) slips in all the seeds of atheism."[287]

The Dutch theologian and biographer Colerus summed up the general reaction:

> this wicked book does altogether overthrow the Christian religion by depriving the sacred writings of the authority on which it is solely grounded and established.[288]

The outrage provoked by the book had something to do with inflaming the attitude of the Dutch people against Jan de Witt, since he was clearly linked with its author. Thus, instead of helping to strengthen the forces of liberty and freedom in the Netherlands, Spinoza may have been one of the many reasons for de Witt's fall from power and subsequent lynching. After his collapse, religious orthodoxy and the House of Orange were stronger than ever.

Spinoza was utterly crushed by this turn of events. It is unquestionable that, if he had ever suspected the terrible consequences that would flow from writing his book, he would never have done it. At least, he would never have published it during his lifetime. He was carried away by naive optimism and an urgent impulse to help his champion de Witt. But as a foreigner who knew very little about his adopted country, Spinoza seriously miscalculated the depths to which his arguments would outrage Dutch conservatives, giving them a perfect excuse to link the forces of liberalism with the program of ungodly atheism.

As noted in the biographical sketch at the beginning of this chapter, Spinoza immediately withdrew into seclusion, rarely venturing out into public after the debacle of 1672. Whatever plans he had to publish the *Ethics* were dropped. It is usually said that he died of consumption not long after; I think it was a broken heart.

Conclusion

In the decades and centuries following the publication of the *Tractatus Theologico-Politicus,* the arguments so trenchantly defended and elaborated in its pages gradually came to be regarded with increasing respect, as the new middle class took up the banner of modern reform. Spinoza's ideas were especially influential in Germany, reappearing in the philosophy of Leibniz and the biblical hermeneutics of G. E. Lessing. Among biblical scholars, his pioneering "historical method" was taken up, elaborated, and developed, so that it is not too much to say that, today, "Spinozist" methods and goals are commonly followed by biblical scholars everywhere in the world, particularly in Euro–North America, Israel, and Japan. A modern French scholar, A. Lods, has written in his *History of Hebrew and Jewish Literature* (1950) that the *Tractatus Theologico-Politicus* outlined every major branch of subsequent modern biblical research, setting forth the

> program of biblical science almost precisely in the way it was conceived and realized in the 19th century. Spinoza defined the method, which

must be philological, historical and critical. He distinguished the different branches: history of the language, history of the text, history of the canon, history of the formation of each book, study of the ideas of the different authors. Passing in review the principal points of this grand program, Spinoza, with a marvelous intuition, divined a major part of the conclusions from which science must not deviate if it is to remain secular activity.[289]

Ernst Cassirer, the eminent historian of the Enlightenment, stated:

> Spinoza was the first who dared to raise the really incisive question (regarding biblical history). His *Tractatus theologico-politicus* is the first attempt at a philosophical justification and foundation of biblical criticism.[290]

A prominent German theologian and New Testament scholar, Peter Stuhlmacher of the Protestant Faculty in Tübingen, echoed the same view:

> Spinoza's *Theological-Political Treatise* reveals most clearly the new points of departure as well as the major results of the then-developing critical investigation of the Bible.[291]

What such estimates fail to mention, and what has been generally overlooked in most histories of modern biblical scholarship, is the *destructive intent* of Spinoza's biblical hermeneutics. He was not interested in helping the Bible present its own point of view. He wanted to defend the forces of democracy and modern science in Holland, just when the powerful coalition representing monarchy and traditional religion was about to regain control. To this end, he consciously created a method of biblical interpretation that would *disembowel the Bible,* rendering it useless as a weapon in the arsenal of traditional monarchist politics and state religion.

Schweitzer saw it clearly, as I pointed out at the beginning of this chapter. The only other person to see clearly what was happening was, ironically enough, no friend of Christianity: Friedrich Nietzsche. In the mid-1870s, two hundred years after Spinoza had concocted his subtle poison and it was being eagerly drunk in great doses all over Europe, Nietzsche let out this derisive laugh: "Recent theology," he wrote in 1874—just when the best German theological faculties were insisting on scientific, historical knowledge—

> seems to have entered quite innocently into partnership with *history* and scarcely sees even now that it has unwittingly bound itself to the Voltair-

ian "*écrasez!*" . . . (The result is that) Christianity has become denaturalized by this historical treatment . . . until it has been resolved into pure knowledge and destroyed in the process![292]

It was within the crucible of Spinoza's hatred of religious tyranny and longing for a better way that the central elements of the Third Form of the Synoptic Problem were forged. But before we go on with the story of its rise from inchoate, bitterly contested rumblings to a final victory, we must consider one other significant contributor to the story: the noted English statesman and philosopher John Locke. He will explain the *economic rationale* of the new historical method.

CHAPTER 17

John Locke and the Economic Agenda of Modern Historical-Critical Interpretation

John Locke was born at Wrington, Somersetshire, near Bristol, on 29 August 1632, the same year as Baruch D'Espiñosa. He was the oldest son of John Locke, clerk to the local justices of the peace in Somerset. Both parents came from the newly affluent class of Puritan traders, his mother's father being a tanner (in this case a member of the smaller gentry), his father's father a well to do owner of a thriving clothing and piece-goods business.[1] There were relatives living in the area, owners of numerous farms and businesses.

It was not a peaceful time. The great Civil War between Puritans and royalists was only ten years away and the forces which would inevitably bring it about were gaining in intensity. As Locke wrote later, "I no sooner perceived myself in the world but I found myself in a storm which has lasted almost hitherto."[2]

One of the justices, Alexander Popham, was particularly friendly to John Locke's father. Popham's father was an eminent justice and his grandfather, Sir John Popham, had been chief justice of the King's bench when Guy Fawkes was tried.[3] Alexander Popham was a member of Parliament when in 1641 it issued the Grand Remonstrance against Charles I, challenging his right to rule.[4] Thus, almost on John Locke's tenth birthday, the Civil War erupted. Popham was made a colonel in the Parliamentary Army, and he made John Locke's father a captain. They saw some action locally and Popham's house was burned to the ground. By 1647, the war was almost won and Popham moved into his father's residence in nearby

Wiltshire. This was close enough to enable him to retain John Locke's father's services as his personal attorney, and he repaid his friend with a small favor that was to have fateful consequences for his son. As a member of Parliament, Popham was entitled to nominate young lads to the preparatory Westminster School adjacent to Westminster Abbey. He nominated John Locke Jr., and in the fall of 1647 young John was admitted to that school and began his long academic career.[5]

At that time, Westminster School was under the headmastership of the royalist Richard Busby. Locke took to Busby's rigorous academic discipline well and eventually distinguished himself sufficiently to receive election to Busby's own college, Christ Church, Oxford.

When Locke moved to Oxford in November 1652 at age twenty, England was again on the verge of civil war. Charles II had fled to France, and England was under the complete control of the Puritans. Among other changes, the Puritan Parliament at first considered abolishing all of England's universities, but instead it purged them, causing more than two-thirds of Oxford's heads, fellows, chaplains, tutors, and undergraduates to quit the university.[6] New men took their places: John Owen, Cromwell's personal chaplain, became dean; other positions were filled with Cromwell's friends and relatives. In this way, Locke found himself in a school having a split personality: staunch Puritans on the one side and a few old-line royalists on the other. The resulting theological turbulence made him sympathetic toward the Latitudinarian Anglicans at Oxford, who held that only a few essentials necessary for salvation were taught in the Bible, everything else (particularly Church government) being categorized as "indifferent" (*adiaphora*), that is, open to each individual's conscience to decide. In particular, he began to study the recently imported "medical philosophy" as taught by Cromwell's brother-in-law John Wilkins, the new warden of Wadham College.

The medical curriculum at Oxford in those days still held to the medieval approach: the study of books by Aristotle and Galen, the aphorisms of Hippocrates, with some herbal lore thrown in.[7] Wilkins, eagerly aided by a few other members of the faculty, resorted instead to direct experimentation. He held a weekly "experimental philosophy club" which was, in time, to become the Royal Society. Members of this club did the unheard-of thing, obtaining actual corpses to cut open so as to observe the circulatory system and internal organs directly. Because of these fascinating studies, Locke chose the new empirical study of medicine as his life's vocation.

Upon completion of his undergraduate degree, on 28 June 1658, Locke qualified as a master of arts and was elected a senior student at Christ Church.[8] However, the political situation in England was steadily growing more chaotic. That September, Oliver Cromwell died and the days of the Cromwellian Protectorate were numbered. On 29 May 1660, Charles II returned to London amidst general rejoicing. Locke himself welcomed the King's return. He wrote to a friend:

> All the freedom I can wish my country or myself is to enjoy the protection of those laws which the prudence and providence of our ancestors established and the happy return of his Majesty has restored.[9]

There is little in Locke's writings from these early years to foreshadow the antiroyalist, political liberal that he was to become.

Shortly after the Restoration, Locke was elected lecturer in Greek at Christ Church. He had just begun his duties when his father became very ill and died a few months later, leaving his eldest son some land and a few cottages from which he received a modest income for the rest of his life.[10]

During this period, Locke continued to attend the weekly meetings of the Experimental Philosophy Club and improving his knowledge of medicine. However, a new star had arrived in their midst: Robert Boyle. From his residence on High Street, Boyle was to exercise great influence over English and European scientists through his inventions as well as his writings. It was primarily from Boyle that Locke absorbed the physical, mechanistic view of nature then fashionable in science.

About the time Locke's post as lecturer ended, his younger brother died, leaving him alone in the family. Temporarily abandoning his academic pursuits, he obtained a minor diplomatic post and spent two years abroad as the secretary to the diplomatic mission of Sir Walter Vane to Brandenburg.[11] Upon return, he was offered a similar post to Spain and another to Sweden; he refused both. Returning instead to Oxford in 1667, he began to collaborate with Thomas Sydenham, a famous English physician.[12] Also at this time, he met Anthony Ashley Cooper, Earl of Shaftesbury and later Lord High Chancellor of England. Lord Ashley was in Oxford to visit his son and came down with a minor illness. Locke treated it successfully and the two became good friends.[13]

Continuing his studies in medicine, at some point in the winter of 1666–1667 he began to read Descartes with great excitement and interest.[14] Then a major event occurred. In the spring of 1667, Lord Ashley invited Locke to join him in London as his personal physician. Locke accepted immediately; the new Royal Society had just been formed in London, Boyle was preparing to move there, and Sydenham had already gone.[15]

Locke was with the Shaftesbury household less than a year when Lord Ashley became deathly ill from an infected cyst on his liver. Locke bravely decided to have a surgeon cut open Ashley's abdomen whence he drained off a copious amount of pus. Before closing him up, Locke installed a silver tube to permit future seepage, and it stayed there the rest of Ashley's life. The patient recovered and Locke was hailed as a medical genius.

Under Ashley's tutelage and encouragement, Locke began to flower as a statesman and scientist. Above all, it was from Ashley that Locke began to appreciate the enormous commercial benefits to be gained from religious tolerance. Locke's biographer Maurice Cranston observes:

> Ashley's "specialty" was trade. Though a considerable landowner, he was chiefly interested in stock-holding and colonial expansion; he was the part-owner of slave-ships and "plantations," he was the leading member of the Committee for Trade, and when the province of Carolina was founded in America in 1663 and put under the control of a board of Lords Proprietors, Ashley seized most of the strings.
>
> Ashley's own zeal for religious toleration was but an aspect of his interest in trade. It was not simply a case of his desiring toleration of dissenters because of his own Presbyterian views, still less a case of having achieved a Christ-like forbearance beyond the range of the average sensual man. Ashley opposed religious persecution because religious persecution divided a nation, drove many of its most industrious citizens to emigrate, and generally impeded commercial development. He saw more clearly than most Englishmen of his time how colonial expansion and international trade could be made to bring enormous fortunes to investors like himself and at the same time increase the wealth and power of the country as a whole. The example of Holland had taught him how trade and toleration could flourish splendidly together.[16]

Locke became caught up in Ashley's practical-minded vision, and, when pressed to accept a minor post on the board of the lords proprietors of Carolina, Locke accepted. His assignment was to find ways to advertise the new province so as to attract settlers who would develop its rich resources. To this end, the board, assisted by Locke, drew up a constitution to govern the lives of the hoped-for settlers. This was Locke's first taste of international politics in the "real world."[17]

By now, John Locke was thirty-six years old and far from his humble birthplace in Wrington. He was circulating daily among men who possessed enormous political power and great wealth. It was clear he could get both if he played his cards right. Thus we find him moved, at this momentous juncture in his life, to set down on paper a few ideals to guide his conduct:

Thus, I think:—it is a man's proper business to seek happiness and avoid misery. Happiness consists in what delights and contents the mind, misery is what disturbs or torments it. I will therefore make it my business to seek satisfaction and delight and avoid uneasiness and disquiet.[18]

Epicurus would have found nothing to object to in what Locke had written so far. He went on:

Let me see then wherein consist the most lasting pleasures of this life:—

1st Health, without which no sensual pleasure can have any relish.

2nd Reputation, for that I find everybody is pleased with and the want of it is a constant torment.

3rd Knowledge, for the little knowledge I have, I found I would not sell at any rate, nor part with for any other pleasure.

4th Doing good. For I find the well-cooked meat I ate today does now no more delight me . . . but the good turn I did yesterday (or a year ago) . . . continues to please me as oft as I reflect on it.

5th The expectation of eternal and incomprehensible happiness in another world is that also which carries a constant pleasure with it.[19]

Locke ends by swearing that he will seek only "the most lasting pleasures" and resolutely avoid all *vicious* and *unlawful* pleasures, since "afterward I would certainly suffer."

Many adjectives have been used to characterize Locke's aspirations here set forth: materialistic, pagan, utilitarian—everything except Christian. We look in vain for any reference to the Bible or the Ten Commandments or the teachings of Christ.[20]

Note that the vague gesture in the direction of "doing good" is in no sense an expression of Locke's altruistic concern for others. Doing good brings *him* pleasure; therefore it is rational to do good. This hedonistic rationale was still quite novel at the time within the new commercial class to which Locke aspired. It still had not found a way to provide its new "capitalism" with a veneer of moral respectability. It did eventually find the perfect motto: "enlightened self-interest." And beyond all this, to anticipate eternal bliss when one is finished with one's pleasurable life? Who could acquire anything more?

Before long, however, such dreams went a-glimmering for the young Locke. King Charles II was busily forcing Puritans out of the government and the Church of England as fast as he could, causing widespread disaffection. Thousands of Puritans and Presbyterians went outside the Established Church into Dissent. The King also passed a number of measures favorable to the Roman Catholic Church, eventually participating in Mass upon his deathbed.

The great Whig families, led by Lord Ashley, were enraged by these measures and plotted revenge. During this period, Ashley urged Locke to go to France for "reasons of health." Rumor has it that he entrusted Locke with certain top-secret proposals for the French court. Whatever the reason, in November 1675, Locke and a friend set sail for Montpelier.[21]

During his travels in France, Locke kept a diary of his impressions (it reveals nothing about any political intrigue). Apart from a number of belittling observations regarding the Roman Catholic clerics he encountered, his journal entries are a mass of trivial facts. John Locke was a surprisingly uninterested and unperceptive traveler. "He had no gift for describing natural beauty, no sense of history, and his immediate response to splendid architecture was to measure the building,"[22] Cranston notes. In this, Locke was not unlike other Enlightenment scientists. The whole new ethos of mechanistic logic and physical science which they believed in

> wanted to get away from the imagination, away from the vague glamour of medieval things, from reverence for tradition, from mysticism, enthusiasm and *gloire;* away from all private visionary insights and down to the plain, measurable, publicly verifiable facts. This desire was central to Locke's whole mission as a philosopher and reformer.[23]

He returned from his tour of France about fifteen months later, in the spring of 1677. Whatever the purposes for his trip, Lord Ashley continued to scheme against the King until he was arrested and imprisoned in the Tower of London. Released some months later, Ashley and others decided the time had come to act. A plot was formed to overthrow the King, but it backfired and Ashley fled to Holland. There, on 21 January 1683, he suddenly fell ill and died.[24] The King's agents began rounding up Lord Ashley's accomplices and, although there is no evidence that Locke was involved in anything, he knew he was under constant surveillance. In September 1683 he also left for Holland.

Locke arrived in Amsterdam in 1684, where he made contact with a number of Dutch physicians and freethinkers, especially Jean Le Clerc and Philip Limborch, members of the faculty of the Arminian (Remonstrant) seminary in Amsterdam. When it was learned that English envoys were in Amsterdam demanding Locke's extradition, Limborch immediately arranged for him to secretly move into the home of the dean of the medical college, Egbert Veen, where he remained in total isolation for almost two years. His only visitor was Limborch, and the many long talks between the two of them about the ravages of religious intolerance in Holland as well as England were undoubtedly the cause of Locke's writing his first tract, the *Epistola de Tolerantia,* during this period. France's Louis XIV had just revoked the Edict of Nantes, causing tens of thousands of French Protestants to flee the country at great loss to France and to themselves.[25] There was ample reason for Locke to write something on a topic that he had studied for years.[26] The *Epistola* was published anonymously in Latin in Holland several years later (1689).

Eventually, the King's agents left and Locke was able to travel about more freely. He fell in love with Amsterdam—prosperous, independent, thrifty, and—clean. Locke—the future prophet of liberty, equality, and tolerance—felt right at home.[27] In 1687 a prominent English Quaker merchant named Benjamin Furly living in Rotterdam invited Locke to be his paying guest. Locke accepted the invitation and stayed with Furly until 1689. He started a philosophical club named the Lantern, to which many leading freethinkers came, including a number of Collegiants and Spinozists. It was during this time that Locke completed his *Essay on Human Understanding.* He also stayed in contact with his friend in Amsterdam Jean Le Clerc, who was favorably disposed toward Spinoza's historical method of biblical criticism and advocacy of freedom of thought.[28] But Limborch—who had met Spinoza in the year before his death—remained adamantly opposed to Spinoza's thinking, always referring to him as an "atheist" and denouncing his "impious" works at every opportunity.[29] I suspect that Limborch's opposition was not so much because Spinoza had insisted on reason over theology, but because his *Tractatus Theologico-Politicus* had caused such an uproar in Amsterdam and elsewhere that it contributed to the fall of the Dutch champion of liberalism, toleration, and science Jan de Witt.[30] Locke may well have learned the whole story from Limborch and others and taken due note of *what not to do.* In any case, as we will see, Locke's method of dealing with the Bible and the Gospels in *The Reasonableness of Christianity* is poles apart from Spinoza.[31]

In February 1689, Locke returned to England after nearly six years' exile, on the same ship that brought the Princess Mary to England. William II of Orange and the great Whig families had negotiated the throne away from James II three months earlier and Locke's long career of opposition to James was now to be rewarded. As a loyal subject of William and Mary, Locke was offered a number of important diplomatic posts, but his health had suffered in Holland, so he had to turn them down, accepting instead a powerful position at the Board of Trade. His *Epistle on Toleration,* the *Essay concerning Human Understanding,* and the *Two Treatises on Civil Government* were all published shortly after his return, prompting a number of attacks on him.[32] Locke had been graciously invited to reside with Sir Francis and Lady Masham in Essex, and there he wrote several defenses of his work.

In the controversies that ensued, Locke was made aware of a number of flaws in his reasoning, and, toward the end of his life, he wrote a final book, the very important *Reasonableness of Christianity,* to rectify the impression that he meant to destroy both religion and ethics by his utilitarian and materialistic philosophy.[33]

Retiring from all activities in 1700, he maintained his connections with the outside world with a constant flow of visitors until he died in 1704.

With this brief biographical sketch as background, let us examine two of Locke's writings to see what he thought of the Bible in general and the Gospels in particular. We shall see that, as was the case with Baruch Spinoza, Locke's proposals regarding the correct way to interpret the Gospels were part of a larger political and economic agenda. To make this clear, we must start with his description of the state or national government and its relation to religious groups called churches.

The Proper Relation between Churches and State Government

I will not examine the *Epistle on Toleration* in the same kind of detail that I used with Spinoza's *Treatise,* instead Locke's views will be arranged under a number of topics.[34] Let us begin with his famous definition of the state or commonwealth.

> The commonwealth seems to me to be a society of men constituted only for the procuring, preserving, and advancing of their own civil interest (*bona civilia*). Civil interests I call life, liberty, health, and freedom from pain (*indolentia*) and the possession of outward things, such as money, lands, houses, furniture, and the like. It is the duty of the civil magistrate, by the impartial execution of equal laws, to secure unto all the people in general, and to everyone in particular, the just possession of these things belonging to this life.[35]

This definition was later given extended treatment in his *Two Treatises on Civil Government* (1689). Parallel with this definition of the state, Locke explains the nature and place of organized religion as follows:

> Let us now consider what a church is. A church, then, I take to be a voluntary society (*societas libera*) of men, joining themselves together of

their own accord in order to the public worshipping of God in such a manner as they judge acceptable to Him, and effectual to the salvation of their souls.[36]

And what is the chief end or purpose of a church?

> The end (or goal) of a religious society (*societas religiosa*) . . . is the public worship of God and, by means thereof, the acquisition of eternal life (*vitae aeternae acquisitio*).[37] All discipline ought therefore to tend to that end, and all ecclesiastical laws to be thereunto confined.[38]

In other words, just as the commonwealth is a voluntary association of men (sic) whose only aim is the acquisition of physical goods (*bonae*), namely, money, property, and land, a church is a voluntary association of the same men whose only goal is the aquisition of a spiritual good, namely, eternal life. And for these two voluntary societies to function properly, they must be kept completely separated from each other.

> (Just as the civil magistrate's authority is strictly defined, so also) ecclesiastical authority ought to be confined within the bounds of the church, nor can it in any manner be extended to civil affairs, because the church itself is a thing *absolutely separate and distinct from the commonwealth and civil affairs.*[39] The boundaries on both sides are fixed and immovable. He jumbles heaven and earth together, the things most remote and opposite, who mixes these two societies, which are in their origin, end, business (*materia*), and in everything perfectly distinct and infinitely different (*toto caelo diversas*) from each other.[40]

The civil magistrate (elected politician) must avoid meddling in the internal affairs of the churches.

> The magistrate has no power to impose by his laws the use of any rites and ceremonies in any church, (nor) has he any power to forbid the use of such rites and ceremonies as are already received, approved, and practiced by any church; because if he did so, he would destroy the church itself, the end (goal) of whose institution is only to worship God with freedom after its own manner.[41]

The reason why there must be complete freedom of worship lies in the very nature of faith itself.

To impose (certain rites or ceremonies) upon any people, contrary to their own judgment, is in effect to command them to offend God, which, considering that the end of all religion is to please Him, and that liberty is essentially necessary to that end, appears to be absurd beyond expression . . . (Hence, whatever is done) in the church and worship of God is removed out of the reach of the magistrate's jurisdiction, because in that use they have no connection at all with civil affairs. *The only business of the church is the salvation of souls,* and it in no way concerns the neighborhood or the commonwealth[42] whether this, that or the other ceremony be there made use of.[43]

It might seem from the foregoing that Locke advocated a complete division and separation between churches and state government. Such a conclusion would be erroneous. Although he does stress that they are two distinct kinds of groups, they both stem from one and the same moral root.

Uprightness of conduct (*morum rectitudo*), which constitutes not the least part of religion and sincere piety, concerns civil life also, and in it lies the salvation (*salus*) both of men's souls and of the commonwealth. Moral actions belong therefore to the jurisdiction of both the outward and the inward court,[44] and are subject to both dominions, of the civil as well as the domestic governor: I mean both of the magistrate and of the conscience.[45]

Locke was well aware that he was treading on thin ice, given what he had already said, and so he warns the reader:

Here there is great danger, lest one of these jurisdictions entrench upon the other and discord arise between the keeper of the public peace and the overseer of souls (the church leader).[46]

But in fact, there are certain situations when the civil magistrate or elected government official has no choice but to step in and take control of the internal affairs of a church.

(What) if some congregations should have a mind to sacrifice infants, or . . . lustfully pollute themselves in promiscuous uncleanliness, or practice any other such heinous enormities? Is the magistrate obliged to tolerate them because they are committed in a religious assembly? I answer no.[47]

What about religious assemblies that plot the overthrow of the government? Here again, the publicly elected official must intervene.

> If anything pass in a religious meeting seditiously and contrary to the public peace, it is to be punished in the same manner and no otherwise than as if it had happened in a fair or market.[48]

The initial clear-cut distinction between state government and the churches has begun to blur, has it not? Nor is Locke finished. Toward the end of his *Epistle,* he insists that no Roman Catholic should be granted freedom of religion. Sharing the view of all Protestants of his age, Locke says that all Roman Catholics by definition are loyal to "a foreign prince" and therefore necessarily traitors to the country they live in.[49]

> That church can have no right to be tolerated by the magistrate which is so constituted that all who enter it *ipso facto* pass into the allegiance and service of another prince (*alterius princeps*).[50]

Since both government and churches coexist in the same nation, share the same moral standards, and share the same public laws, no church can be permitted to do anything that will threaten the government's security, just because it claims it is "religious."

> Whatsoever is lawful in the commonwealth cannot be prohibited by the magistrate for the church . . . And those things that are prejudicial to the commonweal of a people in their everyday use, and are thereby forbidden by laws, those things ought not to be permitted to churches in their sacred rites.[51]

Statements like this could lead one to think that, contrary to his initial separation, Locke actually subsumed the churches under the control of the state, leaving them just enough liberty to perform meaningless esoteric rituals. Again, this would be erroneous. Rather than churches quietly coexisting under government control in a passive, ingrown way, Locke envisioned a dynamic, ideological cooperation between the churches and the government. In addition to their particular sacred rituals, he thought the churches should vigorously inculcate religious tolerance among their members. He hoped to see the day when

> a law (would be) passed granting toleration to (all) so that all churches were obliged to teach and to lay down as the foundation of their own liberty the principle of toleration for others, even for those dissenting

from them on sacred questions, and that nobody should be coerced in matters of religion by any law or force.[52]

Indeed, says Locke, the Lord Jesus Christ will personally punish every single church leader who disregards his (Locke's) advice regarding tolerance.

> How happy and how great would be the fruit, both in church and state, if the pulpits everywhere sounded with this doctrine of peace and toleration ... And if anyone that professes himself to be a minister of the Word of God, a preacher of the gospel of peace, teach otherwise, he either understands not or neglects the business of his calling, *and shall one day give account thereof unto the Prince of Peace!*[53]

By now it seems as if Locke has totally reversed himself and the original "secular" government is actually a theocracy. Another indication of his theologized view of the state is his insistence that atheism is not to be tolerated under any circumstances.

> Those are not to be tolerated at all who deny the being of a God (*nullo modo tolerandi sunt qui numen esse negant*). Promises, covenants, and oaths, which are the bonds of human society, can have no hold upon an atheist. The taking away of God, though even but in thought, dissolves everything.[54]

Locke's need for a state theology appears here very clearly. Having begun by insisting that there is nothing in common between the national government and religious groups, he now says that all citizens—including government officials—must believe in a divine being guarding the nation who will hold them accountable for their deeds on a "Day of Judgment." Only if there is a common dread of getting caught, says Locke, will citizens in their public and private actions honor their oaths and contracts. Locke would have readily agreed with Lord Acton who said, "Nothing has contributed more to the breakdown of morals in our time than the growing disbelief in immortality."

By now, Locke appears almost medieval in his outlook. Now he says every nation is founded on the existence and will of a divine being whose moral law functions as the all-encompassing sphere within which the citizens live and move and conduct their business. Locke makes this same view explicit at another point when he comes to the problem of what to do with evil magistrates. For instance, what if an evil government official orders people to do things against their religious convictions? Locke replies:

> The principal and chief care of everyone ought to be of his own soul first, and, in the next place, of the public peace.[55]
>
> Every man has an immortal soul, capable of eternal happiness or misery, whose happiness depends upon his believing and doing those things in this life which are necessary to the obtaining of God's favor,[56] and are prescribed by God to that end. It follows from thence ... that the observance of these things is the highest obligation that lies upon mankind, and that our utmost care, application, and diligence ought to be exercised in the search and performance of them. Because there is nothing in this world that is of any consideration in comparison with eternity.[57]

Now Locke says that each person's religious obligation takes complete precedence over his civil obligations! We are now at precisely the opposite of the view expressed just moments ago.

Many attempts have been made to resolve these well-known tensions within Locke's political theory.[58] For the purposes of this discussion, we must leave them in place and proceed to our next topic: Locke's basic theological ideas and method of biblical exegesis.

We have already seen something of Locke's concept of "God" (I will use quotation marks to refer to Locke's use of this term and "god" for a generic designation). Running like a steady bass accompaniment throughout the *Epistle,* Locke's "God" is described as a cosmic lawgiver and hidden divine power behind the government (every government has such a god). For Locke, this invisible divine power is the Primary Fact of human existence. Obedience to this national god is the first obligation of every citizen.

> Everyone should do what he in his conscience is persuaded to be acceptable to the Almighty, on whose good pleasure and acceptance depends their eternal happiness. For obedience is due, in the first place, to God, and afterwards to the laws (of the state).[59]

In Locke's writings, this national god inclines toward strictness. One looks in vain for anything more than the barest hint of a doctrine of "divine grace" in Locke's *Epistle.* Instead, he seems to think that this god will be rather strict on the Day of Judgment with the miserable humans huddled before him. In a passage dealing with the foolhardiness of obeying a mere government official's command regarding "indifferent"[60] religious observances, Locke scornfully remarks:

> Things that are in their own nature indifferent (*res sua natura indifferentes*) cannot, by human authority, be made part of divine worship ... Nor when an angry Deity shall ask (on Judgment Day), "Who has required this (ceremony)?" will it be enough to reply "the *magistrate* commanded it!"[61]

In short, the state god John Locke describes in his *Epistle* is a cosmic orderer and final judge. But how are people to know how to live so as to please this god? Locke replies: read the Bible. There the "bulk of mankind" will find "God's Law of Morality."

The Bible and God's Law of Morality

It was primarily in *The Reasonableness of Christianity* that John Locke explained how ordinary people can discover the moral obligations required by the national god, so we will turn now to that writing.[62]

Locke portrays the God of the Christian Bible as becoming so irritated with the human world that he decided it was time for a decisive reform.

> In darkness and error, regarding the true God, Our Savior found the world. But the clear revelation he brought with him dissipated this darkness; made the one invisible true God known to the world; and that with such evidence and energy that polytheism and idolatry hath no where been able to withstand it.[63]

> Christ's coming into the world was ... to reform the corrupt state of degenerate man; and ... (to) a erect new kingdom.[64]

There are two qualifications for those who wish to belong to this "new kingdom":

> Faith and repentance, i.e., believing Jesus to be the Messiah, and a good life, are the indispensable conditions of the new covenant, to be performed by all those who would obtain eternal life.[65]

So far, this all sounds rather Jewish. What about the Reformation doctrine of "justification by faith"? Locke is familiar with this doctrine but he doesn't much like it—it weakens moral resolve. It ends up playing a rather minor role in his thinking, kind of like "God will let us off some *only if* we have done everything we can on our own first."

> The rule of right (Locke's term for God's Law of Morality) is the same that ever it was; the obligation to observe it is also the same. The difference between the law of works (Judaism) and the law of faith (Christianity) is only this: the law of works makes no allowance for failing on any occasion ... *But by the law of faith, faith is allowed to supply the defect of full obedience* (i.e., if anything is lacking after full obedience, "faith" supplies what is lacking); and so the believers are admitted to life and immortality *as if* they were righteous.[66]

This "forensic" or juridical conception of justification by faith[67] appears to be the same doctrine as taught by St. Paul, but it isn't. Locke never mentions the forgiveness of his national god as being made possible by the familiar New Testament concept of the sacrificial death of Jesus Christ on the cross (known in Christian theology as "substitutionary atonement"). The closest Locke comes is to insist that a person must "believe that" Jesus was "the Messiah, the Son of God." However, this kind of "faith" is simply *intellectual assent* to a proposition, like "believing that" the Big Bang theory is true.[68] This intellectual assent appears to function in Locke's thinking as a kind of necessary precondition to sincere obedience to the laws of Christ ("I believe that Jesus is the Son of God and he is therefore entitled to give me rules that I will obey").

As far as the Bible is concerned, Locke is primarily interested in the teachings of Jesus in the Gospels. As such, he is typical of seventeenth- and eighteenth-century rationalists who thoroughly disdained the Old Testament and ignored the New Testament epistles. Even in the Gospels they paid little attention to Jesus' "life and ministry"; none of them ever wrote a "life of Jesus." That came later with the rise of Romanticism. However, Locke was very interested in the harmony of the Gospels produced by Le Clerc since it assumed the same kind of literal historicism Locke preferred. Within the Gospels, Locke placed a tight focus on Jesus' moral teaching and disregarded the repeated apocalyptic predictions, the arguments over the Law of Moses, the trial and crucifixion, and so forth. In this, he is quite typical of early rationalism. Their main concern was Jesus' "law of morality," although even here there is a catch. These sublime teachings *were already known* to universal human reason.

> Let us take a view of the promulgation of the gospel by our Savior himself, and see what it was he taught the world and required men to believe ...[69]

Whatsoever should thus be universally useful as a standard to which men should conform their manners, must have its authority either from reason or revelation ... Such a *law of morality* Jesus Christ hath given us in the New Testament; but by the latter of these ways, by revelation. We have from him a full and sufficient rule for our direction *conformable to that of reason.*[70]

Thus informed of what God expects of us, all we have to do is obey.

Can anyone who reads the Savior's sermon on the mount—not to mention all the rest—doubt that a sincere obedience, as well as faith, is a condition of (belonging to) the new covenant?[71]

Now, like Spinoza and the other rationalists of his time, Locke believed that the geniuses among the human race, those who possessed truly advanced reasoning powers, have always known the true God (Locke cites Socrates and Plato). But for 99.9 percent of the human race, God must use revelation, i.e., he must explicitly tell humans what to do. The tiny amount of divine reason the 99.9 percent possessed, far from being a moderating influence, in fact turned them toward evil and wickedness.

Though the works of nature ... sufficiently evidence a Deity, yet the world made so little use of their reason that they saw him not. Sense and lust blinded their minds in some, and a careless inadvertency in others, and fearful apprehension in most, gave them up into the hands of their priests, to fill their heads with false notions of the deity and their worship with foolish rites as they pleased. And what (religious) awe or craft once began, devotion soon made sacred and religion (made) immutable ... And in the crowd of wrong notions and invented rites, the world had almost lost sight of the one only true God.[72]

So God had to adopt a more direct approach. And what could be more direct than for God to take on human form and, in the person of Jesus Christ, prove he was the divine Son of God by performing all sorts of amazing miracles and then directly instruct men on how they ought to live?

I ask whether one coming from heaven in the power of God, in full and clear evidence and demonstration of miracles, giving plain and direct rules of morality and obedience, be not likelier to enlighten the bulk of mankind, and set them right in their duties, and bring them to do them, than by reasoning with them, from general notions and principles of human reason?[73]

So Locke turns to the Gospels where the Son of God sets forth the "plain and direct rules of morality and obedience." But how must one read the Gospels so as to interpret them correctly?

Locke's Method of Interpreting the Bible

Locke prefaces his *Reasonableness of Christianity* with a brief biographical explanation to the reader:

> The little satisfaction and consistency that is to be found in most of the systems of divinity I have met with, made me betake myself to the sole reading of Scripture, to which they all appeal, for the understanding of the Christian religion. What from thence, by an attentive and unbiased search, I have received, dear reader, I here deliver to thee.[74]

This statement is classic. Locke's rejection of "most of the systems of divinity" in favor of his own individual "unbiased" reading of the Scripture was a tactic first made famous by Martin Luther in his confrontation with the emperor and the Roman Catholic Church at Worms. After him, it became the hallmark of Protestant disputations, and one always claimed to be "unbiased." In case the reader missed it the first time, Locke repeats the claim twice more on the same page: "through a diligent and *unbiased* search" and "To one that, thus *unbiased,* reads the Scriptures."[75]

We might wonder how Locke could be so naive as to think he actually was unbiased in his reading of the Bible. He had already prepared for this with his description of the nature of human understanding: external sense impressions strike the mind, *which is like a blank page* (he used the term *tabula rasa* "blank tablet"), and there the impressions are combined to form ideas. The mind has no ideas other than those arising from sense impressions or combinations of the ideas formed by sense impressions ("ideas about ideas"). Thus conceived, it is easy to think of oneself as unbiased—one's mind is a blank tablet and one just lets the biblical words impress the mind in a direct, simple way, without mixing in extraneous thoughts.

> (The Bible must) be understood in the plain direct meaning of the words and phrases, such as they may be supposed to have had in the mouths of the speakers, who used them according to the language of that time

and country wherein they lived; without such learned, artificial, and forced senses of them as are sought out and put upon them in most systems of divinity (theological systems).[76]

We should remember that the "systems of divinity" he rejects here are both Roman Catholic and Protestant; Locke had heard enough of their boring logic-chopping. Is he thinking of Spinoza's "historical method" in his definition of "plain, direct meaning" as the *original* sense the biblical words had "in the mouths of the speakers, who used them according to the language of that time and country wherein they lived"? Probably not. Locke could have found this definition in any Protestant treatise on biblical interpretation. In them, "literal" or "plain" meaning usually included, beyond such definitions as "grammatical sense" and "obvious" meaning, the historical meaning the words had for the original speakers. One indication that Spinoza is not hovering in the background is Locke's supreme confidence that it is a simple matter to ascertain the original meanings (see below).

So Locke insists that the Gospels should be interpreted literally. For example, the descriptions of Christ's miracles are accounts of literal, historical facts. Anyone can understand their meaning.

> The healing of the sick, the restoring sight to the blind by a word, the raising and being raised from the dead, *are matters of fact* which (anyone) can without difficulty conceive. He who does such things must do them by the assistance of a divine power. These things lie level to the ordinariest apprehension; he that can distinguish between sick and well, lame and sound, dead and alive, is capable of (understanding) this doctrine.[77]

These miracles prove the historical reality of Jesus Christ's divine Sonship. They were performed for no other reason than to give the masses convincing evidence who Christ was, so that everyone would want to (i.e., be afraid not to) obey his moral laws. Locke continues:

> To one who is once persuaded that Jesus Christ was sent by God to be a King and a Savior of those who do believe in him, all his commands become principles; there needs no other proof for the truth of what he says but that he said it.[78]

Once one is sufficiently impressed by Christ's miracles so as to become willing to obey him, then there is nothing left to do but read the Gospels to find his "moral laws." Nor are they at all hard to understand.

There needs no more but to read the inspired books to be instructed. All the duties of morality lie there clear and plain and easy to understand . . . (The gospel writers mixed in) no pride or vanity, no trace of ostentation or ambition . . . It is all pure, all sincere; nothing too much, nothing wanting; but such a complete rule of life as the wisest men must acknowledge, (and tending) entirely to the good of mankind; (indeed,) all would be happy if all would practice it.[79]

Locke's Radical Individualism

So far everything Locke has been saying is core Protestantism, going back to the Reformers. Luther had told Charles V and the Roman Catholic officials gathered to examine him, "Unless I am convicted by Scripture and plain reason—for I do not accept the authority of popes and councils for they have contradicted each other—my conscience is captive to the Word of God, and to go against conscience is neither right nor safe."[80] Locke's position was identical. What is different is the political consequences he drew from it.

After Luther's break with Rome, powerful Protestants and Roman Catholic nobles reached a compromise at the Peace of Augsburg in 1550 whereby each prince could determine the religion of his own little territory (*cujus regio ejus religio*). But far from producing an era of peace, this compromise opened the door to the bloodiest, most destructive series of wars Europe had ever experienced. In the Thirty Years' War, Catholic prince fought Calvinist, Lutheran fought Anabaptist, Catholics and Lutherans fought other Catholics and Lutherans, *ad nauseam.* When the carnage dragged to a halt around 1648—because of exhaustion and lack of arms and money, more than anything else—people all over Europe were in a state of shock because of the massive amounts of grief, destruction, brutality, and hypocrisy they had witnessed. "Is *this* what we can expect if kings and princes have the power to decide the religion of their own states?" they asked. It had been a dreadful mistake. Why? Because

every church is orthodox to itself; to others, erroneous or heretical. For whatsoever any church believes, it believes to be true; and contrary unto those things it pronounces to be in error. So that the controversy between churches about the truth of their doctrines is on both sides equal; *nor is there any judge upon the earth by whose sentence it can be determined.*[81]

They had inadvertently opened the door to a war of all upon all which quickly turned to a war of the strong against the weak. They had mistakenly believed that government officials possessed a superior insight and thus had a right to decide their subjects' fate in matters of religion.

> Princes, indeed, are born superior to other men in power, but in nature equal (*natura vero reliquis mortalibus*). Neither the right nor the art of ruling necessarily carries along with it the certain knowledge of other things, *and least of all of true religion.* For if it were so, how could it come to pass that the lords of the earth should differ so vastly as they do in religious matters?[82]

And with that unanswerable question, Locke—and every Enlightenment thinker before and after him—grimly squashed once and for all the ancient prerogative of kings and princes to decide for their subjects in matters pertaining to religion. Better to allow each individual to make up her or his own mind and to bear with the mass confusion that would certainly follow than to let government officials ever again use their authority to settle theological disputes.

> (It is the height of stupidity) to ignore the dictates of one's own reason and conscience and blindly accept the doctrines imposed by one's prince and worship God in the manner laid down by the laws of one's country. Amid all the variety of opinions that different princes hold about religion, the way . . . that leads to Heaven would inevitably be open to very few and they in one country only. And what would heighten the absurdity and ill suit the notion of God even more, *people would owe their eternal happiness or misery simply to the accident of their birthplace.*[83]

Thus Locke and other Enlightenment thinkers advocated a radical individualism in all things: self-direction in political matters (democracy), self-direction in accumulating personal wealth (capitalism), and self-direction in personal faith (freedom of religion). The great banner leading the charge said: *Liberty & Equality for All!* All monarchies and religious dictatorships—abolished! All archaic religious ceremonies and doctrines—abolished! All excessive controls over commerce—abolished! Where did they mount the attack? On the grim old knot binding Throne to Altar.

> Who sees not how frequently the name of the church, which was venerable in the time of the apostles, has been made use of to throw dust in the eyes of the people in the following ages?[84] . . . To speak the truth, we

must acknowledge that the church—if a convention of clergymen, making canons, must be called by that name—is for the most part more apt to be influenced by the court (of the King) than the court by the church. How the church was (controlled) under the vicissitude of the orthodox and Arian emperors is very well known. Or if these things be too remote, our modern English history affords us fresh examples in the reigns of Henry VIII, Edward VI, Mary and Elizabeth, how easily and smoothly the clergy changed their decrees, their articles of faith, their forms of worship, and everything according to the inclination of those kings and queens. Yet were those kings and queens of such different minds in point of religion, and enjoined thereupon such different things, that no man in his wits will presume to say that any sincere and upright worshiper of God could, with a safe conscience, obey (all of) their several decrees.[85]

No, it was time for a new beginning. It was time for men to pay attention to the evidence coming to their minds from their own firsthand observation of nature. It was time for businessmen to be released from their bondage to the King's excessive taxes and the stranglehold of the landed aristocracy. New wealth was not to be gained by owning land; it was to be gotten from trade and colonial development. Enormous fortunes were there to be made, if only those willing to risk their fortunes in getting them were freed from crippling taxes and from confiscatory government controls (an economic principle later known as laissez-faire). These sweeping changes demanded a new type of democratically elected government with power over the king and the old aristocracy. Thus considered, Locke's ideas were terrifying to those entrenched powers, but music to the ears of American revolutionaries.

Locke's Legacy in America

If Spinoza tried to advance the goals and aspirations of the powerful Dutch middle-class burghers, Locke did his best to advance the goals and aspirations of the new middle class in England. Members of each group had a lot in common and were in constant contact with the other. In stark contrast to the methods and objectives of their enemies in their respective countries, the political, commercial, and religious convictions of the Dutch Remonstrants and the English Whigs were identical: trade unimpeded by royal or ecclesiastical interference, colonial expansion (and in precisely the same areas on the planet), a strong, democratically elected central government composed primarily of their kind of people, a moralistic deism centered on Jesus Christ as the Great Example, and dedication to the goals and methods of mechanistic science.

If Spinoza's writings became widely read in Europe (especially in nineteenth-century France and Germany), Locke's writings were read primarily in Great Britain, whence they emigrated to the American colonies. There Locke's ideas took deep root and flourished unimpeded by Old World institutions or constituencies. His writings became the fountainhead of the essential concepts as well as the very wording of the Declaration of Independence. The Constitutional Congress wove his ideas into the new Constitution as well as the Bill of Rights. It may be said without any danger of exaggeration that John Locke's doctrines, transported to America's frontier settlements, small farms, towns, and cities, were, more than any other single source, the constitutive concepts shaping eighteenth- and nineteenth-century America and have continued to play a dominant role in American culture down to the present. Consider this list of his key concepts.

Politics

- The only purpose for a government is to enable individuals to acquire physical pleasure: health, wealth, and security.[86]
- The government should be run not by kings or aristocrats but by democratically elected professional men (doctors, lawyers, clergy), businessmen, and such farmers and landed gentry as agree with the new capitalist economic system and the principle of religious toleration.

Commerce

- Free-market capitalism will make the state thrive as no other economic system has in the past, provided that the state regulate it as little as possible. However, the individual must try do what is morally right *and* try to make money simultaneously. Overemphasis on one or the other will lead to failure in business.

State religion

- Each nation must have its own god and every citizen must sincerely believe that there will be a "Day of Judgment" when the national god will punish all evildoers who don't keep their oaths and contracts.

· Atheists are malicious deviants who must not hold public office, nor can they be trusted in business dealings.

· Roman Catholics cannot be allowed to be citizens since they will not be loyal to the nation or its god but to a "foreign prince" (the Pope). Therefore, Roman Catholics must either change their beliefs or leave the country.

· Foreigners can become citizens only if they accept the basic national creed, political system, and business methods.

Private religion

· Within the broad citizens' faith in the national god, individuals may associate in any private religious groups they want. No one should be compelled to conform to any previous creeds, decisions of church councils (Roman Catholic or Protestant), or institutions of traditional Christianity. Christians may worship however they wish and adopt whatever religious ceremonies they can afford, provided that

—they never preach the overthrow of the nation's government,
—they never commit acts during worship that are crimes under civil law,
—they never attack, persecute, or otherwise hinder other religious groups that differ from them,
—and in general, they never encourage any action that interferes with the common good or civil order.

· These private religious associations have one basic purpose: to perform such ceremonies as will predispose their god to give them eternal life.

· Membership in a particular private religious association must always remain voluntary. It must never be either coerced or suppressed by anyone in government, because no government official is better equipped to decide ultimate religious questions than any private citizen.

· From the government's point of view, membership in these private religious associations needs no prior qualification of any kind, whether educational attainment, landownership, or political orientation. Conversely, each religious association shall be completely free to establish any membership requirements it deems appropriate to its own ends. If members become disaffected with the way things are going in their religious association, they may begin another. The government shall not impose any limits on the number of private religious associations within the country.

· Jesus Christ is the divinely sent Moral Example. Little attention need be paid either to the Old Testament or to the Epistles or Book of Revelation in the New Testament.

· In these private religious associations, the Bible is best interpreted literally, so that all members have the same access to and authority over biblical interpretation. Doctrine, polity, and public conduct of members must be established from the Bible using rational methods of argument. As stated before, no traditional creeds or other institutional usages are necessary to the accomplishment of these ends.

The Political Value of Locke's Biblical Literalism

A concluding note about the political value of Locke's biblical literalism. Locke's insistence on the "plain, direct meaning" of the Bible is in no sense based on a carefully spelled-out theory of scriptural interpretation such as we saw in Spinoza. In his *Essay on Human Understanding*, Locke described mental understanding in physical terms. Ideas are images created by sense impressions acting on the human receptor called the empty mind (the *tabula rasa*). Quite apart from the logical and physical problems inherent in this definition (which were immediately pointed out by Locke's opponents), it did have an important *political* value. Like Descartes' systematic doubt, it permitted one to wipe one's memory clean of—*to completely forget*—centuries of accumulated tradition and start over with one's own, freshly made, empirical observations.

When Locke's ideas were transposed to the American scene, which was itself a large-scale attempt to "wipe the slate clean" and start over, and were combined with Thomas Reid's "common sense philosophy" (the orthodox Presbyterian rebuttal to Hume's corrosive skepticism),[87] Lockean biblical literalism fit into the American populist temperament perfectly.[88] In a land that aspired to political equality in participation in government and commercial equality of opportunity—exclusively for white males, of course—there must also be religious equality in the freedom to worship as one pleased.

But how to bring these significant freedoms to pass when the Bible (and not tradition) is to be the sole source of theology and morals? Answer: interpret the Bible literally, according to its "plain meaning." No "systems of divinity," no creeds, are needed. Any Christian, equipped with a Bible and common sense, is the equal of any other person, regardless of educational attainment, financial power, or political standing.

> In a century committed to an exaggerated emphasis upon the rights and liberties of the individual, . . . many found in the absolute authority of the Bible a reinforcement to their demand for liberty, because they could appeal to it as an authority not only absolute, but immediately accessible. They could set their personal interpretations of the Bible against what they regarded as the subordinate or spurious authorities of synod and creed.[89]

Thus equipped with the "Great Equalizer," biblical literalists were everywhere to be seen in eighteenth- and nineteenth-century America's religious controversies.

> Countless and colorful debates (took place) between Disciples of Christ and Presbyterians, Methodists and Baptists, Mormons and almost every other religious species, both sides using the Bible and dissecting it with the cold logic of eighteenth-century rationalists.[90]

From this perspective, a comparison of Locke's literal exegesis with Spinoza's historical exegesis is most instructive. Locke eradicated at one stroke all intermediaries between the individual Christian and God's Word. While Spinoza *claimed* he wanted to free every individual to read the Bible for himself or herself, those ten chapters of densely packed methodological instructions proved that his real intentions were very different. As it turned out, Spinoza's complicated hermeneutical program eventually spawned a huge international network of elite "biblical experts" who are viewed with intense distrust by Lockean democratic literalists to this day.

In a country where all white males were deemed to be equal politically and to have equal opportunity, an intense struggle broke out among the descendants of the strictly traditional Puritans of New England, the hierarchical Episcopalians in the states of New York, Maryland, and Virginia, and the religious individualists everywhere else. Locke's principle made it possible for the latter to maintain their cherished freedom and religious independence: let everyone interpret the Bible literally, according to his or her own commonsense understanding of the words. If done this way, no hierarchy could ever be able to develop. Every person, regardless of educational attainment or lack thereof, would have equal access to the Absolute Norm. In this way, all people could do whatever they thought would benefit them spiritually, just as they all did in the business world. All could preach and worship and argue theology and church politics to their heart's content—just don't let the government get mixed up in it.

Locke did not spell out how the Bible could be interpreted literally because to do so would have been self-contradictory. He had to assume that everyone would know instinctively how to do it.

Thus it remains to this day among fundamentalists. The repeated insistence that "the whole Bible is literally true from cover to cover" is matched by massive silence as to how to cope with all of the poetry, hymns, mystical visions, and cultic texts in the Old Testament or the abstruse theological arguments in Paul's letters (which occasionally rely on allegory for their main points) or, not least of all, Jesus' teaching in metaphorical parables about his most important subject: the Kingdom of God. But such questions never seem to matter. They can be ignored for one obvious reason: Locke's literalism is necessary for personal religious freedom. By the same token, there must be no creeds in these religious assemblies, since they impose a standard of belief upon the members.

In America, fundamentalists belong to private, voluntary, *democratic* associations having minimal hierarchy. In these groups, the aversion to all creeds, the aversion to lateral or hierarchical authority so that congregations are joined with other congregations only in the loosest of coalitions, the universal suspicion of educational standards for their clergy—all spring from one and the same core value: the need to remain politically and religiously equal. As such, these groups—however different they may seem to be on the surface from religious groups espousing modern historical criticism—are equally as much rationalist children of the Enlightenment.

One final point. It is among these biblical literalists that Augustine's Second Form of the Synoptic Problem—the harmonistic approach to the differences among the Gospels—thrives and is maintained, albeit in modified form, in the modern world. Based on the traditional fourfold Gospel canon, no decade goes by without a new crop of rationalistic, historicizing harmonizations.

In other words, it is possible to perceive two main groups in modern Enlightenment-style Gospel interpretation. On the one hand are the fundamentalist Lockeans clinging to a modified Second or Augustinian Form of the Synoptic Problem, typified by their use of gospel harmonies. On the other hand are the modern Spinozist historical critics, typified by their use of Gospel synopses, working with a Third Form of the Synoptic Problem. This distinction is discussed more fully in Chapter 20, "The Emergence of a Third Form of the Synoptic Problem."

CHAPTER 18

The Gospel Canon Is Rejected;
John Toland and the Gospel of Barnabas

$\smile$

*A*fter the Protestant Reformers had successfully challenged the legitimacy of certain books in the Old Testament, the issue of the biblical
canon receded in importance. It was the noted Deist John Toland (1670–
1722) who brought it back into the discussion, shining the searchlight of
skeptical reason squarely on the Gospels.

An ardent admirer of Baruch Spinoza[1] and John Locke, Toland became instantly notorious with his first book, *Christianity Not Mysterious*
(1696), in which he proved that Christianity was perfectly conformable to
reason, as defined by John Locke. He thought he was defending the faith,
but not everyone agreed with him. The Irish Parliament voted to have the
book publicly burned by the hangman of Dublin, prompting Toland to
move hastily to London. There he switched to less inflammatory subjects,
for a few months.

In 1699, he troubled the waters again. *Amyntor* questioned the validity of the New Testament canon by listing all of the apocryphal writings
ascribed to Christ's Apostles that had not been included.

This list was remarkably complete by modern standards. Called "A
Catalogue of Books Mentioned by the Fathers and Other Ancient Writers,
As Truly or Falsely Ascrib'd to Jesus Christ, His Apostles, and Other
Eminent Persons," the list began with the writings of the so-called Apos-
tolic Men (*Epistle of Barnabas,* 1 Clement, etc.). Then Toland methodi-
cally listed apocryphal writings under the names of famous persons: Jesus,
Mary, each Apostle, and so forth. It was a lengthy catalog based on materi-

als collected from the *Codex Apocryphus Novi Testamenti* by the indefatigable classical scholar Johannes Fabricius of Hamburg (1668–1736), the anonymous *Decretum Gelasianum* (sixth century), and other sources. He ended with a list of Gospels omitted from the orthodox New Testament canon: "the Gospels of Valentine, Basilides, Marcion, Appelles [*sic*], Cerinthus, Tatian and others."[2]

Toland also described *other canons* of sacred writings that existed in the early centuries, such as those used by the Manichaeans, the Gnostics, the Marcionites, and the Ebionites. From this evidence, he charged that the final selection of no more than four Gospels by the Roman Catholics was undoubtedly an error—there should have been many more.[3] Then he set to work to rectify this error.

Two years later, Toland published his results. *Nazarenus; or Jewish, Gentile, and Mohametan Christianity* (1718) claimed that the long-lost, *original* "Gospel of Jesus" had just been discovered. Its title was the *Gospel of Barnabas.*[4] Never mind that Toland recently found it in *Amsterdam* and that it was written in *Italian* and that in this Gospel Jesus repeatedly denies that he is the Messiah of Israel or the Son of God, that not he but Judas Iscariot is the one who is crucified, and that the One to come will be named not Jesus but *Mohammed.* Not fazed in the least by these *outré* features, Toland was excited beyond bounds. "I have found," he triumphantly announced in his Preface,

> a Mohametan Gospel never publicly made known among Christians . . . The learned gentleman who was so kind as to show it to me had it out of the library of a person of great name and authority in that city (Amsterdam) . . . There is but one copy of it in all of Christendom, accidentally discovered by me in Amsterdam.[5]

The meaning of this boast is unclear, as a number of other people in Amsterdam had obviously seen it.[6] Perhaps Toland meant that he was the first person *to perceive its true historical significance,* which he proceeded to make clear in the rest of the book.

The *Gospel of Barnabas* was especially attractive to Toland because it rejected all supernatural features in the traditional Gospel portraits of Jesus, beginning with his place as the Second Person of the Trinity. Moreover, it emphasized a strict morality that corresponded to what Toland had already proclaimed was the true message of Jesus in *Christianity Not Mysterious* (1696).

In short, Toland must have thought that he had found, by an incredible stroke of good fortune, the historical proof of his hunch that the orthodox Gospel canon was a late, flawed artifact. Here was a Gospel possibly written before the canonical Gospels, that is, the *original* Gospel of Jesus Christ. What was the evidence in favor of this conclusion? Toland devoted most of *Nazarenus* to a discussion of the evidence linking the *Gospel of Barnabas* to the ancient Ebionites or Nazarenes, who had rejected the idea that Jesus was the Son of God and who were, in Toland's estimation, that much more likely to be reliable sources of earliest tradition.

Two years later, in 1720, Toland published *Tetradymus,* an elaborate attempt to salvage the intellectual respectability of the Old Testament by proving that the miracles could be provided with rational explanations. Toland's aim was to rescue the Bible from superstitious believers on the right and outright skeptics on the left. "The discoveries I have made," said Toland, "created in me a higher veneration for Moses than ever was instill'd by my instructors, and on better grounds."[7] In so doing, Toland set the example for generations of skeptical rationalists after him who tried to safeguard the Bible's more incredible narratives by means of elaborate explanations of "what really happened."[8]

Conclusion

By the mid-eighteenth century, Enlightenment *philosophes* in France and England had methodically picked apart everything in orthodox Christianity and subjected it to their rationalist, historical scrutiny. The previous two chapters disclosed a total transvaluation of traditional biblical hermeneutics, based on revolutionary political and religious ideas.

Until John Toland, however, the *canon of the Gospels* had received little direct attention. It was he who inaugurated a frontal assault on the legitimacy of the entire biblical canon. Toland went much further than the Protestant Reformers had, rejecting all decisions of the Church councils as prejudiced conclusions designed to protect a narrow orthodoxy, based on woefully incomplete evidence. As for the fourfold Gospel canon, Toland scoured the Fathers and ancient lists of banned books for signs of other Gospels, repeatedly asking, Why isn't this or that in our New Testament?

Then in *Nazarenus,* Toland held out the *Gospel of Barnabas* as the original Gospel of Jesus Christ, antedating—and therefore pure of—the corrupt and superstitious legends contained in the Gospels of Matthew, Mark, Luke, and John In short, John Toland was one of the earliest Enlightenment figures responsible for arousing widespread skepticism regarding the credibility of the four canonical Gospels. He called for a thorough review of the potential canonical status of all other Gospels as well, a process which hit full stride over a century later in the nineteenth century, when a number of major studies of the canonization process were published. The debate over the canonical status of the Gospels continues unabated to this day, as we will see in Chapter 21.

Although he did not extensively discuss the differences among the canonical Gospels or hazard theories as to how they were composed, Toland did begin the scholarly practice of considering all known Gospels, not just the four in the Bible. In this way, he helped to create the preconditions for the Third Form of the Synoptic Problem, where the assignment would be to provide an adequate intellectual explanation of the differences among the Gospels without regard to canonical restrictions.

CHAPTER 19

The Establishment of a "New Standard Text" of the Gospels

⌒

*I*f the question of the canon of the Gospels became more and more hotly debated during the nineteenth century, without finding much of a satisfactory solution, just the reverse was the case concerning the text of the New Testament, including the Gospels. Decades passed and scores of scholars devoted their lives to painstaking comparison of thousands of manuscripts. Out of this prodigious labor there eventually emerged an answer to Spinoza and the skeptics: a scientifically constructed text of the New Testament is not only possible but has largely been established.

During the course of the nineteenth century, the attainment of a "critical text" made possible certain scientific assumptions about the degree of proximity between what scholars read and what the original authors wrote. Except for the ultra-skeptical, this degree of proximity was considered to be close enough to support detailed analysis of the Gospels, in what I call the Third Form of the Synoptic Problem. That story will be told in the next chapter. This chapter will describe the rise out of the textual chaos in the early nineteenth century to a time of triumph toward the end of the twentieth.

The First Tentative Corrections in Erasmus' Text

By the late eighteenth century, scholars had compared hundreds of biblical manuscripts against Erasmus' Greek New Testament (first published in

1516) and had compared thousands of quotations from the Church Fathers (themselves in the process of obtaining critical texts!) and had discovered and compared dozens of early translations of the New Testament (Latin, Syriac, Coptic, Armenian, etc.).

The result was tens of thousands of differing words and phrases. Despite Erasmus' claims to the contrary,[1] the manuscripts he used were neither early nor reliable. They were very late and extremely unreliable, compared with others that were eventually discovered in libraries and monasteries in Europe and the Middle East. All of the evidence pointed to one conclusion: in a large number of places, the Greek text Erasmus published was different from what the original Apostles had written. Pressure began to build to correct his flawed text.

The scholar who by all accounts was the first person to propose actual changes in Erasmus' Greek New Testament was Johann Jakob Griesbach, professor of New Testament in Jena (1745–1812). A student of Johann Salomo Semler (1725–1791), the Old Testament scholar at Halle, Griesbach as a young man went on a trip through England, Holland, and France, collecting textual evidence and collating manuscripts. He took over and improved Mill's and Wettstein's massive collection of alternative words and phrases, comparing them with manuscripts he studied on his travels.[2] He distributed the variant readings geographically, using Bengel's and Semler's reconstruction of the history of the New Testament text.[3] Finally, he refined Bengel's scientific guidelines for identifying the most likely words or phrases of the original text.[4] After decades of careful work, Griesbach published three successive editions of the Greek New Testament (1774, 1796, 1803) in which, for the first time, he inserted a few changes in the wording of Erasmus' *textus receptus.*[5]

They did not go unchallenged. Roman Catholic and Protestant clergy rose to the defense of the *textus receptus,* saying that its text was akin to the great majority of medieval manuscripts.[6] Most specialists, intent on finding "the original Greek," were not impressed by this argument. Thus it was Griesbach who finally broke the spell of the *textus receptus.* A number of other New Testament scholars soon brought out student editions of his Greek text for use in their teaching and research.[7]

Attempts to Completely Replace the Textus Receptus

Griesbach's brave action spurred scholars to an ever more intensive search for the best ancient manuscripts of the New Testament. Individuals and teams pored over dusty old manuscripts in countless libraries tucked away in ancient schools and monasteries in Greece, the Holy Land, Italy, Russia,

Turkey, and Egypt. By 1830, when a German scholar published a list of all known manuscripts of the New Testament, the total exceeded six hundred, a far cry from Erasmus' original four or five, semi-incomplete manuscripts.[8]

The first scholar to abandon the *textus receptus* completely in favor of a blended text composed of words and phrases pulled together from a number of early manuscripts was a German classical scholar named Karl Lachmann (1793–1851). Convinced that, in the present state of knowledge, it was wishing for the impossible to dream of reconstructing "the original text," Lachmann set out instead to reconstruct the Greek New Testament in use during the *mid-fourth century,* the great age of Constantine.[9] To this end, he used only a few fourth- and fifth-century manuscripts, Jerome's Latin New Testament (largely based on earlier Latin versions), and biblical quotations from a few fourth-century Church Fathers.[10] The resulting text was totally independent of the texts used in the *textus receptus.*

As before, when Lachmann's New Testament came out in 1831, it was greeted with anger, but this time Lachmann was himself largely responsible. Not only was the revered text of Erasmus cast aside, but Lachmann had rearranged the books of the New Testament to conform to the order prevalent in his fourth-century exemplars: Gospels and Acts, Catholic Epistles, Pauline Epistles, Revelation.[11] Nor did Lachmann include any explanation for the drastic rearrangement. He just published the text and left his readers to find an obscure article he had published some time earlier setting out his goals and methods.[12] A second edition appeared in 1842 remedying these shortcomings and it became widely consulted.

The High Point in German Research on the Text of the New Testament

The peak in nineteenth-century German scholarship and genius as far as the text of the New Testament was concerned came during the early 1870s.

> The man to whom modern textual critics of the New Testament owe most is without doubt Lobegott Friedrich Constantin von Tischendorf (1815–1874), who sought out and published more manuscripts and produced more critical editions of the Greek Bible than any other single scholar (has ever done).[13]

By the time he was finished in 1872, Tischendorf had published no less than eight successive editions of the Greek New Testament, each one containing new manuscript evidence and representing more refined attempts to get behind the fourth-century barrier (where manuscript evidence begins to become nonexistent) to the "original Greek New Testament."

The most famous of Tischendorf's discoveries was an extremely ancient manuscript he found in the Greek Orthodox monastery of St. Catherine's, situated at the base of Mt. Sinai in the Judaean desert, hence its name: Codex Sinaiticus. Convinced that the monks had no idea of the extreme antiquity and value of this manuscript, Tischendorf tried to "borrow" it, only to be refused by the monks. Eventually he succeeded in getting it away from the monastery through a subterfuge and "sold" it to Tsar Alexander II of Russia, who sent a "contribution" to St. Catherine's. In the 1930s, the Russian Communist government had no use for it and, being hard pressed for funds, sold it for £100,000 (today, about $10 million) to the British government, which deposited it in the British Museum, where it is today.[14]

Tischendorf's several editions became legendary for their increasingly full collections of alternative words and phrases. To produce this enormous collection of evidence, he personally compared more ancient manuscripts, collected more Church Father quotations, and considered more words from ancient translations than anyone before had done. Most amazing of all, his citations of alternative words and phrases rarely contain any mistakes. He thus established an unparalleled standard for accuracy and completeness.[15]

The English Seize the Palm of Victory

During this period of German activity, French, Italian, and Spanish Roman Catholic scholars were not particularly interested in recovering the "original Greek" of the New Testament. The Roman Catholic Church continued to use the Latin version of the New Testament, so there was little demand for "the original Greek" except by a few scholars.[16]

Not so among the Protestant nations. Indeed, the English were determined not to be outdone by the Germans, especially by Tischendorf. In 1881, ten years after the publication of Tischendorf's massive eighth edition of the Greek New Testament, two Cambridge scholars named Brooke Foss Westcott (1825–1901) and Fenton John Anthony Hort (1828–1892) brought out "the most noteworthy critical edition of the Greek Testament ever produced by British scholarship."[17] After almost thirty years' close collaboration, the two scholars gave their two-volume masterpiece the significant title *The New Testament in the Original Greek.* In giving it this title, they announced their belief that they had succeeded in capturing the long-sought-after prize: the New Testament, not in its fourth-century or third-century form, but in its first-century *"original* Greek."[18]

This claim may seem odd (not to say premature) in view of the fact that neither Westcott nor Hort ever personally examined a single ancient manuscript.[19] Working entirely from previous *editions* (e.g., Griesbach, Lachmann, Tischendorf), where the task of comparison had been done for them, Westcott-Hort's contribution came in the application of a systematic approach to the mass of data others had collected.

Their system rested on a sophisticated reconstruction of the history of the geographical diffusion of the original Greek text of the New Testament, combined with a sensitive case-by-case weighing of all alternative variants of a dubious word or phrase. In practice, their system leaned heavily on one concept: wherever Tischendorf's Codex Sinaiticus agreed with the equally ancient Codex Vaticanus, that was the "original Greek." Where the two split, Westcott-Hort attempted to guess from the available variant words "what the original author would have written."[20]

Having reconstructed the "original Greek New Testament," Westcott and Hort took the next logical step and called for the end of any further use of the *textus receptus,* as well as the King James Version that was based on it.[21] To provide an alternative, they helped bring out in 1881 a "revised version" of the King James that was based on their text.

As before, denunciation was not long in coming. Especially outraged was John W. Burgon (1813–1888), the dean of Chichester Cathedral. He categorically refused to accept the suggestion that the *textus receptus,* which the Church had trustingly used for centuries, could be as mistaken and inaccurate as Westcott and Hort claimed. If the Bible had in fact been verbally inspired by God in the first place, then God must have safeguarded the later text of the biblical books from all admixture of non-inspired words and phrases by later copyists.[22] Nonetheless, biblical scholars on both sides of the Channel hailed Westcott and Hort's epoch-making achievement as "doubtless the oldest and purest text that could be attained with the means of information available."[23]

Westcott and Hort's approach may seem too subjective to be called scientific, but consider the example of the eminent German scholar Bernhard Weiss (1827–1918). Weiss published an edition of the Greek New Testament in 1894 based on *no knowledge* of the ancient manuscripts *nor any acquaintance* with the history of the transmission of the text. Weiss was a theologian who thought he could detect, by means of his *great familiarity* with the New Testament, what the original authors *would have written.* Taking Tischendorf's enormous list of alternative words and phrases, Weiss went through the text using one question to guide him to the right decision: "Which would be *the most appropriate word* in this context?" Weiss' choices were based on nothing more than his *feeling* for the "intrinsic probability."[24]

If we are looking for examples of the "godlike reason" Enlightenment scholars liked to boast of, fearlessly making fundamental, intuitive decisions about the original text of the Gospels based on no knowledge of the manuscript tradition or any systematic textual training of any kind, Weiss would have to rank near the top.

However, Weiss exemplified something textual scholars well knew: occasionally, the manuscript evidence alone is not sufficient for a final decision. Sometimes the cluster of evidence is so complicated and the value of individual readings can shift from valuable to dubious *within the same manuscript* that the textual specialist has no choice but to make educated guesses as to the best reading, based on nothing more than her or his feelings as to the intrinsic probabilities of each particular case.

Von Soden's "Magnificent Failure"

Then came one of the greatest disappointments in the entire history of the struggle to acquire an accurate text of the New Testament. A German scholar named Hermann Freiherr von Soden (1852–1914) obtained sufficient financial backing to make possible a comprehensive review of all the evidence obtained thus far. Hiring some forty assistants, von Soden sent them out across Europe and the Middle East to reexamine nearly every existing manuscript of the New Testament. Then, after twenty years of comparing, sifting, and codifying manuscripts, quotations, and versions, he published in 1913 an enormous, two-volume Greek New Testament bearing the daunting title *The Writings of the New Testament in the Oldest Form Attainable through an Historical Investigation of Its Text.*[25]

Von Soden and his assistants had left no stone unturned, and his two-volume work was nothing less than a complete reinvention of the field: all manuscripts had new, unfamiliar names and numbers on them, the generally accepted history of the text of the New Testament was largely recast in peculiar ways, and, worst of all, he abandoned the idea of recovering the "original" text. All this in 2,200 pages of tiny print.[26] He defended the last position by asserting that a scientist should not attempt to go back any further than the actual, physical copies. Even at that, the text he came up with seemed peculiar, an eccentric mixture of early and medieval readings.

Specialists everywhere had known of von Soden's great endeavor and looked forward eagerly to his results. When his book finally appeared in

1913, everyone was shocked—and then angry. Reviewers complained that not only did he high-handedly demand that everyone learn an entirely new nomenclature for all manuscripts, but the numbers and symbols were extremely cumbersome and confusing. Others complained that the Greek text he produced was eccentric and too heavily influenced by *medieval* evidence, a glaring error in their eyes. Worst of all, when scholars began detailed examinations of his data, they discovered that his lists of thousands of alternative words and phrases were so riddled with mistakes and omissions and misspellings that his results could not be used without laborious rechecking.[27] It was unbelievable. All that work for nothing! Within months of its appearance, von Soden's great effort was reluctantly set aside with the sorrowful verdict "a magnificent failure." He died a year later, in 1914. Modern specialists still claim that his evidence is unsurpassed in comprehensiveness, but, for all intents and purposes, most scholars detour around the huge pile of wreckage, which is all that is left of von Soden's dream.[28]

The Modern Period and the Establishment of a New Standard Text

The critical editions produced by Tischendorf and Westcott-Hort had the effect of making it unwise to use Erasmus' Greek New Testament for serious scholarship.[29] Its text was understood to be defective, unsafe for detailed investigation of the Gospels by theologians and historians. Where did this leave clergy and laypeople who relied on translations based on this defective text for preaching and personal devotion? What should the Bible Societies do who were responsible for producing Bible translations used around the world?

It was a double dilemma. On the one hand, it was realized that it would be very difficult, if not impossible, for a new translation to come up to the power and beauty of Luther's German version or the King James Version. On the other hand, which of several better Greek texts should the agencies adopt? Who could say which was the best? Faced with these perplexing questions, it is understandable that the various national Bible Societies did nothing as long as the specialists argued over who had the best "original text."

A way out of the text dilemma was proposed by the Württembergische Bibelanstalt in Stuttgart. In 1898 it commissioned a German scholar to produce a *consensus text* combining the best of the recent critical editions.[30] Thus Eberhard Nestle (1851–1913) produced a text based not on any ancient manuscripts but simply on the shared words of Tischendorf and Westcott-Hort. Where they clashed (which was not that often), he looked to the text of Bernhard Weiss for a deciding vote.[31]

Six years later, the British and Foreign Bible Society (by far the largest and most influential producer of Bibles in the world) officially adopted Nestle's text.[32] That decision represented the decisive abandonment of Erasmus' *textus receptus* on the part of both German and British Church officials, nearly four hundred years after it first appeared in 1516.[33] Henceforth, each Bible Society began producing new translations into modern languages based on Nestle's consensus Greek text. In this way, the Nestle text signaled the arrival of the period of triumph in the centuries-old struggle for a truly reliable text of the New Testament.

During this entire period, the Roman Catholic Church officially stood aloof, although a small number of Roman Catholic scholars did publish a few studies on the Greek text. But by and large, most Roman Catholic scholars still used the Vulgate for scholarship as well as worship.[34]

In 1914, the lengthy period of international cooperation and peaceful scholarly competition ended with the outbreak of World War I. When the military hostilities ended in 1918, a large residue of mistrust and hatred hindered international scholarly cooperation. Soon other problems loomed as the entire western world plunged into a disastrous economic decline preventing further work on large-scale projects. During this dire period, Erwin Nestle took over the task of improving his father's consensus Greek text. Then the Second World War erupted in 1939, stopping all international activity completely.

After the Second World War ended, work continued on Nestle's text, with the addition of the gifted researcher Kurt Aland.[35] Aland's first task was to go through the text and the list of alternative readings in the footnotes and verify them against photocopies and microfilms of the original manuscripts.[36]

Eventually, Aland took over the project and founded what came to be known as the Institute for New Testament Textual Research at the University of Münster. In 1955, Eugene Nida, translations secretary for the American Bible Society, suggested to Aland that an international, ecumenical committee be established to prepare a Greek New Testament designed specifically for the hundreds of Bible translation committees around the world.[37] Aland agreed, and the Joint Committee of the newly formed United Bible Societies came to be, composed of well-known specialists: Matthew Black (St. Andrews), Bruce Metzger (Princeton University), Allen Wikgren (University of Chicago), and Kurt Aland (Münster University). After a few years, Carlo Cardinal Martini (at that time rector of the Pontifical Biblical Institute in Rome) was added. This committee was charged with preparing an edition of the Greek New Testament suitable for use by translators. It was not asked to carry out fundamental research on the text; that task continued independently at Aland's Institute for Textual Research in Münster and other seminaries and universities in Europe and North America.

One innovation Nida insisted upon, against the opposition of the entire committee,[38] was a system of indicating the level of confidence on the part of the committee regarding its decisions on problematic textual passages: {A} represents a high level of confidence, {B} a moderate level, and so on, down to {D}, which signifies a high level of doubt that the words in the text are correct.[39]

This notation provides important information to users of the United Bible Societies text. Since not all decisions were equally complex, what level of certainty attended each decision? As we can see from the detailed commentary provided by Bruce Metzger, most decisions were fairly straightforward while others were so intractable that the Committee found itself split into two or even three factions, unable to reach any consensus.[40]

Another important by-product of this notation system is that it has the effect of reducing even further the number of *important* uncertainties in the text. For example, if the Committee was unanimous in 90 percent of the cases of textual variation, Nida's scheme divides the remaining 10 percent into a series of progressively uncertain decisions. This isolates the number of cases where there still is serious disagreement about the text.

Aland and his co-workers propose a different way to look at the question of the certainty or reliability of the text. They have compared their text with previous editions of the Greek New Testament: Tischendorf, Westcott-Hort, von Soden, and three other popular editions. They found that

- there was a complete similarity in 56 percent of the text of the Gospels,
- a 77 percent similarity in the text of the letters of Paul,
- about 70 percent for the Catholic Epistles,
- and 52 percent for the Revelation of John.[41]

Further examination revealed why this surprising degree of similarity might exist. The two most diametrically opposed text types are the early-fourth-to-sixth-century manuscripts and the Byzantine manuscripts produced throughout the Middle Ages. Comparison of the two produces an average difference of 20 percent.[42] So even when allowing for the widest latitude of variance in all known manuscripts, there still is an 80 percent degree of complete similarity.

But such broad comparisons do not do justice to the real situation. The vast majority of differences are no more than simple scribal mistakes (repetition of words, omission of words or lines, misspelling, etc.). If these are set to one side, probably less than 5 percent of the remaining variants involve a point of Christian doctrine.[43] In other words, the modern Nestle/Aland editions in use by the United Bible Societies represent approximately 95 percent of the "original text."

The "New Standard Text"

At the present time, scholars around the world are generally satisfied with the text of the United Bible Societies/Aland Institute.[44] The claim of the committee to have largely identified the "original Greek text" is—for the most part—not contested.[45] Rather, a movement has sprung up to call the latest Nestle/Aland edition the "New Textus Receptus" or "New Standard Text."[46] This claim is all the more appropriate since not only have the main Protestant Bible agencies endorsed this text, but it is "the text officially published and distributed by the [Roman] Catholic Church" as well.[47]

In short, the doubters and skeptics have had their day. Now the proponents of the "New Standard Text" can say:

> A hundred years after Westcott-Hort, the goal of an edition of the New Testament "in the original Greek" seems to have been reached ... (We now have) the writings of the New Testament in the form of the text that comes nearest to that which, from the hand of their authors ... set out on their journey in the church of the first and second centuries.[48]

Kurt Aland was aware what a momentous triumph this text represents. It has become nothing less than the authoritative text of the New Testament used by churches around the world. Aland again:

> A peculiar kind of responsibility is involved in preparing an edition of the Greek New Testament. It is not just any random text, but the very foundation for New Testament exegesis by churchmen of all confessions and denominations throughout the world. Further this Greek text serves as the base for new translations as well as for revisions of earlier translations in modern languages, i.e., it is the foundation to which the whole contemporary Church looks in formulating expressions of faith ... The new "standard text" is a reality and as the sole text distributed by the United Bible Societies *and* by the corresponding offices of the Roman

Catholic Church—an inconceivable situation until quite recently, it will soon become the commonly accepted text for research and study in universities and churches.[49]

The tumultuous process begun by Erasmus' publication of the first Greek New Testament in over one thousand years has reached at least one definitive goal: a widely disseminated critical text enjoying broad acceptance. In Chapter 21, I describe a few contemporary challenges to the hegemony of the Nestle/Aland text.

There is a striking parallel between this historical process and the one to be described next in Chapter 20, the gradual emergence of a broad consensus regarding the way in which the Gospels were composed. It is to that fascinating story we turn next.

CHAPTER 20

Emergence of a Third Form of the Synoptic Problem and Its Preferred Solution

$\sim$

The revolutionary ideas spreading through Europe as part of the cultural movement known to us as the Italian Renaissance, Deism in England and France, and the Enlightenment generally had an immediate, if unintended, impact on the interpretation of the Gospels. The broad outlines of the modern, historical method were sketched in Chapter 11. Chapter 12 focused on the application of this historical method to the interpretation of the Bible in general and the Gospels in particular. Chapter 13 documented the differences between Luther and Calvin in their reactions to the differences among the Gospels, showing how they straddled the divide between the traditional Roman Catholic approach going back to Augustine (Luther) and a more modern, literalist, still harmonistic approach clearly echoing the new mechanistic worldview (Calvin).

Subsequent chapters spelled out the progressive breakdown of the great medieval synthesis with respect to three of the main aspects of the Synoptic Problem: the *text* of the Gospels (14 and 15), the *canon* of the Gospels (18), and the emergence of a radically different, skeptical *hermeneutical approach* to the Scripture based on new political (16) and economic (17) values. Chapter 19 led the discussion toward the time of consolidation, describing the gradual establishment of a new critical consensus regarding the text of the New Testament (including the Gospels). This chapter will follow suit and describe the establishment of a critical consensus regarding the fourth aspect of the Synoptic Problem: a new *compositional theory* explaining the differences among the Gospels by means of a hypothetical scenario explaining how and in what order the Gospels were written. In this way, Part Two has presented the hypothesis that the modern worldview created a radically different, *Third Form* of the Synoptic Problem.

Chapter 11 made it clear that these momentous changes did not happen quickly. They required some five hundred years from beginning to end. First there was an early, inchoate stage of deepening confusion and turmoil (including a lengthy period of full-scale war and bloodshed in Europe and Great Britain) that took up most of the sixteenth and seventeenth centuries.

After this, the period of emerging consolidation of a new, historical approach to Gospel studies took place in two stages: an early rationalist stage lasting most of the seventeenth and eighteenth centuries, marked by the appearance of many Gospel harmonies as its chief symptom, and a later Romantic stage in the nineteenth and twentieth centuries, with the Gospel synopsis as its preferred instrument.

During this latter or Romantic phase, Gospel source theories appeared in great profusion, borne upon the wings of free, god-like imagination, as scholars rejected, refashioned, and invented biblical and Church history however they saw fit. All of these theories were characterized by a rampant atomization of the Gospel texts, accompanied by all sorts of conjectures as to the origin of this or that bit of text. Most of these source hypotheses eventually fell by the wayside or were consolidated into later mega-theories.

This exploratory period lasted from the late eighteenth century until the mid-nineteenth. It was followed by a period of consolidation that reached down to the late twentieth century, as one particular approach, the Two Source Hypothesis (*Zwei-Quellen Theorie*), beat back all rivals to emerge as the master scenario preferred by the majority of Gospel scholars in Europe, Great Britain, North America, South Africa, Australia, Korea, and Japan.

With this as an overview, let us now turn to a more detailed account of these events. I begin with the transitional period (sixteenth through seventeenth century), when the traditional, medieval harmony was repeatedly recast in ever more literal interpretations of the differences among the Gospels.

The New Spirit of Literal Historicism in Biblical Interpretation

The first phase of the modern approach to the differences among the Gospels did not seem revolutionary or dangerous at the time: I refer to the striking number of historicizing Gospel harmonies that appeared during the Reformation and after.[1] This period ended in 1776 when J. J. Griesbach published a radically different instrument for comparing the Gospels, called a *synopsis*. These two instruments dealt with the differences among the Gospels starting from very different hermeneutical presuppositions. I will identify some of the main presuppositions for the Gospel harmony here and the Gospel synopsis later when we come to it.[2]

First, traditional Gospel harmonists proceeded on the basis of Augustine's assumption that all four Gospels were uniformly true and without admixture of the slightest degree of error. The traditional way of stating this assumption was to claim that each had been written with the aid of the Holy Spirit, or the Spirit of Christ, so that all four were evenly true in all parts and passages. However, Origen to a great extent and Augustine to a lesser extent approached the Gospels using a *dual conception* of scriptural truth. They said that the Bible in general and the Gospels in particular contained both symbolic truth (ἀληθεῖα πνευματικὴ *mystica locutio*) and literal truth (ἀληθεῖα σαρκικὴ *res gestae*). In this way, differences and discrepancies among the Gospel narratives were still *all true;* they just weren't all literally true.[3] This dual notion of truth disappeared—especially among Protestants—in the sixteenth- and seventeenth-century biblical interpretation, in favor of a modern, flat literalism. We saw the beginning of the process of interpreting everything in the Gospels in terms of "historical fact" in our comparison of Luther and Calvin[4] and the full flowering of it in John Locke.[5]

Second, where Origen had said that each Evangelist had received a unique vision of God, such that the narratives' harmony existed in the spiritual level, not the literal (causing him to avoid harmonizing them beyond a certain point), Augustine took the approach that the Gospel authors—aided by the Holy Spirit—had composed their writings by remembering various things and making use of the accounts that preceded theirs. As such, he believed that all of them *knew more* than what they had written. Therefore, it was entirely appropriate to combine their accounts into a larger *composite* narrative.

The Augustinian approach remained the model for more than a thousand years. During the Middle Ages, only a handful of new harmonizations were published.[6] Then, between 1525 and 1600, more than thirty Gospel harmonies were printed.[7] How can we account for this sudden spurt of Gospel harmonies?

Several factors were at work. The recent invention of movable type and the printing press made the process of publishing books cheaper, easier, and faster. All kinds of books appeared in greater numbers, not just harmonies.

Did the heightened religious activity associated with the Reformation have anything to do with it? The widespread religious controversy undoubtedly stirred up fresh interest in the Gospels, but most of the new Gospel harmonies were not created by Protestants, and the prefaces reveal little interest in the theological issues of the Reformation. They express the usual concerns: protect the Gospels' credibility by removing inconsistencies and describe Christ's life in one continuous narrative.[8] Something else was involved.

The New Harmonies Reflect
the Modern, Physical View of the Universe

These sixteenth- and seventeenth-century harmonies share one significant characteristic: they are without exception strikingly literal in their understanding of the Gospel narratives. Every detail points to a real event in physical space-time. The modern, mechanistic concept of history has crept in and taken over. The Gospels have become literal records of causally connected chains of historical facts. The harmonists disjoined these chains and recombined them into one perfectly consistent super-chain.[9]

This approach resulted in an increasingly *atomistic* analysis of the Gospel narratives. With the modern view of the divinity of human reason, anyone could disjoin the Gospel chains and recombine them with nothing more to guide him than the divine light of human reason. Indeed, a sort of rivalry sprang up to see who could produce the most precise, most detailed harmony. Given the modern understanding of reason in terms of the analogy with mathematics, the harmonists perceived the Gospels to be clear, easily understood writings (Locke) that could be recombined with ever increasing degrees of satisfying precision, as they calculated the chronology of the Lord's activities by the year, month, day, and even hour.

The best example of the new ultra-literal harmony was created by Andreas Osiander (1498–1552), the learned Lutheran theologian. Osiander had kept abreast of the latest scientific discoveries, even writing the Preface to Nicolaus Copernicus' *De revolutionibus orbium caelestium* (1543). Just as Copernicus applied strict mathematical reasoning to discover a unified structure for the solar system, so Osiander sought to apply a strict logical approach to the Gospels, in order to create an objective, unified structure of the Gospel history. What did he accomplish?

His *Harmoniae Evangelicae*, published at Basel in 1537, contained several new features. For one thing, he did not simply create a single composite narrative out of the four Gospels, the way Tatian had. Instead, he placed similar Gospel accounts next to each other in four vertical columns on each page. This allowed the reader to see distinctly the similarities and differences among the Gospel accounts. These were important to him, as we shall soon see.

How did he know which accounts to place next to each other? Did he use the Eusebian sections and canons or follow Augustine's harmony? Possibly, but his understanding of the literal inspiration of the biblical writers required not only that every detail of every story be historically true, but also that the *order* of each Gospel be carefully preserved where it differed from the others.[10] If Osiander spotted any differences of either content *or order of placement,* no matter how minute, this meant different historical events were being recounted. As a result, the tens of thousands of slight differences among the Gospels caused Osiander to create a picture of Christ's life and ministry filled with repeated events: Jesus was tempted three different times; cleansed the temple three times; healed the centurion's servant once, twice, and thrice; gave the Sermon on the Mount (Matthew) as well as the Sermon on the Plain (Luke) in two different places; was betrayed twice by Judas; anointed by three different women; ate two Last Suppers; and so on.[11] The resulting "life of Christ" appalled John Calvin:

> Osiander thinks he is very clever to make one blind man into *four.* In fact, there is nothing sillier than his idea. Because he sees that the Evangelists disagree in a few words, he imagines that sight was restored to one blind man at the entry into the city (of Jericho), then to a second (in the city), and to two others when Christ went away from Jericho again. But all the details hang together so well that no sane man can believe that these are different stories.[12]

However, many admired Osiander's harmony and it was widely imitated, especially by Protestants.[13]

The same physical literalism was applied to other parts of the Bible during this same period. I mentioned earlier John Toland's rationalistic explanation of the miracles in the Old Testament.[14] James Ussher produced a strict chronology of world history based solely on the Bible, in his famous *Annales Veteris Testamenti* (1650). Similarly, William Whiston proved that the story of Moses was historically accurate down to the last detail, in his *New Theory of the Earth* (1696).[15]

The Disappearance of the Gospel Harmony

This historical confidence was not universally shared, however. These attempts to prove the factual accuracy of the Bible were exercises in damage control over against rising skepticism regarding the Bible and Christian doctrine. Where did this spirit of skepticism come from?

Martin Luther's rejection of the medieval criterion had sent a shock across all of Europe and Great Britain, causing traditional allegiances and institutions to crack open, releasing a growing skepticism toward all things traditional.[16]

Since the earliest days of the Italian Renaissance, intellectuals in England, France, and Italy scoured the classics for the criticism of traditional religion in Sextus Empiricus, Lucretius, and Cicero, just to name the most important writers. This criticism was given up-to-date clothing and then turned against the Roman papacy, the Protestant establishment, and traditional Judaism. In a particularly ironic twist, the new skepticism joined hands with the historical literalism employed by the defenders of the Bible to drive out all traditional symbolic interpretation of the biblical writings. Instead, as Klaus Scholder noted, a whole range of mediating positions sprang up in response to the new scientific skepticism, adopting *some* of the modern skepticism and mixing it with traditional Christian/Jewish piety.[17]

In its more extreme form, modern skepticism produced two conclusions regarding the Gospels. First, taking their cue from Spinoza, but as refined by Reimarus (Lessing) and others, the modern skeptics saw the Gospel authors as fraudulent, illiterate knaves who invented the Gospel stories for their own self-aggrandizement. In contrast, *Jesus himself*, that is, the "historical Jesus" as reconstructed by these modern historians, was viewed in a different light. Once the bulk of the Gospel sources had been properly criticized (i.e., dispensed with as unreliable), the "historical Jesus" was seen to have taught a few noble truths (which any decent European already knew anyway).

Second, the view soon sprang up that it was impossible—indeed, untruthful—to indulge in the traditional harmonizing of the Gospels to reproduce the original chronological scheme supposedly hidden within the four Gospels. A different approach was called for, one that did not pretend to find chronological links that were not there. This skepticism regarding the chronological value of the Gospel accounts became the first main root of the *Third Form* of the Synoptic Problem.

A second main root of the Third Form of the Synoptic Problem was the cult of objectivity (read: hatred of all forms of "enthusiasm") in the modernist agenda. The goal here was scientific knowledge, i.e., pure knowledge that was objectively true, like a geometric proof. As we saw in Spinoza's elaborate discussion, scientific knowledge was completely free of emotion, desire, enthusiasm, faith, or religion. The new breed of *natural philosophers,* as they preferred to call themselves, refused to base anything on the Bible, or Church tradition, or religious impulse. Objective truth, obtained by direct, physical experimentation, was the new standard. One of the best examples of this outlook is Francis Bacon's *Novum Organum* (1620).

This quest for objective, scientific knowledge produced prodigious feats of data accumulation and hypothetical explanation, as we have seen in earlier chapters on Gospel text and canon. In this chapter, I suggest that it caused the demise of the Gospel harmony and led directly to the invention of the Gospel synopsis, an instrument intended to facilitate the objective investigation of the differences among the Gospels.

The Emergence of a Romantic Redefinition of History—The Third and Final Root of the New View of the Synoptic Problem

By the beginning of the eighteenth century and on into the nineteenth, philosophers and others had grown tired of the static, machinelike view of nature/the universe propounded by the early rationalists and called for a very different conception of nature, history, God, and the universe.

This second phase is widely known as Romanticism. While still clinging to a nonsupernatural view of nature, Romanticism rejected the machine metaphor of nature in favor of the view that nature/the universe resembled a living organism. Romanticism viewed nature as alive, changing, growing, developing. In sharp contrast to the view of rationalism, nature was not comfortably predictable or reassuringly clear and distinct. Rather, nature was perceived as terrifyingly unpredictable, overpowering, opaque—and interesting.

As a result, the Romantic conception of nature produced a completely different definition of history. If the rationalists were interested in past history at all (which most of them were not), it was viewed in the same static fashion as nature/the universe. Did Kant ever write a "life of Jesus"? Hardly. The rationalist philosophers were, at best, vaguely interested in his moral example and ethical teachings—which they conveniently summarized in a few moral axioms already known by their innate reason.

In the Romantic view, history—still resolutely nonsupernatural—became a complex chain of nonrepeatable, unique events, a dynamic continuum dominated by *change*. Historical *development* became the favorite new category in terms of which to view Europe's past, indeed, the world's past and even the universe's past. The secular concept of *progress* (itself a blend of the traditional idea of Divine Providence mixed with a classical Greek idea of the natural superiority of scientific knowledge over mere opinion) became widely used to explain how "modern" Europe could be so superior to all previous ages in art, technology, science, and civilization.

With the past viewed in terms of dynamic change and development, *history* suddenly took on immense new importance, both as the record of unrepeatable events that needed to be remembered in order to see how much better the modern world was and also as the story of humans who struggled heroically against the forces of superstition, bigotry, and ignorance in their own day, as an inspiration to those in the modern day doing the same.

The developmental view of nature and history typical of Romanticism produced a new developmental approach toward the differences among the Gospels. Keeping the rationalist view of Jesus and the Apostles as human beings, the Romantics went on to view the history of the early Church in dynamic terms, with strife and tension on all sides—similar to their view of history generally. Keeping the earlier view that the Gospel authors wrote for specific audiences and in different locations (Spinoza), the Romantics went on to ask specifically what sources they had used. Out of such dynamic historical considerations emerged the distinctively Romantic image of the Synoptic Problem, the third and final root of the Third Form of the Synoptic Problem.

Early Approaches to the Third Form of the Synoptic Problem

Once the Gospel authors were seen in terms of *historical change*, the main task of the scientific modern Gospel scholar was exactly *not* to harmonize their products, that is, destroy the evidence of their being genuinely unique expressions of the faith and development of the early Church. Now the main task became one of inventing a plausible historical past that would picture the Gospel authors as actual men who had lived in four different place/time situations, writing to four different audiences, for four very different reasons. In this way, a real, living picture of the dynamic development of the early Church could arise.

Given this new task, it was obvious that a *new instrument* was needed to study the Gospels, one that would place similar Gospel texts next to each other so that the minute differences would stand out sharply, one that would permit extensive comparison and contrast and yet would not alter the narrative orders of the respective Gospels in the slightest. It must be an *objective* tool.

The first scholar to devise such an instrument was Johann Jakob Griesbach of Jena and he named it a *synopsis* of the Gospels.[18] How and why did Griesbach come to make this decisive invention?

Johann Griesbach was born on 4 January 1745 in Butzbach, Germany. He was the only son of Konrad Kaspar Griesbach and Dorothea Rambach, the daughter of Professor Johann Jakob Ramsbach. Konrad had met Dorothea while studying with her father at the Pietist Lutheran Institute Francke in Jena. After graduating in 1747, Pastor Konrad Griesbach became a successful and popular preacher in the Church of St. Peter in Neustadt, Frankfurt, remaining there his whole life.

At that time, Frankfurt was a flourishing center of international trade, wealthy banks, a thriving intellectual community, a large annual book fair, and numerous publishers. As a result, the new German bourgeois spirit had taken root in Frankfurt, despite the powerful presence of the traditional German aristocracy and conservative Lutheran clergy, given the central role each played in the election and coronation of German emperors in Frankfurt since the ninth century. But at this time, Frankfurt was a free imperial city, and the impulses of modern trade and modern thought found a ready home there.[19] We will see signs of the new spirit of bourgeois independence in young Griesbach.

As a student, Johann was educated in Lutheran Pietistic orthodoxy during five semesters at the University of Tübingen. He transferred to Halle in 1764, where he came under the decisive influence of the great modernist New Testament scholar Johann David Michaelis (1717–1791) and his younger but equally brilliant contemporary Johann Salomo Semler (1725–1791), in whose house Griesbach lived as a student.[20] Griesbach took a year out to go to Leipzig, where he read the Church Fathers and studied with the eminent New Testament critic Johann August Ernesti, whose literalist, historicist exegetical principles became the cornerstone of Griesbach's own hermeneutics later.[21]

He returned to Halle where he continued to apply himself to the modern, critical New Testament text criticism, exegesis, and biblical theology.[22] After gaining his master's degree in 1768, he set off—at age twenty-three—to visit other great libraries and centers of learning in Europe and Great Britain: the Royal Library, Paris; the British Museum in London; and the Bodleian at Oxford. In Holland he encountered scientific biblical criticism and saw the famous Gospel harmony of Jean Le Clerc. In short, Johann received the best education in Pietist and modernist biblical studies that Germany and other countries of his day had to offer.

Returning to his parents' home in October 1770, he prepared a treatise on the importance of the Church Fathers (especially Origen) for the original text of the New Testament. He submitted it to the faculty in October 1771, earning an instructor's position as a result. Two years later, he was promoted to *extraordinarius*.[23] It was during these years in Halle and on his extensive tour of Europe and England that Griesbach prepared the broad intellectual and scholarly foundation that served him the rest of his life.

In April 1775, Johann married the sister of a close friend in Halle, Friederike Schütz. At the time, he was considering an invitation to join the faculty of the Princely Saxon Comprehensive (Lutheran) Academy at Jena. When the curator at Halle was reluctant to permit Griesbach to abandon "his (instructional) duties to the Prince (i.e., the Academy)," as the curator put it, Griesbach became offended and immediately accepted the new position in Jena without further ado. German biographer Gerhard Delling comments, "Here one sees the *bourgeois* pride of the son of a free, imperial city."[24]

Griesbach was installed at Jena in December 1775. In ensuing years, he lectured in Church history, New Testament exegesis, and the biblical foundations of "popular dogmatics."[25] He soon rose to become the preeminent member of the Jena faculty. As such he was active in the administration of the university and even took on additional duties as the deputy for the district of Jena in the provincial diet at Weimar.[26] Widely respected and trusted, Griesbach lived a long and productive life that was a seamless blend of local and provincial politics and scientific biblical research. In the former he was noted for his judicious, but modern political agenda, and in the latter he was noted for his blend of liberal (modernist) biblical exegesis and Pietist "popular dogmatics." It was in the fields of text criticism and synoptic source criticism that Griesbach made contributions for which he is still famous. His younger rationalist theologian and colleague on the Jena faculty H. E. G. Paulus said in a eulogy for Griesbach that he had been "a paragon of scholarly discernment and patriotic industry."[27]

Griesbach's Hermeneutical Principles

Given his family background and academic training, Johann Griesbach's approach toward the Bible and theology was complex and nuanced. On the one side, throughout his life he remained in close contact with Germany's leading Romantic thinkers—Goethe and Schiller—and, through them, the new German bourgeois political and economic agenda.[28] From his student days with Semler and Michaelis, Griesbach had been exposed to Europe's skeptical, historicist interpretation of the New Testament and

Church history. At the same time, he remained a true son of his religious heritage, never relinquishing in his lectures, publications, and ecclesiastical activities a marked Lutheran Pietism.

Government officials and Church leaders may have viewed Griesbach as a liberal, but Griesbach himself noted that he never pleased either the liberals or the conservatives.[29] If he adopted a number of modern, critical principles and conclusions in his biblical exegesis, he also publicly rejected the extreme rationalist conclusions of his younger colleague Paulus.[30] This is not the occasion for a complete examination of all of the different strands in Griesbach's hermeneutical methodology, but the main outlines of Griesbach's hybrid approach are evident enough. I have laid them out in two lists: modern historicist presuppositions and Lutheran Pietistic presuppositions.

Griesbach's Modern Historicist Presuppositions

- Secular and skeptical: the Bible and the New Testament are to be studied like any other ancient book. "The N.T. must be explained as every ancient book is explained."[31]
- Objective: theological concerns should not intrude into the exegetical process. The Bible's meaning must be discovered by an analysis of the literal and historical context, like any other ancient book.[32]
- Literal: every word, every sentence, every passage has one meaning: the literal, historical sense.[33]
- Psychologizing: attention must be paid to the time, place, and purpose of the biblical authors.[34]
- Historicizing (i.e., cultural relativism; note the appearance of Spinoza's "nominalist barrage"):[35] to understand the New Testament, one must have accurate and detailed historical knowledge of the Jewish culture, the Greek culture, and the Roman, as well as geography, archaeology, linguistics, and philology.[36]
- Rationalist critique of biblical inerrancy: "The N.T. writers . . . often err." The biblical writers ascribed to divine agency events that modern science knows to have natural causes. "The truth of the Christian religion rests not on miracles but partly on its (moral) excellence, partly on its history."[37]
- Modernist distinction between essential and nonessential doctrine: "The Bible contains much temporally conditioned data due to the limited perspective of its writers. This is simply the garment in which the universal truth is contained."[38]
- Atomizing approach: every word must be interpreted according to

its context. "One and the same expression in different circumstances can have a totally different meaning."[39]

· Spinozist disjunction between historical exegesis and theology in the quest for scientific objectivity: "First the philologian and exegete must speak; after the completion of his work, then the theologian and the philosopher come (to do theirs)." Again, "Theology must be based on the results of sound (objective) historical research."[40]

Griesbach's Lutheran Pietistic Presuppositions

· The Bible is a unique book and all interpretations must honor what is unique about it. It contains the *facts* of God's revelation in history, especially Christ's birth, crucifixion, resurrection, and ascension. These "historical facts" are the basis for theology and preaching. "God has caused something extraordinary to happen (in Jesus Christ) which is beyond human power to do, thus confirming his revelation."[41]

· The New Testament writers were not inspired by the Holy Spirit *in the act of writing*. Rather, the Apostles received a onetime gift of the Spirit at Pentecost which "surpassed the powers of nature, . . . (making it possible for them later on) both to understand and transmit doctrine without danger of error."[42] Note that this left out biblical writers like Luke and Mark,[43] as well as those responsible for what Luther had labeled the "inauthentic" books, e.g., the Epistle of James and the Revelation of John (a book Griesbach never discussed in print).

· The Holy Spirit works in Christians through the word of the Apostles, coming alive through the Gospel. In this context, Griesbach stressed the Gospels by the two Apostles, Matthew and John. These were of preeminent importance for giving reliable testimony to the "historical facts" of Jesus' ministry.[44]

· God's *summa beneficia* come to the whole of Christendom through faith, prayer, worship, and good works. In these ways, "all Christians are given a share in all the benefits and privileges granted by God to the members of the community of Christ collectively."[45] Here we may glimpse Griesbach's vision of the Christian state.

· It was in connection with the great feast days of the Christian year that Griesbach published every year for over thirty years specimen exegeses of the relevant Scripture passages, for the benefit of clergy and laity alike.[46]

The tension and discontinuity between these two sets of hermeneutical principles are obvious. One is reminded of Klaus Scholder's comment, quoted at the beginning of Chapter 11:

> In the great controversy over the understanding and significance of the Bible which began with the rise of modern thought in the West, the most important positions were staked out around 1680 ... Orthodoxy died out slowly (over the next 250 years) and with it the last group which held resolutely to the universal claim of scripture. By contrast, rational criticism was extended and made more radical. *In between, there were mediating positions of all degrees and shades* ... (By the late twentieth century) the Bible has become a handbook of morality whose doctrines are acceptable to any reasonable person.[47]

Griesbach was a perfect example of such a hybrid or mediating position. He himself was aware that there were all sorts of tensions, not to say contradictions, within his arguments. His basic, more or less petrified *theologoumenoi* were inconsistently yoked to a soft historicist skepticism. What was the outcome? Judging from his more popular writings, Griesbach's Bible became—in good Enlightenment, i.e., Spinozist, fashion—a handbook of morality whose doctrines were acceptable to any reasonable person.

Griesbach's Historical Scenario of How the Gospels Were Composed

Griesbach's lifelong ambition was to find the most objective, historically accurate information he could about Jesus Christ's life and ministry. He was drawn to the two Gospels believed to have been written by Apostles because he had been taught that they were granted at Pentecost supernatural assistance to record the historical, literal truth. Where did this leave the Gospels of Luke and Mark? To answer this question we must make a small digression and focus on Griesbach's visit to London in 1769–1770.

A few years before Griesbach set off for his tour of Europe and England in 1768, an English clergyman named Henry Owen published a little book on the Gospels in 1764 in London entitled *Observations on the Four Gospels*. In it, Owen proposed an explanation of how each of the Gospels was composed in relation to the others. We know from the list of books in Griesbach's library that he owned a copy of this book, but there is no evidence that he actually met Owen while he was in England in 1769–1770. But he could have.[48] Griesbach's later statements on the relationships among the Gospels is so similar to Owen's and not to his teachers Michaelis and Semler that we may wonder whether—although Griesbach never explicitly mentioned Owen in any of his writings—Owen's ideas were the starting point for many of Griesbach's on the relations among the Gospels.

What might a conversation between the elderly Reverend Henry Owen and the young German scholar have been like, if they had met and talked over matters of mutual scientific interest? Perhaps something like the following.

Owen might have begun by insisting that scholars need to know how the Gospel authors—understood as mortal men—had done their work. Such knowledge would be of great value in arriving at an accurate understanding of the many differences among the Gospels, which are at present a major stumbling block to Christian certainty.

> Could we truly discover at what time, for whose use, and on what occasion the Gospels were respectively written, we should doubtless be able, not only to understand them more perfectly, but also to read them with more profit, than we have the happiness at present to pretend to. For such a discovery, as it would throw light on the difficult passages, and help us to reconcile the seeming contradictions, that obstruct our progress in these sacred studies, so would it impart an additional lustre, force and propriety to the several arguments that the Scripture offers for the confirmation and improvement of our faith.[49]

Griesbach would undoubtedly have thought this statement entirely reasonable. Owen might then have continued, switching with dazzling ease to a totally rationalist idea: "To be of any value, such examinations must be strictly objective and free of any taint of dogmatic prejudice, should they not? Well, my own

> disquisitions, if they can plead no other merit, may yet at least lay claim to this—that they were formed with a good Design, and *conducted with the utmost impartiality*. For the Author, having no hypothesis to serve nor any other end in view but the investigation of Truth, suffered himself to be carried along as the tide of evidence bore him."[50]

Griesbach might have nodded sagely at this display of Owen's selflessness in the pursuit of truth.

Then Owen might have come to his master stroke: this purely objective quest for truth seems to have opened the door to a *previously un-known field of Gospel study.* "Herr Griesbach, I think I have discovered the secret of how the Gospels were written, that is, how the Evangelists used each other in composing their own accounts! That is why I wrote this book. And if my

> plan (of the Gospels' relations to each other) herein exhibited be just in the main ... then *there is a new field of Criticism opened,* where the learned may usefully employ their abilities in comparing the several Gospels together and raising observations from that comparative view."[51]

If the Reverend Henry Owen shared *this* thought with the young biblical scholar from Germany—a man at the very beginning of his scholarly career, eager to learn the latest scientific results from the learned scholars of Cambridge and Oxford—it might have been a life-defining moment. Had not his teacher Semler taught him to meticulously compare the texts of the Gospels to each other? Had not he, Johann Griesbach, decided to make this his lifework? But now he could see that Semler and the rest were unwittingly overlooking a major type of evidence. What if the Gospel authors' *copying from each other* could be accurately sorted out, with the same minute attention to detail already used in text criticism? If a scholar could thereby learn the *direction of dependence* among the Gospels themselves, would this not aid immeasurably in obtaining a more reliable estimate of each Gospel author's *original text* than any number of later manuscripts and patristic quotations?

Even more important, with this kind of scientific approach producing a solid text of the Gospels, it should be possible to go on and—by closely comparing later with earlier accounts—establish with objective certainty what *the original historical facts* of Christ's life and ministry were, upon which the Gospels were based!

Owen was still talking. "The Gospels differ from each other, not because the Evangelists were ignorant of the original facts or wayward in their representation of them.

> In penning their Gospels, the sacred Historians had a constant regard, (not only) to the several particulars of Christ's life, but also to the circumstances of the persons for whose use they wrote. It was *this* that regulated the conduct of their narration—that frequently determined them in their choice of materials—and, when they had chosen, induced them either to contract or enlarge, as they judged expedient. In short, it

was *this* (concern for their audiences) that *modified* their Histories and gave them their different *colourings.*"[52]

Of course! The skeptics had it all wrong! In a flash, the young German saw that by correctly discovering the original order of composition of the Gospels, by means of a minute examination of the "literary footprints" of each author's language and style in the accounts of his successors, the biblical critic would be able to simultaneously provide a rational explanation of the many differences among the Gospels *and* identify the most reliable historical facts about Jesus! It was a thrilling prospect.

Maybe this conversation never took place. Be that as it may. But if we compare the actual discussions of the Gospels by Owen and Griesbach, we can see that they share the same new Romantic conception of a developmental history of early Christianity, in terms of which to *justify* the differences among the Gospels. Furthermore, each has precisely the same source theory: Matthew was written first to convince the Jews that Jesus was the Messiah. Luke was written second, based on Matthew, for use in Paul's missionary churches (his congregations would not have understood many of Matthew's most important passages).[53] Mark was composed third, based on both Matthew and Luke, to bridge the two and focus on their shared material.[54]

We know of two occasions when Griesbach utilized this hypothesis for the instruction of pastors and theologians:

In 1783, Griesbach published a lecture given in Jena defending the historical reliability of the Easter texts, entitled: "That Easter may be celebrated with solemn piety . . . an inquiry into the sources that the Evangelists used in (creating) their narrations of the resurrection of the Lord."[55] Far from being unreliable, said Griesbach, the simple explanation for the many differences among the resurrection accounts is that each Evangelist used *different sources:* the Apostle Matthew based his account on the eyewitness account of Mary, the mother of James; the Apostle John got his account from the eyewitness account of Mary Magdalene; Luke (not an eyewitness) simply made use of the Gospel of Matthew, and Mark (also not an Apostle) wrote down what the Apostle Peter said who combined elements from the Gospels of Matthew and Luke.

Six years later, in 1789, during the feast of Pentecost, Griesbach published another explanation of the differences among the Gospels. This time it was a complete (if brief) statement of the sources used by the author of the Gospel of Mark, entitled: *A Demonstration That the Whole of the Gospel of Mark Was Extracted from the Commentaries of Matthew and Luke.*[56] This, Griesbach's most sustained treatment of the source question, began with an assertion that could have come straight out of Owen's book:

> It is above all important to know the sources from which historical writers have drawn the things that they have put into their commentaries, in order to interpret correctly their books, to evaluate justly the trustworthiness of the authors, and to perceive and judge skillfully the true nature of the events that they have recorded.[57]

Beyond their common starting point, Griesbach's detailed discussions differed markedly from Owen's, however. Before long, Griesbach began to explore this "new field of Gospel studies" in his own way. One of the very first things Griesbach discovered was that he needed a new tool, a new instrument to facilitate this kind of developmental comparison in lectures and speeches, and it was *not* a Gospel harmony. But what was it?

The Hermeneutical Assumptions upon Which Griesbach's Synopsis Was Based

Why did Griesbach produce a synopsis and not another harmony of the Gospels? I suggest that at least three factors were involved. In the process of elaborating them, the fundamental differences between these two instruments for dealing with the differences among the Gospels will stand out sharply and we will see how the Third Form of the Synoptic Problem required the instrument for Gospel study Griesbach invented.

First, Griesbach tells us he was familiar with a large number of Gospel harmonies. In the Preface to his *Synopsis* he said that he was "not unaware of how much trouble very learned men have taken to build up a well-ordered harmony according to self-imposed rules."[58] But something prevented him from making use of any of them. What was it? He was too much of a modern skeptic regarding the general historical reliability of the Gospels. "What if," asked Griesbach,

> *none* of the Evangelists followed the chronological order exactly everywhere? And (what if) there are not enough indications from which could be deduced which one departed from the (original) chronological order and in what places?[59]

Aware that these two questions led to extreme doubt regarding the chronological reliability of the Gospels, putting him outside the pale of his more optimistic contemporaries—even his liberal teacher Michaelis had included a Gospel harmony in his famous *Introduction to the New Testament*—Griesbach stubbornly insisted: "Well, I confess to this heresy!" (*atque in hac me esse haeresi fateor*).[60]

Griesbach spelled out in the preface to his *Synopsis* precisely how chronologically lacking he thought the Synoptic Gospels were.

> Matthew very often departed from the chronological order of things narrated and much less of the time (than the others) has (any) method (at all), such that things seem to be related to themselves, such as his (chapters on) the parables or Christ's sermons.[61] Mark, on the other hand, in order to compile his little commentary from Matthew and Luke, except for a few little narratives, used Matthew as his literary model keeping unchanged Matthew's order of narration (here Griesbach inserted a footnote to the treatise mentioned above proving that Mark was completely compiled from Matthew and Luke). But just as he chose Matthew, he also followed Luke's footsteps so accurately that he preserved the same sequence of events (told by him as well).[62] Finally, Luke is seen to have deviated from the chronological order a little later than the others (e.g., at the Travel Narrative, or in the Passion Narrative). But there appears no real reason (to think) that he most religiously adhered to it (the chronological order in other parts of his narrative) either.[63]

Was all lost? Could no way out of this skeptical impasse be found? This brings us to the second factor behind Griesbach's rejection of the traditional Gospel harmony.

Griesbach firmly believed that he could unravel the riddle of the Gospels because he had discovered the secret of how they had been composed. When *rightly compared with each other,* he felt, what few chronological hints there were in the Gospel narratives made perfect sense.

> There are little indications (or notices) of time, embedded in the individual narratives of the Evangelists, which are sufficient to remove all doubts (about the actual history of Christ's life).[64]

What was needed was a new kind of instrument that would objectively display these little chronological notices in each of the Gospel narratives. The problem with the traditional harmony was that, once the harmonist had used each narrative to create his composite account, these little time indicators were, as it were, obliterated. The harmonist both forced his specific chronology on the reader and destroyed the evidence in the process. For an Enlightenment scholar like Griesbach, this was not acceptable. He knew enough about the intricacies of Gospel interpretation to realize that many alternative approaches were possible. He meant to present the Gospel data in such a way as to preserve as much freedom for alternative interpretations as possible.

Out of this aspiration came Griesbach's *Synopsis*. Parallels will be placed next to each other but transpositions will be clearly indicated so that the original order of each Gospel will be obvious. Here is how Griesbach described his revolutionary new instrument:

> I decided that the order of each individual Evangelist should be retained undisturbed, so that Matthew, Mark, or Luke can be read in their separate order in our little book. (In this way), the judgment of each reader is able by whatever way to choose any hypothesis (he wants of the historical events), based on (his own) comparison of the Evangelists ... But, since a different order of many accounts is used in Matthew as well as Mark and Luke, and since the method of my project demanded that all three of the Evangelists be displayed on the page when they have the same subject matter, some changes of position (of pericopes) must be permitted.[65]

Looking at Griesbach's statements in the light of two hundred years' struggle to accomplish these goals, we can see that the task he took on was more difficult than he realized. He may have thought he was creating an objective arrangement of the texts, but in actuality that was not the case. In the conclusion of the Preface, Griesbach had to explain a number of "judgment calls" where he departed from these objectives.

Did Griesbach use his synoptic theory to guide him in creating his synopsis? It would seem so. His theory said that Mark had made use of Matthew and Luke where the latter two both agreed; in between, he followed one or the other, sometimes abruptly switching from the one to the other.[66] Griesbach's synopsis tends to follow either the order of Matthew and Luke where they coincide, or one or the other where they differ, fitting in the Markan parallels where they belong.[67] In his writing on the composition of Mark, Griesbach expressly warned *harmony* makers never to use Mark as the guide, since Mark had the least concern for chronological order of all.[68]

Third, Griesbach was unable to adopt the traditional Gospel harmony since he felt drawn toward the modern Romantic notion of a developmental view of the Gospels' history, a conception that was intrinsic to the epistemological rationale of the synopsis, as distinguished from the harmony.

Augustine's harmonistic approach viewed the composition of the Gospels in an essentially static way, as the story of Christ revealed from all eternity. Griesbach, on the other hand, had a developmental understanding of the history of the early Church. Like Owen, he believed that the Gospels were written at different times for different audiences. His *Synopsis,* he said, would facilitate the study of that *developmental history.*

> Beyond the usefulness (of gathering together similar passages in the Gospels to facilitate consideration of them in lectures), there are other matters (for which this Synopsis should prove useful). For not only does a comparison help identify the little synonymous phrases used by the evangelists, it also helps to identify the *native character and arrangement* of each Gospel.[69]

As long as the Gospels were viewed as a divinely inspired, inerrant, timeless block, or, more precisely, as four accurate but incomplete chronologies of the original events, the obvious gaps and apparent chronological inconsistencies among the Gospels had to be explained. It was an obvious choice to break up the narratives and realign the pieces in as close an approximation to the original holy events as possible.

As soon as the Gospels were seen to be *human* books written at *different* times for different audiences, their differences and inconsistencies took on a wholly new significance; they were important clues to the shifts and changes in the vital development of the early Christian Church. "The native character and (unique) arrangement of each Gospel" would be of critical significance to the historian in reconstructing that dynamic story.

One immediate result of this approach was to open the door to the possibility that not all of the Gospels were equally reliable. The big question then became how to distinguish the more reliable from the less reliable Gospels. Only if the biblical exegete could solve this prime riddle could the theologian and the preacher be shown how to read the Gospels correctly for accurate and reliable information about the historical Jesus. Hence the need for the *right hypothesis.*

Griesbach solved this riddle by pointing to the Gospels of Matthew and John as the most reliable historical accounts, since they had been written by Apostles who had received the Holy Spirit at Pentecost. This guaranteed their general historical accuracy. The Gospel of Luke, in contrast, was not written by an eyewitness; it was based largely on Matthew. Last and certainly least in Griesbach's view, came the Gospel of Mark. It was not written by an eyewitness either. In fact, 98 percent of his material came directly from the Gospels of Matthew and Luke. "All those who argue that Mark wrote under the influence of divine inspiration," Griesbach said, "must surely regard it as a very meagre one (*satis exilem informent necesse est*)."[70]

What about the Gospel of John? Even Augustine had admitted that the first three Gospels were more similar to each other than any of them was to the Gospel of John. John Calvin had abandoned John entirely when he wrote his *Commentary on a Gospel Harmony*. Griesbach went a step further and confessed to the "heresy" that he could see no chronological common ground among all four Gospels. Consequently, in his synopsis, except for marginal cross-references, he left the Gospel of John out until he got to the passion narrative. This omission of John, based on an explicit expression of Griesbach's skepticism regarding its chronological value, set the pattern for all later synopses.

As a pioneering effort Griesbach's *Synopsis Evangeliorum Matthaei, Marci et Lucae una cum Joannis pericopis* (Halle 1776; 2nd ed. 1797; 3rd ed. 1809) was quickly recognized as a major advance over the Gospel harmony. It signaled the advent of a radically new approach toward the differences among the Gospels. As such, it inaugurated the beginning of the full development of the Third Form of the Synoptic Problem. As was the case with Erasmus' pioneering effort concerning the Gospel text, Griesbach's instrument opened the door to all sorts of theories on how the Gospels had been composed.

Griesbach/Owen's Source Theory Disappears from the German Scene

In 1794, Griesbach published an expanded version of his *Demonstration That the Gospel of Mark Was Extracted from ... Matthew and Luke* to answer a number of attacks on it. A look at his survey of the *status quaestionis* will provide a glimpse of the main trends in the source discussion at the end of the eighteenth century in Germany. It is striking to see the underlying modern historicist assumption just taken for granted—that these authors all wrote in an entirely human fashion. There is no mention of divine inspiration anywhere.

Griesbach began his survey by going all the way back to what Papias had said about Mark.[71] Next he mentioned Augustine's view that Mark was the abbreviator of Matthew (like everyone else, Griesbach evidently knew nothing of what Augustine said in Book 4).[72] Then he jumped to the eighteenth century with an oblique reference to "some" who had propounded the view he favored:

More recently some have shrewdly observed that the conformity of Mark with Luke is also as great (as that with Matthew so) that he would seem to have had his (Luke's) Gospel (also) on hand (besides Matthew).[73]

Griesbach next noted that an English attack on the Augustinian position (Mark the abbreviator of Matthew) had induced a German scholar, Johann Benjamin Koppe of Göttingen, to bring out a publication in 1782 denouncing the idea that there had been any *direct* literary utilization by the canonical authors of each other's writings. Koppe insisted that the Preface to the Gospel of Luke was proof that the canonical Gospels were based on earlier Greek and Hebrew narratives.[74]

Koppe's arguments, continued Griesbach, induced his own teacher Michaelis—the tone of injury is still noticeable—to abandon his previous view.

By these clearly specious arguments (of Koppe), even Michaelis, previously a defender of the common (= Augustinian) view, was induced in the latest edition of his introduction to the NT to reconsider this opinion and to deny that the Gospel of Matthew was available to Mark when he wrote.[75]

Then Griesbach briefly noted the work of Gottlob Christian Storr of Tübingen, published in 1786, who said that Mark was the common *source* of Matthew and Luke—the direct opposite of Griesbach's view. This is the first appearance of the hypothesis of the priority of Mark in the modern German discussion.

Finally, Griesbach came to a book published in 1794 by his own student and former colleague at Jena, Johann Gottfried Eichhorn of Göttingen. The fact that his own student publicly disagreed with him was the main reason Griesbach reissued his *Demonstration*.[76] Eichhorn agreed with Koppe.

Matthew did not use either Mark or Luke; Mark did not use either Matthew or Luke; and Luke did not use either Matthew or Mark. The reason for their agreement is therefore to be sought from *some common source* from which they all drew. Many indications suggest that this source was Hebraic.[77]

The notion of a common (lost) source had been first suggested by Richard Simon in 1689. Soon other scholars were using the idea, notably Gotthold Ephraim Lessing, in a paper published after his death in

1784 entitled "New Hypothesis concerning the Evangelists Regarded as Merely Human Historians."[78] Eichhorn combined Lessing's Hebraic proto-Gospel with Koppe's idea that the Gospels were based on numerous earlier narratives of varying sizes to produce a complicated, multiple-source scenario that somehow accounted for all of the differences among the canonical Gospels.[79]

In his answer to this survey of the field, Griesbach was impatient; to him the truth was obvious:

> We cannot but wonder at such extensive disagreement of these scholars, since in our judgment it is abundantly clear merely from the close comparison of the three Gospels with one another what degree of relationship binds them together.[80]

Griesbach's Preface is evidence that the modernist *developmental* approach had clearly caught hold in Germany and was proving to be an exceptionally creative approach. All sorts of historical scenarios appeared, claiming to explain the differences among the Gospels. Griesbach's hypothesis, though popular at first, did not continue to attract adherents.[81] Ironically, Griesbach's *Synopsis* was more popular than ever.[82]

In 1848, Eichhorn's student Heinrich Ewald, who also taught at Göttingen, produced an even more complicated hypothesis in which he attempted to synthesize elements from many previous theories.

Like Eichhorn, Ewald began with G. E. Lessing's hypothetical common (lost) source, to which he added D. F. Schleiermacher's 1832 suggestion that Papias' statement "Matthew composed the (Lord's) oracles (λόγια) in the Hebrew language and each one interpreted (or translated) them as he was able"[83] may have consisted solely of Jesus' teachings. To this sayings source Ewald added Storr/Koppe's idea that Mark was the nucleus of Matthew, citing evidence gathered by the Berlin classical scholar Karl Lachmann to show that Mark stood in the closest relationship to the presumed Hebraic Ur-Gospel. Ewald was also influenced toward the priority of Mark by J. G. Herder's Romantic evocation of the beautiful simplicity and freshness of Mark's style—sure signs of its early date.[84] To these elements Ewald added Christian Hermann Weisse's conjecture that both Matthew *and Luke* had independently combined Mark with the *Logia* source.[85]

Ewald's nine-document hypothesis was dismissed by his contemporaries as too complicated, but it is possible to perceive, already at this early stage, the embryonic outlines of the later Two Source Hypothesis (*Zwei-Quellen Theorie*).

Incidentally, when Ewald got around to a discussion of the Gospel of Luke, he said the author of this Gospel had made use of every one of the earlier hypothetical sources, including canonical Mark, *but not Matthew.*[86] Ewald's consensus hypothesis was clear evidence of the wall beginning to rise in scholars' minds between the Gospels of Luke and Matthew.

Heinrich Ewald's book was part of a veritable explosion during the mid-nineteenth century of developmental historical scenarios inventing the way the Gospels had been composed, coming from France, Germany, and England. Meanwhile, Griesbach's theory was fading from sight. This was partly because it had become associated with the Tübingen radicals such as F. C. Baur and his notorious disciple David Friedrich Strauss.[87]

It must be admitted that Griesbach's scenario had serious intrinsic problems. One of them was that it ran counter to the widely held belief that the Gospel tradition always tended to grow, never to contract; the shorter form of anything was always more original than the longer. From this perspective, scholars could not believe that the author of Mark, confronted by such treasures in Matthew and Luke as the Beatitudes, the Lord's Prayer, the temptation story, and so on, would have left them out of his Gospel. It seemed much more probable that the shorter Gospel of Mark *was combined with* the *Logia* sayings source by the creators of Matthew and Luke (each adding still other material of his own).

Furthermore, Mark's poorer Greek compared with the other two, its lack of the major dogmatic elements found in the other Gospels (such as the virgin birth), and its seeming freshness of inconsequential historical detail convinced many scholars that it was the first and that the other two had augmented it.

Owen's and Griesbach's other claim, that Luke was created by someone who had access to canonical Matthew, faced even tougher opposition. If Luke used Matthew, scholars asked, why were there places where Luke seemed to preserve a more original form of a saying than its parallel in Matthew? And why were the same sayings of Jesus located in such different contexts in Luke as compared with Matthew? Did Luke actually dismember Matthew's great speeches just to scatter Jesus' sayings about in other locations? Why would he do that? Above all, why was Luke's infancy account (1–2) and Last Supper, trial, and resurrection so different from Matthew's? If Luke made use of Matthew as a source, he must have abandoned it just when he came to the most important parts of the story—a strange way to use a source!

The Griesbachian school did not provide convincing answers to any of these questions. Instead, some of its adherents publicly abandoned ship. The University of Berlin New Testament scholars W. M. L. De-Wette[88] and Friedrich Bleek[89] adopted the emerging consensus that both Luke and Matthew had made independent and differing use of a mass of earlier written and oral sources. This was similar to Lessing's Ur-Gospel concept as modified by Eichhorn and Ewald.[90] True, neither gave up the claim that Luke had *also* made use of canonical Matthew, but their hybrid position contributed to the growing consensus that Luke had been created independently of the Gospel of Matthew. When E. von Simons published, late in the century, a defense of the contrary idea that Luke had indeed used canonical Matthew, it caused a brief flurry but was soon ignored.[91]

So it was that, by the mid-nineteenth century, all four aspects of the Synoptic Problem—text, canon, composition, and hermeneutics—were each embroiled in wide-ranging research and debate, especially in Germany and England, as the Third Form of the Synoptic Problem gradually took shape. The pressures to limit the proliferation of theories as to text, canon, and composition of the Gospels were mounting also. We have seen in Chapter 19 how the debate over the text of the Gospels was resolved during the latter part of the nineteenth and first half of the twentieth centuries. The same process of consensus building took place during the same time period within the sphere of Gospel source criticism. Let us now see by what means that consensus was forged, and by whom.

Heinrich Julius Holtzmann and the Period of Consolidation

By 1860, German universities were caught up in the tremendous controversy provoked by David Friedrich Strauss' *The Life of Jesus Critically Examined* (1835), which carried modern skepticism into the heart of the New Testament and denied the historical reliability of the Gospels.[92] Heinrich Julius Holtzmann joined the fray while still a junior member of the theological faculty at Heidelberg. In 1863, he published *Die synoptischen Evangelien: Ihr Ursprung und geschichtlichen Character,* a meticulously argued vindication of the historical quality of the Gospels based on a brilliant but somewhat artificial synthesis of modern, historicist Gospel scholarship.

What were the elements of Holtzmann's synthesis? First, he kept to Ewald's basic starting point, that the existing Gospels were not directly related to each other but all went back to a primitive *Grundschrift.* But he simplified Ewald's complex nine-source hypothesis, dividing his *Grundschrift* into *two* primitive sources, a narrative source he called "Alpha" (which resembled Mark most closely and which later came to be known as Ur-Markus), and a sayings source, which he labeled "Lambda" (later known as Q). At first Holtzmann agreed with the consensus in Germany that Matthew and Luke were not dependent directly on canonical Mark but on the lost original narrative source Alpha, although he later retracted this view. He also agreed with the consensus that Luke was not directly related to Matthew. Instead, Matthew and Luke independently obtained their additional common material from the hypothetical source Lambda. The conclusion was a brief chapter entitled "The Synoptic Gospels as Sources of History," with a paragraph called "Picture of the Life of Jesus according to Source A," i.e., essentially the Gospel of Mark.[93]

Holtzmann's book, with few exceptions, was greeted as a masterpiece, not only because it seemed to proceed with such caution and deft mastery of the best of modernist Protestant Gospel scholarship, but also because it appeared to give a solid answer to the doubts raised by Strauss about the historical Jesus.[94] However, there is more to this picture than meets the eye. The final chapter, giving a historical reconstruction of Jesus' life and character, was shaped in such a way that it harmonized perfectly with the economic and political aspirations of the rising German bourgeoisie, and it was this part of his book that received the most immediate acclaim.[95]

This brings us to a side of Heinrich Julius Holtzmann not mentioned in previous histories of the Synoptic Problem: the contribution Holtzmann's synthesis made to the national political agenda.

From his earliest days as a student and young faculty member at Heidelberg, Holtzmann had been active in the tumultuous political struggles of the time. A central national issue was whether the numerous small German estates should align themselves with Protestant Prussia, shutting out the huge Roman Catholic Austria-Hungary to form a Protestant dominated "Small Germany," or whether they should strive for unity with all the German states, including Roman Catholic Austria-Hungary, to form a "Greater Germany."

In 1863 (the same year his book was published), Holtzmann helped found an organization known as the Protestant Union (opposed to Catholic tendencies) and he ran for office in the Baden provincial parliament, where he advocated liberal educational policies. In 1866, the great Prusso-Austrian War broke out over the question of German unification. Holtzmann immediately took the lead in his faculty to plead in favor of Prussian hegemony and a Protestant dominated Small Germany.[96] Prussia quickly won the war. Several years later, Holtzmann, having turned down an invitation to come to Vienna, was under consideration by the Prussian Emperor Wilhelm I and the German Reich Chancellery for a major position at the new *German* University of Strasbourg, Alsace having been seized from the French during the Franco-Prussian War of 1870–1871.

However, there was a problem. While Holtzmann's support of Prussian hegemony among the north German states was gratifying to the emperor and was undoubtedly taken into consideration when he was considered for the theological faculty at Strasbourg, he was too outspoken in other liberal political causes. Consequently, the Emperor Wilhelm, acting through his Reich Chancellor Otto von Bismarck, refused to grant Holtzmann the appointment until Holtzmann had produced not one but two written promises to the emperor that in future he would curtail his political activities and stick to academic duties.[97] Holtzmann finally agreed and, in 1874, Bismarck permitted him to be appointed to a chair in the Theological Faculty at the new Kaiser-Wilhelm Universität in Strasbourg. A last-minute petition from sixty local Lutheran pastors, opposing Holtzmann on the grounds that he was too liberal politically and theologically, was ignored.[98]

Holtzmann's scholarly prestige was clearly enhanced by his prominent position at Strasbourg. Some of the Protestant scholars whose works Holtzmann had chosen to synthesize in his magnum opus of 1863 also did well. In 1876, Bernhard Weiss was called from Kiel to be professor at the University of Berlin. With Carl Heinrich von Weizsäcker replacing F. C. Baur at Tübingen, Holtzmann in Strasbourg, and Bernhard Weiss in Berlin, the Two Source Hypothesis became dominant at these leading German universities, borne upon the academic shoulders of the carefully nuanced synthesis of Holtzmann and the influential *Lehrbuch der biblischen Theologie des Neuen Testaments* (1868) of B. Weiss.[99]

As a major sign of this trend, during this same period the leading theologian Albrecht Ritschl published *The Origin of the Early Catholic Church* (1857), in which he announced a radical break with his prior Hegelian agenda and his original acceptance of the Griesbachian hypothesis, in favor of a different, more sociological approach and Markan priority. In 1864, he was called to the theological faculty at Göttingen, Bismarck's alma mater.[100] The early Ritschl and Strauss are evidence that, if the Hegelians belonged to Germany's minuscule left wing theologically and politically, adherents to the Markan hypothesis tended to belong to Germany's intellectual right wing, supporting the Kaiser and a strong central government ruled by the Prussian aristocracy.

The political unity of Protestant-dominated Germany was now matched by a corresponding unity of Germany's leading Protestant centers of theological scholarship, both under the watchful eyes of the Reich Chancellor Bismarck. This was all the more important since, from 1871 on, Bismarck and the Protestant Churches in Germany were embroiled in a furious battle with the Vatican and German Roman Catholics (the *Kulturkampf*).[101] The Reich ministries of the interior, education, and religious affairs poured out decrees, inquiries, and edicts, all intended to harass and punish Roman Catholic priests and university faculty and to create a powerful, Prussian-controlled *Staatskirchentum*. In this highly charged climate of national crisis, it was *politically* important for Protestant theologians to be able to say in effect to the Roman Catholics, "Not only is your recent (1870) doctrine of papal infallibility utter nonsense, your tradition regarding the priority of the Gospel of Matthew is equally mistaken. We German Protestants have proved scientifically that *Mark* was written first!"

What was the *political* value of the priority of Mark? With Mark and Q in hand as the earliest and therefore the most reliable witnesses, German Protestants had a weapon with which to deliver a fatal blow against the famous Matthean text traditionally used by Roman Catholics to support their claim to have inherited the Keys of St. Peter, namely, Jesus' reply to Peter at Mt 16:17f.:

> And Jesus answered him, "Blessed are you, Simon Bar-jona! For flesh and blood has not revealed this to you, but my Father who is in heaven. And I tell you, you are Peter, and on this rock I will build my church, and the powers of death shall not prevail against it. I will give you the keys of the kingdom of heaven, and whatever you bind on earth shall be bound in heaven, and whatever you loose on earth shall be loosed in heaven."

Since this saying of Jesus was found neither in the earliest Gospel—Mark—nor in the equally early Sayings Source (Q), German biblical scholars argued that *the historical Jesus never said it.* In this way they cut the heart out of Roman Catholicism's scriptural warrant for papal infallibility precisely when it was being reaffirmed at Vatican Council I (1870). Nor, we may be sure, was this powerful argument unnoticed by the Reich Chancellor Bismarck as he led the fight against the Vatican in Italy and Ultra-Montanist Roman Catholics in Germany, not least among his university faculties.

In short, the magnificent summary presentation by Heinrich Julius Holtzmann in favor of the Gospel of Mark (so much for the Roman Catholics and their priority of Matthew) and defending the historicity of the (earliest) Gospel (Mark—so much for Strauss and the Tübingen school), became a powerful, defining text in the history of German politics and biblical *Wissenschaft*. In the late twentieth century, German historians can still speak of Holtzmann with great reverence, as the man who almost single-handedly forged the theological and political consensus that, one hundred years later, still unites liberal German Protestant New Testament scholars.[102]

The Two Source Theory Is Studied in England

Not surprisingly, the publications advocating the Two Source Hypothesis, coming from several German universities simultaneously, attracted international attention, particularly in England. On the Roman Catholic side, books written by leading German scholars were bought *and given away* by the indefatigable Baron Friedrich von Hügel, a leader in the Roman Catholic modernist movement at the turn of the century. Von Hügel made his home in London, but his family connections made it possible for him to circulate around Europe at the highest levels, and he used these tours to hold salons with eminent biblical scholars. He also took these opportunities to disseminate what he believed to be the best of modern German biblical scholarship, above all the publications of Heinrich Julius Holtzmann.[103]

Holtzmann's work attracted the attention of leading Protestant scholars in England as well, notably the Cambridge scholar E. A. Abbott and William Sanday, a don at Oxford. However, it would be a serious mistake to think that Holtzmann's results were simply taken over intact by these scholars, the way von Hügel did. On the contrary, they became the springboard for extensive comparative study of the Gospels, particularly among the participants in the sixteen-year, ongoing seminar on the Synoptic Problem at Oxford led by Sanday (1894–1910). As their eventual publication *Studies in the Synoptic Problem* indicates, many alternative routes were explored.[104]

As the Oxford Seminar pursued its work, a fateful trend developed in both countries. In Germany, during the twenty years following the publication of his book, Holtzmann's hypothesis underwent a series of modifications with the result that he issued a series of important changes to his original theory. He mentioned the most important ones in his *Lehrbuch der historisch-kritischen Einleitung in das Neue Testament* (1885).

For clarity's sake I shall list here the points where I have changed my previous position as a result of discussions with D. F. Strauss (a Griesbachian), A. Hilgenfeld (Augustinian hypothesis), Carl Heinrich von Weizsäcker (priority of Mark), Eduard Simons (Luke used Matthew), and others:

1. It is possible that the (so-called *sayings* source Alpha) contained *narrative sketches* undetachable from the sayings of the Lord.
2. *Luke knew Matthew* as well as Mark.

3. Consequently, at least *most of the motives for distinguishing be-tween an ur-Mark and Mark must be dismissed.*[105]

The theory that Matthew and Luke were primarily dependent on canonical Mark, and not some earlier version of it, was given decisive formulation by the young Swiss scholar Paul Wernle in a book entitled *Die synoptische Frage* (1899). Examining the arguments for an Ur-Markus of Lachmann, the early Holtzmann, and others, Wernle roundly declared:

> Evidence of a longer ur-Markus has never been produced and cannot be produced . . . I cannot see anything missing in the stories of John the Baptist and the Temptation; I would not know where to find a gap that would be fitting for the centurion from Capernaum. Also, to me, the conclusion of the parousia speech appears so powerful and effective that a longer presentation would only detract from it. In fact, all of these sections have been assigned to ur-Markus solely for the purpose of alleviating the synoptic problem. Such an undertaking which underestimates the uniqueness and intelligibility of our Mark is doomed to failure . . . There is no compelling reason to postulate a shorter or longer ur-Markus as distinct from our canonical Mark. From this point of view, the ur-Markus hypothesis simply collapses.[106]

A year after this book was published, Wernle was invited to a professorship at the University of Basel. Later scholars judged Wernle's book to have given the clearest presentation of the Two Source Hypothesis in general, and the Sayings Collection in particular (he was among the first to name it Q).[107] So much for Ur-Markus in Germany until it was revived in the mid-twentieth century by Bultmann and some of his students.

Meanwhile, a similar trend was occurring in England. Led by Abbott and Burkitt, Sanday's Oxford Seminar also saw no reason to preserve the carefully nuanced German distinction between an Ur-Markus and the canonical Gospel of Mark. These scholars also began to make a hard identification between canonical Mark and the primary Gospel source used by Matthew and Luke.[108]

Holtzmann noted this dual trend in both countries. In a publication brought out three years before his death in 1910, Holtzmann said:

> No one who has really read the simultaneously-published books by Paul Wernle (*Die synoptische Frage*) and J. Hawkins (*Horae Synopticae*) can doubt any longer that the common root of the synoptic texts, the actual stock of our Gospels, is to be found in Mark.[109]

Although not evident to these men at the time, this fateful modification proved to be disastrous for the Markan hypothesis. As we will see in Part Three, it was no accident that every earlier critic from Lachmann to the early Holtzmann, no matter how carefully he described the precanonical source in terms *resembling* canonical Mark, somehow knew he should never take this final, fatal step. The British scholars, however, never seemed aware of the logical trap awaiting them.

When what must be considered as the final judgment of these Oxford and Cambridge scholars was published by Canon Burnett Hillman Streeter in 1924, *The Four Gospels: A Study of Origins*,[110] it is clear that the German *Zwei-Quellen Theorie* had become England's "Four Source Hypothesis."[111] Streeter's monumental work was based on the massive amounts of research carried out by F. C. Burkitt,[112] Sir John Hawkins,[113] and E. A. Abbott[114] and is unthinkable apart from the impressive colored plates in W. G. Rushbrooke's *Synopticon*.[115] The almost crushing weight of all this scholarship, combined with Streeter's masterful rhetoric, has succeeded in convincing generations of English-speaking scholars in Great Britain and North America that they should agree with their German colleagues and accept, as an "assured result of modern biblical science," the priority of Mark and Q.

The Role of Synopses in Procuring the Acceptance of the Two Source Hypothesis

The mention of Rushbrooke's *Synopticon* brings us to another nevermentioned feature in histories of the Synoptic Problem: the significant role played by the Gospel synopses.

We noted above that when Griesbach published his first three-column synopsis in 1774, he explained in his Preface his understanding of the order of composition of the Gospels of Matthew, Mark, and Luke. His theory helped him to arrange the parallels and construct his synopsis.[116] During the first half of the nineteenth century, a number of new synopses appeared improving on his in various ways: Planck (1809), De Wette and Lücke (1818), Rödiger (1829), Clausen (1829), and Anger (1852).[117]

But in the 1860s, after Holtzmann's magnum opus appeared and the hypothesis of Markan priority was increasing in favor, Holtzmann eventually decided that the many Griesbachian synopses in circulation were not suited to illustrate his theory. Nor was the widely used Gospel harmony[118] published by Constantin von Tischendorf in 1851. It did have his important new critical text, but Tischendorf's pericope divisions were much too large for Holtzmann's atomistic approach. Even worse, the parallels were arranged according to Tischendorf's outmoded chronological scheme. Worst of all, from Holtzmann's perspective, *Tischendorf had not arranged Matthew's and Luke's pericopes according to Mark's order.*

If Tischendorf's harmony was primarily intended for use in text criticism as well as for the old dream of reconstructing the chronology of Christ's ministry,[119] Holtzmann wanted a modern synopsis, one specifically intended to illustrate his source theory. Therefore, shortly after he published his investigation of the Gospels in *Hand-Commentar zum Neuen Testament* (1889), Holtzmann commissioned a young Lutheran pastor living in the area, Albert Huck, to create a synoptic display that would illustrate his Two Source Hypothesis of Gospel origins.[120]

Since histories of the Synoptic Problem say nothing about the origins of Huck's famous *Synopse der drei ersten Evangelien,* it might be best to let him explain how it came to be. In the opening words to the Preface of the first edition, Huck said:

> The present *Synopsis of the first three Gospels* makes no claim to independent scholarly significance. In the first place, it is intended only to form a supplement to the well-known *Commentary* of Holtzmann, and to facilitate the study of this book. Correspondingly, the entire arrangement is governed by it. The pericope titles are, apart from a few insignificant changes, taken over from Holtzmann's *Commentary.* Also with respect to the arrangement of pericopes, this synopsis deviates from the *Commentary* perhaps in only three places. Otherwise, the order of (Holtzmann's) *Commentary* is strictly observed.[121]

What Huck did was to place Mark in the left-hand column and distribute the Matthean and Lukan parallels—out of their original order when necessary—to match the Markan parallels. In addition, each pericope had Holtzmann's page number where it was discussed. Nothing could be clearer than that, in the first instance, Huck was no more than an elaborate illustration of Holtzmann's source theory.

A few years later, Holtzmann decided to make some revisions in his theory and asked Huck to rearrange his synopsis correspondingly. Huck demurred and, separating himself from Holtzmann's project, launched out on his own. His third edition still retained the order of Mark as its basic organizing principle, as well as the unusually small pericope divisions and detailed parallelization of words and lines found in the Holtzmannian first two editions. But in the Preface to the third edition, Huck inserted the following seriously misleading assertion:

The connection to (Holtzmann's) *Hand-* or indeed any commentary *or any synoptic source theory* has been given up for this edition. It follows only one idea: to leave the individual Gospels as much as possible in their natural order and in their context and still offer parallels to similar places (in the other Gospels) to make possible a synoptic treatment.[122]

How could he be so naive?

Apparently, as far as Huck was concerned (and he had no great knowledge of the history of the Synoptic Problem), if he presented all three Gospels in their original order and, where matching parallel pericopes required printing something out of order, to indicate this by the use of italics, then he thought he had left behind all connections to any source theory. Technically, all three Gospels could be read in their entirety, in their original order. This, he believed, made his synopsis "objective." What he did not realize was that by continuing to use largely unchanged Holtzmann's pericope divisions and Holtzmann's parallels, he unwittingly ignored hundreds of alternative ways to divide the material into pericopes and hundreds of alternative ways to set up the parallels. It may have seemed to him that his synopsis was quite straightforward, but that was because he never dealt with hundreds of important "judgment calls" that are inevitable at every step of the synopsis construction process *if* one makes it completely from scratch. But Huck was far from doing this. A careful examination of the third edition (and all subsequent editions) proves that he preserved Holtzmann's fundamental rule of using Mark's order as his guide for both pericope divisions and fundamental order of pericopes. In this way, Huck unwittingly built into his synopsis a *de facto* argument for Markan priority.[123] The sense he had that his synopsis was neutral may actually have been increased by its dependence on the order of Mark, since Huck was an ardent if naive supporter of Markan priority.

Nor did Huck's claim to neutrality strike anyone as peculiar at the time; his synopsis seemed to fit perfectly with the newly popular Two Source Hypothesis, giving both a sense of correctness. Moreover, the claim to neutrality seemed quite appropriate, given the current belief in "historical objectivity," at that time a popular pretense among "scientific" biblical scholars in Europe, Great Britain, and North America.

For these reasons, Huck's *Synopse* soon became the most widely used synopsis. After the First World War, Martin Dibelius, Karl Ludwig Schmidt, and Rudolf Bultmann invented a new discipline in Gospel studies called *form criticism* which further heightened Huck's popularity. His small pericope divisions lent themselves perfectly to the atomistic analysis of the text employed by the form critics, as they sought to identify the source of each and every *word* in the Gospels.

Was Huck ever used in the Oxford Seminar led by Sanday? Yes. Sanday lists in the Preface to his report the following books regularly consulted by the members of his Seminar:

> It has been our custom to take the Synoptic Gospels section by section, with Tischendorf's handy *Synopsis Evangelica* as our basis, but of course calling in the many excellent Synopses that are in use, especially Rushbrooke and Wright, and, among the Germans, *Huck*.[124]

It wasn't their favorite synopsis, however. The British scholars were immensely proud of the beautifully produced, multicolor *Synopticon* published in 1880 by their own colleague W. G. Rushbrooke, fellow of St. John's, Cambridge, and student of E. A. Abbott.[125] As he had brought about the creation of Huck's *Synopse*, did Holtzmann's presentation of the Markan hypothesis by any chance also influence the creation of Rushbrooke's *Synopticon*? Possibly. First, a bit of background information is needed.

Far from pretending to give an objective presentation of the synoptic evidence, Rushbrooke had taken great pains to create his charts so that they would *refute Griesbach's theory* that Mark was based on Matthew and Luke.[126] In the first part of his volume he gave pride of place to the "triple tradition," i.e., the common material shared by Mark, Matthew, and Luke, which his mentor Abbott[127] had insisted was historically the most reliable. The entire Gospel of Mark was printed in the left-hand column, next to which the Matthean and Lukan parallels were placed, *out of order when necessary,* so that they could be brought into parallel with Mark's account. Where all three agreed, this "bedrock tradition" was printed in lowercase red letters, signifying the historically most reliable material (the surrounding text was in black).[128]

In Part Two, Rushbrooke placed the "double tradition." Where Matthew and Luke had identical words, this was printed in capital letters, Finally, material unique to Matthew and to Luke were printed separately in two final parts (in black). Material from the Gospel of John was included only where it agreed with all three other Gospels (*capital* red letters) or just two of them (*gold* letters!). Although it was published in 1880, long before Streeter's solution to the Synoptic Problem was published in 1924, it is not hard to see the general outlines of Streeter's "four source hypothesis" in its pages.[129] Streeter was effusive in his praise of it:

> The happy possessor of W. G. Rushbrooke's magnificent *Synopticon* will find the work (of distinguishing the Gospel texts) done for him by the use of different types and colours.[130]

Abbott thought Rushbrooke's *Synopticon* was "indispensable," which is understandable since he basically suggested the entire plan to him.[131] Likewise, the Oxford guru of Gospel minutiae, Sir John Hawkins, said of Rushbrooke:

> (The best way to begin studying the Gospels is) by collecting all the parallels for which there is any probability at all of a documentary origin. (In this) we cannot do better than adopt as a ground work the very complete and minute statement of them provided in Rushbrooke's *Synopticon*.[132]

Observe what is happening. Hawkins has compiled lists and comparisons illustrating Markan priority which are based at least in part on Rushbrooke's charts, which were created at least in part on the basis of Abbott's theory of Markan priority. Hawkins' lists, in turn, were then used by Streeter and the others to dispense with residual objections against Markan priority, such as the problem of the minor agreements. If anyone objected, Streeter urged them to consult Rushbrooke's *Synopticon*. The supposedly scientific and objective study of the Gospels has unwittingly become a completely circular process.[133] Confidence in the Two Source Hypothesis was unshakable as long as it was grounded on these biased synopses.

Back to Holtzmann. What was *his* reaction to Rushbrooke's beautiful *Synopticon*? He was so impressed that he put it at the top of his short list of essential tools for advanced research on the Gospels.[134] Was this because Rushbrooke had *consciously* arranged everything so that it facilitated studying the synoptic material precisely according to Holtzmann's two source theory? As far as I know, Rushbrooke never mentioned Holtzmann's work explicitly, but Abbott, his mentor, was quite familiar with it. Whatever the lines of influence may have been, Rushbrooke's charts in Parts One and Two reflected Holtzmann's theory precisely: a narrative *Grundschrift* (Alpha) and a sayings source (Lambda), as the bases for Matthew and Luke.[135] Small wonder Holtzmann liked it. In fact, it is still popular in Germany; the historian of modern New Testament research Werner Georg Kümmel—an ardent supporter of Markan priority—still thinks Rushbrooke's is "the most clearly arranged" of all synopses.[136]

It is evident that the same circular process of argument emerged in Germany that appeared later in England. A source theory was invented and a synopsis created to illustrate it. Charts were then created based on that synopsis which were held to "prove" the theory. This *circulus in probando* was camouflaged in Germany by Huck's claim that his synoptic arrangement was "neutral" with respect to all source theories. Thus, whenever scholars raised some objection to the priority of Mark or the existence of Q, they would be told to consult Huck and/or Rushbrooke. Q.E.D.

Extra-Scientific Factors in the Consolidation of the Two Source Hypothesis

By the middle of the nineteenth century, hatred of the Jews and all things Jewish was a thousand-year-old tradition in Germany.[137] Thus, at a time when the new bourgeois intelligentsia in Germany were searching for ways to incorporate a "German Christianity" into the "new Germany"— one thinks above all of the writings of the theologian D. F. Strauss in this regard[138]—this hatred took on new and more virulent forms.

In particular, one notes increasing attacks on the role of the Old Testament within Christian faith. As early as 1821, the famous Berlin theologian David Friedrich Schleiermacher had dismissed the Old Testament because it was "too Jewish." In his influential *Christliche Glaube*,[139] he said, "the Old Testament appears as a *superfluous* authority for (Christian) Dogmatics."[140] "*Everything* in the Old Testament is but the husk and wrapping of its prophecy; whatever is *most definitely Jewish* has *least value*."[141] When he got to the section discussing Jesus Christ, he said that whatever was most important about Jesus had *nothing in common with the Jewish culture of his time.*

> The beginning of Jesus' life cannot in any way be explained (by his Jewish descent) but only and exclusively by (his God-consciousness); so that from the beginning He must have been free from *every influence* of earlier generations.[142]

Again,

> Jesus' spiritual originality (was) set free from every prejudicial influence of natural (Jewish) descent.[143]

In other words,

> Christian piety, in its original form, cannot be explained by means of the *Jewish piety* of that or of an earlier time, and so Christianity cannot *in any wise* be regarded as a remodeling or a renewal and continuation of Judaism.[144]

Hatred of Jews and things Jewish was prevalent among German biblical scholars. Nor was the attack directed solely at the Old Testament. For example, the eminent Göttingen biblical critic and expert in Oriental languages Paul de Lagarde published an essay in 1873, during the height of the *Kulturkampf,* entitled "*Über das Verhältnis des deutschen Staates zu Theologie, Kirche und Religion,*" in which he called for the complete repudiation of the *New* Testament. It was, he said, nothing more than a "collection of books which the early (Roman) Catholic Church found suitable for service as weapons in its conflict with the heretics and sects of the second century."[145] Five years later, Lagarde published another programmatic tract, entitled *Die Religion der Zukunft* (1878), in which he called for

> a new German national religion composed of authentic Christianity and the noble elements of the German soul, but purified of all un-German vices. The Old Testament had no place in this religion . . . because of all the Jewish elements in it.[146]

The German quest for an Aryan Christ included such prominent figures as Adolf von Harnack, the eminent Church historian and New Testament critic. At various times chancellor of the University of Berlin and director of the prestigious Kaiser Wilhelm Institute, Harnack published in 1922 a monograph on the second-century Church figure Marcion in which he said:

> the rejection of the Old Testament in the second century was a mistake which the great church rightly avoided; to maintain it in the sixteenth century was a fate from which the Reformation was not yet able to escape; but *still to preserve it in Protestantism as a canonical document since the nineteenth century is the consequence of a religious and ecclesiastical crippling.*[147]

Harnack went on to lament that Luther, who had made so many bold decisions to free the Christian Church from its "Babylonian Captivity" to Roman Catholicism, had somehow lost his nerve when it came to the canon and never rejected the canonical status of the *entire Old Testament.*

> Had not Luther, ever since the Leipzig debate and all the way down to his writing concerning the councils and churches, pronounced one critical judgment after another upon the church's historical tradition? And with respect to the Old Testament, were not all the premises at hand for finally *withdrawing from it its canonical recognition in Christianity?*[148]

Such views may seem extreme to us, but they were not unusual in Germany at the end of the nineteenth century. Harnack's colleague on the theological faculty K. Holl fully agreed with his position on the Old Testament. Indeed, many names could be given to indicate the breadth and depth of the hatred of the Jews and things Jewish in German biblical scholarship and theology prior to the 1930s.[149] Theodore Fritzsch claimed—like Marcion—that the Jewish God was utterly different from the Christian God. J. K. Niedlich argued that Jesus was the true representative of Aryan religion, while Jews were the elect people of Satan. Franz Delitzsch claimed that all key figures of the Old Testament were morally inferior, and so on.[150]

It is not surprising, therefore, to see German Protestant biblical scholars, in the midst of the violent, national struggle with the forces of Roman Catholicism, create a *Gospel source hypothesis* that will sever "German Christianity" from its *Jewish roots*. With the Two Source Hypothesis in hand, that is, a historical scenario that locates the beginning of the Christian faith in the un-Jewish, pro-Pauline Gospel of Mark, accompanied by a theoretical Sayings Source having a conveniently non-Jewish message, German biblical scholars could *decanonize* the very Jewish Gospel of Matthew *and split* the New Testament from the Old in biblical theology. With Matthew effectively locked up in the basement, liberal German scholars—going all the way back to Schleiermacher and before—could feel natural in looking to the Hellenistic world for antecedents and parallels to the Gospels, as if early Christianity had had nothing to do with Judaism or the Old Testament.

My experience has taught me that biblical scholars think their work is free of cultural, political, and economic agendas. It is one of the main concerns of this entire book, and Part Two in particular, to show that this has never been true. Scholarly naiveté (or tacit collusion) about this aspect of Gospel scholarship during the Second Reich in Germany proved to have disastrous consequences later. I do not have to remind the reader of the horrible outcome that resulted from this denigration of all things Jewish by biblical scholars and theologians in Germany during the Holocaust of the 1930s and 1940s. I do not need to mention all of the German scholars who were swept along by the pernicious tide and supported it with their scholarship: Emmanuel Hirsch, Friedrich Gogarten, Paul Althaus, Gerhard Kittel, to name only a few.[151] I do not need to recall to the reader's memory the obscene "Appeal to the World of Culture" that appeared in 1914 defending the German invasion of Belgium, signed by such prominent theologians as Adolf von Harnack, Wilhelm Herrmann, Adolf von Schlatter, and Reinhold Seeberg.[152] I do not need to mention the evil "95 theses" of the *Deutschchristentum auf reinevangelischer Grundlage*, adopted in 1917 during the jubilee of the Reformation, which called for a *final separation from the legacy of Judaism,* so that *die deutsche Kristen* could achieve pure "*Germanhood.*"[153]

All this is mentioned only to emphasize the point—one that is never mentioned in the histories of the Synoptic Problem—that the great German universities, so widely admired and envied for their outstanding scientific achievements, were always closely linked to the political and cultural agenda of the Second Reich.[154] Although definitive evidence is not yet in hand, this government seems to have openly or covertly placed or supported adherents of the Two Source Hypothesis in key German universities. Even if direct evidence is never found, this much can be said: the widespread preference for the priority of Mark *did nothing to stem* the terrible tide of German hatred of the Jews and things Jewish. Indeed, it opened the door to it and gave a tacit biblical warrant for it by destroying the credibility of the Gospel of Matthew.

This assessment of the influence on biblical scholars of a wider cultural agenda is not unique to Germany. Hatred of the Jews also existed in the other two countries that welcomed the Two Source Hypothesis during the latter part of the nineteenth and early part of the twentieth century: Great Britain and the United States. This is not to say that since French scholars have not, for the most part, ever accepted this hypothesis, it proves that anti-Semitism did not exist in France. On the contrary. But something else acted as a bulwark against the Two Source Hypothesis in France; namely, after the French Revolution, French scholars rarely took over or used *any* philosophical or theological concepts that originated in Germany or England (let alone the United States). I will have more to say about the French biblical scene in Part Three.

Conclusion: the Two Source Hypothesis Becomes the Consensus Research Paradigm

Until the 1950s, with a few exceptions, the main publications on the Synoptic Problem emanated from Protestant scholars in Germany and England. Within Roman Catholicism, Alfred Loisy and the modernist controversy had induced Pope Leo XIII to issue the apostolic letter *Vigilantiae* in 1902, creating a watchdog committee that prevented Roman Catholic scholars from adopting such blasphemous ideas as the priority of Mark. This situation changed in 1943 when Pope Pius XII issued the famous encyclical *Divino Afflante Spiritu,* creating a more open environment for Roman Catholic biblical scholarship.[155] Since then, many important contributions to the Synoptic Problem have been published by Roman Catholics. Some of these will be discussed in Part Three.

By the end of World War II, the Two Source Hypothesis, in various formulations and modifications, had become the dominant scenario used by Gospel scholars in many parts of the world. Relying on a biased critical *text* of the Gospels (Erwin Nestle never admitted this—later the United Bible Societies' textual committee openly stated its bias in favor of the priority of Mark) and using a biased synopsis for purposes of "verification" (Huck and its imitators[156]—it claimed to be *neutral,* deceiving many), the Two Source Hypothesis arrived at the ultimate status of an "assured finding" of modern biblical science.[157] Philip Vielhauer spoke for many when he announced in 1955, "Source critical analysis of the Gospels has in fact *reached its goal* with the Two-Source Theory."[158]

This brings us to the end of our account of the rise of the Third Form of the Synoptic Problem: the modern historical approach to the differences among the Gospels. We have seen the creation of a new critical text, the abandonment of the traditional four-Gospel canon, the invention of a new (Romantic) historical hermeneutics, and an intellectual justification for the differences among the Gospels (i.e., a dynamic scenario explaining how they were composed). The sign of the new form of the Synoptic Problem was the Gospel *synopsis,* in contrast to the Gospel *harmony,* which was the sign of the Second Form. Part Three will take up the story of each aspect of the Synoptic Problem following World War II to the present.

PART THREE

*Current Trends
in the Post-Modern Period*

CHAPTER 21

The Synoptic Problem Today

*A*s discussions of the history of the Synoptic Problem go, Part Two probably set a record for long-windedness. This was due to three factors. First, I wanted to present evidence that the modern historicist Third Form of the Synoptic Problem—the one taken for granted in all current discussions—was in fact radically unlike the First (Origen) or the Second (Augustine), both treated in Part One, because it arose within an attitude of extreme hostility toward the Bible and traditional Christian beliefs and values. The main objective in Part Two was to provide ample evidence to support the claim that the Third (or modern) Form of the Synoptic Problem should under no circumstances be considered either normal or beneficial, as far as the history of the Christian faith is concerned.

Albert Schweitzer warned more than eighty years ago that the modern historical-critical approach arose not from any dispassionate interest in history but as a *weapon in the struggle against the tyranny of dogma.*[1] No wonder Enlightenment biblical scholars dealt with the differences among the Gospels in such an unprecedented manner! They weren't interested in the Gospels for their own sake. They wanted to accomplish something else entirely: the complete destruction of Europe's Thrones and Altars—*Écrasez l'infame!* They wanted to bring in secular democracy, secular merchant capitalism (based on a rapacious attitude toward the environment), and complete freedom of religion. To accomplish these sweeping changes, they invented, among other weapons, a slash-and-burn hermeneutics that gutted the Bible of its core values and symbols so that it could not condemn their actions.

Since contemporary histories of the Synoptic Problem begin with the eighteenth century,[2] biblical scholars think that the historical-critical method is ideologically neutral, innocent, and objective. To counteract this widespread illusion, I spelled out its belligerent ideological mission in Part Two. Neutral and innocent? Spinoza's method is more like a sugar-coated poison pill.

Second, Part Two is lengthy because I attempted to give a brief summary of the developments that took place in *all four* of the basic aspects of the Synoptic Problem—another unusual step. Most think that the Synoptic Problem is confined to the question of how the Gospels were composed. As I have noted previously, the Synoptic Problem viewed holistically is much more inclusive. It begins with a basic question that proceeds toward a solution along four closely related investigations. The basic question is: Where may I obtain reliable testimony to the Lord Jesus? The four closely related investigations are these:

- · Which Gospels must I consult? (canon)
- · Which text(s) of those Gospels must I use? (text)
- · How must I understand how these Gospels were created? (composition)
- · So that I may interpret them correctly? (hermeneutics)

Chapter 7 sets out the evidence to show that Origen was the first to attempt to give answers to all four questions in a tightly knit chain of reasoning. Consequently, I made him the paradigm for all later attempts.

Part Two began at the historic point near the end of the fourteenth century where the first of these basic aspects of the whole Synoptic Problem burst open and had to be completely rebuilt. Within a hundred years, the other three were also under heavy attack. From 1500 onward, a time later ages have labeled the Reformation and the Enlightenment, bold minds sought to reinvent every major aspect of European society. Four hundred seventy years later, in the late nineteenth century, the Third Form of the Synoptic Problem finally emerged within the modern historical-critical method, based on assumptions and bearing answers radically unlike anything ever seen before.

Third, Part Two was lengthy because, as I had done in my discussions of Origen and Augustine, I included a look at the economic and political considerations which played a constitutive role in shaping the way the differences among the Gospels were interpreted by the new class of bourgeois historians aspiring to use "modern" methods. No contemporary histories of the Synoptic Problem mention the decisive political and economic agenda animating the modern, historical-critical approach to the Bible and, with it, the Third Form of the Synoptic Problem (see Chapters 16 and 17). Late-twentieth-century biblical scholars are generally ignorant of this aspect of the history of their Bible industry. Spelling out these matters required attention to numerous, perhaps unexpected, issues.

These many features made Part Two unusually lengthy as discussions of the Synoptic Problem go. My treatment is undoubtedly uneven and tendentious in many places. As a first attempt, it will need to be corrected by more able scholars.

One last question before I turn to an overview of Part Three. We saw in Chapter 16 what Spinoza said he hoped to accomplish. Did he succeed? Recall that I said his main objective was to eviscerate traditional Christianity and the Bible of their core symbols and values and put in their place a pious moralism—love God and your neighbor—so that the clergy and the masses would never again engage in religious oppression or be able to use the Bible to thwart the rise of laissez-faire capitalism, political democracy, and the establishment of a secular nation-state.

Was Spinoza successful? Partly. His bourgeois agenda is flourishing today in Europe and North America as never before. But that is not the whole story. What about "loving God and your neighbor" among these same nations during the past three hundred years?

Consider this summary of the effects of Spinoza's historical-critical method on Germany, the country which more than all the others wholeheartedly adopted his toxic technique. I will draw at some length on the remarks of Edgar Krentz's *The Historical-Critical Method*, directing attention to certain points by means of italics.

Near the end of his historical survey, Krentz says this about the Church's situation in Germany at the end of two hundred years of soaking in the acids of Spinozist hermeneutics:

> The problem of the *relation of faith to historical knowledge* (Spinoza's familiar polar opposites) became acute at the end of the (nineteenth) century. The domination of the History-of-Religions School raised the problem to the level of a major theological debate. (Krentz next summarizes their findings.) . . .
>
> (They) saw a sharp difference between the Old and the New Testaments. (To begin with,) Old Testament scholars were immersed in the world of Near Eastern religion being uncovered by archeologists. Although New Testament scholarship recognized the influence of post-Old Testament apocalyptic Judaism, it stressed (instead of the Old Testament) the influence of Hellenistic popular piety, mystery religions, and

above all gnosticism. (Both groups) sought for the sources of biblical religion in the (religions of the) surrounding world (rather than from divine revelation). *The basic outlook was positivistic.* (That is,) the Bible, firmly anchored in its own world, was interpreted as an *amalgam of various borrowed motifs,* and thus became a book *strange to modern men.* The wandering (Hebrew) nomad, the cultic prophet, and the apocalyptic Preacher Jesus, were far removed from what piety and religious art had pictured for centuries. *The objectified Bible had become a foreign book....*

(They drew the theological) implications in drastic form. Franz Overbeck called for a "purely historical investigation" that had *nothing to do with faith* (1871), since scientific study of the Bible demands historical criticism, and that makes the *Christian use of the Bible impossible.* A quarter of a century later (1897) Wilhelm (*sic*) Wrede concluded that *the inevitable result of historical criticism is to remove all distinctive elements from the New Testament,* place its study into the history of religions, and make *New Testament theology impossible.* The gap between university lectern and church pulpit *cannot be bridged ...*

Alfred Loisy raised (these issues within) Roman Catholicism ... (but) his work was condemned by Pius X in *Pascendi dominici gregis* (1907), thus delaying for decades the formal acceptance of historical methods by the Catholic church....

Historical criticism reigned supreme in Protestantism on the continent at the end of the century. *It had been radicalized to a strictly historical discipline, free, independent, and in no way responsible to the church.* Although there was opposition from such men as Martin Kähler (and) Adolf Schlatter ... Troeltsch's view that *history had triumphed* was correct.[3]

So far, Spinoza's agenda was succeeding remarkably. What Krentz does not mention is that precisely at the same time that this method triumphed, the world-famous Adolf von Harnack was leading the most prominent scientists and theologians of his day in an act of utter betrayal of the Protestant Church in Germany, by issuing a brazenly hypocritical manifesto defending the German government's 1914 invasion of little Belgium.[4] As such, he became the forerunner and archetype of "the good German," paving the way for the infamous *deutsche Christen* of the 1930s. What Krentz does not mention is that these scholars so thoroughly denatured German Protestantism that its leaders included some who led Germany into National Socialism and unfathomable evil. What Krentz and other historians of the historical-critical method never explain is how this historical method *could continue* after the war, in eastern Germany under Communist totalitarianism and in western Germany under the Christian

Democrats, while the biblical scholars just resumed where they left off before they joined Hitler's *Wehrmacht,* as if nothing had happened in the meanwhile.[5] How could this method be so politically malleable?

Spinoza (and his followers) succeeded—too well. Like Francis Bacon, who was absolutely convinced that the new scientific method would usher in an era of peace and plenty, never dreaming that the actual result would be planetary pollution and destruction, Spinoza succeeded in one sense, but failed to bring about the desired utopia of a decent clergy and populace. Instead, into the house from which it had "cleansed" all traditional biblical values and institutions moved a pack of demons: greed justified as "enlightened self-interest," race hatred, exploitation of earth, water, and sky, fanatical nationalism, and imperialism: "Rule Britannia!" *"Deutschland über alles!"* "America, *right or wrong!"*

When the Enlightenment philosophers enthusiastically banished the concepts of sin and redemption from their worldview,[6] they had no idea what a terrible price their descendants would pay for it. Viewed within the context of the bloody twentieth century, is it surprising that the great majority of Asian, African, and South American biblical scholars and theologians are loath to use the West's wonderful historical-critical method in *their* biblical interpretation?

Overview of Part Three

Part Three will not attempt the sort of comprehensive and detailed discussion of the Synoptic Problem presented in Parts Two and One. It will not be a survey of major trends, figures, and contributions in the current scene. As interesting as that might be, such a discussion would fill another book, since each of the four areas of the Synoptic Problem is bursting with activity today. Instead, I have decided that Part Three will take up each of the four areas and point to a few selected developments illustrating certain trends within it.

1. Which Gospels Must Be Consulted? (Canon)

New Testament scholars have tended to give three different answers to this question in the post–World War Two period:

- Exclusively the four canonical Gospels
- The four plus the Q source (increasingly referred to as a "sayings Gospel")

· The four plus Q plus *all other* Gospels, especially the Coptic Gospel of Thomas

The first group includes those who still work within the Second Form of the Synoptic Problem, i.e., Augustine's harmonistic approach, intensified in the direction of traditional Protestant (Lockean) ultra-literalism. Despite the increasing popularity of the Gospel synopsis, these scholars continue to produce harmonies of the four canonical Gospels.[7] The best recent example in English is Robert L. Thomas and Stanley N. Gundry, *The NIV Harmony of the Gospels* (1988).[8]

Within the Third Form of the Synoptic Problem going back via Griesbach to Spinoza, the fourfold Gospel canon has been decisively abrogated in favor of a less or more open-ended approach, the choice of Gospels to consider depending on the whims and reasons of each individual scholar. All known Gospels were sooner or later brought into the picture. Then hypothetical sources and theoretical recensions of Gospels—at times resting on nothing more substantial than the mere supposition of the scholar's fertile imagination—were combined in wonderfully Byzantine developmental scenarios. Like early airplanes with three, four, and five wings, these over-complex hypotheses were abandoned, particularly in Germany and England, with the triumph of the Two Source Hypothesis. Today, the preference for wonderfully complicated hypotheses is typical mainly of French scholarship.

Despite its seeming adherence to the three canonical Gospels, even the Two Source Hypothesis involved a decisive break with the traditional fourfold Gospel canon in two ways. Huck's synopsis dispensed with most of the Gospel of John, as prevailing opinion held it to be totally unhistorical. Today, Huck is no longer in print (and Greeven's revision of it did not win wide acceptance)[9] but Huck's replacement, Kurt Aland's *Synopsis Quattuor Evangeliorum* (1964), took the open canon approach several steps further. All significant apocryphal Gospel parallels are printed in full after the relevant canonical texts at the end of each pericope. Even more striking is the text of the entire Coptic Gospel of Thomas in *three languages* at the back. Second, the Q hypothesis, now raised to the status of a "sayings Gospel" (see Chapter 22), contains an implicit breach of the fourfold Gospel canon.

The logical result of the open canon approach is the radically novel Gospel synopsis prepared by Robert W. Funk, *New Gospel Parallels* (1985).[10] It contains *six columns* across two pages: Matthew, Mark, Luke, John, Coptic Thomas, and *Other,* namely, parallels from all extant apocryphal Gospels, patristic quotations, important papyri, and two imaginary sources: the Signs Source (allegedly used by the author of the Gospel of John) and Q (allegedly used by the authors of Luke and Matthew).

Finally, some French scholars, for example Marie-Émile Boismard, also refuse to be restricted to the traditional Gospel canon in the investigation of text and composition. Any and all evidence from apocryphal Gospels, plus any number of lost sources and hypothetical recensions of canonical Gospels, must be taken into consideration. I will discuss Boismard's approach in the next two sections.

2. Which Text of the Gospels Must Be Used? (Text)

The long process that began with Erasmus' publication of the first, flawed text in Greek of the New Testament (described in Chapter 14) turned into a protracted and arduous struggle to obtain a better text, i.e., one more closely resembling what the original New Testament authors had written (described in Chapter 15). This process reached a plateau of sorts with the appearance of what was called by some in the 1980s the "New Standard Text" (see Chapter 19).[11]

Challenges to the "New Standard Text" have emerged from three directions: North American text critics, such as Eldon Epp,[12] Dutch and American *Diatessaron* experts, and French advocates of the "Western" text. I will discuss the last two, beginning with the last.

French text critics have long maintained that the heavy reliance of Westcott-Hort on the great fourth-century uncials, Vaticanus and Sinaiticus, in creating their critical text—and all later editors who followed their example: Nestle, Aland, the UBS committee—constituted an untenable methodological restriction. Unfortunately, the discovery of the beautifully preserved, early-third-century Bodmer Papyrus P[75] containing a text virtually identical to Vaticanus but created two hundred years earlier ironically made matters worse in the eyes of these critics. The following assessment of that papyrus illustrates the dilemma:

> The striking and highly significant fact that the texts of P[75] and Codex Vaticanus (B) are almost identical . . . demonstrates that there is virtually a straight line from the text of a papyrus dated around 200 to that of a major, elegant MS of 150 years later . . . The close affinity of P[75] and B . . . demonstrates that an early papyrus can stand very near the beginning point of a clearly identifiable and distinctive textual group that has been preserved with a high degree of accuracy over several generations and through a period that often has been assumed to have been a chaotic and free textual environment.[13]

This scholar concludes that the papyrus reveals the existence of a text type very faithful to the originals which should be foundational for preparing the critical text of the Greek New Testament.[14]

Expressing the view of French text critics, Léon Vaganay and Christian-Bernard Amphoux responded to this argument as follows:

> The discovery of the Bodmer papyri, in particular P[75], ... *served to hinder careful thought,* providing as it did an argument in favour of the non-recensional nature (i.e., the nontendentious quality) of Codex Vaticanus ... Thus for many people the question of the original text was henceforth resolved: Codex Vaticanus was its best representative. The existence of the "Western" text was not ignored but its enigmatic quality was forgotten ... The old theory of the "neutral" text gained ground; it became more or less the inevitable choice. It was on these assumptions that the editions of the Bible societies were made (since) *the editorial committee* of the new "textus receptus" has no convinced supporter of the "Western" text. And yet the facts were there. The "Western" text is widely attested in the second century, even before AD 150, whereas P[75] is probably no earlier than AD 230.[15]

A similar objection to the heavy reliance of the Aland Institute/UBS Editorial Committee on Vaticanus and Sinaiticus comes from Dutch and American Tatian scholars. They point to the fact that the *Diatessaron* contains many excellent *early-second-century* "Western" readings (cf. the last paragraph of Chapter 4) and that when these are backed up with good Syriac and Old Latin versional evidence, a solid case exists to prefer these readings *against all later evidence.*

Perhaps the clearest statement of this objection can be found in the recently published study of Tatian's *Diatessaron* by William L. Petersen. Concerning its text, he observed:

> Some of the traditions in the Diatessaron ... antedate our oldest canonical manuscripts and can be fixed to the (mid-) second-century. (They) demonstrate that the traditions found in the Diatessaron are neither capricious nor egregious: one cannot assume that Tatian is responsible for all the Diatessaron's deviations from the text of the canonical gospels, for in some instances he is reliably transmitting ... *the most primitive stratum of the gospel tradition.*[16]

About these second-century readings, the early-twentieth-century English text critic and historian F. C. Burkitt said:

We must recognize that *the earliest texts of the Gospels are fundamentally "Western" in every country of which we have knowledge, even Egypt.* If we have any real trust in antiquity, any real belief in the continuity of Christian tradition, we must be prepared to admit many "Western" readings as authentic, as alone having a historical claim to originality.[17]

This is precisely "the textual family to which the Diatessaron belongs," says Petersen.[18] He then goes on to make this striking observation.

At this point, the reader must be apprised of a pertinent fact ignored by most handbooks of New Testament textual criticism, and by the editors of the critical editions of the Greek New Testament. In the second edition (1896) of the second volume of their *New Testament in the Original Greek,* B. F. Westcott . . . acknowledged that "The discovery of the Sinaitic MS of the Old Syriac raises the question whether the combination of the oldest types of the Syriac and Latin texts can outweigh the combination of the primary Greek texts (of Vaticanus and Sinaiticus). A careful examination of the passages in which Syr.*sin* and *k* are arrayed against ℵ B would point to that conclusion."[19]

Petersen goes on to say, "This is a stunning concession, for it was the edition of Westcott and Hort which championed the idea that the most primitive recoverable form of the text—indeed, the 'original' text as they put it in their title—was to be found in B (Vaticanus)!"[20] The problem was, new evidence kept being discovered that challenged their principle.

By 1896 the evidence to the contrary was so compelling that Westcott himself states he would favour the readings of the "combination of the oldest . . . Syriac and Latin texts" over the "combination of the primary Greek texts," namely his beloved B with ℵ.[21]

Westcott's concession was immediately taken up and seconded by two other English text critics, F. C. Burkitt and Alexander Souter. Souter's view was even more emphatic:

The combination of Syr.*sin* and *k* would now generally be regarded as sufficient to upset the combination of B ℵ or, in other words, the *versions may sometimes have retained the correct text, where all known Greek MSS have lost it. This is a principle of the highest importance,* and likely to be increasingly fruitful.[22]

The noted Oxford scholar of Markan style C. H. Turner agreed with his English colleagues. The opinion went across the Channel where it was seconded by the leading German text critic, Eberhard Nestle. Recently, the Finnish scholar Arthur Vööbus has accepted it, saying that it is confirmed by his lifetime study of Syriac literature.

Given this remarkable array of early-twentieth-century scholarly unanimity on a principle of such fundamental importance, Petersen asks, how did it happen that this view has recently just disappeared from the scholarly literature?

> The position of these scholars . . . has been assiduously and inexplicably ignored by virtually all text critics since . . . The principle is not even mentioned as an historical oddity by B. M. Metzger (in his *Text of the New Testament* 1964), or, to my knowledge, by any other post–Second World War handbook on the NT text.[23]

One cause of this apparent lack of interest in the "Western" text is that Kurt and Barbara Aland have categorically stated that the "Western" text is a "phantom."[24] However, French Gospel scholars strongly oppose this idea. The *only variant readings* provided in the apparatus to the widely used French synopsis prepared by P. Benoit in 1973 are "Western" readings.[25] The same is true of the apparatus for the Greek synopsis created thirteen years later by M. E. Boismard and A. Lamouille.[26]

This issue should find its way back to the forefront of Gospel text criticism, since one of the precious aspects of the second-century "Western" readings is their "Jewish" character. In a time when Gospel scholars are becoming increasingly sensitized to perceived anti-Jewish (not to say anti-Semitic) aspects of the *current critical text* of the canonical Gospels, advocates of the "Western" text have an additional reason to call for a thorough reexamination of the heavy reliance of the Aland Institute and the UBS committee on third-, fourth-, and fifth-century texts. The Gospels in these manuscripts were systematically purged of Jewish traits during *two centuries* of anti-Jewish hatred, such as we can see welling up already in the mid-second-century theologians and bishops as Justin Martyr, Melito of Sardis, and especially Marcion of Pontus (see Chapter 5).[27]

Dissatisfaction of another kind with the Nestle/Aland critical text has prompted Reuben Swanson to produce a revolutionary new kind of text-critical tool. The *New Testament Greek Manuscripts* (1995)[28] is a four-volume set (one for each Gospel) presenting the full texts of each Gospel in a wide variety of the most important early manuscripts. Not in any sense a critical text, because there are no text-critical judgments involved, Swanson's material consists of the base text of Codex Vaticanus, against which are compared the texts of all of the most important papyri, twenty-eight of the earliest uncials, eighteen of the most important minuscules, the Gospel quotations of Clement of Alexandria, and the critical editions of UBS[4] and Westcott-Hort. Swanson prints the full texts of these other witnesses *where they differ* from the Vaticanus base text. The lines containing Vaticanus and the variant readings are laid out horizontally, since the eye can see the variants much more easily when they are stacked up vertically and given in full.

Why did Swanson go to such lengths in preparing this new tool? By way of an answer, he gives in the Introduction a historical review of previous text editions, coming to four main conclusions:

- Critical editions rest on several generations of scholarly choices that are rarely or never explained; hence one often has no idea what supports a particular choice.[29]
- The Aland text has mistakes, omissions, and inexplicable readings.
- The typical text apparatus is virtually impossible for the nonspecialist to read intelligently.
- Variant readings are presented in tiny, abbreviated fragments, so that one has no idea what the context is *around the variant* that could shed light on it.

Swanson's wealth of material—especially after it is released in user-searchable electronic form—should encourage nonspecialists to look more critically at the critical editions to which they are presently bound. Second, he has performed the inestimable service of giving the rest of us (much of) the data *conveniently collated but uninterpreted,* something no text critic ever did before.

Finally, the Jesus Seminar led by Robert Funk has attained an unheard-of level of Enlightenment-style precision regarding the quest for a reliable Gospel text, or, to be more precise, reliable *words* of Jesus. The Seminar's approach to the problem of ascertaining a reliable text is, to say the least, unorthodox.

First, they tossed aside the traditional canon; "canonical boundaries are irrelevant in critical assessments of the various sources of information about Jesus."[30] Thus unrestrained by any patristic guidance regarding spurious and reliable Gospels, or any critical assessment of the best manuscripts to follow, the Seminar examined tens of thousands of alleged *words* of Jesus, culled from all kinds of documents, and even *hypothetical* sources, written prior to 312. These had mostly already been collected for them in a convenient English translation in Funk's *New Gospel Parallels.*

Selecting such Enlightenment saints as Galileo and Thomas Jefferson to inspire them,[31] and guided by nothing more than their godlike reason, participants in a particular Seminar (the scholars present varied considerably from meeting to meeting) *voted*—using colored balls—to indicate whether they personally thought this or that *word* had actually been uttered by their historical Jesus. The resulting red (yes), pink (maybe), gray (doubtful), and black (no) colored print of their Jesus' *words* can be found in their best-selling report *The Five Gospels: The Search for the Authentic Words of Jesus* (1993).[32]

Judging from the results, the intended scientific objectivity of the Seminar seems to have gotten lost somewhere along the way. The picture of Jesus that emerges in *The Five Gospels* is little more than an idealized reflection of their own white, middle-class, American Protestantism. In other words, they fell right into the trap identified eighty years ago by Albert Schweitzer:

> There is no historical task which so reveals a man's true self as the writing of a Life of Jesus . . . *Each individual creates him in accordance with his own character.*[33]

They made the same elementary mistake all must make who set out to discover the "historical Jesus" by starting with the Gospels and then immediately rejecting *all* previous authorities on the subject, beginning with the Gospel writers and Paul. When one accepts nothing else to guide one's choices save one's own experience and intuitions, the results are always predictable.[34]

3. How Must the Creation of the Gospels Be Understood? (Composition)

One line of investigation from the late second century down to the present has been to give a credible account of the differences among the Gospels, while preserving their integrity as authoritative sources for the life and ministry of Jesus Christ.

Chapter 20 described the lengthy and arduous climb out of the morass of conflicting source hypotheses, constantly changing critical instruments, and shifting hermeneutical methods, to the point in the first half of the twentieth century where the Two Source Hypothesis, based on the biased Huck/Rushbrooke synopses, emerged as the most widely accepted account of the creation of the Gospels. However, once this theory achieved wide acceptance, a number of challengers came forth.

Using the three forms of the Synoptic Problem as a guide, they can be divided into three types:

- The First Form, created by Origen, has all but disappeared in white, Euro–North American biblical interpretation. It is to be found only among those who avoid the issue of composition beyond insisting that the evangelists received whatever they got directly from God, *and who go on to interpret the Gospels symbolically as well as literally.* This latter dual type of interpretation is what distinguishes them from practitioners of the Second Form, who begin at the same place but then attempt to interpret the Gospels in strict literal terms (Lockean fundamentalists).
- The Augustinian or Second Form of the Synoptic Problem thrives among fundamentalists. Although they may be aware that some scholars think the Gospels were composed in a certain historical order and borrowed material from each other, such thoughts play no role in their interpretation of them. Like Augustine, fundamentalists prefer to publish traditional harmonies, rather than synopses, which are then interpreted as literally—i.e., historically in the *ancient* sense—as possible.[35]
- The Third Form of the Synoptic Problem, going back to Spinoza and Griesbach, is by far the most active in the latter part of the twentieth century. I treat this subject at greater length in Chapter 22.

4. How Must the Gospels Be Interpreted So As to Be Understood Properly? (Hermeneutics)

As noted in the case of Origen and all biblical interpreters after him, a tight correlation always exists between one's understanding of how and under what conditions the Gospels were created and what one thinks is the correct way to interpret them. They are two sides of the same hermeneutical coin.

Origen stated that the Evangelists received "visions of God" and wrote in diverse ways according to the grace given to them, while agreeing on all essentials, both spiritually and literally. This viewpoint has all but disappeared among Gospel scholars today. A sophisticated statement of this traditional hermeneutic, fully cognizant of modern historical criticism but refusing to grant its ideological presuppositions, is the position paper published in 1993 by the Pontifical Biblical Commission entitled *L'inter-*

prétation de la Bible dans l'Église. I will discuss this important report more fully in Chapter 23.

As for the Second Form, I suggested in the conclusion to the discussion of John Locke that the best contemporary representatives of Augustine's literal, harmonizing approach to the Gospels are modern fundamentalists, both Roman Catholic and Protestant. One of the best examples of this approach is Thomas and Gundry's harmony, *The NIV Harmony of the Gospels* (1988).[36] Their defense of the literal truth of the Gospels could almost have been written by Augustine himself.[37]

Strikingly missing in Thomas and Gundry's volume is any reference to a creed, a *regula fidei,* or any sort of doctrinal magisterium to guide interpretation. This is not an accident. It is the result of their adherence to Locke's epistemology, which functions to sever all reliance on traditional authority. Similarly, they never mention Augustine's important distinction between the order of recollection in the Gospels and the original historical order of events. To them, the Gospels are entirely factual records of what actually happened. As such, they stand within a long tradition of Protestant ultra-literalism going back to the sixteenth century, but it has been reinforced by the authors' Lockean democratic ecclesiology (both are Baptists), according to which the Bible can be sufficiently understood (literally) by anybody, no expert help required. Thomas and Gundry cannot *on principle* accept any hint of the need for interpretive sophistication to read the Bible properly, because to do so would just open the door once again to hermeneutical elitism.

An example of a borderline hermeneutical approach that attempts to combine Augustine literalism with modern historical criticism is Gordon Fee's *New Testament Exegesis* (1993).[38] Fee is quite unaware of the original subversive intent behind modern historical criticism. Consequently, his hybrid approach naively walks down two paths simultaneously, never logically connecting one to the other. He begins by capitulating to modern historical criticism, namely, in saying that the purpose of exegesis is historical investigation of the physical thing, i.e., the *text.*[39] Then he reverts to the traditional starting point, saying that the goal is to understand the intention of the original writer.[40] But this is impossible in the absence of any hermeneutical bridge between the physical text and the interpreter, a bridge Fee leaves out since he never mentions the activity of the Word of God or the Holy Spirit or Church tradition aiding the interpreter in his interpretive task.[41]

Fee's hermeneutics are spelled out in two versions: a long method for full-scale historical exegesis and a short method for sermon preparation. In the latter, he suggests that the pastor, having arrived at an accurate historical interpretation of the text, should "allow 30 minutes" (!) to decide whether his interpretation "fits within the full system of truth contained in Christian theology."[42] Although this may seem to be similar to Augustine's insistence that biblical interpretations must not depart from the *regula fidei*, Fee never pins down precisely what "the full system of truth contained in Christian theology" contains. He cannot do this, since that would contravene his Baptist latitudinarian assumptions. Fee assumes that this abstract admonition will be given concrete content by each interpreter as he or she sees fit. In short, his hermeneutics is a classic example of Luther's pious subjectivism reinforced by Locke's middle-class democratic politics.

The Third Form of the Synoptic Problem—despite all of the talk that we are living in a postmodern era—is still the norm in the latter part of the twentieth century, vastly overshadowing all other approaches. Innumerable handbooks, Bible study guides, and dictionary articles on biblical interpretation, in a score of modern languages, all testify to the fact that the modern historical-critical method remains the standard in all places influenced by Euro–North American middle-class values.

The dominant feature in all of these handbooks and discussions is the classic Spinozist ploy of changing the subject, so that the interpreter seeks not to engage the theological referent of the biblical text on its own terms but instead takes on the materialistic, skeptical investigation of progressively atomized aspects of the *physical history* of the biblical text, as advocated in Spinoza's hermeneutical method. Associated with this ploy is the classic rationalists' dichotomy between the constantly shifting and irresolute results of "historical" knowledge of the Bible (understood in terms of modern mechanistic physics) on the one side and emotionally based (i.e., irrational) faith in or theological interpretation of the Bible on the other.

Two prime examples of Spinoza's method are the famous German Protestant guide to New Testament interpretation by the Göttingen scholars Hans Conzelmann and Andreas Lindemann, *Interpreting the New Testament* (1988). Similar to it is the American handbook by John H. Hayes and Carl R. Holladay, *Biblical Exegesis* (1987).[43] I will briefly examine each for signs of the Spinozist agenda.

Conzelmann begins with the classic Spinozist starting point: New Testament exegesis, he says, is the historical "interpretation of the NT *text*."[44] That is, the focus of attention is transferred to a physical thing: the history of the text. In Chapter 12, I characterized this as Step 1: "changing the subject." Conzelmann's exegete must not set out to discover the Mind of God or ascertain, guided by the Holy Spirit, the inspired intention of the biblical writer. Conzelmann bars the door against such traditional hermeneutical concerns on the very first page.

The goal of exegesis is the understanding of the *text* . . . (However) the text and the reader never encounter one another directly; rather, they are always separated from one another by a distance determined by time and subject matter. There is no unmediated, let alone "direct," understanding . . . (For example,) the reader needs to be informed about the language in which the text is written (etc.).[45]

And with that, Conzelmann has changed the subject and turned the interpreter away from a spiritual/literal hermeneutics, consistent with the biblical writings, toward the endless process of overcoming the supposed distance between the interpreter and the biblical *text* by learning its language, history, cultural presuppositions, and so forth. Diverting attention to these topics is precisely Spinoza's nominalist subterfuge: focus all attention on an infinitely divisible list of physical questions, so as to thwart the entire theological enterprise.

Conzelmann's defense, that "the text and the reader never encounter one another directly" and "there is no unmediated understanding," are modern epistemological presuppositions flowing from his history-of-religions ideology. Consistent with this approach, Conzelmann naively upholds the rationalists' myth of scientific neutrality as well; e.g., "questions of methodology must in no wise be regarded as questions of world-view."[46]

Having cast aside traditional assumptions about the proper way to understand the origins and contents of the Bible and inserted in their place a secular, materialist investigation of the *text* modeled on modern, mechanistic physics, Conzelmann is prepared to take the Step 2 I described in Chapter 12. This consists of the modern interpreter, thought to be endowed with divine reason and with no trace of original sin, setting herself or himself up to be the sole judge *and source* of the meaning and truth of the biblical accounts.

Conzelmann accomplishes this step in two customary moves. First, he deprives the Bible of its unique position within traditional Christian faith.

The biblical texts are to be treated no differently than other literary sources, especially those of classical antiquity.[47]

This methodological step has always been a favorite of modern rationalists because it destroys at one stroke the Bible's authority and relativizes its contents. The intended result of such a step is to demolish all traditional biblical interpretations based on the Bible's unique place within Christian faith.

Having cast the traditional status of the Bible overboard, the modern historical critic is left with a giant hermeneutical vacuum, into which this divinely gifted rational interpreter is free to project any meaning he or she wishes, i.e., bound only by one's own physical sense experience. This yawning conundrum is immediately broken down into specific, manageable activities, which is the second customary move in Step 2: turn on the nominalist data fire hose.

> The scientific study of the Bible utilizes the same formal methods as those used of antiquity, namely, classical philology, archeology, and ancient history.[48]

To be more specific, the interpreter must master the methods and results of biblical text criticism, biblical translation, literary analysis, historical analysis, sociopolitical analysis, canonical criticism, linguistic analysis, and historical theology.[49] Furthermore, the Gospels are a special case for which additional disciplines are needed: source, form, and redaction criticism.[50]

The sense of feeling overwhelmed by this torrent of questions and "results" is precisely the goal of Spinozist biblical hermeneutics. Conzelmann alludes to this sensation in his Preface:

> For the (beginning) student, the multiplicity of methods and especially of findings raises the impression that NT exegesis contributes more to a general uncertainty than to understanding.[51]

Conzelmann also knows how destructive of the Bible and traditional Christian faith his hermeneutical program is. In his discussion of method, he says:

> For the beginner in this discipline, this observation (that the Bible is to be treated no differently than any other ancient document) may already cause initial problems to surface. Anyone who expects "edification" from his encounter with the OT and the NT is at once confronted with the questions of authenticity, unity, and historical reliability (observe the nominalist barrage immediately brought in to prevent "edification" from taking place). He has to ask whether the certainty of his own faith may be jeopardized by questioning the historical reliability of certain traditions concerning Jesus, or whether such dangers can be avoided on the premise that (here comes the Spinozist dichotomy) faith and historical insight belong on two entirely different levels.[52]

Conzelmann even preserves Spinoza's careful duplicity. On the one hand, Conzelmann is not overtly concerned with any theological or moral outcome from his hermeneutical method—his guide to biblical interpretation says exactly nothing on either subject—but he can on the other hand disingenuously claim in the Preface, "the historical-critical interpretation of the NT cannot be an end in itself but *is to contribute especially to the clarification of what is Christian belief.*"[53] One cannot have it both ways.

The closest parallel to Conzelmann's handbook in the American scene is *Biblical Exegesis: a Beginner's Handbook* by John H. Hayes and Carl R. Holladay. These authors also adopt the prime Spinozist materialistic starting point, namely, confining biblical hermeneutics to the interpretation of a thing, i.e., the *text* of the Bible: "Exegesis is best thought of as a systematic way of interpreting a *text.*"[54] There is no mention anywhere in their book of encountering the Word of God, or attempting to learn the will of God from the Bible, or listening to the Holy Spirit as one reads the text. Instead, the authors insist that (Enlightenment-style) historical investigation is the central task.

> The radical impact on biblical studies of the post-Enlightenment (why post?) period can be seen in the way it forced (forced?) interpreters to take history and historical perspectives seriously... *This involves a more critical stance toward the sources*... a biblical text must be thoroughly exegeted and evaluated as to how it can be used for historical reconstruction ... (this means) reconstruct the history (of the event referred to in the text) without appeal either to special divine intervention in history or miraculous occurrences which might have altered the course of events.[55]

Having thus rejected the Bible's own core assumptions, Hayes and Holladay are unusually candid in admitting that the basic assumptions of their historical-critical method are definitely foreign to the Bible's own point of view.

> This (method) represents a rather radical break with the outlook of the sources themselves, which speak of divine involvement in historical events.[56]

Having adopted a method that clashes at every key point with the central assumptions within the Bible, Hayes and Holladay *change the subject* to focus on the history of the *text* rather than the Referent of the text. They then proceed with the familiar Spinozist nominalist barrage: a series of chapters explain text criticism, historical criticism, grammatical criticism, literary criticism, form criticism, tradition criticism, and finally redaction criticism. "The goal," they say, "is to make sure that one has tackled *all those aspects of a passage* which might *conceivably* be related to producing an overall interpretation."[57] The infinite extent of their nominalist barrage is obvious from this statement, and also the following explanation of the need to atomize the text into tinier and tinier "components."

> These initial levels of investigation (listed above) may be viewed as analysis, in the strict sense of "breaking down" the exegetical work into its component parts. Here the exegete's task is to "break down" the passage, examine its language, structure, and *all its various components* (here is the infinite extent again), with a view to seeing them both in isolation and in relation to each other.[58]

Hayes and Holladay claim that there is no need to worry about following any kind of *logical order* in pursuing these "levels of investigation":

> By arranging these various aspects of the exegetical process in this order (namely, the series of chapters beginning with text criticism), we do not mean to suggest that exegesis is a mechanical undertaking which one can accomplish in a stair-step order as if one method or stage of exegesis always leads to the next. Normally, questions may arise from the text in an unsystematic order.[59]

This helter-skelter approach, when combined with the sheer number of disciplines and particular inquiries, results in the desired Spinozist goal of overwhelming and immobilizing the interpreter. At the end of their book, the authors extend their heartfelt personal sympathy to the student struggling to come to terms with all of these requirements as he or she reads the Bible.

> At this point the student may feel a bit overwhelmed by the diversity of critical approaches which can be utilized in understanding a text.[60]

Hayes and Holladay, however, do not want students to feel *completely* overwhelmed, or they might drop out of seminary and join some fundamentalist church where none of this arduous study is required. Then the authors would have shot themselves in the foot by making their hermeneutics so difficult that ordinary pastors would never use it. Are we now looking at the real reason why William Barclay's commentaries are so popular among pastors?

Yet part of the student's sense of frustration could be because she or he has the uneasy sense that something fishy is going on, but can't quite figure out what it is. Perhaps I can help.

One of the main points to emerge from the discussion of Spinoza's hermeneutics in Chapter 16 is that his method was an elaborate hoax on the pious, a carefully prepared trap for those who wanted to read the Bible for edification. As with Conzelmann's text, evidence of Spinoza's duplicity is also visible in Hayes and Holladay. For example, we noted above that they said that their method "represents a rather radical break with the out- look of the sources themselves."[61] A few pages later they state, in the chap- ter entitled "Employing the Fruits of Biblical Exegesis," that the biblical text *should critique the interpreter's own understanding of reality,* allowing the Bible

> to inform, sharpen, and challenge one's own understanding of reality, . . . *to call into question one's own self-understanding and one's understand- ing of the world.*[62]

Well, which is it? Do they mean that the Bible should "inform the inter- preter's understanding of reality" or should the modern interpreter be free to insist on "a radical break with the outlook" of the Bible so as to impose his or her own view of reality upon it?[63] The Enlightenment principle of autonomous reason and the scientist's unquestioned right to universal skepticism has crashed head-on into the Protestant principle of *sola scriptura* and destroyed it. The authors' feeble effort to bring the authority of Scripture back in at the end of their book when it is time to talk about preaching a sermon based on the Bible is no more than a nostalgic echo of the traditional approach.

Again, what is the student to make of the statement that, before preaching, one must "make sure to tackle *all those aspects* of a pas- sage which *might conceivably* be related to producing an overall inter- pretation"?[64] How can such an infinitely open-ended requirement be accomplished? When will the student ever feel justified in saying, "Now I understand this passage"? Hayes and Holladay do more than Conzel- mann did in speaking to the student about using historical-critical exegesis in sermon preparation (which wasn't difficult, since the latter said noth- ing), but they might as well have spared themselves the effort. They have passed on to their generation a biblical hermeneutics fundamentally in- imical to any religious use of the Bible, sermon preparation or otherwise. In this respect, Conzelmann and Lindemann's book is more consistent.

Be that as it may, once Hayes and Holladay do get into the question of sermon preparation, it is possible to see an example of what I described in Chapter 12 as Step 2 of the modern hermeneutics: i.e., make oneself the ultimate judge and source of the truth of the Bible (complete subjectivism). Hayes and Holladay, in true Spinozist fashion, treat all theological statements, ancient and modern, as nothing more than expressions of the *pious imagination.* Regarding the biblical authors, they say:

> The modern historian tends to consider this theological dimension in the texts to be a reflection of the *faith and theology* (read subjective emotion) of the communities and the authors rather than a datum of (the modernist conception of) history itself which can be (rationally) studied and confirmed.[65]

Regarding the modern theologian or preacher, they say, "In *attempting to construct an imaginative theological statement about God ...*"[66] Such statements show that the authors view faith in the modern rationalist manner, i.e., as totally subjective projections of the human imagination, devoid of all rationality. Nor do they ever mention such traditional concepts as the Holy Spirit aiding the exegete or the pastor to make *objectively true statements* about the will of God or help the preacher to receive objectively true interpretations of the Bible.

The American Roman Catholic epitome of modern historical criticism of the Bible is the *Jerome Biblical Commentary.*[67] Its account of the Gospels is fully supportive of the Third Form of the Synoptic Problem, even going so far as to place the Gospel of Mark first in the section on the New Testament. Frederick Gast wrote the article on the Synoptic Problem for the first edition.[68] His account of the history of "the Syn Problem as we know it" goes back as usual only to the eighteenth century; Augustine's discussion is dismissed as "naive." Frans Neirynck wrote a far more detailed, original, and sophisticated account of the Synoptic Problem for the 1990 *New Jerome Biblical Commentary.*[69]

John Kselman wrote the article on the history of biblical criticism for both editions, basing his account largely on well-known German histories, notably those by Albert Schweitzer and Werner Georg Kümmel.[70] As a result, he is totally unaware of the pernicious effects of modern historical criticism or its political/economic agenda. For him, this method is the great new standard, wholly without flaw. At one point he suggests that all "pre-critical" (his term) study of the Bible was not "*real* criticism":

> Although the Middle Ages, especially the great scholastic period, contributed to the better understanding of Scripture, the contributions to *real* NT criticism were not major.[71]

Much more sophisticated is the article by Raymond E. Brown on hermeneutics.[72] Indeed, it is quite unlike anything in the modern Protestant discussion. He does not automatically begin with the usual pseudo-scientific focus on the *written text,* but instead looks at the broad range of ancient uses of the term *hermeneuein* having to do with all acts of interpretation and clarification: of human speech, of the divine will, of translation from a foreign tongue, and conveying past meaning to the present.[73] In fact, Brown emphasizes that hermeneutics existed long before there were any written texts at all; "neither Israel nor the Christian community was originally a 'religion of the book.'"[74]

With this much richer beginning point, Brown goes on to correctly note that all early Christian interpretation, as well as the canonization process itself, took place within the guidelines provided by the *regula fidei.*[75] In this way, Brown is unique in firmly rooting his definition of biblical hermeneutics within the Bible itself, that is, within the canonization process. This decisively places his entire discussion of hermeneutics within the historic community of Christian faith, and thus he avoids the modern Cartesian mirage of individualistic objectivity (which turns out to be unrestrained subjectivism).

Brown can do this since, unlike Kselman or the Protestant authors we have discussed, he is aware of the hostile intention of classical rationalist biblical hermeneutics. He takes pains to distance true Roman Catholic hermeneutics from it.

> Critical exegesis, especially in the 17th and 18th cents., originated in antagonism to a dogmatic theology that imposed later doctrinal issues on biblical texts. An exaggerated ideal developed of a search for objective truth, ruling out the issue of religious relevance. Note, however, that historical-critical exegesis did *not* find acceptance in this way in 20th-cent. Roman Catholicism; it was encouraged by popes (specifically Pius XII and Paul VI, to whom the *NJBC* is dedicated) and was *not* marked by a desire to be free from dogmatic and ecclesiastical guidance.[76]

A typical feature of Protestant historical-critical hermeneutics (going back behind Spinoza to the Reformers) is an exclusive focus on the literal meaning. Brown rightly begins by *not* assuming that this sense is self-evidently foremost. Instead, he notes that, historically, there has been a broad oscillation between greater preference for "literal" and then greater preference for the "more than literal" approaches to the biblical text. Given this historical picture of the quest for *two fundamental kinds of truth in the Bible,* Brown divides his article into two parts, one for each kind, and thus avoids naively privileging the literal sense. Even here,

Brown is careful to point out that the understanding of the literal sense itself changed considerably down through history, thus preventing the reader from making any naive assumptions about the meaning of the term "literal."

Finally, Brown is rare in being clearly cognizant of the pernicious effect of loading the biblical interpreter down with Spinoza's massive list of preliminary historical questions. Rather than immediately launching into them the way Conzelmann et al. do, Brown takes the remarkable step of asking first whether *any antecedent (historical) knowledge is necessary* to read the Bible with benefit for personal faith.[77] Since he is aware of the fundamentalist habit of doing precisely this, Brown goes on to give a carefully balanced answer in the affirmative, to avoid "fundamentalist confusion" when *mis*interpreting the texts without realizing it.

Brown says that there are three antecedent questions which any reader in the community of faith must consider:

- What *kind* of writing is this? (E.g., whether the book of Jonah is a literal history or a parable will have an enormous impact on how I interpret it.)
- How is the text I am reading related to its surrounding parts—are they all by one and the same author? (If not, then the process must be reset and begin over for them.)
- For what purpose did the final editor of the book I am reading include this portion with the others? (This introduces the fundamental question of reading New Testament meaning into Old Testament passages—a critical concern for Christian canonical interpretation.)

After these basic steps have been attended to, says Brown, one is prepared to interpret the text literally, to find its historic meaning, or to go on to the other senses contained within it. At that point, Brown devotes the rest of his article to the many "more than literal" senses of Scripture.

This exquisitely nuanced and original explanation of biblical hermeneutics, rooted in the best of the Church's tradition and in the Scripture itself (which obviously has more than one kind of truth in it, as Origen and Augustine well knew), is worlds apart from contemporary Protestant historical-critical hermeneutics. This makes it all the more difficult to understand why Brown—his concern to rediscover the literal sense of the Bible for the Roman Catholic church of today notwithstanding—did not find a way for his rich Roman Catholic presentation of biblical hermeneutics to inform the actual commentaries contributed to the *JBC* and the *NJBC*.

CHAPTER 22

Current Trends in Understanding How the Gospels Were Created

*In the previous chapter I commented on selected developments within each of three of the four aspects of the Synoptic Problem: text, canon, and interpretation. In this chapter, I will discuss current developments in the remaining aspect: Gospel composition.

Chapter 20 argued that it was not until the Romantic revolt against the earlier static view of history typical of Enlightenment rationalism that a developmental view of human history could become possible.[1] This enabled scholars to invent theories of inevitable progress or decline in human history, depending on the evidence selected. Similar theories were applied to the Bible, both Old and New Testaments, as scholars sought to arrange disparate biblical texts along evolutionary trajectories. In Gospel research, a revolutionary new tool for displaying Gospel parallels was invented by J. J. Griesbach, called a *synopsis,* to replace the traditional Gospel harmony. The genius of his invention was that all of the minute differences among the Gospels were preserved rather than obliterated, thereby providing scholars with the concrete evidence they needed to create the intricate developmental scenarios that have become the hallmark of modern Gospel research.[2]

This new approach was labeled the Third (or modern) Form of the Synoptic Problem, since neither Origen (the First Form) nor Augustine (the Second Form) viewed the differences among the Gospels as valuable evidence of the development of the faith of early Christianity. Origen tended to look past them in order to find the static spiritual truth, while

Augustine wove the disparate details into a single, literally true, chronologically consistent narrative of Jesus' life, death, and resurrection.

In the post–World War II period, representatives of both the First and Second Forms of the Synoptic Problem typically do not spend much time worrying about how the Gospels were created since this topic, along with the Bible as a whole, is covered in their doctrine of literal inspiration. Why dwell on the human mechanics of Gospel creation per se, since the block of divinely inspired fourfold Gospel text that resulted from the work of the Holy Spirit is the really important thing? Given the veil of glory concealing the writing of the Gospels, further historical inquiry is neither appropriate nor helpful.

Thus, all of the activity discussed in this chapter falls under the Third Form of the Synoptic Problem. Chapter 20 described the rise of the Third Form and the eventual consolidation of scholarly approval around a particular historical scenario: the Two Source Hypothesis. This chapter will examine challenges or alternatives to the Two Source Hypothesis and current trends within that theory. The first challenge to be considered will be the revival of Griesbach's hypothesis, followed by a short discussion of the modified Augustinian hypothesis proposed by B. C. Butler and Austin Farrer, French multiple-source scenarios, and, finally, current developments within the Two Source Hypothesis in response to these challenges and alternatives.

Opposition to the Two Source Hypothesis in England

The Two Source Hypothesis was never without its critics and gadflies, either on the Continent or in England.[3] For instance, three years after Holtzmann published his study of the Gospels in 1863, a Dutch scholar at the University of Groningen named Hajo Uden Meijboom published *A History and Critique of the Marcan Hypothesis* (1866) that surveyed the rise of the theory of Markan priority, with particular attention to Holtzmann. After carefully dissecting Holtzmann's logic, Meijboom concluded that his conclusions were entirely based on circular reasoning and that his adherence to the priority of Mark was due to extraneous factors: "In sum, Holtzmann has attached himself to the Marcan Hypothesis *for extrinsic reasons* and attempts now to present it as a necessary consequence of Gospel criticism."[4]

In England, opposition to the Two Source Hypothesis was not lacking either. In 1915, E. W. Lummis published *How Luke Was Written,* an attack on the view that Luke and Matthew had been composed independently of each other.[5] A few years later, H. G. Jameson published *The*

Origin of the Synoptic Gospels. He said that the mere comparison of the orders of pericopes in all three Gospels was quite *inconclusive,* being open to at least four simple interpretations.[6] Jameson preferred Augustine's solution. Moreover, he said that the numerous agreements between Luke and Matthew against Mark, not only in passages where they are supposedly following Mark but differ slightly from him in precisely the same way in hundreds of cases (the minor agreements),[7] but also in passages where Matthew and Luke share large blocks of identical material not found in Mark constituted prima facic evidence that Luke knew and used the Gospel of Matthew.[8] Neither Lummis nor Jameson was ever adequately answered.[9]

Opposition tended to be muted for a time after Canon Burnett Hillman Streeter published his landmark study on the Two Source Hypothesis, *The Four Gospels: A Study of Origins, Treating of the Manuscript Tradition, Sources, Authorship, and Dates* (1924).[10] Indeed, this massive book effectively silenced the opposition for decades. When, in 1937, the research of a former abbot of the Benedictine Abbey of Downside, John Chapman, was published posthumously under the title *Matthew, Mark, and Luke: A Study in the Order and Interrelation of the Synoptic Gospels,* it was met with a resounding silence. Chapman decided that the arguments of Lummis and Jameson pointing away from Markan priority to a hypothesis similar to Augustine's was right, but there was little academic response.[11]

Such was not the case when a later abbot of Downside, Bishop Christopher Butler, published *The Originality of St. Matthew: A Critique of the Two Document Hypothesis* (1951). Also using some of the arguments of Lummis and Jameson, Butler aimed his most devastating blow straight at the weakest link in the chain of logic supporting the Two Source Hypothesis in its Streeterian form: the statement that the triple order of pericopes was the main reason for thinking that canonical Mark was the primary source of Matthew and Luke.

Butler insisted that Streeter, as well as Abbott, Burkitt, and probably Hawkins, had all fallen victim to "a schoolboyish error of elementary reasoning at the very base of the Two Document Hypothesis."[12] The phenomenon of the triple order of pericopes *by itself* did no more than prove that Mark was some sort of "connecting-link (between the other two Gospels) . . . but not necessarily the *source* of more than one of (them)."[13] Streeter had prominently placed this as the main argument in his list of five basic reasons for holding to the priority of Mark. Having destroyed it, Butler went on to demolish the other four as well, demonstrating that none of them were conclusive or free from the taint of circular reasoning.[14] These arguments, he said, contain "no new *evidence* in proof of the (Two Source) theory, but a series of deductions from it."[15] In the remainder of his book, he went on to defend what he took to be Augustine's view, that Matthew had been written first, that Mark had abbreviated Matthew, and that Luke had used both Matthew and Mark.

Unlike previous attacks on the Two Source Hypothesis, this time there was a reaction. In 1962, the eminent Cambridge scholar C. F. D. Moule published *The Birth of the New Testament*, to which he appended an *excursus* by G. M. Styler entitled "The Priority of Mark."[16] In this brief essay, Styler, while still defending the priority of Mark, became the first scholar in modern history to concede in print Jameson's and Butler's main point, namely, that the Streeterian arguments were essentially circular or inconclusive regarding the theory of the priority of Mark.

Butler's book became a turning point in the English-language discussion of the Synoptic Problem. The two major scholars still actively defending the classical Two Source Hypothesis, Frans Neirynck of Leuven University, Belgium, and Christopher Tuckett of the University of Manchester, have both abandoned the traditional Streeterian arguments in support of the priority of Mark and returned to a modified Lachmannian approach. Neirynck has spoken of Gospel criticism as divided between the pre-Butlerian era and the "post-Butlerian era."[17] Butler's book also spurred an American scholar, William R. Farmer, to examine the evidence for himself.

William R. Farmer and the Revival of Griesbach's Theory

As a graduate student at the Union Theological Seminary in the 1940s and 1950s, William Farmer was taught the standard three verities about the Synoptic Problem: the Nestle text was the most reliable critical text; the traditional canon of the Gospels should be ignored, especially since the Two Source Hypothesis had identified a source *behind* the Gospels (called Q) that was more important than they were; and the historical-critical method was the only scholarly way to interpret the Bible.[18] During two years spent in Cambridge attending C. H. Dodd's seminar on the Fourth Gospel and studying with C. F. D. Moule, Farmer didn't hear anything that conflicted with these three verities. Indeed, there seemed to be an impressive international consensus regarding these major aspects of Gospel study.

After completing his doctorate in 1952, followed by a short stint in the pastorate, Farmer was invited to the theological faculty of Drew University in 1955. It was at Drew that he learned of Butler's attack on the Two Source Hypothesis, and decided to look into it. He created a graduate seminar on the Synoptic Problem that examined the synoptic data from different angles and gathered secondary literature on the Two Source Hypothesis. Out of these activities emerged the conviction that Butler's book had at least undermined the credibility of the theory of Markan priority and, also, that C. F. Burney's book *The Poetry of Our Lord: An Examination of the Formal Elements of Hebrew Poetry in the Discourses of Jesus Christ* (1925), contained strong evidence for the authenticity of the sayings of Jesus contained in Matthew.

In 1959, Farmer was invited to the faculty of Perkins School of Theology, Southern Methodist University, Dallas, Texas. There he found a congenial atmosphere for his uncertainty about the Two Source Hypothesis, since his predecessor, Edward C. Hobbs, had already taught the students to question the existence of Q.

From 1959 to 1964 Farmer continued his intensive analysis of the synoptic literary phenomena and extensive reading in the history of the debate. He began to suspect that some of the supposedly "objective" lists of synoptic data, such as are found in Hawkins and Cadbury,[19] were in fact based on the Two Source Hypothesis. This created a false sense of confidence about the scientific foundations of the Two Source Hypothesis. Working with groups of graduate students, Farmer began to create his own statistics based on more evenhanded methods, creating colored charts of the synoptic phenomena that gave a more objective picture of the Gospels' interrelationships. Meanwhile, he received grants to study in British and European libraries and read deeply in the history of the debate.

The results of these activities were published in 1964 under the title *The Synoptic Problem: A Critical Analysis.*[20] It began with a two-hundred-page analysis of the history of the Synoptic Problem going back to the beginning of the modern discussion in the late eighteenth century. In what was by far the most thorough account to date, Farmer not only identified and accounted for the main figures and theories in that history—mostly German and English—he also documented the repeated occurrence of hypothetical conjectures that began with no evidence whatsoever to support them and later were turned into unquestioned axioms. He discovered eclectic and nebulous hypotheses that were based on erroneous logic and maintained by sloppy methodology. Most damning of all, Farmer documented the repeated use of intimidation to suppress scholarly opposition when scientific arguments failed. In his conclusion, Farmer announced this shocking conclusion:

> The only sound historical judgment that can be rendered in a critical review of the history of the Synoptic Problem is that "extra-scientific"

or "nonscientific" factors exercised a deep influence in the development of a fundamentally misleading and false consensus.[21]

In his last two chapters, Farmer rejected Butler's "Augustinian" solution, briefly sketching in a new demonstration of the Griesbachian hypothesis, namely, that Mark had been composed using material from Matthew and Luke.[22]

In striking contrast to the silence which had, in the past, smothered all voices of dissent, this time the reaction was immediate and visceral. Reviews of Farmer's book fell across a narrow spectrum from righteous indignation to outright derision.[23] He was chided for questioning the combined wisdom of one hundred years of scholarly labor. He was regarded with anger for having dared to accuse the famous scholars of the past of allowing themselves to be influenced by "nonscientific" factors. He was accused of "fouling the nest" of Gospel scholarship by daring to make personal accusations. He was jeered at for wanting to "roll back the clock" and "wasting time plowing plowed ground." The form critics laughed his book off as hopelessly outdated; *who cared* when the Gospels were written? The modern quest was to pierce *behind* the Gospels to discover the "most original tradition" of the historical Jesus!

A few years later, Farmer published a copy of the Nestle text of the Gospels, color-coded to indicate parallels, with the title *Synopticon: The Verbal Agreement between the Texts of Matthew, Mark, and Luke Contextually Exhibited.*[24] A pioneering effort to find an alternative to the biased and misleading synopses currently in use, it was generally ignored.

Independent Confirmation of Farmer's Conclusions

It was one thing for an American to criticize the "assured results" of German New Testament scholarship; it was another thing altogether for one of their own to do the same thing, only this time with customary German sarcasm, hyperbole, and rhetorical power.

In 1977, a second, full-length appraisal and critique of the steps by which the Two Source Hypothesis had achieved preeminence was published by Hans-Herbert Stoldt, a German literary historian and New Testament scholar.[25] His book was divided into four parts:

Part One: a critical analysis of the genesis of the Markan hypothesis, describing how the Two Source Hypothesis arose on the basis of untenable and circular arguments.

Part Two: a critical analysis and refutation of each of the seven most commonly used arguments for Markan priority.

Part Three: a presentation of evidence regarding "the *ideological* background of the Marcan hypothesis." Stoldt concluded this part with the statement that Markan priority—as established by Holtzmann—is no longer a scientific theory but a *theologoumenon* of German biblical scholarship.

This part was particularly important in documenting for the first time the extreme use of invective, ridicule, and outright slander—rather than scholarly judgment—against Griesbach's hypothesis by otherwise decent scholars. Lachmann said that Griesbach portrayed Mark as a "tight-rope walker, who now from weariness, now from capriciousness, now from negligence, and finally from blind eagerness swings back and forth between the Gospels of Matthew and Luke."[26] Lachmann went on to vilify his elder colleague. "Some people have let themselves be deceived by a certain treatise by Griesbach, which gives the impression of careful and thorough scholarship; it is, nevertheless, anything but intelligent: it is quite trivial and devoid of content (*minime ingeniosa sit, sed frigida tota et ieiuna*)."[27] Christian Gottlob Wilke was disgustingly graphic: "Mark would be (according to Griesbach) not an excerptor but a castrator of the other texts; or how else should one describe someone who mutilates borrowed passages and mixes up what he had mutilated?"[28] Stoldt quoted other insults by August Tholuck, Johannes Kuhn, Heinrich Julius Holtzmann, and, last but certainly not least, the great Berlin scholar Bernhard Weiss, father of Johannes Weiss. In his Meyer Kommentar on Matthew, Weiss said that according to the Griesbach hypothesis, Mark was no more than "the worthless retouching of a pretentious author" and went on to state that "the Griesbach Hypothesis is the *sole unadulterated aberration in the history of source-criticism.*"[29]

Why such verbal abuse? Stoldt suggested that the real target was David Friedrich Strauss, not Griesbach, but unfortunately "the anathemas of the conservative theologians (against Strauss) struck Griesbach with equal or greater force ... The fact that Strauss took his (Griesbach's) source theory as his point of departure cost Griesbach his scholarly reputation for one hundred and forty years."[30]

Given this powerful ideological animus, Stoldt concluded—as had Farmer before him—that the Two Source Hypothesis *had never been a scientific hypothesis at all.* Rather, it was just a

> vast system of make-shift solutions, a continuing series of experiments with and corrections to the hypothesis, of wrangling and maneuvering and unceasing argumentation and psychologizing.[31]

Part Four: Stoldt surveyed the current scene and noted that despite, or rather precisely because of, the distorted caricatures of Griesbach's hypothesis created and attacked by the "Marcan lions" (Strauss's term for the advocates of Markan priority), the main structure of Griesbach's hypothesis still stood largely unscathed.[32]

One might have thought that Stoldt's attack would elicit an even louder outcry than Farmer's book received, since his critique was much more biting than Farmer's. Instead, there was one brief—misleading—review by Hans Conzelmann.[33] Stoldt was placed under the ban of silence.

Conferences Devoted to Reopening the Discussion of the Synoptic Problem

Not all of the responses to Farmer's book were negative. A few years after it appeared, he was invited by a special committee of the Pitt-Xenia Presbyterian Seminary in Pittsburgh to help plan the 175th anniversary celebration of the seminary. The theme the committee chose was a complete assessment of the whole state of Gospel scholarship (not just the source question). The result was a great, week-long conference in April 1970, attended by more than two hundred scholars from all over the world. The theme was "A Festival of the Gospels," and scholars were invited to debate and discuss the pros and cons of all major Gospel questions.[34] The debate between the Claremont University scholar James Robinson and David Dungan, recently graduated from the Harvard Divinity School, in the seminar dealing with the Gospel of Mark, was particularly intense.[35]

Farmer realized that the partisan reception accorded his book did not represent biblical scholarship at its best. In the years that followed the Pittsburgh conference, he returned to Europe periodically to hold meetings with leading European scholars to gather suggestions on how best to carry on the discussion in a responsible scholarly fashion.[36] Out of these discussions came an unprecedented series of international scholarly conferences that dealt with all conceivable aspects of the Synoptic Problem.

The following list of conferences is not exhaustive; it contains only the more important. It does not include, for example, the many seminars and reports read at the annual meetings of the Society of Biblical Literature in America or the Studiorium Novi Testamenti Societas in Europe, which paralleled and intersected with the agendas of these conferences. Altogether, during the past thirty years, no other problem area in the entire field of biblical research—Old or New Testament—has received this level of concentrated scholarly attention.

1976: Münster Griesbach Bicentenary Colloquium: *J. J. Griesbach, Synoptic and Text-Critical Studies, 1776–1976,* Cambridge University Press 1978 (eds. T. Longstaff & B. Orchard). This conference, attended by some thirty-five scholars from Europe, Great Britain, and North America, reassessed the contribution of Griesbach to text criticism and synoptic source criticism.

1977: San Antonio Colloquy on the Relationship among the Gospels: *The Relationship among the Gospels: An Interdisciplinary Dialogue,* Trinity University Press 1978 (ed. W. Walker). This conference, attended mainly by North American scholars, focused on the characteristics of oral tradition and methodology in source criticism.

1979: Cambridge Conference on the Synoptic Gospels: *New Synoptic Studies: The Cambridge Gospel Conference and Beyond,* Mercer University Press 1983 (ed. W. R. Farmer). This conference was attended by some thirty scholars from India, Europe, Britain, and America, who presented new research based on the Griesbach hypothesis. It was here renamed the "Owen-Griesbach Hypothesis."

1980: Fort Worth Colloquy on New Testament Studies: *Colloquy on New Testament Studies: A Time for Reappraisal and Fresh Approaches,* Mercer University Press 1983 (ed. B. Corley). This was a smaller conference featuring a presentation by Helmut Koester, in which he argued that the Gospel of Mark contained evidence of having been written in five different stages. He was refuted by David Peabody, who proved that Koester's five recensions contained identical stylistic characteristics.

1982 and 1983: Ampleforth Conferences: *Synoptic Studies: The Ampleforth Conferences of 1982 and 1983,* Sheffield Academic Press 1984 (ed. C. Tuckett). These two conferences, attended by approximately twenty scholars, mainly from Great Britain and North America, received a number of different reports on text criticism (Kilpatrick), the Augustinian hypothesis (Goulder), examinations of the argument from order (Dungan, Tuckett), and so on.

1984: Jerusalem Symposium on the "Interrelations of the Gospels": *Interrelations of the Gospels,* Peeters/Mercer University Press 1990 (ed. D. Dungan). This was a major watershed conference that met in Jerusalem in April 1984 for two weeks. Five years in the planning, the conference aimed to get the best possible representatives of the three main source hypotheses (five each: Two Source Hypothesis led by Frans Neirynck; the Griesbach hypothesis led by William Farmer; and the Multiple Stage Hypothesis led by Marie-Émile Boismard) to debate three preselected texts for one week. During the second week, a "jury" of fifteen other New Testament scholars assessed the debates and proposed an "agenda for future research" that would point the way out of the current methodological and source-critical deadlock. This conference was unique in having carefully selected New Testament scholars from Nigeria, Korea, and Japan as observers.

1986: Dallas Colloquy on "New Critical Approaches in Synoptic Studies": *Perkins Journal,* April 1987 and July 1987. This conference was attended primarily by scholars from the American Southwest. It heard reports analyzing Christopher Tuckett's critical response to the "Neo-Griesbachian School."[37]

1986: Decatur Conference on "Textual Criticism and the Making of Gospel Synopses," held at Columbia Seminary, Decatur, Georgia, August 1986 (there was no published report). This conference, attended by the field's foremost English, Belgian, German, and American text critics and synopsis editors, examined Dungan's contention, published in two articles in *Biblica,*[38] that all critical texts and Gospel synopses are necessarily biased toward a particular source hypothesis.

1987: Cambridge Conference on the Eucharistic Texts: *One Loaf, One Cup,* Mercer University Press 1990 (ed. B. Meyer). This conference, attended by about a dozen European and North American scholars, examined the Eucharistic texts in Gospels and Paul.

1988 and 1989: Dublin and Gazada, Italy. Two Conferences on "Oral Tradition and the Gospels": *Jesus and the Oral Gospel Tradition* JSOTSS 64, Sheffield Academic Press 1991 (ed. H. Wansbrough). These conferences brought together some of the world's leading experts in oral tradition, from Scandinavia, Israel, Europe, Great Britain, and North America, to critically examine the claims regarding the Gospel oral tradition by Harald Riesenfeld and Birger Gerhardsson.

1990 and 1992: Latrobe, Pennsylvania, and Bochum, Germany. Two Conferences on the "History of Gospel Studies in the 19th Century": *Biblical Studies and the Shifting of Paradigms, 1850–1914,* JSOTSS 192, Sheffield 1995 (ed. H. Reventlow and W. Farmer). These conferences brought together leading experts from Germany, Canada, Switzerland, and the United States to hear reports on the relation between the German universities and the German government in the nineteenth century, with particular attention to Strasbourg in the 1870s.

1991: Göttingen Conference on "the Minor Agreements": *The Minor Agreements,* Göttinger theologische Arbeiten 50, Vandenhoek and Ruprecht 1993 (ed. G. Strecker). Organized by Strecker and Farmer, this conference was attended by about forty scholars from Europe, England, and the United States to hear reports on ways of interpreting the "minor agreements" using different theoretical approaches: Ur-Markus (Strecker), Augustinian (Goulder), Two Source (Neirynck), Griesbach (Farmer/Peabody).

Naturally, these conferences proved different things to their many different participants. One purpose was universally agreed to, however: the importance of making available to the wider scholarly world a solid body of *new scholarly research* on every aspect of each of the main source theories, so that colleagues and graduate students everywhere could begin to have a less one-sided secondary literature on current source theories and the data that support them.

Publications Advocating the Neo-Griesbachian or "Two Gospel" Hypothesis

I will conclude this account of the revival of the Griesbach hypothesis by identifying the main writings which were produced after Farmer's book of 1964 until the present. These publications can be conveniently divided into four categories:

1. Critiques of previous scholarship from the perspective of the Two Gospel Hypothesis
2. Writings that provided new scholarly foundations for the Owen-Griesbach hypothesis in the primary evidence
3. Writings that used the hypothesis to give a rational account of the differences among the Gospels
4. Writings that examined the pastoral, economic, and political aspects of solutions to the Synoptic Problem

There is considerable overlap among the writings. For example, many attempts to "clear the air" (category 1) involved extensive analyses of Gospel passages (category 3). Still, these categories are generally applicable. For the sake of easier readability, the list consists of the name(s) of the scholar(s) followed by a brief explanation (publication information is in the notes).

1. Critiques of Previous Scholarship from the Perspective of the Two Gospel Hypothesis

- E. P. Sanders proved that the usual criteria used by all form critics to calculate the relative earliness or lateness of synoptic material— namely, shorter or greater length; more or less detailedness; more or less "Semitism"—were in fact *completely inconclusive* when tested against documents whose actual dates were well established.[39]
- Lamar Cope examined ten passages in Matthew and found that they made better sense if it was assumed that Matthew was *independent* of Mark. Moreover, he discovered many instances of redactional phrases typical of Matthew in the parallel passages in Mark and Luke.[40]
- Thomas R. W. Longstaff set up an objective test of conflated writing using documents of known dates. His conclusions revealed that many of the phenomena found in his conflated test documents could also be found in Mark.[41]
- Joseph B. Tyson and Thomas Longstaff attempted to provide an *objective* description of the phenomenon of sequential parallelism among the Synoptic Gospels.[42]
- Bernard Orchard and David Dungan examined dozens of synopses and collected evidence to prove that *the two most commonly used synopses—Huck and Aland—were biased toward the Two Source Hypothesis* in their presentation of the synoptic parallels. Both went on to suggest that it was not possible to create a synopsis that was neutral with respect to all source theories.[43]
- Thomas R. W. Longstaff and Page A. Thomas created a comprehensive bibliography on the Synoptic Problem.[44]
- David B. Peabody pioneered a new type of stylistic analysis of the Gospel of Mark as part of Farmer's doctoral program at Southern Methodist University. He broke with all previous tradition by making *no assumptions* as to whether Mark was a single, unified document or a compilation, or what sources he had used.[45] Peabody discovered a number of significant phrases and stylistic formulae characteristic of the final redactor. After him, Dennis Gordon Tevis did the same thing for the Gospel of Matthew.[46]
- David B. Peabody also published an article examining the logic of arguments for priority based on linguistic characteristics by three prominent German scholars: Eduard Zeller, Christian Gottlob Wilke, and Heinrich Julius Holtzmann. He demonstrated that Wilke—widely regarded as one of the founders of the Two Source

Hypothesis—had discussed the synoptic phenomena in such a way as to methodologically exclude any examination of the data from the perspective of the Griesbach hypothesis.[47] He also showed that the careful presentation of data by Eduard Zeller, leading him to claim that it favored the Griesbach hypothesis, was turned on its head by Holtzmann to support the priority of Mark.[48] Peabody also showed that Holtzmann lifted—without attribution—the skewed data of Wilke.[49] These things led Peabody to conclude that two contemporary defenders of the Two Source Hypothesis, W. G. Kümmel in Germany and C. Tuckett in England, were mistaken in their claims that the linguistic arguments of Wilke and Holtzmann were "conclusive proof" of Markan priority.[50]

· William R. Farmer published a reexamination of the evidence for the fourfold Gospel canon and found that it had its roots in the willingness of the orthodox leaders of the early Christian Church to uphold the tradition of the martyrs' witness following Christ's example.[51]

· Henning Graf Reventlow, noted for his histories of German biblical scholarship, and William Farmer worked together for more than a decade to probe further into the alleged independence of German biblical scholarship from the political and ecclesiastical agenda of the German government during the latter part of the nineteenth century. Their results found that the German government kept a tight rein on the universities, particularly the theological faculties, during this period, but more work needs to be done.[52]

2. *Writings Providing the Owen-Griesbach Hypothesis with a New Foundation in the Primary Evidence*

· J. G. Franklyn Collison carried out an exhaustive analysis of the stylistic characteristics of the Gospel of Luke, although he did assume the Two Gospel Hypothesis as an aid to his analysis.[53]

· Bernard Orchard created a synopsis based on the Two Gospel Hypothesis, to aid in the examination of the synoptic phenomena from the point of view of that hypothesis.[54]

· Bernard Orchard reexamined all of the evidence from the patristic period regarding the composition of the Gospels. Because of the contemptuous attitude of Enlightenment scholars toward the early Church, this evidence had been generally dismissed by German and British scholars. By the nineteenth century, the earliest evidence bearing on the order of composition of the Gospels was not generally known. Orchard uncovered slim but unmistakable evidence that some Church Fathers in fact knew that the Gospels were composed in the order Matthew, Luke, Mark, John.[55]

· David Peabody found that Augustine, in Book IV of his *de consensu evangelistarum* (this final chapter was rarely read during the Middle Ages or later), came to the conclusion that Mark had abbreviated and combined *both* Matthew *and* Luke—precisely the same result that Owen and Griesbach independently reached 1,200 years later.[56]

· David L. Dungan prepared a report linking the Gospel of Mark with other literature in the New Testament traditionally associated with the Apostle Peter, especially 1 Peter. He found that both documents exhibited conflationary literary techniques and inclusive (pro-Jewish and Gentile) outlooks.[57]

· David L. Dungan, in consultation with W. R. Farmer, B. Orchard, L. Cope, A. McNicol, D. Peabody, and P. Shuler, responded to a widely perceived need to make a brief but comprehensive restatement of the Griesbach hypothesis available to scholars, since opponents constantly misunderstood it and misinterpreted it. This restatement was published in the *Anchor Bible Dictionary* under the title "The Two Gospel Hypothesis,"[58] using the new title to indicate that the theory now rested on completely new scholarly foundations.

3. *Writings That Used the Hypothesis to Give a Rational Account of the Differences among the Synoptic Gospels*

· Allan McNicol, together with L. Cope, W. R. Farmer, D. L. Dungan, D. B. Peabody, and P. L. Shuler, carried out a comprehensive redactional analysis of the Gospel of Luke, based on the assumption that the main source of the final redactor of Luke was the canonical Gospel of Matthew. This report is a first; there is no other attempt in the literature that gives a consistent description of Luke's compositional activity on the basic assumption that Matthew was the author's major source. Even the Griesbachians of the previous century (e.g., DeWette and Bleek) could not do this; Griesbach never tried. Instead, it has been a widely shared conviction that it is "inconceivable" (Kümmel) that the final redactor of Luke made use of Matthew. The group above discovered on the contrary that it was not difficult to observe Luke's compositional activity on this hypothesis, *provided no modern synopses were used to examine the evidence.*[59]

· Allan McNicol provided a detailed explanation of one of the most complicated of all synoptic texts, the apocalyptic traditions in Mt 10–11, 24–25; Mk 13; Lk 17, 21; and Paul (1 and 2 Thess). Using the Two Gospel Hypothesis, McNicol was able to provide a simple, straightforward explanation of the basic trends in these traditions, from Matthew/Paul to Luke, and from both of them to the Markan redaction.[60]

4. *Writings That Examined the Pastoral, Economic, and Political Aspects of Solutions to the Synoptic Problem*

· The new name for the former Griesbach hypothesis came into being primarily to emphasize its pastoral orientation and to convey a political message to scholars and laypeople alike. The best explanation of the reason for this change in names was given by W. R. Farmer in an article addressed to pastors. In the 1984 Spring edition of the *Perkins Journal,* Farmer wrote:

> What is meant by Two Gospel Hypothesis? Why not "priority of Matthew"? or as some have proposed, "Posteriority of Mark"? Why this emphasis on two Gospels? "Two-Gospels" is meant to be contrasted with Two Documents (i.e., Two Sources). As you stand in the pulpit today, armed with a theory of Markan priority, you are under some academic constraint to rely mentally on a hypothetical document, "Q," in order to communicate critically about Christian faith with those sitting in the pew. But the layperson in the pew has never seen "Q." This creates a mental gulf, whether you are fully conscious of it or not, between you and the person in the pew.
>
> Therefore, the first import of the Two-*Gospel* Hypothesis is that *it restores to the person in the pew the same scriptures that the clergy have.* The clergy do not have some esoteric or elitist advantage in knowing about some unknown document or documents not readily available to the person sitting in the pew. This is a boon to communication. It contributes to a mutual respect and trust between laypeople and clergy. How does it do this? Well, for example, it does this by removing any feelings of insincerity we may have for withholding from our congregations what we have been taught by our professors.

In this case, that there was once a "Q" document which no longer exists. And that Matthew and Luke were dependent upon this now lost hypothetical document for much of Jesus' teachings.

Second, *Two* Gospel Hypothesis takes the focus off the question of which Gospel is first. To speak of Matthew as first in time can be taken to imply that Matthew is also first in importance. The Two Gospel Hypothesis avoids the difficulty of suggesting that any one Gospel is more important than any other. This is a very real gain, since all four Gospels in our canon are actually four clearly related, but distinctive, written versions of one and the same Gospel.[61]

· William R. Farmer published a book that is unique in the entire history of the debate over the Synoptic Problem. It asks the question What is the *pastoral impact* of the different source hypotheses on the living community of faith? Entitled *The Gospel of Jesus: The Pastoral Relevance of the Synoptic Problem* (Louisville: Westminster/John Knox 1994), the work examined such matters as the effect of the Two Source Hypothesis versus the Two Gospel Hypothesis on the Lord's Prayer, the Eucharist, the doctrine of justification by faith, the faithful witness of women in the Gospels, God's special commitment to the poor, and the keys of the Kingdom. Farmer noted that the Two Source Hypothesis assumes the dismantling of the canon to make room for the Q hypothesis (Part 5). He concluded with a social history of the Markan hypothesis, showing its roots in the late-nineteenth-century *Kulturkampf*, when German anti–Roman Catholicism made a source hypothesis that broke with the traditional emphasis on Matthew desirable.

This concludes the survey of the contemporary attempt to establish the hypothesis of Owen-Griesbach on new scholarly foundations. However, despite the considerable effort just described, this hypothesis is unlikely to draw wide scholarly interest and support, for a number of reasons.

Most important, the Neo-Griesbachian challenge to the Two Source Hypothesis involves the claim that the synopses most widely used (Huck and Aland) should be given up and scholars should "go back to the drawing boards" and reexamine the synoptic phenomena from the basic Gospel texts themselves.[62] This enormous task alone is enough to stop most would-be source critics from even reexamining the question, let alone adopting a new hypothesis. As one scholar put it to me, "It is not that I am lazy, there just are so many other far more interesting things to study. I don't want to spend *my* life staring down *that* black hole!"

Second, there is an ingrained reluctance—quite understandable—to accept the Neo-Griesbachian verdict that "so many scholars could be so wrong." For a scholar to move to the point where she or he is finally convinced that the Two Source Hypothesis is indeed untenable involves considerable independence of judgment, a trait biblical scholars are not usually noted for.

Third, the hypothesis just seems highly unlikely. It was so in the beginning and still is today. Two main problem areas can be mentioned. First, that Mark would omit so much material that Matthew and Luke both contained just does not seem likely. The problem here is that scholars cannot conceive of a situation in early Christianity where this kind of editorial activity would have been appropriate. Far easier is the hypothesis that lets them simply view the Gospel-creating activity as one of accretion: the "snowball" effect. Added to this is the second problem, namely, understanding how Luke could have used Matthew as his main source and still changed it so drastically. That does not fit with what scholars understand about authorial activity in early Christianity.

Finally, the Neo-Griesbachian attention to the Gospels as wholes seems old-fashioned in a day when form criticism has long since bypassed the Gospels for examination of tiny fragments possibly going back to the prewritten stage. This tendency has recently received heavy emphasis within the American quest for the historical Jesus of the 1980s and 1990s. However, recent efforts at diachronic reading of the Gospels seems to be changing this situation.

Taking all of these difficulties together, the Neo-Griesbachian endeavor seems simultaneously obsolete and insulting, it demands far too much work in return for a reward that looks dubious at best, and it means leaving behind the safe and comfortable waters of the happy majority for a life out on the cold fringes of the guild, a place which can definitely be bad for one's career. In other words, whatever its merits may be in the eyes of its proponents, the Owen-Griesbach hypothesis will not gain many adherents until the disadvantages of the Two Source Hypothesis seem much greater and the advantages of the Owen-Griesbach hypothesis seem much more apparent.

The Continuation of B. C. Butler's Proposed Solution

After B. C. Butler attacked Streeter's defense of the Two Source Hypothesis, a small number of English scholars sought to develop his arguments further. Foremost among them has been Austin Farrer[63] and his student Michael Goulder, whose *Luke: A New Paradigm*, 2 vols. (1989) is the most extensive redactional analysis of the Gospel of Luke from this perspective in the literature.[64]

French Scenarios Involving Multiple Sources

In the history of French source criticism, there has never been much enthusiasm for the German (or English) Two Source Hypothesis. Owing to the continuing influence of the Augustinian approach to the Gospels and basic antipathy toward Protestantism in all its forms (cf. the "modernist controversy"), the Protestant Two Source Hypothesis was largely ignored by French Roman Catholic scholars. This avoidance was reinforced by an official ban placed on it by the magisterium during the first half of the twentieth century.

Following the cautious lead of the eminent archaeologist and biblical scholar M. J. Lagrange,[65] French scholars such as X. Léon-Dufour,[66] L. Vaganay, A. Gaboury,[67] and M.-É. Boismard[68] have pursued a completely different approach. They insist that the historical process that gave birth to the canonical Gospels (and most of the others) was a more complicated process than is envisioned by the various "simple" solutions.[69] Vaganay's reaction to all "simple" theories, such as the Two Source and the Griesbach, is typical of this group: "*Quant aux différances entre les synoptiques, s'expliquent simplement par la personnalité de leurs auteurs.*"[70]

A basic presupposition of the French approach toward the source question, as E. P. Sanders has noted, is to regard every difference between the Gospels as the result of the compiler utilizing *different sources.* That is, the Gospel compilers themselves never made any alterations in the material they received. Ergo, any difference between two or more accounts of the same event must be due to different versions circulating prior to the writing of the Gospels. In his survey of contemporary source criticism, Sanders wrote,

> Boismard's theory (takes) the view that *nothing was ever omitted and nothing was ever created* . . . For everything (i.e., for every slight difference between the Gospel narratives) there was a source. The "authors" of our gospels wrote a few introductions, but for the most part simply conflated sources . . . It is clear that Boismard does not think of creativity on the part of the communities, transmitters, or authors.[71]

Since there are numerous differences among the Gospels, both in content and in order, these French scholars posit numerous sources, with corresponding overlappings, cross-pollinations, and recensions.[72] At the 1984 Gospel Symposium in Jerusalem described above, Boismard explicitly stated that he viewed those responsible for the Gospels as basically just scribes, not authors in the modern sense.[73]

This strictly circumscribed conception of the Gospel creators is not limited to French scholarship. It has a lengthy history, going back through both German and Scandinavian Gospel scholarship to Johann Gottfried Herder's conception of an oral Ur-Gospel.[74] At the 1984 Jerusalem Symposium, the Swedish scholar Bo Reicke of Basel declared at one point: "it is *inconceivable* that the Gospel authors would omit anything."

Current Developments in the Two Source Hypothesis

Despite these challenges and alternatives, the dominant fact of the latter half of the twentieth century is that the Two Source Hypothesis continues to expand its sphere of influence among biblical scholars, Old and New Testament, liberal and conservative, in every country where there is a seminary or Church-related institution. Commentaries, introductory textbooks, and Bible study guides, published within the past twenty years in virtually every language, after a brief nod to the alternatives, all subscribe to the Two Source Hypothesis. Given this widespread support, one would think that fundamental scholarship on its scholarly foundations would no longer be necessary and would cease. Precisely the opposite has happened. I will mention here only a few of the most important developments.

First, a new synopsis appeared in 1963 that indirectly supported the Two Source Hypothesis, Kurt Aland's *Synopsis Quattuor Evangeliorum*, based on the Nestle-Aland Greek NT[25]. It contained even smaller pericope divisions and a rather different arrangement of the synoptic parallels than the existing favorite synopsis of Albert Huck.[75] But the really new features were the inclusion of the Gospel of John, the addition of an enormous collection of patristic quotations as well as quotations from all relevant apocryphal Gospels at the end of each pericope (the entire text of the Coptic Gospel of Thomas was printed in an appendix in three languages). Other useful features included a collection of relevant patristic texts dealing with the history of the text at the back of the book and a much larger text-critical apparatus. Taking all of these major additions into consideration, the new Aland synopsis represented a huge advance in modern synopsis construction, soon supplanting Huck as the favorite of scholars.

Second, a number of defenses of the Two Source Hypothesis appeared in the wake of Butler's and Farmer's critiques. In 1972, Frans Neirynck of the University of Leuven responded to the assertion of the Neo-Griesbachians that Mark's wordy style was a sign of its being a conflated writing. They published studies to show that Mark often combined words and phrases found in Matthew and Luke. Neirynck countered this argument by explaining that the frequent "dual expressions" in Mark were simply a prominent feature of Mark's periphrastic style and that Matthew and Luke frequently abridged his wordy style.[76]

Two years later, Neirynck—with help from Theo Hansen and Frans van Segbroeck—took up a long-standing problem area for the Two Source Hypothesis, the so-called minor agreements of Matthew and Luke against Mark. Neirynck adopted the approach of Hawkins and Streeter and said that these agreements were just accidental coincidences where Matthew and Luke simultaneously and independently altered their text of Mark in precisely the same way, dozens and dozens of times, for precisely the same reasons.

Neirynck's explanation did not seem convincing, even to some who accepted the Two Source Hypothesis. Georg Strecker of Göttingen and Albert Fuchs of Linz, both Markan priorists, thought that the piecemeal approach was not adequate.[77] It ignored evidence that the minor agreements in Matthew and Luke sometimes seemed to be linked together into *networks of minor disagreements* over against the text of Mark. Strecker and Fuchs decided that these networks were clear-cut evidence that Matthew and Luke had copied from *a slightly revised version of Mark* that later disappeared.[78]

This view was later given the most extensive treatment to date by Andreas Ennulat, a student of Ulrich Luz, Bern University, in his doctoral dissertation. Ennulat set aside the piecemeal solution saying that its credibility depended on believing too many happy coincidences. Conducting a much more evenhanded and sophisticated investigation, he found that the minor agreements (both positive and negative) (a) were distributed throughout the triple tradition and (b) often formed significant patterns or networks. These conclusions led him to state that 97 percent of the more than one thousand minor agreements indicated that Matthew and Luke probably used a modified version of Mark (known as Deutero-Markus) and not the canonical Mark we now have (hence the "minor agreements" against *it*).[79]

Frans Neirynck also led the defense against the criticism, first stated by Butler and subsequently repeated by William Farmer, that the argument from order of pericopes contained in Streeter's list of proofs for the priority of Mark was based on "an elementary error in logic." Neirynck conceded the point but said that Lachmann's argument from order was still valid for the priority of Mark:

> In fact the basic phenomenon to be reckoned with is the common order between Mark and Matthew (on the one hand) and between Mark and Luke (on the other) . . . Lachmann's . . . argument for the priority of Mark's order is still a valuable one insofar as an acceptable explanation can be given for Matthew's and Luke's transpositions.[80]

Lachmann's argument referred to here states that, instead of looking at all three of the Gospels simultaneously, the way to begin is by taking them in pairs: Matthew/Mark and Luke/Mark. In this way, the number of pericopes "out of order" requiring explanation is greatly reduced.[81] In a number of publications, Neirynck has proposed "acceptable explanations" for the few transpositions seen to exist between *pairs of Gospels*.[82]

Neirynck's new way of defending the priority of Mark—undoubtedly based on W. G. Kümmel's discussion[83]—was adopted by the English scholar Christopher Tuckett of Manchester. In 1983, he published *The Revival of the Griesbach Hypothesis: An Analysis and Appraisal*, the first comprehensive critique of the Neo-Griesbachian school. Early in his book, Tuckett attacked Farmer's use of the argument from order of pericopes, defending Lachmann's approach.[84]

Noticing this new (or old) use of Lachmann's approach to defend the priority of Mark, an Australian scholar, David Neville of Perth, examined the arguments of Neirynck and Tuckett and the replies of Farmer and Dungan. Neville came to the conclusion that Lachmann's approach *begins* by "disallowing any literary connection between Matthew's and Luke's Gospels and *thereby discounts Griesbach's hypothesis without having to argue against it on its own terms*."[85] Neville said that Lachmann's proposal to split the Gospels into two pairs at the outset "was designed to achieve a predetermined result" and resembled "an invisible hand rolling loaded dice."[86] Neville ended with this categorical statement:

> The methodological procedure adopted by Lachmann, Kümmel, Neirynck, and Tuckett determines to some extent what one's conclusion will be. Griesbach's procedure is more neutral.[87]

Note what has happened. First Butler and then Farmer pointed out the logical fallacies in Streeter's main argument from order of pericopes, an argument that he said was the main reason for adhering to the priority of Mark. The correctness of Butler's and Farmer's critique was subsequently acknowledged in print by Styler, Neirynck, and Tuckett. Not long after, Neirynck, followed by Tuckett, switched to Lachmann's approach, saying that it now "constitutes *the main reason* for positing Marcan priority."[88] But David Neville uncovered the logical fallacies within Lachmann's approach as well, leaving the main defenders of the Two Source Hypothesis without any formal arguments to support it.

One might think that in the wake of this kind of crippling criticism, proponents of Markan priority would finally admit that it is an untenable hypothesis. Not at all. It continues to be used far and wide as if nothing had happened, resembling the headless horseman who rides across the countryside every Halloween in the light of the full moon.

A close reading of the most recent comments by Neirynck and Tuckett reveal that they have given up trying to provide any formal arguments to justify the idea that Mark was written first. In his article "The Synoptic Problem" for the *New Interpreters Bible,* Tuckett wrote:

> Contemporary debate has highlighted the weak and inconclusive nature of some of the arguments in the past that have been used to promote the two-source theory. This applies especially to some of the more "formal" arguments (Neville's term), referring to global patterns in the overall set of agreements. For example, in arguing for Mkan priority, some (here he refers to Streeter) have appealed to the fact that nearly all of Mk is paralleled in Mt or Lk or both. Yet all this shows is that some literary relationship exists; it does not prove that the only possibility is that Mk's Gospel was the *source* of Mt and Lk. Similarly, the much discussed appeal to the failure of Mt and Lk ever, or hardly ever, to agree against Mk in order and wording (another reference to Streeter) does not prove that Mt and Lk independently used Mk as a source; it only shows that Mk is some kind of "middle term" (this is Butler's term) between the other two in any pattern of relationships.[89]

Nothing daunted, Tuckett went on to suggest that the truth of Markan priority could still be demonstrated by what Neville called "compositional" arguments, i.e., explaining "specific details in the texts of the gospels."[90] In Tuckett's words:

> Probably *the most important kind of arguments* are based on concrete comparison of individual texts, asking which way the tradition is likely to have developed.[91]

He immediately provided an illustration: "For example, in Peter's Confession it is more likely that Mt expanded Mk's shorter form."[92] Unwittingly, Tuckett hereby revealed the key shortcoming in this kind of compositional argument: namely, there is little agreement among scholars as to what constitutes certain and unambiguous evidence of early versus late forms of the synoptic tradition. E. P. Sanders demonstrated long ago in *Tendencies of the Synoptic Tradition* (1969) that it developed in many different ways simultaneously, so that general principles like "the shorter form is always earlier" can never be taken for granted.

In conclusion, it would seem that we live in the ironic situation where confidence in Markan priority rises to ever new heights despite the fact that, after forty-five years of steady criticism, knowledgeable defenders of the hypothesis have been forced to abandon one basic argument after another, to the point where there are, at present, no formal arguments left that will justify it and the compositional arguments are just as questionable.[93] It has rightly earned the sobriquet "the Teflon hypothesis."

Reconstructions of the Q Source

Another example of the impregnability of the confidence in the Two Source Hypothesis is revealed by the fact that, as scholars find it harder and harder to defend the priority of Mark, trust in the Q hypothesis is more confident than ever. Books and articles pour out containing elaborate reconstructions of its contents,[94] reconstructing the history for the "Q community" to account for the many recensions scholars think they can see in the "history of Q"—complete with rival factions, each sporting its own version of Q, its heroes and theological agendas. Most exciting of all is the recent appearance of the dazzling ultimate idea championed by a small but determined group of scholars: "Q-Thomas Christianity," i.e., Q (properly reconstructed) and the Coptic Gospel of Thomas (properly reconstructed) contain the true message of the historical Jesus for today's alienated world.[95]

This great interest in Q is in part a side effect of the discovery of the Nag Hammadi library, with the sayings Gospel of Thomas.[96] This document was immediately interpreted by James M. Robinson and others as confirmation of the Two Source Hypothesis' postulate of an early collection of Jesus sayings.[97] After leading an international team to produce in record time a complete, critical edition and translation of the Nag Hammadi materials,[98] in 1983 Robinson created a research project under the auspices of the Institute for Antiquity and Christianity at Claremont, California, to reconstruct, translate, and provide a commentary on the text of Q.[99] Over the years, reports have been published recounting the project's progress.[100] Simultaneous with the publication of the "critical text" of Q,

Robinson will bring out a commentary on Q in the *Hermeneia* series. There are even rumors of a pew-rack edition for use in Christian worship.

This brief discussion hardly does justice to the many important publications that have appeared since the end of the Second World War dealing with the composition of the Gospels. However, a fuller discussion will have to be undertaken elsewhere. Perhaps it may serve as an introduction to a more extended discussion of current trends in understanding how the Gospels were created, within the Third Form of the Synoptic Problem.

CHAPTER 23

Conclusion

The dawn of the twenty-first century, and with it the third millennium of the Christian calendar, is an appropriate time for retrospective soul-searching and stocktaking. At the end of this history of the main attempts, from the first century to the twenty-first, to explain the creation of the Gospels, a few general conclusions are in order.

Perhaps most important, the profound changes which took place during the Protestant Reformation and the Enlightenment can hardly be overestimated. Protestant Christianity, modified by Enlightenment ideals and concepts, represents a great sea change over against all earlier forms of traditional Christianity—and the changes were by no means all for the better. If Martin Luther and the Reformers succeeded in breaking through the crust of centuries of misguided and corrupt ecclesiastical dogma and practice to discover a purer, more spiritual form of the Christian faith, at the same time they unleashed an unrestrained individualism and arid scholasticism every bit as destructive as the evils they opposed.

If the Enlightenment rightly perceived and fiercely attacked certain aggravated abuses of entrenched power—religious, political, and economic—in the name of religious tolerance, political freedom, and scientific objectivity, the arrogance and rigid materialism typical of many Enlightenment thinkers either exacerbated or at least did nothing to prevent some of the bloodiest and most destructive wars the world has ever seen. And we now stand on the brink of an environmental crisis whose specific details and awful dimensions are only just beginning to be grasped, caused by certain scientific assumptions that have blinded us to what we have been doing to our planet.

It would seem that this history of the repeated attempts to provide an adequate explanation of the differences among the Gospels, while still preserving their credibility as authoritative witnesses to Jesus Christ, must end on a note of considerable irony. It seems as if the farther we go, the greater the confusion, error, and disintegration. But such a conclusion overlooks the manifold evidence of strong movements for reform, reintegration, and renewal.

As we saw in Part One, the presence of competing, very dissimilar accounts of the Lord Jesus at first led to attempts to suppress rival Gospels by a number of Church leaders. After the canonization process got well under way (by the mid-second century), the orthodox faction found itself ineluctably in possession of *four* rather diverse documents. This resulted in more and more elaborate attempts at justification, culminating among the orthodox in the magisterial work by Augustine *On the Harmony of the Evangelists.*

Part Two described the eclipse of the great Augustinian medieval synthesis and its replacement by the Enlightenment historical-critical method, within a broad cultural revolution leading to the establishment in western Europe of market capitalism, secular political democracy, and religious toleration and freedom of the individual. Within this cultural revolution, every aspect of traditional Christian worship and theology was replaced. In biblical studies, each of the four main aspects of the Synoptic Problem—canon, text, composition, and interpretation—were likewise replaced.

While these great changes seemed advantageous at the time—at least to some—today they need a searching critique. This critique is indeed going on, right now, with great fervor and industry in Christian seminaries, universities, and schools all over the planet. Everywhere the inquiring eye looks, it sees an astonishingly complex vista of scholarly activity, at unprecedented levels of sophistication.

An example of these concerted efforts at renewal is the one-volume commentary on the Bible, entitled *International Bible Commentary: A Catholic and Ecumenical Resource for the Twenty-first Century.* Editions will appear by the year 2000 in Spanish, English, French, Italian, Dutch, and Polish. Intended primarily for pastors all over the world, it was created by an ecumenical, international team of scholars, with contributors from every continent and more than 150 countries. This commentary pioneers a number of new approaches to biblical interpretation. As such, it addresses many of the issues raised in this book.

The Synoptic Problem: Part of the Church's Conversation with God

The Synoptic Problem has been—from the beginning—one of the most sensitive and complex areas in biblical study. It has been the foremost goal of this history to present, in some respects for the first time, a complete (if not comprehensive) history of the debate on this issue from its inception, not just from the eighteenth century. Moreover, this history has examined the Synoptic Problem within a rigorous and consistent methodological perspective, so as to clarify the subtle nuances of its different forms.

This history has documented the heretofore unknown fact that there are not one but three clearly defined, strikingly different forms of the Synoptic Problem. The latter two forms still are active today among the Augustinian/Lockean fundamentalists with their Gospel harmonies (Second Form) and the Spinozist historical critics with their synopses (Third Form). Given their sharply differing assumptions about the Gospel canon and the appropriate method for interpreting the Bible, they clash head-on wherever they meet. Perhaps the account given here of the primary assumptions more or less unwittingly taken for granted by each group will help to remove some of the animosity and confusion in future encounters.

It is striking to observe that, from the first century until now, one and the same basic question has animated all participants in this great discussion in all of its forms, namely: "Where may I find reliable testimony to the Lord Jesus?" Even the Jesus Seminar, which is not noted for its adherence to any traditional norms or institutions, can publish a book, *The Five Gospels,* with the subtitle *The Search for the Authentic Words of Jesus.* Whether it be Justin Martyr or Origen, Celsus or Porphyry, Eusebius or Augustine, Martin Luther or John Calvin, Erasmus or John Toland, Baruch Spinoza or John Locke, Johann Jakob Griesbach or Heinrich Julius Holtzmann, Burnett Hillmann Streeter or Basil Christopher Butler, Frans Neirynck or William Farmer, James Robinson or Robert Funk—they have all sat down at the same table and looked at the same mysterious Gospels and asked the same fundamental question. Clearly, it is the answer that divides us.

At one level, the Synoptic Problem is not really a "problem" at all. That is, it is not like a scientific riddle that can be given this or that solution, which then must be reexamined by later investigators. At its deepest level, the Synoptic Problem is not a scientific "problem" but part of the Church's never-ending conversation with the God of Jesus Christ. At its deepest level, the quest for the correct solution to the Synoptic Problem, like the Church's quest for the correct canon of the Gospels, and the correct text of the Gospels, and the correct way to interpret the Gospels, is a vital aspect of the Church's perennial quest for the Word of Life.

Notes

1 This translation of οἱ ἀπ᾽ ἀρχῆς αὐτόπται seems to me to be what the author means. Some other translations are "eye-witnesses from the beginning" (RSV, NAB); "from the first" (NIV); "from the outset" (JB). To me the Greek implies that these men were some of the original Twelve Apostles or their associates who were with them from the beginning.

2 The usual translation "ministers of the word" (RSV, NAB, JB; cf. "servants of the word" NIV) is more technically correct but less expressive in English.

3 The Greek is Ἐπειδήπερ πολλοὶ ἐπεχείρησαν ἀνατάξασθαι διήγησιν περὶ τῶν πεπληροφορημένων ἐν ἡμῖν πραγμάτων, καθὼς παρέδοσαν ἡμῖν οἱ ἀπ᾽ ἀρχῆς αὐτόπται καὶ ὑπηρέται γενόμενοι τοῦ λόγου, ἔδοξε κἀμοὶ παρηκολουθηκότι ἄνωθεν πᾶσιν ἀκριβῶς καθεξῆς σοι γράψαι, κράτιστε θεόφιλε, ἵνα ἐπιγνῷς περὶ κατηχήθης λόγων τὴν ἀσφάλειαν.

4 There are no other occurrences in the New Testament. There are fifteen occurrences of ἐπιχείρ-words in the LXX, all from the later Hellenistic period: 2 Chron 20:11; Ezra 7:23; 1 Esd 1:26; Esth 9:25, 16:3; Ezra 7:23; 2 Macc 2:29, 7:19, 9:2, 10:15, 15:33; 3 Macc 6:24, 7:5; 4 Macc 1:5; Sir 9:4. A few examples indicate its range of meaning. (The translation is RSV.)

> Sir 9:4: "Do not associate with a woman singer, lest you be caught in her intrigues (ἐν τοῖς ἐπιχειρήμασιν αὐτῆς)."

> 2 Macc 7:19: But do not think that you will go unpunished for having tried to fight against God (θεομαχεῖν ἐπιχειρήσας)."

> 2 Macc 9:2: "For he (Antiochus) had entered the city called Persepolis, and attempted to rob the temples (ἐπεχείρησεν ἱεροσυλεῖν) and control the city."

> 2 Macc 10:15: "Besides this, the Idumeans, who had control of important strongholds, were harassing the Jews; they received those who were

banished from Jerusalem, and <u>endeavored to keep up the war</u> (πολεμο-τροφεῖν ἐπεχείρουν)."

Esth 9:25: "... but when Esther came before the king, he gave orders in writing that Haman's <u>wicked plot which he had devised</u> (ἐπιχειροῦσι μηχανᾶσθαι) against the Jews should come upon his own head, and that he and his sons should be hanged on the gallows."

There are two examples where the word has a positive connotation:

Ezra 7:23: "Whatever is commanded by the God of heaven, let it be <u>done in full for the house of the God</u> (ἐπιχειρήσῃ εἰς οἶκον θεοῦ) of heaven, lest his wrath be against the realm of the king and his sons."

2 Macc 2:29: "For as the master-builder of a new house must be concerned with the whole construction, while the one who undertakes its painting and decoration has to <u>consider only</u> what is suitable for its <u>adornment</u> (ἐπιχειροῦντι τὰ ἐπιτήδεια πρὸς διακόσμησιν), such in my judgment is the case with us."

5 For Origen's interpretation of πολλοὶ ἐπεχείρησαν ἀνατάξασθαι διήγησιν, see below, p. 70.
6 For the classic discussion of this question, see Birger Gerhardsson, *Memory and Manuscript: Oral Tradition and Written Transmission in Rabbinic Judaism and Early Christianity,* Acta Sem. Neotest. Upsal. 22 (Lund: Gleerup 1961). Further, Harald Riesenfeld, "The Gospel Tradition and Its Beginnings," in *The Gospel Tradition,* ed. Harald Riesenfeld, trans. E. M. Rowley (Philadelphia: Fortress Press 1970) 1–30.
7 For a representative collection of such prefaces, see David R. Cartlidge and David L. Dungan, *Documents for the Study of the Gospels,* 2nd ed. (Philadelphia: Fortress Press 1994) 121–127; 206 (Philostratus, *Life of Apollonios*); 251f. (Philo, *Life of Moses*). For the most recent comprehensive discussion of Luke's preface, see Loveday Alexander, *The Preface to Luke's Gospel: Literary Convention and Social Context in Luke 1:1–4 and Acts 1:1,* SNTS Monogr. Ser. 78 (Cambridge: University Press 1993). Alexander points to special affinities between Luke's preface and Greek medical treatises. While these are important and informative, I am inclined to note the close similarities with the prefaces mentioned here.
8 On the much disputed question of the uniqueness of the canonical gospel genre in general, see most recently the review of the literature by Willem S. Vorster, *ABD* 2:1077–1079; "Gospel Genre." As for the genre of Luke (or Luke/Acts), see especially Richard I. Pervo, *Profit with Delight: The Literary Genre of the Acts of the Apostles* (Philadelphia: Fortress Press 1987); further, Philip L. Shuler, *A Genre for the Gospels: The Biographical Character of Mat-*

thew (Philadelphia: Fortress Press 1982); Richard A. Burridge, *What Are the Gospels? A Comparison with Graeco-Roman Biography*, SNTS Monogr. Ser. 70 (Cambridge: University Press 1992); Charles H. Talbert, *What Is a Gospel? The Genre of the Canonical Gospels* (Philadelphia: Fortress Press 1977); and David E. Aune, *The New Testament and Its Literary Environment* (Philadelphia: Westminster Press, 1987); cf. Aune, "Greco-Roman Biography," in *Greco-Roman Literature and the New Testament*, ed. David E. Aune, SBL Sources for Biblical Study 21 (Atlanta: Scholar's Press 1988) 107–126.

9 For a detailed analysis of the Gospel of Luke as a Hellenistic portrait of Jesus of Nazareth in the type of the wandering philosopher/savior, see Allan J. McNicol et al., *Beyond the Q Impasse: Luke's Use of Matthew* (Philadelphia: Trinity Press International 1996). For a discussion of the early Christian portrayal of Jesus of Nazareth as "the savior of the world," see "Savior Gods in the Mediterranean World," in Cartlidge and Dungan, *Documents*, 5–16.

10 For the presence of both, see the preface to the Sacred History of Asklepios (Pap. Oxy. 1381), cited in David R. Cartlidge and David L. Dungan, *Documents for the Study of the Gospels*, 2nd ed. (Philadelphia: Fortress Press 1980) 122–124.

11 The author did not give the titles of any of the rival narratives, probably because none of them had titles at this point (cf. Mt 1:1; Jn 1:1).

NOTES TO CHAPTER 3

1 See Eusebius, *Eccl. hist.* 3.37.1; cf. 5.17.2–4. Recent scholarship has correctly shown that Eusebius and others have confused two Philips; one is the disciple of Jesus and the other is "Philip the Evangelist" mentioned in Acts 6:5, 21:8–9. Similarly, it is doubtful if this Quadratus is the author of the famous Apology named after him; see Johannes Quasten, *Patrology*, 3 vols (Utrecht-Antwerp: Spectrum 1966) 1:190f.

2 Irenaeus, *adv. haer.* 5.33.4. "These things are borne witness to in writing by Papias, the hearer of John and a companion of Polycarp" (Ἰωάννου μὲν ἀκουστής, Πολυκάρπου δὲ ἑταῖρος).

3 This translation is taken from Eusebius, *Ecclesiastical History*, ed. and trans. A. C. McGiffert, *Nicene and Post-Nicene Fathers*, Vol. 1, 2nd ser. (Grand Rapids: Eerdmans 1952) 171. I realize that Eusebius' purpose in giving this quotation was to prove that Papias did *not* interact with the disciple John himself, but with those who were *followers* of John and the other disciples. It is well known that Eusebius was biased against Papias for theological reasons, so we must look for some corrective of what he says about Papias. For example, he was less biased against Irenaeus, another native of Asia. He had no difficulty agreeing with Irenaeus' tradition that Polycarp, the friend of

Papias and the Bishop of Smyrna (a city not far from Hierapolis), was not only a direct hearer but a fervent disciple of John the disciple "and the others who had seen the Lord" (*Hist.* 5.20.6; cf. 4.14.3). Thus Eusebius' statements boil down to the curious position that Eusebius agrees with Irenaeus' statement that Polycarp interacted with the disciple John but disagrees with Irenaeus' statement that Papias, Polycarp's contemporary and bishop of a neighboring city within walking distance of Ephesus, did the same thing.

I suggest that we accept Irenaeus' testimony quoted above in n.2, namely, that Papias had in fact spoken directly with the disciple John and gotten numerous traditions from him, such as this report on the origin of the Gospel of Mark. On the whole question of the necessity of taking into account Eusebius' hostility toward Papias when interpreting the Papias fragments, see most recently Bernard Orchard and Harold Riley, *The Order of the Synoptics: Why Three Synoptic Gospels?* (Macon: Mercer University Press 1987) 169–194.

4 Greek: ἔλεγεν = iterative imperfect, "customarily said, used to say." The point is that "the Elder" said the following things repeatedly, as a matter of custom.

5 Greek: ἑρμηνευτὴς Πέτρου. The term probably means "interpreter" as in "linguistic translator." We have no information where Peter was when Mark first became his interpreter.

6 Greek: ὥσπερ + participle II: to limit or modify an assertion ... frequently with participles; e.g., ὥσπερ ἐξόν "as if it were in our power," Xenophon, *Anab.* 3.1.14; see Liddell-Scott-Jones, *Lexicon* ὥσπερ.

7 The manuscripts are about evenly divided between λόγων "words" and λογ-ίων "oracles." The majority of manuscripts favor the latter, but recent translators prefer the former as the rougher reading; see McGiffert, op. cit. n.3, 1:173 n.24. However, I think λογίων is more likely because (a) it is the term Papias uses elsewhere to refer *generically* to the sayings and actions of the Lord in the fragment concerning Matthew, as well as in the title of his *Commentary* (see below, n.31); (b) Polycarp also uses it in the same generic sense, τὰ λόγια τοῦ κυρίου "and whosoever shall pervert *the oracles of the Lord*, etc." 7:1 (Lightfoot); cf. 1 Clem. 62:3 τὰ λόγια τῆς παιδείας τοῦ Θεοῦ "people ... who had made a study of *the oracles of God's teaching*," basically referring to the whole of Scripture; cf. Bauer-Arndt-Gingrich, *Lexicon* λόγιον.

8 Greek: ἔνια γράψας ὡς ἐπεμνημόνευσεν. The word ἔνια means "some, some of (a larger totality)," cf. Latin *aliqui*. This word refers to Peter's not recounting the whole Gospel tradition but only some of it—according to the needs of the moment. Mark, the next sentence says, "was careful not to omit anything he heard" Peter say. So it was not *Mark* who was responsible for the truncated Gospel named after him, but Peter.

9 Eusebius, *Eccl. Hist.* 3.39.15. The Greek text is ... ἀναγκαίως νῦν προσθήσο-

μεν . . . παράδοσιν ἦν περὶ Μάρκου τοῦ τὸ εὐαγγέλιον γεγραφότος ἐκτέθειται διὰ τούτων »καὶ τοῦθ' ὁ πρεσβύτερος ἔλεγεν· Μάρκος μὲν ἑρμηνευτὴς Πέτρου γενόμενος, ὅσα ἐμνημόνευσεν, ἀκριβῶς ἔγραψεν, οὐ μέντοι τάξει τὰ ὑπὸ τοῦ κυρίου ἢ λεχθέντα ἢ πραχθέντα. οὔτε γὰρ ἤκουσεν τοῦ κυρίου οὔτε παρηκολούθησεν αὐτῷ, ὕστερον δέ, ὡς ἔφην, Πέτρῳ· ὃς πρὸς τὰς χρείας ἐποιεῖτο τὰς διδασκαλίας, ἀλλ' οὐχ ὥσπερ σύνταξιν τῶν κυριακῶν ποιούμενος λογίων, ὥστε οὐδὲν ἥμαρτεν Μάρκος οὕτως ἔνια γράψας ὡς ἐπεμνημόνευσεν. ἑνὸς γὰρ ἐποιήσατο πρόνοιαν, τοῦ μηδὲν ὧν ἤκουσεν παραλιπεῖν ἢ ψεύσασθαί τι ἐν αὐτοῖς. Ταῦτα μὲν οὖν ἱστόρηται τῷ Παπίᾳ τοῦ Μάρκου.« Text taken from Kurt Aland, *Synopsis quattuor evangeliorum* (Stuttgart: Württembergische Bibelanstalt 1964) 531. Compare the translations by McGiffert, op. cit. n.3, 1:172f.; also Helmut Koester, *Ancient Christian Gospels: Their History and Development* (Philadelphia: Trinity Press International 1990) 274.

10 Koester, ibid., 274.

11 Cf. Xenophon, *Mem.* 4.2, 25 πρὸς τὴν ἀνθρωπίνην χρείαν "for human use." Xenophon is comparing things a human is "used" for with "a horse's use" πρὸς τὴν τοῦ ἵππου χρείαν; see Liddell-Scott-Jones, *Lexicon* χρεία. Cf. Moulton-Milligan, *Vocabulary of the Greek Testament* χρεία: "necessity," "need," or "occasion of need"; further, Bauer-Arndt-Gingrich, *Lexicon* χρεία, Phil 4:19 εἰς τὴν χρείαν τινὶ πέμψαι "to send something to someone to supply his need(s)."

12 Greek: οὐχ ὥσπερ σύνταξιν τῶν κυριακῶν ποιούμενος λογίων. The term σύνταξις means a systematically arranged or prepared treatise; cf. Bauer-Arndt-Gingrich, *Lexicon* σύνταξις. Luke 1:1 uses a synonym, ἀνατάξασθαι, when speaking of others who have "drawn up, compiled" a narrative, i.e., "repeat in the proper (*scil.* chronological) order"; Bauer-Arndt-Gingrich, ἀνατάσσομαι. Recently, another interpretation has been proposed by J. Kürzinger, *Papias von Hierapolis und die Evangelien des Neuen Testaments* (Regensburg: Pustet 1983) 51–56. He suggests that πρὸς τὰς χρείας should be translated "in *chreia* form." A *chreia* was a Greek rhetorical *topos* which referred to a brief story, saying, or memoir, commonly used in Hellenistic storytelling to illustrate a famous person's character. This interpretation fits perfectly with the next statement, that Peter did not make a σύνταξις, a connected narrative, of the Lord's oracles. On this interpretation, "the Elder" says that Peter used to tell χρεῖαι, "stories, anecdotes" in no particular order, which Mark accurately remembered and recorded. Kürzinger's argument is very plausible and may be correct. However, he says nothing about the *source* of this description of Mark, nor the curiously negative tone of "the Elder's" report. Hence I am inclined toward the other interpretation of the Greek: "according to necessity," "as need arose."

13 New Jerusalem Bible. Cf. the portrait of Peter in Acts 11 where he is accused of eating Gentile food when away from Jerusalem. The author of Acts glori-

fies Peter's action by recounting a vision sent from God complete with a *bath Qol* telling him not to be bound by Jewish restrictions against "unclean foods" (Acts 11:1–10).

14 I am aware that this interpretation is not the usual understanding of "elder." See, for example, J. Munck, "Presbyters and Disciples of the Lord in Papias," *HTR* 52 (1959): 223–244, who argues that this was a "teaching elder" named John, not the disciple of Jesus. This is the consensus; cf. Kürzinger, op. cit. n.12, 65 n.5. However, this view is too willing to take at face value Eusebius' attempt to drive a wedge between Papias and John the disciple of Jesus and should not be accepted.

15 For a concise statement of the sharp contrast between Peter and John in the Gospel of John, see Arthur J. Droge, "The Status of Peter in the Fourth Gospel," *JBL* 109/2 (1990): 307–311; the quote is from p. 311. For a more bureaucratic discussion, see R. E. Brown, K. P. Donfried, and J. Reumann, *Peter in the New Testament* (Minneapolis: Augsburg 1973), 130–139.

16 This means that presumably the "correct" order would be the order found in John's Gospel.

17 The question of the authorship and date of writing of the Gospel of John is intricately bound up with the question of its history of composition. At present, there is little consensus as to how much of the existing version of the Gospel of John was written by the disciple John and how much was added by later members of his "school." On this whole subject see Raymond E. Brown, *The Gospel according to John*, 2 vols., Anchor Bible Commentaries (New York: Doubleday 1966) 1:xxiv–xl. For a presentation of the Bultmannian approach to the composition of the Gospel of John, see Koester, op. cit. n.9, 246–271.

18 Koester 246.

19 See Funk-Bihlmeyer, *Die apostolischen Väter*, 2nd ed., W. Schneelmelcher (Tübingen: J.C.B. Mohr/Paul Siebeck 1956) 114–120; cf. Cyril C. Richardson, *Early Christian Fathers*, Library of Christian Classics (Philadelphia: Westminster Press 1953), 1:131–137; my statistics are based on Richardson's footnotes. A clear allusion to 1 Jn 4:2–3 can be found in *Ep. Pol.* 7:1: "whosoever does not confess that Jesus Christ has come in the flesh is antichrist"; cf. "by this you know that you have the Spirit of God: every spirit which confesses that Jesus Christ has come in the flesh is of God, and every spirit which does not confess Jesus is not of God. This is the spirit of antichrist" 1 Jn 4:2–3; cf. 2 Jn 7. An unmistakable allusion to 3 Jn 8 occurs in *Ep. Pol.* 10:1: "Stand firm, therefore, in these things and follow the example of the Lord, . . . loving the brotherhood (cf. 1 Pet 2:17), cherishing one another (cf. 1 Pet 3:8; also Rom 12:10), *fellow companions in the truth*"; cf. 3 Jn 8: "so that we may be fellow workers in the truth." I realize that modern scholars believe that the second

two letters are not by the same person as the author of the first letter or the Gospel, but the allusion to 1 Jn does support my point.

20 See Koester, op. cit. n.9, 246: "Ignatius of Antioch, although his theological language is closely related to that of [the Gospel of] John, does not seem to know [it]."

21 So William L. Petersen, *Tatian's Diatessaron: Its Creation, Dissemination, Significance, and History in Scholarship*, Suppl. Vig. Christ. 25 (Leiden: Brill 1994) 16: "Scholarship acknowledges that . . . Justin [used] the synoptics and/or their traditions and not the Gospel of John (which Justin cites once, if at all)." This fact is all the more striking since Justin did make extensive use of a Logos Christology similar to that found in the Gospel of John. For this reason, it is at least probable that he *knew* of the Gospel of John even if he never quoted from it. See further Arthur Bellinzoni, *The Sayings of Jesus in the Writings of Justin Martyr*, Suppl. Nov. Test. 17 (Leiden: Brill 1967) 140; Koester, op. cit. n.9, 360–402, esp. 391.

22 Epiphanius, *Panarion* 51.17.11–18.1. Translation from Philip R. Amidon, *The Panarion of St. Epiphanius, Bishop of Salamis* (Oxford: University Press 1990) 181.

23 Ibid. 51.22.1.

24 A. Bludau, *Die ersten Gegner der Johannes-Schriften*, Biblische Studien 22/1, 2 (Breslau: Herder 1925), tries to sort out the various references, most explicitly in Epiphanius, *Panarion* 51.17.11f., 51.22.1, Irenaeus and Hippolytus.

25 Translation: J. B. Lightfoot, *The Apostolic Fathers* (New York: Macmillan 1891; reprint Grand Rapids: Baker Book House 1967) 265. The Greek text is ταῦτα μὲν οὖν ἱστόρηται τῷ Παπίᾳ τοῦ Μάρκου· περὶ δὲ τοῦ Ματθαίου ταῦτ᾽ εἴρηται »Ματθαῖος μὲν οὖν Ἑβραΐδι διαλέκτῳ τὰ λόγια συνετάξατο, ἡρμήνευσεν δ᾽ αὐτὰ ὡς ἦν δυνατὸς ἕκαστος.« Text taken from Kurt Aland, *Synopsis quattuor evangeliorum* (Stuttgart: Württembergische Bibelanstalt 1964) 531.

26 Johannes Quasten, *Patrology*, 3 vols. (Utrecht-Antwerp: Spectrum 1966) 1:83.

27 Liddell-Scott-Jones, *Lexicon* διαλέκτος. This interpretation has most recently been urged by J. Kürzinger, op. cit. n.12, 20–22.

28 J. Kürzinger 22: "Diesen Ἑβρᾶς διάλεκτρος den Papias also vom griechischen AT her kennen muste, erkennt er in der literarischen Art des Mt-Ev wieder."

29 For a list of the earliest Matthew papyri fragments and related writings, see Koester, op. cit. n.9, 314–315.

30 As such, it was synonymous with such technical terms as μαντεῖον and χρηστήριον.

31 It is in this sense that Luke portrays Stephen using it in his speech: "(Moses) received *living oracles* (λόγια ζῶντα) to give to us" (Acts 7:38 NRSV). Paul

used the term in the same broad sense in his letter to the Christians at Rome: "Then what advantage has the Jew (over the Gentiles)? Or what is the value of circumcision? Much in every way! To begin with, the Jews (alone) are entrusted with *the oracles of God* (τὰ λόγια τοῦ θεοῦ)" (Rom 3:1–2 NRSV). The writer of 1 Clement uses it in the same broad sense when, coming to the end of his lengthy exhortation to the Corinthian Church, after he has summarized all sorts of passages from the Hebrew Scripture, he says: "We were all the more delighted to remind you of these things, since we well realized that we were writing to people who ... had made a study of the *oracles of God's teaching* (τὰ λόγια τῆς παιδείας τοῦ θεοῦ)" (1 Clem 62:3 Richardson translation); cf. Bauer-Arndt-Gingrich, *Lexicon* λόγιον, for further references.

32 Koester seems unaware of the broader meaning in his discussion of Papias; he says that λόγια cannot include "actions"; op. cit. n.9, 316. But this untenable opinion may be caused by his desire to identify the Matthean λόγια with the alleged Sayings Source Q (see 318). For the broader interpretation adopted here, see the discussion of Kürzinger where he rightly points out that it is parallel to τὰ ὑπὸ τοῦ κυρίου ἢ λεχθέντα ἢ πραχθέντα; 47, 51. Cf. Acts 1:1; cf. also J. Munck, op. cit. n.14, 228.

33 McGiffert, op. cit. n.3, 1.173.

34 Koester, op. cit. n.9, 317 n.1: "Papias's reference to a 'Hebrew' composition by Matthew is extraordinary because it is certain there never was a Semitic (Hebrew or Aramaic) original of the Gospel of Matthew." However, Koester's reasoning is based on the Two Source Hypothesis, not on any historical evidence: "The Greek literary style of the Gospel of Matthew and its use of Greek sources (Mk and Q) exclude this."

NOTES TO CHAPTER 4

1 See *1 Apol.* 1. I wish to thank William L. Petersen for his helpful critique of this chapter.

2 Hence it is clear that Justin was not a Jew. In any case, he says in *Dial.* 28 that he is "an uncircumcised man."

3 See *Dialogue with Trypho* 2–8. E. R. Goodenough, *The Theology of Justin Martyr* (Amsterdam: Philo Press 1968) 58f., gives evidence of the traditional or formalistic nature of this "survey of all schools of thought until the True Way is found," in Lucian's *Menippus and Necromancy* chs. 4–6. Goodenough (59–61) also notes that Justin's criticisms of the different philosophical schools are conventional critiques revealing minimal knowledge and understanding of them.

4 *Dial.* 8. Goodenough notes that Justin's conversion on the basis of proof from prophecy remained for him the major compelling argument in favor of Chris-

tianity (cf. *1 Apol.* 30–53), a characteristic he shared with Tatian, Theophilus of Antioch, and Hilary; ibid. 73f.

5 Goodenough is particularly good on this point; see 72f.

6 Cf. *2 Apol.* 8, which refers to Musonius as being "among those of our own time."

7 *2 Apol.* 3.

8 J. B. Lightfoot, *The Apostolic Fathers* (New York: Macmillan 1891; reprint Peabody, MA: Hendrickson 1989) Pt 2, vol. 1, 530f., makes a convincing case for the likelihood of Celsus' familiarity with the situation in Rome during the reigns of Antoninus Pius and Marcus Aurelius, writing the *True Doctrine* during the reign of the latter; cf. further 2.1.526f. See also Henry Chadwick, *Origen: Contra Celsum* (Cambridge: University Press 1965) xxiv–xxix. For a summary of Celsus' attacks, see chapter 6.

9 See *ABD*, s.v. "Valentinus" 6:783f.

10 Cf. Irenaeus, *adv. haer.* 1.24.1–2.

11 See *ABD*, s.v. "Basilides" 1:624f.

12 See further below, chapter 5.

13 Cf. Eusebius, *Hist. eccl.* 4.11; for Justin's references to these other Christian teachers, see *Dial.* 35; also *1 Apol.* 26.

14 Eusebius, *Hist. eccl.* 4.14.1.

15 Cf. the discussion in Goodenough, op. cit. n.3, 76f.

16 Antoninus Pius was not one to take lightly the scolding Justin gave him in the *First Apology*. Moreover, Justin was well aware of the potential consequences of angering him. Pius had had Telesphorus, the Bishop of Rome, executed not long before Justin wrote his *First Apology* (Irenaeus, *adv. haer.* 3.3.3). Indeed, Telesphorus' execution may have been one of the factors prompting Justin to protest against the way the government was treating Christians.

17 Eusebius, *Hist. eccl.* 4.16.7f.; cf. *Chronicon Paschale.* See also Epiphanius, *Pan.* 46.1. For a possibly apocryphal account containing the "court transcript" of his arrest, trial, and beheading, see *Martyrdom of Justin, Chariton et al., ANF* 1:305–306.

18 *1 Apol.* 66–67; Greek: καὶ τῇ τοῦ ἡλίου λεγομένῃ ἡμέρᾳ πάντων κατὰ πόλεις ἢ ἀγροὺς μενόντων ἐπὶ τὸ αὐτὸ συνέλευσις γίνεται, καὶ τὰ ἀπομνημονεύματα τῶν ἀποστόλων ἢ τὰ συγγράμματα τῶν προφητῶν ἀναγινώσκεται, μέχρις ἐγχωρεῖ. εἶτα παυσαμένου τοῦ ἀναγινώσκοντος ὁ προεστὼς διὰ λόγου τὴν νουθεσίαν καὶ πρόκλησιν τῆς τῶν καλῶν τούτων μιμήσεως ποιεῖται . . . οἱ γὰρ ἀπόστολοι ἐν τοῖς γενομένοις ὑπ' αὐτῶν ἀπομνημονεύμασιν, ἃ καλεῖται εὐαγγέλια, οὕτως παρέδωκαν ἐντετάλθαι αὐτοῖς . . . *1 Apol.* 67.4–5; 66.3.

19 In the *Dialogue with Trypho,* he uses the term *memoirs* thirteen times: 100.4; 101.3; 102.5; 103.6, 8; 104.1; 105.1, 5, 6; 106.1, 3, 4; 107.1. In 106.3, there is a reference to something found only in the Gospel according to Mark; hence it

is clear from this and other similar quotations precisely which Gospels Justin meant. See further the discussion in Helmut Koester, *Ancient Christian Gospels: Their History and Development* (Philadelphia: Trinity Press International 1990) 37–40.

20 Cf. Diogenes Laertius, *Vitae phil.* (Loeb Library) 3.34; the term used by Xenophon is ἀπομνημονεύματα. We do not know which writings of Plato may be meant. It is possible that Diogenes Laertius is referring to writings known to us under other titles: e.g., the *Laches,* the *Charmides;* see Diogenes Laertius, *Vitae phil.* 1:308 n.1.

21 I do not agree with the suggestion that the Pythagorean tradition should be sharply distinguished from the Platonic simply because the Pythagoreans used the slightly different term ὑπομνήματα (*pace* Koester, op. cit. n.19, 39 n.4). The basic idea seems the same. For the significance of this literary category among the Pythagoreans, see F. R. Levin, *The Harmonics of Nicomachus and the Pythagorean Tradition,* American Classical Studies no. 1 (State College, PA: Commercial Printing 1975) 14: "ὑπόμνημα (was) a term of more than passing significance in Pythagorean doxography ... (It was) the technical term denoting the writings of the early Pythagoreans who purportedly had direct contact with the teachings of the Master." See further Holger Thesleff, *An Introduction to the Pythagorean Writings of the Hellenistic Period,* Acta Academiae Aboensis Humaniora 24.3 (Abo: Abo Akademi 1961) 77 n.5. This is precisely the significance of ἀπομνημονεύματα in the Platonic tradition.

22 See W. Burkert, *Lore and Science in Ancient Pythagoreanism,* trans. E. L. Minar, Jr. (Cambridge: Harvard University Press 1972) 53: "the most important later sources for Pythagorean philosophy are the Πυθαγορικὰ ὑπομνήματα (*Pythagorika hypomnemata*) excerpted by Alexander Polyhistor and the many fragments quoted by Sextus Empiricus" (fl. 200, possibly also in Rome).

23 The term used here is ὑπομνήματα; see *De vita Pythag.* 157 (Deubner-Katz ed. 88.12–18); translation by Levin, op. cit. n.21, 15.

24 The Greek term is ἀπομνημονεύματα; see Diog. Laert. 4.2.

25 The Greek term is ἀπομνημονεύματα; see Diog. Laert. 1.63.

26 The Greek term is ἀπομνημονεύματα; see Diog. Laert. 3.48; for other examples, see 8.53, 63, 73, et passim.

27 The original names of the "three holy children" in Dan 1:17; cf. Cyril C. Richardson, *Early Christian Fathers* (Philadelphia: Westminster Press 1953) 272 n.34.

28 *1 Apol.* 46; Richardson 272.

29 *Dial.* 103.6; *ANF* 1:251.

30 For a discussion of Luke's Preface, see above chapter 2.

31 Chadwick, op. cit. n.8, 2.14, 80. Note that Origen has no problem using ὑπομνήματα not ἀπομνημονεύματα.

32 So also Koester, op. cit. n.19, 39f.

33 For examples of Justin's exegesis of the Old Testament, see his *First Apology*. This blending of "Greek" and "barbarian" religious traditions was not at all uncommon in Justin's day. Numenius of Apamea (ca. 150–200 C.E.) blended Platonic, Pythagorean, and Jewish elements in his philosophy; cf. H. Chadwick, *Christian Thought and the Classical Tradition* (Oxford: Oxford University Press 1966) 21. The *Chaldean Oracles*, composed by one Julianus the Chaldean during the time of Marcus Aurelius, was another mixture of Neoplatonic and "oriental" mythology. On the Christian side, Irenaeus of Lugdunum, Clement of Alexandria, Marcion of Pontus, and all of the Gnostic theologians blended Greek, Jewish, and other modes of thought during this period. In the previous century, Philo, Plutarch, and others did the same thing.

34 For an example of Justin's hermeneutics, see *1 Apol.* 30–53, esp. 36.

35 *Oratio* 29.

36 *Oratio* 19.1. The Greek is θανάτου δὲ ὁ καταφρονεῖν συμβουλεύων οὕτως ἐδεδίει τὸν θάνατον ὡς καὶ Ἰουστῖνον <u>καθάπερ καὶ ἐμέ</u>.

37 For an exquisite statement of this aspiration of Christians from this time period, nothing surpasses Ignatius' *Letter to the Romans*.

38 No scholars with whom I am familiar mention this perspective. Indeed, it is commonplace for them to emphasize Tatian's harshness as compared with Justin's more gentle attitude. This is a result of naively taking what the western orthodox fathers said about Tatian at face value and also of making no attempt to grasp the possible psychological situation Tatian was in following the death of his teacher, as he wrote the *Oration*.

39 Greek: κατὰ βαρβάρους = following a norm or standard; cf. 1 Pet 1:15 κατὰ τῆς Ἕλληνας = "in the manner of the Greeks"; Bauer-Arndt-Gingrich, s.v. κατά + Acc. 5a. Cf. Ignatius, *Trall.* 2:1 κατὰ Χριστὸν Ἰησοῦν = "in Christ Jesus' way"; also at *Mag.* 8:2; *Phil.* 3:2; *Eph.* 1:3. Tatian is about to parallel κατὰ βαρβάρους with κατὰ Θεόν = "according to God's way."

40 *Oratio* 42.1; my translation. Greek: ἕτοιμον ἐμαυτὸν ὑμῖν πρὸς τὴν ἀνάκρισιν τῶν δογμάτων παρίστημι μενούσης μοι τῆς κατὰ θεὸν πολιτείας ἀνεξαρνήτου. Typical of Tatian's florid style, the final phrase is very important. He has just addressed "you Greeks" and defiantly proclaims his alternative citizenship rights (πολιτεία, Lat. *civitas*) over against theirs. Cf. Molly Whittaker, *Tatian, Oratio ad Graecos* (Oxford: Clarendon Press 1982) 77: ". . . I offer myself to you, prepared for my doctrines to be examined while holding to my way of life in following God with no possibility of denial."

41 Irenaeus, *adv. haer.* 1.28.1.

42 Loc. cit.

43 Scholars generally believe that neither was written by Justin Martyr; see Quasten, *Patrology* 1.205f. I am inclined to take them as genuine. For the texts of both writings, beautifully translated by Marcus Dods, see *ANF* 1:271–289.

44 See especially the autobiographical section: "My soul was taught by God and I understood that some parts (of the barbarian writings) had a condemnatory effect *while others freed us from many rulers and countless tyrants,* etc." *Oration* 29.2 (trans. Whittaker).

45 *1 Apol.* 14.3; Greek: οἱ κατὰ τὰς τοῦ Χριστοῦ καλὰς ὑποθημοσύνας βιώσαντες.

46 *1 Apol.* 15.6.

47 Clement of Alexandria, who was Tatian's contemporary, mentions a (now lost) writing of Tatian's called *On Discipline according to the Savior,* which forbids sexual activity for married couples who wish to join together in prayer; cf. Clem. Alex., *Strom.* 3.12. The title Tatian used—Περὶ τοῦ κατὰ τὸν σωτῆρα καταρτισμοῦ—is reminiscent of a Pauline phrase in Eph 4:12: "But grace was given to each of us according to the measure of Christ's gift . . . some apostles, some prophets, etc., to equip (train, discipline πρὸς τὸν καταρτισμόν) the saints for the work of ministry." As for restraint of sexual activity in marriage for the sake of prayer, Tatian is simply repeating what Paul taught in 1 Cor 7:5. What is heretical about any of this?

48 *Oration* 11.1.

49 Compare this statement of Paul's: "Not that I complain of want; for I have learned, in whatever state I am, to be content (Greek αὐτάρκης; a major technical term in Stoic ethics; cf. the references to Epicurus, Aristotle, and Plato in Liddell-Scott, *Greek Lexicon, s.v.* αὐτάρκεια). I know how to be abased, and I know how to abound; in any and all circumstances I have learned the secret of facing plenty and hunger, abundance and want" (Phil 4:11–12).

50 This is no accident. It has long been recognized that many of Paul's ethical teachings are very similar to the popular Cynic-Stoic philosophical lifestyles of his day. For a comparative analysis, see especially Ragnar Hoïstad, *Cynic Hero and Cynic King* (Uppsala: Gleerup 1948); and, more recently, A. J. Malherbe, *Paul and the Popular Philosophers* (Minneapolis: Fortress 1989).

51 *Oration* 7.1.

52 *Oration* 5.1 (twice); 7.2.

53 For this whole discussion, I am relying on E. R. Goodenough, *The Theology of Justin Martyr* (Amsterdam: Philo Press 1968) 64–66. He points out that the νοῦς βασιλικός of Justin is similar to Philo of Alexandria's concept of the *Logos* and that both are related to the doctrines of the Neoplatonist Albinus (21–31).

54 *Dial.* 4.2 (italics added).

55 In Hellenistic Orphism, "an ascetic life featuring specific abstinences, especially vegetarianism," would have been required; see Burkert, op. cit. n.22, 125. Peter Brown, *The Body and Society: Men, Women, and Sexual Renunciation in Early Christianity* (New York: Columbia University Press 1988) 87, says, "While Tatian's break with the Church in Rome in 172 was long remem-

bered . . . he merged back without remark into Syrian Christianity that may always have been as radical as himself . . . (There) his own sharp views in favor of sexual abstinence were taken for granted in the Syrian world" (cf. further on Tatian's "encratism" 92f.).

56 Greek: δογμάτων ἐναντιότης ἐστὶ πολλή.

57 Tatian, *Orat. ad graec.* 8; translation from *Ante Nicene Fathers* 2:68. Cf. translation of Molly Whittaker, *Tatian, Oratio ad Graecos* (Oxford: Clarendon Press 1982) 15.

58 Irenaeus, *adv. haer.* 1.10.2; *ANF* 1:331.

59 *Contra Apionem* 1.29.38 (Loeb translation).

60 On the harmonizations of Gospel texts in Justin's quotations, see especially Arthur Bellinzoni, *The Sayings of Jesus in the Writings of Justin Martyr,* Suppl. Nov. Test. 17 (Leiden: Brill 1967); further, Koester, op. cit. n.19, 360–402; and most recently William L. Petersen, *Tatian's Diatessaron: Its Creation, Dissemination, Significance, and History in Scholarship* (Leiden: Brill 1994) 16.

61 Petersen's account of the amazing diffusion of Tatian's *Diatessaron* is the best account at present. My father knew of a harmony of the Gospels in Chinese used by missionaries during his activities in the China Inland Mission (Presbyterian) from 1926 to 1943.

62 The assumption by H. Koester and others that the Gospel quotations in Justin Martyr should be taken at face value as coming from *actual Gospel texts* represents a comprehensive misunderstanding of their origin and purpose. Much more likely is the suggestion of Plooij that the *Diatessaron* "had from the beginning a missionary and a private character"; cf. the citation of Plooij in Petersen, op. cit. n.60, 176. It may be that few Western scholars understand this point since so few of them have worked in a mission context and therefore have no sense of how difficult it is to make Christian theology understandable in a foreign cultural milieu, let alone give a credible explanation of why the Christian God caused four different Gospels to be written. A brilliant example of a Gospel harmony composed for missionary purposes is the famous Saxon *Heliand,* composed near Werden during the latter part of the ninth century. For an analysis of it as a missionary outreach tool, see G. Ronald Murphy, S.J., *The Saxon Savior: The Germanic Transformation of the Gospel in the Ninth-Century Heliand* (Oxford: University Press 1989). Even though it was enormously popular, no one thought the *Heliand* was meant to replace the canonical Gospels. By the same token, Justin Martyr's harmony did not signify the existence of a *rival authoritative text* of Matthew, Mark, and Luke. See further Petersen 105f., 329.

63 Cf. Justin, *1 Apol.* 30–53, esp. 31, 33, 43, 47, 52.

64 He may have been influenced by Ammonius of Alexandria, whose harmonization was a synopsis-like chart with Matthew broken up into paragraphs

and the parallel texts of Mark, Luke, and John rearranged to correspond to Matthew's order (see further below, pp. 109ff.). For a comprehensive account of the impact of the Gospel of Matthew during the second century, see Éduard Massaux, *The Influence of the Gospel of Saint Matthew on Christian Literature before Saint Irenaeus,* trans. N. J. Belval, S. Hecht, ed. A. J. Bellinzoni, New Gospel Studies 5/1, 2, 3 (Peeters/Leuven & Mercer University Press 1990–93).

65 So Petersen, op. cit. n.60, 16: "Scholarship acknowledges that . . . Justin (used) the synoptics and/or their traditions and not the Gospel of John (which Justin cites once, if at all)." This fact is all the more striking since Justin did make extensive use of the Johannine Logos Christology; hence it is highly likely that he knew of the Gospel of John. See also Bellinzoni, op. cit. n.60, 140; Koester, op. cit. n.19, 360–402, esp. 391. For an explanation of this widespread avoidance of the Gospel of John, see above, pp. 23f.

66 The consensus now is that Tatian's *Diatessaron* was originally produced in Syriac, not Greek; see Petersen, op. cit. n.60, following A. Baumstark 237. However, there is still considerable confusion as to its relationship to the very early *Latin* diatessaronic readings found in the West since these can hardly have been Latin translations of Tatian's Syriac. Hence there must have been an original *Greek* harmony of at least the first three Gospels; see Petersen 221. On Tatian carrying out Justin's work, cf. Koester, op. cit. n.19, 402. For a fascinating speculation about the contents of Justin's *Greek* harmony, see Petersen 347.

67 This is not a merely rhetorical question. Surprisingly enough, there is very little in the scholarly literature dealing with Tatian's choice of title; for the relevant bibliographical references, see Petersen, 49–51.

68 *New Grove Dictionary of Music and Musicians,* ed. S. Sadie (New York: Macmillan 1980) *s.v.* "diatessaron."

69 See *Oxford Classical Dictionary, s.v.* "music." For those familiar with popular American speakers, Robert Bly is an example of this method, a conscious throwback to the old bardic style.

70 J. A. Philip, *Pythagoras and Early Pythagoreanism* (Toronto: University of Toronto Press 1966) 123: "The word *harmonia* . . . is not (originally) a musical concord but a 'fitting together' produced by a craftsman such as to result in a unified object, or 'perfect fit.'"

71 Ibid. 128 n.1.

72 Ibid.

73 E.g., Lydian, Phygian, Doric, Ionian; cf. Philip op. cit. 123. The intervals differed according to the type of music desired. Again, modern Western interpreters must guard against inaccurate assumptions. In modern Western music, there are basically only two scales, the major and the minor; in ancient Greek

music, as in Arabic and Indian music, there were numerous alternative scales available to the musician, depending on the occasion and type of emotion appropriate to it.

74 Quote in Petersen, op. cit. n.60, 39.

75 Many aspects of ancient Greek music were believed to go back to certain fundamental discoveries by the philosopher and mathematician Pythagoras of Samos (ca. 520–460 B.C.E.). It was he, tradition said, who first related the two basic elements in music, sound and note, to the two basic elements in geometry, line and point. Sound was viewed as an infinite continuum, like the line in geometry; the discrete tone (Greek: ὁ τόνος from τείνω "to stretch," hence "a stretched," scil. sinew or length of cat gut χορδή, producing a pitch or note) was thought to resemble a specific point (anywhere) on a line. Separate points were "whole" tones resembling "whole" numbers and, like points on a line, could be placed anywhere on the sound continuum; cf. W. Burkert, *Lore and Science in Ancient Pythagoreanism,* trans. E. L. Minar, Jr. (Cambridge: Harvard University Press 1972) 350ff., 387. It was considered one of Pythagoras' main achievements to have calculated precisely the numerical ratios for each tone in the human voice's sound continuum (the diapason or octave). S. K. Heninger, Jr., *Touches of Sweet Harmony: Pythagorean Cosmology and Renaissance Poetics* (San Marino, CA: The Huntington Library 1974) 100, says:

> "Pythagoras had shown how to set apart the diapason from the endless continuum of sound, which stretches from the immeasurably low to inexpressibly high. Neither the diapason nor the tone admits a numerical mean of any sort—the mean between 2 and 1 and the mean between 9 and 8 are both irrational—so neither the diapason nor the tone can be divided into equal parts. This fact allied them with odd numbers, indicating their limited and ordered nature. Pythagoras had demonstrated how to know this unit with its discrete parts and how to manipulate it for human ends. He had revealed a dependable relationship between the finite and the infinite, some manageable way of dealing with the infinite through knowledge of the finite. The diapason with its numerical ratios and its harmonies exposed in small to moral comprehension the divinely proportioned structure of the universe."

76 Pythagorean mathematical speculation on the octave was endlessly creative. As Levin, op. cit. n.21, 65f., says, "(The) octave was defined by the outer limits of the construct—6:8:9:12. The internal components, 6:9 (fifth) and 9:12 (fourth) and conversely, 6:8 (fourth) and 8:12 (fifth), when extended beyond the limit of the octave construed as 6:12, and added to it, compassed a double octave, thus yielding a new application of the original Pythagorean tet-

raktys—1, 2, 3, 4—which contained all the components of 6:8:9:12 extended over two full octaves, for it comprises 1:2 (6:12), the lower octave; 2:3 (6:9), the fifth; 3:4 (6:8), the fourth; 2:4 (6:12), the upper octave and 1:4, the double octave." All of this would have been rich with significance. Oddly, in his monumental study of Tatian's *Diatessaron,* Theodore Zahn missed the possible Pythagorean connection completely, although he did notice that the term was a *terminus technicus* from Greek music; see Zahn, *Tatian's Diatessaron: Forschungen zur Geschichte des neutestamentlichen Kanons und der altchristlichen Literatur,* I Theil (Erlangen: Verlag Andreas Deichert 1881) 239.

77 The first written discussions of these concepts does not occur in the writings of Pythagoras (who left nothing in writing), or his followers, but in the writings of *Plato.* The *Timaeus* contains the earliest metaphysical analysis of the *diapason,* and the *Republic* contains the earliest extant discussion of the relation between the notes of the *diapason* and the sounds made by the planets as they whirled in their celestial orbits; see Plato, *Republic,* the myth of Er (617B): "and from all eight (Sirens) there was the concord of a single harmony ἐκ (*n.b.,* not διά) πασῶν δὲ ὀκτὼ οὐσῶν μίαν ἁρμονίαν συμφωνεῖν. The oldest extant treatise on music *per se* is by the quasi-Pythagorean philosopher Aristoxenus of Tarentum in Magna Graecia (fl. 320 B.C.E.). It is a moot issue within philosophical debate today to what extent both Plato and Aristotle were attracted to the doctrines of Pythagoras.

78 For the presence of Pythagoreanism in Palestine generally during this period, see especially I. Lévy, *La légende de Pythagore de Grèce en Palestine* (Paris 1927). For a more recent account of the history of the Pythagorean tradition and especially the upsurge of activity during the first century C.E. in the eastern Mediterranean, see John Dillon and Jackson Hershbell, *Iamblichus, On the Pythagorean Way of Life: Text, Translation, and Notes,* Texts and Translations/Graeco-Roman Series No. 11, ed. H. D. Betz (Atlanta: Scholars Press 1991) 4–16, esp. 9.

79 On Nichomacus' treatise, see most recently Levin, op. cit. n.21, especially 46f., 64ff.

80 Ibid. 32.

81 On this combination, see H. J. Cadbury, *The Making of Luke–Acts* (London: SPCK 1958) 60; also H. Conzelmann, *Commentary on the Acts of the Apostles* Hermeneia Series, trans. and ed. J. Limburg et al. (Philadelphia: Fortress Press 1987) xxxviii–xl; also W. C. van Unnik, "Luke's Second Book and the Rules of Hellenistic Historiography," in J. Kremer, ed., *Les Actes des Apôtres,* BETL 48 (1977) 37–60, esp. 41.

82 Cf. the careful reconstruction in Koester, op. cit. n.19, 422–427; further 427f.: "the sources of the Diatessaron." Petersen notes a strong Jewish-Christian component in the noncanonical material in the *Diatessaron;* see op. cit. n.60, 257–259. For a detailed account of how Tatian supposedly combined his

sources, see A. Augustus Hobson, *The Diatessaron of Tatian and the Synoptic Problem* (Chicago: University of Chicago Press 1904).

83 On the avoidance of the Gospel of John in Rome, see above, pp. 23f.

84 For an excellent account of the astonishing history of Tatian's *Diatessaron,* see most recently Petersen, op. cit. n.60. For a briefer discussion of the same material, see Petersen in Koester, op. cit. n.19, 406–419.

85 See further below, pp. 352f.

86 Leading text critics prior to World War II agreed that the oldest Syriac (including the *Diatessaron*) and Latin manuscripts can preserve a more original text than all of the great fourth- and fifth-century uncials combined. This view has been tacitly abandoned since World War II, however. See Petersen, op. cit. n.60, 20. This point is discussed more fully below, pp. 352f.

NOTES TO CHAPTER 5

1 This is the reaction Stephen gets at precisely the point where he accuses the Jerusalem mob of murdering their Messiah; cf. Acts 7:51–54.

2 This dual characterization is of course based upon the statement of the Apostle Paul: "We preach Christ crucified, a stumbling block to Jews and folly to Gentiles" (1 Cor. 1:23). Cf. Justin Martyr, *1 Apol.* 13, "It is for this reason people charge us with *madness,* saying that we give the second place after the unchanging and ever-existing God . . . to a crucified man, not knowing the mystery involved." Cf. Pliny, *Ep. X,* "There were others of the same *insanity* but as they were Roman citizens, I had them sent to Rome (for trial)." See further below what Celsus says about the pathetic figure Jesus cut at his trial (below pp. 62f.).

3 After the disastrous fire in the center of Rome in July 64, Nero managed to deflect blame onto the Christians: "Nero fastened the guilt . . . on a class hated for their abominations, called Christians by the populace . . . They were arrested not so much for the crime of arson as of hatred of the human race (*odium humani generis*)." Tacitus, *Annals* XV. 44.3–5.

4 Eusebius, *Hist. Eccl.* 3.5.3.

5 For the correct dating of this rebellion, see T. D. Barnes, "Trajan and the Jews," *Journal of Jewish Studies* 40 (1989) 145–62.

6 For this precise dating, see ibid. 153.

7 This reconstruction is admittedly quite speculative, but it is based on recent Israeli archeological research. See especially Benjamin Isaac and Aharon Oppenheimer, "The Revolt of Bar Kokhba: Ideology and Modern Scholarship," *Journal of Jewish Studies* 36 (1985) 33–60; Alexander Fuks, "Aspects of the Jewish Revolt in A.D. 115–117," *Journal of Roman Studies* 51 (1961) 98–104; Victor A. Tcherikover and Alexander Fuks, *Corpus Papyrorum Judaicarum*

(Cambridge: Harvard University Press 1957) 1:78–94; Doron Mendels, *The Rise and Fall of Jewish Nationalism*, ABRL (New York: Doubleday 1992) chap. 13 "The 'Polemus Quietus' and the Revolt of Bar Kokhba, 132–135 C.E."; Gedalyahu Alon, *Jews, Judaism and the Classical World* (Jerusalem: Magnes Press 1977) "Rabban Johanan B. Zakkai's Removal to Jabneh" (269–313) and "The Patriarchate of Rabban Johanan B. Zakkai" (314–343); Shim'on Applebaum, *Jews and Greeks in Ancient Cyrene*, Studies in Judaism in Late Antiquity 28 (Leiden: Brill 1979) 201–327; and E. Mary Smallwood, *The Jews Under Roman Rule from Pompey to Diocletian*, Studies in Judaism in Late Antiquity 20 (Leiden: Brill 1976).

8 See A. Kloner, "Underground Hiding Complexes from the Bar Kochba War," in *Biblical Archeologist* 46 (1983) 210–221.

9 For a good summary of popular anti-Jewish sentiment at this time, see Smallwood, op. cit. n.7, 123ff.

10 Cf. Justin Martyr, *1 Apol.* 31 "In the Jewish War recently past, Bar Cochba, the leader of the revolt of the Jews, ordered Christians only to be subjected to terrible punishments unless they would deny Jesus the Christ and blaspheme (him)." Yigael Yadin, *Bar-Kokhba: The Rediscovery of the Legendary Hero of the Second Jewish Revolt Against Rome* (New York: Random House 1971) 137, is not inclined to read Bar Kokhba's letter containing the demand to "destroy (?) the Galileans who are with you" as a reference to Christians.

11 Suetonius, *Life of Claudius* 25.4.

12 For a helpful summary of what is known of Melito, see Johannes Quasten, *Patrology* (Utrecht-Antwerp: Spectrum 1966) 1:242–248.

13 The discoverer of the text was Campbell Bonner, ed., *The Homily on the Passion by Melito Bishop of Sardis*, Studies and Documents 12 (London and Philadelphia: Christophers 1940). For a more recent edition, see S. G. Hall, *Melito of Sardis "On Pascha" and Fragments* (Oxford: Clarendon Press 1979). There has been a striking reluctance on the part of Christian scholars to focus on the vicious hatred of Jews in Melito's sermon. A noteworthy exception is A. T. Kraabel, "Melito the Bishop and the Synagogue at Sardis: Text and Context," in *Studies Presented to George M. A. Hanfmann*, ed. D. G. Mitten et al., (Cambridge: Fogg Art Museum 1971) 77–85. For some of the more bitter, anti-Jewish passages in Melito's sermon, where "he seems to be thinking of real flesh and blood Jews," see Kraabel 81f. Kraabel noted that Melito's Quartodeciman theology may have given him an additional reason for distancing himself from the Jews of Sardis: "Additional pressure to take a position (of hostility toward the large and powerful Jewish community in Sardis) would come from the fact that—as a Quartodeciman—he was liable to the charge that his Christianity was little different from Judaism. The *Peri Pascha* is then a strong attempt on Melito's part to establish and preserve the identity of his religion over against the Jews" (84). For the most recent general discussion of

Melito in English, see Stephen G. Wilson, *Related Strangers: Jews and Christians 70–170* C.E. (Minneapolis: Fortress Press 1995) "Melito's Paschal Homily" 241–256.

14 Epiphanius, *Panarion* 41.1.4. There is no firsthand information about Marcion from any extant copies of his writings or those of his followers. All information regarding Marcion and his movement comes from statements and descriptions by his bitter enemies. The best sources are Irenaeus, Hippolytus, Tertullian, and Origen.

15 For a reference to the amount, see Tertullian, *de praescr. haer.* 30.2 (*ANF* 3:257); cf. *adv. Marc.* 4.4.4. A sestertius was a silver coin, equal to one-quarter denarius (Cassell's *New Latin Dictionary, s.v.* "sestertius"). In New Testament writings, a denarius was roughly equivalent to a day's wage (cf. Mt 20:2, 9f.); so Bauer *Greek-English Lexicon of the New Testament, s.v.* If we divide 200,000 by 4 to get the number of denarii, the result is 50,000. This would then be the equivalent of 50,000 work days. If we calculate approximately 50 Sabbaths and 15 other nonwork days, we obtain the figure of 300 work days per year. $50,000 \div 300 = 166.66$, that is, approximately $166\frac{2}{3}$ work years.

16 Justin Martyr, *1 Apol.* 26, trans. Cyril C. Richardson, *Early Christian Fathers,* Library of Christian Classics no. 1 (Philadelphia: Westminster Press 1953) 258.

17 J. J. Clabeaux, "Marcion," *ABD* 4:515b.

18 *Pan.* 42.1.1.

19 Tertullian, *adv. Marc.* 1.8.1.

20 Tertullian, *adv. Marc.* 1.19.1.

21 Tertullian, *adv. Marc.* 1.27.5, 1.17.4.

22 Tertullian, *adv. Marc.* 2.12.3.

23 Tertullian, *adv. Marc.* 1.23.2.

24 Tertullian, *adv. Marc.* 1.17.1. For the doctrine that the Good God never created flesh, see 3.9.3: *(Hic) autem deus, eo quod carnem nullam omnino produxerit . . .*

25 Tertullian, *adv. Marc.* 1.24.3; cf. 3.24.1. Cf. Irenaeus, *adv. haer.* 1.27.3.

26 Tertullian, *adv. Marc.* 1.26.2.

27 Tertullian, *adv. Marc.* 1.27.6: "What will happen on that day to every sinner? The Marcionites answer that they will be cast away, as it were, out of sight" *respondent ibici illum quasi ab oculis,* "where they will be overtaken by the Creator's fire" (1.28.1).

28 Tertullian, *adv. Marc.* 1.27.2: *atque adeo prae se ferunt Marcionitae quod deum suum omino non timeant. Malus autem, inquiunt, timebitur, bonus autem diligetur.*

29 Tertullian, *adv. Marc.* 1.51.1.

30 Tertullian, *adv. Marc.* 1.11.9.

31 Tertullian, *adv. Marc.* 1.13.5: *sordidum artificem pronuntiabit tibi creatorem.*

32 Tertullian, *adv. Marc.* 1.15.5: *malum materiae deputans, innatum innatae, infectum infectae et aeternum aeternae . . .*

33 Tertullian, *adv. Marc.* 1.14.3: *in hac cellula creatoris.*

34 Tertullian, *adv. Marc.* 2.11.1: *iudex et severus et . . . saevus;* cf. 2.27.8.

35 Tertullian, *adv. Marc.* 3.4.5.

36 Tertullian, *adv. Marc.* 3.12.1–2; cf. 3.13.1; 3.14.7: *bellipotens et armiger Christus creatoris . . .*

37 Tertullian, *adv. Marc.* 3.18.1. The Creator's Christ was never predicted to be crucified: "You try to suggest a contradiction, alleging that the passion of the cross was never prophesied of the Creator's Christ, with the further argument that it is quite incredible that the Creator should have exposed his son to that form of death on which he himself had laid a curse": *diversitatem temptatis inducere, negantes passionem crucis in Christus creatoris praedicatam, et argumentantes insuper non esse credendum ut in id genus mortis exposuerit creator filium suum quod ipse maledixerat.* Cf. also 3.19.7.

38 Tertullian, *adv. Marc.* 3.21.1: "The Judaic Christ (who) was intended by the Creator for the regathering out of dispersion of the people (of Israel) and no others."

39 Tertullian, *adv. Marc.* 3.6.1.

40 Tertullian, *adv. Marc.* 3.6.2: *ipsi alium fuisse qui venit.*

41 Tertullian, *adv. Marc.* 3.8.1: *phantasma vindicans Christum.* Cf. 3.10.1, 1.24.5.

42 Tertullian, *adv. Marc.* 3.11.8: *Si (non) vere ista passus est Christus . . . si mendacio passus est ut phantasma . . .*

43 Tertullian, *adv. Marc.* 3.8.6: *Negata vero morte, dum caro negatur, nec de resurrectione constabit. Eadem enim ratione non resurrexit qua mortuus non est.* On all of this, cf. Hippolytus, *Ref. omn. haer.* 10.19: "(Marcion) asserts that he appeared as a man though not being a man, and as incarnate though not being incarnate . . . and that he underwent neither generation nor passion except in appearance" (Macmahon; *ANF* 5:146). Greek: ὡς ἄνθρωπον φανέντα λέγων οὐκ ὄντα ἄνθρωπον, καὶ ὡς ἔνσαρκον οὐκ ἔνσαρκον, δοκήσει πεφηνότα, οὔτε γένεσιν ὑπομείναντα οὔτε πάθος, ἀλλὰ τῷ δοκεῖν.

44 Tertullian, *adv. Marc.* 3.9.7: *Qui in Christo . . . perierunt sane resurrectuari sed phantasmate forsitan, sicut et Christus.*

45 Tertullian, *adv. Marc.* 3.9.2, 4: "And truly if your god promises to men some time the true substance of angels—'they will, he says, be as the angels'" (Lk 20:36).

46 It should be noted that this saying is recorded in Luke alone; the parallels in Mt 22:29–30/Mk 12:24–25 record something quite different.

47 Hippolytus, *adv. omn. haer.* 8.16 (*ANF* 8.9) γάμον δὲ φθορὰν εἶναι παραπλησίως Μαρκίωνι λέγει (Τατιανός); cf. *ANF* 10.15. See also Irenaeus, *adv. haer.* 1.28.1; Tertullian, *adv. Marc.* 1.29.5: *Unde iam dicam deum Marcionis cum matrimonium ut malum et impudicitiae negotium reprobat;* cf. also 1.24.4.

48 Tertullian, *adv. Marc.* 1.29.1: *Non tinguitur apud illum caro nisi virgo, nisi vidua, nisi caelebs, nisi divortio baptisma mercata.* Cf. 1.29.5: *Unde iam dicam deum Marcionis cum matrimonium ut malum et impudicitiae negotium reprobat;* cf. also 1.24.4.

49 Cf. Hippolytus, *ref. omn. haer.* 10.15: "(Marcion) leads his disciples in a very abstemious (κυνικός) lifestyle. By these means he imagines that he annoys the Creator (by) abstaining from the things that are made or appointed by Him" (MacMahon; *ANF* 5:146). N.B.: the reference is to the text of the *ANF,* which differs from the paragraph numbering of the *GCS* edition.

50 For the Antitheses as not a separate writing but rather a brief "preface" to Marcion's Scripture book, see the comment in Tertullian, *adv. Marc.* 4.6.1: *Certe enim totum* (scil. *liber*) *quod elaboravit etiam Antitheses praestruendo* ... For the accusation that the Apostles had falsified the other Gospels, see *adv. Marc.* 4.3.4.

51 Although I will use some of Tertullian's direct references to the Antitheses in *adv. Marc.* 2.21–27 to reconstruct something of its contents, Tertullian's references are usually nonverbatim allusions. It is possible to gain some idea of Marcion's rhetorical power from Origen's quotations of the words of the pagan philosopher Celsus, who may have quoted Marcion's Antitheses in his attack on Genesis; cf. Henry Chadwick, *Origen: "Contra Celsum"* (Cambridge: University Press 1965) 6.74, p. 387. For an interesting and typically ingenious reconstruction of other parts of Marcion's Antitheses, see J. Rendel Harris, "Marcion's Book of Contradictions," *Bulletin of the John Rylands Library* 6 (1921) 289–309.

52 Origen, *contra Cels.* 6.60; Chadwick 375.

53 Origen, *contra Cels.* 6.60; Chadwick 375.

54 Origen, *contra Cels.* 6.36; Chadwick 211.

55 Origen, *contra Cels.* 5.28; Chadwick 343f.

56 Tertullian, *adv. Marc.* 1.6.1 (trans. Evans): *Marcionem dispares deos constituere, alterum iudicem, ferum, bellipotentem, alterum mitem, placidum et tantummodo bonum atquae optimum.* Cf. *de praescr. haer.* 34.3. Tertullian regularly uses the Latin term *optimus* for Marcion's term ἀγαθός. Cf. Irenaeus, *Adv. Haer.* 1.27.1: Κέρδων ... ἐδίδαξε τὸν ὑπὸ τοῦ νόμου καὶ προφητῶν κεκηρυγμένον θεόν, μὴ εἶναι Πατέρα τοῦ Κυρίου ἡμων Ἰησοῦ Χριστοῦ. Τὸν μὲν γὰρ γνωρίζεσθαι, τὸν δὲ ἀγνῶτα εἶναι· καὶ τὸν μὲν δίκαιον, τὸν δὲ ἀγαθὸν ὑπάρχειν. Διαδεξάμενος δὲ αὐτὸν Μαρκίων ὁ Ποντικός, ηὔξησε τὸ διδασκαλεῖον, ἀπηρυθριασμένως βλασφημῶν.

57 Origen, *contra Cels.* 7.18; Chadwick 409.

58 Tertullian, *adv. Marc.* 2.14.1 (Evans).

59 Tertullian, *adv. Marc.* 1.27.5 (Evans), *deo optimo;* cf. 1.17.4 "the supremely good one" *maxime optimo;* cf. 2.12.3 "They have dreamed up another god whose sole attribute is goodness" *solummodo bonum.*

60 Tertullian, *adv. Marc.* 1.16.4 (Evans).

61 Tertullian, *adv. Marc.* 2.21.1–2 (Evans).

62 Tertullian, *adv. Marc.* 2.23.1 (Evans).

63 Tertullian, *adv. Marc.* 4.6.3: *Inter hos magnam et omnem differentiam scindit, quantam inter iustum et bonum, quantam inter legem et evangelium, quantam inter Iudaismum et Christianismum.*

64 Tertullian, *adv. Marc.* 3.21.1 (Evans): *Sic nec illam iniectionem tuam potes sistere ad differentiam duorum Christorum, quasi Iudicus quidem Christus populo soli ex dispersione redigendo destinetur a creatore, vester vero omni humano generi liberando collatus sit a deo optimo.*

65 Origen, *contra Cels.* 6.78; Chadwick 391.

66 Tertullian, *adv. Marc.* 1.19.4 (Evans): *separatio legis et evangelii proprium et principale opus est Marcionis ... Nam hae sunt Antitheses Marcionis, id est contrariae oppositiones, quae conantur discordiam evangelii cum lege committere.*

67 Tertullian, *adv. Marc.* 4.2.3.

68 Cf. Epiphanius, *Pan.* 42.10.1: "the one he calls a gospel and (the other part) he calls the letters of the apostle" (trans. Amidon).

69 Cf. Tertullian, *adv. Marc.* 4.3.5: *Aut si ipsum erit verum, id est, apostolorum, quod Marcion habet solus ...*

70 Origen, *Commentary on John* 5:6; trans. Heine, *Origen: Commentary on the Gospel according to John, Books 1–10,* Fathers of the Church (Washington, DC: Catholic University of America 1989) 165.

71 The problems besetting the task of reconstructing the actual wording of Marcion's *Evangelion*, to ascertain its independence from the orthodox version of the Gospel of Luke or lack thereof, are virtually insurmountable. They begin with the fact that our most important source of information about the contents of Marcion's *Evangelion*, Tertullian's *adversus Marcionem*, Book Four, contains mostly *allusions* to Marcion's text, rarely actual quotations. Then there is the even knottier question of whether Tertullian had a *Latin translation* of Marcion's *Evangelion* to compare with the second-century north African *Latin translation(s)* of the orthodox Gospel of Luke in his possession (a Latin translation about which we know little enough in any case) or whether he had a copy of the *original Greek* of Marcion's *Evangelion* and *translated it himself into Latin* as he went along, comparing *his translations* with his Latin *translation* of the orthodox Gospel of Luke. If the former was the case, reconstructing the actual Marcion's *Evangelion* would be foolhardly. If the latter was the case, then a word-by-word reconstruction of Marcion's *Evangelion* is impossible. Added to this problem is the uncertainty regarding our manuscripts of Tertullian's *adversus Marcionem* themselves; we have no idea how accurate they were. So the riddle of the text of Marcion's *Evangelion*

rests on the enigma of Tertullian's *adversus Marcionem*. On this debate, see especially Gilles Quispel, *De Bronnen van Tertullianus' Adversus Marcionem* (Leiden: Burgersdikj en Niemans 1943); cf. further A. J. B. Higgins, "The Latin Text of Luke in Marcion and Tertullian," *Vig. Christ.* 5 (1951) 1–42; and, most recently, T. P. O'Malley, *Tertullian and the Bible: Language-Imagery-Exegesis* (Utrecht: Dekker & Van de Vegt 1967) 37–63. An agnostic position regarding the reconstruction of Marcion's text can be found in Joël Delobel, "Extra-Canonical Sayings of Jesus: Marcion and Some 'Non-Received' Logia," in *Gospel Traditions in the Second Century: Origins, Recensions, Text, and Transmission,* ed. W. L. Petersen (South Bend, IN: University of Notre Dame Press 1989) 105–116. For a recent attempt regardless of the difficulties, see Robert M. Grant, "Marcion, Gospel of," in *ABD* 4:516–520.

72 Cf. Tertullian, *adv. Marc.* 4.7.1.

73 Throughout his discussion of Marcion's Gospel, Tertullian's position is that Marcion produced his text by mutilating the orthodox Gospel according to Luke. This view he got from Irenaeus (cf. *adv. haer.* 1.27.2, 4). He was, however, well aware that the Marcionites categorically rejected this accusation (cf. Tertullian, *adv. Marc.* 4.4.1). In fact, one gets the distinct impression in reading Book Four that Tertullian actually *did not know* where Marcion got his *Evangelion* and is simply arguing that he obtained it by high-handedly emending the orthodox Gospel according to Luke. An example of his ambivalent attitude can be found in the curiously elliptical phrasing of *adv. Marc.* 4.2.4: "Out of the (Gospel) authors whom we possess, Marcion is seen to have chosen Luke as the one to mutilate"—*Lucam videtur Marcion elegisse quem caederet.*

74 Cf. Tertullian, *adv. Marc.* 4.4.4; *de praescr. haeret.* 18.3. Historians in the past have tended to accept this verdict of the orthodox Church Fathers uncritically. However, this view was challenged by a number of scholars in the nineteenth century and in the twentieth, especially by John Knox, in *Marcion and the New Testament: An Essay in the Early History of the Canon* (Chicago: University of Chicago Press 1941). For bibliographical references to earlier scholars supporting this view, see Knox 78–83. For a more recent discussion, see David S. Williams, "Reconsidering Marcion's Gospel," in *JBL* 108 (1989) 477–496.

75 Cf. Tertullian, *de praescr. haer.* 18.3. Cf. *adv. Marc.* 4.4.4: "that gospel which among us is ascribed to Luke . . . is the same that Marcion in his Antitheses accuses of having been falsified by the upholders of Judaism with a view to its being so combined in one (book) with the law and the prophets, that they (i.e., the orthodox) might pretend that Christ had that origin (i.e., was Jewish)."

76 See above, n.68.

77 Tertullian, *adv. Marc.* 1.20.2 (Evans); cf. 1.20.1: *non tam innovasse regulam separatione legis et evangelii quam retro adulteratam recurasse;* further 4.3.2.

78 John J. Clabeaux, "Marcionite Prologues to Paul," *ABD* 4:520–521.

79 For a handy list of alleged Marcionite alterations to the Pauline epistles, see Ernest Evans, *Tertullian: adversus Marcionem* (Oxford: Clarendon Press 1972) 2:644–646.

80 I am not convinced by recent attempts to provide this Gospel with an early first-century date, parallel to and independent of the synoptic Gospels; for arguments to support this conclusion, see J. D. Crossan, *The Cross That Spoke: The Origins of the Passion Narrative* (San Francisco: Harper & Row 1988); further Helmut Koester, *Ancient Christian Gospels: Their History and Development* (Philadelphia: Trinity Press International 1990) 218–240.

81 See the report of Eusebius on Serapion, sixth bishop of Antioch, who found this Gospel being used by a Docetic congregation in Rhossus under the leadership of a certain Μαρκιανός; *hist. eccl.* 6.12.5. I am inclined to think that this was a *Marcionite* congregation (as the Armenian version of Eusebius spells the name of its leader).

82 Justin Martyr urged the Emperors Antoninus Pius et al. to consult the *Acts of Pilate* to verify the facts of the crucifixion of Jesus Christ; cf. *1 Apol.* 35, 48. For text and discussion of the *Acts of Pilate/Gospel of Nicodemus,* see Felix Scheidweiler, "The Gospel of Nicodemus, Acts and Pilate and Christ's Descent into Hell," in *New Testament Apocrypha,* rev. edition, ed. by W. Schneemelcher, ET by R. McL. Wilson (Cambridge: James Clarke & Co./Louisville: Westminster/John Knox Press 1991) 1.501–536.

83 For an overview of this literature, see J. Juster, *Les juifs dans l'empire romain,* 2 vols. (Paris: Guenther 1914) 1:43–76; further Marcel Simon, *Verus Israel: A Study of the Relations between Christians and Jews in the Roman Empire (135–425)* (Oxford: Oxford University Press 1986); and John G. Gager, *The Origins of Anti-Semitism: Attitudes Toward Judaism in Paganism and Christian Antiquity* (Oxford: Oxford University Press 1983) "controversies and debates" 153–159.

84 Some of the Church Fathers influenced by Melito are mentioned by Eric Werner, "Melito of Sardes, the First Poet of Deicide," *Hebrew Union College Annual* 37(1966) 203: e.g., Apollinaris, Hippolytus, Ps. Cyprian, Ephrem Syrus, Proclus, Epiphanius, and Chrysostom. For a more complete list see the introduction to Campbell Bonner's edition of the *Peri Pascha,* op. cit. n.13. Werner 199 contends that Melito was the *fons et origo* of the later Roman Catholic custom of condemning the Jews for Christ's death during the Easter Liturgy (the *Improperia*). Some (but not all) of the most vicious anti-Jewish language was repudiated by Vatican Council II; see the discussion in Wilson, op. cit. n.13, "Patterns of Christian Worship" 222–257.

85 For a summary of Saturninus' doctrines, see Irenaeus, *adv. haer.* 1.24.

86 See Irenaeus, *adv. haer.* 1.27.1–2.

87 For a general discussion of this critical period, see Judith M. Lieu, *Image and Reality: The Jews in the World of the Christians in the Second Century* (Edinburgh: T & T Clark 1996).

88 For the continuation of this story and the role played in it by Adolf von Harnack, the modern popularizer of Marcion, see below p. 338.

89 Cf. Sura 4 157f., "And for their saying, Verily we have killed the Messiah, Jesus the Son of Mary, the Apostle of God;—for they killed him not, nor crucified him, but (so) it appeared to them . . . and there is none of the people of the Book—(the Christians)—but must believe in (his crucifixion) . . . but on the day of resurrection he will be a witness against them." Quoted from Mirza Abu'l-fazl, *The Koran: A New Translation from the Original* (Bombay: Reform Society 1955) 98f. For a full discussion of the complex and ambiguous gamut of traditions about Jesus in the Qur'an, see most recently Geoffrey Parrinder, *Jesus in the Qur'an* (Oxford: One World Publications 1995).

NOTES TO CHAPTER 6

1 For a brief biography and account of Celsus, see Henry Chadwick, *Origen: Contra Celsum* (Cambridge: University Press 1965) xxiv f. For an excellent overview of Celsus' critique of the Christian religion, see Robert L. Wilken, *The Christians as the Romans Saw Them* (New Haven: Yale University Press 1984) 94–125.

2 For an overview of Justin's arguments, see above, chapter 4.

3 Chadwick, op. cit. n.1, dates the writing of the *Contra Celsum* around 245 during Origen's final years, when he was over sixty years of age and living in Caesarea; see further Henri Crouzel, *Origen: The Life and Thought of the First Great Theologian;* trans. A. S. Worrall (San Francisco: Harper & Row 1989) 48. Origen was prominent enough that this writing may have attracted the attention of the emperor's philosophers, who would not have taken it lightly. In any case, Origen was arrested not long after during the Decian Persecution of 250, tortured, and died in 253.

4 The brief summary given here is based on Henry Chadwick's reconstruction. My use of quotation marks corresponds to Chadwick's use of italics to set off words he considers to be actual quotations from Celsus' work.

5 The bullet list is found in Chadwick, op. cit. n.1, xxf. The rest of the examples are about all that Celsus says on this subject as far as I could discover. The longer quotations set forth below are mostly words of Celsus (i.e., they correspond to italicized text in Chadwick's edition).

6 Ibid. 6.71.

7 Ibid. 6:18–20; cf. Plato, *Epist.* 312E.

8 Chadwick, op. cit. n.1, 7.28.

9 Ibid. 6.21f.

10 Ibid. 3.16.

11 Ibid. 6.42–43.

12 Ibid. 140.

13 Ibid. 142.

14 Ibid. 144.

15 Ibid. 140 (my translation).

16 Ibid. 109.

17 Ibid. 134.

18 Ibid. 311–313.

19 Ibid. 386.

20 Ibid. 388f.

21 Ibid. 28.

22 Ibid. 31. For a discussion of the possible Jewish sources referenced by Celsus, see Stephen G. Wilson, *Related Strangers: Jews and Christians 70–170 C.E.* (Minneapolis: Fortress Press 1995) 186f.

23 Ibid. 62f.

24 Ibid. 94.

25 Ibid. 88.

26 Ibid. 118; cf. 95. For the account of Apollonios' sudden disappearance during his trial before the Emperor Domitian, see *Vit. Apol.* 8.5; an abbreviated version can be found in David R. Cartlidge and David L. Dungan, *Documents for the Study of the Gospels,* 2nd ed. (Philadelphia: Fortress Press 1994) 233.

27 Chadwick, op. cit. n.1, 73.

28 Ibid. 101.

29 Ibid. 97.

30 Ibid. 93.

31 Ibid. 109.

32 Ibid. 90.

33 Ibid. 162.

NOTES TO CHAPTER 7

1 The Christian philosopher Justin Martyr made his own list of parallels and similarities between Christian beliefs about Jesus and those of other religions as part of an argument that the emperor should stop attacking Christians because "we do not say anything different from what you do about the Sons

of Zeus"; see Justin, *1 Apol. 24.* This risky line of argument was never, to my knowledge, attempted again by later Christian apologists.

2 Most of our information regarding Origen's life and literary output comes from the biography in Book 6 of Eusebius' *Ecclesiastical History.*

3 This is the *Debate with (Bishop) Heraclides and the Bishops His Colleagues on the Father, the Son, and the Soul;* see Henri Crouzel, *Origen,* trans. A. S. Worrall (San Francisco: Harper & Row 1989) 32f. For a brief extract, see Quasten, *Patrology* 2:63–64.

4 Crouzel, ibid. 35, reports that Jerome is the source of this information. Later, Origen was reburied in the wall of the Cathedral of the Holy Sepulchre at Tyre. His tomb could still be seen as late as the thirteenth century.

5 This was the estimate of Jerome; Quasten, *Patrology* 2:43.

6 Modern critical scholarship has long since learned to relativize (if not ignore altogether) this Greek translation of the Old Testament. But if we are to understand anything about the early Church use of the term *Scripture,* we must remember that this Greek translation was universally regarded as a bona fide miracle that occurred during the time of Ptolemy Philadelphus II (285–247 B.C.E.) in Alexandria. According to the well-known story, seventy translators, hired at royal expense to make a translation of the Hebrew Scriptures into Greek, produced seventy identical translations. This astonishing result was interpreted as proof of the Jewish God's approval of the otherwise questionable act of translating divinely inspired Hebrew writings into a foreign language. For the standard account, see *Epistle of Aristeas,* ed. Moses Hadas (New York: KTAV 1973). For evidence of the widespread acceptance of this account, see Philo, *de vit. Mos.* 2.25–43; Josephus, *Antiquities* 12.2; Justin Martyr, *1 Apol.* 1.31; Clem. Alex., *Strom.* 1.22; Tertullian, *Apol.* 18; Irenaeus, *adv. haer.* 3.21.1 (retold in Eusebius, *Hist. eccl.* 5.8.11–15).

7 See below, n.37 for Origen's explanation of his method.

8 Crouzel, op. cit. n.3, 41; see further below, p. 108.

9 Crouzel considers the *Commentary on John* Origen's "masterpiece" (42).

10 See above, chapter 6.

11 *Commentary on Matthew,* Book 2; *ANF* 10:413 (Menzies trans.); this extract is preserved in Greek in the *Philocalia* 100.6 and is all that remains of Book 2. The words in parentheses in this quote, and those that follow, have been added by me to improve the sense.

12 Frank Pack, "The Methodology of Origen as a Textual Critic in Arriving at the Text of the New Testament," unpubl. diss., University of Southern California 1948, 66f., lists the apocryphal Gospels used by Origen: the *Gospel according to the Hebrews* (although noting that it is not accepted in the orthodox *ekklesia*) in his *Commentary on John* 2.6; the *Gospel according to Peter* and the *Protevangelium of James* to support the belief that Jesus' brothers

and sisters were by Joseph's former marriage, in his *Commentary on Matthew* 10.17.

13 In the quotations that follow, I translate the familiar Greek term ἐκκλησία by the word "Assembly" (capitalized) since the usual translation "church" has long since lost all of its *original specific technical meaning* of the self-styled "orthodox Assembly" within the whole spectrum of the Christian movement. The term ἐκκλησία was the orthodox faction's most widely used *self-designation*. It frequently functioned to set the "orthodox" apart from the "heresies," usually naming them after their leaders, e.g., Carpocratians, Marcionites, etc. Thus, when I use the term "orthodox," I use it in the same sense, i.e., not as my own historical judgment but as this faction's self-description.

It is important to notice the various usages of this term. It could be used absolutely, e.g., "the ἐκκλησία never accepted such and such," as when Origen retorts to Celsus in 5.54, "the books entitled Enoch are not generally held to be divine by *the assemblies*," ἐν ταῖς ἐκκλησίαις οὐ πάνυ φέρεται ὡς θεῖα τὰ ἐπιγεγραμμένα τοῦ Ἐνὼχ βιβλία. Again: "Jesus is not described as a carpenter anywhere in the Gospels accepted in the Assemblies" οὐδαμοῦ τῶν ἐν ταῖς ἐκκλησίαις φερομένων εὐαγγελίων (*contra Cels.* 6.36).

The term ἐκκλησία could function as a group designator to set it off from other Christian factions, e.g., "The Scriptures accepted in the Assembly of God ἐκκλησία τοῦ θεοῦ do not declare that there are seven heavens, etc." (*contra Cels.* 6.21). Some of the clearest examples of this contrastive use of ἐκκλησία are to be found in Hippolytus, *Philosophumena* 9.7. In his attack on his Roman rival Callistus, Hippolytus said: "The impostor Callistus ... established a school διδασκαλεῖον against the Assembly κατὰ τῆς ἐκκλησίας." Again, "they (the followers of Callistus), lost to all shame, attempt to call themselves (by *our* name) a 'General Assembly' καθολικὴν ἐκκλησίαν." In another place, Hippolytus distinguished the "sects" from the ἐκκλησία as follows: "Many persons were gratified with (Callistus' lax) regulations, ... and having been rejected by numerous sects (αἱρέσεις), were later by our condemnatory sentence ... forcibly ejected from the Assembly ἐκ τῆς ἐκκλησίας as well (and then they were welcomed by him)"; trans. J. H. Macmahon, *ANF* 5.131.

As we saw in Hippolytus' second example, ἐκκλησία could be used with a modifier, such as καθολικὴ ἐκκλησία, or μεγάλε ἐκκλησία, which should be translated "(the) *general* or *great Assembly*," labels that may have denoted the comparatively greater size and inclusiveness of the orthodox faction.

14 Cf. Pack, op. cit. n.12, 59. The translation here is my own based on the fragment in Greek and a parallel Latin "translation" in M. Rauer, ed., *Origenes Werke.* Bd. 9 *Die Homilien zu Lukas,* Griech. christl. Schriftst. (Leipzig: Hinrichs 1930) 3–4. The Greek of the last sentence is Φέρεται γὰρ καὶ τὸ κατὰ

Θωμᾶν εὐαγγέλιον καὶ τὸ κατὰ Ματθίαν και ἄλλα πλείονα. Ταῦτα ἐστι τῶν »ἐπιχειρησάντων« τὰ δὲ τέσσαρα μόνα προκρίνει ἡ τοῦ θεοῦ ἐκκλησία.

15 This full phrase probably meant "the whole orthodox Assembly everywhere it is found in the (Mediterranean) world."

16 This statement has been preserved only in Eusebius, *Hist. eccl.* 6.25.3–6. Another important technical term is found in this quotation: "undisputed," Greek ἀναντίρρητα "without objection." It meant that *no orthodox Assembly anywhere in the entire Mediterranean world objected*, a very significant demographic claim.

17 Irenaeus, *adv. haer.* 3.1.1.

18 Ibid. 3.2.2.

19 Ibid. 3.3.1.

20 Ibid. 3.1.1.

21 Tertullian, *adv. Marc.* 4.2; trans. from E. Evans, ed. and trans., *Tertullian adversus Marcionen* (Oxford: Clarendon Press, 1972). It is worth noting that, immediately following this brief catalog, Tertullian gave precisely the same creedal summary of their contents as is found after Irenaeus' catalog of the four Gospels in *adv. haer.* 3.1.2. Tertullian then went on to concede that the Gospels thus created did differ from each other somewhat. His reply to this problem was the same one used by everyone from Origen to Augustine: "It matters not if the arrangement of their narratives varies (*si narrationum dispositio variavit*) so long as there is agreement on the *essentials of the faith* (*dummodo de capite fidei conveniat*)."

22 Origen would have obtained what information he could about Irenaeus on his visit to Rome during the episcopate of Zephrynus, or around 211 (Eusebius, *Hist. eccl.* 6:14). Additional evidence for this pattern could be given from Justin Martyr, Clement of Alexandria, Tatian, and many others—precisely the "chain" of apostolic succession bishops and theologians later documented by Eusebius in his monumental *Ecclesiastical History* (see below, p. 100f.).

23 *Commentary on Matthew* 15.14 (my translation); for the Greek text, cf. Erich Klostermann, *Origenes Werke: Matthäuserklärung*, rev. ed., Griech. Christl. Schriftst. (Leipzig: Hinrichs 1935) 10:387f.; also Migne, *Patrologia graeca* tom. 13 col. 1293A.

24 *Apol.* 18; *ANF* 3:32: "So the king (Ptolemy Philadelphus) left these (Hebrew) works unlocked to all, in the Greek language. To this day, at the temple of Serapis, the libraries of Ptolemy are to be seen, with the identical Hebrew originals in them." The Serapeum in question would probably have been the great Temple of Serapis dedicated by Ptolemy Euergetes I. It was situated on Rhacotis hill some distance from the former east harbor and overlooking Alexander's canal that debouched into Lake Mareotis; see P. M. Fraser, *Ptolemaic Alexandria* (Oxford: Clarendon Press 1972) 1:268f. I wish to thank

David Tandy, Classics Department of the University of Tennessee, Knoxville, for drawing my attention to this reference.

25 Plutarch, *Vit. Ant.* 58 (Loeb 9:271): "Calvisius, who was a companion to (Julius) Caesar, brought forward against Antony the following charges regarding his behavior towards Cleopatra: he bestowed upon her the libraries from Pergamum in which there were two hundred thousand volumes . . ."

26 For a description of the link between the Alexandrian Museion and the Lyceum of Athens, see Fraser, op. cit. n.24, 1:312–314.

27 Strabo, *Geography* 17.1.8; cf. Fraser, op. cit. n.24, 1:315.

28 Alexander Souter, *Text and Canon of the New Testament*, rev. ed. (London: Duckworth 1954) 75.

29 As he says in a letter to one of his pupils, "I have paid particular attention to the (text) of the Septuagint lest I might be found to accredit any forgery to the Churches (*sic* = Assemblies) which are under Heaven, and give an occasion to those who seek such a starting-point for gratifying their desire to slander (the Assembly) . . . And I make it my endeavor not to be ignorant of the various readings (of the Septuagint) lest in my controversies with the Jews I should quote to them (something) that is not found in *their* copies (of the Bible)" *Epist. ad Africanus* 5; Crombie trans., *ANF* 4:387.

30 Trans. by Allan Menzies, *Commentary on John* 6.24, in *ANF* 10:371. Most of my quotations are based on Menzies' translation. Menzies' text divisions are based on the Greek edition by Lommatzsch. Where necessary, I will provide the Greek text from E. Klostermann, *Origenes Werke*. Bd. 3 *Das Johanneskommentar*, rev. ed., Griech. Christl. Schrift. (Leipzig: Hinrichs 1901). Another fairly reliable Greek text of the *Commentary* is also available by A. E. Brooke, *The Commentary of Origen on S. John's Gospel*, 2 vols. (Cambridge: University Press 1896). I have also consulted the English translation of Ronald E. Heine, *Origen: Commentary on the Gospel according to John, Books 1–10*, Fathers of the Church 80 (Washington, DC: Catholic University of America 1989). Heine's text divisions are based on Preuschen. References to the passage(s) in Heine will have the form, as in this case, Heine §6.208–211.

31 *Commentary on John* 6.24; *ANF* 10.370; cf. Heine §6.204–205.

32 *Commentary on Matthew* 15.13; cited by Pack, op. cit. n.12, 130. This part of Origen's commentary was never translated for the Ante-Nicene Fathers and will be cited here in Tollinton's translations given by Pack. However, I have in each case compared the English against the Greek text of Klostermann, op. cit. n.23.

33 *Commentary on Matthew*, Series 134; cited by Pack, ibid. 138.

34 Loc. cit.

35 In his *Commentary on Matthew* 15.14, Origen gave this succinct description of his text-critical method: "Where (we found) variations among copies of the Septuagint, we based our judgment (as to the correct reading) upon the

(majority text) of the other (parallel) versions . . . (In some cases) we added words (to the Septuagint) where the readings agreed with the Hebrew text (but the words were missing from the Septuagint)." Greek: τῶν γὰρ ἀμφιβαλλομένων παρὰ τοῖς Ἑβδομήκοντα διὰ τὴν τῶν ἀντιγράφων διαφωνίαν τὴν κρίσιν ποιησάμενοι ἀπὸ τῶν λοιπῶν ἐκδόσεων τὸ συνᾷδον ἐκείναις ἐφυλάξαμεν . . . τινὰ δὲ . . . μὴ κείμενα παρὰ τοῖς Ἑβδομήκοντα ἐκ τῶν λοιπῶν ἐκδόσεων συμφώνος τῷ Ἑβραϊκῷ προσεθήκαμεν; cf. Klostermann, op. cit. n.23, 10:388.

36 *Commentary on Matthew* 15.14: Τὴν μὲν οὖν ἐν τοῖς ἀντιγράφοις τῆς Παλαῖς Διαθήκης διαφωνίαν, Θεοῦ διδόντος, εὕρομεν ἰάσασθαι, κριτηρίῳ χρησάμενοι ταῖς λοιπαῖς ἐκδόσεσιν; cp. Migne *P.G.* tom. 13 col. 1293A.

37 Pack, op. cit. n.12, 124, observes, "this concern for textual accuracy Origen learned from the classical scholars of Alexandria" (125). Origen had a high estimation of the three Greek versions he used next to the LXX, as we can see from the following statement in the passage quoted earlier, where he is commenting on inaccurate place names: "The same inaccuracy (as we find in the Gospels) with regard to proper names is also to be observed in many passages of the Law and the Prophets, as we have been at pains to learn from the Hebrews, comparing their copies with (those of) ours which (are supported by) the versions *which have never been corrupted*, namely, of Aquila and Theodotion and Symmachus" (*Commentary on John* 6.24, Menzies; *ANF* 10:371; cf. Heine, op. cit. n.30, 6.212).

38 The reasoning here is presumably that the statement in Matthew (which is missing from the parallel context in Lk 11:30) is more likely to be authentic—given the traditional three days between death and resurrection—than the strange reference to "Paradise" in Luke; this example comes from Origen's *Commentary on John* 32.19; cited in Pack, ibid. 144.

39 See Mt 26:6–13; Mk 14:3–9; Lk 7:36–50; Jn 12:1–8. This discussion occurs in his *Commentary on Matthew*. For fragments of the original Greek and a lengthy Latin paraphrase, see the text in Klostermann, op. cit. n.23, 10.77; Bd. 11:178–186. Cf. Migne, *P.G.* tom. 13. col. 1721 A–D; cf. the discussion in Robert M. Grant, *The Earliest Lives of Jesus* (London: SPCK 1961) 67–68.

40 Cf. Jn 1:29–34; in John's Gospel Jesus is not baptized, although John testifies to him.

41 *Commentary on John* 10:2; *ANF* 10:382; cf. Heine §10.13.

42 Greek: Δεῖ τὴν περὶ τούτων ἀλήθειαν ἀποκεῖσθαι ἐν τοῖς νοητοῖς; cf. *ANF* 10:2; §Heine 10.10.

43 Greek: ἀφεῖσθαι τῆς περὶ τῶν εὐαγγελίων πίστεως ὡς οὐκ ἀληθῶν οὐδὲ θειοτέρῳ πνεύματι γεγραμμένων.

44 Greek: τὴν δοκοῦσαν διαφωνίαν οἰόμενοι μὴ λύεσθαι διὰ τῆς ἀναγωγῆς.

45 *Commentary on John* 10:2, Menzies, *ANF* 10:382. Cf. Heine §10.10.

46 *On First Principles* 4.3.1 (Latin version; Greer trans.).

47 The following discussion summarizes the series of observations in the *Commentary on John* 10.14–21; *ANF* 10:391–401; cf. Heine, op. cit. n.30, 152–166.

48 See the lengthy series of comparisons of the entry into Jerusalem in all four Gospels in *Commentary on John* 10:15–17; *ANF* 10:391f.; cf. Heine §10.119f.

49 Loc. cit.; cf. *ANF* 10:396; Heine §10.162.

50 *Commentary on John* 10.17; Heine §10.163.

51 *Commentary on John* 10.17, Menzies, *ANF* 10:396; cf. Heine §10.164.

52 Greek: ἐπεκάθισεν ἐπάνω αὐτῶν (Mt 21:7). Cf. *Commentary on John* 10.17, Menzies, *ANF* 10:396; cf. Heine §10.156.

53 *Commentary on John* 10.17, Menzies, *ANF* 10:396; cf. Heine §10.156.

54 *Commentary on John* 10.17, Menzies, *ANF* 10:396; cf. Heine §10.166. The Greek text is οὐκ οἶδα εἰ μὴ βλακείαν τινὰ ἐμφαίνουσε τοῦ ἐπὶ τοῖς τοιούτοις, εἰ μηδὲν ἄλλο ἀπ᾿ αὐτῶν δηλοῦται, εὐφραινομένου. The text I used for this commentary is that of Brooke, op. cit. n.30. The standard critical text is that of Erich Klostermann, *Origines Werke. Das Johanneskommentar*, Bd. 3; Griechische christliche Schriftsteller (Leipzig: Hinrichs 1901).

55 *Commentary on John* 10.18, Menzies, *ANF* 10:397; cf. Heine §10.172–178.

56 *Commentary on John* 10.16, Menzies, *ANF* 10:394; cf. Heine §10.144.

57 *Commentary on John* 10.16, Menzies, *ANF* 10:394; cf. Heine §10.145.

58 Loc. cit.

59 *Commentary on John* 10.16, Menzies, *ANF* 10:394; cf. Heine §10.146.

60 *Commentary on John* 10.16, Menzies, *ANF* 10:394f.; cf. Heine §10.147.

61 *Commentary on John* 10.16, Menzies, *ANF* 10:395; cf. Heine §10.148. Greek: εἴ γε καὶ αὐτὴ γεγένηται. Cf. *Commentary on John* 10.15, Menzies, *ANF* 10:393: "I conceive it to be impossible for those who admit nothing more than the history in their interpretation (of these passages) to show that these discrepant statements are in harmony with each other"; cf. Heine §10.130.

62 *Commentary on John* 10.16, Menzies, *ANF* 10:393; cf. Heine §10.131. "I believe that in these words He (Jesus) indicated also a deeper truth and that we may regard these occurrences as a symbol . . ." loc. cit.; cf. Heine §10.138.

63 In *Contra Cels.* 1.42 (Chadwick op. cit. chap. 6 n.1, 39f.), Origen berates Celsus for finding fault with the Gospels because they contained narratives of impossible events. Pointing out that verifying the truth of any opinion regarding past history "is one of the most difficult tasks and in some cases impossible," Origen asks Celsus how scholars deal with the mixture of miraculous and factual in Homer's account of the Trojan War, or the *Odyssey*. Do they just reject them completely because of some "fictitious stories"? No,

anyone who reads these stories (ἱστορίας) with a fair mind, who wants to keep himself from being deceived by them, will decide what he will accept (as literal truth) and what he will interpret allegorically (τροπο-λογήσει), searching out the meaning of the authors who wrote such fictitious stories (ἀναπλασαμένων), and what he will disbelieve (completely) as having been written to gratify certain people. We have said this by way of introduction to the whole question of the narrative about Jesus in the gospels (τὴν . . . ἐν τοῖς εὐαγγελίοις περὶ τοῦ Ἰησοῦ ἱστορ-ίαν), not in order to invite people with intelligence to a mere irrational faith (πίστιν ἄλογον), but with a desire to show that readers need an open mind and considerable study, and, if I may say so, need to enter into the mind of the writers (εἰσόδου εἰς τὸ βούλημα τῶν γραψάντων) to find out with what spiritual meaning each event was recorded (ἵν᾽ εὑρεθῇ, ποίᾳ διανοίᾳ ἕκαστον γέγραπται.)."

64 In the discussion and quotations that follow, I have translated Origen's term σωματικός by the English word "bodily" wherever possible, otherwise by "literal" or "historical." I have translated Origen's term πνευματικός by "spiritual" most of the time, but also by "symbolic." Other customary translations, such as "material" and "physical," are not as helpful, in my opinion. Origen's thought is deeply influenced by a Neoplatonic body-spirit dualism, and I wish to preserve this terminology wherever possible, even though it sounds peculiar in modern English.

65 *On First Principles* 4.3.4; trans. G. W. Butterworth, *Origen: On First Principles* (New York: Harper & Row 1966) 294–295, following the text (here and in the subsequent notes) of the *Philocalia*, as edited by P. Koetschau, *Origenes Werke*. Bd. 5 *De principiis*. ΠΕΡΙ ΑΡΧΩΝ, rev. ed., Griech. Christl. Schriftst. (Leipzig: Hinrichs 1913). See also the excellent translation of Rowan A. Greer, *Origen: An Exhortation to Martyrdom, Prayer, First Principles: Book IV*, Classics of Western Spirituality (New York: Paulist Press 1979) 192.

66 *On First Principles* 4.3.5 (Butterworth 296). Greek: Ὁ μέντοι γε ἀκριβὴς ἐπί τινων περιελκυσθήσεται, χωρὶς πολλῆς βασάνου μὴ δυνάμενος ἀποφήνασθαι, πότερον ἤδε ἡ νομιζομένη ἱστορία γέγονε κατὰ τὴν λέξιν ἢ οὔ, καὶ τῆσδε τῆς νομοθεσίας τὸ ῥητὸν τηρητέον ἢ οὔ. διὰ τοῦτο δεῖ ἀκριβῶς τὸν ἐντυγχάνοντα, τηροῦντα τὸ τοῦ σωτῆρος πρόσταγμα τὸ λέγον· »ἐρευνᾶτε τὰς γραφάς«, ἐπι-μελῶς βασανίζειν, πῇ τὸ κατὰ τὴν λέξιν ἀληθές ἐστι καὶ πῇ ἀδύνατον . . . κτλ.

67 *On First Principles* 4.2.9 (Latin version; Butterfield trans.).

68 *Commentary on John* 10.17, Menzies, *ANF* 10:396; cf. Heine §10.165.

69 Ibid. 4.3.5 (Butterworth 296–297; cf. Greer trans. 193 n.73). Greek: ἐπεὶ τοί-νυν, ὡς σαφὲς ἔσται τοῖς ἐντυγχάνουσιν, ἀδύνατος μὲν ὁ ὡς πρὸς τὸ ῥητὸν εἰρμός, οὐκ ἀδύνατος δὲ ἀλλὰ καὶ ἀληθὴς ὁ προηγούμενος, ὅλον τὸν νοῦν φι-λοτιμητέον καταλαμβάνειν, συνείροντα τὸν περὶ τῶν κατὰ τὴν λέξιν ἀδυνάτων λόγον νοητῶς τοῖς οὐ μόνον οὐκ ἀδυνάτοις ἀλλὰ καὶ ἀληθέσι κατὰ τὴν ἱστορ-ίαν, συναλληγορουμένοις τοῖς ὅσον ἐπὶ τῇ λέξει μὴ γεγενημένοις. διακείμεθα

γὰρ ἡμεῖς περὶ πάσης τῆς θείας γραφῆς, ὅτι πᾶσα μὲν ἔχει τὸ πνευματικόν, οὐ πᾶσα δὲ τὸ σωματικόν· πολλαχοῦ γὰρ ἐλέγχεται ἀδύνατον ὂν τὸ σωματικόν. διόπερ πολλὴν προσοχὴν συνεισακτέον τῷ εὐλαβῶς ἐντυγχάνοντι ὡς θείοις γράμμασι ταῖς θείαις βίβλοις. In his *Commentary on John*, Origen says somewhat the same thing: "We must not suppose that historical things are types of historical things, and bodily things of bodily. Quite the contrary: bodily things are types of spiritual things, and historical of intellectual" (Heine §10.110; cf. Menzies, *ANF* 10:391.

70 *Commentary on John* 10:2, my translation; cf. *ANF* 10:382. The Greek of this extremely important passage is as follows: καὶ ἐπὶ ἄλλων δὲ πλειόνων εἴ τις ἐπιμελῶς ἐξετάζοι τὰ εὐαγγέλια περὶ τῆς κατὰ τὴν ἱστορίαν ἀσυμθωνίας, ἥτινα καθ᾽ ἕκαστον πειρασόμεθα κατὰ τὸ δυνατὸν παραστῆσαι, σκοτοδεινιά-σας ἤτοι ἀποστήσεται τοῦ κυροῦν ὡς ἀληθῶς τὰ εὐαγγελία, καὶ ἀποκληρω-τικῶς ἑνὶ αὐτῶν προσθήσεται, μὴ τολμῶν πάντη ἀθετεῖν τὴν περὶ τοῦ κυρίου ἡμῶν πίστιν, ἢ προσιέμενος τὰ τέσσαρα εἶναι ἀληθὲς αὐτῶν οὐκ ἐν τοῖς σωματικοῖς χαρακτῆρσιν. Cf. Heine §10.14.

71 Greek: ὑπεθέμην, ἐκληφθεὶς ὁ νοῦς τῶν ἱστορικῶν, χαρακτῆρι βουληθέντων ἡμᾶς διδάξαι τὰ ὑπὸ τοῦ νοῦ αὐτῶν τεθεωρημένα.

72 Greek: ἔσθ᾽ ὅπου καὶ προσυφανάντων τῇ γραφῇ μετὰ λέξεως ὡς περὶ αἰσθητῶν τὸ καθαρῶς νοητῶς αὐτοῖς τετρανωμένον.

73 Greek: οὐ καταγινώσκω δέ που καὶ τὸ ὡς κατὰ τὴν ἱστορίαν ἑτέρως γενόμενον πρὸς τὸ χρήσιμον τούτων μυστικοῦ σκοποῦ μετατιθέναι πως αὐτούς, ὥστε εἰπ-εῖν τὸ ἐν τόπῳ γενόμενον ὡς ἐν ἑτέρῳ, ἢ τὸ ἐν τῷδε τῷ καιρῷ ὡς ἐν ἄλλῳ, καὶ τὸ οὕτωσὶ ἀπαγγελλόμενον μετά τινος παραλλαγῆς αὐτοὺς πεποιηκέναι.

74 *Commentary on John* 10.4, my translation; Greek: προέκειτο γὰρ αὐτοῖς ὅπου μὲν ἐνεχώρει ἀληθεύειν πνευματικῶς ἅμα καὶ σωματικῶς, ὅπου δὲ μὴ ἐνεδε-χετο ἀμφοτέρως, προκρίνειν τὸ πνευματικὸν τοῦ σωματικοῦ, σωζομένου πολ-λάκις τοῦ ἀληθοῦς πνευματικοῦ ἐν τῷ σωματικῷ, <u>ὡς ἂν εἴποι τις, ψεύδει</u>. Cf. Menzies, *ANF* 10:383; Heine §10.18–20. Both translators ignore Origen's consistent use of the passive voice, indicating his obvious conviction that the Gospel authors' alternating use of spiritual and literal senses was controlled by the Holy Spirit, not by their choice. These modes of communication were *given to* the Gospel authors. "It was their intention to speak the truth spiritually and materially at the same time where that was possible" (Heine). Such a translation makes it sound as if the Gospel authors were simply confronted by a choice of authorial conventions, as modern writers believe. This subtle shift destroys a very important point, as I show in the conclusion.

75 *Commentary on John* 10.2, Menzies, *ANF* 10:382; Greek: Δεῖ τὴν περὶ τούτων ἀλήθειαν ἀποκεῖσθαι ἐν τοῖς νοητοῖς, ἢ μὴ λουμένης τῆς διαφωνίας ἀφεῖσθαι τῆς περὶ τῶν εὐαγγελίων πίστεως, ὡς οὐκ ἀληθῶν οὐδὲ θειοτέρῳ πνεύματι γεγραμμένων, <u>ἢ ἐπιτετευγμένως ἀπομνημονευθέντων</u>· ἑκατέρως γὰρ λέγεται συντετάχθαι ἡ τούτων γραφή. In the last of the either/or's, Menzies has "as

records worthy of our faith," which is not what the Greek says (see underlined phrase); cf. Liddel-Scott, *s.v.* ἐπιτετευγμένως. Cf. Heine §10.10 "(We
must, however, set before the reader) that the truth of these accounts lies in
the spiritual meanings, (because) if the discrepancy is not solved, (many) dis-
miss credence in the Gospels as not true, or not written by a divine spirit, <u>or
not successfully recorded</u>. The composition of these Gospels, in fact, is said
to have involved both."

76 *Commentary on John* 10.3, my translation; cf. Menzies, *ANF* 10:382–383.
Greek: ἔστω τισὶ προκείμενον βλέπουσι τῷ πνεύματι τὸν θεὸν καὶ τοὺς τούτου
πρὸς τοὺς ἁγίους λόγους, τήν τε παρουσίαν, ἣν πάρεστιν αὐτοῖς ἐξαιρέτοις
καιροῖς τῆς προκοπῆς αὐτῶν ἐπιφαινόμενος, πλέοσιν οὖσι τὸν ἀριθμὸν καὶ ἐν
διαφόροις τόποις, οὐχ ὁμοειδεῖς τε πάντη εὐεργεσίας εὐεργετουμένοις,
ἑκάστῳ ἰδίᾳ ἀπαγγεῖλαι ἃ βλέπει τῷ πνεύματι περὶ τοῦ θεοῦ καὶ τῶν λόγων
αὐτοῦ, τῶν τε πρὸς τοὺς ἁγίους ἐμφανειῶν, ὥστε τόνδε μὲν περὶ τῶνδε τῷδε
τῷ δικαίῳ κατὰ τόνδε τὸν τόπον λεγομένων ὑπὸ θεοῦ καὶ πραττομένων ἀπαγ-
γέλλειν, τόνδε δὲ περὶ τῶν ἑτέρῳ χρησμωδουμένων καὶ ἐπιτελουμένων, καὶ
ἄλλον περί τινος τρίτου παρὰ τοὺς προειρημένους δύο θέλειν ἡμᾶς διδάσκειν·
ἔστω δέ τις καὶ τέταρτος τὸ ἀνάλογον τοῖς τρισὶ περί τινος ποιῶν. συμφερέ-
σθωσαν δὲ οἱ τέσσαρες περί τινων ὑπὸ τοῦ πνεύματος αὐτοῖς ὑποβαλλομένων
ἀλλήλοις, καὶ περὶ ἑτέρων ἐν ὀλίγῳ παραγγελλέτωσαν . . . κτλ. Heine's translation is particularly garbled and misleading. For example, he has inexplicably
omitted the key phrase at the beginning of the whole passage (in §10.15),
"certain men . . . *see God*."

77 *Commentary on John* 10.4, Menzies, *ANF* 10:383; Greek: καὶ ὁ Ἰησοῦς τοίνυν
πολλά ἐστι ταῖς ἐπινοίαις, ὧν ἐπινοιῶν εἰκὸς τοὺς εὐαγγελιστὰς διαφόρους
ἐννοίαις, λαμβάνοντας. Heine's translation is extraordinarily turgid: "Therefore Jesus too is many things in his aspects. It is likely that the different evangelists took their thoughts from these aspects and wrote the Gospels, sometimes also being in agreement with one another concerning certain things"
(§10.21). Cf. Origen's statement in his *Commentary on John:* "Since (Jesus)
is the one of whom all the evangelists write, so the Gospel, although written
by . . . four is one" (5.4, Menzies, *ANF* 10:348).

78 *Commentary on John* 10.3, Menzies, *ANF* 10:383; Greek: Δόξει τοίνυν τῷ
ἱστορίαν εἶναι νομίζοντι τὴν τούτων γραφὴν, ἢ διὰ εἰκόνος ἱστορικῆς προ-
σθετὰ ὄντα παραστῆσαι πράγματα, καὶ τὸν θεὸν ὑπολαμβάνοντι κατὰ περι-
γραφὴν εἶναι ἐν τόπῳ, μὴ δυνάμενον τῷ αὐτῷ πλείονας ἑαυτοῦ ἐμποιῆσαι
φαντασίας πλείοσιν ἐν πλείοσι τόποις καὶ πλείονα ἅμα λέγειν, ἀδύνατον
εἶναι ἀληθεύειν οὓς ὑπεθέμην τέσσαρας . . . κτλ. Cf. Heine §10.17.

79 *Commentary on John* 10.3, Menzies, *ANF* 10:382; Greek: ὑπὲρ δὲ τοῦ ποσὴν
ἐπίνοιαν τοῦ βουλήματος τῶν εὐαγγελίων . . . λαβεῖν, καὶ τοῦτο ἡμῖν λεκτέον.

80 See below, p. 139.

81 For example, when Origen prepared himself to explain the intricacies locked

inside the cleansing of the temple, he wrote: "We shall ... expound according to the strength that is given to us the reasons which move us to recognize here a harmony (between these extremely discordant descriptions); and in doing so we entreat Him who gives to every one that asks and strives acutely to enquire, and we knock that by the keys of higher knowledge the hidden things of Scripture may be opened to us" (*Commentary on John* 10.16, Menzies, *ANF* 10:393; cf. Heine §10.131). Cf. later, "To perceive the meaning in these matters belongs to that true understanding which has been given to those who say, 'But we have the mind of Christ, that we may see the things that are given to us by God'" (Heine §10.172).

82 *Commentary on John* 10:15, Menzies, *ANF* 10:393; cf. Heine §10.129–130.

83 *Contra Cels.* 8.76 (trans. Chadwick op. cit. chap. 6 n.1, 510f.).

NOTES TO CHAPTER 8

1 Arthur C. McGiffert, ed., *Ecclesiastical History,* Ante-Nicene Fathers, 2nd ser. (Grand Rapids, MI: Eerdmans 1952) 280 n.1.

2 The term "book" in Porphyry's title (and others like it) is equivalent to "part" in modern usage. Porphyry probably wrote on papyrus sheets and had them bound in a codex, or bound sheaf. If so, considering its great length, his writing may have taken some two thousand sheets of papyrus, which might be five hundred modern printed pages. We would say his book consisted of fifteen divisions or parts, each of which contained several chapters. Likewise, all of the replies to Porphyry, consisting of "twenty-five books" or "thirty books" (there may have been a competition to see who could come up with the largest number of sections or topics to discuss), are the same thing; these are all parts or divisions of the total literary work.

3 Hulen estimates that it compared in length to a volume in the Ante-Nicene library (average length five hundred pages); see *Porphyry's Work against the Christians: An Interpretation,* Yale Studies in Religion no. 1 (Scottdale, PA: Mennonite Press 1933) 4; for a list of earlier attacks possibly drawn on by Porphyry, see 31–43.

4 For a good discussion of the probable causes of Diocletian's first and second edicts, see McGiffert, op. cit. n.1, 397–400.

5 Ibid. 400. Cf. T. D. Barnes, *Constantine and Eusebius* (Cambridge: Harvard University Press 1981) 178. For an interesting picture of the uneven enforcement of the persecution in the eastern localities, see Robin Fox, *Pagans and Christians* (New York: Knopf 1987) 596–601.

6 For an abbreviated biography of Apollonios of Tyana by Philostratus of Lemnos, see David R. Cartlidge and David L. Dungan, *Documents for the*

Study of the Gospels, 2nd ed. (Philadelphia: Fortress Press 1994) 203–238; see also 5–16.

7 For the text of this reply, see F. C. Conybeare, *Philostratus: The Life of Apollonios of Tyana,* Loeb Library (Cambridge: Harvard University Press 1960) 2:483–605.

8 Hulen, op. cit. n.3, 4–6.

9 See further below, pp. 115f.

10 McGiffert, op. cit. n.1, 32; cf. Augustine, *City of God* 19.22: "Porphyry, the most learned of the philosophers (and) the bitterest enemy of the Christians."

11 Hulen, op. cit. n.3, 6.

12 Adolf von Harnack was of the opinion that Porphyry was still *the* critic of Christianity to be answered; cf. *The Mission and Expansion of Christianity in the First Three Centuries,* trans. and ed. James Moffatt, 2nd ed. (New York: Putnam & Sons; London: Williams & Norgate 1908) 1:505: "This work of Porphyry is perhaps the most ample and thoroughgoing treatise which has ever been written against Christianity ... The controversy between the philosophy of religion and Christianity lies today in the very position in which Porphyry placed it. Even at this time of day Porphyry remains unanswered." See further, Hulen, "Porphyry's Attitude toward Christianity," in ibid., 25–31.

13 Barnes, op. cit. n.5, 211; 377 n.14.

14 For an older list of attempts to collect the fragments and arrange them, see Hulen, op. cit. n.3, 56. Probably the most famous reconstruction was by Adolf von Harnack, *Porphyrius 'Gegen die Christen' 15 Bücher; Zeugnisse, Fragmente und Referate* (Berlin: Königl. Akademie der Wissenschaften 1916). Harnack argued that the *Apocriticus* of Macarius Magnes could be used to reconstruct the wording of Porphyry's writing. For a critique of Harnack's position, see T. W. Crafer, "The Work of Porphyry against the Christians, and Its Reconstruction," in *Journal of Theological Studies* 15 (1913–14) 360–374. For a more recent refutation of the use of Macarius Magnes, see Timothy D. Barnes, "Porphyry against the Christians: Date and the Attribution of Fragments," *Journal of Theological Studies* 24 (1973) 424–42. This chapter is based on Crafer's list of relatively certain fragments, see Crafer, 483–499. For an equally cautious summary overview of Porphyry's arguments, see Robert L. Wilken, *The Christians as the Romans Saw Them* (New Haven: Yale University Press 1984) 126–163. For the most recent attempt to translate the fragments into English based on Harnack's unreliable reconstruction, see R. Joseph Hoffmann, *Porphyry's Against the Christians. The Literary Remains* (Amherst: Prometheus Books 1994).

15 Crafer, ibid. 499.

16 Henry Chadwick, *Origen: Contra Celsum* (Cambridge: University Press 1965) 211f.

17 Ibid. 375.

18 Ibid. 370.

19 This list comes from Crafer, op. cit. n.14, 502–507. He gives the appropriate references to the *Apocriticus*.

20 The reconstruction gives specific chapter and verse references; of course, these were not in the original.

21 Crafer, op. cit. n.14, 510.

22 Hulen, op. cit. n.3, 40f.

23 Barnes, op. cit. n.5, 179.

NOTES   TO   CHAPTER   9

1 Arthur C. McGiffert, ed., *Ecclesiastical History,* Ante-Nicene Fathers, 2nd ser. (Grand Rapids, MI: Eerdmans 1952) 1.6.

2 Eusebius, *Vit. Const.* 1.19.

3 See above, chap. 6.

4 Timothy D. Barnes, *Constantine and Eusebius* (Cambridge: Harvard University Press 1981) 174.

5 See above, pp. 96f.

6 Barnes, op. cit. n.4, 178–186. See also Quasten, *Patrology* 3.331f.: "Although nominally directed against pagans and Jews, the *Praeparatio* as well as the *Demonstratio* is really aimed at Porphyry's treatise *Against the Christians.* Eusebius refers to him again and again ... However, Eusebius refrains from meeting the objections of Porphyry point by point, as Origen did with Celsus. He follows a different course, which does not permit the opponent to draw the author aside from his well-ordered and systematic program of Scriptural exposition into fruitless controversy on points of minor importance. This method proves far more effective and does much toward making his work not only a codification of the results achieved by his predecessors but probably the most important apologetic contribution of the early Church." I propose to add to this view the possibility that Eusebius' *Ecclesiastical History* and *Canons of the Gospels* played similar roles in the same general strategy. On the meaning of "Book" in these titles, see above, p. 430 note 2.

7 See above, p. 96.

8 For these dates, see McGiffert, op. cit. n.1, 33–35. Barnes, op. cit. n.4, 178, dates both after the persecution ended.

9 See above, p. 97.

10 Cf. McGiffert, op. cit. n.1, 33.

11 Ibid. 45.

12 See above, p. 97.

13 If not otherwise indicated, the translation of the *Ecclesiastical History* that I quote is that by Arthur C. McGiffert, op. cit. n.1. At certain clearly indi-

cated points I use instead the translation by C. F. Cruse, *The Ecclesiastical History of Eusebius Pamphilus* (1850; reprint Grand Rapids: Baker Book House 1966), or the one by Kirsopp Lake, *Eusebius: The Ecclesiastical History,* Loeb Library (Cambridge: Harvard University Press 1959).

14 Greek: Τὰς τῶν ἱερῶν ἀποστόλων διαδοχάς; cf. 3.37.1; 4.22.3; 5.11.2. The concept διαδοχῆ was a widely used technical term. In this case it reflects the usage of the Greek philosophical schools and means the succession of appointed or elected heads of the philosophical schools going back to the founder. The historian Diogenes Laertius wrote a compendium of the philosophical schools of his day entitled *Lives of Eminent Philosophers* (written ca. 225). It contained numerous successions of the heads of the major Greek philosophical schools; see 1.13: "Philosophy, the pursuit of wisdom, has had a two-fold origin: it started with Anaximander on the one hand, with Pythagoras on the other . . . The one school was called Ionian, . . . the other was called Italian . . . The succession (of the Ionian) passes from Thales through Anaximander, Anaximenes, Anaxagoras, (etc.) to Socrates." Laertius mentioned other authors who preserved succession lists, e.g., "Sosicrates in his Successions of the Philosophers" (8.8) and "Alexander (Polyhistor) in his Successions of Philosophers" (8.24). Rabbinic Judaism showed the influence of this custom, cf. *Pirke Aboth* chap. 1, which identifies the succession of orthodox Torah interpreters back to Moses; see R. Travers Herford, trans. and commentary, *Pirke Aboth: The Ethics of the Talmud: Sayings of the Fathers* (New York: Schocken Books 1962); see p. 36 for a chart of the succession in the "House (=School) of Hillel."

15 Eusebius actually discussed in detail fewer than ten "prominent parishes," and these not at all systematically. Those commented on most fully were Jerusalem (up to a point), Antioch, Laodicea, Ephesus, Corinth (in part), Rome, Lugdunum (Lyons), Alexandria, and Caesarea. However, in between Eusebius inserted references to the actions and writings of many orthodox bishops, theologians, and historians in other orthodox centers.

16 Eusebius, *Hist. eccl.* 1.1.1–2.

17 Because of the dearth of records for some of these successions, Barnes notes that "after Book Three of the *Eccl. Hist.,* the idea of (recording all of the) apostolic successions fades away" and the narrative becomes a disjointed collection of episodes on various subjects with the successions worked in here and there; see Barnes, op. cit. n.4, 128–140, for an overview of the many different themes Eusebius touched on.

18 Eusebius, *Hist. eccl.* 5.6, refers to the apostolic succession at Rome provided by Irenaeus in *adv. haer.* 3.3.3.

19 More familiarly known from its Latin title as *Against All Heresies.* My references will use the familiar abbreviation *adv. haer.*

20 *Adv. haer.* 1.23.2 et passim. Cf. 3.pref.: "You have enjoined upon me, my dear

friend, that I should bring to light the Valentinian doctrines ... that I should exhibit their diversity and compose a treatise in refutation of them. I therefore have undertaken (to prove) that they (the heretics) spring from Simon the father of all heretics (and) to exhibit both their doctrines and their successions." This view of Simon was a commonplace among the orthodox; cf. Justin Martyr, *Apol.* 1.26; Eusebius, *Hist. eccl.* 2.13.

21 E.g., *adv. haer.* 1.14.2–6.

22 Ibid. 1.10.1.

23 Ibid. 1.10.2.

24 1 Clem. 42.1–3; trans. Cyril C. Richardson, *Early Christian Fathers*, rev. ed., Library of Christian Classics (Philadelphia: Westminster Press 1953) 1:62.

25 Ibid. 1.1.4–5.

26 Ibid. 3.1.1–2.

27 A somewhat misleading translation. The Greek is: τὴν δὲ φερομένην δευτέραν οὐκ ἐνδιάθηκον μὲν εἶναι παρειλήφαμεν. I suggest "but we have received (the tradition) that the (epistle) named 'the Second' is not to be covenanted (with 'the First')." Cruse *ad loc* tries to warn the reader about the difficulty of translating the strange technical Greek term ἐνδιάθηκον by inserting it *in Greek* next to his translation: "embodied with the sacred books," which scarcely resembles the Greek. McGiffert's translation: "belong to the canon" is the right idea, but it is not what the Greek says.

28 "Used" is another technical term. When it occurs absolutely (as is the case here), i.e., without any qualifier, it means precisely *to read with the other scriptures in public worship*, cf. 2.15.2; 3.16. However, it frequently has a broader sense, namely, to quote something as a scriptural authority when expounding or defending orthodox theology; *passim*. There is an occasional third meaning of "use," namely, to employ in catechetical instruction. Note that the following excerpt from Eusebius' discussion of the *Shepherd of Hermas* contains all three meanings of "use":

> The Shepherd of Hermas ... has been disputed by some and on that account cannot be placed among the acknowledged books; while by others it is considered quite indispensable, especially to those who need instruction in the elements of the faith. Hence ... it has been publicly read in churches and I have found that some of the most ancient writers used it. (3.3.6)

The term never means "used" for private edification.

29 Greek: τῶν ἀλλῶν γραφῶν.

30 The *Gospel of Peter;* see Eusebius' further discussion of it at 6.12; cf. also 3.25.

31 For text and discussion of the *Preaching of Peter* (usually referred to as *Ke-*

rygma Petri), see Edgar Hennecke, *New Testament Apocrypha*, rev. ed., Wilhelm Schneemelcher, trans. R. M. Wilson, 2 vols. (Philadelphia: Westminster Press 1964) 2.102–127; for the text and discussion of the *Apocalypse of Peter*, see ibid. 2.620–641.

32 Greek: ὅλως ἐν καθολικοῖς (γραφαῖς). McGiffert's translation is seriously deficient. He mistranslates ἐν καθολικοῖς as "universally," i.e., as an adverb. But it is an adjective and refers to "catholic writings." Moreover *katholikos* had been used, at least since the time of Irenaeus, as a self-chosen *name* for the orthodox Christian assemblies to set them apart from the heretical Christian churches (whom the orthodox named after their heretical leaders; e.g., Valentinians, Carpocratians, Nicolaitans, Marcionites, etc.). For further clarification of the specific, technical meaning of ἐκκλησία, see above, p. 422 n.13.

33 Greek: τις ἐκκλησιαστικός. The Greek word "ecclesiastical" is another technical term and is used to refer *exclusively* to orthodox bishops and theologians; it is never used to refer to heretical Christians. Eusebius' book title could be translated *History of the Orthodox Assembly.*

34 *Hist. eccl.* 3.3.1–2. This final statement implies two arguments simultaneously: use by an ancient orthodox writer not only certified a writing's orthodoxy by someone close to the source of all orthodoxy, Jesus Christ, it also provided critical information about the date of a writing—important in a day when copyright records and central archives didn't exist.

35 Greek: σὺν ταῖς διαδοχαῖς. Cruse: "with the successions of the apostles." Lake ad loc. inexplicably omits the critical words in his translation, thereby destroying the logical base of Eusebius' whole argument regarding the canon.

36 *Hist. eccl.* 3.3.3. Again, McGiffert's use of "canonical" is misleading. The Greek is περὶ τῶν ἐνδιαθήκων καὶ ὁμολογουμένων. Cruse's translation is better: "respecting the incorporated (ἐνδιαθήκων) and acknowledged writings." Again, I suggest that "covenanted" is closer to the Greek than "incorporated." Note Eusebius' addition of a clarifying parallel term "acknowledged." But here again, we must remember: acknowledged—by the right authorities.

37 For the names of these churches, see above, n.15.

38 These three categories, and the basic logical structure of the canonization process, were not invented by the Christian authorities. These categories had been widely used by the philosophical schools in canonizing their own writings. Cf. Diogenes Laertius, *Lives of Eminent Philosophers* 2:64: "Panaetius thinks that, of all the Socratic dialogues, those by Plato, Xenophon, Antisthenes and Aeschines are genuine (ἀληθεῖς); he is in doubt (διστάζει) about those ascribed to Phaedo and Euclides; but he rejects (ἀναιρεῖ) the others one and all"; cf. further the same three categories used of the writings of Phaedo 2:105 and Plato 3:57f.

39 Greek: τῆς καινῆς διαθήκης γραφάς. This is a rare, early occurrence of this set of technical terms ("new testament or covenant" used absolutely in conjunction with "scripture"). Later, these terms will become standard.

40 I get this translation from Lake; McGiffert's translation, "the extant former epistle of John," is astonishingly misleading.

41 Again for this clause, I am following the translation of Lake rather than McGiffert's confusing "and likewise the epistle of Peter must be maintained."

42 Greek: ταῦτα μὲν ἐν ὁμολογουμένοις. Cruse's "these then are acknowledged as genuine" goes beyond the Greek but clarifies the sense intended. Lake's use of capital letters, "These belong to the Recognized Books," conveys the technical category intended.

43 Greek: τῶν δ᾽ ἀντιλεγομένων.

44 Greek: ἐν τοῖς νόθοις. The word νόθος means "illegitimate, counterfeit, spurious"; see Liddell-Scott-Jones *Lexicon ad voc.* McGiffert's translation, "Among the rejected writings," is misleading, giving the result rather than the reason, which, for this discussion, is of critical significance. I here follow Cruse's translation.

45 Greek: ὧν οὐδὲν οὐδαμῶς ἐν συγγράμματι τῶν κατὰ τὰς διαδοχὰς ἐκκλησιαστικῶν τις ἀνὴρ εἰς μνήμην ἀγαγεῖν ἠξίωσεν. This passage occurs at *hist. eccl.* 3:25. McGiffert's translation, "which no one belonging to the ecclesiastical writers has deemed worthy of mention in his writings," once again omits the all-important term "succession," nullifying the logical basis of the canonization process. Eusebius' language here is exceedingly emphatic: "not one single man ever . . ."

46 If one looks at the list of "acknowledged" writings given by Eusebius, 3.25, one must avoid two calculated ambiguities introduced by Eusebius himself. The clear-cut cases are four Gospels, the Acts of the Apostles, 1 Peter, and 1 John. The ambiguous cases are first: "the epistles of Paul," where he does not specify whether or not the Epistle to the Hebrews is to be included among "the epistles of Paul," leaving it unmentioned. If it is not included (and it shouldn't be, as Eusebius well knows, since he will go on to give vivid evidence that it was "disputed," although oddly enough he does not put it in that category), that would add only thirteen epistles of Paul to the previous seven, for a total of twenty "acknowledged" writings. Eusebius also coyly dangles the Apocalypse of John in front of this category but a moment later dangles it in front of the group of "spurious" writings. Then he does not even mention it in the list of "disputed" writings, which is where it obviously belonged. This is one of the more blatant examples of Eusebius' intentional or unintentional obfuscation.

47 I am not aware of the existence of an up-to-date, comprehensive list of all candidate writings which were held to be sacred Scripture by all groups con-

sidering themselves to be Christians, prior to the Council of Nicaea. This number is my estimate, based on the texts presented and discussed in the following: Hennecke, op. cit. n.31; James Robinson, ed., *The Nag Hammadi Library in English* (New York: Harper & Row 1977); Bentley Layton, *The Gnostic Scriptures* (Garden City, NY: Doubleday 1987); Walter Bauer, *Orthodoxy and Heresy in Earliest Christianity*, rev. ed., ed. R. A. Kraft and G. Krodel (Philadelphia: Fortress Press 1971); and Helmut Koester, *Ancient Christian Gospels: Their History and Development* (Philadelphia: Trinity Press International 1990).

48 This fundamental assumption was shared by virtually all of the philosophers belonging to the Great Assembly, as well as their pagan philosophical critics, from the middle of the second century onward. It was not a concept that can be found prominently displayed in the thinking of the first generation of Palestinian-Syrian-Jewish Christians. However, it was fundamental in the logic of the canonization process from the mid-second century on.

49 For the expression of this idea by Irenaeus, see above, p. 102; cf. Eusebius *Hist. eccl.* 4.7.13.

50 Johannes Quasten, *Patrology* (Utrecht-Antwerp: Spectrum 1966) 2:269–273, calls this writing "the most finished, the most valuable of Tertullian's works."

51 *De praescr. haer.* 32; *ANF* 3.258.

52 Ibid. 28; *ANF* 3.256. Latin: *Nullus inter multos eventus unus est exitus . . . Caeterum, quod apud multos unum invenitur, non est erratum sed traditum.*

53 Viewed in terms of modern logic, there are a number of unresolved problems inherent in Tertullian's argument, such as the system-boundary dilemma, the illegitimate use of an argument from silence to prove a historical fact (at one level, this objection applies to the entire canonization process), and others. Nevertheless, while recognizing these difficulties, it still has considerable merit, given the realities faced by the Great Assembly as it searched—without centralized archive or authority, without the benefits of modern printing and electronic storage—for the authentic apostolic writings. I might rephrase it this way: what is the statistical probability that a long series of *accidental* historical judgments (e.g., Jesus' disciple Matthew wrote the Gospel called by his name) made by a statistically significant number of different authorities in congregations scattered around the Mediterranean world, stretching over a time span of more than two hundred years, resulting in a self-identical pattern across them all, would be totally fallacious? The probability would be virtually nil, says Tertullian, because a series of accidental, independent judgments by a large group of separated individuals never produces a consistent pattern. Therefore, he concludes, the pattern proves that these decisions are not the result of error or accident but carefully preserved *tradition* shared by all of these more or less independent churches. Taken as it stands, the argu-

ment is worth careful study. Remember, *a single negative vote* was in theory sufficient to cast a candidate writing into the "disputed" category or to knock it out of contention altogether (e.g., the negative decision of Antioch's Bishop Serapion regarding the Gospel of Peter).

54 *Vit. Const.* 4.36.

55 Ibid. 4.37.

56 For a discussion of the relationship between these fifty copies and the early-fourth-century parchment volumes of the Scripture which we have today, e.g., the magnificent Codex Vaticanus and the equally magnificent Codex Sinaiticus, see Bruce M. Metzger, *The Canon of the New Testament: Its Origin, Development, and Significance* (Oxford: Clarendon Press 1989) 207; cf. also Kurt Aland and Barbara Aland, *The Text of the New Testament: An Introduction to the Critical Editions and to Modern Textual Criticism*, trans. E. F. Rhodes (Grand Rapids: Eerdmans 1987) 66. For a helpful clarification of the occasionally mistranslated phrase τρίσσα καὶ τέτρασσα, see Barnes, op. cit. n.4, 124: "three or four at a time."

57 Discussed above, pp. 90f.

58 Barnes, op. cit. n.4, 122.

59 These and other examples can be found in Barnes, ibid. 122f. He suggests that these little, relatively unsophisticated writings may have been "school exercises" stemming from the catechetical school in Caesarea. If so, they reveal a depth and breadth of customary analysis that approaches modern Gospel study and that makes more understandable Augustine's sophisticated series of explanations.

60 Barnes, ibid. 123.

61 Barnes, ibid.

62 William L. Petersen, *Tatian's Diatessaron: Its Creation, Dissemination, Significance, and History in Scholarship*, Suppl. Vig. Christ. 25 (Leiden: Brill 1994) 32f. and 38, calls Ammonius' creation "a type of synopsis" rather than a harmony. He says "no trace is known to survive" (33).

63 Eusebius' sections and canons were taken over into the Syriac copies of the Tetraevangelium at a very early date, probably during his lifetime. Interestingly, the learned Syrian doctors in the great Scripture school at Edessa immediately introduced a thorough refinement of the Eusebian approach. G. H. Gwilliam discovered that the Syriac sections and parallels are far more numerous than were those of Eusebius (Syriac total 1,389; Greek total 1,165). "The latter only sought to place in harmony those paragraphs in one Gospel which are in historical or perhaps only verbal agreement with paragraphs in one or more of the other Evangelists: the Syriac aimed at a complete tabulation of the more minute resemblances between the several statements within the compass of such paragraphs. Thus it often appears that the Syriac section

is but a few words, only half a verse, or less, but it forms a distinct division, because it bears a resemblance to some longer or shorter passage in another Gospel"; see Gwilliam, "The Ammonian Sections, Eusebian Canons, and Harmonizing Tables in the Syriac Tetra-evangelium," in *Studia Biblica et Ecclesiastica* 2 (1890) 246. Gwilliam goes on to note that the Syriac parallels were also collected in a small table at the bottom of each page, a sort of "Foot Harmony." This excellent feature is never seen in Western Gospel manuscripts.

64 The translation of this letter is that of Barnes, op. cit. n.4, 121–122; cf. H. H. Oliver, "The Epistle of Eusebius to Carpianus: Textual Tradition and Translation," *Nov. Test.* 3 (1959) 138–145. The Greek text followed by the Eusebian canons is available in K. Aland, ed., *Greek-English New Testament,* 3rd rev. ed. (Stuttgart: Deutsche Bibelgesellschaft 1986) 35*–40*.

65 Greek: τὸ διὰ τεσσάρων ἡμῖν καταλέλοιπεν εὐαγγέλιον. Barnes has inexplicably ignored this technical term. For a discussion of the significance of the title διὰ τεσσάρων, see above, pp. 41f.

66 Greek: τὰς ὁμοφώνους περικοπάς.

67 Greek: ὡς ἐξ ἀνάγκης . . . τῶν τριῶν διαφθαρῆναι ὅσον ἐπὶ τῷ ὕφει τῆς ἀναγνώσεως; literally: "so that the fabric of the text of the (other) three is necessarily completely destroyed." The term ὕφη was used of a spider's web; Barnes' translation "continuous" is weak. Moreover, the term διαφθείρω means "to break up, destroy utterly, ruin"; it is a very emphatic term, to which Barnes' "broken" does not do justice. Gwilliam, op. cit. n.63, 255f., provides the text of the Syriac translation of Eusebius' letter, followed by a Latin translation: *ita ut fiat ut necessario perdatur nexus ordinatorum verborum Evangelistarum* . . . (257).

68 Greek: τοὺς οἰκείους ἑκάστου εὐαγγελιστοῦ τόπους.

69 Greek: σωζομένου καὶ τοῦ τῶν λοιπῶν δι ' ὅλου σώματός τε καὶ εἱρμοῦ: "preserving the wholeness (δι ' ὅλου i.e., the integrity) of both the body (i.e., the matter, the contents) and the order of the others."

70 Greek: καθ' ἑτέραν μέθοδον.

71 Greek: ἐφ' ἑκάστῳ τῶν τεσσάρων εὐαγγελίων.

72 Greek: καθ' ἕκαστον δὲ ἀριθμὸν ὑποσημείωσις πρόκειται διὰ κινναβάρεως. The word κιννάβαρις means "vermilion, (deep) red." Oliver's translation: "and for each number a rubricate note is given" is a marvel of obfuscation for "red mark."

73 Greek: ὁποιονδήποτε ἐπιστῆσαί τινι ᾧ βούλει κεφαλαίῳ. Translating κεφαλαίῳ by "chapter" is anachronistic. Note the very small κεφαλαίαι in the *Vit. Const.* They are usually rather small divisions, corresponding to what we mean by pericope or passage in modern Gospel research.

74 For further discussion of this critical point, see above, pp. 84f.

NOTES TO CHAPTER 10

1 Augustine, *Retractions* 42, trans. M. I. Bogan, The Fathers of the Church (Washington, DC: Catholic University of America Press 1968) 60:152.

2 Ibid. 60:150.

3 Eugène Portalié, *A Guide to the Thought of Saint Augustine,* trans. R. J. Bastian (Chicago: Library of Living Catholic Thought 1960) 123.

4 Eugene TeSelle, *Augustine the Theologian* (New York: Herder & Herder 1970) 237. Cf. Jerry H. Bentley, *Humanists and Holy Writ: New Testament Scholarship in the Renaissance* (Princeton: Princeton University Press 1983) 51: "Most students of Jerome today believe that he translated afresh no part of the New Testament, that he revised earlier versions of the gospels, and that he only slightly amended earlier translations of the Acts, Epistles, and Apocalypse."

5 See *Realencyclopedie für Prot. Theologie und Kirche* 3te Aufl. 1907 *s.v.* "synopse." Augustine was familiar with some of Eusebius' historical writings; note the reference to the *Chronicon* in his *de doctr. christ.* 2.39.59.

6 *De cons.* 1.7.10; *NPNF* 6:81.

7 His critique of the morals of the Manichaean community in Rome was written in 388; his critique of the Manichaean doctrine of two souls appeared in 391; his *Disputation against Fortunatus the Manichaean* appeared in 392; and his critique of Mani's *Epistle Called The Fundamental* in 397.

8 *Contra epist. Manich. q.v. fund.* 3.3; *NPNF* 4:130.

9 *Contra Faustus* 1.1; *NPNF* 4:155: "Faustus was an African by race, a citizen of Mileum; he was eloquent and clever but he had adopted the shocking tenets of the Manichaean heresy."

10 *Contra Faustus* 2.1; *NPNF* 4:156.

11 *Contra Faustus* 3.1; *NPNF* 4:159.

12 See ibid. Books 7, 23, 28.

13 Ibid. 17.1; *NPNF* 4:234.

14 TeSelle, op. cit. n.4, 257. See Epistle 102 addressed to Deogratias. The questions were six in number, and the last five occasionally reflect Porphyry's language.

    Question 1 asked what the resurrection body was going to be like.

    Question 2: "Concerning the Christian religion, they have advanced some of the . . . arguments of Porphyry against the Christians: 'If Christ,' they say, 'declared himself to be the way of salvation . . . and only to souls believing in him is the way of return to God, what has become of men who lived in the many centuries before Christ came?'"

    Question 3 asked about Christian rituals.

    Question 4 found a contradiction between the words of Christ where he threatened eternal punishment for all who did not believe in him (Jn 3:18) and where he also said, "with the measure you measure so will it also be measured unto you" (Mt 7:2).

Question 5 noted that the preceding two were from Porphyry and added another: "The objector who has brought forward these questions from Porphyry has added this one in the next place: 'did Solomon say that God has no son?'"

Question 6 dwelt on the absurdity of the story of Jonah, about which Porphyry had devoted an entire book (i.e., chapter).

15 In *Retractions* 42 he mentions "others," i.e., other treatises.

16 *Retractions* 38; for the date of these writings, see Bogan's comment on p. 142.

17 TeSelle, op. cit. n.4, 252.

18 Eusebius, *Eccl. hist.* 6.25.4.

19 See above, page 70.

20 *De doctr. christ.* 2.8.13. This list was ratified at the Councils of Carthage in 397 and 419; Portalié, op. cit. n.3, 121.

21 *De doctr. christ.* 2.7.9–11; 2.41.62

22 TeSelle, op. cit. n.4, 84.

23 Portalié, op. cit. n.3, 122.

24 *De doctr. christ.* 1.2.2; *NPNF* 2.523: "No one uses words except as signs of something else."

25 *De doctr. christ.* 1.1.1; *NPNF* 2.522: "There are two things on which all interpretation of Scripture depends: the mode of ascertaining the proper meaning, and the mode of making known the meaning when it is ascertained."

26 *De doctr. christ.* 2.5.6; *NPNF* 2.537.

27 *De doctr. christ.* 1.36.41: "whoever understands in the Sacred Scriptures something other than what the writer had in mind is deceived."

28 *De doctr. christ.* Book 2 passim.

29 *De doctr. christ.* 3.29.40; 2.10.15–11.16.

30 Cf. the seven rules of interpretation of Tyconius given in Book Three.

31 For examples where Augustine explicitly avoids a particular interpretation because it offends "the rule of faith," see *de doctr. christ.* 3.2.3–4; cf. 3.27.38.

32 *De cons.* 1.1.2; *NPNF* 6.78.

33 Latin: *in auctoritatem canonicam sanctorum librorum eorum scripta reciperet.*

34 Latin: *quae catholica adque apostolica regula fidei et sana doctrina condemnat.*

35 *De cons.* 1.1.2; *NPNF* 6.78.

36 See chap. 18.

37 *De cons.* 1.2.3; *NPNF* 6.78. Note that there is no reference to Irenaeus, possibly the originator of this explanation; but Augustine may not have known where it came from. The character of Augustine's explanation suggests that he had no historical information as to why God caused exactly four canonical

Gospels to be written, and so he invented an explanation that would not offend the rule of faith (see n.32).

38 Ibid.

39 Ibid.

40 Ibid.

41 *De cons.* 1.4.7; *NPNF* 6:79.

42 *De cons.* 1.2.3; *NPNF* 6:78.

43 Ibid. Note the lack of attribution to Papias, or any other source, for this information.

44 Ibid.

45 The first scholar in modern times to emphasize this change in Augustine's perception of the Gospels was David B. Peabody, "Augustine and the Augustinian Hypothesis: A Reexamination of Augustine's Thought in *de consensu evangelistarum*," in *New Synoptic Studies: The Cambridge Gospel Conference and Beyond*, ed. William R. Farmer (Macon: Mercer University Press 1983) 37–64. See further below, pp. 136, 140.

46 *De cons.* 1.7.10.

47 Ibid.

48 Ibid. 1.7.11. It is precisely at this weak point that the Enlightenment rationalists, led by Hermann Samuel Reimarus, launched their attack on the New Testament in their efforts to destroy Christianity (see below, p. 307).

49 *De cons.* 1.7.11; *NPNF* 6:81f.

50 *De cons.* 1.7.12.

51 *De cons.* 1.35.54.

52 Ibid.; *NPNF* 6:101.

53 *De cons.* 2.66.128.

54 *De cons.* 1.2.3; *NPNF* 6:78.

55 *De cons.* 2.19.44; *NPNF* 6:124. Latin: *sed ut solent praetermissa recordari vel posterius facta praeoccupari, sicut divinitus suggerebantur quae ante cognita postea recordando conscriberent.*

56 *De cons.* 2.21.51; *NPNF* 6:127. Latin: *satis probabile est quod unusquisque evangelistarum eo se ordine credidit debuisse narrare, quo voluisset deus ea ipsa quae narrabat eius recordationi suggerere in eis dumtaxat rebus.*

57 Lk 4:23.

58 *De cons.* 2.42.90; *NPNF* 6:145.

59 Latin: *fluitat enim humana memoria per varias cogitationes.* The pun is lost in the translation. Literally: "For human memory *flows* through various thoughts," echoing the reference to God who rules over the "flowing waters" (an allusion to Gen 1:2).

60 *De cons.* 3.14.48; *NPNF* 6:202.

61 Mt 13:1.

62 *De cons.* 2.41.88; *NPNF* 6:144. Latin: *post illud quod narratum est de matre*

et fratribus domini hoc continuo gestum esse et eum ordinem Mattheum etiam in narrando tenuisse ea res insinuat, quia, cum illic transiret, ita conexuit, ut diceret: in illo die ...

63 Ibid.; Mk 4:1. Note the use of the principle of multiple attestation as evidence for historical fact.

64 Ibid.; Lk 8:22 says "One day"—it could have been any day—and tells the story of the stilling of the storm, which occurs elsewhere in the order of Matthew and Mark.

65 Ibid.; Latin: *in ipso ordine.*

66 Ibid.; Latin: *partim gestarum rerum.*

67 Ibid.; Latin: *partim recordationis suae.*

68 Ibid.; Latin: *video quid vel cui quisque adversetur.*

69 *De cons.* 1.2.4. Latin: *pedisequus et breviator.*

70 Ibid.

71 *De cons.* 4.10.11; *NPNF* 6:231 (italics added). Latin: *Marcus* ... *vel Matthei magis comes videtur* ... *quod in primo libro commemoravi, vel, quod probabilius intellegitur, cum ambobus incedit. nam quamvis Mattheo in pluribus, tamen in aliis nonnullis Lucae magis congruit.* For a discussion of the significance of this passage in the history of the Synoptic Problem, see Peabody, op. cit. n.46.

72 See Calvin, 182; Griesbach, 317; Butler, 370; Goulder, 384f.

73 *De cons.* 1.2.4; *NPNF* 6:78 (my translation). Latin: *et quamvis singuli suum quendam narrandi ordinem tenuisse videantur, non tamen unusquisque eorum velut alterius praecedentis ignarus voluisse scribere repperitur vel ignorata praetermisisse, quae scripsisse alius invenitur, sed sicut unicuique inspiratum est non superfluam cooperationem sui laboris adiunxit.*

74 *De cons.* 2.25.58; *NPNF* 6:131 (italics added). Latin: *sicut in multis ita faciunt praetermittentes media, tamquam hoc continuo sequatur quod sine ulla praetermissionis suae significatione subiungunt.*

75 *De cons.* 2.5.16; *NPNF* 6:108 (italics added). Latin: *tacitus enim quae non vult dicere sic ea quae vult dicere illis quae dicebat adiungit, ut ipsa continuo sequi videantur.*

76 *De cons.* 2.25.58.

77 Latin: *alia narrationis via.*

78 *De cons.* 2.45.94; *NPNF* 6:147f. Latin: *et iste qui sermonum domini alta consecutans per alia quae illi tacuerunt curcumvolavit quodammodo et eis ad miraculum de quinque panibus pariter commemorandum non multo post ab eis rursus in altiora revolaturus occurrit.*

79 Latin: *cum ergo illi sancti et veraces viri quasi fortuita recordationum suarum propter narrationis ordinem occultae dei potestati, cui nihil fortuitum est, commisissent.* The "casual-casualties" translation is a superb rendering of the important *fortuitum-fortuita* pun.

80 Latin: *longe abiectum ab oculis dei et longe Peregrin antem.* A noteworthy echo of Origen's statement (which Augustine undoubtedly never read) that the Gospel authors had had *visions of God* and hence they wrote what they did; see above, pp. 84f.

81 *De cons.* 3.13.48; *NPNF* 6:202.

82 *De cons.* 2.21.52; *NPNF* 6:128.

83 *De cons.* 2.42.89; *NPNF* 6:144.

84 *De cons.* 2.21.51; *NPNF* 6:127.

85 *De cons.* 2.5.16; *NPNF* 6:109. Augustine goes on in 2.5.17 to provide a complete harmonization of the material in Mt 1–2 and Lk 1–2. Other examples of Augustine's use of this principle can be found in 2.17.34, 2.19.43, 2.29.46, and throughout Book Three.

86 *De cons.* 2.32.77; *NPNF* 6:139.

87 *De cons.* 2.19.43–47. Interestingly, Augustine sees a "space" in Mark's text for this sermon at Mk 1:39, as did Huck but not Griesbach.

88 *De cons.* 2.50.105.

89 *De cons.* 2.67.129.

90 *De cons.* 2.79.154; Matthew, John, and Mark describe one occasion involving a Pharisee named Simon, Luke describes another occasion, also involving someone named Simon, but it was the same Mary both times.

91 *De cons.* 3.24.67.

92 *De cons.* 2.31.78; *NPNF* 6:139. Latin: *non quidem ipso ordine, sed quis eorum recordationis suae, quis rerum ipsarum hic ordinem teneat, non apparet.*

93 *De cons.* 3.13.46–47; *NPNF* 6:201.

94 *De cons.* 2.21.52; *NPNF* 6:127f.

95 *De cons.* 2.21.51; *NPNF* 6:127.

96 *De cons.* 2.21.52; *NPNF* 6:6:127.

97 *De cons.* 3.14.48; *NPNF* 6:202.

98 *De cons.* 2.14.31; *NPNF* 6:120. Latin: *quamquam in antiquioribus codicibus Graecis non inveniri.* However, in this case, Augustine does not go on to reject the apparently secondary reading but says, "If it can be established by any copies worthy of credit (that this version is original), what results but that we suppose *both* voices to have been heard from heaven, in one or the other verbal order?"

99 Mt 21:1–9.

100 Mk 11:1–10; Lk 19:28–38.

101 *De cons.* 2.66.128; *NPNF* 6:160.

102 *De cons.* 2.12.28; *NPNF* 6:118.

103 Ibid.

104 *De cons.* 2.20.50; *NPNF* 6:127.

105 Ibid.; Latin: *etiam sancti evangelistae altitudo mysticae locutionis.*

106 Latin: *quod ad doctrinam fidelem maxime pertinet.*

107 Latin: *intellegeremus non tam verborum quam rerum quaerendam vel amplectendam esse veritatem.*

108 *De cons.* 2.12.28; *NPNF* 6:118. Latin: *quando eos qui non eadem locutione utuntur, cum rebus sententiisque non discrepant, in eadem veritate constitisse adprobamus.*

109 *De cons.* 2.12.28; *NPNF* 6:118.

110 Latin: *ut enim quisque meminerat et ut cuique cordi erat . . .*

111 *De cons.* 2.12.27; *NPNF* 6:117f.

112 Latin: *res quae discenda est.*

113 *De cons.* 2.66.128; *NPNF* 6:160. Latin: *si eam sine his (sermonibus) nosse possemus, sicut illam nouit deus et in ipso angeli eius.*

114 Latin: *quisquis autem putat non putuisse dominum in uno sermone quaedam figurate, quaedam proprie ponere eloquia, cetera eius inspiciat: videbit. quam hoc temere adquae inerudite arbitretur.*

115 *De cons.* 2.32.76; *NPNF* 6:139.

116 *De cons.* 2.14.31.

117 *De cons.* 2.14.31; *NPNF* 6:119.

118 Latin: *quid horum potius Christo dictum sit.*

119 Latin: *sive alia verba quae nullus evangelistarum commemoravit.*

120 *De cons.* 2.24.55; *NPNF* 6:129 (italics added). Latin of the final question: *quid ad rem interest?*

121 Mt 27:9–11.

122 Zech 11:11–12; cf. Jer 32:6–13.

123 *De cons.* 3.7.29; *NPNF* 6:191. Augustine goes on to reject this easy way out, in the process giving a superb statement of the text-critical principle of following the *lectio difficilior:* "Let others adopt this method of defence if they are so minded. For my part, I am not satisfied with it, and the reason is a majority of codices contain the (specific) name of Jeremiah, (including) the more ancient Greek exemplars. I look also to this further consideration, namely, that there was no reason why this name should have been added and a corruption thus created; whereas there was certainly an intelligible reason for erasing the (wrong) name from . . . the codices."

124 *De cons.* 3.7.30; *NPNF* 6:191. Latin: *auctoritatem spiritus sancti a quo mentem suam regi plus nobis ille utique sentiebat, ita hoc scriptum relinqueret, sicut eum admonendo constituerat ei dominus.*

125 *De cons.* 2.12.28; *NPNF* 6:118.

126 *De cons.* 2.12.28 (my translation). Latin: *cum enim fas non sit evangelistarum aliquem mentitem fuisse vel existimare vel dicere, sic apparebit nec eum fuisse mentitum cui recordanti tale aliquid acciderit, quale illis accidisse monstratur.* This argument grows directly out of Augustine's concept of the incarnation of the Word of God.

127 *De cons.* 2.66.128; *NPNF* 6:160.

128 *De cons.* 2.46.97 (my translation; cf. *NPNF* 6:149). Latin: *ex qua universa varietate verborum, rerum autem sententiarumque concordia satis apparet salubriter nos doceri nihil quaerendum in verbis nisi loquentium voluntatem . . . cum de homine vel de angelo vel de deo.*

129 See below, pp. 303f.

130 TeSelle, op. cit. n.4, 202f., gives this quote from the *Confessions* about the soul's final vision of God:

> In your Gift (grace) we rest . . . Love bears us there, and your good Spirit delivers us, lowly though we are, from the doors of death . . . By your Gift we are kindled and borne aloft; burning with your fire, onward we go toward the peace of Jerusalem. (*Conf.* 13.9.10)

For Augustine, "the terminus of this pilgrimage of the spirit," says TeSelle, "is the unceasing vision of God" (203).

NOTES TO CHAPTER 11

1 Robert Anchor, *The Enlightenment Tradition* (Berkeley: University of California Press 1967) 3.

2 Louis Dupré, *Passage to Modernity: An Essay in the Hermeneutics of Nature and Culture* (New Haven: Yale University Press 1993) 1–12.

3 Klaus Scholder, *The Birth of Modern Critical Theology: Origins and Problems of Biblical Criticism in the Seventeenth Century* (London: SCM Press and Philadelphia: Trinity Press International 1990) 143.

4 I am thinking of such naive (i.e., unself-consciously ideological) histories as Werner Georg Kümmel, *The New Testament: The History of the Investigation of Its Problems,* trans. S. McLean Gilmour and Howard C. Kee (Nashville: Abingdon Press 1972), or, more recently, William Baird, *History of New Testament Research,* Vol. 1: *From Deism to Tübingen* (Minneapolis: Fortress Press 1992). Baird also wrote "New Testament Criticism," *ABD* 1:730–736; and cf. J. C. O'Neill, "Biblical Criticism—Criticism in the Modern Era," *ABD* 1:728f. The same naive presentation can be found in articles on "historical criticism" in recently published Bible commentaries such as John S. and Alexa Suelzer Kselman, "Modern New Testament Criticism," *NJBC* 1130–1145; cf. Robert Wilken, "The Bible and Its Interpreters: Christian Biblical Interpretation—the Modern Period," *HBC* 63f. Two of the most important voices to sound a warning recently have been Hans Frei, *The Eclipse of Biblical Narrative: A Study in Eighteenth and Nineteenth Century Hermeneutics* (New Haven: Yale University Press 1974), and Ben Meyer, *The Aims of Jesus*

(London: SCM Press 1979). This chapter is dedicated to Meyer's memory (†December 28, 1996).

5 Albert Schweitzer, *The Quest of the Historical Jesus: A Critical Study of Its Progress from Reimarus to Wrede,* trans. W. Montgomery (New York: Macmillan 1968) 4.

6 Dupré, op. cit. n.2, 3.

7 Ibid. 66.

8 Ibid. 58.

9 Quoted from ibid. 105. Ibid. 68 says that the "homogenization of the cosmos by universal mathematical laws was Galileo's most revolutionary achievement."

10 Ibid. 78; cf. 67, 76.

11 Scholder, op. cit. n.3, 65.

12 Dupré, op. cit. n.2, 118; cf. George Heffernan, *René Descartes, Meditationes de prima philosophia/Meditations on First Philosophy* (Notre Dame: University of Notre Dame Press 1990) IV. 1: "I have a . . . distinct idea of the human mind . . . as a cogitating thing . . ." (*habeo ideam mentis humanae, quatenus est res cogitans*) (151).

13 Dupré, op. cit. n.2, 69.

14 Ibid. 75.

15 Ibid. 71.

16 Ibid. 151f.

17 Ibid. 145f.

18 Ibid. 147.

19 Ibid. 120f.

20 Ibid. 121f.

21 Ibid. 123.

22 Ibid. 97.

23 Ibid. 97 (italics added).

24 Ibid. 124.

25 Ibid. 125.

26 Ibid. 125; cf. 168.

27 Sophocles, *Antigone* 332–374.

28 For an excellent discussion of this whole topic, see Richard H. Popkin, *The History of Skepticism from Erasmus to Spinoza* (Berkeley: University of California Press 1979), and, further, Richard H. Popkin and Charles B. Schmitt, eds., *Skepticism from the Renaissance to the Enlightenment,* Wolfenbütteler Forschungen No. 35 (Wiesbaden: Otto Harrassowitz 1987).

29 Popkin, ibid. 3.

30 Ibid. 2.

31 Ibid. 4. Scholder, op. cit. n.3, 9–25, gives an excellent discussion of the attempts by two Roman Catholics to challenge Luther's *criterion.*

32 Scholder, ibid. 10.

33 George Heffernan, *René Descartes, Discours de la méthode/Discourse on the Method* (Notre Dame: University of Notre Dame Press 1994) II.7, 35.

34 For John Locke's withering critique of this principle in favor of pure religious individualism, see below, pp. 272f.; 280.

35 Scholder, op. cit. n.3, 112.

36 Dupré, op. cit. n.2, 81, notes that this solution to absolute skepticism had already been propounded by the fourteenth-century French nominalist Nicholas d'Autrecourt, who said: "Nothing is known with certitude except knowledge itself."

37 Ibid. 116f.

38 Ibid. 86–87.

39 Ibid. 83.

40 Ibid. 84.

41 Ibid. 76: "The universal homogeneity of nature presupposes a common measure that, according to Galileo and Descartes, consisted in a common quantifiability . . . Reliable cognition of Nature becomes limited to the quantifiable."

42 Ibid. 38–40.

43 Ibid. 88.

44 Ibid. 88.

45 Ibid. 89.

46 Ibid. 118.

47 Ibid. 131: "Freedom of the will is what Descartes considers the most godlike thing of being human."

48 Ibid. 89.

49 Ibid. 89. Cf. *Discourse* V.5, 9, Heffernan 69, 79. "Since Descartes believed that animals were comparable not to human beings but to machines . . . he engaged in experimentation with, and dissection of, *live* animals" (Heffernan 139; emphasis in original).

50 Dupré, ibid. 131.

51 Ibid. 118: "This disconcerting emptiness of the foundational self announces its primarily functional future in modern thought . . . The modern self possesses little content of its own. This poverty contrasts with Augustine's conception of the soul which to him was the richest of all concepts." For references to Nietzsche's and Kierkegaard's reactions, see ibid. 119.

52 Ibid. 132.

53 Cf. Cicero, *On the Commonwealth* 1.25: "The commonwealth, then, is the people's affair (*res publica*) and the people is not just any group of men associated in any manner, but is the coming together of a considerable number of men who are united by a common agreement about law and rights and by the desire to participate in mutual advantages. The original cause of this coming

together is not so much weakness as a kind of social instinct natural to man. For the human kind is not solitary ... (but) impelled by nature to live in social groups" (trans. G. H. Sabine and S. B. Smith, Bobbs-Merill Publ. Indianapolis 1976).

54 Dupré, op. cit. n.2, 139–140.

55 *Leviathan* 1.6; quoted in Dupré 120.

56 Dupré 133f.

57 This simple generalization does not do justice to the complexity of Hobbes' discussion of civil law and "natural law" (which he at times equates with "divine" law). Nor does it take into account the situations Hobbes discusses when "natural right" required citizens to disobey the sovereign; see *Leviathan* 2.20.

58 Anchor, op. cit. n.1, 28–33.

59 Ibid. 30.

60 Ibid. 70.

61 Raymond Klibansky and J. W. Gough, trans. and ed., *John Locke, Epistula de Tolerantia: A Letter on Toleration* (Oxford: Clarendon Press 1968) 67.

62 The wording of this quotation is taken from the more pointed seventeenth-century translation by William Popple, ed. Patrick Romanell, *John Locke: A Letter concerning Toleration* (Indianapolis: Bobbs-Merrill 1955) 22; cf. Klibansky and Gough, ibid. 77.

63 Anchor, op. cit. n.1, 75.

64 Ibid. 9.

65 The brief sketch given in this section is based on Geoffrey Barraclough, *An Introduction to Contemporary History* (London: Penguin Books 1967) 43–64.

66 Ibid. 50.

67 Ibid. 52.

68 Ibid. 52f.

69 Ibid. 54.

70 Anchor, op. cit. n.1, 9f.

71 Ibid. 19f. Anchor devotes a long section to Rousseau's critique of "modern" society, 84–100.

72 By far the best account of the shock to Europe's optimistic self-esteem is Paul Fussell, *The Great War and Modern Memory* (New York: Oxford University Press 1975). The powerful aftershocks of that cataclysm continued long afterward; witness the premier performance of Benjamin Britten's *War Requiem*, expressing rage and grief at the horrible destruction caused by World War I, at the dedication ceremonies for the partially rebuilt Coventry Cathedral, *in 1962.*

73 Albert Schweitzer, *The Decay and Restoration of Civilization*, trans. C. T. Campion, 2nd Engl. ed. (London: A & C Black) 1, 3.

74 Fussell, op. cit. n.72, 7–35.

75 For an early (1957) high-level warning of the utter futility of using nuclear weapons for any political purposes, see George F. Kennan, *The Nuclear Delusion* (New York: Pantheon Books 1976) 6f. "A Sterile and Hopeless Weapon." For the classic 1980s description of "nuclear winter" and planetary destruction likely to result from a massive nuclear exchange between the U.S. and Russia, see Jonathan Schell, *The Fate of the Earth* (New York: Avon 1982).

76 Dupré, op. cit. n.2, 90.

NOTES TO CHAPTER 12

1 I first encountered a clear explanation of these two fundamentally different styles of biblical interpretation in Ben Meyer, "A Tricky Business: Ascribing New Meaning to Old Texts," in *Gregorianum* 71 (1990) 743–760.

2 Cf. Edgar Krentz, *The Historical-Critical Method,* Guides to Biblical Study (Philadelphia: Fortress Press 1975) 17.

NOTES TO CHAPTER 13

1 Luther's suggestion that these writings be placed in a deuterocanonical category was not based solely on his theological preferences. He knew of their "disputed" status in Eusebius' *Ecclesiastical History* (see above, p. 105).

2 For the text, see *Luther's Works,* ed. Jaroslav Pelikan, vol. 21, *The Sermon on the Mount* (St. Louis: Concordia 1956).

3 Ibid. 70.

4 Ibid. 72; cf. 66, 91, 99, 102f.

5 Ibid. 105. The discussion extends to p. 113.

6 Ibid. 106.

7 M. H. Bertram, trans., *Sermons on the Gospel of St. John Chapters 1–4,* Luther's Works, ed. Jaroslav Pelikan, vol. 22 (Saint Louis: Concordia 1957) 160 (italics added).

8 Ibid. 182.

9 Ibid. 218.

10 Loc. cit.

11 Loc. cit. (italics added).

12 Ibid. 218f. (italics added).

13 Thomas H. L. Parker, *Calvin's New Testament Commentaries* (Grand Rapids: Eerdmans 1971) 69.

14 Ibid. 70.

15 For Calvin's theological argument for the freedom of God with respect to the canon of the Bible, see Parker, op. cit. n.13, 71f.

16 John Calvin, *A Harmony of the Gospels Matthew, Mark, and Luke,* trans. A. W. Morrison, *Calvin's Commentaries,* ed. David W. Torrance and Thomas F. Torrance, 3 vols. (Grand Rapids: Eerdmans 1972).

17 Ibid. 1:xiiif.

18 Ibid. 1:xiv.

19 Ibid. 1:xiif.

20 Ibid.

21 Ibid. 1:xiii.

22 Ibid. 64; cf. 66.

23 Ibid. 67.

NOTES TO CHAPTER 14

1 For a brief survey of New Testament text criticism during the late Middle Ages and early Renaissance, see Jerry H. Bentley, *Humanists and Holy Writ: New Testament Scholarship in the Renaissance* (Princeton: Princeton University Press 1983) 4–31.

2 Bruce Metzger, *The Text of the New Testament: Its Transmission, Corruption, and Restoration* (New York and London: Oxford University Press 1964) 95.

3 Ibid.

4 Ibid. 96.

5 See the map of Europe with major universities and their dates of founding in D. Matthew, *Atlas of Medieval Europe* (New York: Facts on File 1983) 165. For a list of chairs of oriental languages founded in universities in the fourteenth and fifteenth centuries, see Bentley, op. cit. n.1, 15. But already in the late thirteenth century, Roger Bacon had insisted that biblical scholars should learn Hebrew and Greek, work with accurate texts of Scripture, and base their theological pronouncements on the Greek and Hebrew, not the Latin texts of the Bible; cf. Bentley 15.

6 Valla prepared a careful annotation of Jerome's Vulgate in light of the Greek New Testament, although the Greek manuscripts he used have never been identified; cf. Bentley's discussion of Valla's contribution to New Testament textual criticism in ibid. 32–69.

7 Metzger, op. cit. n.2, 96. For an excellent history of the production of the *Complutensian Polyglot,* see Bentley, op. cit. n.1, 70–111.

8 Bentley 73.

9 Ibid.

10 For a photograph of a page of the New Testament text (Rom 1:27–2:15), see Metzger plate xvi. The use of quotations around the word "original" indicates

the fact that no one has been able to fully identify the origins of the texts used in this edition; so Metzger 97f. Bentley mentions five or six possible manuscripts, but none are known to modern scholars and there are no manuscripts on display in the library of the College of San Ildefonso (University of Madrid) where the Hebrew, LXX, and Vulgate manuscripts used in creating the Old Testament volumes are still preserved; cf. Bentley 93.

11 Bentley 91f.

12 Ibid. 71.

13 The process by which the Greek New Testament was constructed is still shrouded in obscurity. But this much is apparent: the Greek text (whatever it was) was usually conformed to the Vulgate translation, but not always; cf. ibid. 102f. Sometimes it is unclear whether any principles of selection were followed (107). A recently discovered set of notes, apparently prepared by the scholars responsible for the New Testament, for the first time throws some light on their methods (98f.).

14 Kurt Aland and Barbara Aland, *The Text of the New Testament: An Introduction to the Critical Editions and to the Theory and Practice of Modern Textual Criticism,* trans. E. F. Rhodes (Grand Rapids: Eerdmans 1987) 4. The name requires some explanation. The project was controlled from the new University in Alcalà, Spain. Its Latin name was Complutem. Then, since there were a number of languages involved, it was given the jaw-breaking title *Complutensian Polyglot* (the term "polyglot" comes from the Greek word *poly* meaning "many" and *glottos* meaning "language or tongue").

15 Metzger, op. cit. n.2, 98.

16 Bentley, op. cit. n.1, 35.

17 Ibid. 115.

18 Ibid. 116–117, 119.

19 Ibid. 117f.

20 Literally: "I will give you an amount (equal to) whatsoever another might promise." Cf. Metzger, op. cit. n.2, 98f.

21 Ibid. 99. For photocopies of a manuscript with Erasmus' corrections, now on permanent display in the University Library, Basel, see Aland and Aland, op. cit. n.14, 5 (showing Mt 16); cf. Metzger, plate 15 (showing Lk 6).

22 Bentley, op. cit. n.1, 120.

23 Metzger 99; Aland and Aland 4.

24 Latin: *praecipitatum verius quam editum;* for this translation, see Aland and Aland 4; cf. Metzger 99; Bentley 122.

25 Aland and Aland 4 n.2; cf. Metzger 99.

26 Aland and Aland 4. For the best recent assessment of Erasmus' detailed work with texts of the Greek New Testament, see Bentley, op. cit. n.1, 115–161. Bentley goes a long way toward righting the usually jaundiced view of Erasmus to be found in handbooks on the history of text criticism.

27 Metzger 103.

28 Ibid. 100 n2.

29 Bentley 191.

30 For a history of this reaction, see Bentley 194–213.

31 Earlier editions (1546 and 1549) were closer to the *Complutensian Polyglot,* but for the 1550 edition Estienne returned to the text of Erasmus; cf. Metzger 104.

32 Estienne drew alternative readings from the *Complutensian Polyglot* as well as fourteen Greek codices; cf. Metzger 104.

33 Here again there are signs of haste: numerous verse divisions make no sense. Metzger mentions the rumor that Estienne did it while traveling from Paris to Lyons on horseback, and that the horse's motions caused his pen to jump around on the page (104).

34 Metzger 105.

35 Metzger 106.

36 Ibid.

37 Ibid. (italics added).

NOTES TO CHAPTER 15

1 Leon Vaganay, *An Introduction to New Testament Textual Criticism,* rev. ed., ed. Christian-Bernard Amphoux, trans. J. Heimerdinger (Cambridge: University Press 1986) 131 (italics added).

2 Bruce Metzger, *The Text of the New Testament: Its Transmission, Corruption, and Restoration* (New York and London: Oxford University Press 1964) 106.

3 Ibid. 107.

4 For the date of the original Elzevir edition, see above, p. 190.

5 Metzger 107.

6 Ibid. For a history of the Gothic versions, see Bruce M. Metzger, *The Early Versions of the New Testament: Their Origin, Transmission and Limitations* (Oxford: Clarendon Press 1977) 375–393.

7 Metzger, *Text* 107 n.1.

8 Ibid. 108; Vaganay, op. cit. n.1, 138.

9 Metzger, loc. cit.

10 Ibid. 109.

11 Vaganay 138f.

12 Metzger, *Text* 109f.; cf. Vaganay 139.

13 Vaganay 139.

14 Metzger, *Text* 112; cf. Vaganay 140.

15 Metzger, loc. cit.

16 Ibid.

17 Ibid.

18 For an explanation of these marks, see ibid. 113.

19 Ibid.

20 Ibid. 114; Vaganay 140f.

21 Metzger, loc. cit. There is a team of German scholars currently working to bring out a "New Wettstein."

22 Vaganay 141.

23 Metzger, *Text* 115.

NOTES TO CHAPTER 16

1 The analysis of Spinoza in this chapter departs from traditional Spinoza scholarship in a number of ways, principally by refusing to follow the usual custom of discussing his thought mainly in terms of the intellectual content of his *Ethics.* Oddly enough, even historians of philosophy or biblical scholars who do pay attention to his *Theological-Political Treatise* seem unwilling or unable to examine its political agenda; see Leo Strauss, *Die Religionskritik Spinoza als Grundlage seiner Bibelwissenschaft* (Berlin 1930), translated as *Spinoza's Critique of Religion,* trans. E. M. Sinclair (New York: Schocken Books, 1965); Sylvain Zac, *Spinoza et l'interpretation de l'écriture* (Paris 1965); André Malet, *Le Traité théologique-politique de Spinoza et la pensée biblique,* Publications de l'université de Dijon 35 (Paris: Sociéte les belles lettres 1966); Martin Greschat, "Bibelkritik und Politik: Anmerkungen zu Spinozas Theologisch-Politischem Traktat," in *Text-Wort-Glaube: Festschrift für Kurt Aland* (Berlin 1980) 324–343. There are also distinct "Spinoza orthodoxies" flourishing in the many European and American Spinoza societies and clubs. After working on this chapter for some twenty years, I discovered the holistic approach of the Israeli scholar Yirmiyahu Yovel and his superb *Spinoza and Other Heretics,* 2 vols. (Princeton: Princeton University Press 1989). Yovel is one of the rare interpreters who is fully aware of the fundamental *irony* within Spinoza's biblical hermeneutics. He has given it—in my judgment—its correct *Sitz im Leben* in Bento D'Espiñosa's identity as a Portuguese Marrano refugee. I wish to express my appreciation for the helpful critique of this chapter by my friend and colleague Sam Preus, Department of Religion, Indiana University, *emeritus.*

2 See Yovel, ibid. 2:3.

3 Albert Schweitzer, *The Quest of the Historical Jesus: A Critical Study of Its Progress from Reimarus to Wrede,* trans. W. Montgomery (New York: Macmillan 1968) 4.

4 Cf. Yovel 2:3: "(Spinoza's) biblical hermeneutics is not only an independent science; it is also—and primarily—a weapon in combating historical religion and a vehicle in constructing a purified substitute for it."

5 In 1654, the Dutch governor of New Amsterdam, Peter Stuyvesant, tried to forbid Jewish colonists from joining his community. Protests from the Jewish shareholders forced him to change his policy; see Lewis S. Feuer, *Spinoza and the Rise of Liberalism* (Boston: Beacon Press 1958) 27. For a description of the various commercial activities of the Jewish colony in Amsterdam at the time of Spinoza, see especially 2–4.

6 For a description of Michael D'Espiñosa's commercial activities, see Feuer 17.

7 Henry E. Allison, *Benedict de Spinoza: An Introduction* (New Haven: Yale University Press 1987) 5; for a fuller account, see Feuer 2f.

8 Feuer 12.

9 Ibid. 13f.

10 Ibid. 7.

11 Ibid. 17.

12 It was here that he met the Marrano theologian and biblical scholar Isaac La Peyrère, whose book *Men before Adam* contained a number of ideas Spinoza was to use later in his *Theological-Political Treatise;* see Brad S. Gregory, ed., *Baruch Spinoza: Tractatus Theologico-Politicus,* trans. Samuel Shirley (Leiden: E. J. Brill 1989) 33f. It was also here that he probably met the Quaker freethinker Samuel Fisher (Gregory 35f.; see further below, p. 216). Because of rising opposition to his ideas, Van den Enden had to leave Amsterdam. He closed his school and went to France, where he tried to found a utopian community in which all men would be equal; Allison op. cit. n.7, 6; cf. Feuer, op. cit. n.5, 18–21. For a discussion of the Dutch reception of Descartes and critique of his thought in the direction of a materialist pan-psychism, later taken up in modified form by Spinoza, see Feuer, op. cit. n.5, 230–233.

13 Allison 7.

14 The Latin equivalent of Baruch, which means "blessed."

15 Allison 9; Feuer 45.

16 Allison 9.

17 See ibid. 11f. for a brief summary.

18 Cf. *Short Treatise* Part One 2.[12], Edwin Curley, ed. and trans., *The Collected Works of Spinoza* (Princeton: Princeton University Press 1985) 1:68; for the Latin critical edition, see Carl Gebhardt, *Spinoza Opera,* 4 vols. (Heidelberg: Carl Winter 1925) 1/22/9–12 (all references to Gebhardt's edition will be in this format: volume number/page number/line numbers); Part Two 22.[5] (Curley 1:139; Gebhardt 1/101/20f.). In April 1662, Spinoza wrote a lengthy letter to his friend Henry Oldenburg commenting on some experiments of the English scientist Robert Boyle (1627–1691). He concluded by mentioning two short works he recently completed—the *Treatise on the Emendation of the Intellect* and the *Short Treatise*—adding that all of the theologians and philosophers he had read confused attributes of God with "creatures," i.e., creations of God. As for me, he says, "I do not separate God

from nature, as everyone known to me has done." (Letter 6, IV/36/23f. Curley 1:188); cf. Feuer, op. cit. n.5, 55.

19 *Emendation* [76]: "But as for the knowledge of the origin of Nature . . . (we must not confuse it) with abstractions . . . for the origin of Nature can neither be conceived abstractly nor universally . . . for it is a unique and infinite being, beyond which there is no being" (Curley 1:34; Gebhardt 2/29/5–17).

20 Cf. *Emendation of the Intellect* [13]: "The true good consists in the knowledge of the union that the mind has with the whole of nature" (Curley 1:11; Gebhardt 2/8/26f.); cf. [10], [13], [40], [42], [99]; also *Short Treatise*, Part Two 22.[2] (Curley 1:139; Gebhardt 1/100/16–22).

21 "God" was primarily to be known through scientific study of material phenomena (with which "God" is identical). This thought must be kept in mind while reading everything Spinoza has to say about the Bible. Cf. *Short Treatise*, Part 2 24.[10] (Curley 1:144; Gebhardt 1/106/9–20): "To make himself known to man God neither can, nor needs, to use words, miracles, or any other created thing, but only himself" (*ST* 25.13; Curley 1:145; Gebhardt 1/107/14f.). For a good introduction to the very complex subject of Spinoza's concept of God, see Allison, op. cit. n.7, 44–83.

22 Cf. *Emendation of the Intellect* [12], [99]: "Everything that happens happens according to the eternal order and according to certain laws of Nature" (Curley 1:10; Gebhardt 2/8/15–18). Cf. *Emendation* [99]: "To unite and order all our perceptions, it is required and reason demands that we . . . deduce all our ideas from physical things . . . proceeding according to the series of causes from one real (physical) being to another" (Curley 1:41; Gebhardt 2/36/7–17). Cf. *Short Treatise*, Part One 3.[2].5 (Curley 1:80f.; Gebhardt 1/36/1–5); 6.[7] (Curley 1:87; Gebhardt 1/43/6–8); Part Two 24.[4]: "God's laws are not of such a nature that they could ever be transgressed. For the rules that God has established in Nature, according to which all things come to be and endure . . . are such that they can never be transgressed" (Curley 1:142; Gebhardt 1/104/20–29). Nor is there such a thing as Divine Providence; cf. *Short Treatise* ch. 5: "God's 'Providence' is nothing but that striving we find in the whole of nature and in particular things to maintain and preserve their being" (Curley 1:84; Gebhardt 1/40/3–6).

23 Cf. *Short Treatise*, Part One 6.[7]: "All things and actions which are in Nature are perfect" (Curley 1:87; Gebhardt 1/43/34); cf. 7.[8]: "They (traditional philosophers and theologians) call (God) the greatest good. But if they understand anything other than . . . that God is immutable and a cause of all things, then they are confused" (Curley 1:89; Gebhardt 1/44/29–31).

24 Cf. *Short Treatise*, Part One 10.[3]: "All things which exist in Nature are either things or actions. Now good and evil are neither things nor actions. Therefore, good and evil do not exist in Nature" (Curley 1:93; Gebhardt 1/49/30–32).

25 *Short Treatise,* Part Two 25.[1] (Curley 1:145; Gebhardt 1/107/20f.).

26 According to *Short Treatise,* Preface to Part Two, 12, if the soul has no knowledge of eternal nature, it will die when the body dies. But if it has become
one with eternal nature, it will be eternal (15): "(Since the soul) is a mode in
the thinking substance (called nature), it has been able to know and love this
[substance] . . . and uniting itself with (it) has been able to make itself eternal"
(Curley 1:96; Gebhardt 1/53/38–41). Cf. Part Two 19: "Of our blessedness";
also 23: "Of the immortality of the soul": "if it is united with the body only
and the body perishes, then it must also perish" (Curley 1:141; Gebhardt
1/103/9f.). Cf. Allison, op. cit. n.7, 10.

27 Cf. *Emendation of the Intellect* [14]: "This then is the end I aim at: to acquire
such a nature (knowing the highest good) and to strive that many acquire it
with me. That is, it is part of my happiness to take pains that many others
may understand as I understand, so that their intellect and desire agree entirely with my intellect and desire. To do this it is necessary first to understand as much of Nature as suffices for acquiring such a nature, next to form
a society of the kind that is desirable so that as many as possible may attain
it as easily and surely as possible" (Curley 1:11; Gebhardt 2/8/28–2/9/3).

28 For an explanation of the love of the Enlightenment for geometry, see Ernst
Cassirer, *The Philosophy of the Enlightenment,* trans. F. C. A. Koelln and
J. P. Pettegrove (Princeton: Princeton University Press 1951) 19. Cassirer
quotes Fontanelle as saying in the preface to his *On the Usefulness of Mathematics and Physics,* "The geometric spirit is not so exclusively bound to geometry that it could not be separated from it and applied to other fields.
A work on ethics, politics, criticism, or even eloquence, . . . (would be) much
more beautiful and perfect if it is written in the geometric spirit." Cf. Allison,
op. cit. n.7, 38–43. Allison suggests that Spinoza was influenced to use this
geometrical style of reasoning from both Descartes and Hobbes, 228 n.13.

29 He wrote to a friend at this time, "The authority of Plato, Aristotle and Socrates has not much weight with me. (The orthodox Christian and Jewish
theologians love to) rave with the Greeks (and believe) the speculations of
Platonists and Aristotelians. (But as for me, I prefer the writings of) Epicurus,
Democritus, Lucretius"; quoted in Feuer, op. cit. n.5, 54. Cf. 272 n.47: "Spinoza regarded Plato's theory of ideas and Aristotle's theory of universals as
nonsense." Spinoza was a thoroughgoing nominalist. "For it is precisely the
particular things, and they alone, that have a cause, and not the general, because they are nothing" (*Short Treatise* I/43/6–8 [Curley 1:87]).

30 Cf. Feuer 54: "During this time the ancient materialists were coming into
their own. A *History of Philosophy* published in 1656 by Sir Thomas Stanley
devoted 112 pages to Epicurus, more than any other philosopher received,
and that same year appeared John Evelyn's *Essay on Lucretius.*" Cf. Yovel, op.
cit. n.1, 2:8f. For a discussion of Spinoza's relation to Stoicism, see K. H. E.

De Jong, *Spinoza en de Stoa* (Leiden: E. J. Brill 1939). For a list of common expressions, cf. Martial Gueroult, *Spinoza,* Studien und Materialien zur Geschichte der Philosophie #7–8, 2 vols. (Hildesheim: Georg Olms Verlagsbuchhandlung 1968): "Les notions communes stoïciennes et spinozistes"; Appendice No. 12; 2:581f.

31 Feuer 54.

32 For a summary description of Samuel Fisher's teachings, see Gregory, op. cit. n.12, n.11, 35f.

33 Leo Strauss, "On the Spirit of Hobbes's Political Philosophy," in *Hobbes Studies,* ed. K. C. Brown (Cambridge: Harvard University Press 1965) 10f.

34 Cf. *Tractatus Politicus* 5:7.

35 Cicero, *de re publica* 3.13.23, gives this fragment from the doctrine of Carneades on how states were originally formed. Note the psychological rationale; this is the hallmark of the Sophistic tradition, to reappear again in Enlightenment skepticism in the theories of Hobbes, Locke, Hume, and others. "When there is mutual fear, man fearing man and class fearing class, then, because no one is confident in his own strength, a sort of bargain is made between the common people and the powerful . . . Thus not nature or desire (for human fellowship) but weakness is the mother of (civilized society)" (Loeb).

36 *Leviathan* chs. 6, 11. Hobbes secularized the Christian concept of "original sin" or "fallen nature," calling it "the state of nature" which was "nasty, brutish, and short." He likewise secularized the Christian doctrine of redemption, arguing that what was needed was not divine grace but civil society, i.e., the right kind of government; cf. Strauss, op. cit. n.33, 15.

37 Michael Oakeshott, ed., *Thomas Hobbes' Leviathan or the Matter, Forme, and Power of a Commonwealth Ecclesiasticall and Civil* (Oxford: Basil Blackwell n.d.): "It followeth that there is on earth no such universal Church as all Christians are bound to obey, because there is no power on earth to which all other commonwealths are subject . . . There is no other government in this life, neither of state nor religion but temporal . . . (and) one chief pastor . . . according to the law of nature . . . (namely) the civil sovereign" (39; cf. 42, 43). For a comparison of Hobbes and Spinoza on the state of nature and civil society, see Allison, op. cit. n.7, 178–187.

38 See *Leviathan* chs. 33–43.

39 In fact, there are a few striking verbal correspondences between the *Leviathan* and the *Treatise* that we will point out in due course. For other aspects of Hobbes' influence on Spinoza, see above, n.27. He did not read Hobbes in English. Cf. letter dated 26 May 1666 and sent to Henry Oldenburg from Voorburg; Spinoza says he would be most delighted to read young Boyle's treatise on colors "if I could read English" (Curley 1:394).

40 For evidence of the wide circulation of these ideas in Spinoza's time, see

Feuer, op. cit. n.5, 52–57, "Spinoza's pantheism and the radical thought of the seventeenth century."

41 Allison, op. cit. n.7, 14f.

42 Feuer 76–80. At one point de Witt even worked on a scheme he called "social mathematics" that envisioned all social problems as modeled on the then fashionable style of geometry.

43 Ibid. 73–75.

44 Petrus Johannes Blok, *History of the People of the Netherlands,* trans. O. A. Bierstadt and R. Putnam, 5 vols. (New York: AMS Press 1970) 4:308.

45 Curley, op. cit. n.18, 1:350, mentions a lost letter to Henry Oldenburg in which it is evident that Spinoza has begun work on the *Theological-Political Treatise* at this time.

46 For a description of the battle, see Blok, op. cit. n.44, 4:319.

47 Ibid. 4:335f.

48 Ibid. 4:341–343.

49 Feuer, op. cit. n.5, 108–110.

50 "All this Spinoza knew"; Ibid. 110.

51 Ibid. 136–138; Allison, op. cit. n.7, 16.

52 Allison 19.

53 Ibid. 20f.; Feuer, op. cit. n.5, 145–148.

54 Allison 21.

55 Feuer 139.

56 Feuer 40.

57 Allison 16.

58 Ibid.

59 For a discussion of Spinoza's Marrano heritage, see Yovel, op. cit. n.1, vol. 1 passim.

60 Allison, op. cit. n.7, 22.

61 Cf. n.27 above.

62 "The geometrical model . . . stresses the need for rigor, clarity, and step-by-step consequentiality as necessary conditions of rationality, and it also calls for philosophical detachment in dealing with the most passionate issues" (Yovel, op. cit. n.1, 1:139).

63 Ibid. 2:7. This passage comes from Yovel's helpful discussion of the similarities between Kant and Spinoza. The term "legislates" does not mean "legislate to" but that human reason creates "natural laws" *which accurately reflect* the actual or necessary patterns of nature.

64 Cf. the discussion of the "coldness" of Spinoza's concept of God in ibid. 2:7; 1:164f: "In Spinoza's ontology I am, in both body and mind, the product of an impersonal substance—a God which has no humanlike features and may not be anthropomorphized. In other words, the natural processes that produce me bear no resemblance to my own subjectivity: they do not work by

intention or purpose, have no privileged affinity to human affairs, and allow no room or special laws for history as distinguished from the rest of nature. Recognizing this, I may well become emancipated from religious and metaphysical illusions, but I also lose their soothing comforts." Paul Weinpahl, *The Radical Spinoza* (New York: New York University Press 1979) 51, found a pattern in Spinoza's Latin to refer to "God" by words from all three genders, thus producing a "genderless God."

65 Allison, op. cit. n.7, 36.

66 Ibid. For a discussion of this, the "third kind of knowledge," in Spinoza's thought, see Yovel, op. cit. n.1, 1:153–171.

67 Yovel 1:175.

68 For Spinoza's understanding of "reason," see ibid. 1:154–171.

69 *Emendation of the Intellect* 2:823–27; Curley 1:10f.

70 Cf. the illuminating remarks in Rudolf Otto, *Mysticism East and West,* trans. B. L. Bracey and R. C. Payne (New York: Macmillan 1932) 229f.

71 *Treatise,* chap. 16 n.34; Gregory, op. cit. n.12, 308. Cf. James Collins, *Spinoza on Nature* (Carbondale: Southern Illinois University Press 1984) 229; also Yovel, op. cit. n.1, 1:167f.

72 Collins, loc. cit.

73 Yovel 2:4.

74 *Treatise* 67, 70.

75 *Treatise* 70–73.

76 *Treatise* 125.

77 *Treatise* 73, 86.

78 *Treatise* 3.

79 *Treatise* 104f., 122.

80 *Treatise* 105, 112, 119.

81 *Treatise* chap. 12 passim.

82 *Treatise* 247.

83 *Treatise* 235.

84 *Treatise* chap. 11.

85 For a useful list (which could be greatly expanded) of the traditional categories in the Bible and Spinoza's equivalents, see Yovel, op. cit. n.1, 1:147.

86 Ibid. 2:10f. An early statement of this accommodating approach is in Spinoza's *Treatise on the Emendation of the Intellect* [17]: "(We must) speak according to the power of understanding of ordinary people, and do whatever does not interfere with our attaining our purpose. For we can gain a considerable advantage, if we yield as much to their understanding as we can. In this way, they will give a favorable hearing to the truth" (Curley 1:12). For Hobbes' own accommodationism, see Strauss, op. cit. n.33, 27 n.43.

87 For another list, see Yovel 1:147.

88 *Treatise* 1:59.

89 *Treatise* 125.

90 *Treatise* 89.

91 *Treatise* 103.

92 *Treatise* Note 27.

93 *Treatise* 202.

94 *Treatise* 205.

95 *Treatise* 206.

96 *Treatise* 221.

97 *Treatise* 235. While we are in the neighborhood of the Trinity, a remarkable redefinition of the concept "son of God" is to be found in the *Treatise on God, Man, and His Well-Being*, Part 1, ch. 9 [2], where Spinoza defines the extensions of God (*natura naturata*) and says they include "things (like) a Son, product or effect created immediately by God" (Curley 1:92).

98 *Treatise* 226.

99 See *Leviathan* chaps. 33–43.

100 Yovel op. cit. n.1, italics added.

101 It is critical for an adequate understanding of Spinoza's exegetical method that the essentially nominalist, physical nature of his understanding of "history" be constantly kept in mind; cf. ibid. 1:161–163. This was discussed more fully above (pp. 149–154).

102 Cf. Letter 21 to Blijenbergh, 28 January 1665: "As for me, I have learned no eternal attributes of God from Sacred Scripture, nor could I learn them" (Curley 1:381).

103 Yovel 2:12.

104 Ibid. 2:13.

105 For a superb discussion of Spinoza's interest in the various "inner light" groups, see Feuer, op. cit. n.5, 52–57.

106 In the quotations that follow, I will follow the recent translation by Samuel Shirley, *Baruch Spinoza. Tractactus Theologico-Politicus* (Leiden: Brill 1989). I don't find it much superior to Elwes' translation, but it is based on the critical text of Gebhardt. I will give my own translation in those rare instances where I feel Shirley has especially obscured Spinoza's point and indicate this in the accompanying footnotes. As always in this book, words in ( ) within quotations are my additions to clarify the meaning.

107 *Treatise* 49.

108 The psychological approach to political and legal and religious issues was pioneered by the ancient Greek Sophists. "It is characteristic of the Sophists and their period that in approaching this problem (of the origin and meaning of religion) they begin with the nature of the religious subject instead of following the older philosophers of nature and starting with the reality of the Divine." Werner Jaeger, *The Theology of the Early Greek Philosophers*, trans. E. S. Robinson (Oxford: Clarendon Press 1947) 188. The sweeping grandeur

of the opening lines of Spinoza's Preface and immediate focus on superstition as the crushing problem for all humanity may be a conscious imitation of the beginning of Lucretius, *On the Nature of the Universe:* "When human life lay for all to see groveling on the ground, crushed beneath the weight of superstition . . ." (Lucretius, *de rerum natura* 1:63). For a comparison between Epicurus' treatment of superstition and that of Spinoza, see Strauss, op. cit. n.1, 39–45.

109 Cf. Allison, op. cit. n.7, 33.

110 Cf. ibid. 36f.: "Spinoza provided the clearest statement of his basic standpoint in the critique of final causes that he appended to the first part of the *Ethics:* 'All the prejudices I here undertake to expose depend on this one: that men commonly suppose that all natural things act, as men do, on account of an end' (Part One, Appendix)." Allison continues:

> When combined, as it has been since the Middle Ages, with the Judeo-Christian conception of God, this notion leads to the familiar belief that God created all things for the benefit of man . . . Not only does (Spinoza) reject any appeal to (such final causes) on the grounds that it would constitute an inadequate, unscientific mode of explanation, an attitude he shares with all proponents of the new science, but he treats this conception as an important expression of the theistic, pluralistic world view (of Christianity and Judaism) that stands in the way of achieving the desired (objective) understanding of ourselves and our place in nature (in terms of completely natural causes).

111 *Treatise* 50.

112 Ibid.

113 The full text of this reference reads, "Nothing sways the common herd more effectively than superstition; generally uncontrolled, savage, fickle, when they are the victims of vain superstition, they obey the soothsayers better than they do their leaders" (*History of Alexander* 4:10.7; Loeb). It seems plausible that Spinoza is continuing his comment on the current Dutch emergency.

114 *Treatise* 51.

115 For the classical Sophists' theme of deification of humans as a method of political control, we can do no better than recall the famous fragment in Sextus Empiricus attributed to Critias (fl. 400 B.C.E.), the brilliant and cynical student of Socrates, who is reported to have portrayed the stages of human development as first, life among the beasts, then life in cities torn by conflict, and finally life in cities governed by law. What was different about the third stage, said Critias, was an innovation that caused men to obey the law even when no one was looking. God had been invented.

"There is a Spirit," said the ruler of the city,
"Having deathless life,
Knowing and listening and seeing all things,
Aware of and knowing everything . . .
He will hear every word that is spoken,
And he will watch every act (you) do,
And if in secret you plan some evil deed,
It will by no means escape (his) attention . . .
For (his) understanding is immense."

Saying such words as these, he introduced
his teaching most sweetly;
hiding the truth by his lies . . .
And thus by the fear that he aroused among men . . .
Creating in their hearts the idea of Divinity,
He replaced lawlessness by law.

This is my translation; for the Greek text of this passage, see Hermann Mutschmann, *Sexti Empirici Opera*, 4 vols. (Lipsiae: B.G. Teubner 1914), *Adversus Mathematicos* 9:54 (included in Diels-Krantz, *Die Vorsokratiker* 88.B 25) 2:225–228. For another translation and discussion of the fragment, see H. D. Rankin, *Sophists, Socratics, and Cynics* (Totowa, NJ: Barnes & Noble 1983) 72–74; also G. B. Kerferd, *The Sophists and Their Legacy* (Wiesbaden: Franz Steiner Verlag 1981) 97f., who suggests that this fragment is possibly one of the earliest attempts to provide a psychological theory of the origins of civil law. Jaeger, op. cit. n.110, 186–188, mentions other occurrences in early Greek philosophy of the idea that religion was invented by tyrants to control human behavior.

116 *Treatise* 52. Italics added.

117 *Treatise* 52. Latin: *ita ut facilius ex his, quam illis fides uniuscujusque noscatur* (Gebhardt Pref/8/4f.). Shirley: "so that these latter characteristics make known a man's creed more readily than the former"; cf. Elwes: "that this rather than the virtues they claim is the readiest criterion of their faith." The term *fides* is meant ironically in this passage and should somehow be indicated in the translation.

118 Ibid. Latin: *et quod fides jam nihil aliud fit quam credulitas & praejudicia* (Gebhardt Pref/8/23–24). Cf. Shirley: "and that faith has become identical with credulity and biased dogma" (52). Cf. the following similar passage in Hobbes' *Leviathan* Part 4.47: "After the doctrine . . . of the Kingdom of God spoken of in the Old and New Testaments was received into the world, the ambition and canvassing for the offices that belong thereunto, and . . . the

pomp that obtained to the principal public offices became by degrees so evident that they lost the inward reverence due to the pastoral function . . . (Moreover, the church's) ecclesiastics take from young men the use of reason, by certain charms compounded of metaphysics and miracles and traditions and abused Scripture, so that they are good for nothing else but to do whatever they command them." Quoted from Michael Oakeshott, ed., *Leviathan or the Matter, Forme and Power of a Commonwealth Ecclesiasticall and Civil*, by Thomas Hobbes (Oxford: Basil Blackwell n.d.) 457f.

119 *Treatise* 52f.

120 *Treatise* 53.

121 *Treatise* 53f.

122 *Treatise* 59.

123 Ibid.

124 Ibid.

125 *Treatise* 65, 70, 71.

126 *Treatise* 73.

127 *Treatise* 60.

128 Cf. Yovel, op. cit. n.1, 2:10f.

129 *Treatise* 76–85.

130 *Treatise* 86f.

131 *Treatise* 97.

132 *Treatise* 89.

133 *Treatise* 93.

134 *Treatise* 99.

135 *Treatise* 100.

136 Ibid.

137 *Treatise* 103.

138 Ibid.

139 Ibid. (italics added).

140 Ibid.

141 Ibid. (italics added).

142 Ibid. (italics added). At this point, Spinoza adds, "An enquiry as to what these means are and what are the rules of conduct required for this end . . . belongs to a general treatise on Ethics." He might have added: "which I just happen to have ready to publish."

143 *Treatise* 105.

144 Ibid. (italics added).

145 Ibid. Therefore "God" or Nature is not a lawgiver (106f.). "How it came about that (Moses) imagined God as a ruler, lawgiver, king, merciful, just, and so forth . . . are all merely attributes of human nature and not at all applicable to the divine nature" (107).

146 *Treatise* 111.

147 *Treatise* 112.

148 Ibid.

149 Ibid.

150 *Treatise* 117.

151 *Treatise* 119.

152 Ibid.

153 *Treatise* 120–122.

154 *Treatise* 120.

155 *Treatise* 122.

156 *Treatise* 121.

157 Ibid.

158 *Treatise* 124.

159 Ibid.

160 *Treatise* 125.

161 Ibid.

162 *Treatise* 130.

163 *Treatise* 127.

164 For a description of the concept of the universe of Galileo, Newton, Kepler, and Descartes, see Allison, op. cit. n.7, 24–28.

165 Ibid. 27.

166 Latin: *Raro admodum sit, ut homines rem aliquam, ut gesta est, ita simpliciter narrent, ut nihil sui judicii narrationi immisceant* (Gebhardt 3/91/33–35).

167 *Treatise* 134f. Latin of the last sentence: *Hinc sit, ut homines in suis Chronicis & magis suas opioniones, quam res ipsas actas narrent* (Gebhardt 3/92/ 5–6).

168 For two histories of skepticism from the Middle Ages to the end of the seventeenth century, see Charles B. Schmitt, *Cicero Scepticus: A Study of the Influence of the Academica in the Renaissance*, Archives internationales d'histoire des idées 52 (The Hague: Martinus Nijhoff 1972), and Richard H. Popkin and Charles B. Schmitt, eds., *Scepticism from the Renaissance to the Enlightenment*, Wolfenbütteler Forschungen 35 (Wiesbaden: Otto Harrassowitz 1987).

169 *Treatise* 136.

170 *Treatise* 133.

171 *Treatise* 125.

172 *Treatise* 135f. (italics added). The reference here is to Exod 19:18; Deut 5:19. The Latin of this quotation is *Igitur ad miracula Scriptura interpretandum & ex eorum narrationibus intelligendum, . . . necesse est opiniones eorum scire qui ipsa primi narraverunt . . . (et) distinguere . . . quae revera contingerunt cum rebus imaginariis & quae non nisi repraesentationes Propheticae fuerunt*

. . . In Scriptura enim multa ut realia narrantur & quae etiam realia esse crede-
bantur, quae tamen non nisi repraesentationes resque imaginariae fuerunt; ut
quod Deus e caelo descenderit (et cetera). (Gebhardt 3/92/26–93/3).

173 *Treatise* 134f. Spinoza is already giving hints as to the methodological proce-
dures he will outline in Chapters 7–11. Before he concludes Chapter 6, however, he makes a very significant admission. He emphasizes to the reader that
"in the matter of prophecy (chaps. 1–2) I made no assertion that I could not
infer from grounds revealed in Holy Scripture," whereas "in this chapter I
have drawn my main conclusions solely from basic principles known by the
natural light of reason" (137f.). His justification for doing so is somewhat
forced, but what is important is this frank admission that he simply asserted
his own antisupernatural universe over against the supernatural world of the
Bible as well as the great religious edifices erected upon it by Judaism and
Christianity. It is to Spinoza's credit that, at this one point, he drops his mas-
querade and states clearly that he is critiquing the Bible from a foreign point
of view.

174 *Treatise* 140.

175 Ibid.

176 Ibid.

177 *Treatise* 141.

178 My translation. The Latin is *Nam sicuti methodus interpretandi naturam in*
hoc potissimum consistit, in concinnanda scilicet historia naturae, ex qua, ut-
pote ex certis datis, rerum naturalium definitiones concludimus: sic etiam ad
Scripturam interpretandam necesse est ejus sinceram historiam adornare, & ex
ea tanquam ex certis datis & principiis mentem authorum Scripture legitimis
consequentiis concludere (Gebhardt 3/98/18–24). Shirley translates: "The
method of interpreting Scripture is no different from the method of interpreting Nature . . . For the method of interpreting Nature consists essentially in
composing a detailed study of Nature from which, as being the source of our
assured data, we can deduce the definitions of the things of Nature. Now in
exactly the same way the task of Scriptural interpretation requires us to make
a straightforward study of Scripture, and from this, as the source of our fixed
data and principles, to deduce by logical inference the meaning of the authors
of Scripture" (141). A comparison with Elwes' translation is instructive: "I
may sum up the matter by saying that the method of interpreting Scripture
does not widely differ from the method of interpreting Nature—in fact, it is
almost the same. For as the interpretation of Nature consists in the examination of the history of Nature, and therefrom deducing definitions of natural
phenomena on certain fixed axioms, so also Scriptural interpretation proceeds
by the examination of Scripture, and inferring the intention of its authors as a
legitimate conclusion from its fundamental principles" (99). Both translations
seem to me less than optimal, while the final words of Elwes' sentence, "from

its fundamental principles," is seriously misleading. Spinoza uses this kind of terminology only to refer to philosophical and moral knowledge known by natural reason entirely apart from what historical research can find out regarding the Bible. The fundamental moral and philosophical principles in the Bible are already crystal-clear to reason and are about to be listed (see further below).

179 Loc. cit.

180 *Treatise* 142.

181 This ringing declaration sounds very similar to the Protestant Reformers' motto *sola scriptura* and, even more, *sacra scriptura sui ipsius interpres.* It is meant to. But what Spinoza has in mind is light-years away from what the Reformers had in mind; cf. Martin Greschat, "Bibelkritik und Politik. Anmerkungen zu Spinozas Theologisch-politischem Traktat," in *Text-Wort-Glaube. Studien zur Überlieferung, Interpretation und Autorisierung biblischer Texte,* ed. Martin Brecht, Arbeiten zur Kirchengeschichte 50 (Berlin: de Gruyter 1980) 330.

182 *Treatise* 142.

183 Ibid. 142f. (italics added).

184 *Treatise* 143.

185 *Treatise* 144.

186 Ibid.

187 Ibid.

188 *Treatise* 145.

189 Ibid.

190 Ibid.

191 Ibid.

192 *Treatise* 147.

193 *Treatise* 148.

194 *Treatise* 149.

195 *Treatise* 152.

196 Ibid.

197 *Treatise* 153.

198 *Treatise* 154.

199 *Treatise* 153, 159.

200 *Treatise* 160.

201 Ibid. Latin: *Nam cum maxima authoritas Scripturam interpretandi apud unumquemque sit, interpretandi ergo norma nihil debet esse praeter lumen naturale omnibus commune, non ullum supra naturam lumen, neque ulla externa authoritas; non etiam debet esse adeo difficilis, ut non nisi ab acutissimis Philosophis dirigi possit, sed naturali & communi hominum ingenio & capacitati accommodata, ut nostram esse ostendimus* (Gebhardt 3/117/15–22).

202 See his discussion of the place of religion within the state, below, pp. 250ff.

203 *Treatise* 161–167.

204 *Treatise* 167–169.

205 *Treatise* 170.

206 *Treatise* 179–185.

207 *Treatise* 195.

208 Lists like this occur in Curley 1:120, 123, 145, 211, 212, and (the most extensive) 224f.

209 Yovel, op. cit. n.1, 2:5 describes the process thus: "When the mind vacillates back and forth in a state of doubt and confusion, (this) can help *destroy entrenched beliefs* and clear the way for philosophy." There is an excellent illustration of how Spinoza himself uses his barrage of historical questions in Chapter 15. The context is a discussion of views held by famous Jewish authorities, which Spinoza finds deficient in one way or another. Spinoza is discussing one of the most famous Jewish scholastic theologians, a well-known opponent of Maimonides, and quotes the scholar as saying, "We must accept as true or reject as false everything that Scripture affirms or denies, and secondly, ... Scripture never expressly affirms or denies anything that contradicts what it elsewhere affirms or denies." Disgusted with this widely used maxim (not just among Jews but also among Protestants), Spinoza turns the fire hose of "historical method" on him: "The rashness of both these assertions will be apparent to all. I pass by his failure to perceive that Scripture consists of different books written at different times for different men by different authors ... (Nor does he say anything about) the nature of language nor does he consider the context of (scriptural passages), nor (does he discuss the problem whether) Scripture has come down to us uncorrupted (etc.)" (*Treatise* 230). The effect of this "swarm of objections" is obvious (and behind them, there are more). The entrenched idealist/scholastic principle is being eaten away by the sand-blasting hose of thousands of tiny, historical (nominalist) questions until it is nothing.

210 *Treatise* 197.

211 *Treatise* 199. At this point, Spinoza is following the argument of Hugo Grotius, who made the same case regarding the Gospel of Luke as not having been written in the Old Testament prophetic style; see Dean Freiday, ed., *The Bible: Its Criticism, Interpretation, and Use in 16th and 17th Century England*, Catholic and Quaker Studies 4 (Pittsburgh: 1979) 108.

212 *Treatise* 199.

213 Ibid.

214 *Treatise* 202 (italics added). The Latin of this important passage is *Deinde quamvis religio, prout ab Apostolis praedicabatur, nempe simplicem Christi historiam narrando, sub rationem non cadat, ejus tamen summam, quae potissimum documentis moralibus constat, ut tota Christi doctrina, potest unusquisque lumine naturali facile assequi.* Spinoza has a footnote (n.27) to this

passage: "the whole of Christ's doctrine" means the Sermon on the Mount, Mt 5.

215 See the discussion of Spinoza's basic points above, pp. 212ff., especially "through the proper use of intellect . . . to become aware of one's place in the infinite and necessary scheme of things" (Allison, op. cit. n.7, 36).

216 *Treatise* 203 (italics added).

217 *Treatise* 205. Latin: *Dei verbum mendosum, truncatum, adulteratum, & sibi non constans statuerim, nosque ejus non nisi fragmenta habere & denique sygraphum pacti Dei quod cum Judaeis pepigit, perisse* (Gebhardt 3/144/24–27).

218 Ibid.

219 *Treatise* 206.

220 Ibid.

221 Yovel, op. cit. n.1, 2:19.

222 *Treatise* 210.

223 Ibid.

224 Ibid.

225 Ibid.

226 *Treatise* 210f.

227 *Treatise* 211. Latin: *Denique quia quatuor habentur in Novo Testamento Evangelistae, & quis credet, quod Deus quater Historiam Christi narrare voluerit & scripto hominibus communicare?* (Gebhardt 3/150/16–19).

228 See above, pp. 122f.

229 *Treatise* 211.

230 Ibid.

231 *Treatise* 212.

232 Ibid.

233 Ibid.

234 Ibid.

235 *Treatise* 214f.

236 Ibid.

237 *Treatise* 215.

238 Ibid.

239 Ibid.

240 *Treatise* 217. Latin: *hoc est talia Dei attributa quae homines certa vivendi ratione imitari possunt* (Gebhardt 3/170/34).

241 *Treatise* 220.

242 Ibid.

243 *Treatise* 221.

244 Ibid.

245 *Treatise* 221f.

246 *Treatise* 220f.

247 *Treatise* 226.

248 Ibid.

249 *Treatise* 228: "Theology defines its religious dogmas only so far as suffices to secure obedience, but it leaves it to reason to decide exactly how these dogmas are to be understood in respect of truth."

250 *Treatise* 236.

251 *Treatise* 237, 239. The introduction here of Hobbes' theory of the origin of civil society is striking. In a moment, however, Spinoza will branch off from Hobbes when it comes to the issue of monarchy versus democracy.

252 *Treatise* 239.

253 *Treatise* 239. This *negative* version of the Golden Rule comes from the ancient rabbis contemporary with Jesus, not the New Testament, which has it in the positive form. It is another rare hint of Spinoza's Jewish heritage.

254 Ibid.

255 *Treatise* 242.

256 *Treatise* 253.

257 *Treatise* 254.

258 The whole discussion of fraud on people's religious instincts takes place in *Treatise* 251–254.

259 The discussion of the Hebrew state takes place in *Treatise* 254–271.

260 *Treatise* 273, 275.

261 *Treatise* 276.

262 This word is Spinoza's derogatory code name for Jews of traditional belief and lifestyle throughout the *Treatise*. For Spinoza's use of "Pharisee," see Feuer, op. cit. n.5, 36.

263 *Treatise* 276.

264 For the story of these men's fates, see Gregory, op. cit. n.12, 4.

265 *Treatise* 276.

266 Ibid.

267 *Treatise* 283.

268 *Treatise* 286.

269 This concept of the religiously "indifferent" state had already been discussed by Hobbes; cf. Strauss, op. cit. n.33, 27: "Hobbes's is the first doctrine that necessarily and unmistakably points to a thoroughly 'enlightened,' i.e., a-religious or atheistic society as the solution of the social or political problem (of religious strife). This most important implication of Hobbes's doctrine was made explicit not many years after his death by Pierre Bayle, who attempted to prove that an atheistic society was possible."

270 *Treatise* 282f.

271 *Treatise,* Preface 52.

272 *Treatise* 291.

273 *Treatise* 292f.

274 *Treatise* 294f.

275 *Treatise* 295.

276 *Treatise* 297.

277 Ibid.

278 *Treatise* 298.

279 *Treatise* 299.

280 This is the view of Paul Weinpahl, *The Radical Spinoza* (New York: New York University Press 1979) 57.

281 Allison, op. cit. n.7, 17.

282 Gregory, op. cit. n.12, 27.

283 Ibid.

284 Allison 18.

285 Ibid.

286 Gregory 30.

287 Ibid. 31.

288 Ibid. 32.

289 Malet, op. cit. n.1, 301. My translation. Lods' French is "*programme des sciences bibliques tel à peu près que l'a conçu et réalisé le xixe siècle. Spinoza en a défini la méthode, qui doit être philologique, historique et critique. Il en a distingué les différentes branches: histoire de la langue, histoire du texte, histoire du canon, histoire de la formation de chaque livre, étude des idées des divers auteurs. Passant en revue les points principaux de ce grandiose programme, Spinoza, avec une merveilleuse intuition, devine une grande partie des conclusions auxquelles la science ne devait aboutir au'après un travail séculair.*"

290 Cassirer, op. cit. n.28, 184.

291 Peter Stuhlmacher, *Vom Verstehen des Neues Testament,* 2nd rev. ed. (Göttingen: Vandenhoeck/Ruprecht 1986) 119: "*Von welchem neuartigen Ansatz die aufkommende Bibelkritik ausing und wohin sie zielte, lässt sich am klarsten am 'Tractatus theologico-politicus' des . . . Spinoza sehen.*"

292 Friedrich Nietzsche, *Use and Abuse of History,* trans. A. Collins (Indianapolis: Bobbs-Merrill, 1949) 43. For the German text, cf. "Vom Nützte und Nachteil der Historie," in *Friedrich Nietzsche: Werke in drei Bänden,* ed. K. Schlechta (München: Carl Hanser Verlag, 1957), *Unzeitgemässe Betrachtungen,* Zweites Stück (1:253):

> *. . . scheint die neuere Theologie sich rein aus Harmlosigkeit mit der Geschichte eingelassen zu haben und jetzt noch will sie es kaum merken, daß sie damit, wahrsheinlich sehr wider Willen, im Dienste des Voltaire-schen* écrasez *steht . . . Was man am Christentume lernen kann, daß es unter der Wirkung einer historisierenden Behandlung blasiert und*

unnatürlich geworden ist, bis endlich eine vollkommen historische, das heißt gerechte Behandlung es in reines Wissen um das Christentum auflöst and dadurch vernichtert. . .

Just before this, Nietzsche had explained why he thought historical criticism, as practiced in his time (late-nineteenth-century Germany), was so destructive of the religious impulse:

> The *unrestrained* historical sense pushed to its logical extreme, uproots the future, because it destroys illusions and robs existing things of the only atmosphere in which they can live. Historical justice even if practiced conscientiously with a pure heart is therefore a dreadful virtue, because it always undermines and ruins the living thing—its judgment always means annihilation . . . A religion, for example, that has to be turned into a matter of historical knowledge . . . and to be scientifically studied throughout, is destroyed at the end of it all. For the historical audit brings so much to light which is false and absurd, violent and inhuman, that the condition of pious illusion falls to pieces. (Italics added) (42)

German (1:252; emphasis in original):

> *Der historische Sinn, wenn er ungebändigt waltet and alle seine Konsequenzen zieht, entwurzelt die Zukunft, weil er die Illusionen zerstört und den bestehenden Dingen ihre Atmosphäre nimmt, in der sie allein leben können. Die historische Gerechtigkeit, selbst wenn sie wirklich und in reiner Gesinnung geübt wird, ist deshalb eine schreckliche Tugend, weil sie immer das Lebendige untergräbt und zu Fall bringt: ihr Richten ist immer ein Vernichten . . . Eine Religion zum Beispiel, die in historisches Wissen, unter dem Walten der reinen Gerechtigkeit . . . durch und durch wissenschaftlich erkannt werden soll, ist am Ende dieses Weges zugleich vernichtet. Der Grund liegt darin, daß bei der historischen Nachrechnung jedesmal so viel Falsches, Rohes, Unmenschliches, Absurdes, Gewaltsames zutage tritt, daß die pietätvolle Illusions-Stimmung, in der alles, was leben will, allein leben kann, notwendig zerstiebt . . .*

NOTES TO CHAPTER 17

1 Maurice Cranston, *John Locke: A Biography* (New York: Macmillan 1957) 4f.
2 Ibid. 3.

3 Ibid. 14.

4 Ibid. 16.

5 Ibid. 17.

6 Ibid. 30.

7 Ibid. 39.

8 Ibid. 43.

9 Cited in ibid. 59.

10 Ibid. 70.

11 Ibid. 81.

12 Ibid. 91.

13 Ibid. 93f.

14 Ibid. 100.

15 Ibid. 103f.

16 Ibid. 107.

17 Ibid. 119.

18 Ibid. 123.

19 Ibid. 123f.

20 Ibid.

21 Ibid. 158f.

22 Ibid. 103.

23 Ibid.

24 Ibid. 224f.

25 For an excellent survey of how the theme of religious toleration was all around Locke during his early months in Amsterdam, see Raymond Klibansky and J. W. Gough, trans. and eds., *John Locke, Epistola de Tolerantia: A Letter on Toleration* (Oxford: Clarendon Press 1968) x–xvii. For a list of the names of predecessors who had written on toleration collected by Locke for his personal library, see op. cit. xxx.

26 For an account of the four drafts of what became the *Epistola de Tolerantia*, see Klibansky and Gough 14–24.

27 Cranston 231.

28 Lewis S. Feuer, *Spinoza and the Rise of Liberalism* (Boston: Bucan Press 1958) 257f.

29 Klibansky and Gough, op. cit. n.25, xxxii n.3.

30 See above, pp. 256f.

31 Klibansky and Gough, xxxif., observe: "Considering how profoundly different Locke's approach to philosophical problems was from that of Spinoza, his manifest interest in Spinoza's writings is somewhat surprising. Even in one of his earliest notebooks, that of 1674, Locke, having read Spinoza's early treatise on Descartes' *Principia philosophiae*, expressed his intention of finding out what other works there were by this author. When in 1674–5 he was

Lord Shaftesbury's confidential agent (in France), he certainly had the opportunity of perusing the works of Spinoza, for Shaftesbury reimbursed him for a sum spent on acquiring these books for him. Later in 1679, Locke mentioned in his 'Catalogue de livres differends et qu'on trouve avec peine' the *Tractatus theologico-politicus* en francois soubs (*sic*) le nom de 'Ceremonies des Juifs.' An inventory of 1686 of the books belonging to Locke at the time of his stay in the Netherlands shows clearly that he possessed Spinoza's *Opera Posthuma* (1677). In a catalogue of his books drawn up some years later, in 1693, several works of Spinoza in separate editions have been added, among them the *Tractatus theologico-politicus*."

32 For an account of the attacks on Locke and the resulting three more "letters of toleration," see Peter Nicholson, "John Locke's Later Letters on Toleration," in *John Locke: A Letter Concerning Toleration in Focus*, ed. J. Horton and S. Mendus (London and New York: Routledge 1991) 163–187.

33 Henning Graf Reventlow, *The Authority of the Bible and the Rise of the Modern World*, trans. John Bowdon (Philadelphia: Fortress Press 1985) 260.

34 Any attempt to interpret Locke's writings must contend with the surprising fact that a critical edition has only recently begun to appear. The *Epistola de Tolerantia: A Letter on Toleration*, Latin text edited with preface by R. Klibansky and English (facing) translation with introduction and notes by J. W. Gough, came out in 1968 (see n.25). It was followed in 1975 by the *Essay concerning Human Understanding*, ed. P. H. Nidditch (Oxford: Clarendon Press), and then six volumes of Locke's *Correspondence*, ed. E. de Beer (Oxford: Clarendon Press 1976–1981). The *Epistola de Tolerantia*, originally written in Latin and published at Gouda in 1689, was soon translated into English without Locke's permission by an acquaintance of his, a merchant of Unitarian sympathies named William Popple. Popple knew both Benjamin Furly and the Shaftesbury family and he must have learned immediately from one or the other who the author was. Realizing how valuable Locke's views would be in influencing public opinion in the still formative period of William and Mary's reign, he immediately translated it into English, without asking Locke's permission. It came out in 1689 at virtually the same time as Locke's unsigned Latin version. From that time to this, Popple's English translation has been the only one available. The Clarendon Press translation by J. W. Gough avoids Popple's exaggerations and corrects some mistranslations. However, I have decided not to use Gough's translation for the following reasons: (a) in his attempts to be more faithful to Locke's sedate Latin, he has lost some of Popple's fire. (b) Popple's translation is the famous one; it is the one with historic significance, not Locke's Latin original, which few people in England or America ever read. That is, the issue for this study is not pedantic faithfulness to Locke's Latin original but which translation made the widest

impact in the seventeenth and eighteenth centuries. (c) Popple's translation is available in a number of handy editions, especially the widely used edition by Patrick Romanell: *A Letter Concerning Toleration by John Locke* (Indianapolis: Bobbs-Merrill 1980). Hence I have quoted from this translation (as Popple/Romanell) except in four instances, indicating in the footnotes the corresponding page in Gough's translation. In a few cases, I have employed words in parentheses to clarify Popple's meaning. All Latin quotations are from Klibansky's critical text and I give his page and line number(s).

35 John Locke, *A Letter concerning Toleration*, 2nd ed., trans. William Popple, ed. P. Romanell (new York: Bobbs-Merrill 1980) 17; cf. 18, 23. See Klibansky and Gough 66–68.

36 Ibid. 20; cf. Klibansky and Gough 71.

37 Gough's translation (77)—"The end of a religious society ... is the public worship of God and by that means the *gaining* of eternal life"—doesn't convey Locke's relentless acquisitiveness.

38 Ibid. 22; cf. Klibansky and Gough 77.

39 Latin 84:29–30: *a republica rebusque civilibus prorsus sejuncta est et separata.* Popple omitted the three underlined words.

40 Ibid. 27; see Klibansky and Gough 85–87.

41 Ibid. 39; see Klibansky and Gough 109. Latin 108:19f.: *tolleret ecclesiam cujus finis est ut Deum suo more libere colat.*

42 Klibansky and Gough 103 is to be preferred here. Popple's translation (36) "the commonwealth or any member in it" misses the Latin (102:24–25): *ubi solum agitur de salute animarum, nec vicini nec reipublicae interest.*

43 Klibansky and Gough 103 (italics added); cf. Popple/Romanell 36; 18.

44 Latin (122:19): *forum internum* and *forum externum.* Gough notes that the terms were common in moral theology and referred to the conscience and ecclesiastical courts, respectively (161 n.49).

45 Klibansky and Gough 123; cf. Popple/Romanell 46.

46 Popple/Romanell 46; cf. Klibansky and Gough 123.

47 Ibid. 39; cf. Klibansky and Gough 109.

48 Ibid. 56; cf. Klibansky and Gough 143.

49 Ibid. 51; cf. 45, 55, 56. Cf. Klibansky and Gough 133.

50 Klibansky and Gough 133; cf. Popple/Romanell 51.

51 Popple/Romanell 40; cf. 50. Cf. Klibansky and Gough 111.

52 Klibansky and Gough 135–137; cf. Popple/Romanell 52: "liberty of conscience is every man's natural right" goes far beyond the Latin, though it is within Locke's general idea.

53 Popple/Romanell 28; cf. Klibansky and Gough 87 (italics added).

54 Ibid. 52; cf. Klibansky and Gough 135.

55 Ibid. 49; cf. Klibansky and Gough 131.

56 It is fascinating to see Locke give not one hint of the Christian doctrine of grace. He will rectify this in his last writing, *Reasonableness of Christianity* 44, 47.

57 Popple/Romanell 46; cf. Klibansky and Gough 123–25.

58 See most recently John Marshall, *John Locke: Resistance, Religion, and Responsibility* (Cambridge: University Press 1994) and extensive bibliography cited there.

59 Popple/Romanell 48; cf. Klibansky and Gough 127.

60 Religious *adiaphora* was the Latitudinarian doctrine that what is not explicitly commanded in Scripture can be left up to believers in their own time and place, *and not fought over;* see Reventlow, op. cit. n.33, 223–285. Klibansky gives a beautiful example of the Latitudinarian ethos in the Latin motto of Episcopius: *in necessariis unitas, in dubiis libertas, in omnibus caritas* (xv; "often wrongly ascribed to St Augustine" n.1).

61 Klibansky and Gough 105. Popple's translation (37) following Locke's typically convoluted sentence structure, is unusually confusing here.

62 For the text of this writing, I will rely on John Locke, *The Reasonableness of Christianity*, ed. I. T. Ramsey (Stanford: Stanford University Press 1958). It is based on an edition of 1751, but considerably abridged.

63 Ibid. 58.

64 Ibid. 46.

65 Ibid. 44f.

66 Ibid. 30; cf. 31 (italics added).

67 "Forensic" implies the image of a judge in a court of law saying to a defendant, "You have committed all these sins, and you have made restitution on half of them—but I forgive you of the guilt for the rest. You are free."

68 In theological jargon, this type of "faith" is known as *fides qua*, "faith that" such and such is true. It is distinguished from "faith by which" (*fides quae*), meaning the faith by means of which one trusts in God, loves God, etc. The latter is the emotional, affective act; the former is the intellectual act.

69 Ramsey, op. cit. n.62, 39.

70 Ibid. 63.

71 Ibid. 49. The quotation is my rephrasing of his almost incomprehensible statement: "A sincere obedience, how can anyone doubt to be, or scruple to call, a condition of the new covenant, as well as faith; whoever read our Savior's sermon on the mount, to omit all the rest?"

72 Ibid. 57.

73 Ibid. 66.

74 Ibid. 24.

75 Ibid. 25.

76 Ibid.

77 Ibid. 67 (italics added).

78 Ibid.

79 Ibid.

80 Roland H. Bainton, *Here I Stand: A Life of Martin Luther* (Nashville: Abingdon 1950) 185.

81 Popple/Romanell 25 (italics added); cf. Klibansky and Gough 81.

82 Ibid. 31 (italics added); cf. Klibansky and Gough 95.

83 Klibansky and Gough 71 (italics added); cf. Popple/Romanell 19f.

84 Popple/Romanell 32; cf. Klibansky and Gough 95.

85 Ibid. 33–34; cf. Klibansky and Gough 97–99.

86 If this summary statement seems too narrow and materialistic, consider the following repeated definitions of the purpose of the state in the *Epistle on Toleration:* "men (are obliged) to enter into society with one another, that by mutual assistance and joint force they may secure . . . their properties in the things that contribute to the comfort and happiness of this life" (47; cf. Klibansky and Gough 125); and again, "the temporal good and outward prosperity of society, which is *the sole reason of men entering into society and the only thing they seek and aim at in it*" (48; cf. Klibansky and Gough 127). On the materialistic basis of Locke's view of society, see especially Werner Euchner, *Naturrecht und Politik bei John Locke* (Frankfort aM.: Europaosche Verlagsanstalt 1969), and Rainer Rotermundt, *Das Denken John Lockes: zur Logik burgerlichen Bewusstseins* (Frankfort aM.: Campus Verlag 1976); cited in Reventlow, op. cit. n.33, 248, 549 n.179.

87 See S. A. Grave, *The Scottish Philosophy of Common Sense* (Oxford: Clarendon Press 1960).

88 For the connection between Lockean literalism and Reid's "common sense philosophy" in America, see Winfred E. Garrison and Alfred T. DeGroot, *The Disciples of Christ: A History* (St. Louis: Christian Board of Publication 1948) 57; further, David E. Harrell Jr., *Quest for a Christian America: The Disciples of Christ and American Society to 1866* (Nashville: Disciples of Christ Historical Society 1966) 28.

89 Garrison and DeGroot 57.

90 Harrell 28.

NOTES   TO   CHAPTER   18

1 For Spinoza's influence on Toland, see John Redwood, *Reason, Ridicule, and Religion: The Age of the Enlightenment in England, 1660–1750* (London: Thames & Hudson 1976) 143.

2 The materials from *Amyntor* mentioned here have been reissued by Garland Press under the title *John Toland: A Collection of Several Pieces,* 2 vols. (New York: Garland Publishing 1977) 1:350–403.

3 Ibid. 307f.

4 The only English translation is that of Lonsdale and Laura Ragg, *The Gospel of Barnabas: Edited and Translated from the Italian Ms. in the Imperial Library at Vienna* (Oxford: Clarendon Press 1907). A more recent French translation, with photo-facsimiles of the Italian version on facing pages, has been published by Luigi Cirillo, *Évangile de Barnabé: Recherches sur la composition et l'origine. Text et traduction par Luigi Cirillo et Michel Fremaux. Préface de Henry Corbin* (Paris: Éditions Beauchesne 1977). The official designation of the Italian version discovered by Toland is Codex 2662 Eug. For a brief description of its physical characteristics, see Ragg xiii–xv. For another exhaustive analysis of its physical characteristics—paper, ink, binding, orthography, grammatical features, etc.—see Cirillo 39–48. For excellent detective work on a possible author of the *Gospel of Barnabas,* see David Sox, *The Gospel of Barnabas* (London: Allen & Unwin 1984) 49–73, complete with photographs of the *Gospel of Barnabas,* Pope Sixtus V, and the title page of the list of condemned books published in 1549 by the Inquisitor of Venice, Fra Marino. Medieval Italian features of the *Gospel of Barnabas* have been identified. For the most complete list of features from Dante's *Commedia Divina,* see Ragg xl; cf. Cirillo 88f. In addition, Cirillo collected a number of misspellings, added letters, doubling of consonants, etc., which locate the writing style in mid-sixteenth-century Venice; see 77–80. Jan Slomp, "The Gospel in Dispute: A Critical Evaluation of the First French Translation . . . of the So-called Gospel of Barnabas," *Islamochristiana* 4 (1978), compared the *Gospel of Barnabas* with two popular Italian Gospel harmonies composed in the thirteenth and fourteenth centuries, one Venetian and one north Tuscan (126–129). He found that the order of events in the three were similar for Jesus' birth and early ministry. In the Annunciation, the wording of the *Gospel of Barnabas* is closer to a fifteenth-century Venetian harmony than to early Venetian translations of the Gospels. Clusters of the same texts are found in all three writings, and accounts of similar events in the canonical Gospels are harmonized in the same way, especially between the *Gospel of Barnabas* and the Venetian harmony (see evidence laid out, 125f.). For Muslim teachings in the *Gospel of Barnabas,* see Ragg 226f., Sox 33f., and Cirillo 220f.

There was little notice of the *Gospel of Barnabas* among Muslims prior to George Sale's mention of it in his translation of the Koran in 1734; Sox 25. See the brief discussion of the early notice of the Spanish version, *as well as an Arabic version,* by the Dutch scholar Adriaan Reeland in 1717, mentioned by Cirillo 51. This changed dramatically at the beginning of the twentieth century when the Raggs translated the Italian *Gospel of Barnabas* into English. Within a year, pirated English versions appeared in Pakistan and India, and an Arabic translation was published in Cairo. Since then, thousands of copies have been sold, translations into Urdu and Persian have appeared, and it has spread from Indonesia to Morocco—all minus the Raggs' introduction questioning its authenticity. Sox 10f. describes contemporary Muslim argument pro and con regarding the authenticity of the *Gospel*. See also Jan Slomp, "Pseudo-Barnabas in the Context of Muslim-Christian Apologetics," *Al-Mushir* 16 (1974) 129; also Slomp, "The Gospel in Dispute," op. cit., 87f.

5 Sox 26f.

6 For an exhaustive list of earlier references to the Italian version of the *Gospel of Barnabas*, see Cirillo 51f.

7 Quoted from Henning Graf Reventlow, *The Authority of the Bible and the Rise of the Modern World*, trans. John Bowden (Philadelphia: Fortress Press 1985) 294f.

8 Reventlow 308 concluded: "with his many-sided interests, more than any other writer in England, Toland reflects the revolutionary situation (in biblical criticism) in the eighteenth century. He adopted positions ... which proved decisive for the understanding of the Bible in modern Protestantism."

NOTES TO CHAPTER 19

1 In the Preface, Erasmus wrote that he had "used many manuscripts, both Greek and Latin, and not just any sort but the oldest and the most correct"; quoted in Léon Vaganay and Christian-Bernard Amphoux, *An Introduction to New Testament Textual Criticism*, rev. ed., trans. J. Heimerdinger (Cambridge: University Press 1986) 131. Vaganay and Amphoux go on to observe, "in reality, Erasmus' edition is one of the poorer ... (almost) akin to the work of a schoolboy. In order to get it finished as quickly as possible, he gave the printers three manuscripts which he had to hand, namely codex 2e (Gospels), 2ap (Acts and the Epistles) and 1r (Revelation); and he simply used a few other manuscripts (1eap, 4ap, 7p) to make some slight alterations to the text. But all these manuscripts are of a late date (none is from before the tenth century) ... all are of the Byzantine type of text, unquestionably the least good."

2 Bruce Metzger, *The Text of the New Testament: Its Transmission, Corruption, and Restoration* (New York and London: Oxford University Press 1964) 119; cf. Vaganay and Amphoux 142.

3 Metzger 120.

4 See, for example, Metzger's discussion of Griesbach's sophisticated discussion of "the shorter reading"; loc. cit.

5 For a description of what a typical page in Griesbach's New Testament contained, see William Baird, *History of New Testament Research*, 2 vols. (Minneapolis: Fortress Press 1992) 1:142.

6 Vaganay and Amphoux 142. The Majority Text approach still finds adherents; see further below, p. 357.

7 Metzger 121.

8 Johannes Martin Augustinus Scholz (1794–1852), professor at Bonn and a pupil of Johann Leonhard Hug (1765–1846); cf. Metzger 123.

9 Ibid. 124; Vaganay and Amphoux 146f.

10 Metzger, op. cit. n.2, 125.

11 Baird, op. cit. n.5, 321.

12 Metzger 125.

13 Metzger 126.

14 For a brief account of this astonishing story, see Metzger 42–46. As for the amount, Metzger says the Russian government arranged to sell it to the British Museum "for £100,000 (then slightly more than $500,000)" (45). See also Baird, op. cit. n.5, 323; Metzger, op. cit. n.2, 126; Vaganay and Amphoux, op. cit. n.1, 147f.

15 Kurt Aland and Barbara Aland, *The Text of the New Testament: An Introduction to the Critical Editions and to the Theory and Practice of Modern Textual Criticism,* trans. E. F. Rhodes (Grand Rapids: Eerdmans 1987) 11.

16 After the brilliant start with the *Complutensian Polyglot* (see above, pp. 186ff.), Roman Catholic scholars spent their time bringing out more accurate texts of the Vulgate; see Vaganay and Amphoux, op. cit. n.1, 144, 161.

17 Metzger, op. cit. n.2, 129.

18 Naturally, this claim has provoked lengthy criticism; see most recently Aland and Aland, op. cit. n.15, 14.

19 Ibid. 18.

20 Metzger, op. cit. n.2, 129–131; cf. Vaganay and Amphoux, op. cit. n.1, 150f.

21 Metzger 135.

22 Ibid. 135f.

23 Ibid. 137. For a summary of the scholarly critique of their contemporaries, see Vaganay and Amphoux, op. cit. n.1, 151–154.

24 Metzger 137f.

25 German: *Die Schriften des Neuen Testaments in ihrer ältesten erreichbaren Textgestalt hergestellt auf Grund ihrer Textgeschichte* (Göttingen 1913); see Metzger 139.

26 Metzger 140.

27 Ibid. 142; Aland and Aland, op. cit. n.15, 22f.

28 Metzger 139.

29 Aland and Aland 19.

30 Ibid.

31 Ibid.; Metzger 144.

32 Aland and Aland 19.

33 Ibid.

34 See the discussions in Vaganay and Amphoux, op. cit. n.1, 159–161, and Metzger, op. cit. n.2, 143.

35 Aland and Aland 20.

36 Ibid. 30.

37 Ibid. 31.

38 Ibid. 44.

39 Bruce Metzger, *A Textual Commentary on the Greek New Testament: A Companion Volume to the United Bible Societies' Greek New Testament* (3rd ed.) (London and New York: United Bible Societies 1971) xxviii; cf. 2nd edition (1994) 14*. Metzger notes that this kind of system was first pioneered by Bengel; xxviii n.10.

40 For example, see the committee's discussion of the Words of Institution in Lk 22:19b–20. The United Bible Societies committee published a majority decision followed by minority dissenting statement; see Metzger, *Textual Commentary* 2nd ed. 148–150.

41 Aland and Aland, op. cit. n.15, 29.

42 Ibid. 28.

43 Ibid. 29f. For a breakdown of the average number of mistakes there would be *per page,* see 30. It comes out to no more than two or three per page.

44 For a critique from the French perspective, see Vaganay and Amphoux, op. cit. n.1, 167.

45 "On the whole, each of the editors is probably satisfied that the new "Standard Text" is the best that can be achieved in the present state of knowledge"; Aland and Aland 34.

46 For the origin of this claim, see ibid. 30.

47 Ibid.

48 The quote comes at the conclusion of an article published by K. Aland, "Der neue 'Standard-Text' in seinem Verältnis zu den frühen Papyri und Majuskeln" (1981), cited by E. J. Epp in Eldon Jay Epp and Gordon D. Fee, *Studies in the Theory and Method of New Testament Textual Criticism,* Studies and Documents 45 (Grand Rapids: Eerdmans 1993) 121f. The same perspective can be seen in the first edition of the Alands' *Text of the New Testament,* op. cit. n.15, 36: "The (new) 'standard text' is not based on a small group of manuscripts, selected by chance, mostly of late date and poor quality (as was Erasmus' Standard Text), but on a review of *all the evidence* that is in *any way relevant to establishing the original text* . . . All who have participated in its preparation are glad that this immense work . . . *is now finished*" (italics added). These emphatic statements disappeared completely in the revised (1989) edition; see K. Aland and B. Aland, *The Text of the New Testament,* 2nd ed. (Grand Rapids: Eerdmans 1989) 36.

49 Aland and Aland, op. cit. n.15, 35.

NOTES TO CHAPTER 20

1 I am indebted to Harvey K. McArthur, *The Quest through the Centuries: The Search for the Historical Jesus* (Philadelphia: Fortress Press 1966), for the following discussion of Gospel harmonies during the sixteenth and seventeenth centuries. I wish to thank William R. Farmer for his helpful critique of this chapter.

2 See below, pp. 318ff.

3 For Origen's discussion of this issue, see above, pp. 80f.; for Augustine, see above, pp. 133, 135.

4 See Chapter 13.

5 See Chapter 17.

6 And most of these appeared toward the end of the Middle Ages. For a helpful survey, see McArthur, op. cit. n.1, 57–84.

7 Listed and briefly described in ibid. 158–164.

8 Ibid. 87.

9 One of the shortcomings of McArthur's otherwise very helpful discussion is the lack of any discussion of the new conception of history lying behind these harmonies.

10 Ibid. 88–93, 159.

11 Ibid. 93f.

12 Thomas H. L. Parker, *Calvin's Commentaries: A Harmony of the Gospels Matthew, Mark, and Luke,* 3 vols. (Grand Rapids: Eerdmans 1972) 2:278, commenting on Mt 20:29.

13 So McArthur, op. cit. n.1, 94f., who gives a list of Protestants who followed Osiander. He observes that Roman Catholics were more reluctant to use it since Augustine had said the Evangelists did not preserve the historical order but followed the order of recollection (96).

14 See above, p. 289.

15 Henning Graf Reventlow, *The Authority of the Bible and the Rise of the Modern World,* trans. John Bowden (Philadelphia: Fortress Press 1985) 340. The full title of the book is revealing: *A New Theory of the Earth, from its Origin, to the Consummation of all Things, wherein the Creation of the World in six Days, the Universal Deluge and the Great conflagration, as laid down in the Holy Scriptures, are shewn to be perfectly agreeable to Reason and Philosophy;* Reventlow 594 n.61.

16 This topic, with accompanying bibliography, was discussed above, pp. 157f.

17 See above, p. 147.

18 *Libri historici Novi Testamenti Graece. Pars prior, sistens synopsin Evangeliorum Matthae, Marci et Lucae, etc.* (Halle 1774); cf. *Synopsis Evangeliorum Matthaei, Marci et Lucae, etc.* (Halle 1776). It is not appropriate to call earlier

harmonies "synopses" as many do; cf. H. Greeven, "The Gospel Synopsis from 1776 to the Present Day," in *J. J. Griesbach: Synoptic and Text-Critical Studies, 1776–1976,* ed. Bernard Orchard and Thomas R. W. Longstaff (Cambridge: University Press 1976) 23f.

19 Gerhard Delling, "Johann Jakob Griesbach: His Life, Work, and Times," in Orchard and Longstaff 5.

20 Ibid. 7.

21 Ernesti insisted that the New Testament was grammatically, i.e., historically true. Indeed, he said that there was no other way to interpret the New Testament than the grammatical or literal meaning. For further information on Ernesti, see Werner Georg Kümmel, *The New Testament: The History of the Investigation of Its Problems,* trans. S. McLean Gilmour and Howard C. Kee (Nashville: Abingdon Press 1972) 61.

22 Delling, op. cit. n.19, 7.

23 Ibid. Delling notes: "to this period belongs the oil painting of Griesbach by Johann Daniel Bager of Frankfort."

24 Ibid. 8.

25 Delling gives a detailed description of Griesbach's courses; ibid. 8–10.

26 Ibid. 13.

27 Quoted in ibid.

28 These two together with the noted poet and novelist Christoph Martin Wieland (later known as the German Voltaire) and the rationalist New Testament scholar H. E. G. Paulus formed the famous "Jena Circle" which met in Jena until 1803. When Johann Wolfgang von Goethe would be in Weimar on government business at the same time Griesbach was, he would often be a guest in Griesbach's home. Schiller also resided for a time in Griesbach's town house; see ibid. 14.

29 Ibid. 9, 15.

30 Ibid.

31 William Baird, *History of New Testament Research,* vol. 1, *From Deism to Tübingen* (Minneapolis: Fortress Press 1992) 139. Cf. Johann Jacob Griesbach, *Vorlesungen über die Hermeneutik des N.T. mit Anwendung auf die Leidens—und Auferstehungsgeschichte Christi,* ed. by Johann Carl Samuel Steiner (Nürnberg: Zehschen Buchhandlung 1815) 53: "*Das N.T. muß erkläret werden, wie jedes alte Buch erklärt wird.*"

32 Baird 1:140. Cf. Griesbach, *Vorlesungen* 46: "*Man muß den grammatischen und historischen Sinn einer Stelle nicht hinein tragen, sondern aus den Worten und dem Zusammenhange hervorziehen, d.h. man muß keinen andern Sinn mit den Worten verbinden, als erweislich ist, daß der Autor dieß dabei gedacht haben wollte.*" Cf. 50: "*Der biblische Ausleger muß von allem menschlichen Ansehen ganz unbeschränkt sein. Kirchliches Ansehen ist auch blos menschliches, also kann dieß auch nichts entscheiden. Bei den Protestanten entscheidet*

die Kirche nichts; bei den Katholiken ist es die erste Regel, daß man die Bibel nach der Kirche erklären müsse."

33 Baird 1:140; Delling, op. cit. n.19, 10.

34 Ibid.

35 For an explanation of this term, see above, pp. 215f., 233f.

36 Baird 1:140.

37 Ibid.

38 Ibid. 1:140f.

39 Ibid.

40 Ibid. 1:139.

41 Ibid. ascribes this view to Michaelis. It is very similar to Locke's; see above, pp. 278f.

42 Baird 1:139; Delling 11.

43 We will note that Griesbach did not consider the author of the Gospel of Mark, whom he believed to have done little more than combine excerpts drawn from Matthew and Luke, to be very "inspired"; see below, pp. 321f.

44 Delling 12. Griesbach thought the passion narrative in the Gospel of John was the most historically reliable (Baird 1:141; see further Delling 12).

45 Delling 11.

46 Cf. the comment of his student J. P. Gabler: "and year by year, (Griesbach published) specimen exegeses for feast-days"; quoted in Delling 12.

47 Klaus Scholder, *The Birth of Modern Critical Theology: Origins and Problems of Biblical Criticism in the Seventeenth Century* (London: SCM Press; Philadelphia: Trinity Press International 1990) 143 (italics added).

48 In a personal letter to me (24 October 1988), Bernard Orchard wrote, "While he was in England, Griesbach visited Oxford (the Bodleian) and London (the British Museum), chiefly gathering materials for his text-critical research. At the time, Henry Owen, an Oxford man, was the incumbent of St Olave's near the Tower of London. Although there is no written evidence that they ever met, Griesbach must have met many men who knew Owen, whose book *Observations on the Four Gospels* had appeared in London five years earlier in 1764. That Griesbach bought the book at some point cannot be doubted, since it is listed in the catalogue of his library when it was prepared for sale after his death in 1813 ... It seems to me highly probable that Griesbach picked up Owen's book while he was in London and it would not surprise me in the least if they had met during that year." I would just add that nothing in the teachings of Michaelis or Semler, nothing in the doctrines of Ernesti or Le Clerc, in any way resembles the source theory Griesbach propounded in the Preface to the *Synopsis* he published in 1776, six years after his visit to London.

49 This hypothetical conversation is based on Owen's statements in the Preface to his book *Observations on the Four Gospels; Tending Chiefly to Ascertain*

the Times of Their Publication and to Illustrate the Form and Manner of Their Composition (London: T. Payne 1764). This comment comes from the first paragraph.

50 Owen iv; a choice expression of contemporary rationalist optimism.

51 Ibid. vi.

52 Ibid. 15f.

53 Ibid. 23–48; Owen said that Matthew was probably written around the year 38, to brace up the struggling Christian Church as its leaders faced martyrdom, as had Jesus their Lord. The author of the Gospel of Luke, however, wrote a number of years later for a radically different audience. Owen pointed to a number of passages exhibiting similar wording between Matthew and Luke and concluded that there was ample evidence to support the view that Luke had made use of Matthew when he composed his Gospel for the Greek-speaking churches of Paul's missionary area.

54 Having thus accounted for the first two Gospels, Owen went on to suggest that, because the earliest two Gospel "histories" had had to answer many questions and deal with many objections and were quite complicated as a result, a simpler version might be desired for use in the Christian church at Rome.

> When the Christian Religion had gained ground, and the controversies that (first) disturbed it were tolerably settled, it is in no wise unnatural to suppose, that some of its most faithful and serious Professors might wish to see the Gospel exhibited in a more simple form. (ibid. 50)

Out of this desire sprang the Gospel of Mark, said Owen. "But as the things he records to this purpose are chiefly taken from the other Evangelists, so it is to be observed that they are often expressed (by Mark) in their very words" (53).

To document this observation, Owen presented a series of comparative charts containing passages from Matthew next to identical ones from Mark. Along the way, he interspersed notations indicating at which point Mark stopped following Matthew and began copying Luke; see ibid. 53ff. Mk 4:1–9 is parallel with Mt 13:1–9, but the conclusion Mark gets from Lk 8:16–18/ Mk 4:21–25; Mk 14:26–46/Mt 26:30–50.

On this basis, Owen stated that it was clear to him that Mark excerpted both Matthew and Luke simultaneously. Moreover, he said that when Mark did take material from either or both of his predecessors, he frequently *expanded* it "for the sake of the Romans, to enable them the better to understand his accounts" (ibid. 73).

Apart from the brief comment of Augustine (which was in any case lost sight of during the Middle Ages), Owen was the first modern scholar to identify the phenomenon of *conflation* in Mark: "St. Mark makes quick and frequent transitions from the one Evangelist to the other, and blends their *accounts,* I mean their *words,* in such manner as is utterly inexplicable upon any other footing than by supposing that he had both these Gospels before him" (ibid. 74).

Basing his conclusions on the ancient patristic testimony as to the identity of Mark as the companion of Paul and the stenographer of Peter, Owen concluded that the Gospel of Mark was composed in Rome around 62 or 63. After this, he concluded with an account of the origin and audience of the Gospel of John, using the same kinds of arguments In the process, Owen used modern text criticism, citing the *Complutensian Polyglot,* the Syriac versions, and Wetstein's monumental *Novum Testamentum* in support of a disputed reading in Jn 5:2. He was also aware of the recent reopening of the canon of the Gospels, commenting on the significance of the Gospel of the Hebrews and the Gospel of the Egyptians (ibid. 104–105, 112f.).

55 *Paschatos solemnia pie celebranda . . . Inquiritur in fontes, unde Evangelistae suas de resurrectione Domini narrationes hauserint.* Jena: J. C. G. Goepferdt, 1793. Rpr. in *J. J. Griesbachii Opuscula academica,* J. P. Gabler, ed., Jena: F. Frommanni, 1825, 2:241–56.

56 *Commentatio qua Marci Evangelium totum e Matthaei et Lucae commentariis decerptum esse monstratur* (Jena 1789). This was republished five years later in an expanded version which is the one used here: Jena: J. C. G. Goepferdt, 1789–1790. Trans. Bernard Orchard, "A Demonstration that Mark Was Written After Matthew and Luke, in *J. J. Griesbach, Synoptic and Text-Critical Studies, 1776–1976,* Bernard Orchard and Thomas R. W. Longstaff, eds., Cambridge: University Press 1978, 103–135; the Latin text is on pp. 74–102.

57 Ibid., op. cit. n.56, 103.

58 Translation by Heinrich Greeven, "The Gospel Synopsis from 1776 to the Present Day," in Orchard and Longstaff, ibid. 27.

59 Ibid. I am indebted to Brian Carr, classics major, and Professor Thomas Heffernan, of the English Department at the University of Tennessee, Knoxville, for their assistance with these translations.

60 Ibid. That Griesbach's dissenting vote would have been considered not just heresy but an insult to his academic elders can be seen from the title of J. A. Bengel's own harmony: *Richtige Harmonie der vier Evangelien* (Tübingen 1736).

61 Johann Jakob Griesbach, *Synopsis evangeliorum Matthaei Marci et Lucae una cum iis Joannis pericopis quae omnino cum caeterorum evangelistarum narrationibus conferendae sunt,* 3rd ed. (Halle: Officina libraria curtiana 1809), Preface to 2nd ed. ix: *Matthaeus quidem persaepe a chronologica rerum narratarum serie discessit, et multo minus temporis, quam similitudinis cujusdam,*

qua sermones Christi aut eventus cognati inter se esse viderentur, rationem habuit.

62 Griesbach, ibid.: *Marcus vero, uti totum commentariolum suum, paucissimis narratiunculis exceptis, e Matthaeo et Luca compilavit, ita ubi Matthaeo duce usus est, qualemcunque hujus ordinem retinuit immutatum; ubi vero Matthaeo seposito comitem sese adjunxit Lucae, ipsius vestigia tam presse secutus est, ut eandem etiam narrationum seriem servaret.*

63 Griesbach, ibid.: *Lucas denique paulo minus quam caeteri a chronologico ordine aberrasse videtur, verum causa tamen apparet nulla, cur hunc ubique ab ipso religiosissime servatum esse existememus.*

64 Ibid., x: *Nec notae temporis, singulis Evangelistarum narrationibus impressae, dubitationibus tollendis sufficiunt.*

65 Ibid. xf.: *Cum igitur nihil certi quod sequerer invenirem, sed lectorum judicio, quamnam de harmonia Evangelistarum hypothesin amplecti quisque vellet, permittendum esse censerem; uniuscujusque Evangelistae ordinem imperturbatum ita retinendum esse duxi, ut Matthaeus, aut Marcus, aut Lucas suo ordine seorsim in libello nostro legi posset . . . Sed cum alius apud Matthaeum sit multarum narrationum ordo, quam apud Marcum et Lucam; et nostri instituti ratio postularet, ut trium Evangelistarum de eadem re narrationibus simul lectorum oculis exhiberentur, transpositiones nonnullae necessario erant admittendae.*

66 See his discussion of this phenomenon in Orchard and Longstaff, op. cit. n.60, 106f., 113f.

67 Griesbach, op. cit. n.61, x; after pointing out that Matthew has little chronological data at all, Griesbach said: "For the most part I have preferred the order of Mark and Luke, when they are in agreement, to the order used by Matthew, to narrate the deeds of Christ." *Plerumque ordinem Marci et Lucae, ubi hi inter se consentiunt, praetuli ordini, quo Matthaeus res gestas Christi narravit.*

68 See Griesbach, *Demonstration*, IV:11, in Orchard and Longstaff, op. cit. n.56, 135: "Let those who wish to devote themselves to making a harmony of the Gospels take care not to call upon Mark in constructing it for he was clearly not interested in the chronological order of events but passes from Matthew to Luke and back again, taking no account of the time at which each event occurred."

69 Griesbach, op. cit. n.61, vii: *Praeter huncce vero utilitatis fructum, qui academico doctori nulli, Evangelistas interpretaturo, spernendus videbitur, alia simul commoda e tali, quam mente conceperam, synopsi sperari posse putabam. Nam non solum phrasum synonymarum ab Evangelistis adhibitarum comparatio, facillime in hujus generis synopsi instituenda, interpretem magnopere adjuvat; verum etiam indoles et velut oeconomiae cujusque Evangelii . . . etc.*

70 Griesbach, *Demonstration* IV.13, in Orchard and Longstaff, op. cit. n.56, 135.

71 Ibid. 104.

72 See above, p. 140.

73 Orchard and Orchard, op. cit. n.56, 104. There still is no mention of Owen, nor a German scholar, Anton Büsching, who published similar ideas in *Die vier Evangelisten mit ihren eigenen Worten zusammengesetzt und mit Erklär-ungen versehen* (Hamburg 1766).

74 Reicke, "Griesbach's Answer to the Synoptic Question," in Orchard and Longstaff, 72.

75 Griesbach, *Demonstration*, Introduction, in Orchard and Longstaff, ibid. 104.

76 Reicke, op. cit. n.74, 71.

77 Griesbach, *Demonstration*, op. cit. n.68, 105.

78 G. E. Lessing, "Neue Hypothese über die Evangelisten als bloss menschliche Geschichtsschreiber betrachtet," in *Theologischer Nachlass* (1784) 45–72. An English translation by Henry Chadwick is available in *Lessing's Theological Writings* (London: A. & C. Black 1956) 45–72.

79 J. G. Eichhorn, "Ursprung und Wesen der Evangelien," in *Jahrbücher der biblischen Wissenschaft* (Göttingen) 1 (1848) 113–154; 2 (1849) 180–224; 3 (1854) 140–177.

80 Greeven, op. cit. n.58, 106. Griesbach then went on and, in Section I of his reissued *Demonstration*, restated in fifteen theses the kinds of authorial pro-cedures the author of Mark followed on the assumption that Matthew and Luke were his sources. In Section II, he provided three arguments (with charts) to prove that the author of Mark had indeed used Matthew and Luke. In Section III, Griesbach answered a number of objections, mainly those of Storr. In Section IV, he drew a few corollaries.

81 See the account in Reicke, op. cit. n.74, 59–67. Among other followers, Reicke mentions Griesbach's colleague at Jena H. E. G. Paulus, Schleiermacher's stu-dent at Berlin Heinrich Saunier, the Leipzig rationalist theologian Karl Gott-fried Wilhelm Theile, and finally his former pupil Wilhelm Martin Leberecht DeWette, eventually professor at Basel. But, as we will see in a moment, De-Wette seriously modified Griesbach's theory and so was instrumental in its rapid disappearance by the mid-nineteenth century. The Griesbachian source theory was used by a few Roman Catholics, notably Johann Kuhn of Tü-bingen and Adalbert Maier of Freiburg. It was the favored hypothesis of some members of the Tübingen school, led by Ferdinand Christian Baur, including Eduard Zeller, Albrecht Schwegler, the early Albrecht Ritschl, and above all David Friedrich Strauss. For an account of this period, see William R. Farmer, *The Synoptic Problem: A Critical Analysis* (New York: Macmillan 1964) 9f.

82 For a brief account of Griesbach's successors in synopsis construction, see Greeven, op. cit. n.61, 29–34.

83 See discussion of this quotation of Papias above, pp. 25f.

84 Farmer, op. cit. n.81, 25.

85 Hans-Herbert Stoldt, *History and Criticism of the Markan Hypothesis,* trans. Donald L. Niewyk (Macon: Mercer University Press 1980) 49.

86 Eichhorn, op. cit. n.79.

87 So Reicke, ibid., 66.

88 Reicke, ibid., 62, points out that one can account for DeWette's hybrid position from the influence of the oral hypothesis of Herder, DeWette's first teacher, and the direct utilization theory of Griesbach, his second teacher. For DeWette's discussion, see *Lehrbuch der historisch-kritischen Einleitung in die kanonischen Bücher des Neuen Testaments* (Berlin: G. Reimer 1826); see 6th ed. 1860: "Erklärung des Verhältnisses zwischen Matthäus und Lucas," 168–184. ET: *An Historical-Critical Introduction to the Canonical Books of the New Testament,* trans. from the 5th, improved and enlarged edition by Frederick Frothingham (Boston: Crosby, Nichols 1858); "Explanation of the Relation between Matthew and Luke," 148–163.

89 F. Bleek, *Einleitung in das Neue Testament* (Berlin: Reimer 1862). ET: *An Introduction to the New Testament* (Edinburgh: T. and T. Clark 1869–1870); see the discussion in Farmer, op. cit. n.81, 19f.

90 See comments by Reicke, op. cit. n.74, 62.

91 Eduard von Simons, *Hat der dritte Evangelist den kanonischen Matthäus benutzt?* (Bonn: Georgi 1880). See Farmer, op. cit. n.81, 40, 47 n.11; for the reaction in England, see Farmer 81.

92 See Henning Graf Reventlow, "Conditions and Presuppositions of Biblical Criticism in Germany in the Period of the Second Empire and Before: The Case of Heinrich Julius Holtzmann," in Henning Graf Reventlow and William Farmer, eds., *Biblical Studies and the Shifting of Paradigms, 1850–1914* (Sheffield: Sheffield Academic Press 1995) 274–276; further Stoldt, op. cit. n.85, 227f.

93 Reventlow, ibid. 275f. For a very helpful collection in English of some of the most important passages in Holtzmann's book, see Kümmel, op. cit. n.21, 152–155.

94 It was not without critics, however. His senior contemporary Adolf Hilgenfeld wrote a scathing review; see David Peabody, "H. J. Holtzmann and His European Colleagues: Aspects of the Nineteenth Century European Discussion of Gospel Origins," in Reventlow and Farmer, op. cit. n.92, 50–131, esp. 129. Equally significant is the unpublished doctoral dissertation written in 1866 by Hajo Uden Meijboom of the University of Groningen, *Geschiedenis en critiek der Marcushypothese,* trans. and ed. John J. Kiwiet, *A History and Critique of the Origin of the Marcan Hypothesis, 1835–1866,* New Gospel Studies 8 (Leuven: Peeters; Macon: Mercer University Press 1992). Meijboom's dissertation contains a surprisingly sophisticated analysis of the key figures in contemporary French and German Gospel scholarship. He also

found many questionable elements in Holtzmann's work. Peabody concludes, "Meijboom's conclusions about the inadequacy of works by Wilke, Weisse, Ewald, B. Weiss, and Holtzmann in establishing the Markan Hypothesis have been confirmed in modern times by W. R. Farmer, H.-H. Stoldt, and, within a more limited perspective, by me" (60f.). Unfortunately, Meijboom's valuable work hardly got beyond the Groningen library. David Peabody has examined Holtzmann's arguments and found evidence that he seriously misrepresented the research of Eduard Zeller on the use of linguistic characteristics to determine direction of dependence between two writings. Zeller had favored Griesbach's hypothesis, and Holtzmann, by misrepresenting Zeller's work, managed to reverse Zeller's conclusions to support Markan priority, causing academic "slippage" of far-reaching consequences; see David B. Peabody, "Chapters in the History of the Linguistic Argument for Solving the Synoptic Problem," in *Jesus, the Gospels, and the Church,* ed. E. P. Sanders (Macon: Mercer University Press 1987) 61–67. It is not clear why Zeller did not protest (cf. Peabody, "Holtzmann" 126f.).

95 See the excellent quotations about Jesus' character from Holtzmann's conclusion given in Kümmel, op. cit. n.21. For a further discussion of Holtzmann's lifelong pursuit of the values and aspirations of the new German middle class, see most recently Reventlow, op. cit. n.92, 275–285. For an appraisal from his most gifted student, see Albert Schweitzer, *Von Reimarus zu Wrede: Eine Geschichte der Leben-Jesu-Forschung* (Tübingen 1906); ET: *Quest of the Historical Jesus* (New York: Macmillan 1948) 295: "The ideal life of Jesus at the close of the nineteenth century is the Life which Heinrich Julius Holtzmann did not write but which can be pieced together from his commentary on the Synoptics and his New Testament Theology."

96 Reventlow, op. cit. n.92, 283f.

97 Ibid. 286–288. For a more detailed account of the process whereby the Prussian emperor Wilhelm and the Reich Chancellor Bismarck made the choice of Holtzmann, see William R. Farmer, "State *Interesse* and Marcan Primacy, 1870–1914," in Reventlow and Farmer, op. cit. n.92, 15–49. For extracts from the correspondence between them regarding Holtzmann, see Reventlow, op. cit. n.92, 285–288.

98 See Reventlow, ibid. 286f.

99 For the genius of Holtzmann's solution, see Farmer, op. cit. n.81, 44f. Weiss contributed many commentaries on New Testament books in the new *Meyer Kommentar;* Kümmel, op. cit. n.21, 172f.

100 Meijboom, trans. Kiwiet, op. cit. n.94, xxiii.

101 For the most recent account of this period in German, state-controlled university life, see Farmer, op. cit. n.97. Ironically, the best research on the history of the German universities has been done not by German but by English and American scholars; see the Select Bibliography in Farmer, 43–46.

102 As evidence, I point to this paean to Holtzmann in Kümmel, op. cit. n.21, 151: "Heinrich Julius Holtzmann ... summed up all previous research [on the Gospels] in magnificent fashion (*in seinem die ganze bisherigen Forschung souverän zusammen-fassenden Werk*). He not only demonstrated most convincingly, by an appeal to the primitive character of its narrative style and diction, that Mark's Gospel was the source of the two other Synoptics, but also showed just as convincingly that we must assume a second source back of Matthew and Luke, one that consisted mainly of discourses ... Holtzmann grounded the two-source hypothesis so carefully that the study of Jesus henceforth could not again dispense with this firm base (*diesen Boden nicht mehr aufgeben konnte*)."

103 For a fascinating glimpse into this little-known aspect of the dissemination of Holtzmann's influence, see Hans Rollmann, "Baron Friedrich von Hügel and the Conveyance of German Protestant Biblical Criticism in Roman Catholic Modernism," in Reventlow and Farmer, op. cit. n.92, 197–222.

104 W. Sanday, ed., *Studies in the Synoptic Problem: By Members of the University of Oxford* (Oxford: Clarendon Press 1911).

105 H. J. Holtzmann, *Lehrbuch der historisch-kritischen Einleitung in das Neue Testament* 2:339 (italics added); cited in Stoldt, op. cit. n.85, 92. Holtzmann's change of viewpoint was duly noted and welcomed by the Oxford scholar F. H. Woods in 1909; see Farmer, op. cit. n.81, 66.

106 Paul Wernle, *Die synoptische Frage* (1899) 218. Quoted in Stoldt, ibid. 92f.

107 The originator was probably J. Weiss; see F. Neirynck, "The Symbol Q," in *ETL* 54 (1978) 119–125.

108 See the discussion of this process in Farmer, op. cit. n.81, 70f., 90f.

109 "Die Markus-Kontroverse in ihrer heutigen Gestalt," in *Archiv für Religions-wissenschaft* (1907) 18; quoted in Stoldt, op. cit. n.85, 95.

110 B. H. Streeter, *The Four Gospels: A Study of Origins, Treating the Manuscript Tradition, Sources, Authorship, and Dates* (London: Macmillan 1924).

111 The English scholars were thoroughly familiar with the whole spectrum of German research. Cf. Sanday's comparative chart, published in Smith's *Dictionary of the Bible* (1893), of Holtzmann's hypothetical sources with those of Weizsäcker, Weisse, Wendt, and Beyschlag; cited in Farmer, op. cit. n.81, 40 n.5.

112 See especially F. C. Burkitt, *The Gospel History and Its Transmission* (Edinburgh: T. & T. Clark 1906).

113 John C. Hawkins, *Horae Synopticae: Contributions to the Study of the Synoptic Problem* (Oxford: Clarendon Press 1899).

114 See especially his influential *Encyclopaedia Britannica* article "Gospels," 9th ed., 1879.

115 W. G. Rushbrooke, *Synopticon: An Exposition of the Common Matter of the Synoptic Gospels* (London: Macmillan 1880).

116 *Pace* Greeven, op. cit. n.58, 28: "To the honour of Griesbach it must here be stressed that neither in this conspectus nor anywhere else in his synopsis does he lay before the user a particular theory about the mutual relationship of the Gospels." If Greeven had compared Griesbach's synoptic arrangement with that of the Neo-Griesbachians (who *did* use the theory to guide their synopsis construction), he would have discovered a virtually identical arrangement. But Greeven firmly believed that it was possible to create a source-theory-free synopsis; cf. Introduction to his edition of *Albert Huck, Synopse der drei ersten Evangelien mit Beigabe der johanneischen Parallelstellen* (Tübingen: Mohr/Siebeck 1981).

117 For more information on each, see Greeven, ibid. 28–36.

118 Tischendorf called his product a synopsis but the full title reveals his true aims: *Synopsis Evangelica ex Quattuor evangeliis ordine chronologico concinnavit praetexto brevi commentario illustravit ad antiquos testes apposito apparatu critico recensuit* (Lipsiae: Avenarius & Mendelssohn 1851).

119 See his thirty-page chronological outline: "*Conspectus synopsis evangelicae,*" followed by a seven-page "*de rationibus textus criticiis*" in the Prolegomena.

120 Holtzmann explained in his Preface: "Among the synopses in print, the most serviceable is the *Synopticon* of Rushbrooke, which is, at least for scholarly research, indispensable … (But) for normal needs (?) Herr Albert Huck's synopsis, which follows the principles of the present commentary, … should suffice" (quoted in Greeven, op. cit. n.61, 38).

121 My translation. See A. Huck, *Synopse der drei ersten Evangelien* (Freiburg 1892) v: "*Vorliegende Synopse der drei ersten Evangelien erhebt keinen Anspruch auf selfständige, wissenschaftliche Bedeutung. Sie will in erster Linie nur eine Ergänzung zu dem betreffenden Commentar von Holtzmann bilden und das Studium dieses Buches erleichtern. Dem entsprechend ist die ganze Einrichtung getroffen. Die Überschriften sind, von wenigen ungedeutenden Änderungen abgesehen aus dem HC. herübergenommen; auch bezüglich der Eintheilung der Perikopen weicht die Synopse nur an 3 Stellen etwas vom HC. ab. Sonst ist streng der Gang des HC. befolgt.*" An American translation was made of Huck's first edition with an admiring Preface ("the best thing we have in its class") by Ross L. Finney. See *Huck's Synopsis of the First Three Gospels Arranged for English Readers* (Cincinnati: Jennings & Graham 1907).

122 Italics added. Huck's German is "*Der Anschluss an den Hand- oder überhaupt irgend einen Kommentar oder eine synoptische Theorie ist aufgegeben worden. Leitend war nur der Gedanke: die einzelnen Evangelien möglichst in ihrer natürlicher Ordnung und in ihrem Zusammenhang zu belassen und doch das Gemeinsame am gleichen Orte zu bieten um eine synoptische Behandlung zu gestatten*"; see *Synopse der drei ersten Evangelien,* 3rd ed. (Tübingen: Mohr/Siebeck 1906) v; cf. vi. For proof to the contrary of this claim, see D. Dungan, "Theory of Synopsis Construction," *Biblica* 61 (1980) 326;

cf. D. Dungan, "Synopses of the Future," *Biblica* 66 (1985) 468; reprinted in D. Dungan, ed., *The Interrelations of the Gospels,* 326.

123 See Dungan, "Theory," ibid. 316f., 326f.; further, Dungan, "Synopses," ibid. 468.

124 Sanday, op. cit. n.104, viii.

125 Cf. the comment by Sanday on this subject: "It has been our custom to take the Synoptic Gospels section by section, with Tischendorf's handy *Synopsis Evangelica* as our basis, but of course calling in the many excellent Synopses that are in use, especially Rushbrooke and Wright, and, among the Germans, Huck"; see ibid. The reference to Rushbrooke is to Rushbrooke, op. cit. n.115.

126 So Greeven: "The *Synopticon* was not only suggested by E. A. Abbott . . . in his article 'Gospels' in the *Encyclopaedia Britannica* . . . (its) aim is to refute the opinion that Mark compiled his Gospel out of Matthew and Luke, and instead to show that he is their source" (op. cit. n.61, 36).

127 Farmer, op. cit. n.81, 192, quotes this dedication in the front of Rushbrooke's *Synopticon:* "To Edwin Abbott Abbott, DD, the first suggester of this work, who to suggestion added encouragement and to encouragement counsel and assistance, these pages are now dedicated by his former pupil."

128 Rushbrooke gave this rather disingenuous explanation for this procedure: "St. Mark's version, which stands in the left-hand column, *apart from other considerations,* seemed best fitted by its brevity to be adopted as the standard. It has therefore been printed at full length without deviation from its order" (ii; italics added).

129 So Farmer, op. cit. n.81, 194.

130 Burnett Hillman Streeter, *The Four Gospels: A Study of Origins, Treating of the Manuscript Tradition, Sources, Authorship, and Dates* (London: Macmillan 1924) 161 n.1; see further, Farmer, *Synoptic Problem* 191; 194.

131 Greeven, op. cit. n.58; see further the discussion in Farmer, ibid. 193.

132 See Sanday, op. cit. n.104, 96; quoted in Farmer, ibid. 195.

133 Sandays Oxford Seminar liked Tischendorf's fifth edition of his *Synopsis evangelica* (Lipsiae: Hermann Mendelsohn 1884) for his superb critical text. But Tischendorf's pericope divisions were too large. Rushbrooke's *Synopticon* (London: Macmillan 1880) focused attention on the shared matter in the Synoptic Gospels (triple tradition and several kinds of double tradition). Somehow the Seminar ignored the fact that Rushbrooke was constructed to *illustrate* the priority of Mark, prompting the Seminar to use it as objective evidence of Matthew and Luke. The same result came about when they used another of their German favorites, the research of Bernhard Weiss. But here we must distinguish between his *Das Marcusevangelium und seine synoptischen parallelen* (Berlin: W. Hertz/Besser 1872), and his *Die Quellen der synoptischen Überlieferung* (Leipzig: J. C. Hinrichs 1908), which is much

more nuanced. The former would have readily led the Seminar to adopt the Two Source Hypothesis (of which Weiss was an ardent advocate, as was his son Johannes).

Apparently, the Sanday Seminar did not use another well-known English synopsis, Arthur Wright's *Synopsis of the Gospels in Greek* (London: Macmillan 1896, 1903). It would have given them a very different picture of the relations among the Gospels. This avoidance was probably not an accident, since the members of the Seminar generally believed (as did most German scholars by the end of the nineteenth century) that the oral hypothesis (upon which Wright was based) was outdated and obsolete. While his large folio pages were a marvel of the printer's craft equal in every respect to Rushbrooke's *Synopticon*, Wright's *Synopsis* would not have fit in with the tendency of Sanday's Seminar to look to the priority of Mark plus Q.

Finally, since the Seminar undoubtedly used Huck's *third* edition (and not the first) of his *Synopse* (op. cit. n.122), they might have believed they were in possession of a "natural" (Huck's word) arrangement, which, like Rushbrooke, arranged the common "triple tradition" according to Mark's order and, in between, placed the common material shared by Matthew and Luke (the so-called Q source).

In short, the combined use of the synopses of Rushbrooke and Huck—when "confirmed" by the biased charts of Sir John Hawkins—became a circular argument leading ineluctably to the argument from order of pericopes Streeter presented in his 1924 "magnus opium."

134 See Farmer, op. cit. n.91, 192.

135 See Farmer, ibid. 192f.

136 W. G. Kümmel, *Introduction to the New Testament, Founded by Paul Feine and Johannes Behm,* trans. A. J. Mattill Jr. (Nashville: Abingdon Press 1965) 33.

137 A comparison between the Saxon *Heliand,* the ninth-century Gospel harmony prepared for use in missionary work among the Teutonic nations in Friesland, and the canonical Gospels (the *Heliand*'s main source), reveals that already here—*in the very earliest texts of Saxon Christianity*—a violent hatred of "the Jews" has sprung up because they killed the Lord Jesus, even though the Saxons had never met a single Jew. Astonishingly, two recent analyses of the enculturation of the Gospel in northern Europe as represented by the *Heliand* do not even mention the blatantly heightened antagonism toward "the Jews" in it; see G. Ronald Murphy, S.J., *The Saxon Savior: The Germanic Transformation of the Gospel in the Ninth-Century Heliand* (Oxford: Oxford University Press 1989); and James C. Russell, *The Germanization of Early Medieval Christianity: A Sociohistorical Approach to Religious Transformation* (Oxford: Oxford University Press 1994).

138 On the *political* aspirations of Strauss, see the important essay by Friedrich

Wilhelm Graf, "The Old Faith and the New: The Late Theology of D. F. Strauss," in Reventlow and Farmer, op. cit. n.92, 223–245. For a biographical sketch of Strauss's stress-filled life, see Leander E. Keck, trans. and ed., *The Christ of Faith and the Jesus of History*, Lives of Jesus Series, ed. Leander E. Keck (Philadelphia: Fortress Press 1977) xix–1.

139 David Friedrich Schleiermacher, *Der christliche Glaube nach den Grundsätzen der evangelischen Kirche* (Berlin: 1821). All quotations are from Schleiermacher, *The Christian Faith*, 2nd ed., trans. H. R. Macintosh and J. S. Stewart (Edinburgh: T. & T. Clark 1928).

140 Ibid. 115.

141 Ibid. 62 (italics added).

142 Ibid. 388.

143 Ibid. 389.

144 Ibid. 61.

145 Kümmel, op. cit. n.21, 302.

146 Henning Graf Reventlow, *Problems of Old Testament Theology in the Twentieth Century*, trans. John Bowden (Philadelphia: Fortress Press 1985) 29.

147 Adolf von Harnack, *Marcion: The Gospel of the Alien God*, 2nd ed., trans. John. E. Steely and L. D. Bierma (Durham, NC: Labyrinth Press 1924) 134 (italics in original).

148 Ibid. 135 (italics in original).

149 I am indebted for this list to Reventlow, op. cit. n.146, 28ff.

150 Such views were not confined to Germany. The English writer H. S. Chamberlain claimed that "Jesus was not a Jew by blood"; the French Orientalist Ernest Renan said in his extremely popular *Life of Jesus* that it was impossible to know what kind of blood flowed in Jesus' veins; cf. Ernest Renan, *Vie de Jésus*, fifth ed. (Paris: Michel Lévy Frères 1863) 22: "*Cette province (Galilee) comptait parmi ses habitants, au temps de Jésus, beaucoup de non-Juifs (Phéniciens, Syriens, Arabes, et même Grecs). Les conversions au judaïsme n'étaient point rares dans ces sortes de pays mixtes. Il est donc impossible de soulever ici aucune question de race et de rechercher quel sang coulait dans les veines de celui qui a le plus contribué à effacer dans l'humanité les distinctions de sang.*" Cf. (For one of many possible English translations see Ernest Renan, *The Life of Jesus* [New York: A. L. Burt Company nd] ch. 2, third paragraph p. 83).

151 There is a considerable literature on this subject. See especially Robert P. Erickson, *Theologians under Hitler: Gerhard Kittel, Paul Althaus, and Emmanuel Hirsch* (New Haven: Yale University Press 1985); Klaus Scholder, *A Requiem for Hitler and Other New Perspectives on the German Church Struggle*, trans. John Bowman (London/Philadelphia: SCM Press & Trinity Press International 1989); and for the best general history, Scholder, *The Churches and the Third Reich*, 2 vols., trans. John Bowden (Philadelphia: Fortress Press 1988).

152 The signatories also included such world-famous scientists as Max Planck
and Wilhelm Röntgen, literary figures such as Gerhard Hauptmann and Max
Liebermann, and humanists like Karl Lamprecht and Rudolf Eucken. The list
represented the cream of the German universities, including theology faculties. It was the shock caused by this manifesto that caused Karl Barth to break
with German liberal theology. For a brief discussion of this document and
its impact on Barth's development, see George Rupp, *Culture Protestantism:
German Liberal Theology at the Turn of the Twentieth Century,* AAR Studies
in Religion 15 (Atlanta: Scholars Press 1977) 11f.

153 This document is widely regarded as the foundation of the German Christian
Movement; for bibliography, see Reventlow, op. cit. n.146, 29.

154 It is an ironic fact that German scholars seem to know little about the history
of their own universities and have a typically naive understanding about their
real or imagined "academic freedom." For in-depth histories and discussions,
one must consult British and American scholars; see especially Charles E.
McClelland, *State, Society, and University in Germany, 1700–1914* (Cambridge: University Press 1980). Most recently, see Christian Simon, "History
as a Case-Study of the Relations between University Professors and the State
in Germany," in Reventlow and Farmer, op. cit. n.92.

155 Augustin Bea, *The Study of the Synoptic Gospels,* English version edited by
Joseph A. Fitzmyer (New York: Harper & Row 1965) 10f.

156 For a list of all the translations and imitations of Huck, see David L. Dungan,
"Theory of Synopsis Construction," *Biblica* 61 (1980) 319f. This includes the
use of colored charts, such as Allan Barr, *A Diagram of Synoptic Relationships*
(Edinburgh: T. & T. Clark 1938); cf. Preface 2: "In the preparation of this
Diagram I have consulted the works of many writers on the Synoptic Gospels
and I can make only a general acknowledgment of my indebtedness to them.
I wish, however, to mention particularly Huck's *Synopse der drei ersten Evangelien,* in which the Greek text is arranged in a form indispensable for a work
of this kind."

157 Willi Marxsen, *Introduction to the New Testament,* trans. G. Buswell (Philadelphia: Fortress Press 1968) 118: "The Two Source theory has been so widely
accepted by scholars that one feels inclined to abandon the term 'theory' (in
the sense of 'hypothesis'). We can, in fact, regard it as *an assured finding.*"
The German is more cautious: *"Abschließend ist darauf hinzuweisen, daß es
sich bei der Zweiquellentheorie um eine—Theorie handelt. Sie hat sich aber
in der Arbeit an den synoptischen Evangelien so sehr bewährt, daß sie als ein
(relativ) gesichertes Ergebnis der Forschung angesehen werden kann"; Einleitung in das Neue Testament: Eine Einführung in ihre Probleme,* 4te voll. neu
bearb. Aufl. (Gütersloh: Gerd Mohn 1978) 125.

158 Italics added. P. Vielhauer, "Zum synoptischen Problem. Ein Bericht über die
Theorien Léon Vaganay," *Theologische Literaturzeitung* 80 (1955) 652: *"Die*

quellenkritische Arbeit an den Synoptikern hat ... mit der Zwei-Quellen-Theorie tatsächlich ihr Ende erreicht." Reference found in A. Ennulat, *Die »Minor Agreements«. Untersuchungen zu einer offenen Frage des synoptischen Problems.* WUNT 2/62 (Tübingen: Mohr/Siebeck 1994) 1.

NOTES TO CHAPTER 21

1 For further discussion of Schweitzer, see above, p. 148.

2 For example, W. G. Kümmel said, "The Synoptic Problem was not actually recognized until the second half of the eighteenth century"; see Werner Georg Kümmel, *Introduction to the New Testament,* trans. A. J. Mattill Jr., 14th German edition (Nashville: Abingdon Press 1966) 37.

3 Edgar Krentz, *The Historical-Critical Method,* Guides to Biblical Study (Philadelphia: Fortress Press 1975) 28–30 (italics added).

4 For the names of German theologians who signed their names to the manifesto defending the Kaiser's invasion of Belgium, see chap. 20 n.152.

5 Krentz has a naive and narrowly conceived list of the alleged benefits of German historical criticism entitled "By Their Fruits Shall Ye Know Them" (63–67). What "fruits" has Krentz overlooked?

6 For a description of Spinoza's rejection of the category of sin, as well as good and evil, see above, p. 213.

7 For a partial list of Gospel harmonies published down to 1896, see E. Robinson, *A Harmony of the Four Gospels in Greek,* ed. M. B. Riddle (Boston 1896). For a partial list of harmonies from 1896 to the present, see Robert L. Thomas and Stanley N. Gundry, *The NIV Harmony of the Gospels with Explanations and Essays Using the Text of the New International Version: A Revised Edition of the John A. Broadus and A. T. Robertson Harmony of the Gospels* (San Francisco: Harper 1988) 256ff. For the ancient Church, the authors inexplicably skip Augustine, nor do they mention any medieval or modern European harmonies. For a more complete list of the former, see Harvey K. McArthur, *The Quest through the Centuries: The Search for the Historical Jesus* (Philadelphia: Fortress Press 1966). The list of Thomas and Gundry must be used with caution; they do not seem to understand the difference between a synopsis and a harmony.

8 Thomas and Gundry, ibid.

9 Heinrich Greeven, *Albert Huck, Synopse der drei ersten Evangelien mit Beigabe der johanneischen Parallelstellen* (Tübingen: Mohr/Siebeck 1981).

10 Robert W. Funk, *New Gospel Parallels,* vol. 1, *The Synoptic Gospels,* vol. 2, *John and the Other Gospels* (Philadelphia: Fortress Press 1985). Soon after the publication of volume 1, Funk brought out a revision based on a more readable format. It contained just the Gospel of Mark plus parallels: *New*

Gospel Parallels, vol. 1,2 Mark, rev. ed. (Sonoma: Polebridge 1990). Future publications will have Matthew and Luke in separate volumes to reduce the cost and size of the books. A unique publication is the *Sayings Parallels: A Workbook for the Jesus Tradition,* ed. John Dominic Crossan (Philadelphia: Fortress Press 1986). Not restricted to just the so-called Q texts, it contains only the sayings of Jesus in the canonical Gospels with parallels to all other apocryphal Gospels.

11 For Kurt Aland's claim to have produced the "New Standard Text," see above, pp. 297f.

12 See esp. Eldon Jay Epp, "A Continuing Interlude in New Testament Textual Criticism?" in Eldon Jay Epp and Gordon D. Fee, *Studies in the Theory and Method of New Testament Textual Criticism,* Studies and Documents 45 (Grand Rapids: Eerdmans 1993) 109–123.

13 Eldon Jay Epp, "The Significance of the Papyri for Determining the Nature of the New Testament Text in the Second Century: A Dynamic View of Textual Transmission," in Epp and Fee, ibid. 289f.

14 Ibid. 290: "P^{75} is not an editorial adaptation or recension," that is, it is free of tendentious alterations. Epp cites the Alands' decision to apply the term "strict" to this text type, i.e., it was "strictly controlled" and therefore relatively free from tendentious alterations; see Kurt Aland and Barbara Aland, *The Text of the New Testament: An Introduction to the Critical Editions and to the Theory and Practice of Modern Textual Criticism,* trans. E. F. Rhodes (Grand Rapids: Eerdmans 1987) 63, 95; cf. the Alands' contrast with the "free" text type (93) and the "normal" text type (95).

15 Léon Vaganay and Christian-Bernard Amphoux, *An Introduction to New Testament Textual Criticism,* rev. ed., trans. J. Heimerdinger (Cambridge: University Press 1986) 169 (italics added).

16 William L. Petersen, *Tatian's Diatessaron: Its Creation, Dissemination, Significance, and History in Scholarship,* Suppl. Vig. Christ. 25 (Leiden: Brill 1994) 20 (italics added).

17 Ibid. 11f. (italics added).

18 Ibid. 12.

19 Ibid. 20f.

20 Ibid. 21.

21 Ibid.

22 Ibid. 20 (italics added).

23 Ibid. 22.

24 See the discussion by Kurt Aland and Barbara Aland, "Did the West develop its own text type," in Aland and Aland, op. cit. n.14, 54f. However, it is not clear what the Alands mean by their dismissal of this text type, since they seem to reintroduce something very similar to it; see the discussion of the Alands' ambiguous statements in Epp, op. cit. n.14, 293 n.42.

25 See P. Benoit and M.-É. Boismard, *Synopse des quatres évangiles en francais avec parallèls des apocryphes et des pères,* 2nd ed., rev. and corrected by P. Sandevoir, 2 vols. (Paris: Les éditions du Cerf 1973) Tome I Textes. The text for this synopsis was the first edition of the *Bible de Jérusalem.* Boismard had nothing to do with the preparation of this synopsis; his contribution was limited to the explanation of the composition of the Gospels in volume 2.

26 M.-É. Boismard and A. Lamouille, *Synopsis Graeca quattuor evangeliorum* (Leuven: Peeters 1986); see the explanation on xi. The parallelization of pericopes in this synopsis is almost the same as Benoit's, and quite dissimilar to both Huck and Aland (see xi). This synopsis sets a new record for atomizing the material (Benoit has 376 pericopes; Boismard has 404, beating Aland's old record of 367; Huck has only 275), and John is matched up more precisely than Benoit had done, especially in the area between Mt 3–12.

27 It is to be hoped that someone will examine the orthodox *removal of Jewish elements* from the Gospels in the way B. Ehrman demonstrated the orthodox emendation of the Gospels during the Christological controversies; see Bart Ehrman, *The Orthodox Corruption of Scripture: The Effect of Early Christological Controversies on the Text of the New Testament* (Oxford: University Press 1993).

28 Reuben Swanson, *New Testament Greek Manuscripts: Variant Readings Arranged in Horizontal Lines against Codex Vaticanus* (Sheffield: Academic Press and William Carey International University Press 1995).

29 See Bruce Metzger, *A Textual Commentary on the Greek New Testament: A Companion Volume to the United Bible Societies' Greek New Testament,* 3rd ed. (1971; 2nd rev. ed., London & New York: United Bible Societies 1994).

30 See Robert W. Funk, Roy W. Hoover, and the Jesus Seminar, *The Five Gospels: The Search for the Authentic Words of Jesus* (New York: Macmillan 1993) 35.

31 See dedication page in ibid.

32 Funk et al., op. cit. n.31. It is not clear what the number ("five") alluded to in the title means. Funk said the Seminar examined something like "fifteen hundred versions of approximately five hundred items," items being parables, aphorisms, dialogues, and stories containing words of Jesus (35). In the end, the Coptic Gospel of Thomas seems to have gotten a majority of the affirmative votes for authentic words outside the canonical Gospels; perhaps this explains the number five in the title.

33 Albert Schweitzer, *The Quest of the Historical Jesus: A Critical Study of Its Progress from Reimarus to Wrede,* trans. W. Montgomery (New York: Macmillan 1968) 4 (italics added).

34 Cf. L. T. Johnson, "The Jesus Seminar's Misguided Quest for the Historical Jesus," *Christian Century,* 3–10 January 1996, 16–22; R. B. Hays, "The Corrected Jesus" (a review of *The Five Gospels*), *First Things* 4 (1994) 43–48; and, on other writings but with the same criticism, L. E. Keck, "The Second Com-

ing of the Liberal Jesus?" *Christian Century,* 24–31 August 1994, 784–787. One would have thought that someone as hermeneutically knowledgeable as Robert Funk would have seen this coming. But perhaps the Hollywood atmosphere that suffused at least some meetings of the Seminar clouded his better judgment. As the reporter for *GQ for the Modern Man* wrote after visiting one session, "Free to choose whatever suited their fancy, these scholars created a Baskin-Robbins of Jesuses"; *GQ,* June 1994, 116–123; quote on 118.

35 For a partial list of Gospel harmonies published down to 1896, see Robinson, op. cit. n.7. For the most recent harmony in English, see Thomas and Gundry, op. cit. n.7. As evidence of the latter authors' concern for literal truth, note especially the concern for "historical integrity" in the essay "Problems and Principles of Harmonization" (293–299). Thomas lists most of the (English-language) harmonies created since the late nineteenth century down to the present (256ff.). For other comments on this harmony, see n.8.

36 See n.7.

37 Consider the following defense of the historical truth of the Gospels in the chapter entitled "Is a Harmony of the Gospels Legitimate?" Thomas and Gundry list several objections to harmonies, all stemming from the advent of "modern criticism." Regarding the modern charge that the Gospels were not written to be histories but Gospels, they say, "The evangelists intended to give accurate reports based on thorough investigation (Lk 1:3–4); it is unlikely that those who wrote . . . practiced distortions of historical truth in the very books where it is taught" (249). To the charge that modern redaction criticism makes it difficult "to accept the gospels at face value," they insist, "It may be agreed that each gospel writer had a distinctive purpose in mind (as Augustine clearly thought), but it is unwarranted to conclude that he altered the facts at hand in order to attain this purpose. Matthew, Mark, Luke, and John were truthful men writing about a system of truth built around him who is the Truth. To arbitrarily attribute to them an almost endless stream of lies . . . is to impugn the truth itself" (250).

38 Gordon D. Fee, *New Testament Exegesis: A Handbook for Students and Pastors,* 2nd rev. ed. (Louisville: Westminster/John Knox Press 1993).

39 Ibid. 27; cf. 31. A rather striking example of this principle comes out in Fee's insistence that, when interpreting the Gospels, one can have recourse in the final analysis to the text alone: "Given the nature of the Gospels (i.e., their conflicting testimonies) . . . the task of exegesis is primarily to understand a passage in its present context" (47). He goes on to tentatively suggest that the interpreter may hazard some conjectures about the historical Jesus as part of an explanation of the meaning, but ultimately the text must remain the touchstone, since "this is the only *certain* context one has" (48; italics in original).

40 Ibid. 161.

41 When he comes to describe the task of writing the sermon, Fee does suggest that the pastor must rely on God's help (162): "Spend some time in reflection on the text and in prayer (he does not suggest the number of minutes in this step) . . . Let there be time for you yourself to respond to the Word of God . . . Remember: Sermon preparation without personal encounter with the Word and without prayer will probably lack inspiration; and sermons preached by those who have not themselves sat in awful (*sic*) silence before the majesty of God and his Word will probably accomplish very little."

42 Ibid. 160. This time limit is part of a series of timed steps: studying the passage: one hour twenty minutes; determining the meaning: one hour; historical/literary questions: one hour; secondary literature: fifty minutes; biblical/theological framework: thirty minutes; application: forty minutes. This same step is elaborated in the long method as follows: "As you begin to draw together all of your discoveries . . . you will want to fit the 'message' of the text into its broader biblical and theological contexts. How does the passage function dogmatically in the section, book, division, Testament, Bible—in that order? . . . Where does the passage fit within the whole corpus of revelation comprising Christian (dogmatic) theology?" (54f.).

43 Hans Conzelmann and Andreas Lindemann, *Interpreting the New Testament: An Introduction to the Principles and Methods of N.T. Exegesis*, trans. of the 8th German ed. of the *Arbeitsbuch zum Neuen Testament* by Siegfried S. Schatzmann (Peabody, MA: Hendrickson 1988); John H. Hayes and Carl R. Holladay, *Biblical Exegesis: A Beginner's Handbook*, 2nd rev. ed. (Atlanta: John Knox Press 1987).

44 Conzelmann-Lindemann, ibid. 1 (italics added).

45 Ibid.

46 Ibid. xvii.

47 Ibid. 2.

48 Ibid.

49 These methods are spelled out briefly on 2–7.

50 For the discussion of source criticism, see 45–59; for form criticism, see 59–82; for redaction criticism, see 82–87.

51 Ibid. xvii.

52 Ibid. 2f.

53 Ibid. xviif (italics added).

54 Hayes and Holladay, op. cit. n.44, 23 (italics added).

55 Ibid. 143 (italics added).

56 Ibid.

57 Ibid. 139 (italics added).

58 Ibid. 138 (italics added).

59 Ibid. 29.

60 Ibid. 131.

61 Ibid. 143.

62 Ibid. 148 (italics added).

63 Another way Hayes and Holladay put out a double message is to urge the preacher to be open to the text and engage the Bible at a deep, existential level (148) but then also to insist: "under no circumstances should one suspend critical judgment in reading the biblical text" (154). Which is it? Can't do both.

64 Ibid. 139 (italics added).

65 Ibid. 143 (italics added).

66 Ibid. 147 (italics added).

67 Raymond E. Brown, Joseph A. Fitzmyer, and Roland E. Murphy, eds., *The Jerome Biblical Commentary* (Englewood Cliffs, NJ: Prentice-Hall 1968); cf. Raymond E. Brown, Joseph A. Fitzmyer, and Roland E. Murphy, eds., *The New Jerome Biblical Commentary* (Englewood Cliffs, NJ: Prentice-Hall 1990).

68 *JBC* 2:1–6.

69 *NJBC* 587–595.

70 *JBC* 72:7–20; cf. Ronald D. Witherup, *NJBC* 1130–1145.

71 *JBC* 2:8; unchanged in *NJBC* 1131.

72 *JBC* 2:604–623; cf. Sandra M. Schneiders, *NJBC* 1146–1165. I will not discuss the differences between the two versions; the comments in the text are based on the latter.

73 *NJBC* 1147.

74 Ibid.

75 Ibid.

76 *NJBC* 1150f. (italics in original).

77 *NJBC* 1149f.

NOTES TO CHAPTER 22

1 See above, pp. 308f.

2 For an explanation of the revolutionary purposes of the Gospel synopsis, see above, pp. 318ff.

3 For a complete bibliography of all scholarly opposition to the Two Source Hypothesis between 1920 and 1970, see David L. Dungan, "Mark—The Abridgment of Matthew and Luke," in *Jesus and Man's Hope*, ed. David Miller and Dikran Y. Hadidian (Pittsburgh: Pittsburgh Theological Seminary 1971) 1:51–97; reprinted in Arthur Bellinzoni, ed., *The Two-Source Hypothesis: A Critical Appraisal* (Macon: Mercer University Press 1985). Still the most

incisive history of this debate is by William R. Farmer, *The Synoptic Problem: A Critical Analysis* (New York: Macmillan 1964).

4 See Hajo Uden Meijboom, *A History and Critique of the Origin of the Marcan Hypothesis, 1835–1866,* trans. John J. Kiwiet, New Gospel Studies 8 (Leuven: Peeters; Macon: Mercer University Press 1992) 72–73. Meijboom's book is also noteworthy in its presentation of rarely read early French scholarship on the source question. Kiwiet's admirable translation is prefaced by a superb historical introduction locating Meijboom within the main theological currents of his scholarly world.

5 See the discussion of Lummis and Streeter's review in Farmer, op. cit. n.3, 112.

6 H. G. Jameson, *The Origin of the Synoptic Gospels: A Revision of the Synoptic Problem* (Oxford: Basil Blackwell 1922) 10f.

7 The total number of these minor agreements has had a strange inclination to increase each time they are counted. Sir John Hawkins claimed to have discovered over 230 minor agreements but listed only 21 of them as worthy of discussion (see *Horae Synopticae: Contributions to the Study of the Synoptic Problem,* 2nd ed. [Oxford: Clarendon Press 1909] 208ff.). Streeter discussed considerably more (see *The Four Gospels: A Study of Origins, Treating of the Manuscript Tradition, Sources, Authorship, and Dates* [London: Macmillan 1924] 295–331). Frans Neirynck listed over 750 (see Frans Neirynck, ed., with Theo Hansen and Frans van Segbroeck, *The Minor Agreements of Matthew and Luke Against Mark with a Cumulative List,* BETL 37 (Leuven: Leuven University Press 1974), but most recently, Andreas Ennulat conducted the most exhaustive examination ever attempted and he claims to have discovered more than 1,000 distributed throughout all of the material Matthew and Luke have in common with Mark (see *Die "Minor Agreements": Untersuchungen zu einer offenen Frage des synoptischen Problems,* WUNT 2/62 (Tübingen: Mohr/Siebeck 1994; esp. p. 417).

8 For a discussion of Jameson's book and Burkitt's review, see Farmer, op. cit. n.3, 113f.

9 See the comments of Farmer on Streeter's handling of Lummis (ibid. 112) and Burkitt's review of Jameson (113f.). For a detailed discussion of Streeter's arrogant and question-begging treatment of Jameson's arguments, see ibid. 287–293.

10 Equally influential at the time, though rarely mentioned in later histories of the Synoptic Problem, were the massive studies of Markan usage, based squarely on the biased lists and tables of Hawkins' *Horae Synopticae,* by another Oxford scholar, C. H. Turner, in the *Journal of Theological Studies* for 1924 and 1925. For Turner's uncritical use of Hawkins, see Farmer, ibid. 115.

11 For a discussion of Chapman, see Farmer, ibid. 191, 196.

12 Basil Christopher Butler, *The Originality of St. Matthew: A Critique of the*

Two-Document Hypothesis (Cambridge: Cambridge University Press 1951) 63.

13 Ibid. 65.

14 Ibid.

15 Ibid. 67.

16 C. F. D. Moule, *The Birth of the New Testament,* 2nd ed. (San Francisco: Harper & Row 1962) 223–232.

17 Frans Neirynck, "Synoptic Problem," *IDB* Suppl. 845f.: "B. C. Butler has contended that there is a logical error in the traditional argument from order. A number of scholars, among them some who continue to espouse the two-document hypothesis on other grounds (Styler, Fuller), have in fact dismissed the argument as useless." Neirynck, "The Griesbach Hypothesis: The Phenomenon of Order," *Eph. Theol. Lov.* 58(1982) 114: "In a previous study on the argument from order, I observed that for too long this discussion had been characterized by abstract reasoning, which is still the case in the *'post-Butlerian' era"* (italics added).

18 For a more complete biographical history of W. R. Farmer, consult David Peabody, "William Reuben Farmer, a biographical and bibliographical essay," in E. P. Sanders, ed., *Jesus, the Gospels, and the Church: Essays in Honor of William R. Farmer* (Macon, GA: Mercer University Press 1987) ix–xxxviii.

19 Henry J. Cadbury, *The Making of Luke-Acts* (London: SPCK 1958).

20 Op. cit. n.3.

21 Ibid. 190.

22 See ibid. 199–233.

23 For a representative sample of thirteen reviews of Farmer's book, see Dungan, op. cit. n.3, 1:52.

24 William R. Farmer, *Synopticon: The Verbal Agreement between the Texts of Matthew, Mark, and Luke Contextually Exhibited* (Cambridge: University Press 1969).

25 Hans-Herbert Stoldt, *History and Criticism of the Marcan Hypothesis,* trans. Donald L. Niewyk (Macon: Mercer University Press 1980).

26 Ibid. 228.

27 Ibid.

28 Ibid.

29 Ibid. 232 (italics added).

30 Ibid. 233.

31 Ibid. 255. Especially choice is Stoldt's thundering peroration on 253–255.

32 Ibid. 259f.

33 The only review done by an eminent German scholar was by Hans Conzelmann in *Theologische Rundschau* 43 (1978). It contained an intentional misquotation and misrepresentation of Stoldt's book. For the evidence documenting Conzelmann's malicious act, see Farmer's Introduction to Stoldt,

ibid., xiv–xvii. Nor has Stoldt's book had much impact in North America, despite an attempt to emphasize some of its more important conclusions in a debate between Howard Kee and David Dungan with Stoldt present at the 1978 meeting of the Society of Biblical Literature in New Orleans.

34 For the conference proceedings, see Donald G. Miller and Dikran Y. Hadidian, eds., *Jesus and Man's Hope*, 2 vols. (Pittsburgh: Pittsburgh Theological Seminary 1971).

35 Their respective papers are to be found in ibid. vol. 1.

36 A key meeting took place near Basel in 1973 with Bo Reicke acting as host. Scholars Farmer consulted over a period of time included Bishop Eduard Lohse, Erich Grässer of Heidelberg, Heinrich Greeven of the University of Bochum, Otto Betz and Martin Hengel of Tübingen, Karl Rengstorf of Münster, and Kurt Aland of the Institut für Neutestamentliche Textforschung in Münster.

37 Christopher Tuckett, *The Revival of the Griesbach Hypothesis: An Analysis and Appraisal*, SNTS Monogr. Ser. 44 (Cambridge: University Press 1983).

38 See David Dungan, "Theory of Synopsis Construction," *Biblica* 61(1980) 305–329; further, Dungan, "Synopses of the Future," *Biblica* 66(1985) 457–492.

39 See E. P. Sanders, *The Tendencies of the Synoptic Tradition*, SNTS Monogr. Ser. 9 (Cambridge: University Press 1969).

40 See Lamar Cope, *Matthew: A Scribe Trained for the Kingdom of Heaven*, CBQ Monogr. Scr. 5 (Washington: Catholic Biblical Association of America 1976).

41 See Thomas R. W. Longstaff, *Evidence of Conflation in Mark? A Study in the Synoptic Problem* (Missoula: Scholars Press 1977).

42 See Joseph B. Tyson and Thomas R. W. Longstaff, *Synoptic Abstract*, Computer Bible 15 (Wooster: Biblical Research Associates 1978). Also Tyson, "Sequential Parallelism in the Synoptic Gospels," *NTS* 22 (1976) 276–308.

43 See Bernard Orchard, "Are All Gospel Synopses Biassed?" *Theol. Zeitschr.* 34(1978) 149–162. See also Dungan, "Theory" and "Synopses," op. cit. n.37.

44 See T. R. W. Longstaff and P. Thomas, *The Synoptic Problem: A Bibliography, 1716–1988*, New Gospel Studies 4 (Leuven: Peeters; Macon: Mercer University Press 1988).

45 See David B. Peabody, *Mark as Composer*, New Gospel Studies 1 (Leuven: Peeters; Macon: Mercer University Press 1987).

46 See Dennis Gordon Tevis, "An Analysis of Words and Phrases Characteristic of the Gospel of Matthew," unpubl. diss., Perkins School of Theology 1982; available from University Microfilm International of Ann Arbor, Michigan.

47 See David Barrett Peabody, "Chapters in the History of the Linguistic Argument for Solving the Synoptic Problem: the Nineteenth Century in Context,"

in *Jesus, the Gospels, and the Church,* ed. E. P. Sanders (Macon: Mercer University Press 1987) 57–61.

48 Ibid. 61–66.

49 Ibid. 57.

50 Ibid. 58, 61, 65, 66, 67.

51 See William R. Farmer and Dennis M. Farkasfalvy, *The Formation of the New Testament Canon: An Ecumenical Approach* (New York: Paulist Press 1983) esp. 39–74.

52 See especially W. R. Farmer's very important essay "State *Interesse* and Marcan Primacy, 1874–1914," in *The Four Gospels: Festschrift for Frans Neirynck,* ed. F. van Segbroeck, C. M. Tuckett, G. van Belle, and J. Verheyden, Biblio. Eph. Theol. 100 (Leyden: University Press 1992) 2473–2498. This was an earlier version of "Marcan Primacy and the Kulturkampf," in *The Gospel of Jesus: The Pastoral Relevance of the Synoptic Problem* (Philadelphia: Westminster/ John Knox Press 1994) 148–160. The most recent version, with select bibliographies on the history of German universities and on the *Kulturkampf,* is "State *Interesse* and Marcan Primacy, 1874–1914," in *Biblical Studies and the Shifting of Paradigms, 1854–1914,* ed. Henning Graf Reventlow and William Farmer, JSOT Suppl. Ser. 192 (Sheffield: Academic Press 1995) 15–49. This volume contains the reports delivered at two international conferences convened by Reventlow and Farmer and devoted to the subject of the German universities and the German government during the nineteenth century.

53 See J. G. F. Collison, "Linguistic Usages of the Gospel of Luke," unpubl. diss., Perkins School of Theology 1977; available from University Microfilm International of Ann Arbor, Michigan.

54 See Bernard Orchard, *A Synopsis of the Four Gospels in a New Translation: Arranged according to the Two Gospel Hypothesis* (Macon: Mercer University Press 1982). A year later he published *A Synopsis of the Four Gospels in Greek: Arranged according to the Two-Gospel Hypothesis* (Edinburgh: T. & T. Clark 1983).

55 See Bernard Orchard and Harold Riley, *The Order of the Synoptics: Why Three Synoptic Gospels* (Leuven: Peeters; Macon: Mercer University Press 1987), esp. Part Two, "The Historical Tradition," 111–226.

56 See David Barrett Peabody, "Augustine and the Augustinian Hypothesis: A Reexamination of Augustine's Thought in *de consensu evangelistarum,*" in *New Synoptic Studies: The Cambridge Gospel Conference and Beyond,* ed. William R. Farmer (Macon: Mercer University Press 1983) 37–64.

57 See David L. Dungan, "The Purpose and Provenance of the Gospel of Mark according to the Two-Gospel (Owen-Griesbach) Hypothesis," in Farmer, ibid. 411–440.

58 See David L. Dungan, "Two Gospel Hypothesis," *ABD* 6:671–678.

59 Allan J. McNicol, with Lamar Cope, David Dungan, William Farmer, David

Peabody, and Philip Shuler, *Beyond the Q Impasse: Luke's Use of Matthew, a Demonstration by the Research Team of the International Institute for Gospel Studies* (Philadelphia: Trinity Press International 1996).

60 See Allan J. McNicol, *Jesus' Directions for the Future: A Source and Redaction-History Study of the Use of the Eschatological Traditions in Paul and in the Synoptic Accounts of Jesus' Last Eschatological Discourse,* New Gospel Studies 9 (Macon: Mercer University Press 1996).

61 William R. Farmer, "Timeless Truth and Apostolic Faith," *Perkins Journal* 37(1984) 9.

62 Even here there is an additional, daunting challenge: the critical text published by the UBS committee and the Aland Institute is itself corrupted by decades of decisions tacitly or openly based on the Two Source Hypothesis. So even the text must undergo a critical cleansing. But how many of our graduate programs teach their Ph.D. candidates how to think critically about the text of the Gospels?

63 See Austin Farrer, "On Dispensing with Q," in D. E. Nineham, ed., *Studies in the Gospels: Essays in the Memory of R. H. Lightfoot* (Oxford: Basil Blackwell 1955) 55–88; further, *St. Matthew and St. Mark* (Westminster: Dacre Press 1954).

64 For a recent account of Goulder's work by one of his leading students, see Mark S. Goodacre, *Goulder and the Gospels: An Examination of a New Paradigm,* JSOT Suppl. Ser. 133 (Sheffield: Sheffield Academic Press 1996).

65 Lagrange's commentaries on Matthew, Mark, and Luke were especially influential: *Évangile selon saint Marc* (Paris: Gabalda 1911); *Évangile selon saint Matthieu* (Paris: Lecoffre, 1923); *Évangile selon saint Luc* (Paris: Gabalda 1914). Lagrange also produced a Greek synopsis: with C. Lavergne, *Synopsis evangelica* (Paris 1926), and a version in French, C. Lavergne, *Synopse des quatre évangiles en français d'après la synopse grecque du P. M.-J. Lagrange* (Paris 1927).

66 See esp. x. Léon-Dufour, "Autour de la question synoptique," *Rech. Sci. Rel.* 42 (1954) 549–584. His most extensive discussion is in "Les évangiles synoptiques," in A. Robert and A. Feuillet, eds., *Introduction à la Bible,* 2 vols. (Tournai: Desclée 1959) 2:143–334; also available in ET, *Introduction to the New Testament* (New York: Desclée 1965) 139–324. Léon-Dufour also produced a colored synoptic chart: *Concordance of the Synoptic Gospels in Seven Colors,* trans. R. J. O'Connell (Paris & New York: Desclée 1956).

67 See A. Gabourg, *La structure des évangiles synoptiques: la Structure-type à l'origine des synoptiques* (Leiden: Brill 1970).

68 See M.-É. Boismard, "The Two Source Theory at an Impasse," *New Testament Studies* 26 (1979) 1–17. His most important publications dealing with the Synoptic Problem are the position paper defending the multiple stage theories in D. Dungan, ed., *The Interrelations of the Gospels: A Symposium led*

by M.-É. Boismard, W. R. Farmer, F. Neirynck, Jerusalem 1984, BETL 95 (Leuven: University Press 1990) 231–288, and the explanatory volume accompanying the synopsis of P. Benoit; see P. Benoit and M.-É. Boismard, *Synopse des quatres évangiles en français avec parallèls des apocryphes et des pères*, 2nd ed. revised and corrected by P. Sandevoir, ed., 2 vols. (Paris: Les éditions du Cerf 1973).

69 See the discussion of these theories in Dungan, op. cit. n.3, esp. 81–88.

70 L. Vaganay, *Le problème synoptique—une hypothèse de travail*, Bibliotheque d. théol. III, 1 (1954) 2.

71 E. P. Sanders and Margaret Davies, *Studying the Synoptic Gospels* (Philadelphia: Trinity Press International 1989) 117, 119 (italics added).

72 For a graphic illustration of one such hypothesis, see the chart prepared by M.-É. Boismard in Benoit and Boismard, op. cit. n.68, 2.17. This chart should be used with caution, however, since it omits important lines of influence in Boismard's complex hypothesis and is misleading in not revealing major and minor lines of influence (they all look the same). But Document A is the common source of *all three synoptics* (2.31) and also the *major* source of Matt Intermédiaire. Matt Intermédiaire is the *major* source of Proto-Luc (2.392), and Marc Intermédiaire is the *major* source of *all three* canonical Gospels.

Some lines of influence postulated by Boismard do not show up on this chart at all. For example, he says that Matt Intermédiaire contains elements of Q (see 2.33) as well as Proto-Luc, but there is no line connecting them. He says Document A directly influenced Document B (no line on the chart), as well as Mark Intermédiaire (no line). He says that "Luke" was not only the final redactor of canonical Luke but also *the final redactor of Mark and Matthew* (no lines indicating this on the chart). The box labeled "Jn" on the right should be actually labeled "Proto-John"; it was redacted by the same person as "ultimate redactor of John."

Important assumptions that Boismard never defends are (a) these are *all written documents* (2.15 et passim); (b) the most simple is always the most ancient version (2.393 et passim); and (c) nothing is ever lost—it is always a process of accretion. One should think that Boismard would have provided these important assumptions with a scholarly justification.

73 This statement was in an earlier version of his report, but after being roundly criticized for holding this view, he took it out of the final version, although he did not give it up in his argumentation.

74 See William Baird, *History of New Testament Research*, vol. 1, *From Deism to Tübingen* (Minneapolis: Fortress Press 1992) 1:181; cf. Farmer, op. cit. n.3, 30–34; further, Werner Georg Kümmel, *The New Testament: The History of the Investigation of Its Problems*, trans. S. McLean Gilmour and Howard C. Kee (Nashville: Abingdon Press 1972) 82f.

75 See the discussion in Dungan, "Synopses," op. cit. n.37, 463f. To my knowl-

edge, Aland never published an explanation of his methods in dividing pericopes or creating parallels. In an oral communication from Barbara Aland, I
learned that Kurt Aland simply took the Two Source Hypothesis for granted;
be that as it may, it is not as clearly represented in his synoptic arrangement
as it is in Huck's synopsis.

76 See Frans Neirynck, *Duality in Mark: Contributions to the Study of the Markan Redaction*, BETL 31 (Leuven: Leuven University Press 1972). For example, the Neo-Griesbachians claimed that the phrase in Mk 1:32 "in the
evening when the sun was setting Ὀψίας δὲ γενομένης, ὅτε ἔδυ ὁ ἥλιος was a
combination of Mt. 8:16 Ὀψίας δὲ γενομένης and Lk 4:40 Δύνοντος δὲ τοῦ
ἡλίου

77 For the report of Neirnyck, et al., see Frans Neirynck, ed. with Theo Hansen
and Frans van Segbroeck, *The Minor Agreements of Matthew and Luke
Against Mark with a Cumulative List*, BETL 37 (Leuven: Leuven University
Press 1974). Two of the best discussions out of many contributed by Albert
Fuchs are *Die Entwicklung der Beelzebulkontroverse bei den Synoptikern*
(Linz 1980), and "Die 'Seesturmperikope' Mk 4,35–41 parr im Wandel der
urkirchlichen Verkündigung," a report given to the Göttingen Conference on
the Minor Agreements in 1991 organized by Georg Strecker and William
Farmer (see next note for bibliographical reference).

78 For the most recent discussion of this issue from a number of different perspectives, see Georg Strecker, ed., *Minor Agreements: Symposium Göttingen
1991*, Göttingen Theologische Arbeiten 50 (Göttingen: Vandenhoeck &
Ruprecht 1993). Papers at this conference were given by Frans Neirynck, Albert Fuchs, Wolfgang Schenk, Christopher Tuckett, Michael Goulder, William Farmer, and Ulrich Luz. After the conference Neirynck contributed a
list of minor agreements but the list was not discussed at the conference.

79 Ennulat, op. cit. n.7.

80 Neirynck, "Synoptic Problem," op. cit. n.16. Note a similar unequivocal assertion in his article "The Synoptic Problem" in *NJBC* 589: "The argument
from order as understood since K. Lachmann (1835) *constitutes the main reason for positing Marcan priority.* The objection that the argument from order
explains Matt in relationship to Mark on the one hand and then Luke in
relationship to Mark on the other, but that the relationship among all three
remains unexplained (W. R. Farmer, *NTS* 23 [1976–77] 294) is hardly convincing. Mark need not be explained 'in relationship to both Matthew and Luke
taken together,' for it cannot be decided *a priori* that all three Synoptic Gospels should be interrelated. A solution of independence between Matt and
Luke is possible." This argument was later examined by David Neville and
found logically wanting (see next note).

81 Lachmann adopted this approach because of strong disapproval regarding
Griesbach's simultaneous triple Gospel comparison approach, seeing it as un-

necessarily complicated. Far better, he said, to explain the few changes Matthew made over against Mark, and likewise the few changes Luke made. For an excellent explanation of Lachmann's approach, see David J. Neville, *Arguments from Order in Synoptic Source Criticism: A History and Critique,* New Gospel Studies 7 (Macon: Mercer University Press 1994) 39–58.

82 Perhaps the most important example is Neirynck's contribution to the 1984 Jerusalem Symposium on the Gospels; see Dungan, op. cit. n.67, 3–124. Note that in this lengthy discussion, Neirynck considers only the evidence in Matthew and Mark.

83 See Werner Georg Kümmel, *Introduction to the New Testament,* trans. A. J. Mattill, Jr. (Nashville: Abingdon Press 1966) 45f.: "A comparison of all three Synoptics is astonishing chiefly because of the extensive agreement in the range of material between Matthew–Mark and Luke–Mark . . . (Moreover,) the fact that Mark in respect to sequence represents the common ground for Matthew and Luke was recognized by Lachmann . . . (This may rightly be considered evidence for Mark's priority) provided that the divergence of Matthew and Luke from Mark can be made understandable."

84 See Tuckett, op. cit. n.37, esp. 27.

85 David J. Neville, *Arguments from Order in Synoptic Source Criticism: A History and Critique,* New Gospel Studies 7 (Macon: Mercer University Press 1994) 234.

86 Ibid.

87 Ibid. 236.

88 Quoted from Neirynck's article "The Synoptic Problem" in *NJBC* 589.

89 Christopher Tuckett, "The Synoptic Problem," in *The New Interpreters Bible,* ed. Leander Keck et al. (Nashville: Abingdon Press 1995) 8:75f.

90 Neville, op. cit. n.85, 8f.: "The history of synoptic research reveals that a number of arguments from order have been put forward to defend a variety of source theories. Nevertheless, it is possible to classify any specific argument as one of two basic types. The first type is really an inference regarding the direction of dependence between gospels from purely formal considerations . . . The second type of argument goes beyond formal considerations (and) tries to account for specific details in the texts of the gospels."

91 Tuckett, op. cit. n.88, n.87 (italics added).

92 Ibid.

93 Cf. the conclusion of E. P. Sanders and M. Davies in their recent survey of source theories, *Studying the Synoptic Gospels* (Philadelphia: Trinity Press International 1989) 117: "Of all (modern) solutions, the Two Source Theory, which remains the dominant hypothesis, is the least satisfactory."

94 The most important recent attempts are A. Polag, *Fragmenta Q* (1979); W. Schenk, *Synopse zur Redenquelle der Evangelien* (1981); Frans Neirynck, *Q-Synopsis: The Double Tradition Passages in Greek* (1988); and J. S. Klop-

penborg, *Q Parallels: Synopsis, Critical Notes & Concordance* (1987). See also David R. Catchpole, *The Quest for Q* (Edinburgh: T. & T. Clark 1993). For the most important recent collection of essays by current leaders in Q research, see Ronald A. Piper, ed., *The Gospel behind the Gospels*, Supp. Nov. Test. 75 (Leiden: Brill 1995).

95 See John S. Kloppenborg, Marvin W. Meyer, Stephen J. Patterson, and Michael G. Steinhauser, *Q-Thomas Reader: The Gospels before the Gospels* (Chico, CA: Polebridge Press 1990).

96 The Coptic Gospel of Thomas is being reissued in a number of popular editions; cf. Marvin Meyer, trans. and ed., *The Gospel of Thomas: The Hidden Sayings of Jesus* (San Francisco: Harper 1992), in which Harold Bloom wrote that this Gospel "spares us the crucifixion, makes the resurrection unnecessary, and does not present us with a God named Jesus." The theological reductionism implied in such a sentence makes one wonder what precisely is left of Jesus Christ that will appeal to the modern secular world.

97 This reaction was given early formulation by James M. Robinson, "LOGOI SOPHON: On the Gattung of Q," in James M. Robinson and Helmut Koester, *Trajectories through Early Christianity* (Philadelphia: Fortress Press 1971) 71–113; also an ET of "LOGOI SOPHON: zur Gattung der Spruchquelle Q," in *Zeit und Geschichte: Dankesgabe an Rudolf Bultmann zum 80. Geburtstag* (Tübingen: Mohr/Siebeck 1964) 77–96.

98 See James M. Robinson, ed., *The Nag Hammadi Library in English* (New York: Harper & Row 1977).

99 James M. Robinson, "The Sayings of Jesus: Q," *Drew Gateway* 54 (1983) 37.

100 See "The International Q Project Work Session 17 November 1989," *JBL* 109 (1990) 499–501; "The International Q Project Work Session 12–14 July, 22 November 1991," *JBL* 111 (1992) 500–508; "The International Q Project Work Session 31 July–2 August 1992," *JBL* 112 (1993) 500–506.

INDEX